PHILIP'S

STREET ATLAS
Berkshire

Bracknell, Camberley, Maidenhead, Newbury, Reading, Slough, Windsor

www.philips-maps.co.uk

First published in 1990 by

Philip's, a division of
Octopus Publishing Group Ltd
www.octopusbooks.co.uk
2-4 Heron Quays, London E14 4JP
An Hachette Livre UK Company
www.hachettelivre.co.uk

Fourth colour edition 2008
First impression 2008
BERDA

ISBN 978-0-540-09294-9 (spiral)

Data for the speed cameras provided by PocketGPSWorld.com Ltd.

Printed and bound in China by Toppan

Contents

II **Mobile safety cameras**

III **Key to map symbols**

IV **Key to map pages**

VI **Route planning**

VIII **Administrative and Postcode boundaries**

1 **Street maps** at 3½ inches to 1 mile

154 **Index** of towns, villages, streets, hospitals, industrial estates, railway stations, schools, shopping centres universities and places of interest

Digital Data

The exceptionally high-quality mapping found in this atlas is available as digital data in TIFF format, which is easily convertible to other bitmapped (raster) image formats.

The index is also available in digital form as a standard database table. It contains all the details found in the printed index together with the National Grid reference for the map square in which each entry is named.

For further information and to discuss your requirements, please contact victoria.dawbarn@philips-maps.co.uk

On-line route planner

For detailed driving directions and estimated driving times visit our free route planner at www.philips-maps.co.uk

Mobile safety cameras

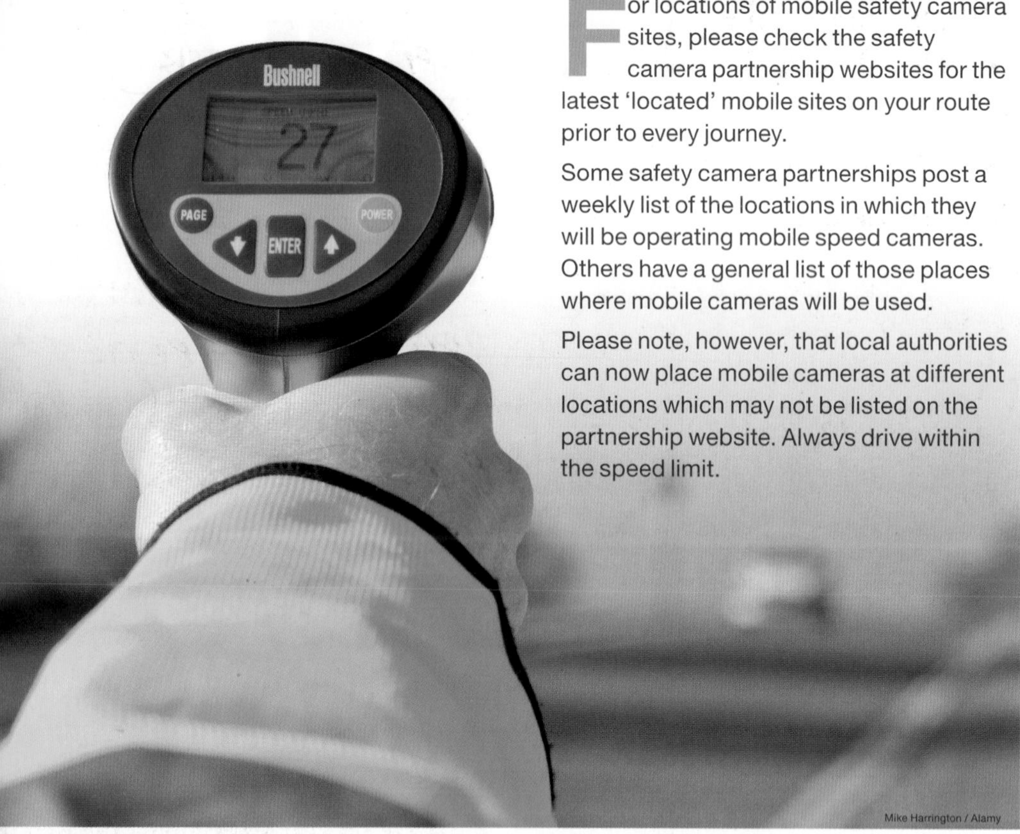

Mike Harrington / Alamy

For locations of mobile safety camera sites, please check the safety camera partnership websites for the latest 'located' mobile sites on your route prior to every journey.

Some safety camera partnerships post a weekly list of the locations in which they will be operating mobile speed cameras. Others have a general list of those places where mobile cameras will be used.

Please note, however, that local authorities can now place mobile cameras at different locations which may not be listed on the partnership website. Always drive within the speed limit.

Useful websites

Thames Valley Safety Camera Partnership
http://www.saferroads.org/

London Safety Camera Partnership
www.lscp.org.uk/

Surrey Safety Camera Partnership
www.surrey-safecam.org

Further information
www.dvla.gov.uk
www.thinkroadsafety.gov.uk
www.dft.gov.uk
www.road-safe.org

Key to map symbols

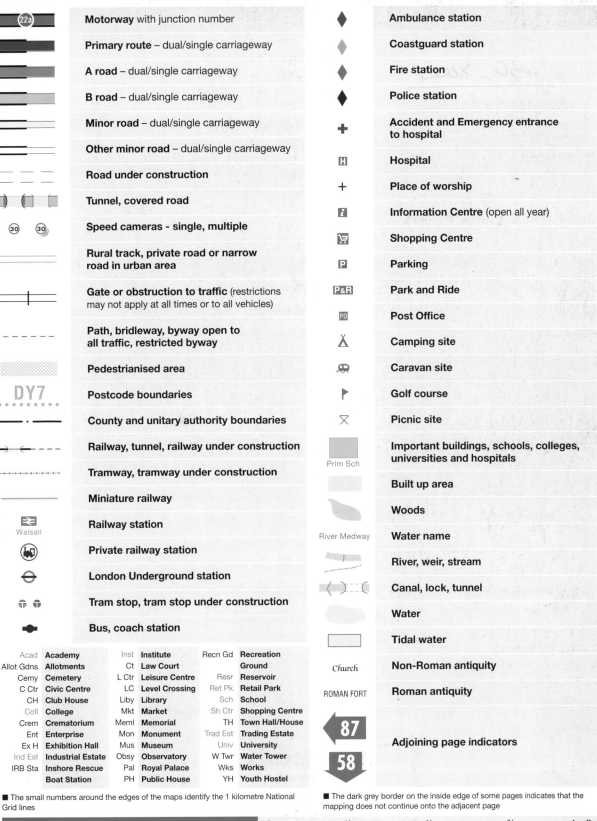

22a	**Motorway** with junction number
	Primary route – dual/single carriageway
	A road – dual/single carriageway
	B road – dual/single carriageway
	Minor road – dual/single carriageway
	Other minor road – dual/single carriageway
	Road under construction
	Tunnel, covered road
30 30	**Speed cameras - single, multiple**
	Rural track, private road or narrow road in urban area
	Gate or obstruction to traffic (restrictions may not apply at all times or to all vehicles)
	Path, bridleway, byway open to all traffic, restricted byway
	Pedestrianised area
DY7	**Postcode boundaries**
	County and unitary authority boundaries
	Railway, tunnel, railway under construction
	Tramway, tramway under construction
	Miniature railway
Walsall	**Railway station**
	Private railway station
	London Underground station
	Tram stop, tram stop under construction
	Bus, coach station
	Ambulance station
	Coastguard station
	Fire station
	Police station
	Accident and Emergency entrance to hospital
H	**Hospital**
	Place of worship
i	**Information Centre** (open all year)
	Shopping Centre
P	**Parking**
P&R	**Park and Ride**
PO	**Post Office**
	Camping site
	Caravan site
	Golf course
	Picnic site
Prim Sch	**Important buildings, schools, colleges, universities and hospitals**
	Built up area
	Woods
River Medway	**Water name**
	River, weir, stream
	Canal, lock, tunnel
	Water
	Tidal water
Church	**Non-Roman antiquity**
ROMAN FORT	**Roman antiquity**
87 58	**Adjoining page indicators**

Acad	**Academy**	Inst	**Institute**	Recn Gd	**Recreation Ground**
Allot Gdns	**Allotments**	Ct	**Law Court**	Resr	**Reservoir**
Cemy	**Cemetery**	L Ctr	**Leisure Centre**	Ret Pk	**Retail Park**
C Ctr	**Civic Centre**	LC	**Level Crossing**	Sch	**School**
CH	**Club House**	Liby	**Library**	Sh Ctr	**Shopping Centre**
Coll	**College**	Mkt	**Market**	TH	**Town Hall/House**
Crem	**Crematorium**	Meml	**Memorial**	Trad Est	**Trading Estate**
Ent	**Enterprise**	Mon	**Monument**	Univ	**University**
Ex H	**Exhibition Hall**	Mus	**Museum**	W Twr	**Water Tower**
Ind Est	**Industrial Estate**	Obsy	**Observatory**	Wks	**Works**
IRB Sta	**Inshore Rescue Boat Station**	Pal	**Royal Palace**	YH	**Youth Hostel**
		PH	**Public House**		

■ The small numbers around the edges of the maps identify the 1 kilometre National Grid lines

■ The dark grey border on the inside edge of some pages indicates that the mapping does not continue onto the adjacent page

The scale of the maps on the pages numbered in blue is 5.52 cm to 1 km • 3½ inches to 1 mile • 1: 18103

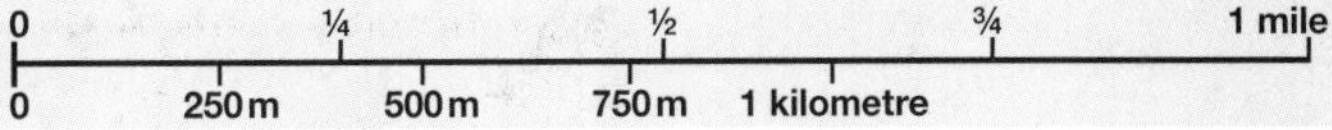

Key to map pages

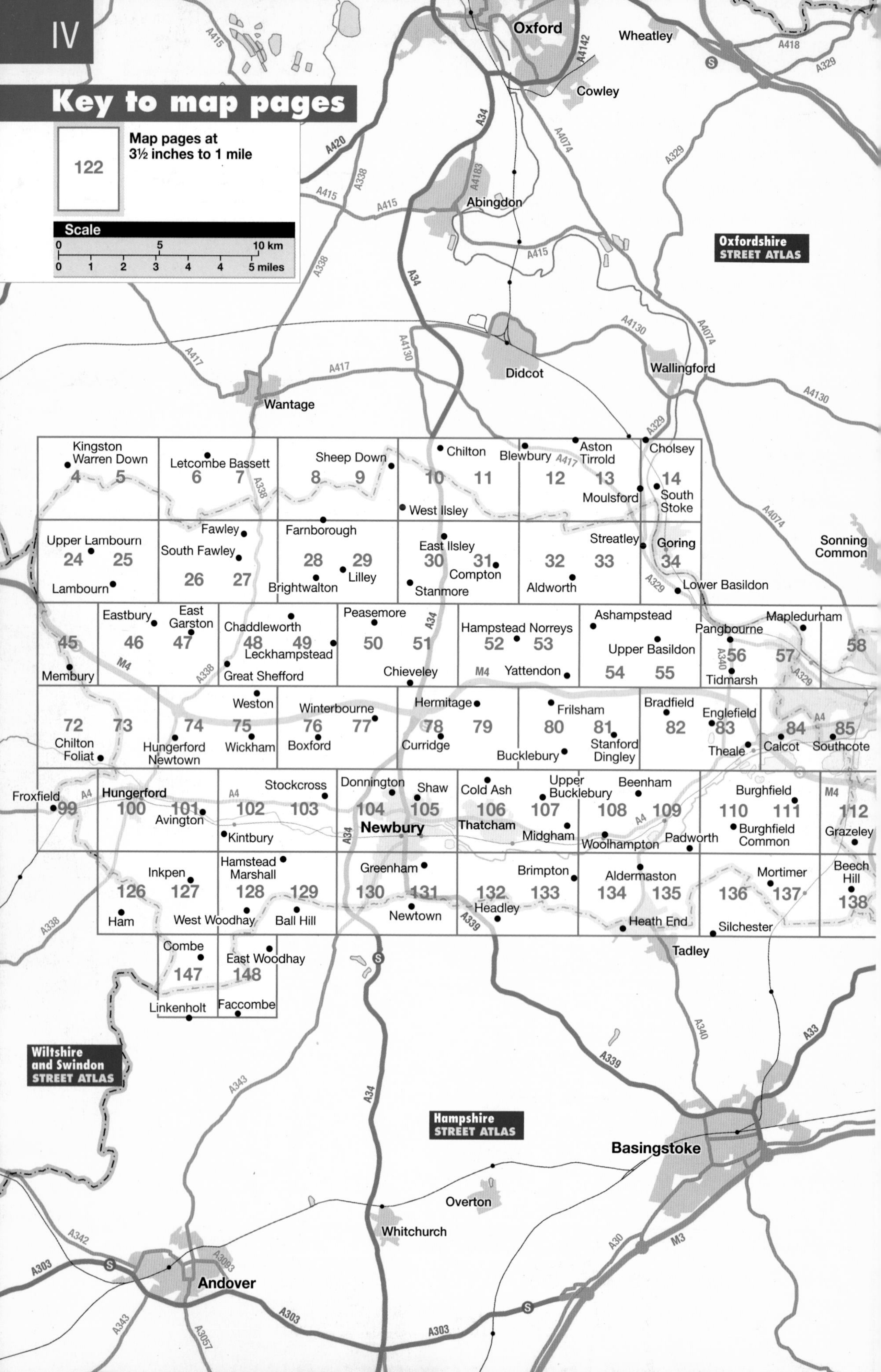

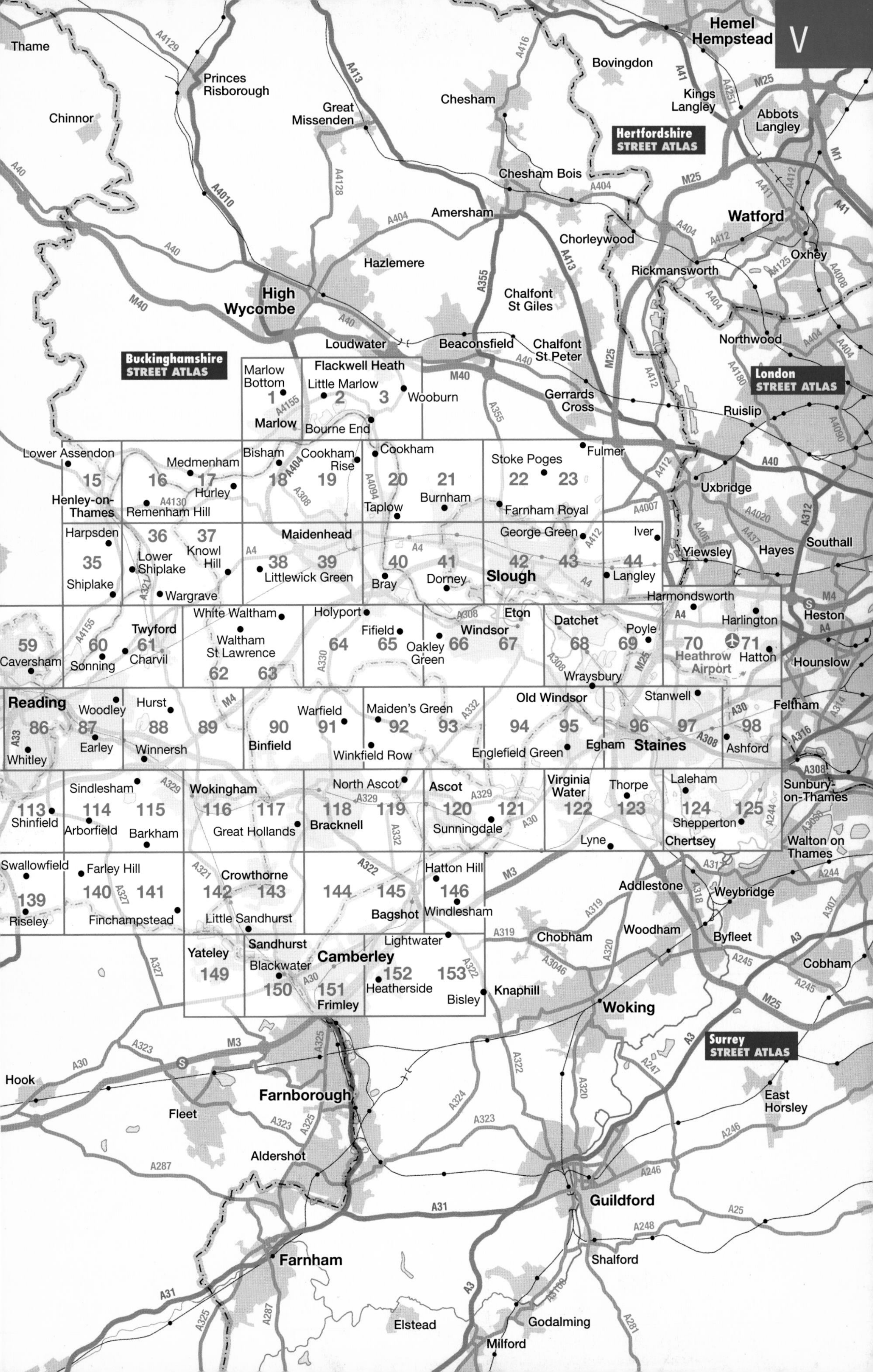
Thame
Princes Risborough
Chinnor
Great Missenden
Chesham
Bovingdon
Hemel Hempstead
Kings Langley
Abbots Langley
Hertfordshire STREET ATLAS
Chesham Bois
Amersham
Watford
Chorleywood
Oxhey
Hazlemere
Rickmansworth
High Wycombe
Chalfont St Giles
Northwood
Loudwater
Beaconsfield
Chalfont St Peter
Buckinghamshire STREET ATLAS
London STREET ATLAS
Gerrards Cross
Ruislip
Marlow Bottom
Flackwell Heath
Little Marlow
Wooburn
Marlow
Bourne End
Lower Assendon
Medmenham
Bisham
Cookham Rise
Cookham
Stoke Poges
Fulmer
Hurley
Henley-on-Thames
Remenham Hill
Taplow
Burnham
Farnham Royal
Uxbridge
Harpsden
Maidenhead
George Green
Iver
Knowl Hill
Lower Shiplake
Shiplake
Wargrave
Littlewick Green
Bray
Dorney
Slough
Langley
Yiewsley
Hayes
Southall
Harmondsworth
Harlington
Heston
White Waltham
Holyport
Eton
Datchet
Twyford
Waltham St Lawrence
Fifield
Windsor
Poyle
Caversham
Sonning
Charvil
Oakley Green
Heathrow Airport
Hatton
Hounslow
Wraysbury
Reading
Woodley
Hurst
Warfield
Maiden's Green
Old Windsor
Stanwell
Feltham
Earley
Whitley
Winnersh
Binfield
Winkfield Row
Englefield Green
Egham
Staines
Ashford
Sindlesham
Wokingham
North Ascot
Ascot
Virginia Water
Thorpe
Laleham
Sunbury-on-Thames
Shinfield
Arborfield
Barkham
Great Hollands
Bracknell
Sunningdale
Shepperton
Chertsey
Lyne
Walton on Thames
Swallowfield
Farley Hill
Crowthorne
Hatton Hill
Addlestone
Weybridge
Riseley
Finchampstead
Little Sandhurst
Bagshot
Windlesham
Woodham
Chobham
Byfleet
Yateley
Sandhurst
Lightwater
Camberley
Blackwater
Heatherside
Frimley
Knaphill
Bisley
Cobham
Woking
Surrey STREET ATLAS
Hook
Farnborough
Fleet
East Horsley
Aldershot
Guildford
Farnham
Shalford
Elstead
Godalming
Milford
1 2 3 15 16 17 18 19 20 21 22 23 35 36 37 38 39 40 41 42 43 44 59 60 61 62 63 64 65 66 67 68 69 70 71 86 87 88 89 90 91 92 93 94 95 96 97 98 113 114 115 116 117 118 119 120 121 122 123 124 125 139 140 141 142 143 144 145 146 149 150 151 152 153
M40 M4 M25 M3 M1 A40 A404 A413 A4010 A4128 A4129 A416 A41 A4251 A412 A411 A4125 A4008 A355 A4155 A4094 A308 A4130 A321 A4 A330 A332 A329 A30 A33 A327 A322 A319 A320 A3046 A318 A317 A245 A3 A323 A325 A324 A287 A31 A246 A25 A248 A281 A3100 A247 A244 A316 A314 A312 A4020 A437 A408 A4180 A4090 A4007

Route Planning

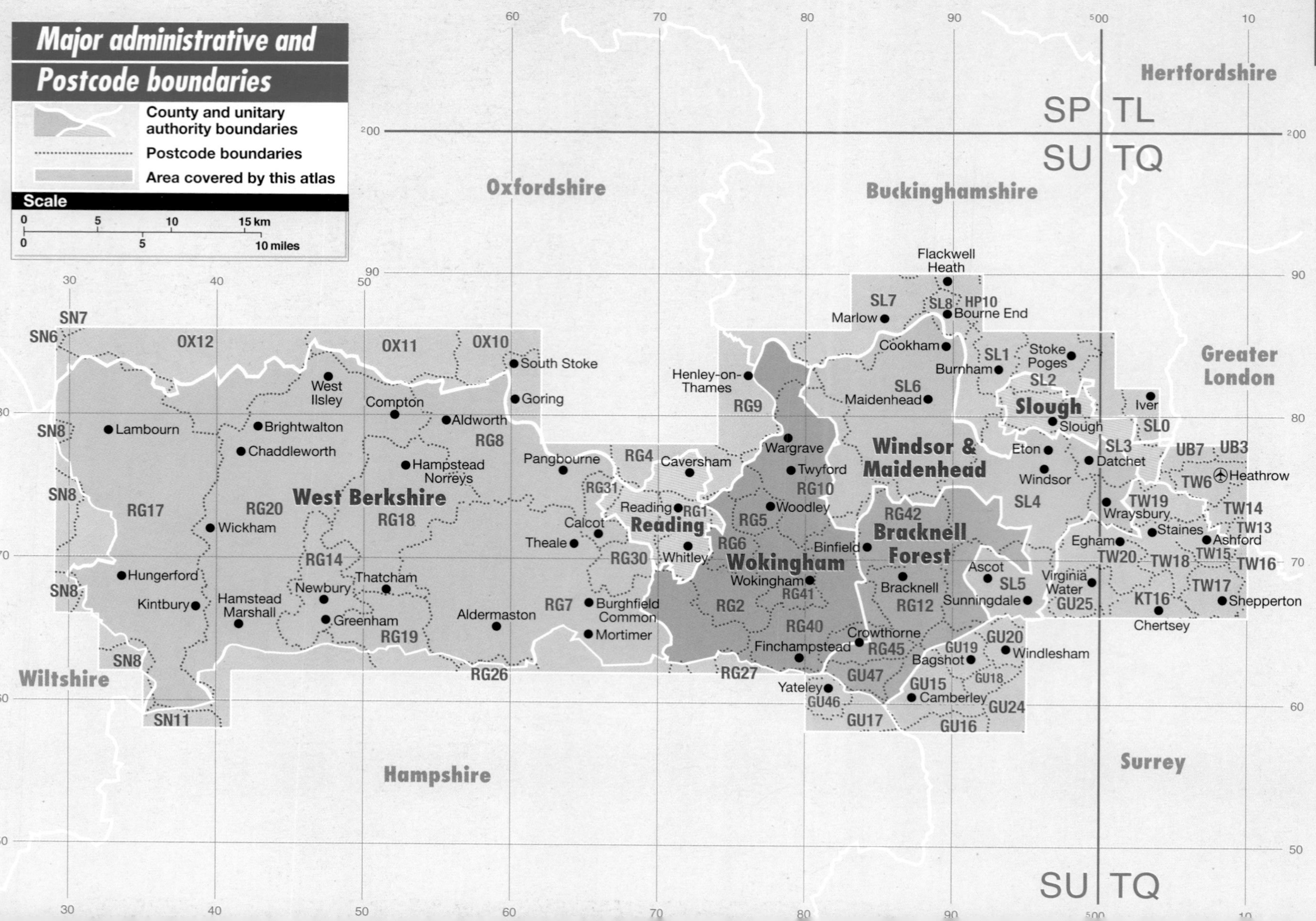
Major administrative and Postcode boundaries
County and unitary authority boundaries
Postcode boundaries
Area covered by this atlas
Scale
0 5 10 15 km
0 5 10 miles
Hertfordshire
SP TL
SU TQ
Oxfordshire
Buckinghamshire
Greater London
Wiltshire
Hampshire
Surrey
West Berkshire
Reading
Wokingham
Bracknell Forest
Windsor & Maidenhead
Slough
SN7
SN6
SN8
SN11
OX12
OX11
OX10
RG17
RG20
RG18
RG14
RG19
RG26
RG8
RG7
RG4
RG31
RG30
RG1
RG6
RG5
RG2
RG27
RG9
RG10
RG41
RG40
RG42
RG12
RG45
GU47
GU46
GU17
GU15
GU16
GU18
GU19
GU20
GU24
GU25
SL5
SL4
SL6
SL7
SL8
HP10
SL1
SL2
SL3
SL0
UB7
UB3
TW6
TW19
TW14
TW13
TW15
TW16
TW17
TW18
TW20
KT16
Lambourn
West Ilsley
Compton
Brightwalton
Chaddleworth
Aldworth
Hampstead Norreys
South Stoke
Goring
Pangbourne
Caversham
Henley-on-Thames
Wickham
Hungerford
Kintbury
Hamstead Marshall
Newbury
Thatcham
Greenham
Aldermaston
Theale
Calcot
Reading
Whitley
Burghfield Common
Mortimer
Finchampstead
Wokingham
Woodley
Twyford
Wargrave
Binfield
Crowthorne
Yateley
Camberley
Bagshot
Windlesham
Bracknell
Ascot
Sunningdale
Virginia Water
Egham
Staines
Ashford
Shepperton
Chertsey
Wraysbury
Datchet
Windsor
Eton
Slough
Iver
Heathrow
Stoke Poges
Burnham
Maidenhead
Cookham
Bourne End
Flackwell Heath
Marlow

2

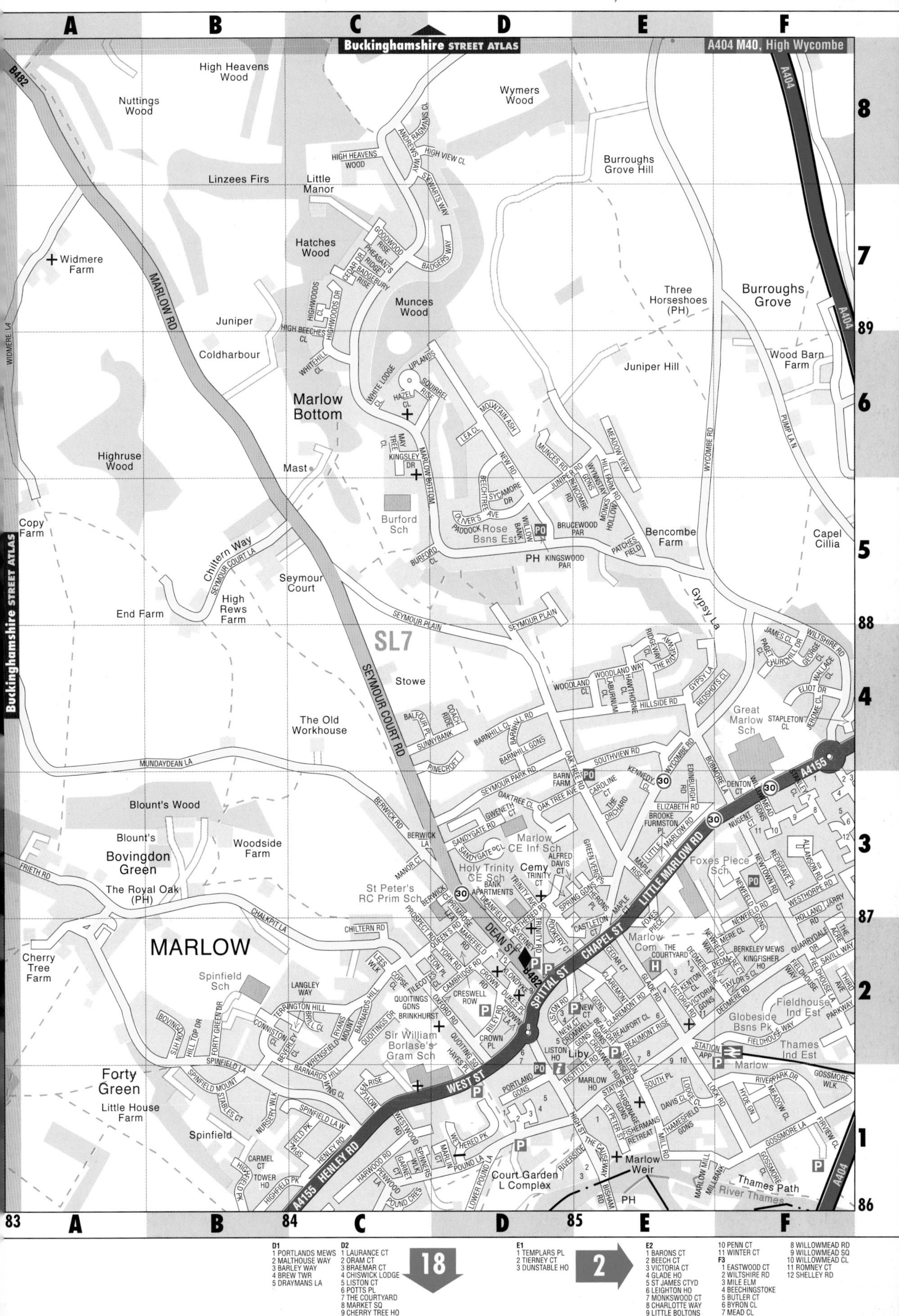

D1
1 PORTLANDS MEWS
2 MALTHOUSE WAY
3 BARLEY WAY
4 BREW TWR
5 DRAYMANS LA

D2
1 LAURANCE CT
2 ORAM CT
3 BRAEMAR CT
4 CHISWICK LODGE
5 LISTON CT
6 POTTS PL
7 THE COURTYARD
8 MARKET SQ
9 CHERRY TREE HO

18

E1
1 TEMPLARS PL
2 TIERNEY CT
3 DUNSTABLE HO

2

E2
1 BARONS CT
2 BEECH CT
3 VICTORIA CT
4 GLADE HO
5 ST JAMES CTYD
6 LEIGHTON HO
7 MONKSWOOD CT
8 CHARLOTTE WAY
9 LITTLE BOLTONS
10 PENN CT
11 WINTER CT

F3
1 EASTWOOD CT
2 WILTSHIRE RD
3 MILE ELM
4 BEECHINGSTOKE
5 BUTLER CT
6 BYRON CL
7 MEAD CL
8 WILLOWMEAD RD
9 WILLOWMEAD SQ
10 WILLOWMEAD CL
11 ROMNEY CT
12 SHELLEY RD

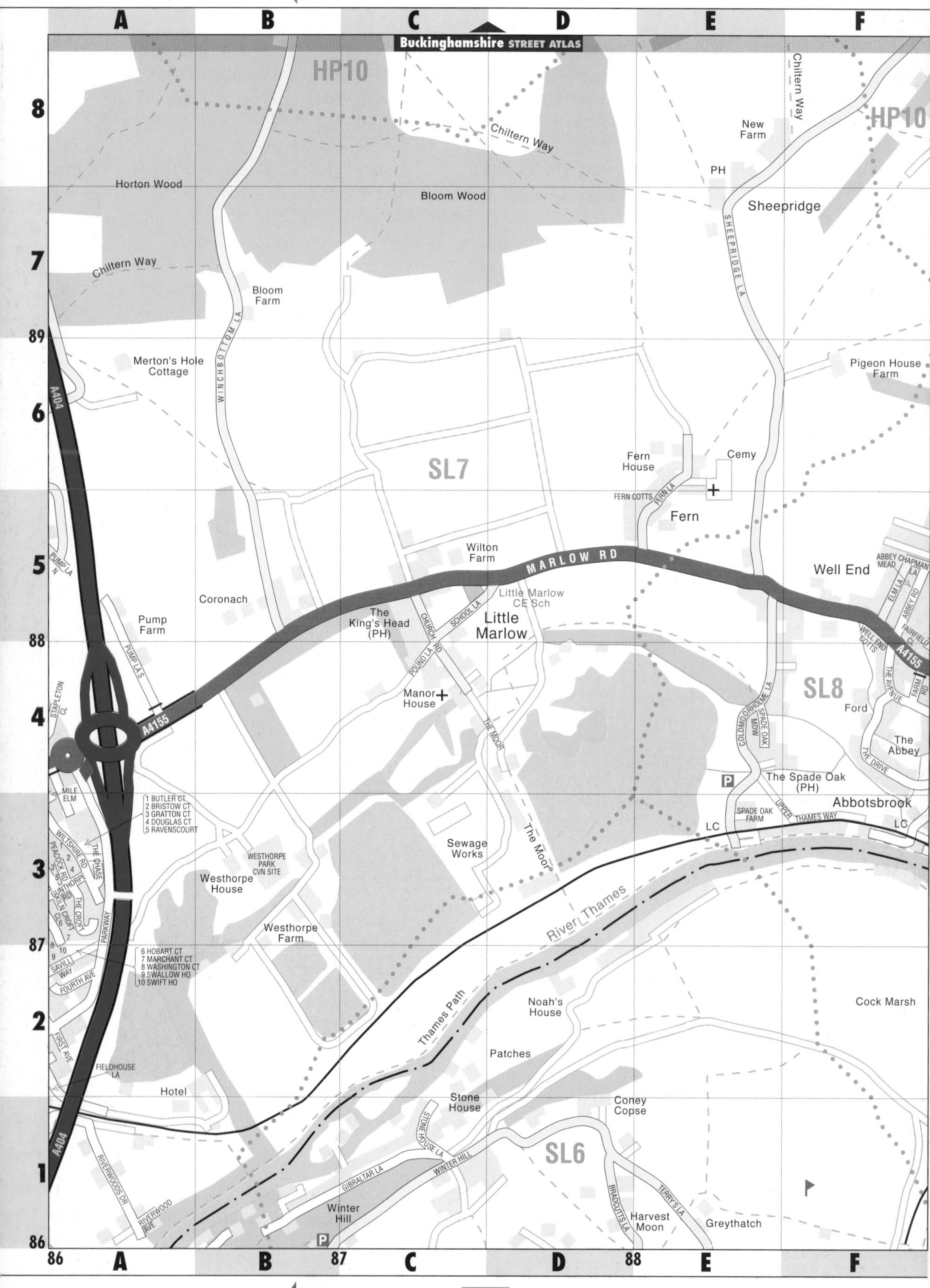
Buckinghamshire STREET ATLAS
HP10
Chiltern Way
Horton Wood
Bloom Wood
Bloom Farm
Merton's Hole Cottage
WINCHBOTTOM LA
New Farm
PH
Sheepridge
SHEEPRIDGE LA
Pigeon House Farm
SL7
Fern House
Cemy
FERN COTTS
FERN LA
Fern
Wilton Farm
MARLOW RD
Well End
ABBEY MEAD
CHAPMAN LA
ELM LA
ABBEY RD
FAIRFIELD CL
WELL END COTTS
A4155
A404
PUMP LA N
PUMP LA S
Pump Farm
Coronach
The King's Head (PH)
CHURCH RD
SCHOOL LA
POUND LA
Little Marlow CE Sch
Little Marlow
Manor House
THE MOOR
The Moor
SL8
Ford
THE AVENUE
FARM RD
The Abbey
THE DRIVE
COLDMOORHOLME LA
SPADE OAK MDW
The Spade Oak (PH)
Abbotsbrook
SPADE OAK FARM
UPPER THAMES WAY
LC
STAPLETON CL
MILE ELM
1 BUTLER CT
2 BRISTOW CT
3 GRATTON CT
4 DOUGLAS CT
5 RAVENSCOURT
WILTSHIRE RD
PEACOCK RD
THE CHASE
GUNTHORPE RD
THE CROFT
PARKWAY
WESTHORPE PARK CVN SITE
Westhorpe House
Westhorpe Farm
Sewage Works
River Thames
SAVILL WAY
FOURTH AVE
6 HOBART CT
7 MARCHANT CT
8 WASHINGTON CT
9 SWALLOW HO
10 SWIFT HO
Thames Path
Noah's House
Cock Marsh
FIRST AVE
FIELDHOUSE LA
Patches
Hotel
Stone House
STONE HOUSE LA
Coney Copse
SL6
RIVERWOODS DR
RIVERWOOD AVE
GIBRALTAR LA
WINTER HILL
Winter Hill
BRADCUTTS LA
TERRY'S LA
Harvest Moon
Greythatch
A B C D E F
8 7 89 6 5 88 4 3 87 2 1 86
86 87 88

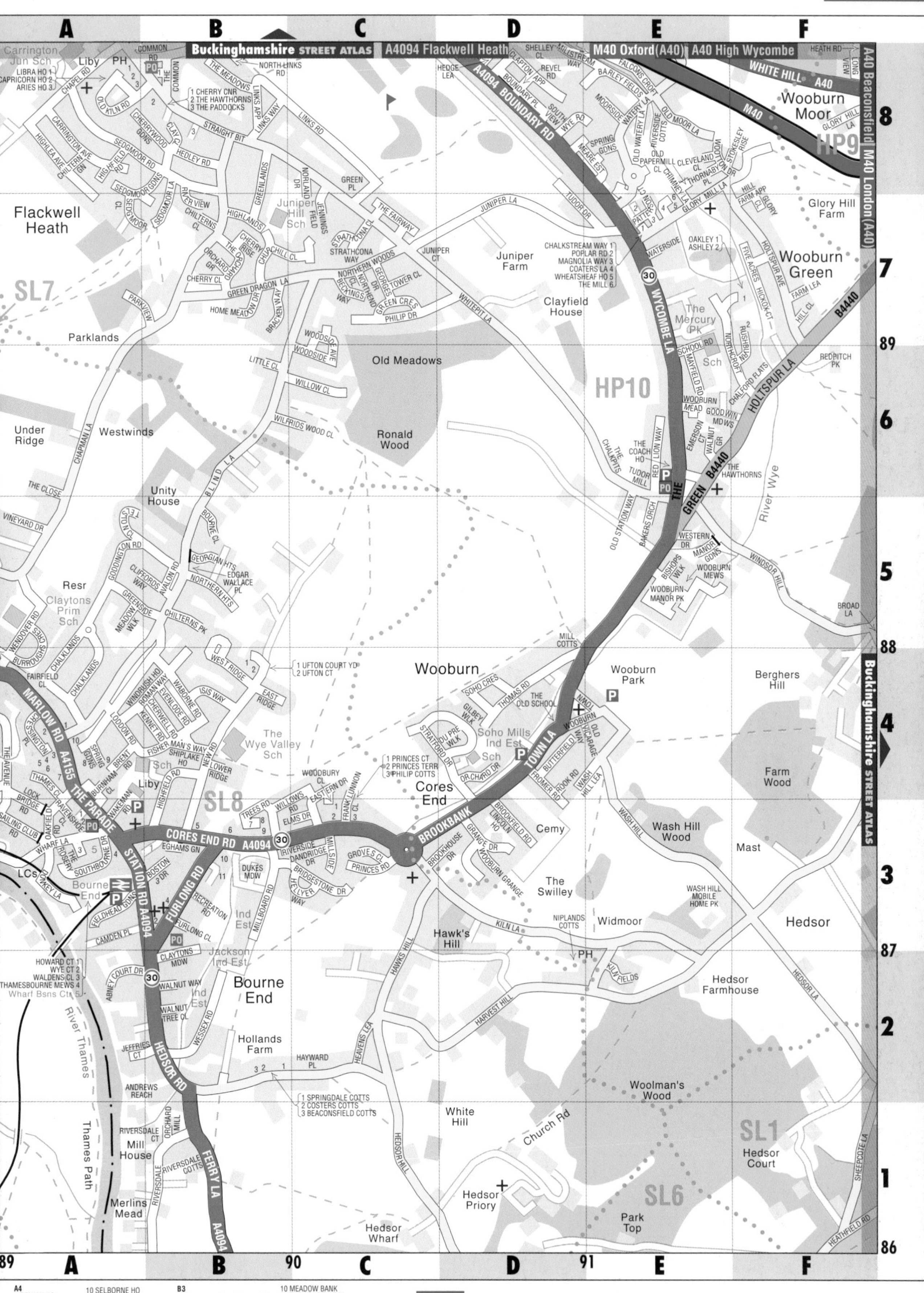

A4
1 ROWAN HO
2 CRESSINGTON CT
3 COKERS CT
4 RUSSELL HO
5 RAY HO
6 GRANT HO
7 PARADE CT
8 ORCHARD HO
9 BAILEY HO
10 SELBORNE HO

B3
1 Bourne End Bsns Pk
2 ALFRED CT
3 EGHAMS CT
4 HYLAND HO
5 FARRIER CT
6 MOUNT PLEASANT COTTS
7 SYCAMORE CL
8 THE WILLOWS
9 THE MAPLES
10 MEADOW BANK
11 THE COURTYARD

20

A
B
C
D
E
F
Oxfordshire STREET ATLAS
Wiltshire & Swindon STREET ATLAS
8
7
85
6
5
84
4
3
83
2
1
82
29
30
31
Ridgeway
SN7
Uffington Down
Long Plantation
Woolstone Hill Barn
SN6
Pingoose Covert
Idlebush Barrow
Gallops
OX12
Kingston Warren
Kingston Warren Down
Gallops
Woolstone Down
Compton Close
Knighton Down
Gallops
Whit Coombe
Wellbottom Down
Knighton Bushes Plantation
RG17
Gallops
Lambourn Valley Way
Baldback Covert
Gallops
Parkfarm Down
Maddle Farm
MADDLE RD
Weathercock Hill
Postdown Border

24

6

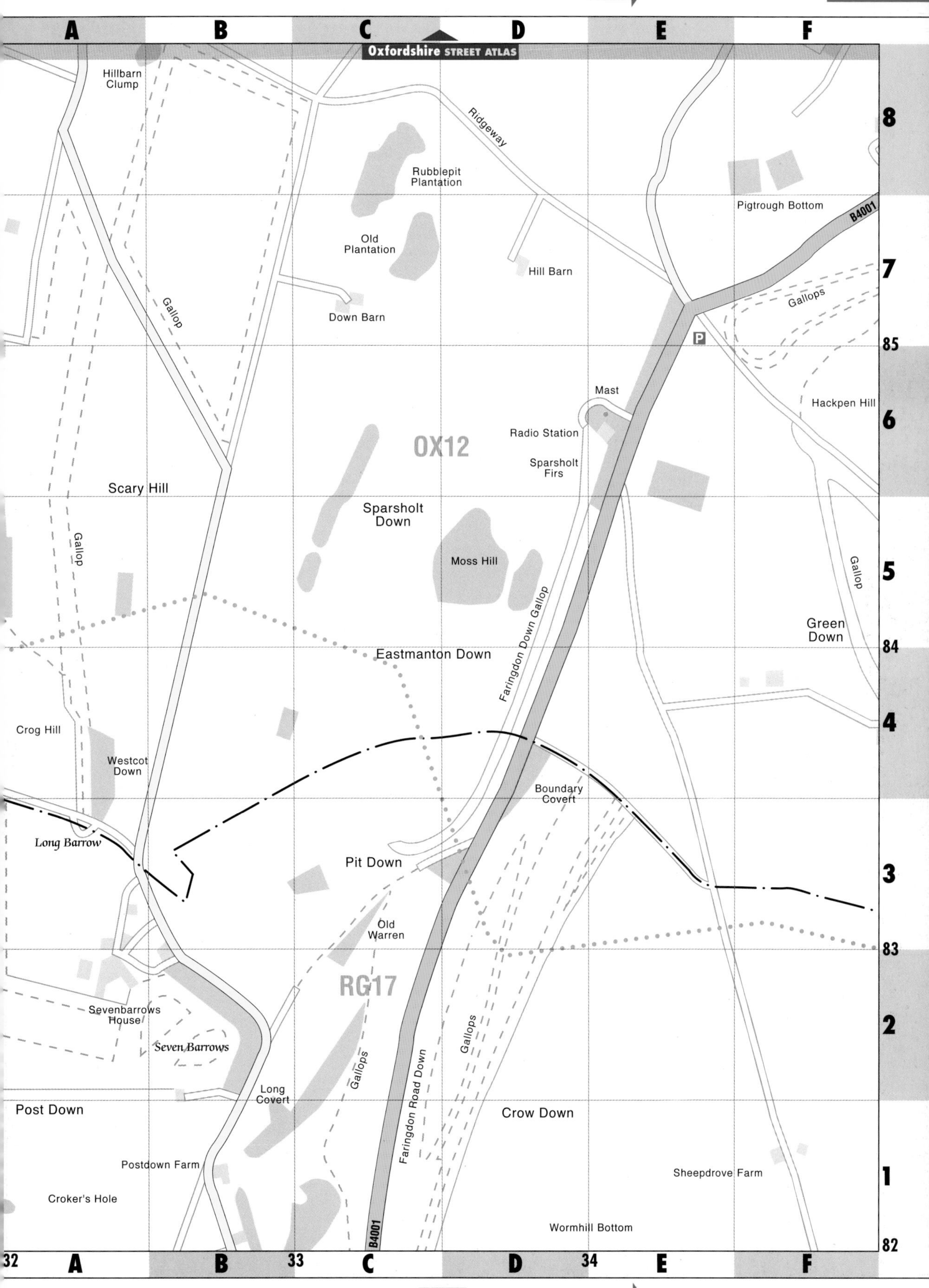
A
B
C
D
E
F
Oxfordshire STREET ATLAS
Hillbarn Clump
Ridgeway
Rubblepit Plantation
Old Plantation
Pigtrough Bottom
B4001
Hill Barn
Gallops
Gallop
Down Barn
Mast
Hackpen Hill
Radio Station
OX12
Sparsholt Firs
Scary Hill
Sparsholt Down
Moss Hill
Gallop
Gallop
Green Down
Faringdon Down Gallop
Eastmanton Down
Crog Hill
Westcot Down
Boundary Covert
Long Barrow
Pit Down
Old Warren
RG17
Sevenbarrows House
Seven Barrows
Gallops
Gallops
Faringdon Road Down
Long Covert
Post Down
Crow Down
Postdown Farm
Sheepdrove Farm
Croker's Hole
Wormhill Bottom
B4001
8
7
85
6
5
84
4
3
83
2
1
82
32
33
34

25
6

5

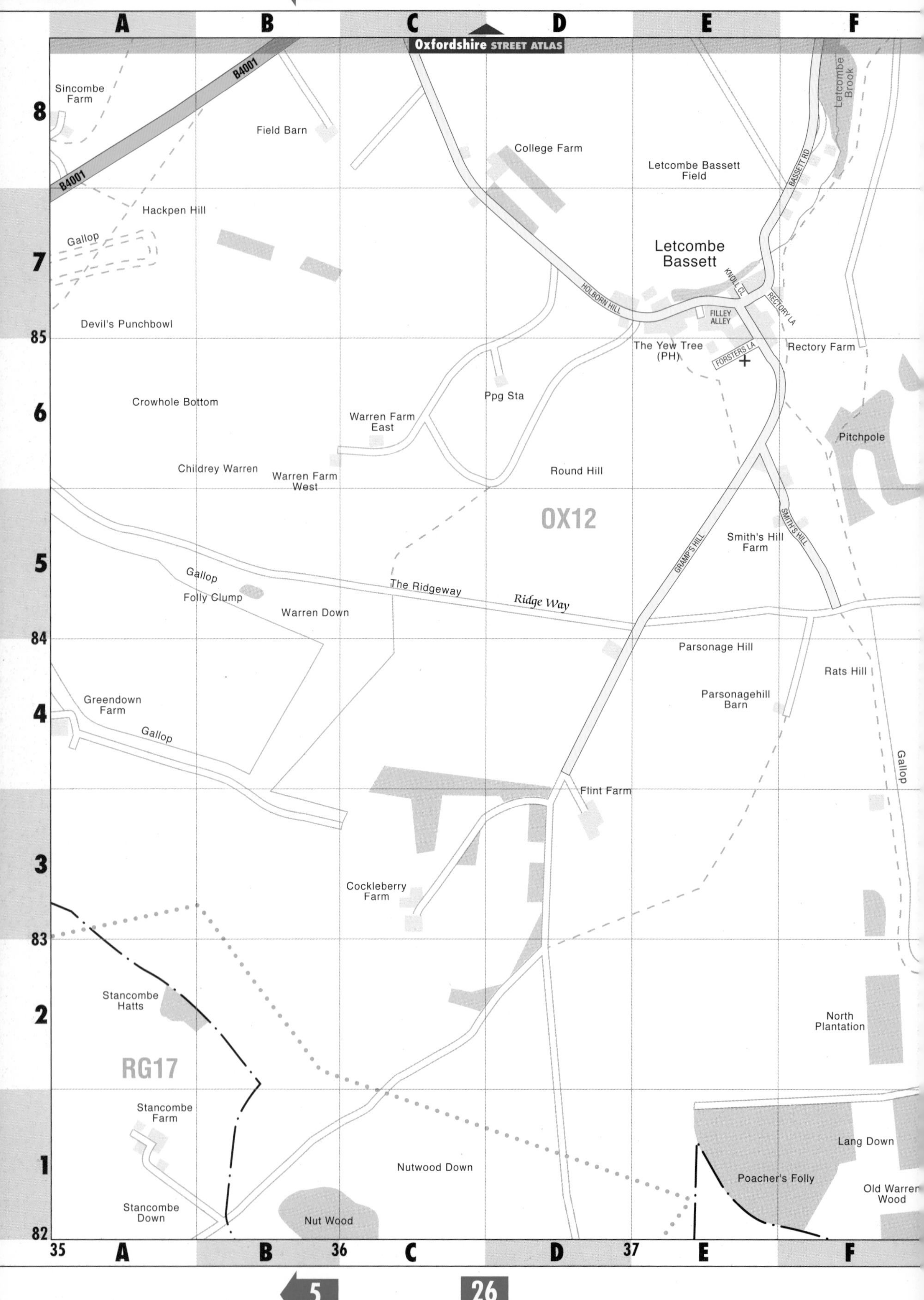
Oxfordshire STREET ATLAS
A
B
C
D
E
F
8
7
85
6
5
84
4
3
83
2
1
82
35
36
37
B4001
Sincombe Farm
Field Barn
College Farm
Letcombe Bassett Field
Letcombe Brook
Hackpen Hill
Gallop
Letcombe Bassett
BASSETT RD
KNOLL CL
RECTORY LA
HOLBORN HILL
FILLEY ALLEY
FORSTERS LA
Devil's Punchbowl
The Yew Tree (PH)
Rectory Farm
Crowhole Bottom
Ppg Sta
Warren Farm East
Pitchpole
Childrey Warren
Warren Farm West
Round Hill
OX12
GRAMP'S HILL
SMITH'S HILL
Smith's Hill Farm
Folly Clump
The Ridgeway
Ridge Way
Warren Down
Parsonage Hill
Rats Hill
Greendown Farm
Parsonagehill Barn
Flint Farm
Cockleberry Farm
Stancombe Hatts
North Plantation
RG17
Stancombe Farm
Lang Down
Nutwood Down
Poacher's Folly
Old Warren Wood
Stancombe Down
Nut Wood

5
26

8

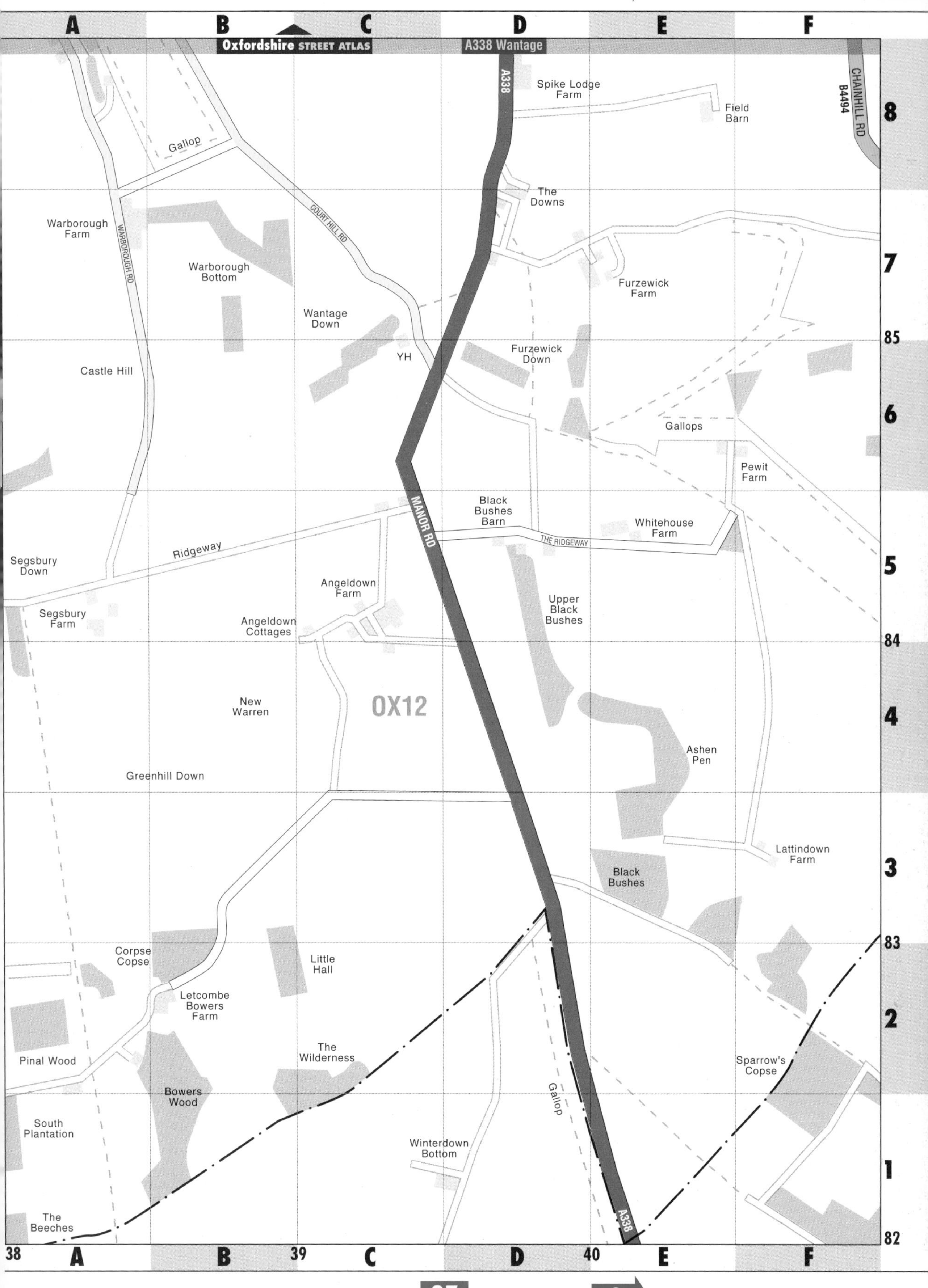
A
B
C
D
E
F
Oxfordshire STREET ATLAS
A338 Wantage
A338
Spike Lodge Farm
Field Barn
CHAINHILL RD
B4494
8
Gallop
The Downs
Warborough Farm
WARBOROUGH RD
COURT HILL RD
7
Warborough Bottom
Furzewick Farm
Wantage Down
85
Furzewick Down
YH
Castle Hill
6
Gallops
Pewit Farm
Black Bushes Barn
MANOR RD
Whitehouse Farm
THE RIDGEWAY
Ridgeway
Segsbury Down
5
Angeldown Farm
Upper Black Bushes
Segsbury Farm
Angeldown Cottages
84
New Warren
OX12
4
Ashen Pen
Greenhill Down
Lattindown Farm
3
Black Bushes
83
Corpse Copse
Little Hall
Letcombe Bowers Farm
2
The Wilderness
Pinal Wood
Sparrow's Copse
Bowers Wood
Gallop
South Plantation
Winterdown Bottom
1
The Beeches
A338
82
38
39
40

27
8

7

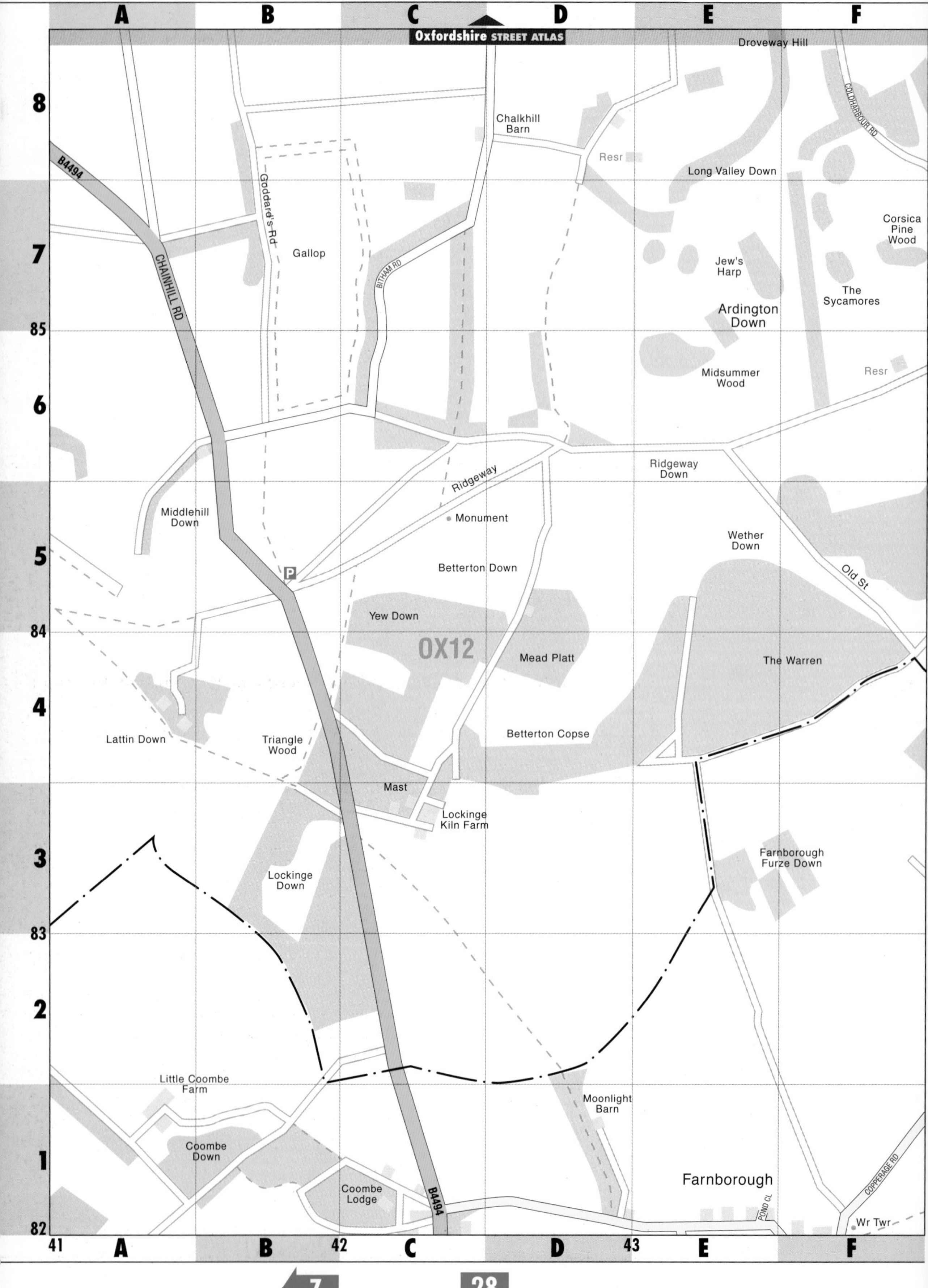
A
B
C
D
E
F
Oxfordshire STREET ATLAS
Droveway Hill
8
Chalkhill
Barn
COLDHARBOUR RD
Resr
Long Valley Down
B4494
Goddard's Rd
Gallop
7
CHAINHILL RD
BITHAM RD
Jew's
Harp
Corsica
Pine
Wood
The
Sycamores
Ardington
Down
85
Midsummer
Wood
Resr
6
Ridgeway
Down
Ridgeway
Monument
Middlehill
Down
Wether
Down
5
P
Betterton Down
Old St
84
Yew Down
OX12
Mead Platt
The Warren
4
Betterton Copse
Lattin Down
Triangle
Wood
Mast
Lockinge
Kiln Farm
3
Farnborough
Furze Down
Lockinge
Down
83
2
Little Coombe
Farm
Moonlight
Barn
Coombe
Down
1
COPPERAGE RD
Farnborough
Coombe
Lodge
B4494
POND CL
Wr Twr
82
41
A
B
42
C
D
43
E
F

7
28

10

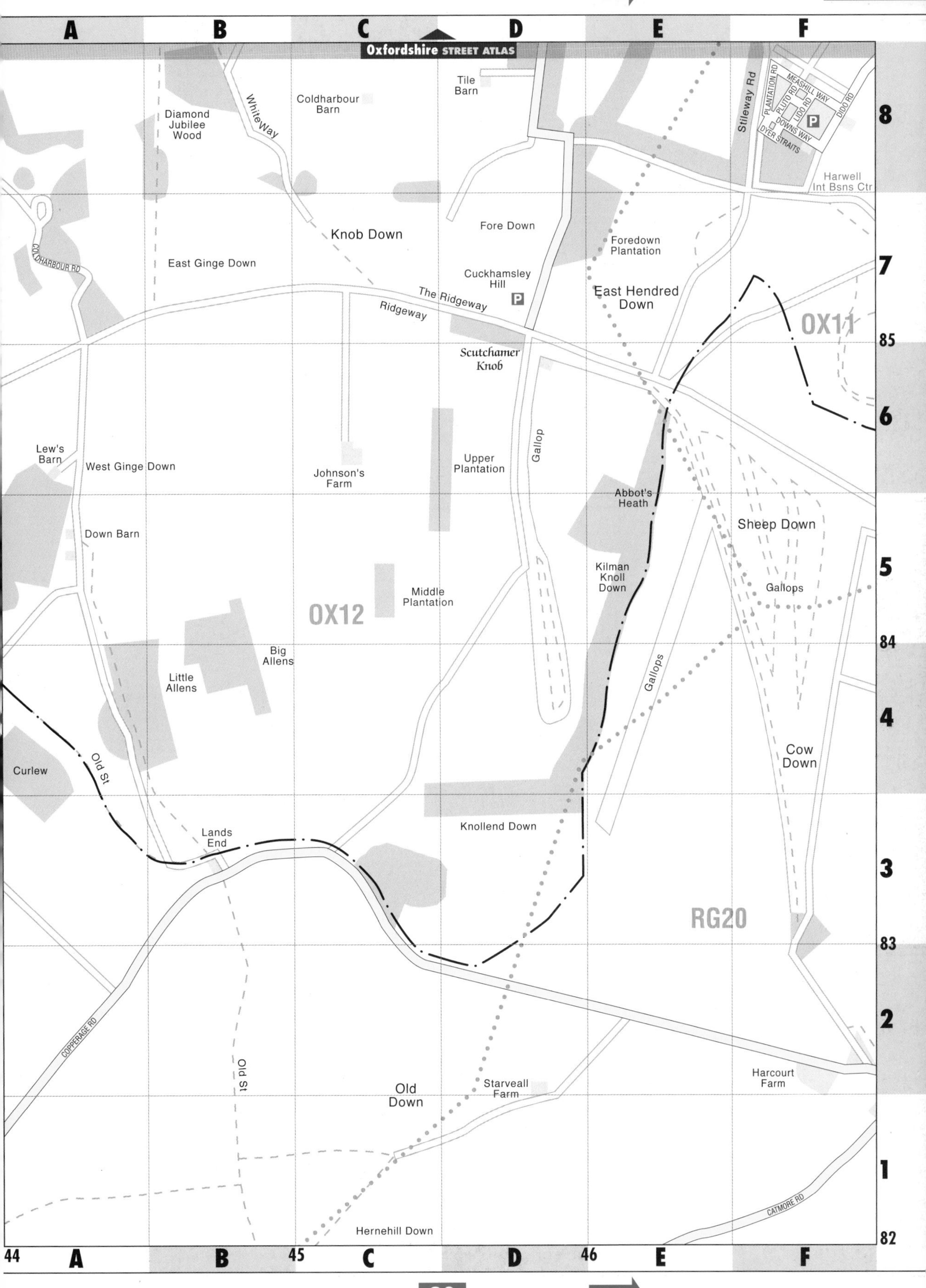

Oxfordshire STREET ATLAS
A
B
C
D
E
F
Diamond Jubilee Wood
White Way
Coldharbour Barn
Tile Barn
Stileway Rd
PLANTATION RD
MEASHILL WAY
PLUTO RD
LIDO RD
DIDO RD
DOWNS WAY
DYER STRAITS
Harwell Int Bsns Ctr
COLDHARBOUR RD
Knob Down
Fore Down
Foredown Plantation
East Ginge Down
Cuckhamsley Hill
East Hendred Down
The Ridgeway
Ridgeway
OX11
Scutchamer Knob
Lew's Barn
West Ginge Down
Johnson's Farm
Upper Plantation
Gallop
Abbot's Heath
Sheep Down
Down Barn
Kilman Knoll Down
Gallops
Middle Plantation
OX12
Big Allens
Little Allens
Gallops
Cow Down
Curlew
Old St
Lands End
Knollend Down
RG20
COPPERAGE RD
Old St
Old Down
Starveall Farm
Harcourt Farm
CATMORE RD
Hernehill Down
8
7
85
6
5
84
4
3
83
2
1
82
44
45
46

29
10

9

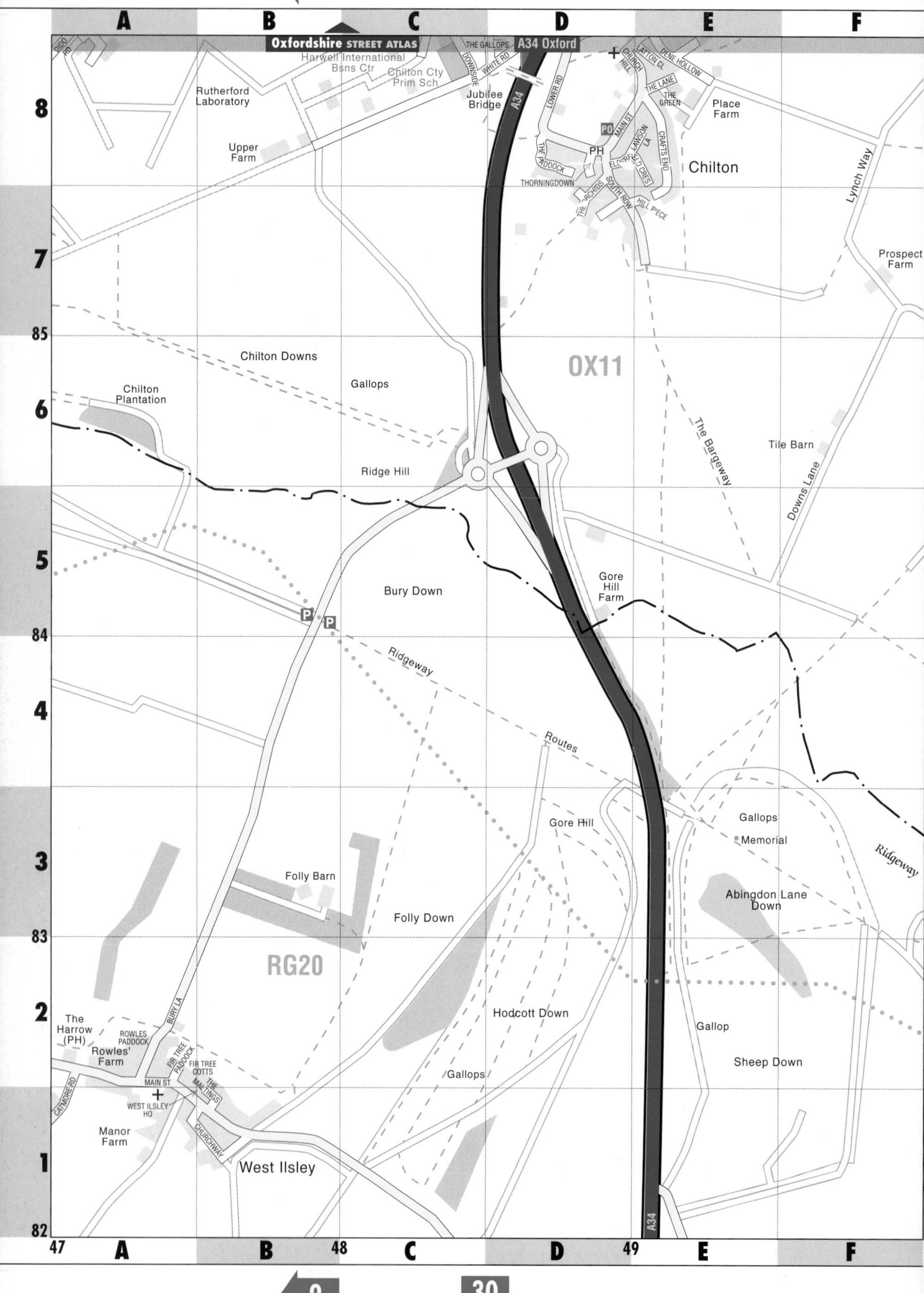
Oxfordshire STREET ATLAS
A34 Oxford
Harwell International Bsns Ctr
Chilton Cty Prim Sch
Rutherford Laboratory
Upper Farm
Jubilee Bridge
Place Farm
Chilton
Lynch Way
Prospect Farm
Chilton Downs
Gallops
OX11
Chilton Plantation
The Bargeway
Tile Barn
Ridge Hill
Downs Lane
Bury Down
Gore Hill Farm
Ridgeway
Routes
Gore Hill
Gallops
Memorial
Folly Barn
Folly Down
Abingdon Lane Down
RG20
Hodcott Down
The Harrow (PH)
Rowles' Farm
Gallop
Sheep Down
Gallops
Manor Farm
West Ilsley
A34

9
30

12

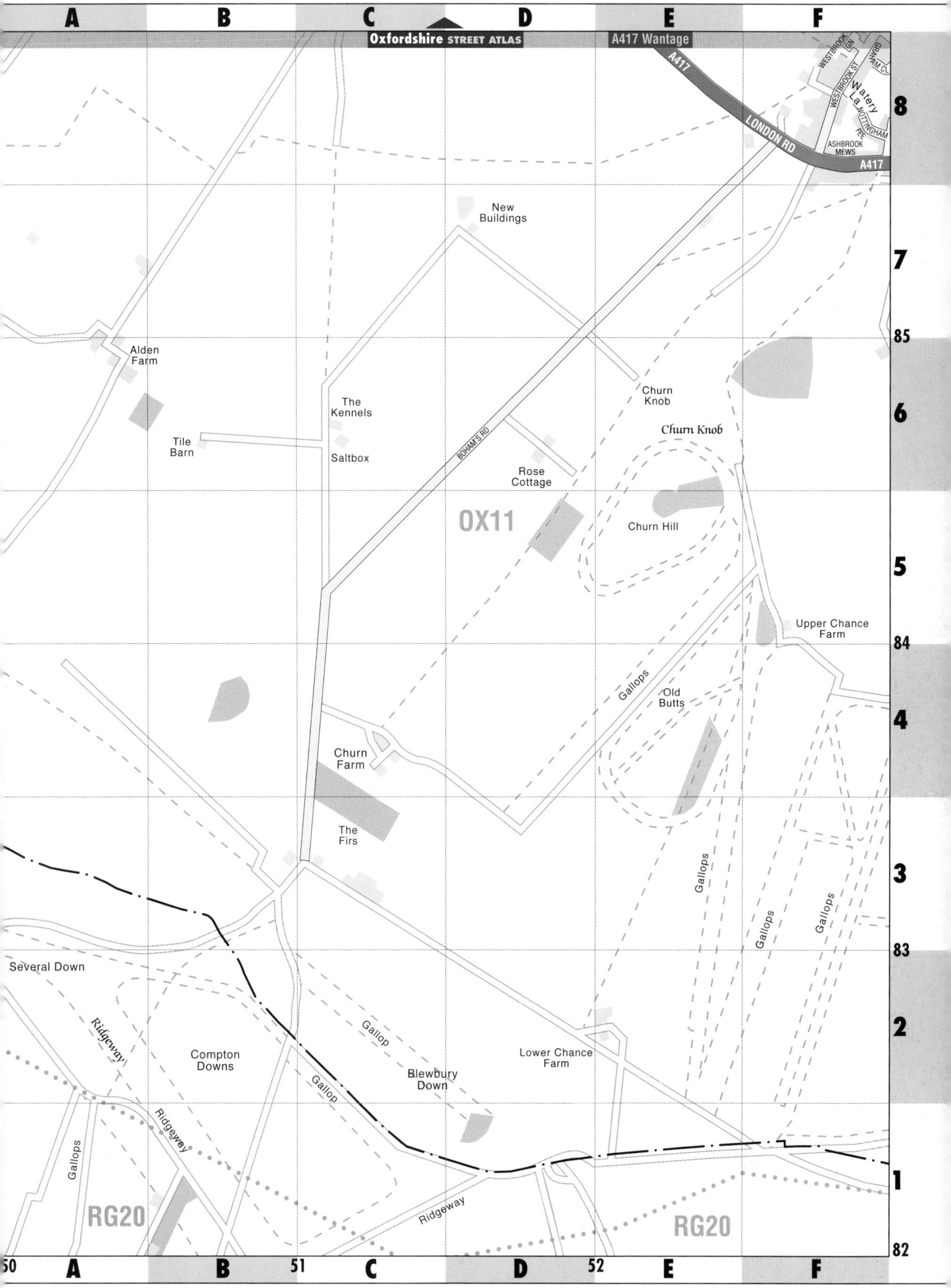

A B C D E F

Oxfordshire STREET ATLAS
A417 Wantage

A417
WESTBROOK GN
GRAHAM CL
WESTBROOK ST
Watery La
NOTTINGHAM FEE
LONDON RD
ASHBROOK MEWS
A417

8

New Buildings

7

85

Alden Farm
The Kennels
Churn Knob
Churn Knob
Tile Barn
Saltbox
BOHAM'S RD
Rose Cottage

6

OX11
Churn Hill

5

Upper Chance Farm

84

Gallops
Old Butts

4

Churn Farm
The Firs

3

Gallops
Gallops
Gallops

83

Several Down
Ridgeway
Gallop

2

Compton Downs
Lower Chance Farm
Blewbury Down
Gallop
Ridgeway
Gallops

1

Ridgeway
RG20
RG20

82

50 A B 51 C D 52 E F

31
12

11

Oxfordshire STREET ATLAS
A
B
C
D
E
F
8
7
85
6
5
84
4
3
83
2
1
82
53
54
55
Blewbury
CHURCH END
WATT'S LA
CHURCH RD
SOUTH ST
ROBINSON CL
EASTFIELD
B4016 BESSEL'S WAY
CHAPEL LA
RUMSEY'S
DIBLEYS
CRICKLEWOOD COTT
PH
A417
LONDON RD
BLEWBURY HILL
TREBLE HO TERR
1 NOTTINGHAM FEE
2 FORTY CROSS
THE PILGRIMS WAY
Huntsgrave Farm
Golf Driving Range
Blewbury Barn
Copse Style Farm
SPRING LA
PO
RECTORY LA
BAKER ST
THE CLOSE
DOWNS VIEW
ASTON ST
Aston Tirrold
CHALK HILL
WOODWAY RD
Downside Farm
Baldon Hill
Lid's Down
Gallop
Carrimers Farm
Riddle Hill
Chalk Hill Bottom
WHITE SHOOT
OX11
Sheepcot Farm
Woodway Hostel
Woodway
Lower Hill Barn
Hogtrough Bottom
Gallop
Upper Hill Barn
Big Bull Hill
Oven Bottom
Langdon Hill
The Plantation
Gallop
Gallops
Aston Upthorpe Downs
The Fair Mile
Unhill Bottom
Gallops
Fuller's Firs
Lowbury Hill
RG8
RG20
Dean's Bottom
Ridgeway

11
32

14

A B C D E F

Oxfordshire STREET ATLAS

PAPIST WAY

8

Westfield Farm

Lollingdon Farm

The Lynch

7

Lollingdon Hill

85

OX11

Bowslade

WESTFIELD RD

6

Offlands Court

OX10

Sheephouse Farm

Breach House

Breach Farm

A329

5

Cranford House Sch

WILLOW COURT LA

Stormerbank Kennels

HALFPENNY LA

WILLOW COTTS

THE STREET

GLEBE CL

Westfield Stables

84

Kingstanding Hill

4

MEADOW CL

Cholsey Downs

SHORTLANDS HILL

NORTH RD

UNDERHILL

Moulsford

North Unhill Bank

Starveall Farm

Moulsford Bottom

3

Greenlands Farm

COW LA

Unhill Bottom

83

Lingley Knoll

2

South Unhill Bank

Moulsford Downs

Well Barn

1

Ickleton Fields

WANTAGE RD A417

RG8

Unhill Wood

Unhill Bottom

82

56 A B 57 C D 58 E F

33

14

13

A
B
C
D
E
F
A329 Wallingford
Oxfordshire STREET ATLAS
WHITE HOUSE RD
CELSEA PL 1
WEEDON CL 2
CHARLES RD 3
ABBOTS MEAD
PAPIST WAY
FERRY WAY
Cholsey
Cholsey Marsh
(Nature Reserve)
B4009
READING RD
WATERLOO CL
Barracks
Farm
OX10
Littlestoke
Manor Farm
Ash
Cottage
HALFPENNY LA
Offlands
Farm
Cottages
Middle
Barn
Swan's Way
THE STREET
THE OAK
Moulsford
Prep Sch
River Thames
Watch
Folly
Ridgeway
White Hill
WALLINGFORD RD
Lower
Farm
Ivol
Barn
WOODCOTE RD
FERRY LA
FERRY RD
NORTH RD
Hotel
THAMESIDE REACH
South Stoke
Prim Sch
The
Bier Path
South
Stoke
UNDERHILL
FERRY LA
CROSS KEYS RD
PH
THE STREET
Sowberry
Court
Lower
Cadley's
CHAPEL CL
THE GARDENS
GLEBE
COTTS
COW LA
Thames Path
The Old
Vicarage
SOUTH
BANK
DEACONFIELD
RG8
Swan's Way
Grove Farm
House
GROVE RD
Sewage
Works
Grove
House
Runsford
Hole
Grove
Farm
Icknield Way
WALLINGFORD RD
PH
Spring
Farm
House
SPRING
FARM MEWS
BEECH LA
Streatley
Farm
Spring Farm
Cottages
ICKNIELD RD
A329
B4009
8
7
85
6
5
84
4
3
83
2
1
82
59
60
61

13
34

16

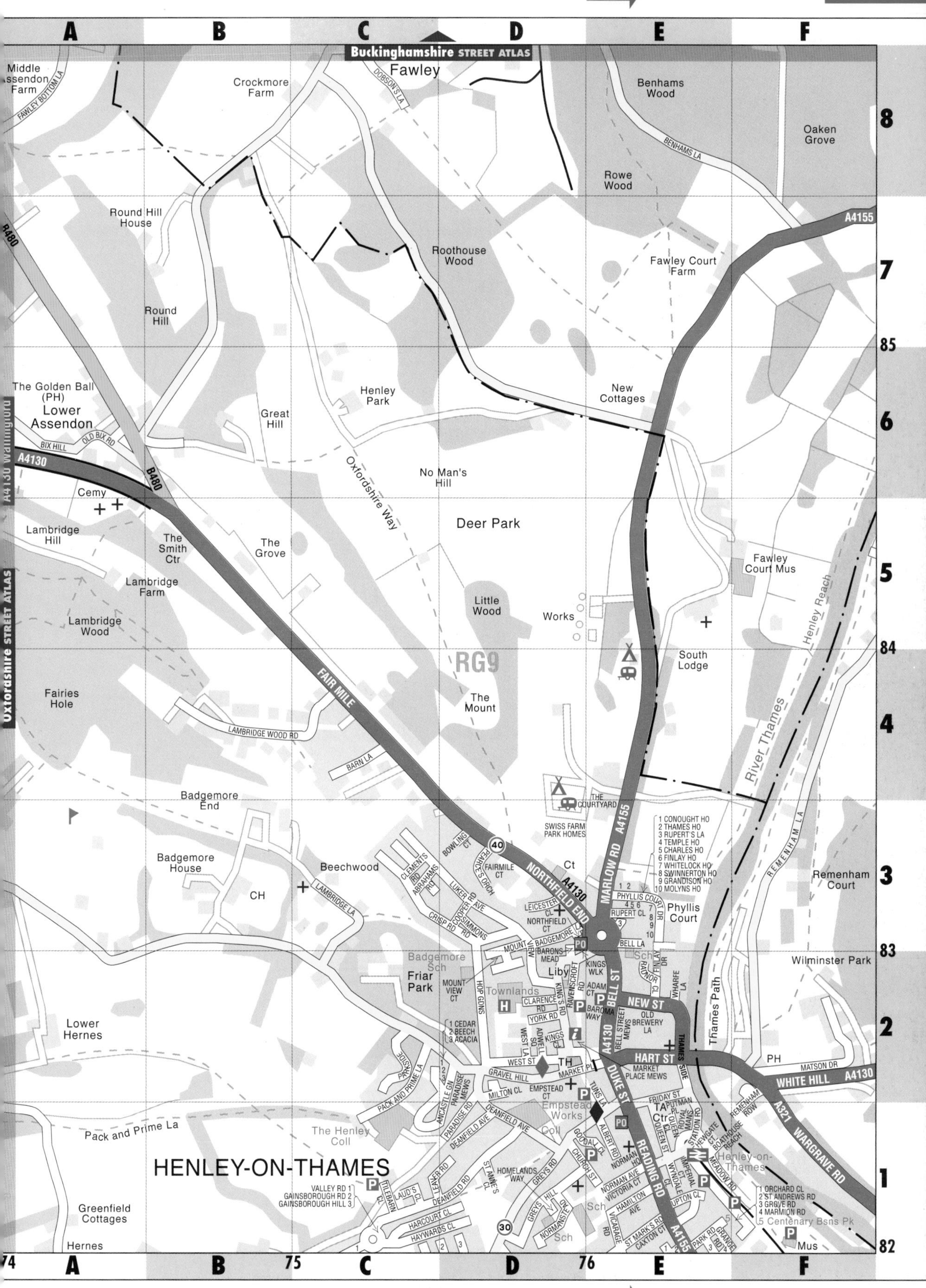
Buckinghamshire STREET ATLAS
Oxfordshire STREET ATLAS
Middle Assendon Farm
Crockmore Farm
Fawley
Benhams Wood
Oaken Grove
Rowe Wood
Round Hill House
Roothouse Wood
Fawley Court Farm
Round Hill
The Golden Ball (PH)
Lower Assendon
Great Hill
Henley Park
New Cottages
No Man's Hill
Oxfordshire Way
Deer Park
Cemy
Lambridge Hill
The Smith Ctr
The Grove
Lambridge Farm
Lambridge Wood
Little Wood
Works
Fawley Court Mus
South Lodge
Henley Reach
RG9
Fairies Hole
The Mount
River Thames
LAMBRIDGE WOOD RD
BARN LA
Badgemore End
THE COURTYARD
SWISS FARM PARK HOMES
Badgemore House
Beechwood
CH
Remenham Court
Phyllis Court
Wilminster Park
Badgemore Sch
Friar Park
Townlands
Lower Hernes
Thames Path
HENLEY-ON-THAMES
Pack and Prime La
The Henley Coll
Empstead Works
Henley-on-Thames
Greenfield Cottages
Hernes
FAIR MILE
NORTHFIELD END
MARLOW RD
BELL ST
NEW ST
HART ST
DUKE ST
READING RD
WHITE HILL
WARGRAVE RD
REMENHAM LA
A4130
A4155
B480
A321
1 CONOUGHT HO
2 THAMES HO
3 RUPERT'S LA
4 TEMPLE HO
5 CHARLES HO
6 FINLAY HO
7 WHITELOCK HO
8 SWINNERTON HO
9 GRANDISON HO
10 MOLYNS HO
1 CEDAR
2 BEECH
3 ACACIA
VALLEY RD 1
GAINSBOROUGH RD 2
GAINSBOROUGH HILL 3
1 ORCHARD CL
2 ST ANDREWS RD
3 GROVE RD
4 MARMION RD
5 Centenary Bsns Pk
Mus
PH
74
75
76
82
83
84
85

35
16

15

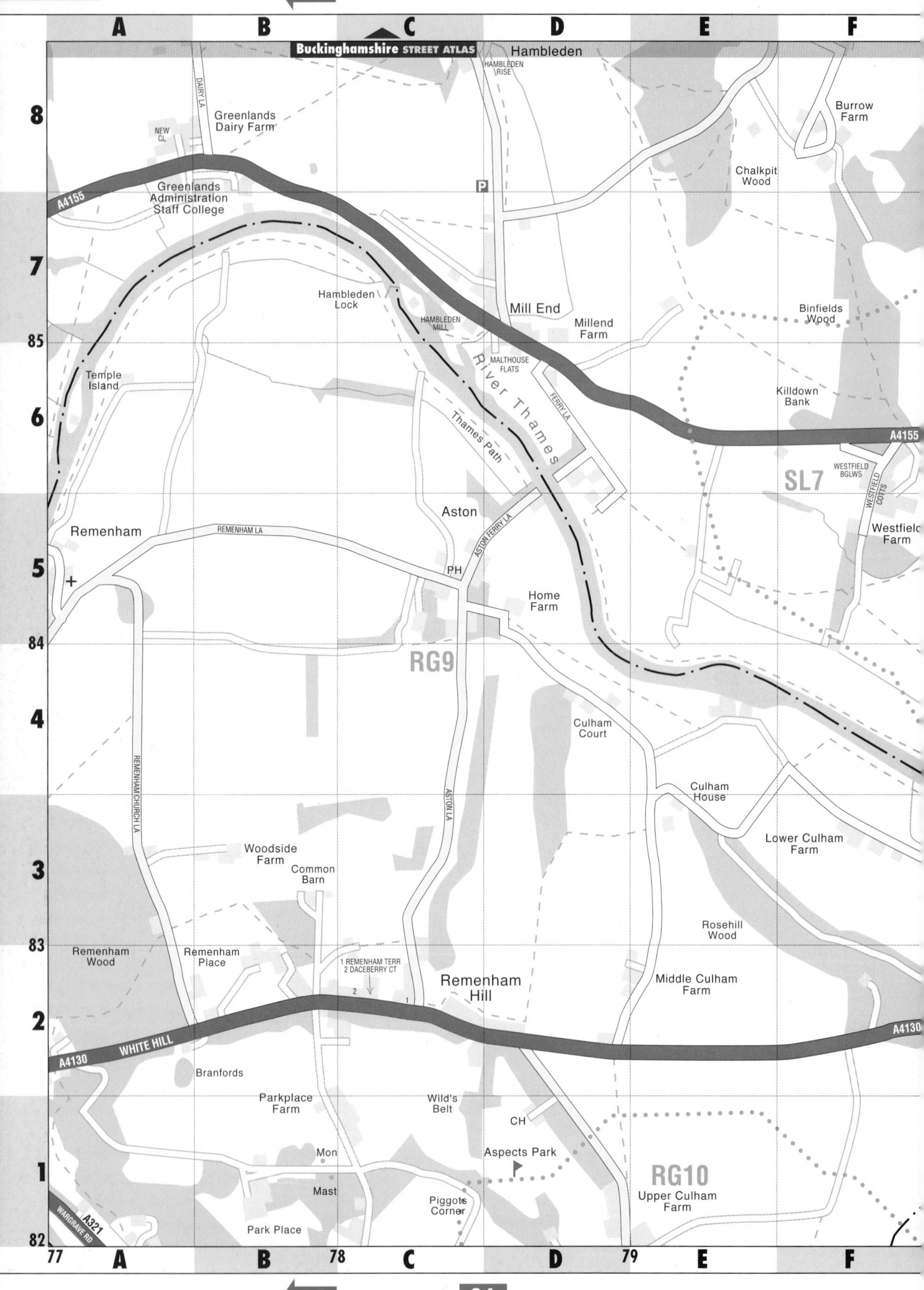

A
B
C
D
E
F
Buckinghamshire STREET ATLAS
Hambleden
HAMBLEDEN RISE
DAIRY LA
Greenlands Dairy Farm
NEW CL
Burrow Farm
8
Chalkpit Wood
A4155
Greenlands Administration Staff College
P
7
Hambleden Lock
Mill End
Millend Farm
Binfields Wood
HAMBLEDEN MILL
85
MALTHOUSE FLATS
River Thames
Temple Island
FERRY LA
Killdown Bank
Thames Path
6
A4155
WESTFIELD BGLWS
SL7
WESTFIELD COTTS
Aston
Remenham
REMENHAM LA
ASTON FERRY LA
Westfield Farm
5
PH
Home Farm
84
RG9
4
Culham Court
REMENHAM CHURCH LA
Culham House
ASTON LA
Lower Culham Farm
Woodside Farm
3
Common Barn
Rosehill Wood
83
Remenham Wood
Remenham Place
1 REMENHAM TERR
2 DACEBERRY CT
Remenham Hill
Middle Culham Farm
2
A4130
A4130
WHITE HILL
A4130
Branfords
Parkplace Farm
Wild's Belt
CH
Aspects Park
Mon
1
RG10
Mast
Piggots Corner
Upper Culham Farm
A321
WARGRAVE RD
Park Place
82
77
78
79

15
36

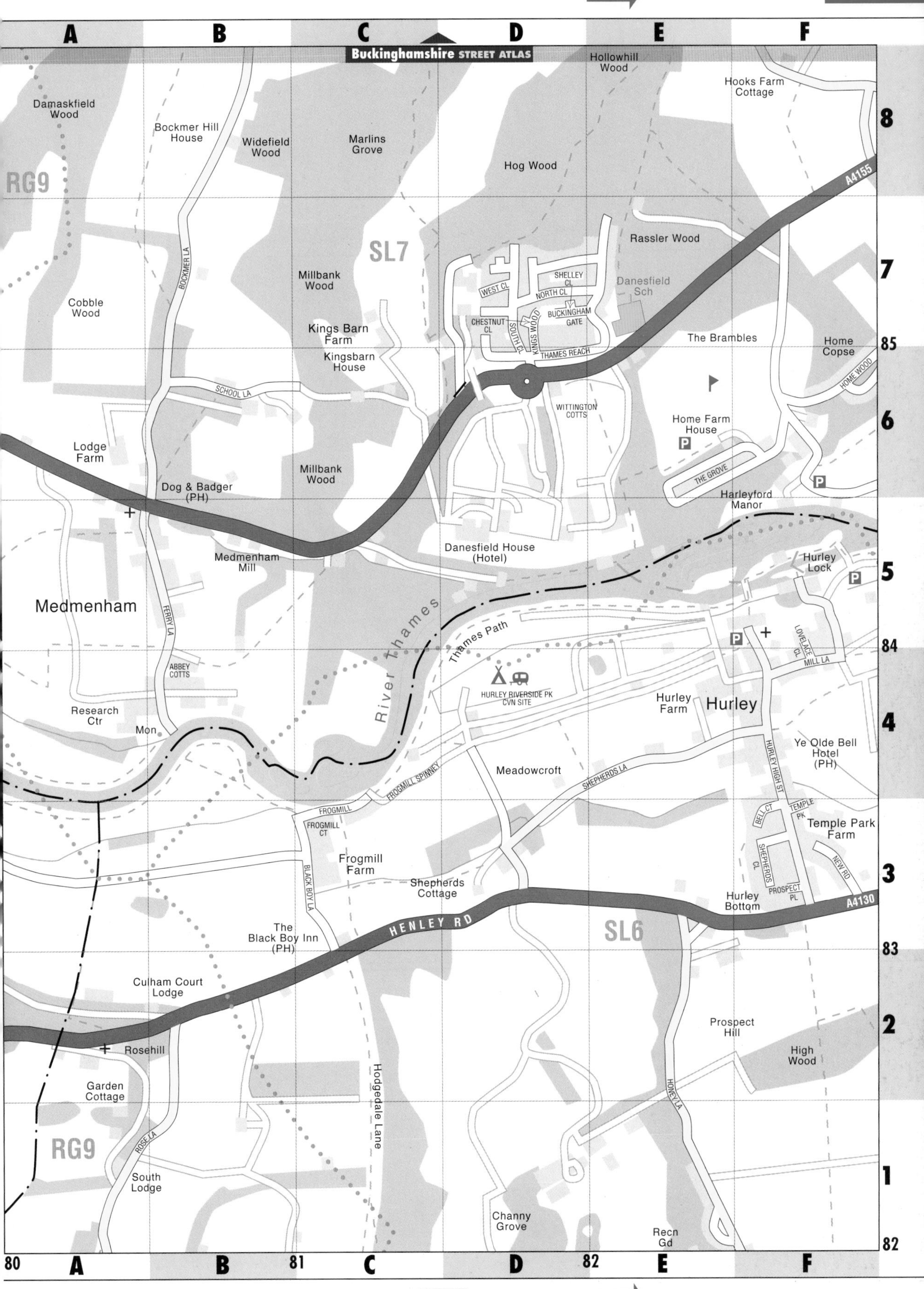
Buckinghamshire STREET ATLAS
A
B
C
D
E
F
Damaskfield Wood
RG9
Bockmer Hill House
Widefield Wood
Marlins Grove
Hollowhill Wood
Hooks Farm Cottage
Hog Wood
A4155
Rassler Wood
SL7
Millbank Wood
Cobble Wood
BOCKMER LA
SHELLEY CL
WEST CL
NORTH CL
Danesfield Sch
BUCKINGHAM GATE
CHESTNUT CL
SOUTH CL
KINGS WOOD
THAMES REACH
Kings Barn Farm
Kingsbarn House
The Brambles
Home Copse
HOME WOOD
SCHOOL LA
WITTINGTON COTTS
Home Farm House
Lodge Farm
Millbank Wood
THE GROVE
Dog & Badger (PH)
Harleyford Manor
Danesfield House (Hotel)
Medmenham Mill
Hurley Lock
Medmenham
FERRY LA
River Thames
Thames Path
LOVELACE CL
MILL LA
ABBEY COTTS
HURLEY RIVERSIDE PK CVN SITE
Research Ctr
Hurley Farm
Hurley
Mon
Ye Olde Bell Hotel (PH)
Meadowcroft
HURLEY HIGH ST
FROGMILL SPINNEY
SHEPHERDS LA
FROGMILL
FROGMILL CT
BELL CT
TEMPLE PK
Temple Park Farm
Frogmill Farm
SHEPHERDS CL
NEW RD
BLACK BOY LA
Shepherds Cottage
PROSPECT PL
Hurley Bottom
A4130
HENLEY RD
SL6
The Black Boy Inn (PH)
Culham Court Lodge
Prospect Hill
Rosehill
High Wood
Garden Cottage
HONEY LA
Hodgedale Lane
RG9
ROSE LA
South Lodge
Channy Grove
Recn Gd
8
7
85
6
5
84
4
3
83
2
1
82
80
81
82

17
1

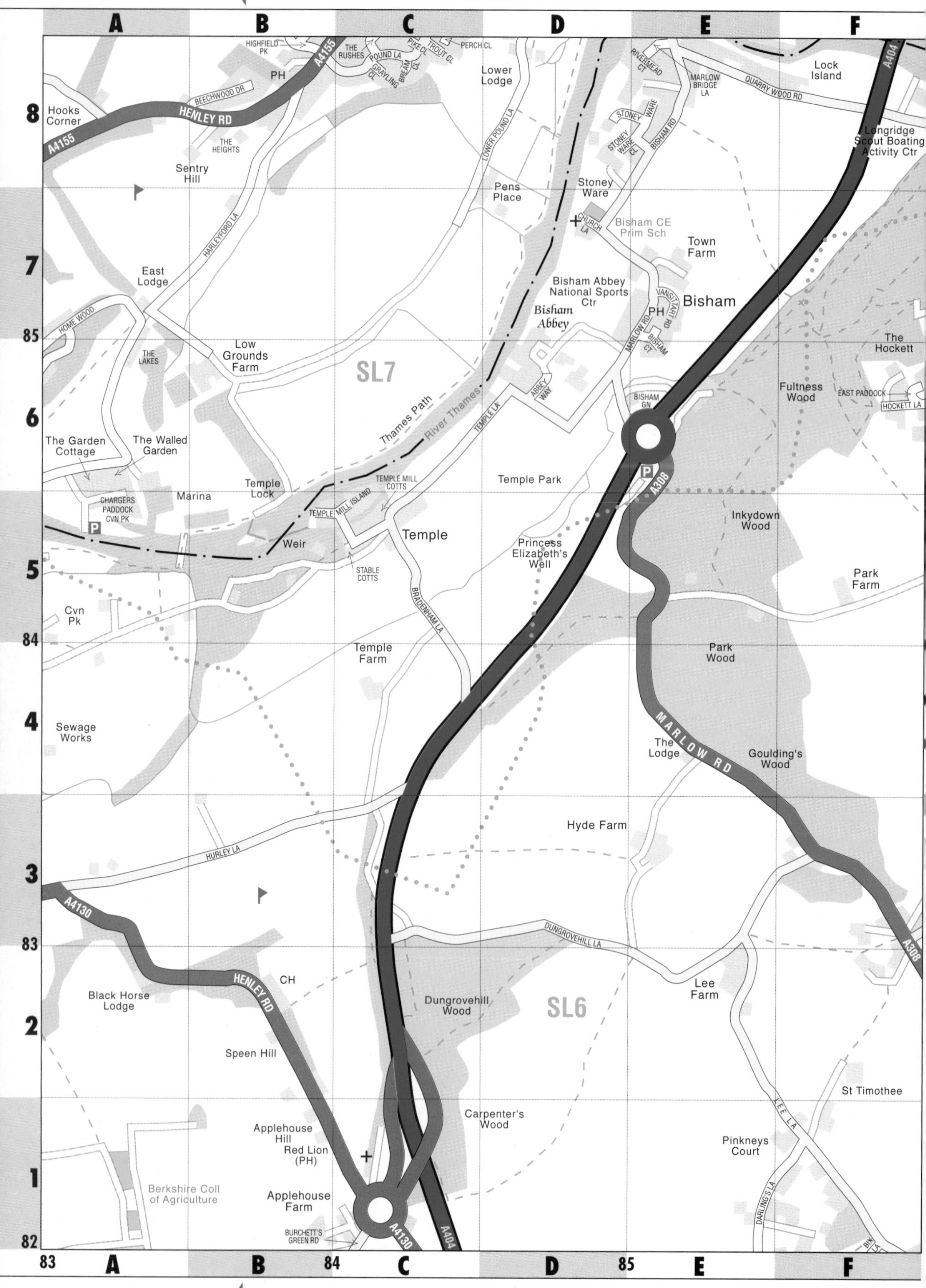
A
B
C
D
E
F
8
7
85
6
5
84
4
3
83
2
1
82
83
84
85
Hooks Corner
A4155
HENLEY RD
BEECHWOOD DR
HIGHFIELD PK
PH
THE RUSHES
POUND LA
PIKE CL
TROUT CL
PERCH CL
GRAYLING CL
BREAM CL
Lower Lodge
LOWER POUND LA
RIVERMEAD CT
MARLOW BRIDGE LA
QUARRY WOOD RD
Lock Island
A404
STONEY WARE
STONEY WARE CL
BISHAM RD
Longridge Scout Boating Activity Ctr
THE HEIGHTS
Sentry Hill
Pens Place
Stoney Ware
CHURCH LA
Bisham CE Prim Sch
Town Farm
HARLEYFORD LA
East Lodge
Bisham Abbey National Sports Ctr
Bisham Abbey
VANSITTART RD
PH
Bisham
MARLOW RD
BISHAM CT
HOME WOOD
THE LAKES
Low Grounds Farm
SL7
ABBEY WAY
The Hockett
Fultness Wood
EAST PADDOCK
HOCKETT LA
BISHAM GN
Thames Path
River Thames
TEMPLE LA
The Garden Cottage
The Walled Garden
Temple Park
Temple Lock
TEMPLE MILL COTTS
Marina
CHARGERS PADDOCK CVN PK
TEMPLE MILL ISLAND
A308
Inkydown Wood
Temple
Princess Elizabeth's Well
Weir
STABLE COTTS
Park Farm
Cvn Pk
BRADENHAM LA
Temple Farm
Park Wood
Sewage Works
MARLOW RD
The Lodge
Goulding's Wood
Hyde Farm
HURLEY LA
A4130
DUNGROVEHILL LA
A308
CH
HENLEY RD
Black Horse Lodge
Dungrovehill Wood
SL6
Lee Farm
Speen Hill
St Timothee
Carpenter's Wood
LEE LA
Applehouse Hill
Red Lion (PH)
Pinkneys Court
Berkshire Coll of Agriculture
Applehouse Farm
DARLING'S LA
BURCHETT'S GREEN RD
A4130
A404
BIX LA

17
38

2
20

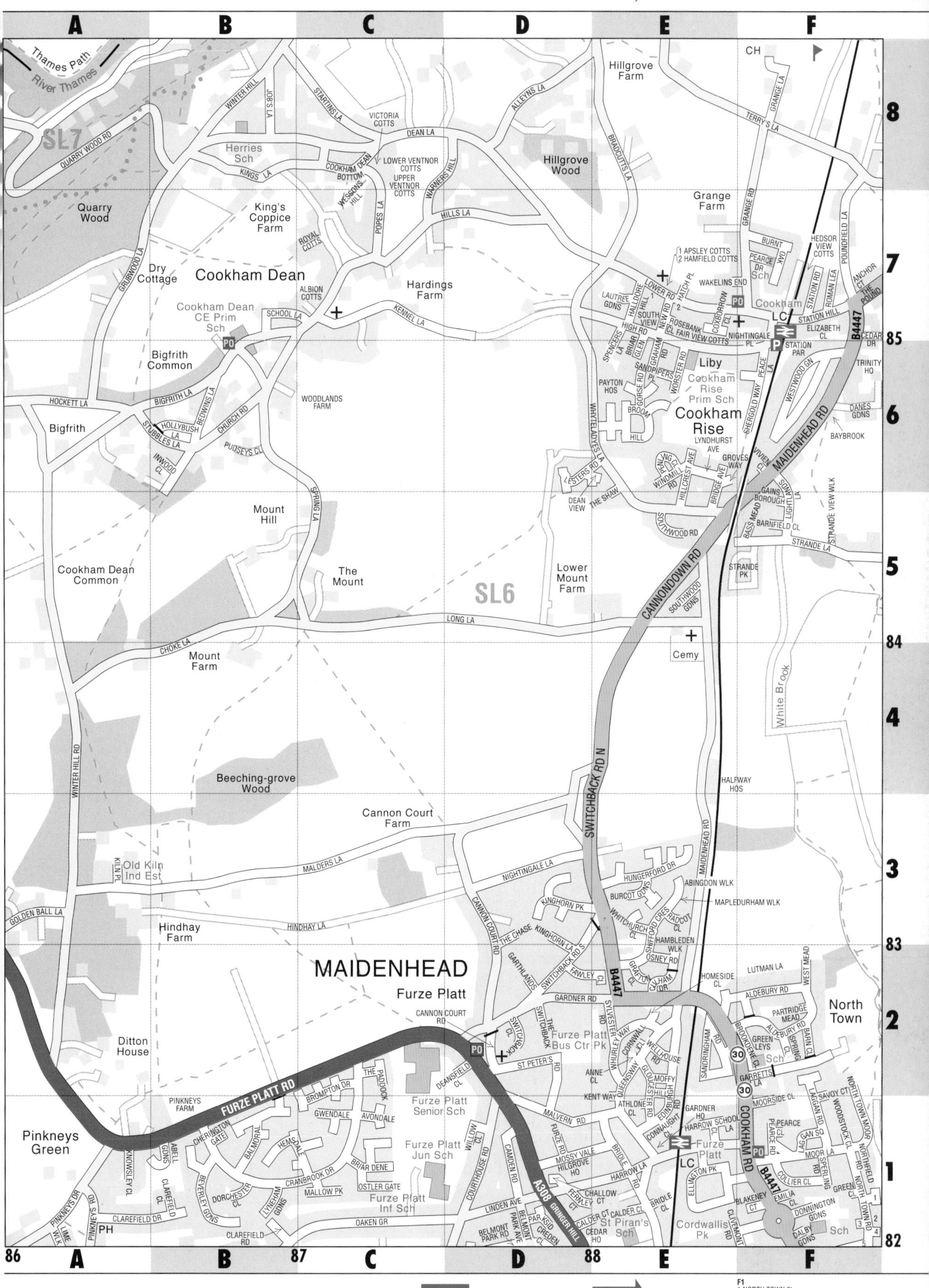
A
B
C
D
E
F
Thames Path
River Thames
SL7
QUARRY WOOD RD
Quarry Wood
Herries Sch
KINGS LA
King's Coppice Farm
Dry Cottage
Cookham Dean
Cookham Dean CE Prim Sch
Bigfrith Common
Bigfrith
HOCKETT LA
VICTORIA COTTS
DEAN LA
LOWER VENTNOR COTTS
UPPER VENTNOR COTTS
HILLS LA
Hardings Farm
KENNEL LA
Hillgrove Wood
Hillgrove Farm
Grange Farm
Cookham
Liby
Cookham Rise Prim Sch
Cookham Rise
MAIDENHEAD RD
B4447
CANNONDOWN RD
Mount Hill
The Mount
SL6
Lower Mount Farm
LONG LA
Cemy
Cookham Dean Common
Mount Farm
White Brook
WINTER HILL RD
Beeching-grove Wood
Cannon Court Farm
SWITCHBACK RD N
Old Kiln Ind Est
MALDERS LA
NIGHTINGALE LA
Hindhay Farm
HINDHAY LA
GOLDEN BALL LA
MAIDENHEAD
Furze Platt
North Town
Ditton House
FURZE PLATT RD
Pinkneys Green
Furze Platt Senior Sch
Furze Platt Jun Sch
Furze Platt Inf Sch
Furze Platt Bus Ctr Pk
COOKHAM RD
A308
St Piran's Sch
Cordwallis Pk
8
7
85
6
5
84
4
3
83
2
1
82
86
87
88
F1
1 NORTH TOWN CL
2 ALYSON CT
3 NORTH GN
4 NORTH TOWN MEAD
5 NORTHDEAN

39
20

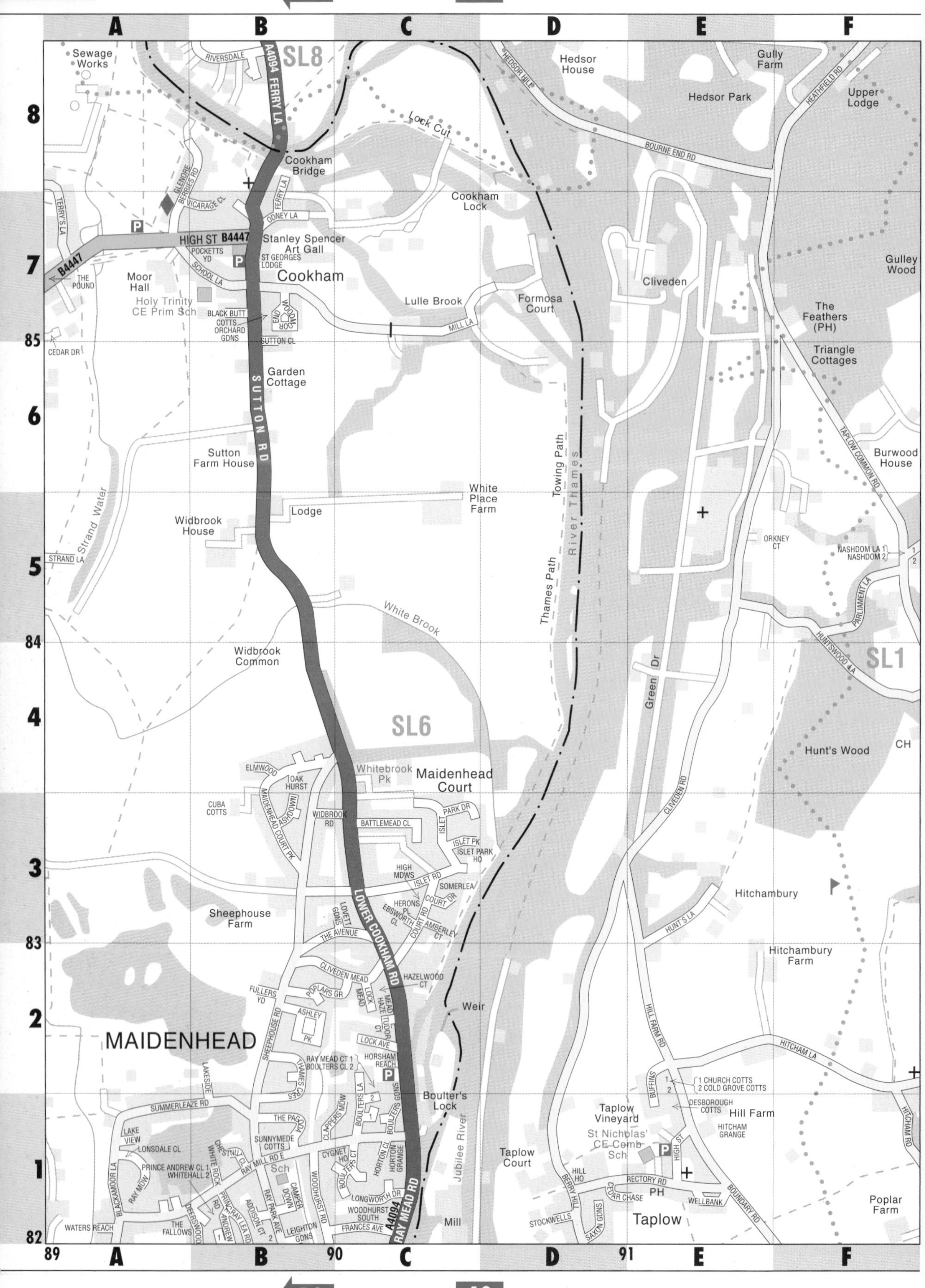
19
3
A B C D E F
Sewage Works
SL8
A4094 FERRY LA
RIVERSDALE
Hedsor House
Gully Farm
Hedsor Park
Upper Lodge
HEDSOR HILL
HEATHFIELD RD
Lock Cut
BOURNE END RD
Cookham Bridge
Cookham Lock
GLENORE
BERRIES RD
VICARAGE CL
FERRY LA
ODNEY LA
TERRY'S LA
HIGH ST B4447
B4447
Stanley Spencer Art Gall
POCKETTS YD
ST GEORGES LODGE
Cookham
SCHOOL LA
THE POUND
Moor Hall
Holy Trinity CE Prim Sch
BLACK BUTT COTTS
ORCHARD GDNS
WOODMOOR END
SUTTON CL
Lulle Brook
MILL LA
Formosa Court
Cliveden
Gulley Wood
The Feathers (PH)
Triangle Cottages
CEDAR DR
Garden Cottage
SUTTON RD
Sutton Farm House
Towing Path
River Thames
White Place Farm
TAPLOW COMMON RD
Burwood House
Strand Water
Widbrook House
Lodge
ORKNEY CT
NASHDOM LA 1
NASHDOM 2
STRAND LA
Thames Path
PARLIAMENT LA
White Brook
HUNTSWOOD LA
SL1
Widbrook Common
Green Dr
SL6
Hunt's Wood
CH
ELMWOOD
OAK HURST
Whitebrook Pk
Maidenhead Court
CUBA COTTS
MAIDENHEAD COURT PK
ASHDOWN
WIDBROOK RD
BATTLEMEAD CL
ISLET
PARK DR
ISLET PK
ISLET PARK HO
CLIVEDEN RD
HIGH MDWS
ISLET RD
SOMERLEA
COURT DR
Hitchambury
Sheephouse Farm
LOVETT GDNS
HERONS PL
EBSWORTH CL
COURT RD
AMBERLEY CT
THE AVENUE
LOWER COOKHAM RD
HUNT'S LA
Hitchambury Farm
CLIVEDEN MEAD
HAZELWOOD CT
FULLERS YD
POPLARS GR
LOCK MEAD
HAZE TUDOR
MEAD CT
Weir
ASHLEY PK
SHEEPHOUSE RD
MAIDENHEAD
LOCK AVE
HILL FARM RD
HITCHAM LA
RAY MEAD CT 1
BOULTERS CL 2
HORSHAM REACH
THAMES CRES
LAKESIDE
BOULTERS LA
BOULTERS GDNS
Boulter's Lock
BUFFINS
1 CHURCH COTTS
2 COLD GROVE COTTS
DESBOROUGH COTTS
Hill Farm
HITCHAM GRANGE
HITCHAM RD
Taplow Vineyard
St Nicholas' CE Comb Sch
SUMMERLEAZE RD
THE PAGODA
LAKE VIEW
LONSDALE CL
SUNNYMEDE COTTS
CLAPPERS MDW
Jubilee River
Taplow Court
HIGH ST
CHESTNUT
WHITE ROCK
RAY MILL RD E
CYGNET HO
HORTON CL
HORTON GRANGE
BOULTERS CT
PRINCE ANDREW CL 1
WHITEHALL 2
Sch
HILL HO
RECTORY RD
BLACKAMOOR LA
RAY MDW
PRINCE ANDREW
RAY LEA RD
ADDISON CT
RAY PARK AVE
CAMPER DOWN
WOODHURST RD
LONGWORTH DR
WOODHURST SOUTH
A4094 RAY MEAD RD
FERRY HILL
CEDAR CHASE
PH
WELLBANK
BOUNDARY RD
Poplar Farm
STOCKWELLS
SAXON GDNS
Taplow
Mill
WATERS REACH
THE FALLOWS
DEERSWOOD
LEIGHTON GDNS
FRANCES AVE
8
7
85
6
5
84
4
3
83
2
1
82
89
90
91
19
40

22

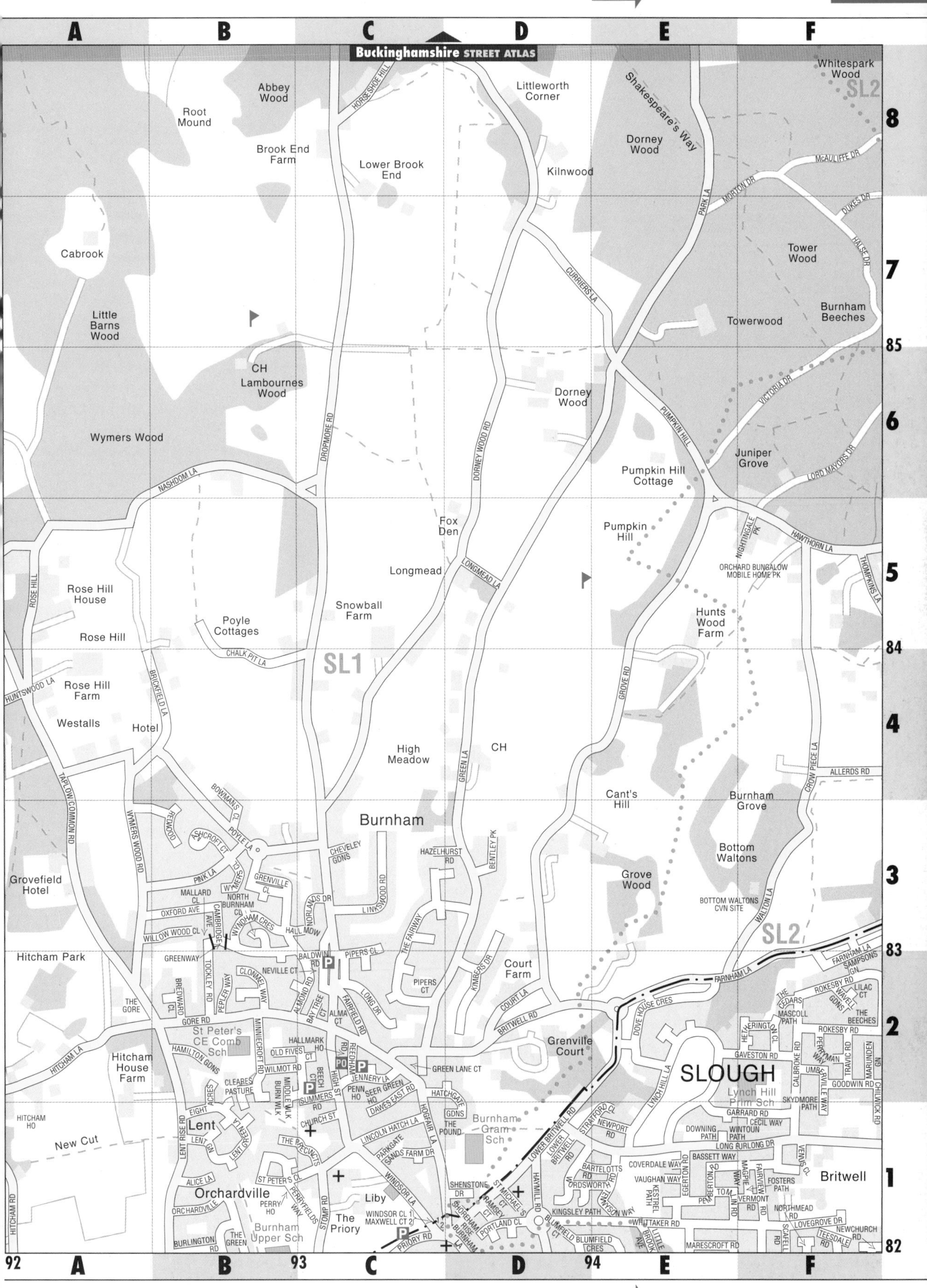

Buckinghamshire STREET ATLAS
Abbey Wood
Root Mound
Brook End Farm
Lower Brook End
Littleworth Corner
Dorney Wood
Kilnwood
Shakespeare's Way
Whitespark Wood
SL2
Cabrook
Little Barns Wood
CH
Lambournes Wood
Wymers Wood
Tower Wood
Towerwood
Burnham Beeches
Dorney Wood
Juniper Grove
Pumpkin Hill Cottage
Pumpkin Hill
Fox Den
Longmead
Snowball Farm
Rose Hill House
Rose Hill
Poyle Cottages
SL1
Rose Hill Farm
Westalls
Hotel
Hunts Wood Farm
Orchard Bungalow Mobile Home Pk
High Meadow
CH
Cant's Hill
Burnham Grove
Burnham
Bottom Waltons
Grove Wood
Grovefield Hotel
Bottom Waltons Cvn Site
SL2
Hitcham Park
Court Farm
Grenville Court
St Peter's CE Comb Sch
Hitcham House Farm
SLOUGH
Lynch Hill Prim Sch
Burnham Gram Sch
Hitcham Ho
New Cut
Lent
Orchardville
Liby
The Priory
Burnham Upper Sch
Britwell

21

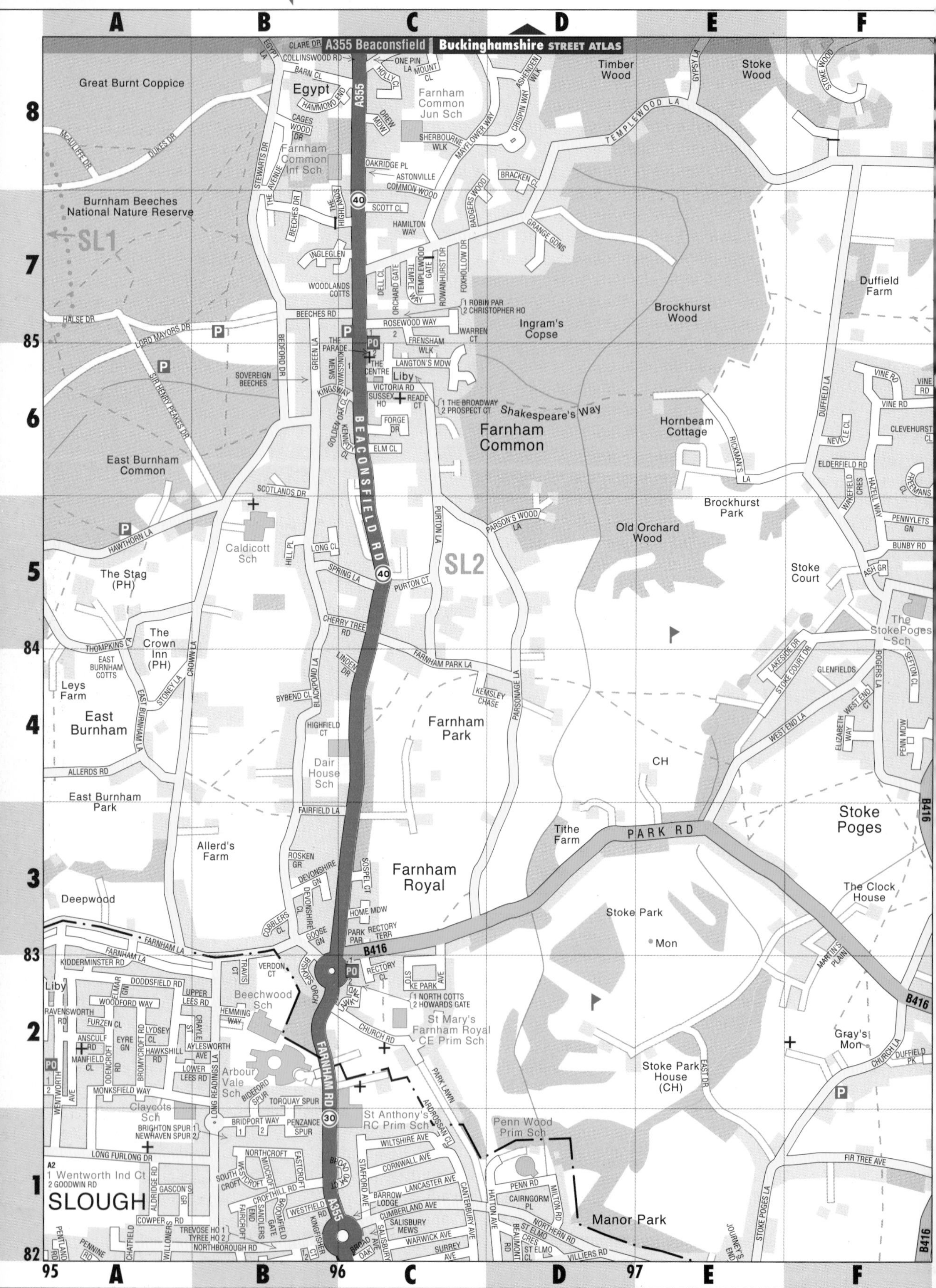
A355 Beaconsfield
Buckinghamshire STREET ATLAS
Great Burnt Coppice
Egypt
Farnham Common Jun Sch
Farnham Common Inf Sch
Timber Wood
Stoke Wood
Burnham Beeches National Nature Reserve
SL1
Brockhurst Wood
Duffield Farm
Ingram's Copse
Shakespeare's Way
Farnham Common
Hornbeam Cottage
East Burnham Common
Caldicott Sch
Brockhurst Park
Old Orchard Wood
SL2
BEACONSFIELD RD
The Stag (PH)
The Crown Inn (PH)
Stoke Court
The StokePoges Sch
Leys Farm
East Burnham
Farnham Park
Dair House Sch
East Burnham Park
Allerd's Farm
Tithe Farm
PARK RD
Stoke Poges
Farnham Royal
Deepwood
Stoke Park
The Clock House
Beechwood Sch
St Mary's Farnham Royal CE Prim Sch
Arbour Vale Sch
Claycots Sch
St Anthony's RC Prim Sch
Gray's Mon
Stoke Park House (CH)
Penn Wood Prim Sch
FARNHAM RD
SLOUGH
Manor Park
A2
1 Wentworth Ind Ct
2 GOODWIN RD
B416
A355

21
42

Buckinghamshire STREET ATLAS
M40 High Wycombe
M40 London (A40)
A412 Uxbridge (A4007)
The Pickeridge
Fulmer Hall
Fulmer
Fox & Pheasant (PH)
Stoke Common
Shakespeare's Way
The Black Horse (PH)
Church Farm
Fulmer Inf Sch
Fulmer House Farm
Furzeney Wood
Watersplash Farm
Alder Bourne
Penn Wood
Fernacres Farm
Frame Wood
Mill House Farm
Fulmer Common
Hollybush Hill
Fairfield Lodge
Teikyo Sch (UK)
Upton Wood
Upton Lake
Upton Farm
Sefton Park
Sefton Park Sch
Twin Trees Farm
The Thames Valley Nuffield
Wexham Street
Rowley Wood
Iver Heath
Sports Ctr
Black Park Country Park
Blackpark Lake
Visitor Ctr
Gallions Wood
Berry Farm
Spring Wood
Rowley Farm
Bell Farm
Rowley Lake
Red Lion (PH)
Wexham Park
Stoke Place
Stoke Green
William Hartley Yd
SL2
SL3
SL9
WINDSOR RD
GERARDS CROSS RD
BELLS HILL
GRAYS PARK RD
STOKE RD
STOKE COMMON RD
WINDMILL RD
FRAMEWOOD RD
FULMER COMMON RD
BLACK PARK RD
ROWLEY LA
WEXHAM ST
UXBRIDGE RD
WEXHAM PARK LA
HOLLYBUSH HILL
FARTHING GREEN LA
Galleons La
8
7
85
6
5
84
4
3
83
2
1
82
98
99
00

4

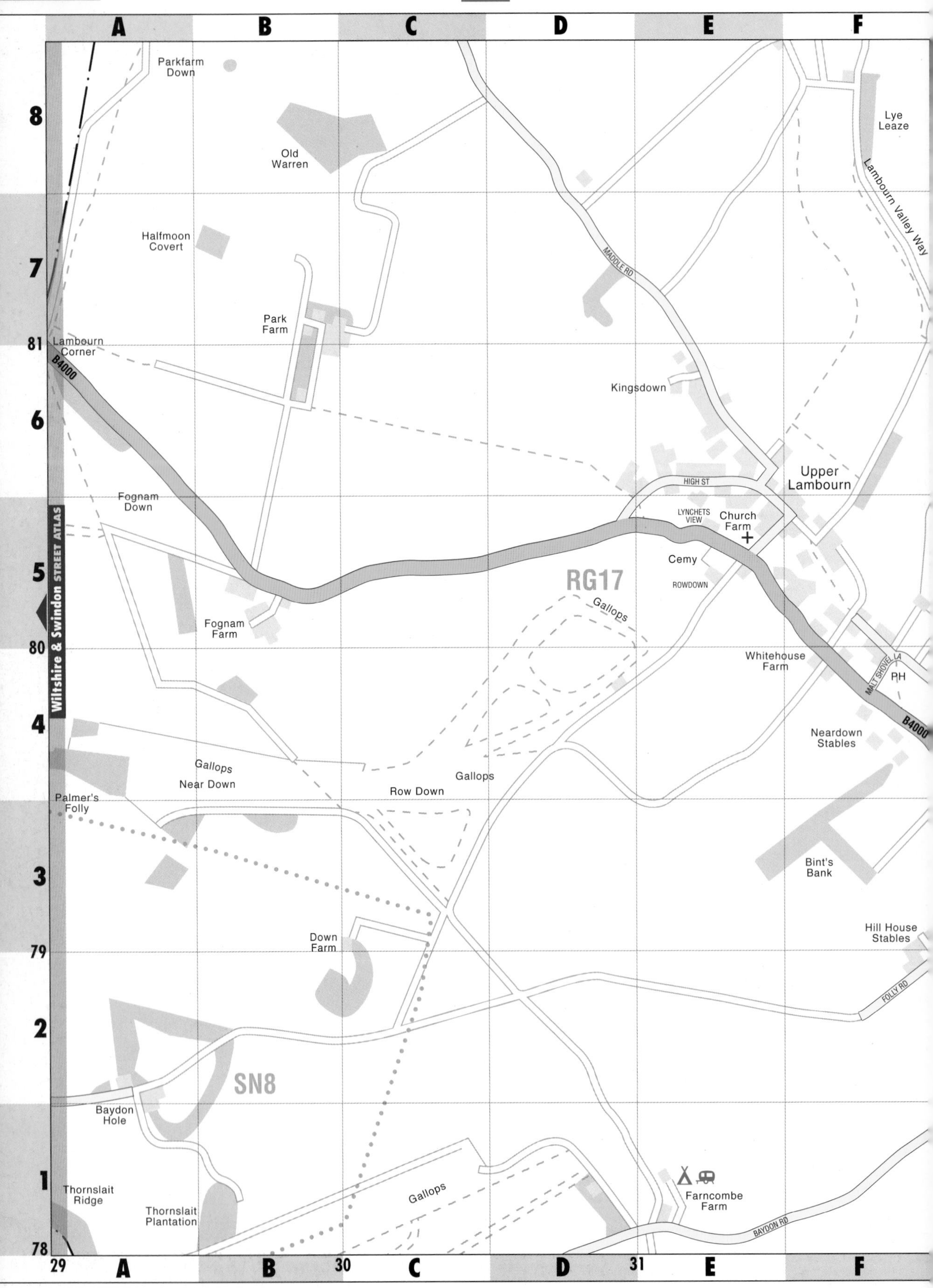

A
B
C
D
E
F
8
7
81
6
5
80
4
3
79
2
1
78
29
30
31
Parkfarm Down
Old Warren
Halfmoon Covert
Park Farm
Lambourn Corner
B4000
Fognam Down
Fognam Farm
Wiltshire & Swindon STREET ATLAS
Lye Leaze
Lambourn Valley Way
MADDLE RD
Kingsdown
HIGH ST
Upper Lambourn
LYNCHETS VIEW
Church Farm
Cemy
RG17
ROWDOWN
Gallops
Whitehouse Farm
MALT SHOVEL LA
PH
B4000
Neardown Stables
Gallops
Near Down
Row Down
Gallops
Palmer's Folly
Bint's Bank
Hill House Stables
Down Farm
FOLLY RD
SN8
Baydon Hole
Thornslait Ridge
Thornslait Plantation
Gallops
Farncombe Farm
BAYDON RD

45

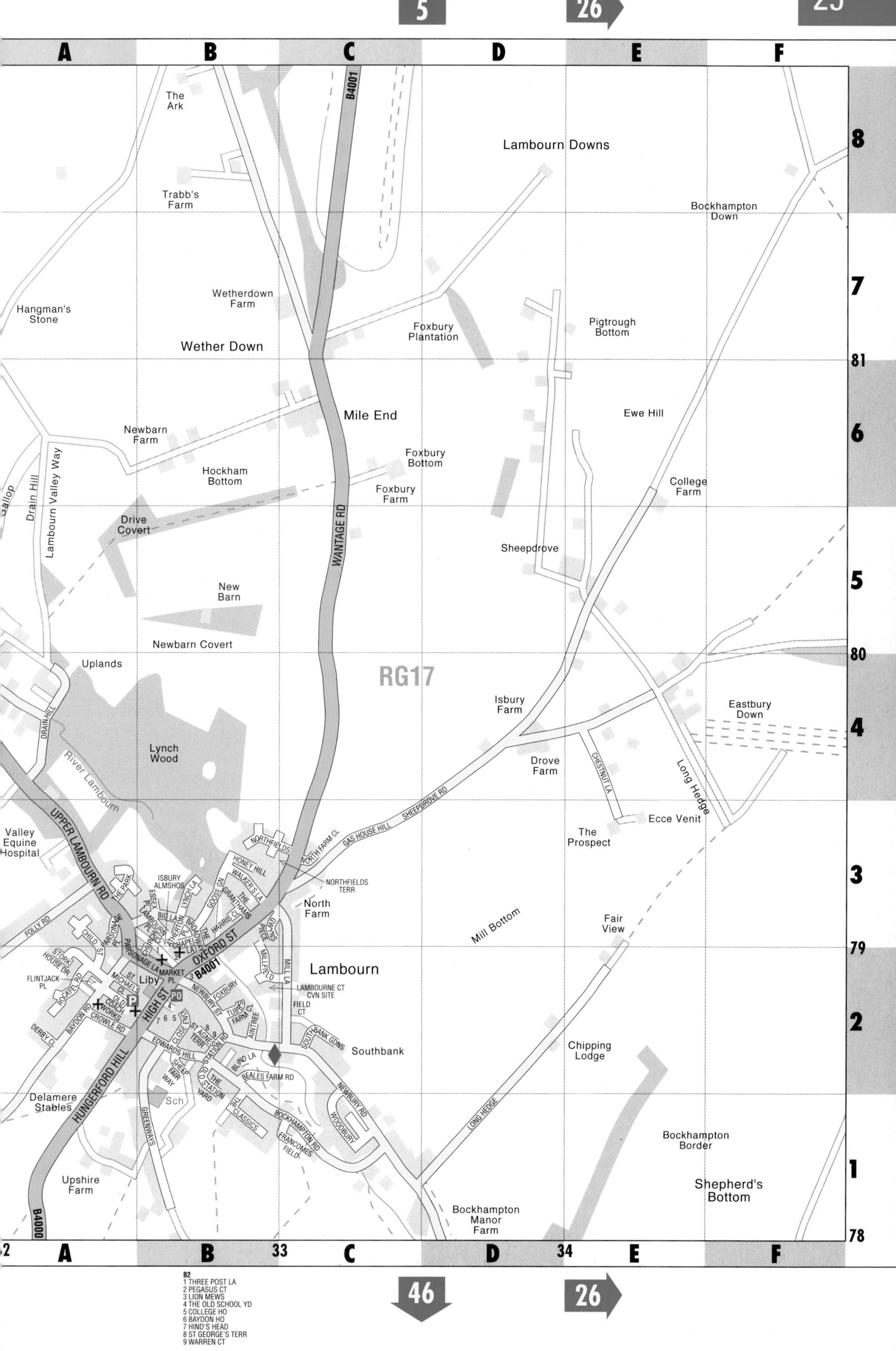
5
26
A
B
C
D
E
F
8
7
81
6
5
80
4
3
79
2
1
78
33
34
46
The Ark
Trabb's Farm
Lambourn Downs
Bockhampton Down
Hangman's Stone
Wetherdown Farm
Wether Down
Foxbury Plantation
Pigtrough Bottom
Mile End
Ewe Hill
Newbarn Farm
Hockham Bottom
Foxbury Bottom
Foxbury Farm
College Farm
Drive Covert
Drain Hill
Lambourn Valley Way
Gallop
Sheepdrove
New Barn
Newbarn Covert
Uplands
RG17
Isbury Farm
Eastbury Down
Lynch Wood
River Lambourn
Drove Farm
Long Hedge
Valley Equine Hospital
UPPER LAMBOURN RD
WANTAGE RD
B4001
CHESTNUT LA
Ecce Venit
The Prospect
SHEEPDROVE RD
GAS HOUSE HILL
NORTH FARM CL
NORTHFIELDS
NORTHFIELDS TERR
HONEY HILL
WALKER'S LA
ISBURY ALMSHOS
THE PARK
North Farm
Mill Bottom
Fair View
FOLLY RD
OXFORD ST
Lambourn
MILL LA
LAMBOURNE CT CVN SITE
FIELD CT
Liby
MARKET PL
HIGH ST
NEWBURY ST
SOUTHBANK GDNS
Southbank
Chipping Lodge
FLINTJACK PL
DERBY CL
BAYDON RD
CROWLE RD
EDWARDS HILL
BLIND LA
BEALES FARM RD
HUNGERFORD HILL
Delamere Stables
Sch
GREENWAYS
NEWBURY RD
WOODBURY
BOCKHAMPTON RD
FRANCOMES FIELD
LONG HEDGE
Bockhampton Border
Upshire Farm
Shepherd's Bottom
Bockhampton Manor Farm
B4000
B2
1 THREE POST LA
2 PEGASUS CT
3 LION MEWS
4 THE OLD SCHOOL YD
5 COLLEGE HO
6 BAYDON HO
7 HIND'S HEAD
8 ST GEORGE'S TERR
9 WARREN CT

25 6

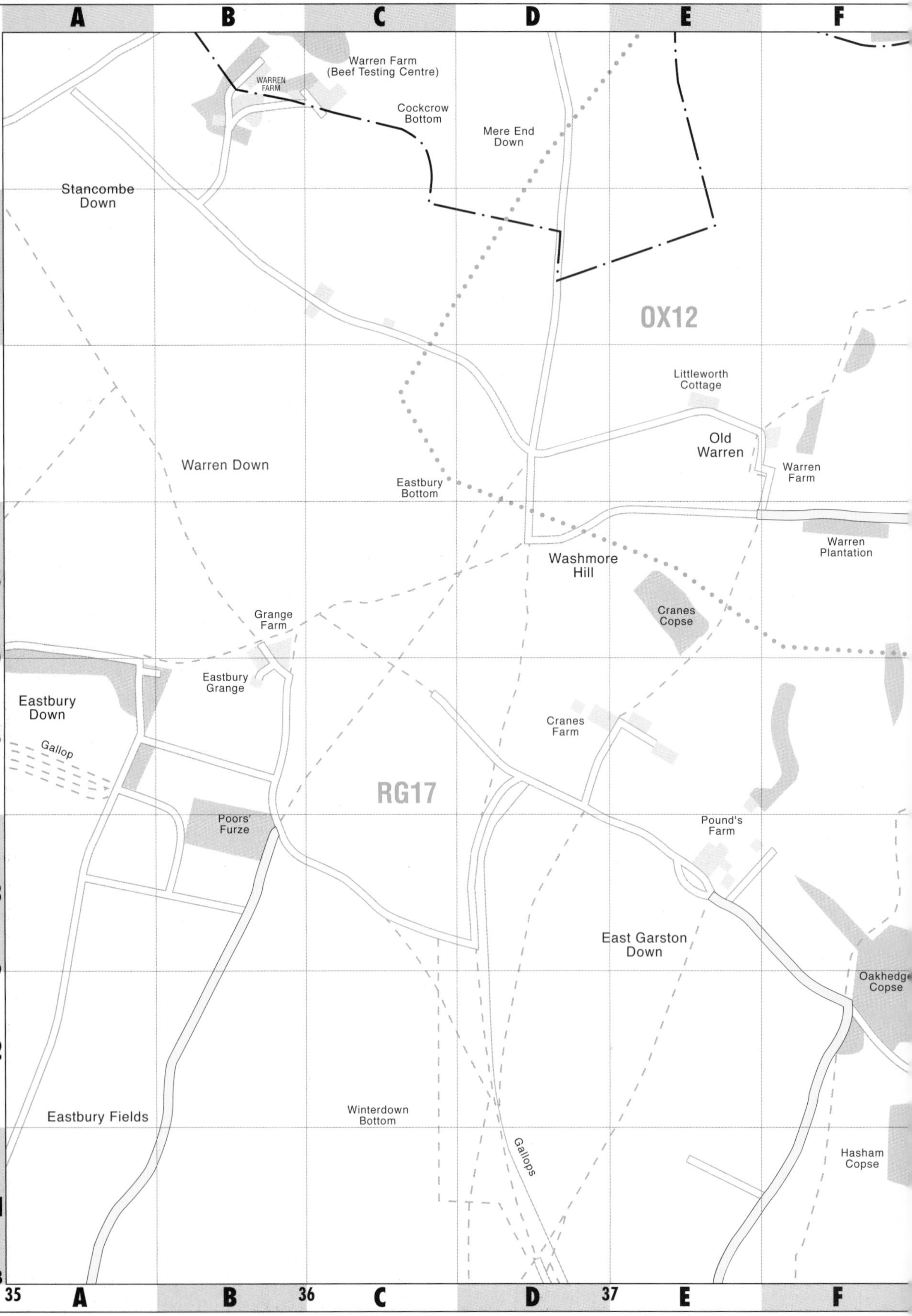

A B C D E F
8
7
81
6
5
80
4
3
79
2
1
78
Warren Farm
(Beef Testing Centre)
WARREN
FARM
Cockcrow
Bottom
Mere End
Down
Stancombe
Down
OX12
Littleworth
Cottage
Old
Warren
Warren
Farm
Warren Down
Eastbury
Bottom
Washmore
Hill
Warren
Plantation
Cranes
Copse
Grange
Farm
Eastbury
Grange
Eastbury
Down
Gallop
Cranes
Farm
RG17
Poors'
Furze
Pound's
Farm
East Garston
Down
Oakhedge
Copse
Eastbury Fields
Winterdown
Bottom
Gallops
Hasham
Copse
35 A B 36 C D 37 E F

25 47

7
28
A
B
C
D
E
F
8
7
81
6
5
80
4
3
79
2
1
78
38
39
40
A338
Pit Plantation
North Farm
CHESTNUT CL
THE GREENWAY
Fawley
Mast
The Beeches
Woolley Down
WELLHILL RD
Greenway Cottages
Gallops
Woolley Down Cottages
Monument
OX12
The Rookery
South Fawley
South Fawley Farm
Lower Barn
Furze Border
Field Border
Dogkennel Cottage
Dogkennel Copse
DOGKENNEL LA
Woolley Farm
Mitchell Copse
Well Copse
Coldharbour Plantation
Two Acre Plantation
Whatcombe
Nun's Walk
Gallop
Whatcombe Copse
RG20
Manor Farm
Kite Hill
RG17
Hasham Copse
Lady Copse
Whatcombe Upper Copse
Henley Farm
BUTTSFIELD RD
48
28

27
8

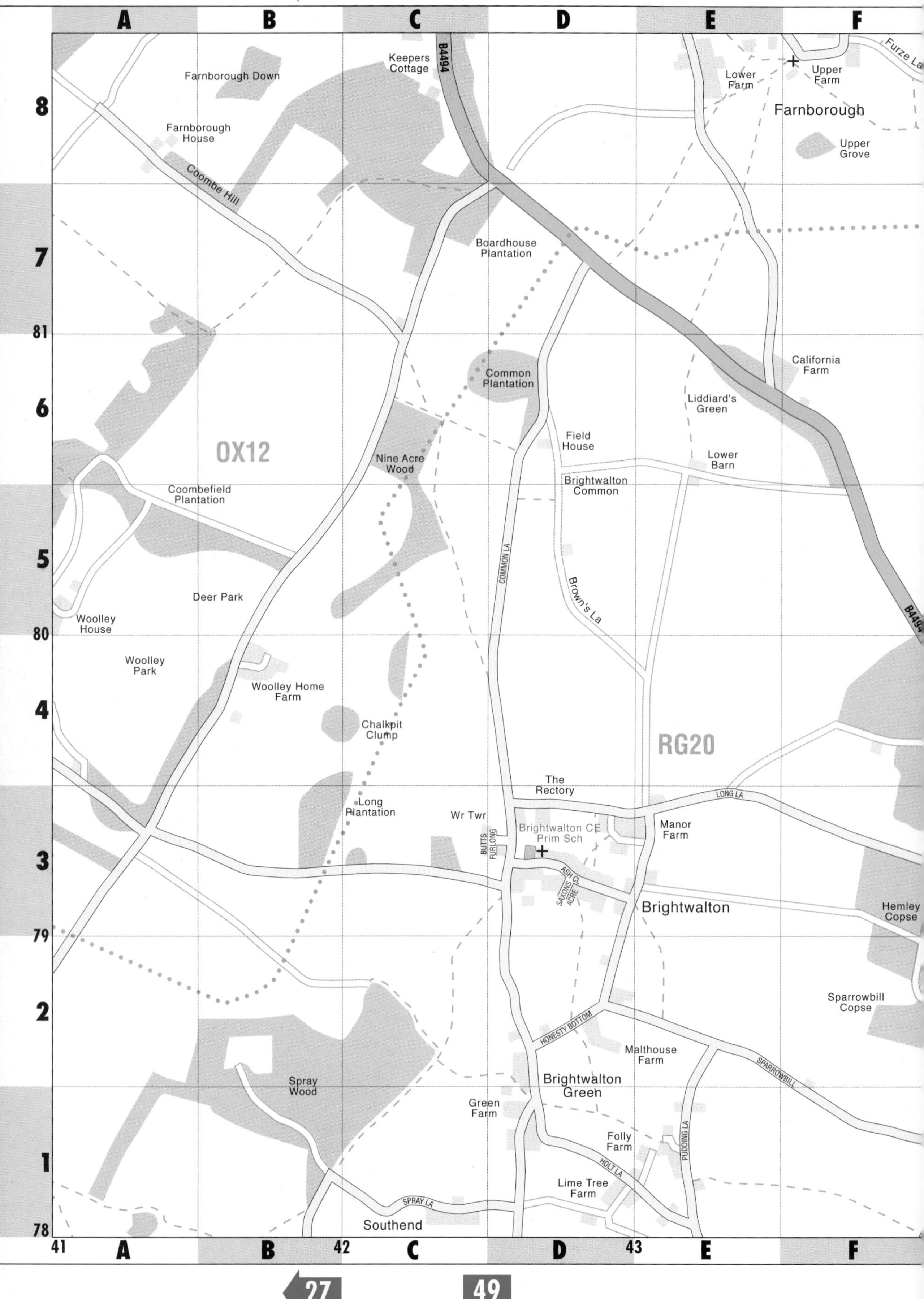
A
B
C
D
E
F
8
7
81
6
5
80
4
3
79
2
1
78
41
42
43
Farnborough Down
Keepers Cottage
B4494
Lower Farm
Upper Farm
Furze La
Farnborough
Upper Grove
Farnborough House
Coombe Hill
Boardhouse Plantation
OX12
Common Plantation
California Farm
Liddiard's Green
Field House
Nine Acre Wood
Lower Barn
Coombefield Plantation
Brightwalton Common
COMMON LA
Deer Park
Brown's La
Woolley House
Woolley Park
Woolley Home Farm
Chalkpit Clump
RG20
The Rectory
LONG LA
Long Plantation
Wr Twr
Brightwalton CE Prim Sch
Manor Farm
BUTTS FURLONG
ASH CL
SAXONS ACRE
Brightwalton
Hemley Copse
Sparrowbill Copse
HONESTY BOTTOM
Malthouse Farm
SPARROWBILL
Spray Wood
Brightwalton Green
Green Farm
Folly Farm
PUDDING LA
HOLT LA
Lime Tree Farm
SPRAY LA
Southend

27
49

9
30
A
B
C
D
E
F
Furze La
OX12
Whiteshute Row
Old St
Old Down Row
Parkwood
The Barracks
8
7
Heath Copse
CATMORE RD
Hodcott Copse
81
Hodcott Buildings
Wickslett Copse
Wickslett Row North
6
Woolvers Borders
High Robins
Catmore
Old St
Woolvers Barn
5
Catmore Farm
Dark La
80
RG20
Parson's Row
Round Copse
4
Lilley
Warren Row
Redlane Barn
The Old Fox & Cubs (PH)
REDLANE RD
Lilley Copse
Hunham Copse
Witnam's Copse
Wilkins Barne
Redlane Wood
Green La
LONG LA
3
The Broadway
Witnam's Barn
79
Earl's Grove
Larches
SHEEP LEAZE LA
Heath Barn
Barrow Hill
2
Old Street La
Whitelands
FIELD RD
HAILEY LA
SPARROWBILL
Rowdown Farm
1
B4494
PEASEMORE HILL
Hailey Copse
78
4
A
B
45
C
D
46
E
F
50
30

29
10

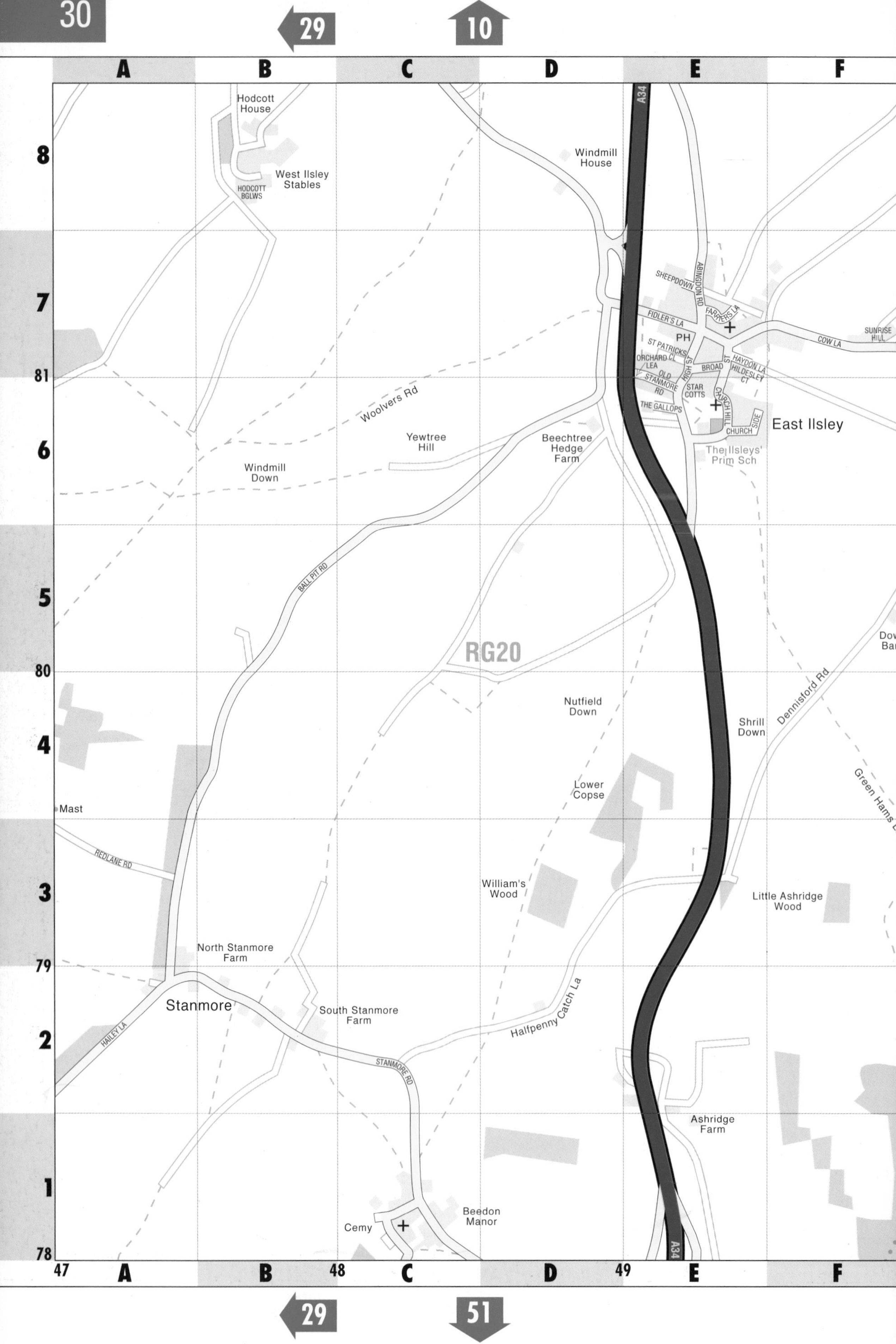
A
B
C
D
E
F
8
7
81
6
5
80
4
3
79
2
1
78
47
48
49
A34
Hodcott House
West Ilsley Stables
HODCOTT BGLWS
Windmill House
SHEEPDOWN
ABINGDON RD
FARRIERS LA
FIDLER'S LA
PH
COW LA
SUNRISE HILL
ST PATRICKS CL
ORCHARD LEA
OLD STANMORE RD
HIGH ST
BROAD
ST HAYDON LA
HILDESLEY CT
STAR COTTS
THE GALLOPS
CHURCH HILL
CHURCH SIDE
East Ilsley
The Ilsleys' Prim Sch
Woolvers Rd
Yewtree Hill
Beechtree Hedge Farm
Windmill Down
BALL PIT RD
RG20
Dow Bar
Nutfield Down
Shrill Down
Dennisford Rd
Green Hams La
Lower Copse
Mast
REDLANE RD
William's Wood
Little Ashridge Wood
North Stanmore Farm
Stanmore
South Stanmore Farm
Halfpenny Catch La
HAILEY LA
STANMORE RD
Ashridge Farm
Beedon Manor
Cemy

29
51

11
32

A
B
C
D
E
F
Ridgeway
Ilsley Barn Farm
East Ilsley Down
Roden Farm
8
7
81
6
5
80
4
3
79
2
1
78
Ilsley Arch
Compton Downs
Superity Farm
SUPERITY COTTS
Stocks Farm
DENISFORD RD
Inst for Animal Health
Thorndown Folly
RG20
CHURN RD
WHITEWALLS CL
WALLINGFORD RD
HOCKHAM RD
MEADOW CL
RODEN DOWN MEWS
CHEAP ST
HORN ST
Hostel
PH
YEW TREE STABLES
Compton
Old Station Bsns Pk
COMPTON MANOR
HIGH ST
PO
ILSLEY RD
MANOR BGLWS
YEW TREE MEWS
CHURCH FARM BARNS
FAIRFIELD
WESTFIELDS
Mayfield Farm
MAYFIELD COTTS
NEWBURY LA
MANOR CRES
GORDON CRES
SCHOOL RD
WILSON CL
Church Farm
Compton CE Prim Sch
BURRELL RD
SHEPHERDS RISE
ALDWORTH RD
The Downs Sch
Recn Ctr
SHEPHERDS MOUNT
CHESERIDGE RD
SHEPHERDS HILL
Warnham's Cottages
Cradlicote Coppice
Hawk Croft Copse
Hill Barn
Ash Close
Woodview
New Farm
COOMBE RD
WARNHAM LA
Cheseridge Farm
River Pang
Green Hams La
Compton Crossing
Compton Wood
Ashridge Wood
Cheseridge Wood
Cow Down
Woodend Farm
RG18
50
51
52

52
32

31
12
A
B
C
D
E
F
8
7
81
6
5
80
4
3
79
2
1
78
53
54
55
Roden Downs
Warren Farm
Town Copse
Ridgeway
Starveall
Streatley Warren
Crows Foot
Bower Farm
Grey Ladies
RG20
RG8
Uplands Stables
DOWNS RD
The Red Lion (PH)
Applepie Hill
AMBURY RD
The Bell Inn (PH)
Hungerford Green
Parsonage Green
BELL LA
B4009
THE GLEBE
TOWNSEND RD
COOMBE RD
Dumworth Farm
Pibworth Farm
READING RD
Aldworth
Woodrows Farm
Fayleys Border
Aces High
Four Points
The Four Points (PH)
Foxborough Copse
Southfield Shaw
HAW LA
Lower Point Cottage
De La Beche
RG18
Thorn Hill
B4009
31
53

13
34

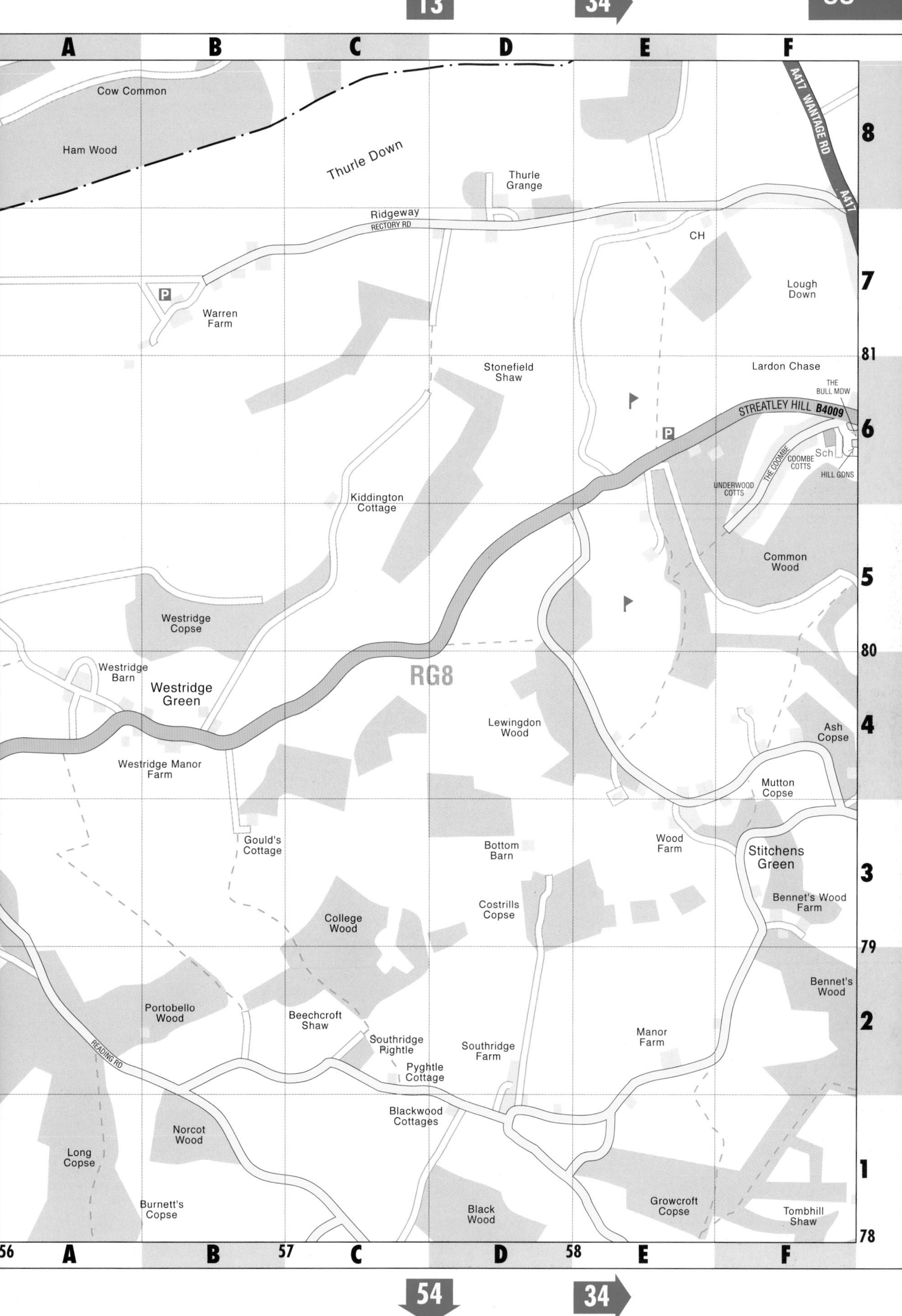
A
B
C
D
E
F
Cow Common
Ham Wood
Thurle Down
Thurle Grange
Ridgeway
RECTORY RD
A417 WANTAGE RD
A417
CH
Warren Farm
Lough Down
Stonefield Shaw
Lardon Chase
THE BULL MDW
STREATLEY HILL B4009
THE COOMBE
COOMBE COTTS
Sch
HILL GDNS
UNDERWOOD COTTS
Kiddington Cottage
Common Wood
Westridge Copse
Westridge Barn
Westridge Green
RG8
Lewingdon Wood
Ash Copse
Westridge Manor Farm
Mutton Copse
Gould's Cottage
Bottom Barn
Wood Farm
Stitchens Green
Bennet's Wood Farm
Costrills Copse
College Wood
Bennet's Wood
Portobello Wood
Beechcroft Shaw
Southridge Pightle
Southridge Farm
Manor Farm
READING RD
Pyghtle Cottage
Blackwood Cottages
Norcot Wood
Long Copse
Burnett's Copse
Black Wood
Growcroft Copse
Tombhill Shaw
8
7
81
6
5
80
4
3
79
2
1
78
56
57
58

54
34

33
14

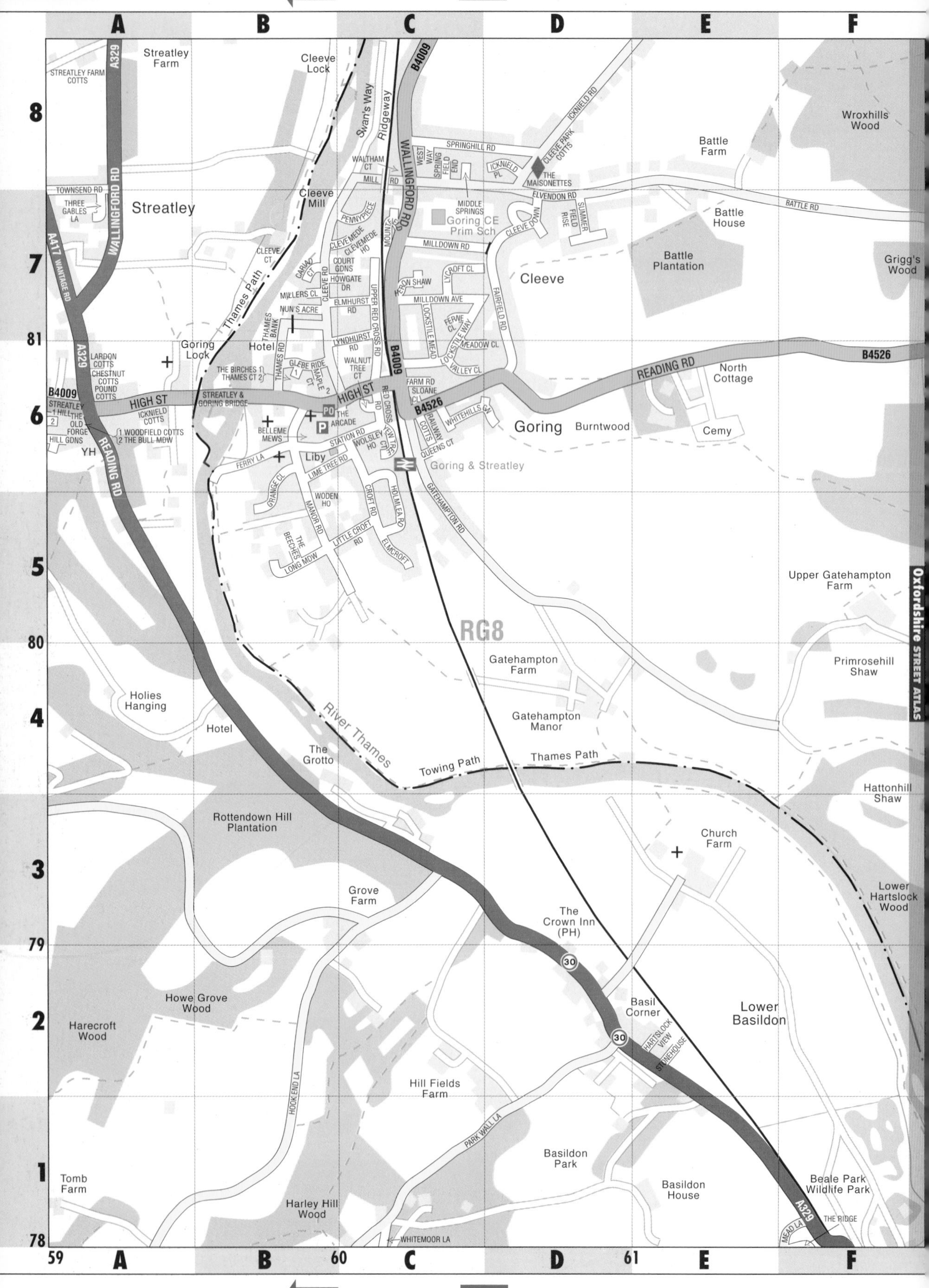
Streatley Farm
Cleeve Lock
Streatley
Cleeve Mill
Goring Lock
Hotel
Cleeve
Goring
Burntwood
Cemy
North Cottage
Battle Farm
Battle House
Battle Plantation
Wroxhills Wood
Grigg's Wood
Goring CE Prim Sch
Goring & Streatley
RG8
Upper Gatehampton Farm
Gatehampton Farm
Gatehampton Manor
Primrosehill Shaw
Holies Hanging
The Grotto
River Thames
Towing Path
Thames Path
Hattonhill Shaw
Rottendown Hill Plantation
Church Farm
Grove Farm
The Crown Inn (PH)
Lower Hartslock Wood
Howe Grove Wood
Harecroft Wood
Basil Corner
Lower Basildon
Hill Fields Farm
Basildon Park
Basildon House
Tomb Farm
Harley Hill Wood
Beale Park Wildlife Park
WALLINGFORD RD
READING RD
HIGH ST
B4009
B4526
A329
A417
Oxfordshire STREET ATLAS

33
55

15
36

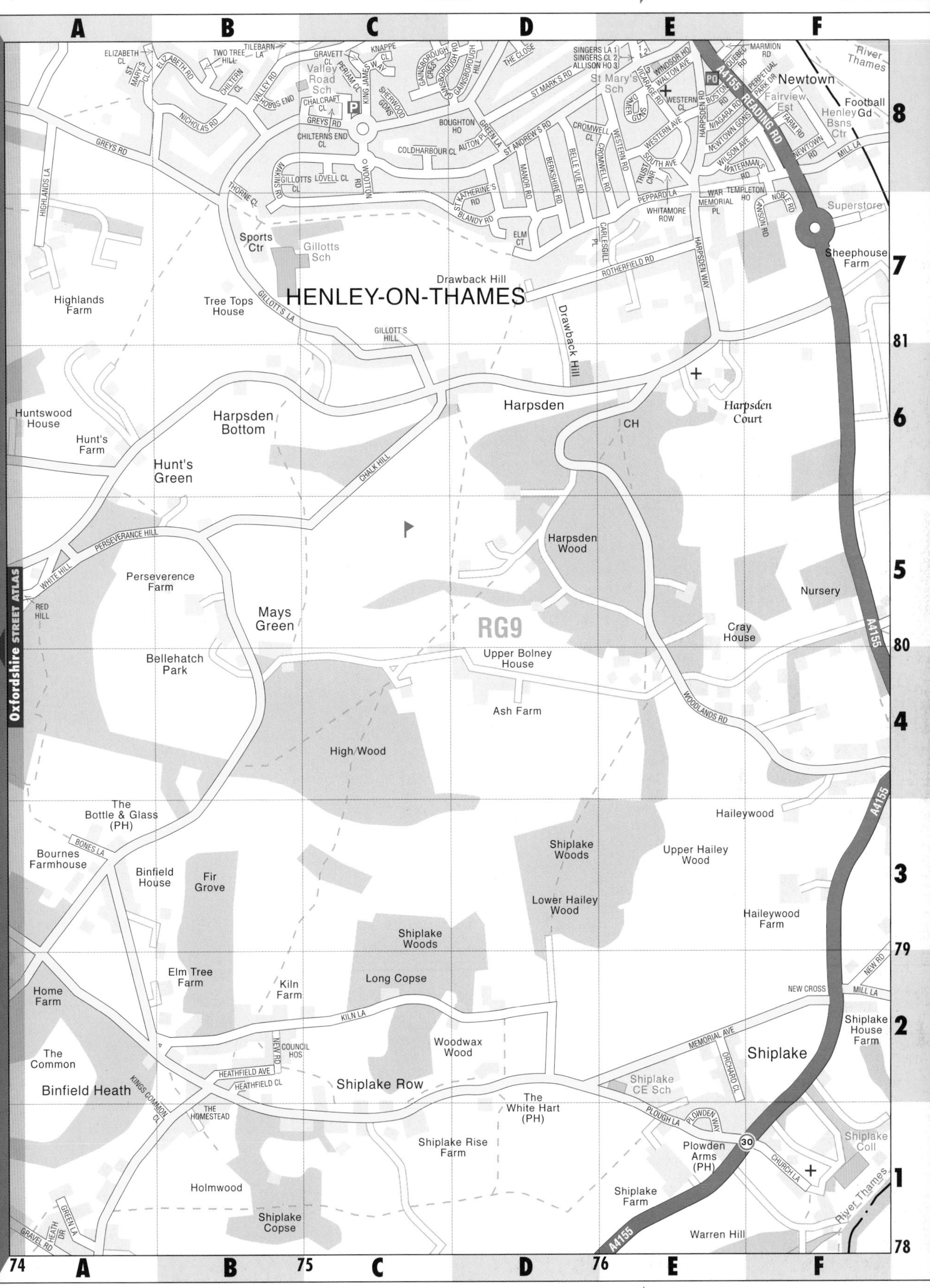
HENLEY-ON-THAMES
RG9
Newtown
Fairview Est
Henley Bsns Ctr
Football Gd
River Thames
Superstore
Sheephouse Farm
St Mary's Sch
Valley Road Sch
Gillotts Sch
Sports Ctr
Drawback Hill
Tree Tops House
Highlands Farm
Harpsden
Harpsden Court
CH
Huntswood House
Hunt's Farm
Harpsden Bottom
Hunt's Green
Harpsden Wood
Perseverance Farm
Mays Green
Nursery
Cray House
Bellehatch Park
Upper Bolney House
Ash Farm
High Wood
The Bottle & Glass (PH)
Bournes Farmhouse
Binfield House
Fir Grove
Haileywood
Upper Hailey Wood
Shiplake Woods
Lower Hailey Wood
Haileywood Farm
Elm Tree Farm
Kiln Farm
Long Copse
Home Farm
Shiplake House Farm
The Common
Woodwax Wood
Shiplake
Binfield Heath
Shiplake Row
Shiplake CE Sch
The White Hart (PH)
Shiplake Rise Farm
Plowden Arms (PH)
Shiplake Coll
Holmwood
Shiplake Farm
Shiplake Copse
Warren Hill
A4155
READING RD
GREYS RD
HIGHLANDS LA
NICHOLAS RD
ST ANDREW'S RD
ST MARK'S RD
WESTERN RD
HARPSDEN RD
HARPSDEN WAY
ROTHERFIELD RD
GILLOTT'S LA
GILLOTT'S HILL
CHALK HILL
PERSEVERANCE HILL
WHITE HILL
RED HILL
WOODLANDS RD
BONES LA
KILN LA
NEW RD
COUNCIL HOS
HEATHFIELD AVE
HEATHFIELD CL
KINGS COMMON CL
THE HOMESTEAD
MEMORIAL AVE
ORCHARD CL
PLOUGH LA
PLOWDEN WAY
CHURCH LA
NEW CROSS
MILL LA
NEW RD
GREEN LA
HEATH DR
GRAVEL RD
Oxfordshire STREET ATLAS
A B C D E F
8 7 81 6 5 80 4 3 79 2 1 78
74 75 76
30

60
36

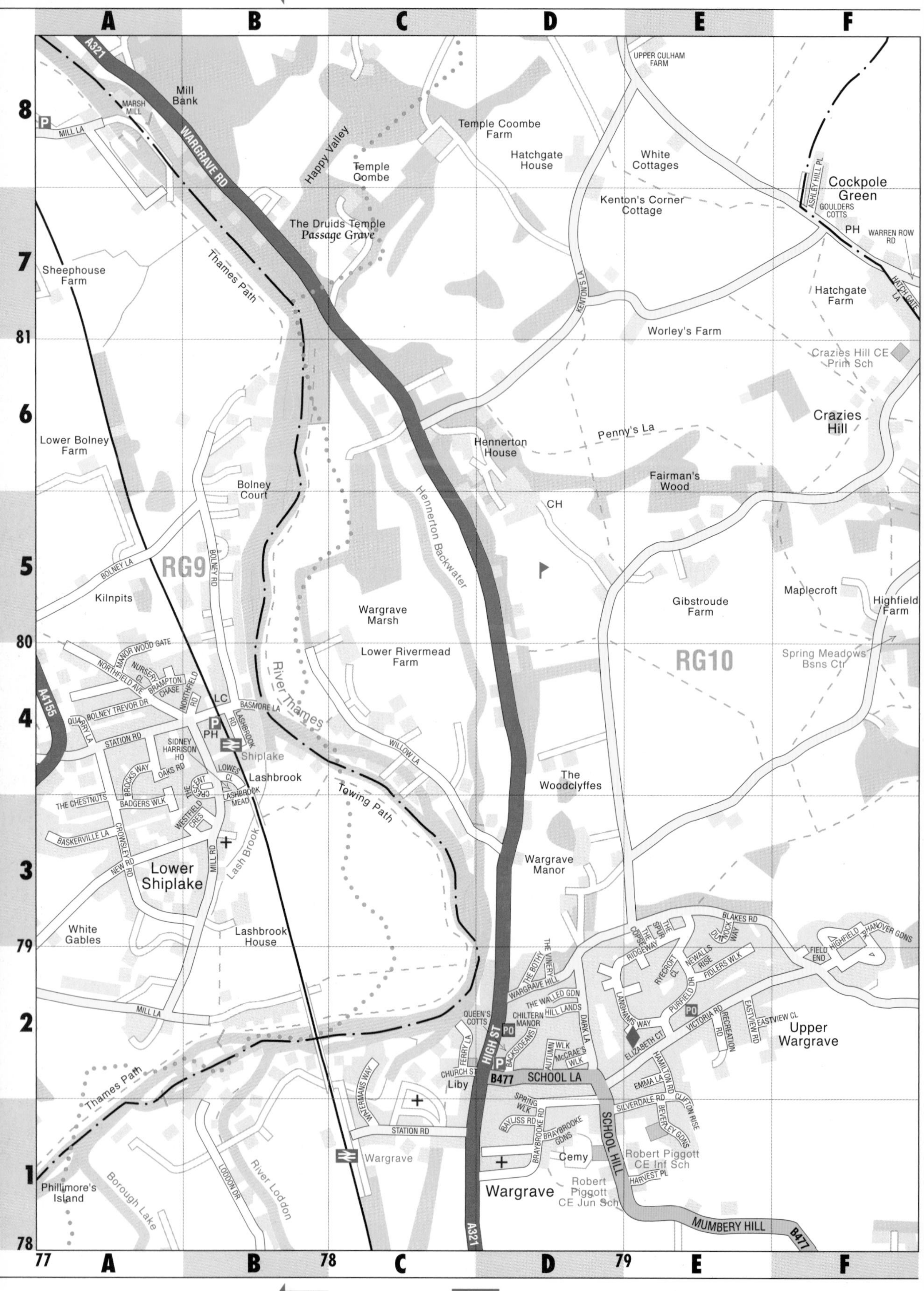
35
16
Mill Bank
Marsh Mill
Mill La
Wargrave Rd
A321
Happy Valley
Temple Combe
Temple Coombe Farm
Hatchgate House
White Cottages
Upper Culham Farm
Cockpole Green
Ashley Hill Pl
Goulders Cotts
PH
Warren Row Rd
Kenton's Corner Cottage
The Druids Temple
Passage Grave
Sheephouse Farm
Thames Path
Kenton's La
Hatchgate Farm
Hatch Gate La
Worley's Farm
Crazies Hill CE Prim Sch
Crazies Hill
Lower Bolney Farm
Hennerton House
Penny's La
Fairman's Wood
Bolney Court
Hennerton Backwater
CH
Bolney La
RG9
Bolney Rd
Kilnpits
Wargrave Marsh
Gibstroude Farm
Maplecroft
Highfield Farm
Manor Wood Gate
Nursery Cl
Northfield Ave
Brampton Chase
Northfield Rd
Lower Rivermead Farm
RG10
Spring Meadows Bsns Ctr
A4155
LC
Basmore La
River Thames
Quarry La
Bolney Trevor Dr
Station Rd
PH
Lashbrook Rd
Sidney Harrison Ho
Oaks Rd
Shiplake
Willow La
Brocks Way
Lowes Cl
Lashbrook
The Chestnuts
Badgers Wlk
The Crescent
Lashbrook Mead
Towing Path
The Woodclyffes
Westfield Cres
Baskerville La
Crowsley Rd
Lash Brook
Mill Rd
New Rd
Lower Shiplake
Wargrave Manor
White Gables
Lashbrook House
Blakes Rd
The Spur
The Copse
Ridgeway
Dunnock Way
Highfield
Hanover Gdns
Field End
The Bothy
The Vinery
Wargrave Hill
The Walled Gdn
Ryecroft Cl
Newalls Rise
Fidlers Wlk
Mill La
Hill Lands
Chiltern Manor
Langhams Way
Purfield Dr
Victoria Rd
Queen's Cotts
PO
Dark La
Recreation Rd
Eastview Rd
Eastview Cl
Upper Wargrave
High St
Backsideans
Autumn Wlk
McCrae's Wlk
Elizabeth Ct
Hamilton Rd
Ferry La
Thames Path
Church St
B477
School La
Liby
Emma La
Spring Wlk
Silverdale Rd
Clifton Rise
Beverley Gdns
Wintermans Way
Bayliss Rd
Braybrooke Gdns
Braybrooke Rd
Station Rd
School Hill
Wargrave
Cemy
Robert Piggott CE Inf Sch
Harvest Pl
Phillimore's Island
Borough Lake
Loddon Dr
River Loddon
Wargrave
Robert Piggott CE Jun Sch
Mumbery Hill
A B C D E F
8 7 81 6 5 80 4 3 79 2 1 78
77 78 79
61

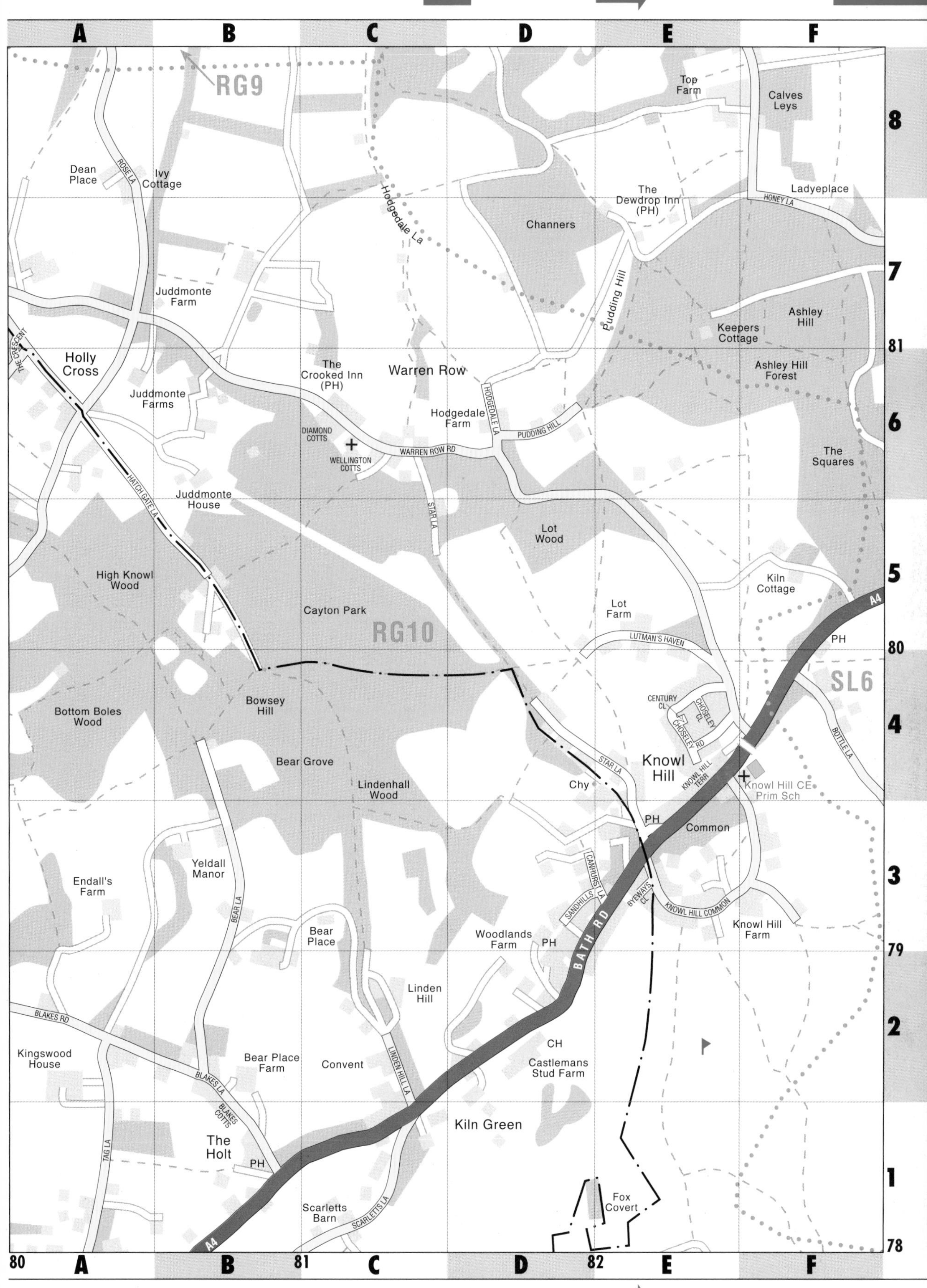
17
38
A
B
C
D
E
F
RG9
RG10
SL6
Top Farm
Calves Leys
Dean Place
Ivy Cottage
ROSE LA
The Dewdrop Inn (PH)
Ladyeplace
HONEY LA
Channers
Hodgedale La
Pudding Hill
Juddmonte Farm
Ashley Hill
Keepers Cottage
Ashley Hill Forest
Holly Cross
THE CRESCENT
The Crooked Inn (PH)
Warren Row
Juddmonte Farms
Hodgedale Farm
HODGEDALE LA
PUDDING HILL
DIAMOND COTTS
WELLINGTON COTTS
WARREN ROW RD
The Squares
HATCH GATE LA
Juddmonte House
STAR LA
Lot Wood
High Knowl Wood
Kiln Cottage
Cayton Park
Lot Farm
A4
PH
LUTMAN'S HAVEN
Bottom Boles Wood
Bowsey Hill
CENTURY CL
CHOSELEY CL
CHOSELEY RD
BOTTLE LA
Bear Grove
Knowl Hill
KNOWL HILL TERR
Lindenhall Wood
Chy
Knowl Hill CE Prim Sch
PH
Common
Yeldall Manor
CANHURST LA
Endall's Farm
SANDHILLS
BYEWAYS CL
KNOWL HILL COMMON
BEAR LA
Bear Place
Woodlands Farm
PH
Knowl Hill Farm
BATH RD
Linden Hill
BLAKES RD
CH
Kingswood House
Bear Place Farm
Convent
Castlemans Stud Farm
BLAKES LA
LINDEN HILL LA
BLAKES COTTS
Kiln Green
The Holt
TAG LA
PH
Fox Covert
Scarletts Barn
SCARLETTS LA
8
7
81
6
5
80
4
3
79
2
1
78
80
81
82
62
38

37
18

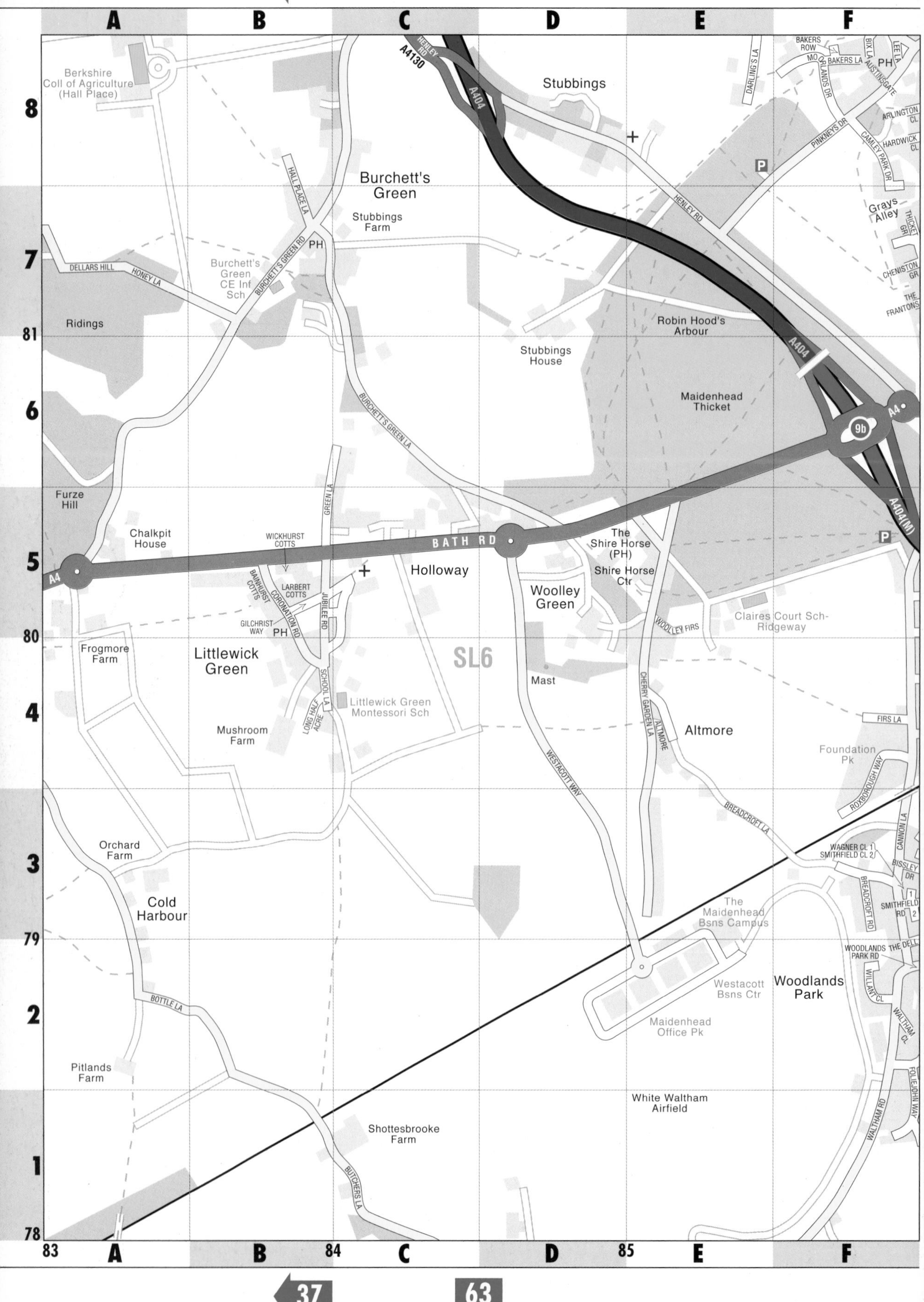
Berkshire Coll of Agriculture (Hall Place)
Stubbings
Burchett's Green
Stubbings Farm
Burchett's Green CE Inf Sch
Ridings
Stubbings House
Robin Hood's Arbour
Maidenhead Thicket
Grays Alley
Furze Hill
Chalkpit House
BATH RD
Holloway
Woolley Green
The Shire Horse (PH)
Shire Horse Ctr
Claires Court Sch-Ridgeway
Frogmore Farm
Littlewick Green
SL6
Mast
Littlewick Green Montessori Sch
Mushroom Farm
Altmore
Foundation Pk
Orchard Farm
Cold Harbour
The Maidenhead Bsns Campus
Westacott Bsns Ctr
Woodlands Park
Maidenhead Office Pk
Pitlands Farm
White Waltham Airfield
Shottesbrooke Farm
HENLEY RD
A4130
A404
A4
A404(M)
HALL PLACE LA
BURCHETT'S GREEN RD
DELLARS HILL
HONEY LA
BURCHETT'S GREEN LA
GREEN LA
WICKHURST COTTS
BANNHURST COTTS
CORONATION RD
LARBERT COTTS
JUBILEE RD
GILCHRIST WAY
SCHOOL LA
LONG HALF ACRE
WESTACOTT WAY
CHERRY GARDEN LA
ALTMORE
WOOLLEY FIRS
BREADCROFT LA
FIRS LA
ROXBOROUGH WAY
DARLING'S LA
BAKERS ROW
BAKERS LA
BIX LA
LEE LA
AUSTINSGATE
ORLANDS DR
PINKNEYS DR
CAMLEY PARK DR
ARLINGTON CL
HARDWICK CL
THICKET GR
CHENISTON GR
THE FRANTONS
CANNON LA
WAGNER CL 1
SMITHFIELD CL 2
BISSLEY DR
SMITHFIELD RD
BREADCROFT RD
WOODLANDS PARK RD
THE DELL
WILLANT CL
WALTHAM CL
WALTHAM RD
FOLIEJOHN WAY
BOTTLE LA
BUTCHERS LA
PH
9b
A
B
C
D
E
F
8
7
81
6
5
80
4
3
79
2
1
78
83
84
85

37
63

B8
1 STIRLING PL
2 GREENLANDS CT
3 MERLIN CT
4 WELLINGTON CL

E7
1 THE FIRS
2 TUSCANY CT
3 LADY ELIZABETH HO
4 ELMSLIE CT
5 SHERINGHAM CT

19

F7
1 HIGH ST MALL
2 WHITE HART RD
3 QUEENS WLK MALL
4 KINGS WLK
5 Nicholsons Ctr
6 BROADWAY MALL

40

F7
7 BROCK LA MALL
8 QUEEN'S LA
9 REGENT CT
10 OLD POST OFFICE LA
11 FROGMORE CT
12 NEW MARKET
13 KIDWELLS PARK DR
14 PROVIDENCE PL
15 WILBERFORCE MEWS
16 ST MARY'S WLK

F8
1 Cordwallis Est
2 SUFFOLK CT

64

40

B8
1 BARBICUS CT
2 SOMERSHAM
3 KIMBOLTON
4 SHERIDAN CT
5 THAMEBRIDGE CT

39
20

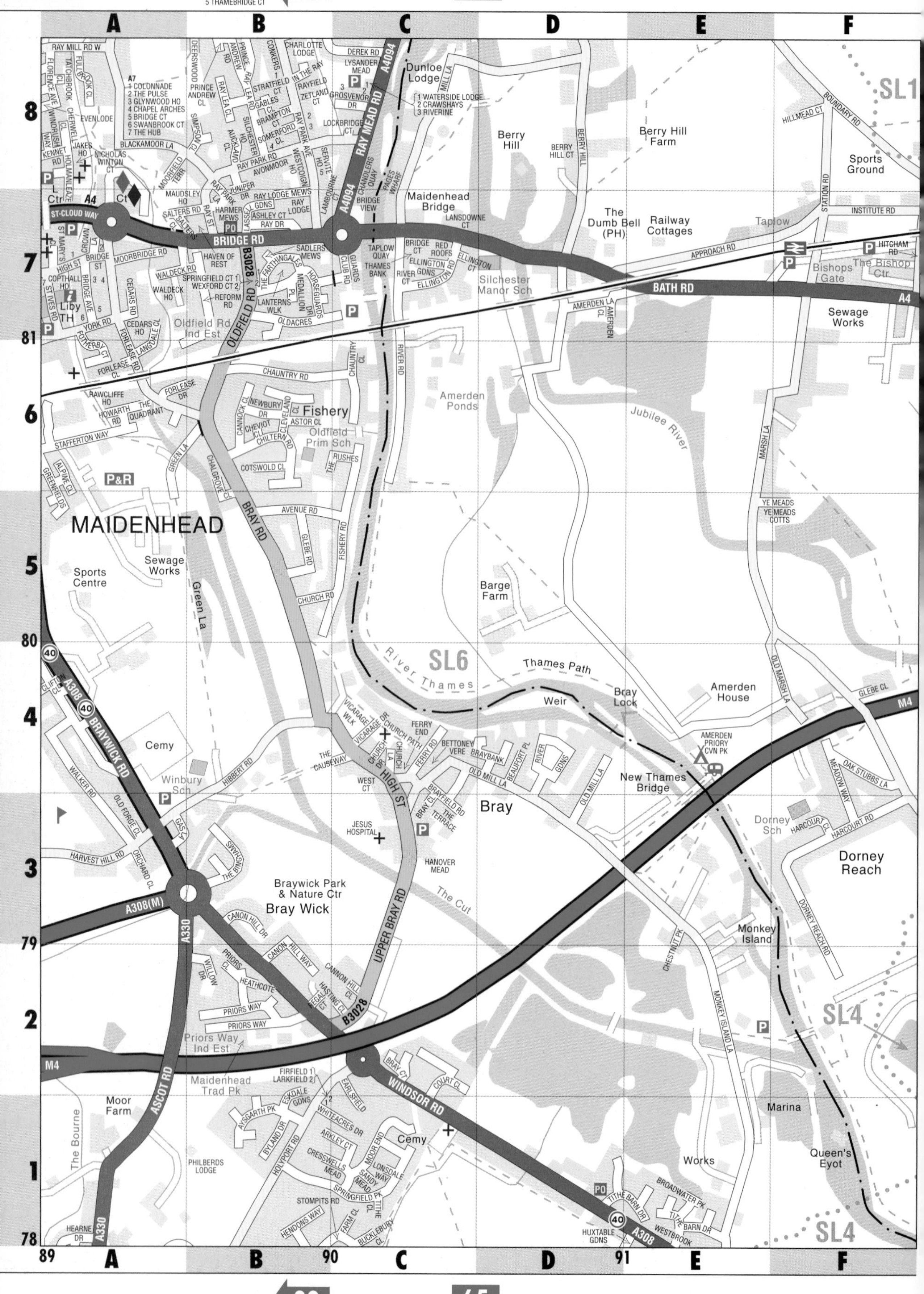

39
65

21
42

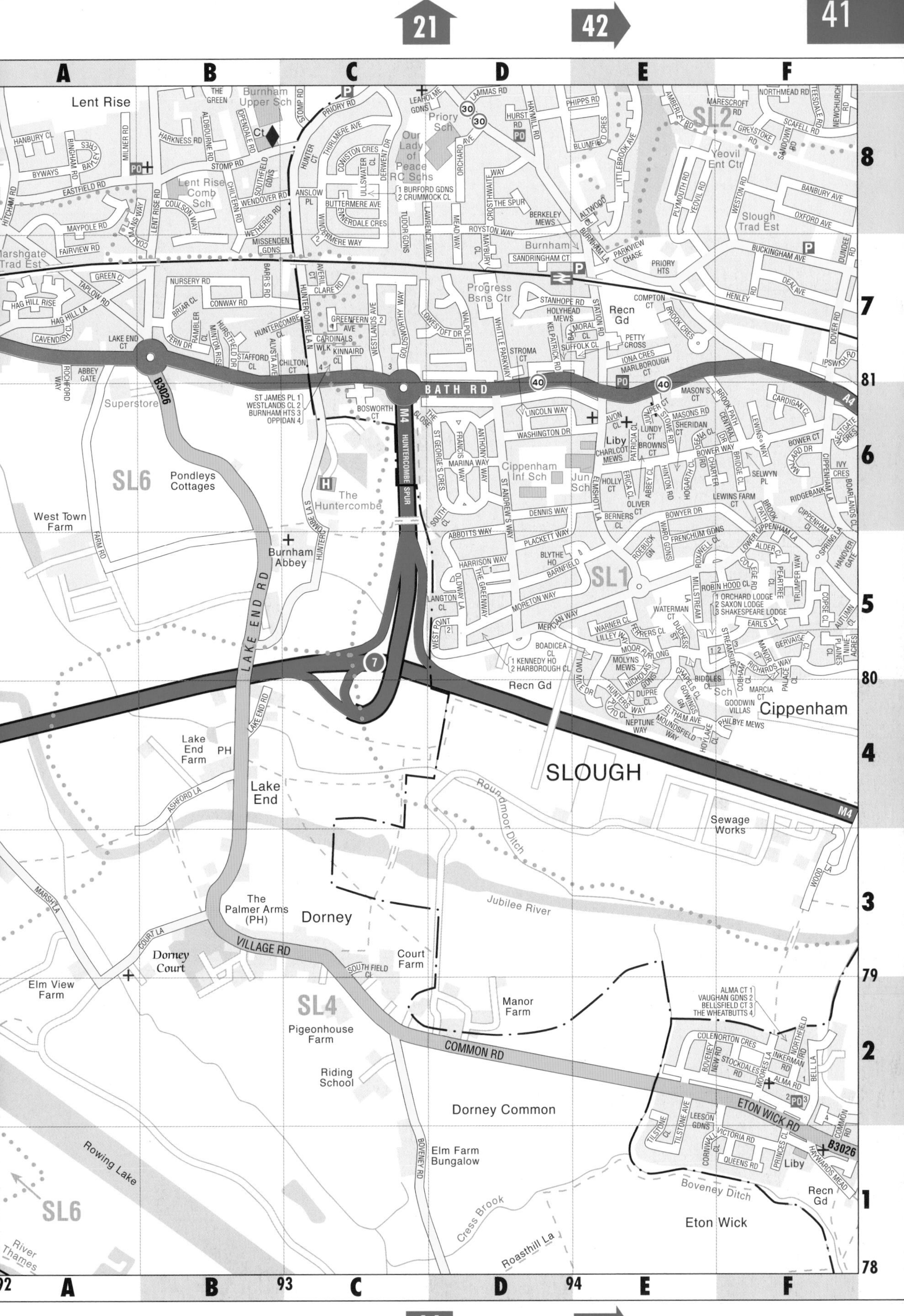
A
B
C
D
E
F
Lent Rise
Burnham Upper Sch
Priory Sch
Our Lady of Peace RC Schs
SL2
Yeovil Ent Ctr
Slough Trad Est
Lent Rise Comb Sch
Marshgate Trad Est
Burnham
Progress Bsns Ctr
Recn Gd
BATH RD
A4
M4
HUNTERCOMBE SPUR
B3026
Superstore
SL6
Pondleys Cottages
West Town Farm
The Huntercombe
Burnham Abbey
Cippenham Inf Sch
Jun Sch
Liby
SL1
LAKE END RD
Lake End Farm
PH
Lake End
SLOUGH
Cippenham
Sewage Works
Roundmoor Ditch
Jubilee River
The Palmer Arms (PH)
Dorney
Dorney Court
VILLAGE RD
Court Farm
Elm View Farm
SL4
Pigeonhouse Farm
Manor Farm
COMMON RD
Riding School
Dorney Common
ETON WICK RD
Elm Farm Bungalow
Rowing Lake
SL6
River Thames
Cress Brook
Roasthill La
Boveney Ditch
Eton Wick
Recn Gd
Liby
1 BURFORD GDNS
2 CRUMMOCK CL
ST JAMES PL 1
WESTLANDS CL 2
BURNHAM HTS 3
OPPIDAN 4
1 ORCHARD LODGE
2 SAXON LODGE
3 SHAKESPEARE LODGE
1 KENNEDY HO
2 HARBOROUGH CL
ALMA CT 1
VAUGHAN GDNS 2
BELLSFIELD CT 3
THE WHEATBUTTS 4
8
7
81
6
5
80
4
3
79
2
1
78
92
93
94

66
42

41
22

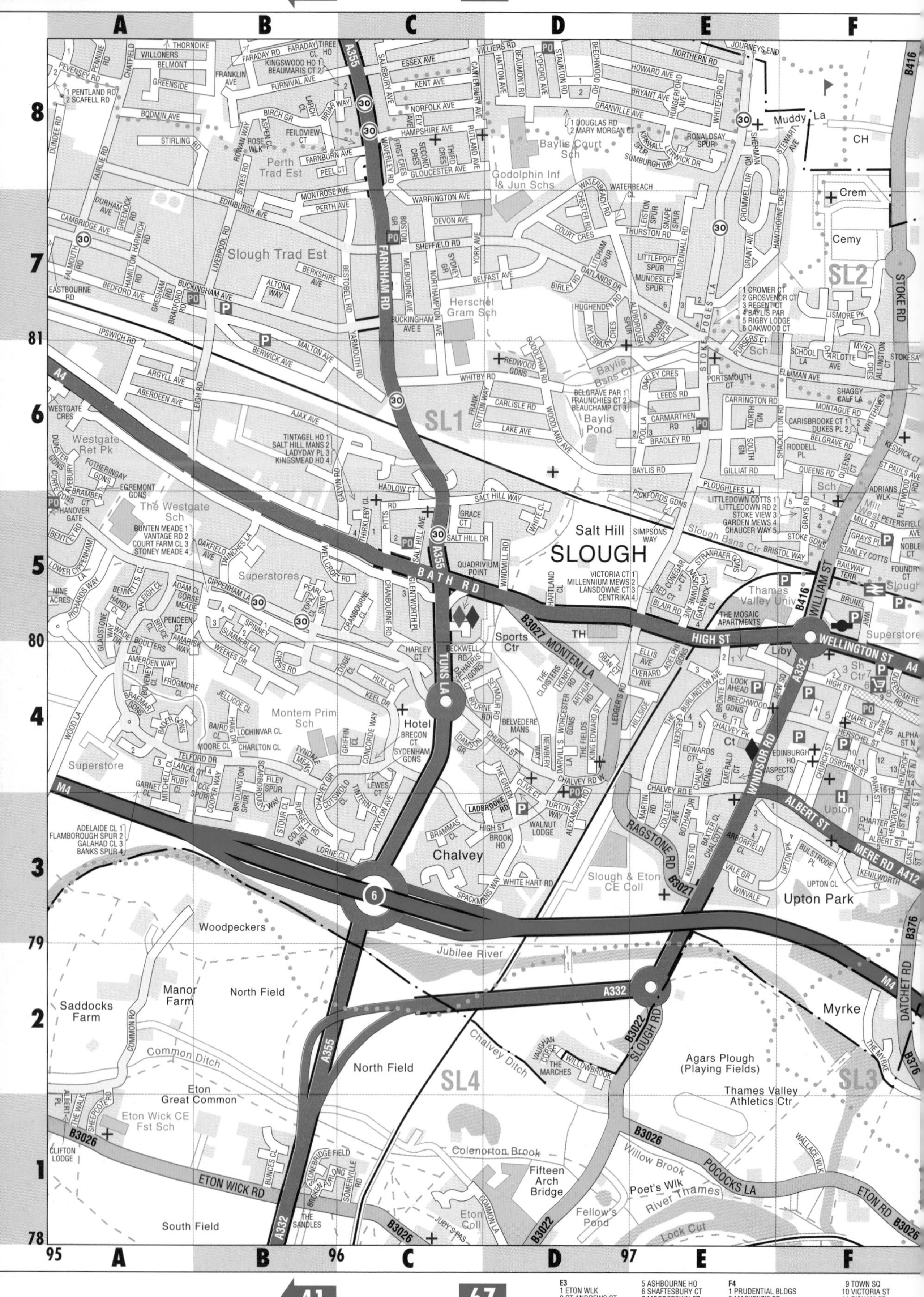

E3
1 ETON WLK
2 ST ANDREWS CT
3 LINCOLN CT
4 LOCKSLEY CT
5 ASHBOURNE HO
6 SHAFTESBURY CT
7 MOORSTOWN CT

E4
1 BURLINGTON CT
2 BURLINGTON RD
3 HILPERTON RD
4 TOWER HO

F3
1 SPRUCE CT
2 DARTMOUTH CT
3 ALBERT CL
4 WINSFORD PAR
5 MANOR CT

F4
1 PRUDENTIAL BLDGS
2 MACKENZIE ST
3 Mackenzie Mall
4 BUCKINGHAM GDNS
5 The Village Sh Ctr
6 Leopold Mall
7 Curzon Mall
8 Chandos Mall
9 TOWN SQ
10 VICTORIA ST
11 BISHAM CT
12 BEMBRIDGE CT
13 STEPHENSON CT
14 HENCROFT MEWS
15 SHAMAA HO
16 RICHARD DODD PL

41
67

23
44

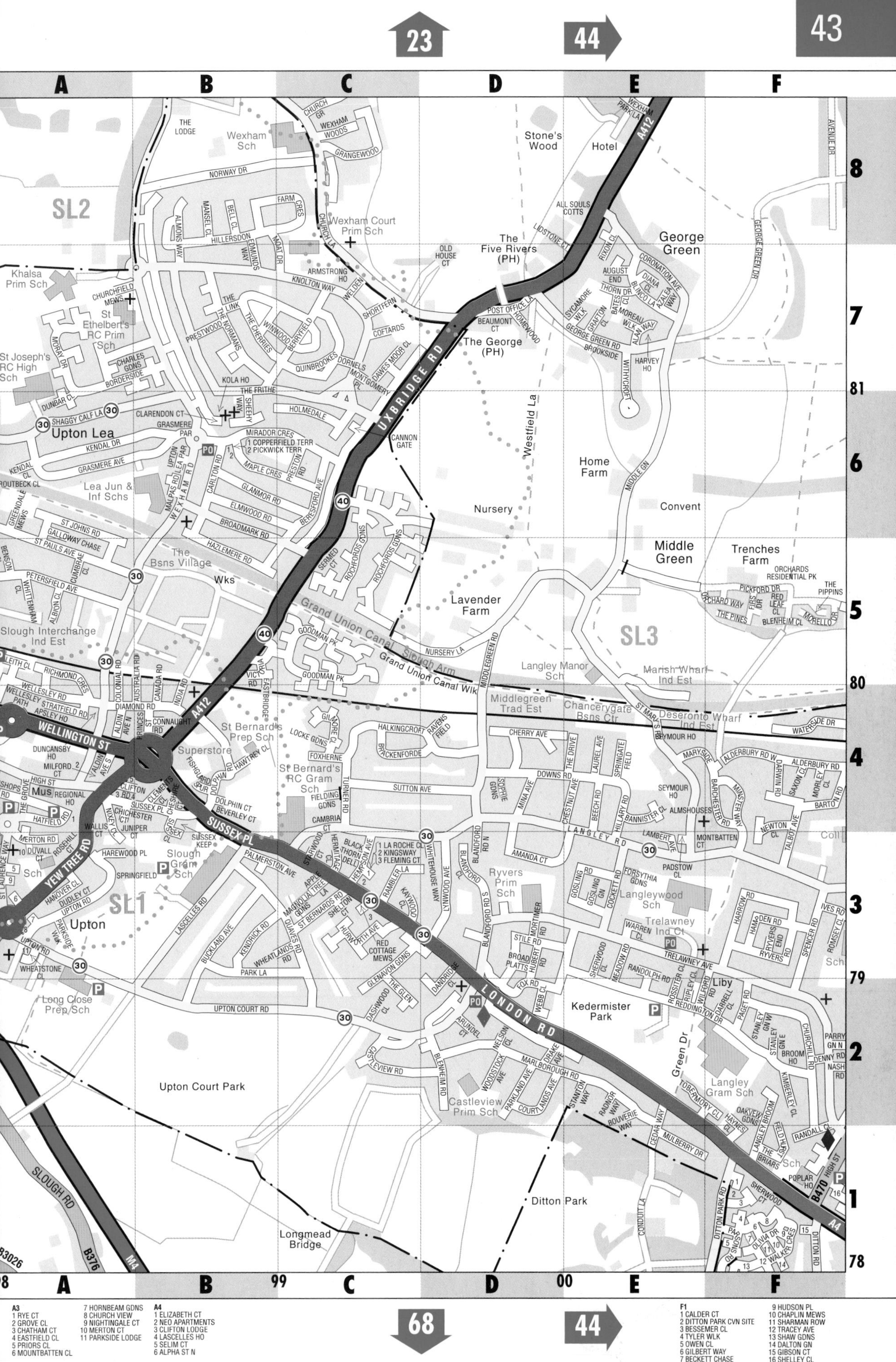

A3
1 RYE CT
2 GROVE CL
3 CHATHAM CT
4 EASTFIELD CL
5 PRIORS CL
6 MOUNTBATTEN CL
7 HORNBEAM GDNS
8 CHURCH VIEW
9 NIGHTINGALE CT
10 MERTON CT
11 PARKSIDE LODGE

A4
1 ELIZABETH CT
2 NEO APARTMENTS
3 CLIFTON LODGE
4 LASCELLES HO
5 SELIM CT
6 ALPHA ST N

68
44

F1
1 CALDER CT
2 DITTON PARK CVN SITE
3 BESSEMER CL
4 TYLER WLK
5 OWEN CL
6 GILBERT WAY
7 BECKETT CHASE
8 DAVIDSON RD
9 HUDSON PL
10 CHAPLIN MEWS
11 SHARMAN ROW
12 TRACEY AVE
13 SHAW GDNS
14 DALTON GN
15 GIBSON CT
16 SHELLEY CL

43

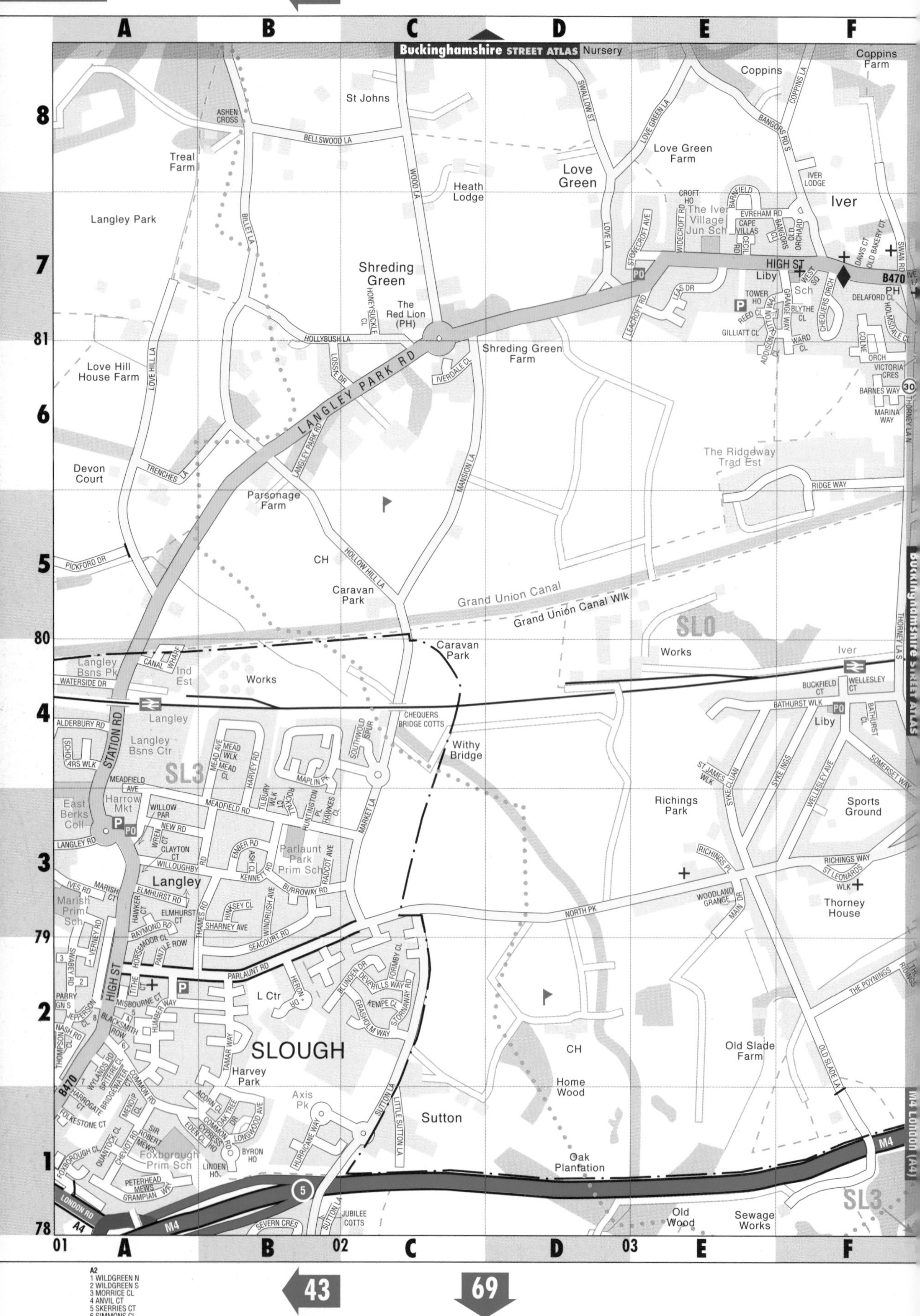

A2
1 WILDGREEN N
2 WILDGREEN S
3 MORRICE CL
4 ANVIL CT
5 SKERRIES CT
6 SIMMONS CL
7 KNIGHTSBRIDGE CT
8 THE LAURELS

43

69

24
46

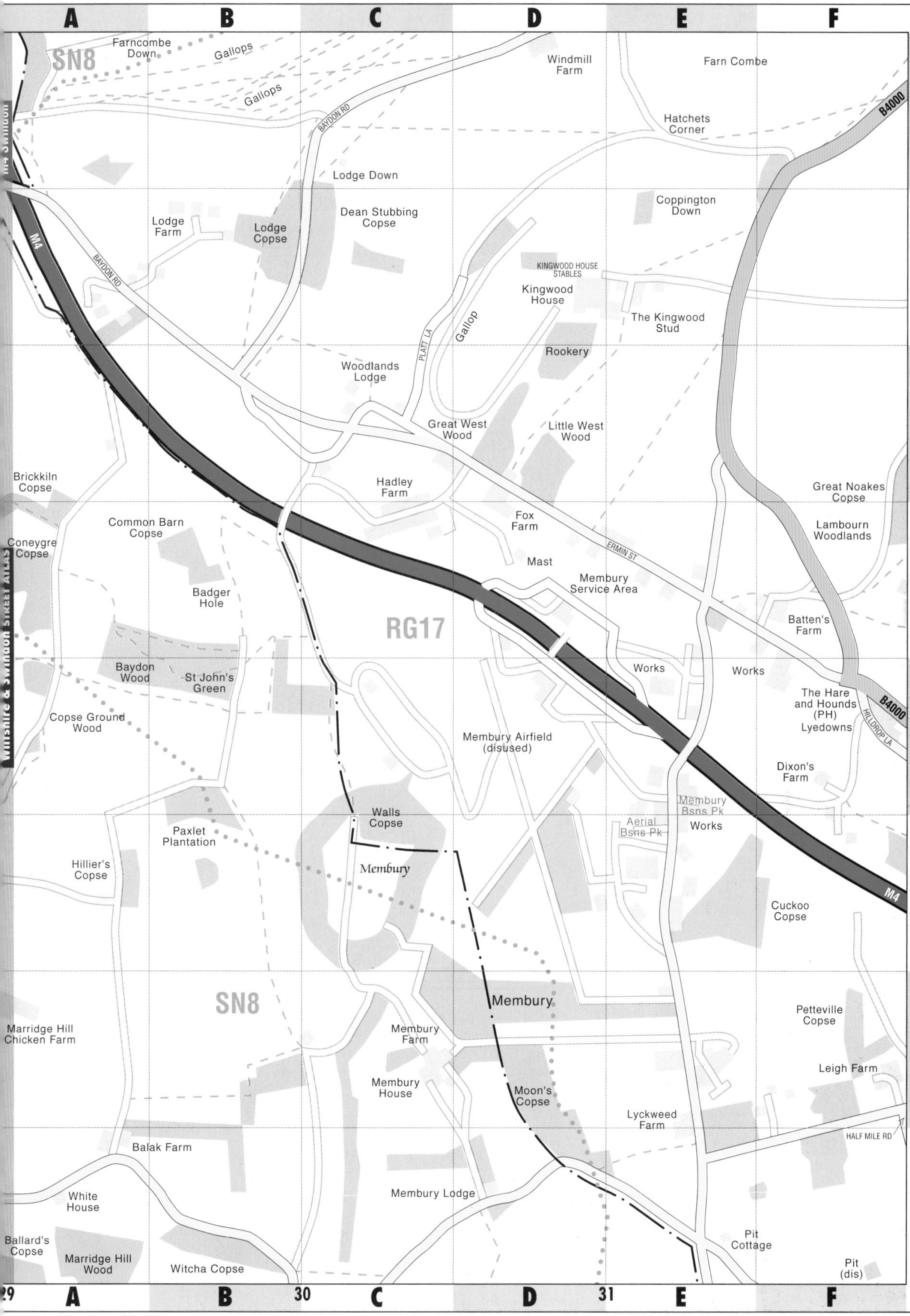

A B C D E F

Farncombe Down
SN8
Gallops
Gallops
Windmill Farm
Farn Combe
BAYDON RD
Hatchets Corner
B4000
8
Lodge Down
Coppington Down
Lodge Farm
Lodge Copse
Dean Stubbing Copse
M4
BAYDON RD
KINGWOOD HOUSE STABLES
Kingwood House
7
The Kingwood Stud
PLATT LA
Gallop
Rookery
77
Woodlands Lodge
Great West Wood
Little West Wood
6
Brickkiln Copse
Hadley Farm
Great Noakes Copse
Common Barn Copse
Fox Farm
Lambourn Woodlands
Coneygre Copse
ERMIN ST
Mast
Membury Service Area
5
Badger Hole
RG17
Batten's Farm
76
Baydon Wood
St John's Green
Works
Works
The Hare and Hounds (PH)
Lyedowns
B4000
HILLDROP LA
Copse Ground Wood
Membury Airfield (disused)
4
Dixon's Farm
Membury Bsns Pk
Walls Copse
Aerial Bsns Pk
Works
Paxlet Plantation
Hillier's Copse
Membury
Cuckoo Copse
M4
3
75
SN8
Membury
Petteville Copse
Marridge Hill Chicken Farm
Membury Farm
2
Leigh Farm
Membury House
Moon's Copse
Lyckweed Farm
HALF MILE RD
Balak Farm
White House
Membury Lodge
1
Ballard's Copse
Marridge Hill Wood
Witcha Copse
Pit Cottage
Pit (dis)
74

29 A B 30 C D 31 E F

45
25

A B C D E F
8
7
77
6
5
76
4
3
75
2
1
74
32 33 34
B4000
Hungerford Gap
Coppington Hill
White Shute
Boldstart Farm
Boldstart Copse
Thorn Hill
Thornhill Copse
Lambourn Valley Way
River Lambourn
THE HERMITAGE
Hall
Eastbury
Manor Farm
The Plough (PH)
DOWNS CL
COUNCIL HOS
HAYFIELD CT
Willis Farm
Clapper Border
Dance's Copse
Gifford's Copse
Cleeve Wood
Shrags Hill
Alms Wood
Dance's Cottage
Lord's Wood
Haycroft Hill
Berry's Wood
Cleeve Hill
RG17
Lowesden Works
Great Park Wood
Rooksnest
Househill Copse
STRAIGHT LA
Patch Copse
Pebblehill Copse
Cymbalcroft Copse
Lambourn Woodlands
Danesfield Copse
Leyatt Copse
Watchcroft Copse
Lyedown Copse
HILLDROP LA
Hilldrop Farm
Burgess's Farm
Peaks Copse
M4
B4001
STONY LA
Bushyleaze Border
ERMIN ST
Hall
May's Copse
EASTBURY SHUTE
Lye Farm Cottages
Woodlands St Mary
Kimber's Border
Riverwood Border
HALF MILE RD
Carols Acre
Holt Copse
Breach Border
GOODINGS LA
B4000
B4001
M4

45
73

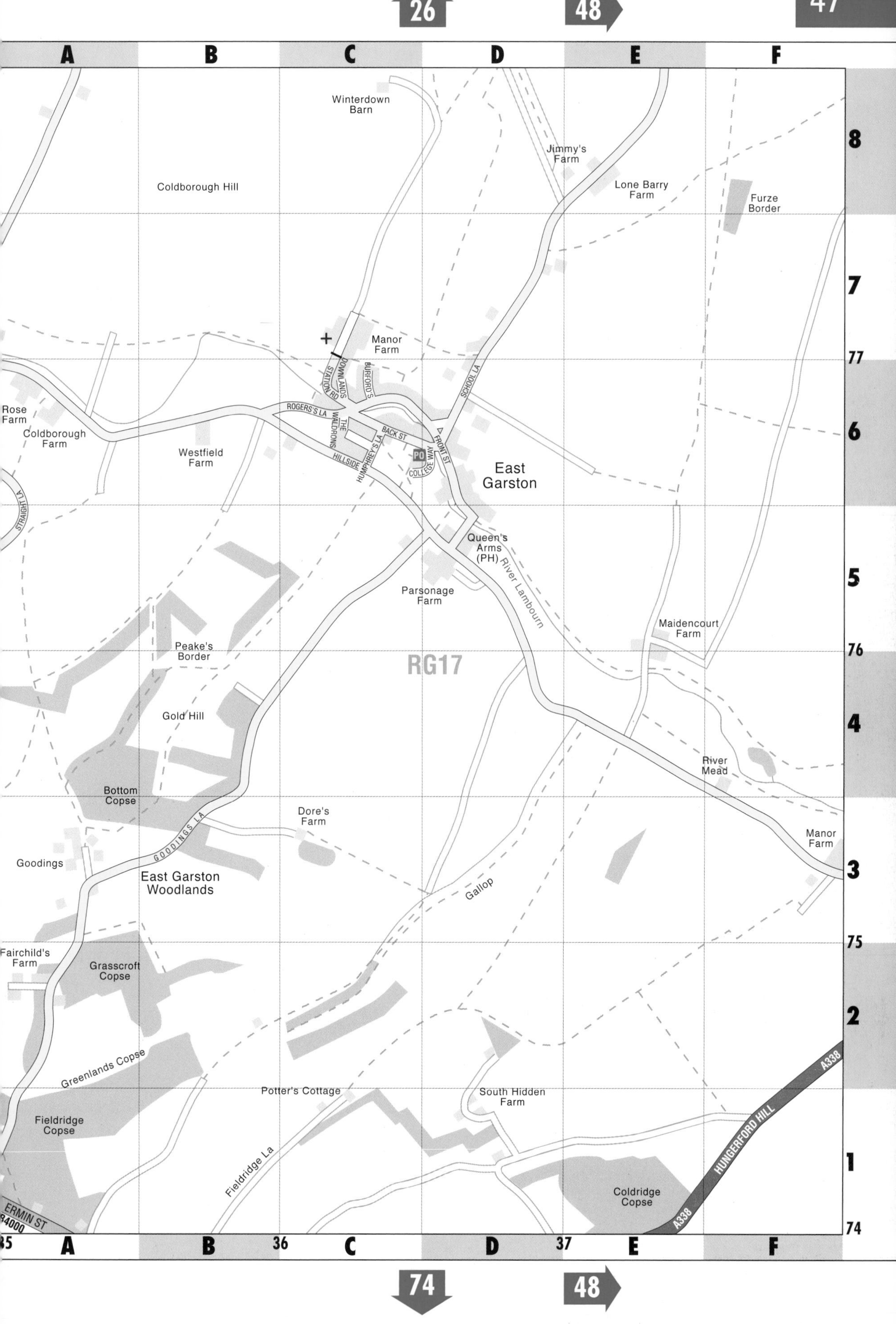
26
48
A
B
C
D
E
F
8
7
77
6
5
76
4
3
75
2
1
74
Winterdown Barn
Coldborough Hill
Jimmy's Farm
Lone Barry Farm
Furze Border
Manor Farm
DOWNLANDS
STATION RD
BURFORD'S
SCHOOL LA
ROGERS'S LA
THE WALDRONS
BACK ST
FRONT ST
HILLSIDE
HUMPHREY'S LA
COLLEGE WAY
PO
Rose Farm
Coldborough Farm
Westfield Farm
East Garston
STRAIGHT LA
Queen's Arms (PH)
River Lambourn
Parsonage Farm
Maidencourt Farm
Peake's Border
RG17
Gold Hill
River Mead
Bottom Copse
Dore's Farm
Manor Farm
GOODINGS LA
Goodings
East Garston Woodlands
Gallop
Fairchild's Farm
Grasscroft Copse
Greenlands Copse
Potter's Cottage
South Hidden Farm
A338
HUNGERFORD HILL
Fieldridge Copse
Fieldridge La
Coldridge Copse
ERMIN ST
B4000
A338
35
36
37
74
48

47
27

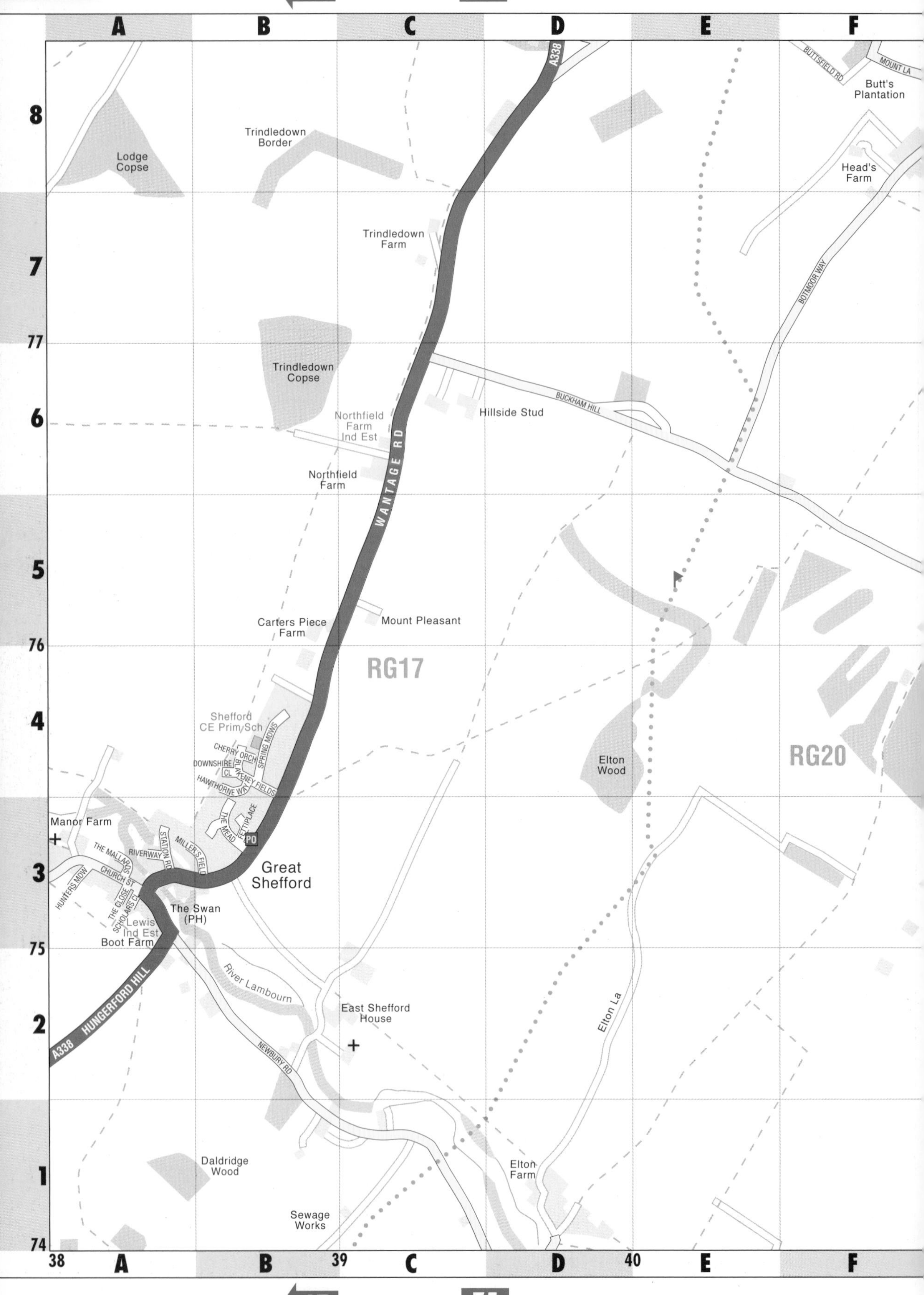
A
B
C
D
E
F
8
7
77
6
5
76
4
3
75
2
1
74
38
39
40
A338
BUTTSFIELD RD
MOUNT LA
Butt's Plantation
Lodge Copse
Trindledown Border
Head's Farm
Trindledown Farm
BOTMOOR WAY
Trindledown Copse
Northfield Farm Ind Est
BUCKHAM HILL
Hillside Stud
WANTAGE RD
Northfield Farm
Carters Piece Farm
Mount Pleasant
RG17
Shefford CE Prim Sch
CHERRY ORCH
SPRING MDWS
DOWNSHIRE CL
BLAKENEY FIELDS
HAWTHORNE WAY
Elton Wood
RG20
Manor Farm
THE MEAD
FETTIPLACE
PO
STATION RD
MILLER'S FIELD
RIVERWAY
THE MALLARDS
CHURCH ST
HUNTERS MDW
THE CLOSE
SCHOLARS CL
Great Shefford
The Swan (PH)
Lewis Ind Est
Boot Farm
HUNGERFORD HILL
River Lambourn
East Shefford House
NEWBURY RD
Elton La
Daldridge Wood
Elton Farm
Sewage Works

47
75

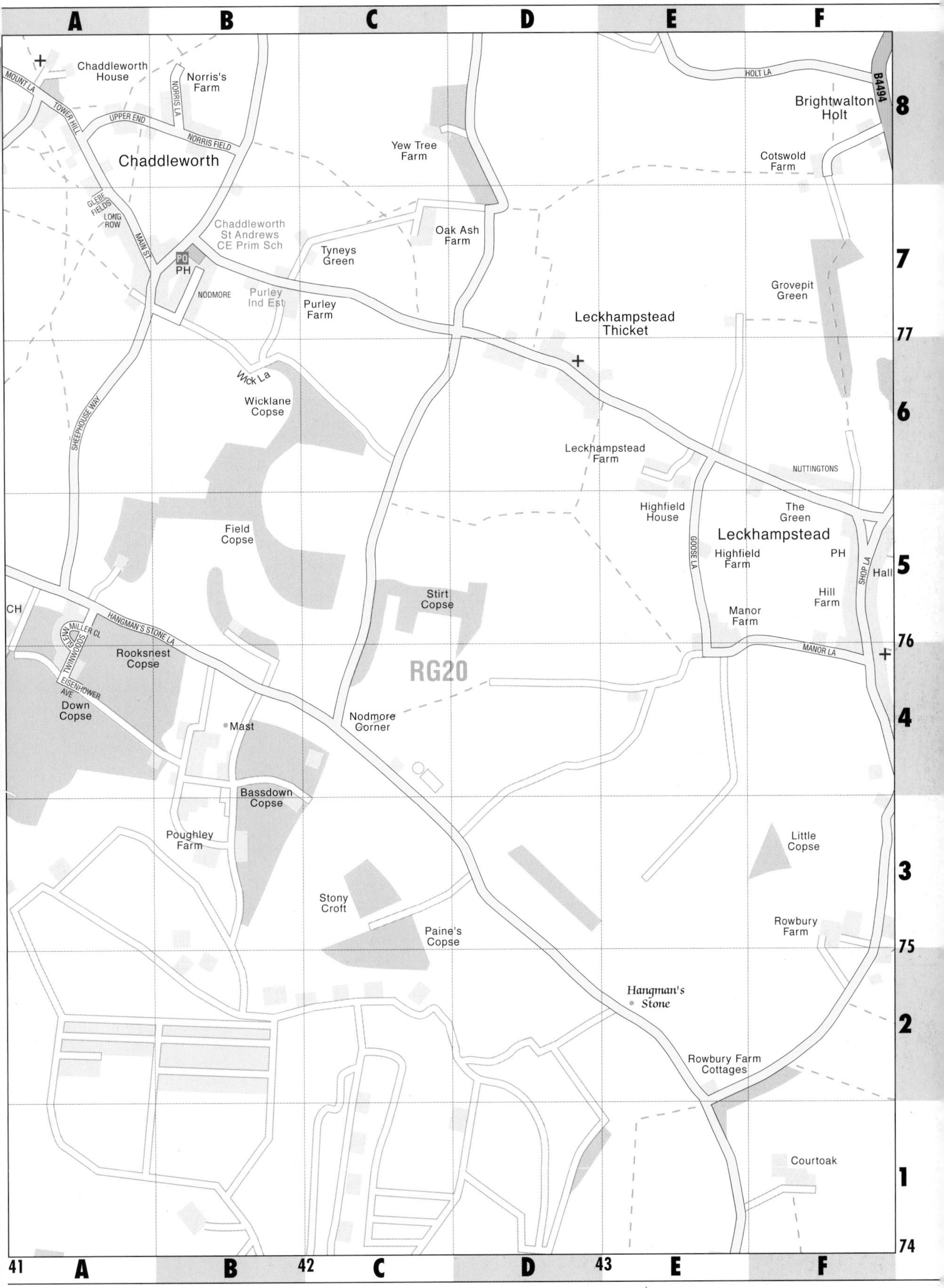

A B C D E F

Chaddleworth House
Norris's Farm
MOUNT LA
TOWER HILL
UPPER END
NORRIS LA
NORRIS FIELD
Chaddleworth
Yew Tree Farm
HOLT LA
B4494
Brightwalton Holt
Cotswold Farm
8
GLEBE FIELDS
LONG ROW
MAIN ST
Chaddleworth St Andrews CE Prim Sch
PO
PH
Tyneys Green
Oak Ash Farm
NODMORE
Purley Ind Est
Purley Farm
Grovepit Green
7
Leckhampstead Thicket
77
Wick La
Wicklane Copse
SHEEPHOUSE WAY
6
Leckhampstead Farm
NUTTINGTONS
Highfield House
The Green
Field Copse
GOOSE LA
Leckhampstead
Highfield Farm
PH
SHOP LA
Hall
5
CH
Stirt Copse
Hill Farm
Manor Farm
HANGMAN'S STONE LA
GLENN MILLER CL
TWINWOODS
Rooksnest Copse
MANOR LA
76
EISENHOWER AVE
RG20
Down Copse
Mast
Nodmore Corner
4
Bassdown Copse
Poughley Farm
Little Copse
3
Stony Croft
Paine's Copse
Rowbury Farm
75
Hangman's Stone
2
Rowbury Farm Cottages
Courtoak
1
74

41 A B 42 C D 43 E F

49
29

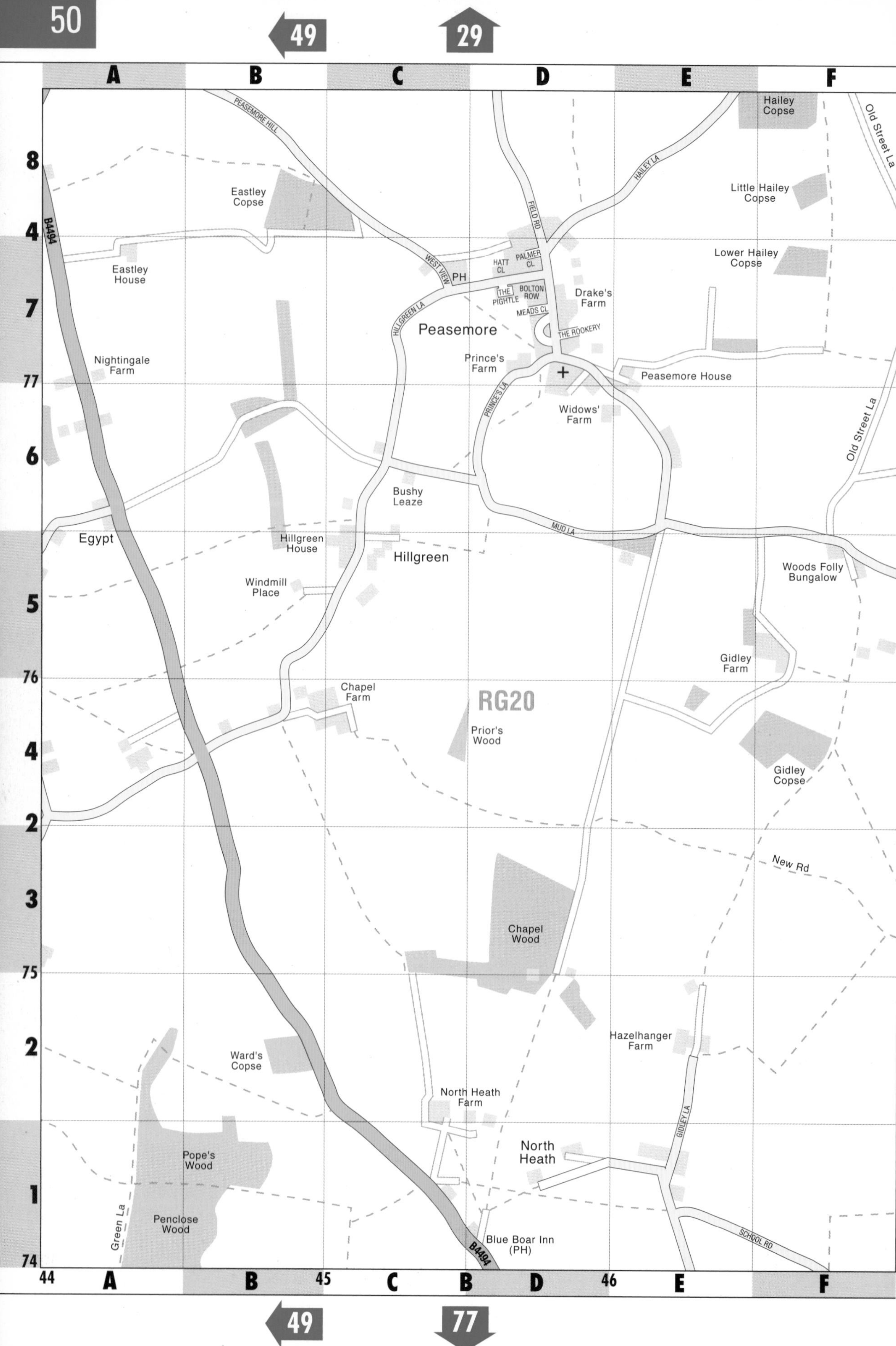
A
B
C
D
E
F
8
4
7
77
6
5
76
4
2
3
75
2
1
74
44
45
46
Peasemore Hill
Eastley Copse
B4494
Eastley House
Nightingale Farm
Egypt
Hillgreen House
Windmill Place
Hillgreen
Hillgreen La
West View
PH
Hatt Cl
Palmer Cl
The Pightle
Bolton Row
Meads Cl
The Rookery
Field Rd
Hailey La
Peasemore
Drake's Farm
Prince's Farm
Prince's La
Widows' Farm
Peasemore House
Hailey Copse
Little Hailey Copse
Lower Hailey Copse
Old Street La
Bushy Leaze
Mud La
Woods Folly Bungalow
Gidley Farm
Gidley Copse
Chapel Farm
RG20
Prior's Wood
New Rd
Chapel Wood
Hazelhanger Farm
Ward's Copse
North Heath Farm
North Heath
Gidley La
Pope's Wood
Penclose Wood
Green La
Blue Boar Inn (PH)
School Rd

49
77

30
52

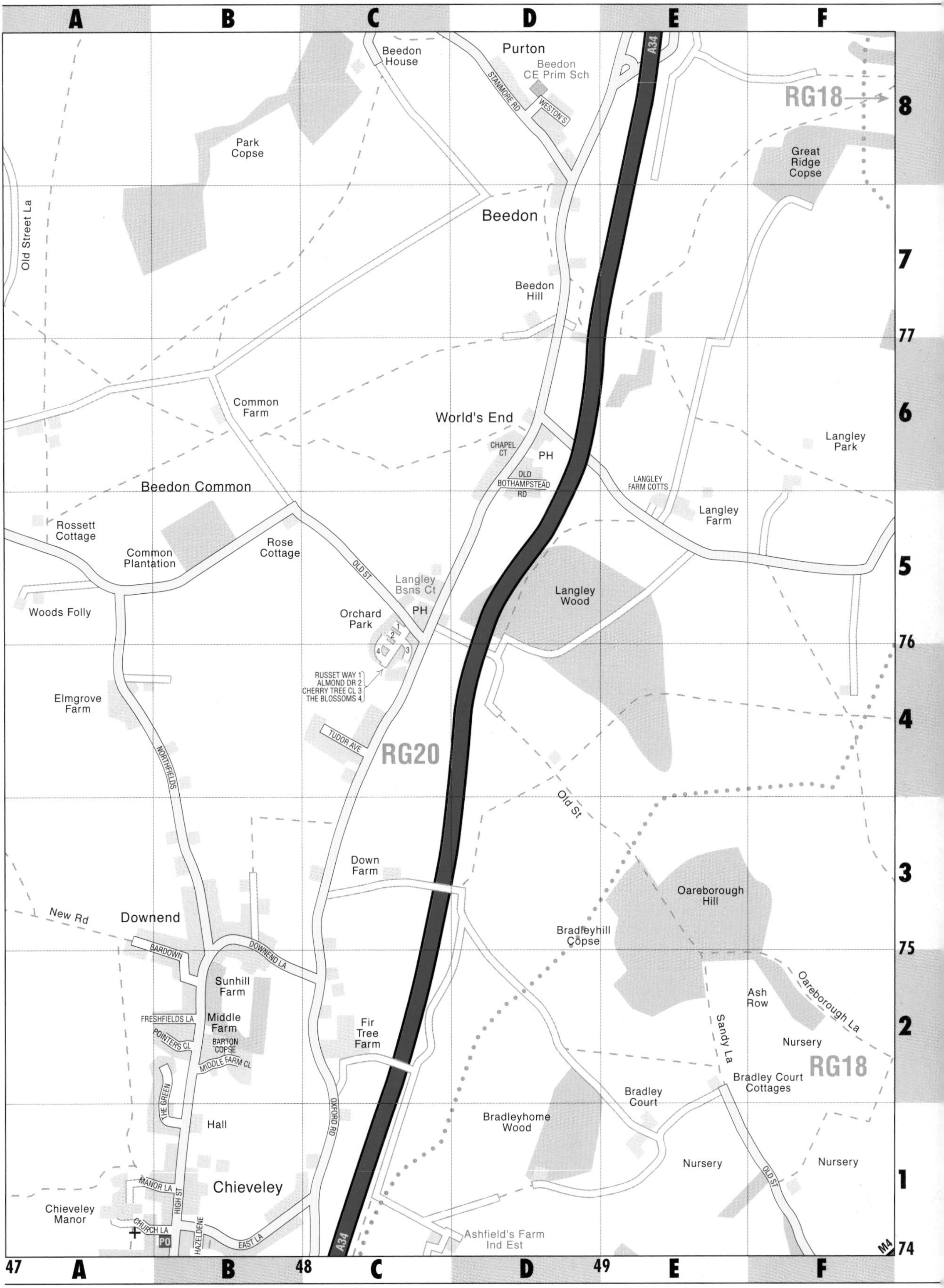

A B C D E F
8 7 77 6 5 76 4 3 75 2 1 74
47 48 49
Purton
Beedon House
Beedon CE Prim Sch
STANMORE RD
WESTON'S
RG18
Park Copse
Great Ridge Copse
Old Street La
Beedon
Beedon Hill
A34
Common Farm
World's End
CHAPEL CT
PH
OLD BOTHAMPSTEAD RD
LANGLEY FARM COTTS
Langley Park
Langley Farm
Beedon Common
Rossett Cottage
Common Plantation
Rose Cottage
OLD ST
Langley Bsns Ct
Langley Wood
Woods Folly
Orchard Park
RUSSET WAY 1
ALMOND DR 2
CHERRY TREE CL 3
THE BLOSSOMS 4
Elmgrove Farm
NORTHFIELDS
TUDOR AVE
RG20
Old St
Down Farm
Oareborough Hill
New Rd
Downend
Bradleyhill Copse
BARDOWN
DOWNEND LA
Sunhill Farm
Ash Row
Oareborough La
FRESHFIELDS LA
Middle Farm
POINTERS CL
BARTON COPSE
MIDDLE FARM CL
Fir Tree Farm
Sandy La
Nursery
RG18
Bradley Court Cottages
THE GREEN
Hall
OXFORD RD
Bradleyhome Wood
Bradley Court
Nursery
Nursery
OLD ST
MANOR LA
Chieveley
HIGH ST
Chieveley Manor
CHURCH LA
PO
HAZELDENE
EAST LA
Ashfield's Farm Ind Est
M4

78
52

51
31

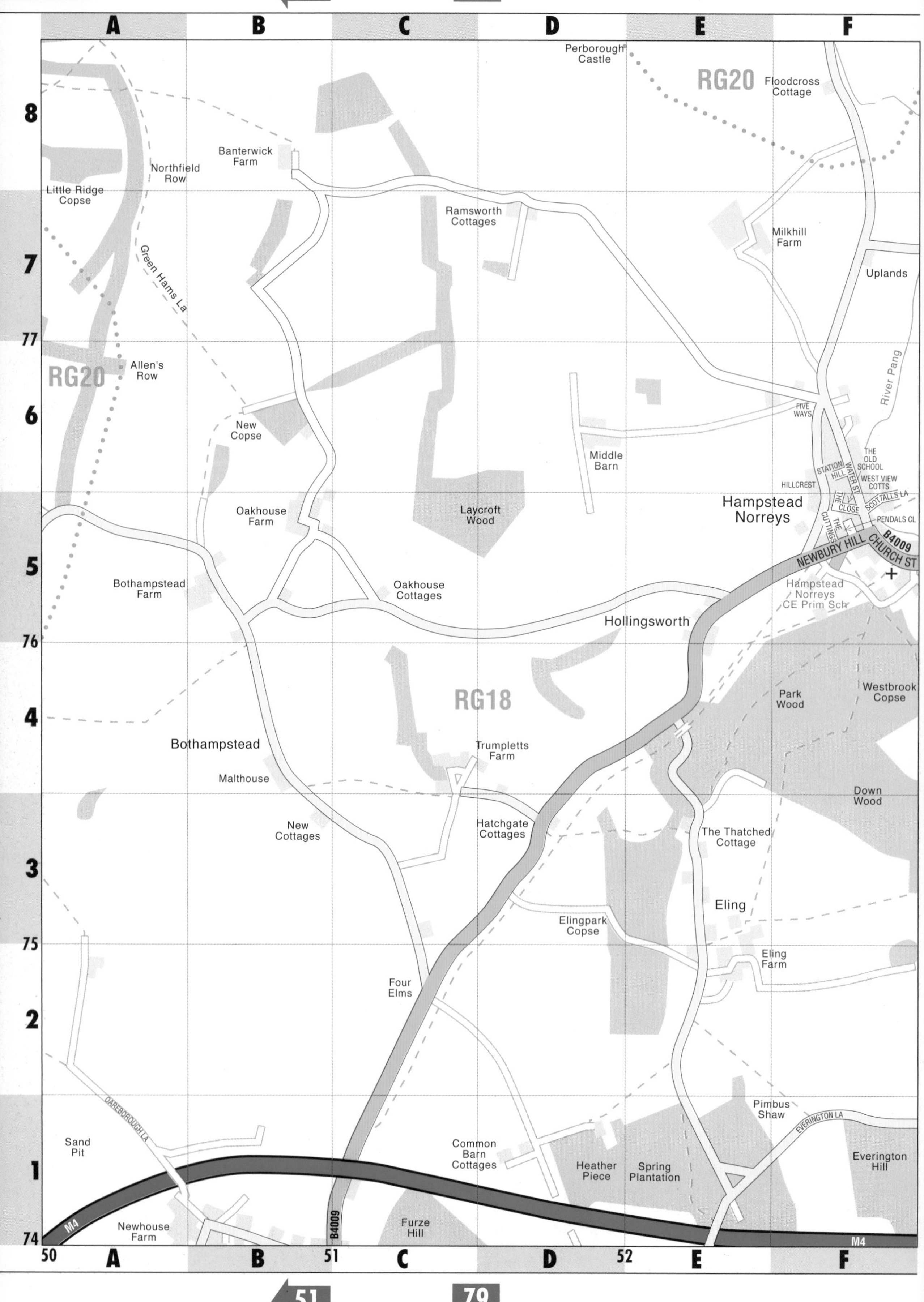
A
B
C
D
E
F
8
7
77
6
5
76
4
3
75
2
1
74
50
51
52
Perborough Castle
RG20
Floodcross Cottage
Banterwick Farm
Northfield Row
Little Ridge Copse
Ramsworth Cottages
Milkhill Farm
Uplands
Green Hams La
Allen's Row
RG20
River Pang
New Copse
FIVE WAYS
Middle Barn
THE OLD SCHOOL
STATION HILL
WATER ST
WEST VIEW COTTS
HILLCREST
SCOTTALLS LA
THE CLOSE
Hampstead Norreys
PENDALS CL
THE CUTTINGS
Oakhouse Farm
Laycroft Wood
B4009
NEWBURY HILL
CHURCH ST
Bothampstead Farm
Oakhouse Cottages
Hampstead Norreys CE Prim Sch
Hollingsworth
RG18
Park Wood
Westbrook Copse
Bothampstead
Trumpletts Farm
Malthouse
Down Wood
New Cottages
Hatchgate Cottages
The Thatched Cottage
Eling
Elingpark Copse
Eling Farm
Four Elms
Pimbus Shaw
OAREBOROUGH LA
EVERINGTON LA
Sand Pit
Common Barn Cottages
Heather Piece
Spring Plantation
Everington Hill
M4
Newhouse Farm
B4009
Furze Hill
M4

51
79

32
54

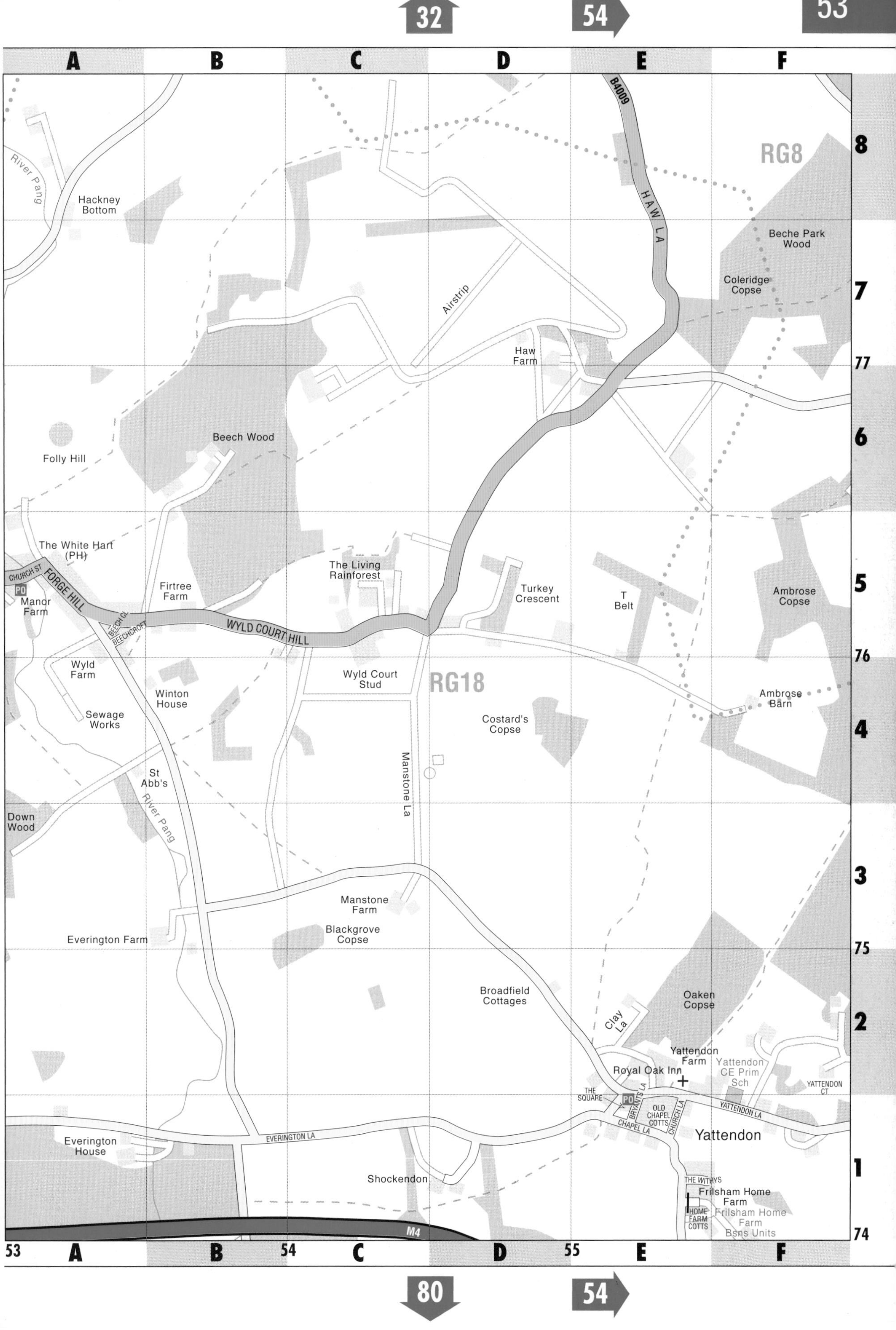
A
B
C
D
E
F
8
7
77
6
5
76
4
3
75
2
1
74
53
54
55
RG8
RG18
B4009
HAW LA
River Pang
Hackney
Bottom
Beche Park
Wood
Coleridge
Copse
Airstrip
Haw
Farm
Beech Wood
Folly Hill
The White Hart
(PH)
CHURCH ST
FORGE HILL
PO
Manor
Farm
Firtree
Farm
BEECH CL
BEECHCROFT
WYLD COURT HILL
The Living
Rainforest
Turkey
Crescent
T
Belt
Ambrose
Copse
Wyld
Farm
Winton
House
Wyld Court
Stud
Sewage
Works
Ambrose
Barn
Costard's
Copse
St
Abb's
Manstone La
Down
Wood
Manstone
Farm
Blackgrove
Copse
Everington Farm
Broadfield
Cottages
Clay
La
Oaken
Copse
Yattendon
Farm
Yattendon
CE Prim
Sch
Royal Oak Inn
THE
SQUARE
BRYANTS LA
OLD
CHAPEL
COTTS
CHURCH LA
YATTENDON LA
YATTENDON
CT
CHAPEL LA
Yattendon
EVERINGTON LA
Everington
House
Shockendon
THE WITHYS
Frilsham Home
Farm
HOME
FARM
COTTS
Frilsham Home
Farm
Bsns Units
M4

80
54

53
33

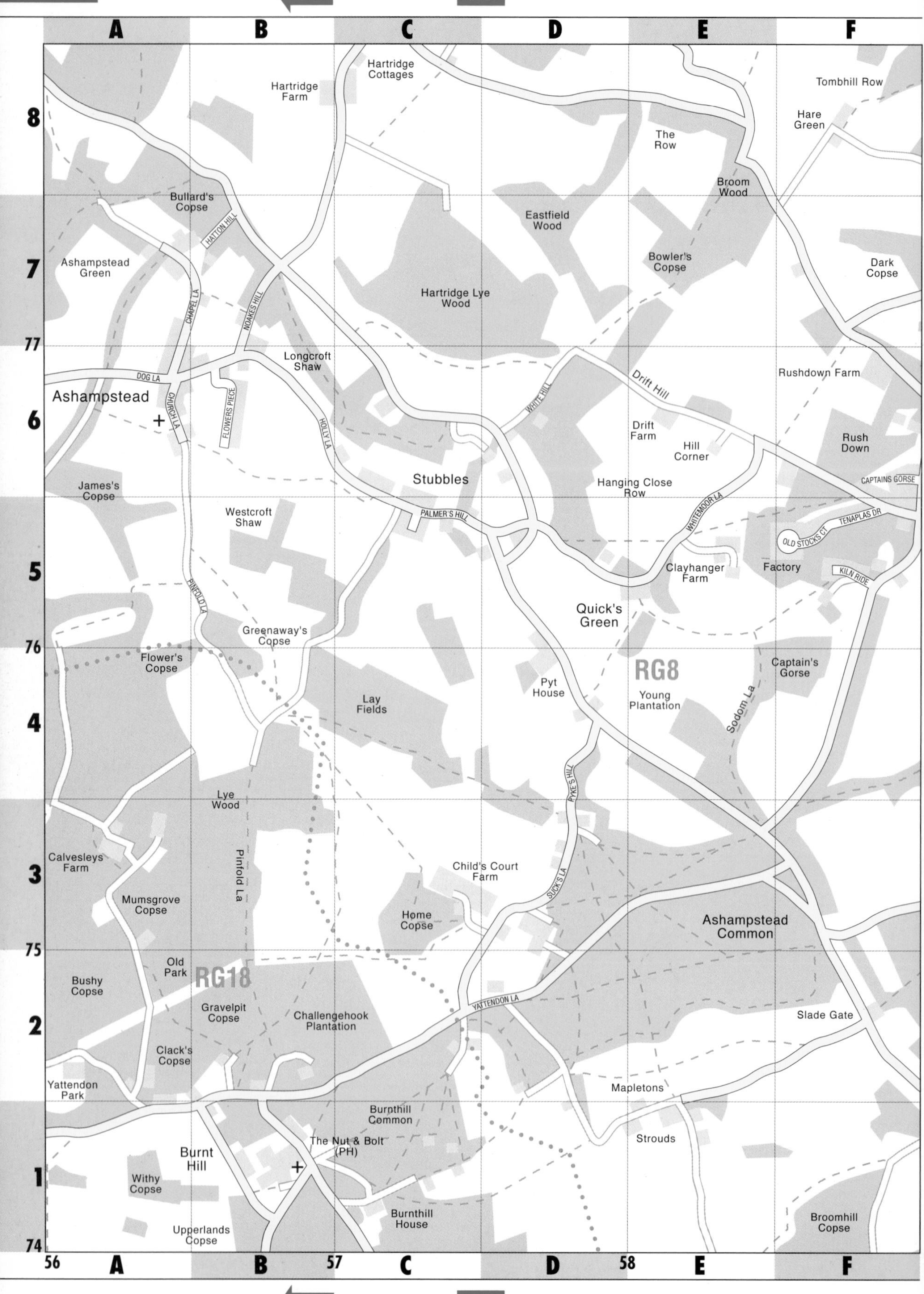
A
B
C
D
E
F
8
7
77
6
5
76
4
3
75
2
1
74
56
57
58
Hartridge Cottages
Hartridge Farm
Tombhill Row
Hare Green
The Row
Broom Wood
Bullard's Copse
HATTON HILL
Eastfield Wood
Bowler's Copse
Ashampstead Green
Dark Copse
CHAPEL LA
NOAKES HILL
Hartridge Lye Wood
Longcroft Shaw
DOG LA
Drift Hill
Rushdown Farm
Ashampstead
CHURCH LA
FLOWERS PIECE
WHITE HILL
HOLLY LA
Drift Farm
Hill Corner
Rush Down
Stubbles
James's Copse
Hanging Close Row
CAPTAINS GORSE
Westcroft Shaw
PALMER'S HILL
WHITEMOOR LA
TENAPLAS DR
OLD STOCKS CT
Clayhanger Farm
Factory
KILN RIDE
PINFOLD LA
Quick's Green
Greenaway's Copse
Flower's Copse
RG8
Captain's Gorse
Pyt House
Young Plantation
Lay Fields
Sodom La
PYKE'S HILL
Lye Wood
Pinfold La
Calvesleys Farm
Child's Court Farm
SUCK'S LA
Mumsgrove Copse
Home Copse
Ashampstead Common
Old Park
RG18
Bushy Copse
YATTENDON LA
Gravelpit Copse
Challengehook Plantation
Slade Gate
Clack's Copse
Yattendon Park
Mapletons
Burnthill Common
Strouds
The Nut & Bolt (PH)
Burnt Hill
Withy Copse
Burnthill House
Broomhill Copse
Upperlands Copse

53
81

A B C D E F

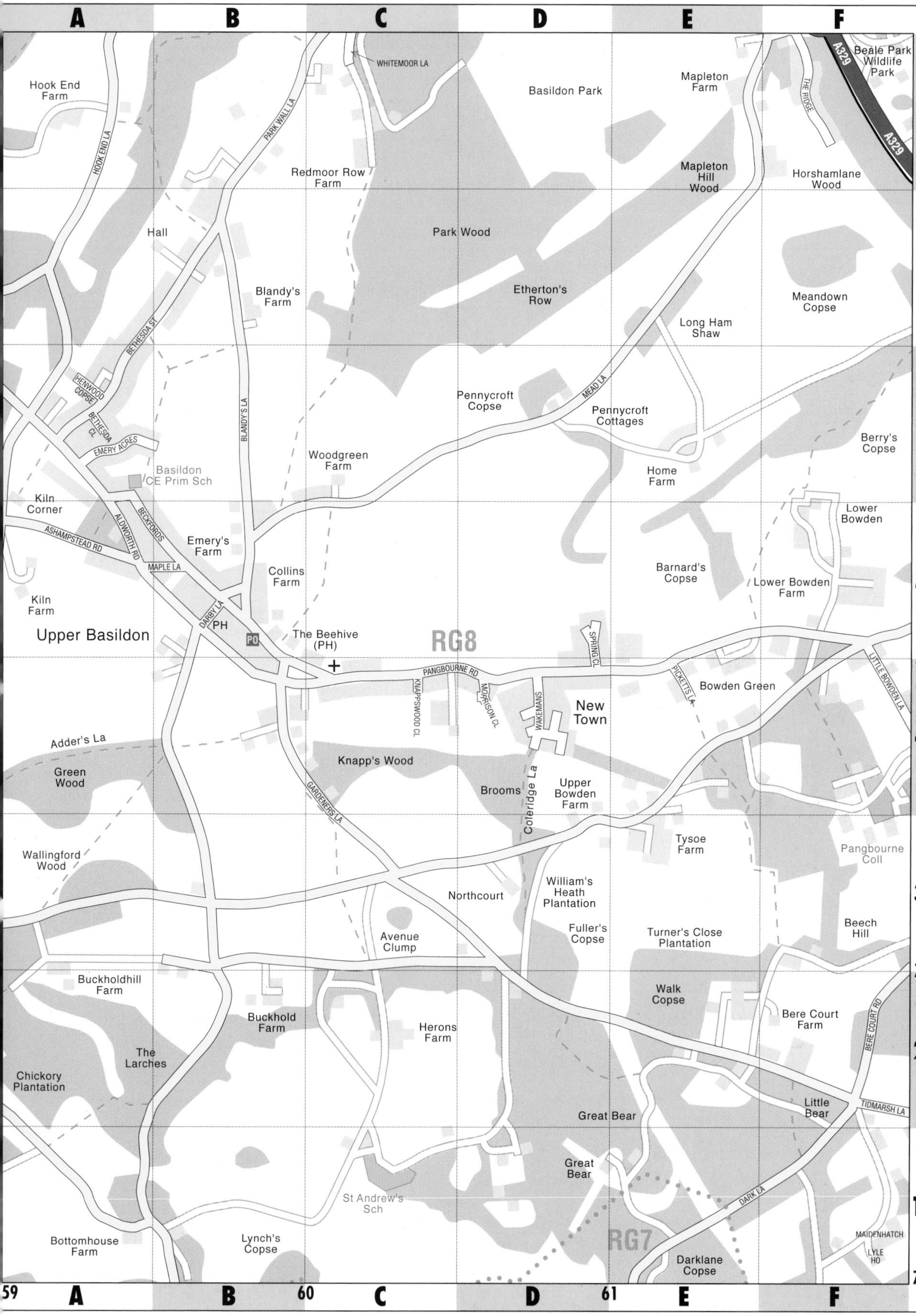

8
Hook End Farm
HOOK END LA
WHITEMOOR LA
PARK WALL LA
Basildon Park
Mapleton Farm
Beale Park Wildlife Park
A329
THE RIDGE
Redmoor Row Farm
Mapleton Hill Wood
Horshamlane Wood

7
Hall
Park Wood
Blandy's Farm
BETHESDA ST
Etherton's Row
Meandown Copse
Long Ham Shaw

77
HENWOOD COPSE
BETHESDA CL
EMERY ACRES
BLANDY'S LA
Pennycroft Copse
MEAD LA
Pennycroft Cottages

6
Berry's Copse
Woodgreen Farm
Basildon CE Prim Sch
Home Farm
Kiln Corner
ASHAMPSTEAD RD
ALDWORTH RD
BECKFORDS
Emery's Farm
MAPLE LA
Lower Bowden

5
Collins Farm
Barnard's Copse
Lower Bowden Farm
Kiln Farm
DARBY LA
PH
PO
Upper Basildon
The Beehive (PH)
RG8
SPRING CL

76
PANGBOURNE RD
KNAPPSWOOD CL
MORRISON CL
WAKEMANS
New Town
PICKETTS LA
Bowden Green
LITTLE BOWDEN LA

4
Adder's La
Green Wood
Knapp's Wood
GARDENERS LA
Brooms
Coleridge La
Upper Bowden Farm
Tysoe Farm
Wallingford Wood
Pangbourne Coll

3
William's Heath Plantation
Northcourt
Fuller's Copse
Avenue Clump
Turner's Close Plantation
Beech Hill

75
Buckholdhill Farm
Buckhold Farm
Herons Farm
Walk Copse
Bere Court Farm
BERE COURT RD

2
The Larches
Chickory Plantation
Little Bear
TIDMARSH LA
Great Bear
Great Bear

1
St Andrew's Sch
DARK LA
RG7
MAIDENHATCH
LYLE HO
Bottomhouse Farm
Lynch's Copse
Darklane Copse

74

59 A B 60 C D 61 E F

82
56

55

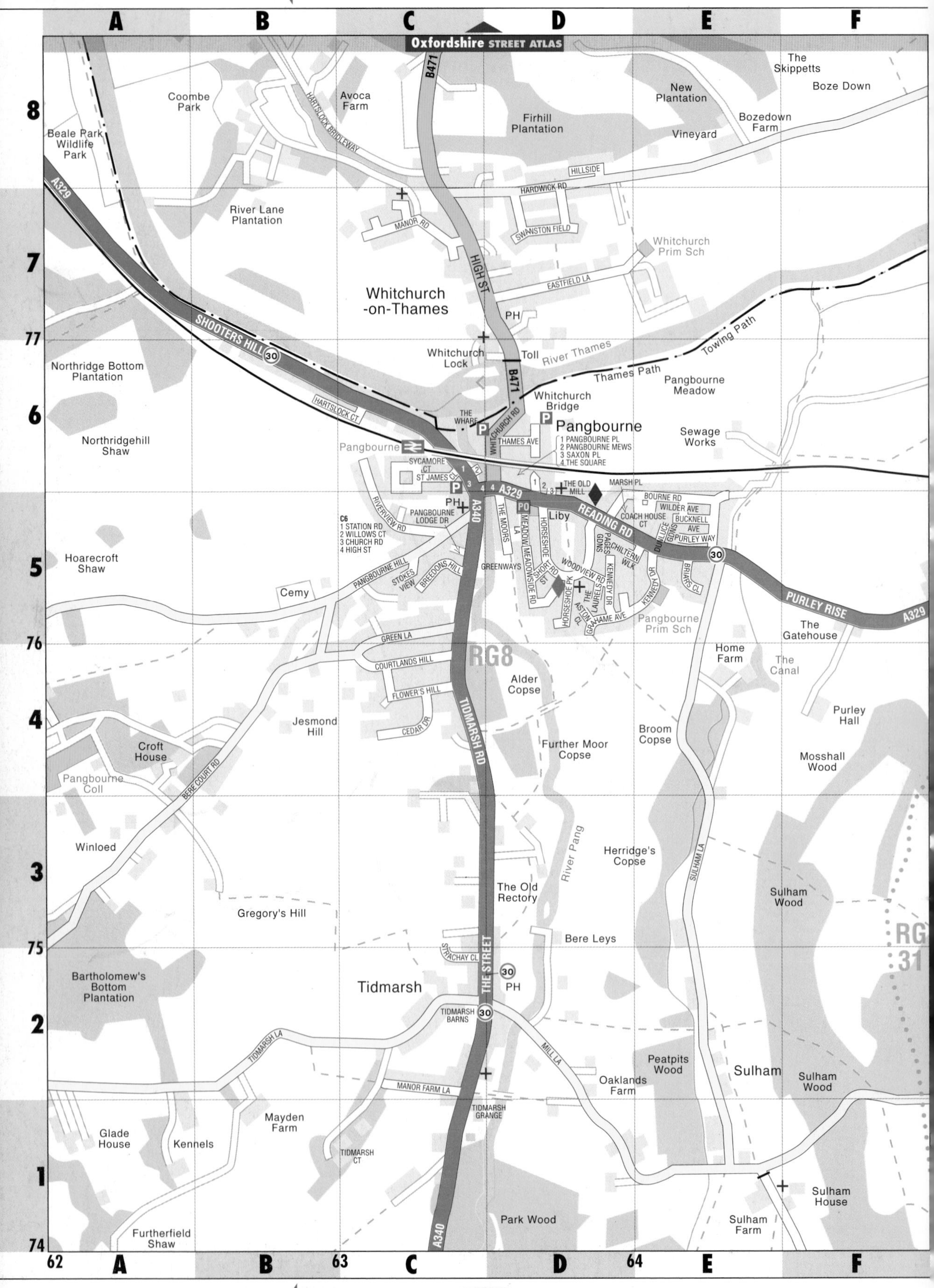

A B C D E F
8 7 77 6 5 76 4 3 75 2 1 74
62 63 64
Oxfordshire STREET ATLAS
B471
Coombe Park
Avoca Farm
HARTSLOCK BRIDLEWAY
Firhill Plantation
New Plantation
The Skippetts
Boze Down
Bozedown Farm
Vineyard
Beale Park Wildlife Park
HILLSIDE
HARDWICK RD
A329
River Lane Plantation
MANOR RD
SWANSTON FIELD
HIGH ST
Whitchurch Prim Sch
EASTFIELD LA
Whitchurch -on-Thames
PH
SHOOTERS HILL
Towing Path
Northridge Bottom Plantation
Whitchurch Lock
Toll
River Thames
Thames Path
Pangbourne Meadow
Whitchurch Bridge
HARTSLOCK CT
THE WHARF
WHITCHURCH RD
Pangbourne
Northridgehill Shaw
Sewage Works
THAMES AVE
1 PANGBOURNE PL
2 PANGBOURNE MEWS
3 SAXON PL
4 THE SQUARE
SYCAMORE CT
ST JAMES CL
THE OLD MILL
MARSH PL
BOURNE RD
WILDER AVE
BUCKNELL AVE
PURLEY WAY
COACH HOUSE CT
READING RD
PO
Liby
RIVERVIEW RD
PANGBOURNE LODGE DR
C6
1 STATION RD
2 WILLOWS CT
3 CHURCH RD
4 HIGH ST
A340
THE MOORS
MEADOW LA
MEADOWSIDE RD
HORSESHOE RD
SHORT ST
PAGES GDNS
CHILTERN WLK
DUNLUCE GDNS
KENNEDY DR
WOODVIEW RD
THE LAURELS
ASTON CL
GRAHAME AVE
HORSESHOE PK
BRIARS CL
Hoarecroft Shaw
PANGBOURNE HILL
STOKES VIEW
BREEDONS HILL
GREENWAYS
PURLEY RISE
Cemy
Pangbourne Prim Sch
The Gatehouse
GREEN LA
COURTLANDS HILL
RG8
Home Farm
The Canal
Alder Copse
FLOWER'S HILL
Jesmond Hill
CEDAR DR
TIDMARSH RD
Broom Copse
Purley Hall
Further Moor Copse
Croft House
Mosshall Wood
Pangbourne Coll
BERE COURT RD
River Pang
Herridge's Copse
SULHAM LA
Winloed
The Old Rectory
Sulham Wood
Gregory's Hill
Bere Leys
RG 31
STRACHAY CL
THE STREET
Bartholomew's Bottom Plantation
Tidmarsh
TIDMARSH BARNS
TIDMARSH LA
MILL LA
Peatpits Wood
Sulham
Sulham Wood
Oaklands Farm
MANOR FARM LA
TIDMARSH GRANGE
Glade House
Kennels
Mayden Farm
TIDMARSH CT
Sulham House
Park Wood
Furtherfield Shaw
Sulham Farm

55

83

58

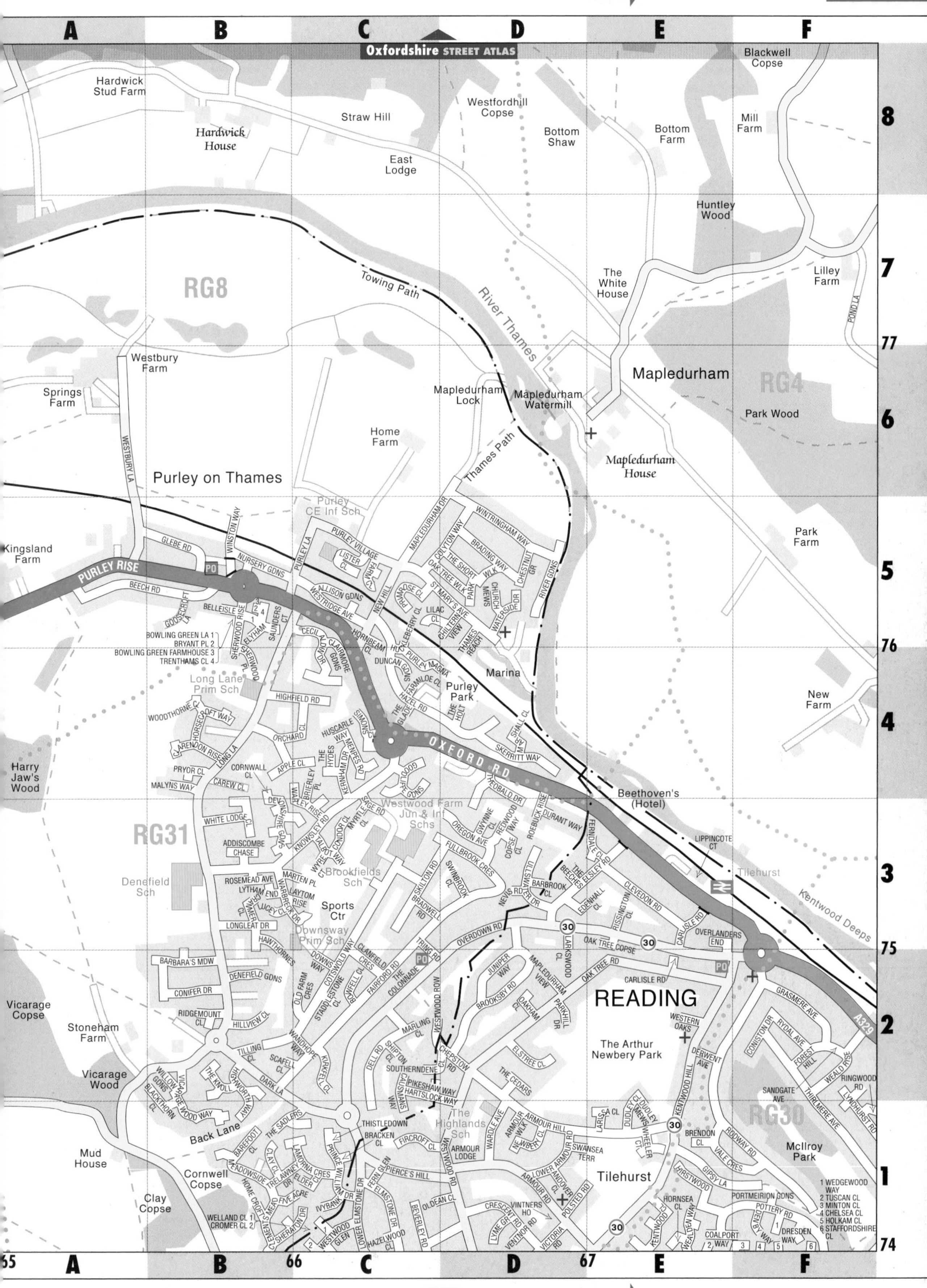
Oxfordshire STREET ATLAS
A
B
C
D
E
F
Hardwick Stud Farm
Hardwick House
Straw Hill
East Lodge
Westfordhill Copse
Bottom Shaw
Bottom Farm
Blackwell Copse
Mill Farm
Huntley Wood
RG8
Towing Path
River Thames
The White House
Lilley Farm
POND LA
Westbury Farm
Springs Farm
Mapledurham Lock
Mapledurham Watermill
Mapledurham
RG4
Park Wood
Home Farm
Thames Path
Mapledurham House
WESTBURY LA
Purley on Thames
Purley CE Inf Sch
Park Farm
Kingsland Farm
PURLEY RISE
GLEBE RD
WINSTON WAY
NURSERY GDNS
PURLEY LA
PURLEY VILLAGE
LISTER CL
BEECH RD
GOOSECROFT LA
BELLEISLE
ALLISON GDNS
WESTRIDGE AVE
NEW HILL
MAPLEDURHAM DR
COLYTON WAY
WINTRINGHAM WAY
BRADING WAY
THE SHORT
OAK TREE WLK
CHESTNUT GR
RIVER GDNS
CHURCH MEWS
WATERSIDE DR
ST MARY'S AVE
LILAC CL
CHILTERN VIEW
THAMES REACH
BOWLING GREEN LA 1
BRYANT PL 2
BOWLING GREEN FARMHOUSE 3
TRENTHAMS CL 4
SHERWOOD RISE
ELYHAM
SAUNDERS CT
CECIL
CLAIRMORE GDNS
HORNBEAM CL
HUCKLEBERRY CL
PURLEY MAGNA
DUNCAN GDNS
FARMILOE CL
Marina
Long Lane Prim Sch
HIGHFIELD RD
HAZEL RD
THE GLADE
THE HOLT
Purley Park
WOODTHORNE CL
HORSECROFT WAY
ORCHARD CL
HUSCARLE WAY
SIMONS CL
SHALL CL
New Farm
CLARENDON RISE
LONG LA
OXFORD RD
SKERRITT WAY
PRYOR CL
CORNWALL CL
APPLE CL
THE HYDES
KERNHAM DR
MENPES RD
GOODLIFFE GDNS
Harry Jaw's Wood
MALYNS WAY
CAREW CL
DEVONSHIRE GDNS
WARLEY RISE
BRIERLEY PL
THEOBALD DR
Beethoven's (Hotel)
Westwood Farm Jun & Inf Schs
GWYNNE CL
REDWOOD WAY
ROEBUCK RISE
DURANT WAY
WHITE LODGE CL
RG31
KNOWSLEY RD
CONDOR CL
OREGON AVE
COPSE CL
FERNDALE CL
LIPPINCOTE CT
ADDISCOMBE CHASE
FULLBROOK CRES
Tilehurst
Denefield Sch
ROSEMEAD AVE
MARTEN PL
Brookfields Sch
SWINBROOK CL
ULLSWATER DR
THE BEECHES
ELSLEY RD
Kentwood Deeps
LYTHAM END
LAYTOM RISE
SKILTON RD
NEVIS RD
BARBROOK CL
EDENHALL CL
CLEVEDON RD
Sports Ctr
BRADWELL RD
RISSINGTON CL
3
LONGLEAT DR
Downsway Prim Sch
OVERDOWN RD
LARKSWOOD CL
OAK TREE COPSE
CARLISLE RD
OVERLANDERS END
75
HAWTHORNES
CLANFIELD CRES
TRING RD
BARBARA'S MDW
DOWNS WAY
FAIRFORD RD
THE COLONNADE
JUNIPER WAY
MAPLEDURHAM VIEW
OAK TREE RD
DENEFIELD GDNS
CARLISLE RD
A329
COTSWOLD WAY
GRASMERE AVE
CONIFER DR
OLD FARM CRES
BOSWELL CL
WESTWOOD ROW
BROOKSBY RD
OAKHAM CL
PARKHILL DR
READING
Vicarage Copse
RIDGEMOUNT CL
STAPLESTONE RD
WESTERN OAKS
RYDAL AVE
CONISTON DR
HILLVIEW CL
MARLING CL
The Arthur Newbery Park
Stoneham Farm
WANDHOPE WAY
KIRKFELL CL
DELL RD
SHIPTON CL
CHEPSTOW RD
ELSTREE CL
DERWENT AVE
FOREST HILL
WEALD RISE
TILLING CL
SCAFELL CL
SOUTHERNDENE CL
THE CEDARS
KENTWOOD HILL
RINGWOOD RD
Vicarage Wood
THE KNOLL
HIGHWORTH WAY
DARK LA
PIKESHAW WAY
HARTSLOCK WAY
SANDGATE AVE
THIRLMERE AVE
LYNDHURST RD
WILLOW GDNS
VICARAGE WOOD WAY
CAUSMANS WAY
The Highlands Sch
WARDLE AVE
ARMOUR HILL
LARISSA CL
DUDLEY MEWS
WHEELER CL
RG30
BLACKTHORN CL
Back Lane
THE SADLERS
THISTLEDOWN
NEWBERY CL
ARMOUR RD
SWANSEA TERR
BRENDON CL
RODWAY RD
Mud House
BAREFOOT CL
CLAY CL
LAMORNA CRES
BRACKEN CL
FIRCROFT CL
ARMOUR LODGE
VALE CRES
McIlroy Park
Cornwell Copse
MEADOWSIDE
TRELAWNEY DR
ELDER CL
PRINCE WILLIAM DR
FERN GLEN
PIERCE'S HILL
LOWER ARMOUR RD
ANDOVER CL
Tilehurst
HIRSTWOOD
GIPSY LA
1 WEDGEWOOD WAY
2 TUSCAN CL
3 MINTON CL
4 CHELSEA CL
5 HOLKAM CL
6 STAFFORDSHIRE CL
Clay Copse
HOME CROFT
FINCH ACRE
IVYBANK
ELMSTONE DR
OLDEAN CL
POLSTED RD
HORNSEA CL
PORTMEIRION GDNS
WELLAND CL 1
CROMER CL 2
CLEMENTS MEAD
SHERATON DR
WESTWOOD GLEN
LOWER ELMSTONE DR
HAZELWOOD CL
BEVERLEY RD
CRESCENT RD
LYME GR
VINTNERS HO
VENTNOR RD
VICTORIA RD
KENTWOOD CL
WEALDEN WAY
COALPORT WAY
POTTERY RD
DENBY WAY
DRESDEN WAY
8
7
77
6
5
76
4
3
75
2
1
74
65
66
67
30

84
58

57

A
B
C
D
E
F
8
7
77
6
5
76
4
3
75
2
1
74
68
69
70
A4074 Wallingford
Oxfordshire STREET ATLAS
Greendene Farm
Newell's Copse
Curr's Copse
Trench Green
Pithouse Farm
Chazey Heath
Tokers Green
Dysons Wood Farm
Tokers Green Farm
Tanners Lane Farm
Fox Hill Farm
Middle Farm
Pack Saddle Inn (PH)
Page's Shaw
Newell's La
Farthingworth Green
Shipnell's Cottages
Noke End Shaw
Rose Farm
RG4
Sandy Hill
Hemdean Bottom
Blagrave Farm House
Grain Store
Chazey Wood
King's Hill
Gravel Hill
Caversham Heights
Chazey Court Farm
The Chase
The Fishery
The Warren
River Thames
St Mary's Island
Poplar Island
Gresham Way Ind Est
Appletree Eyot
Upper Large
Towing Path
Thames Path
Coombe Bank
Thames Side Promenade
Allot Gdns
Rivermead L Ctr
Hotel
RG1
RG30
Little John's Farm
Reading West Junction
The Portman Ctr
Reading Ret Pk
UPPER WOODCOTE RD
WOODCOTE RD
ST PETER'S HILL A4074
OXFORD RD
A329
1 WARREN HO
2 WARREN HOUSE CT
3 WARREN CT

57

85

60

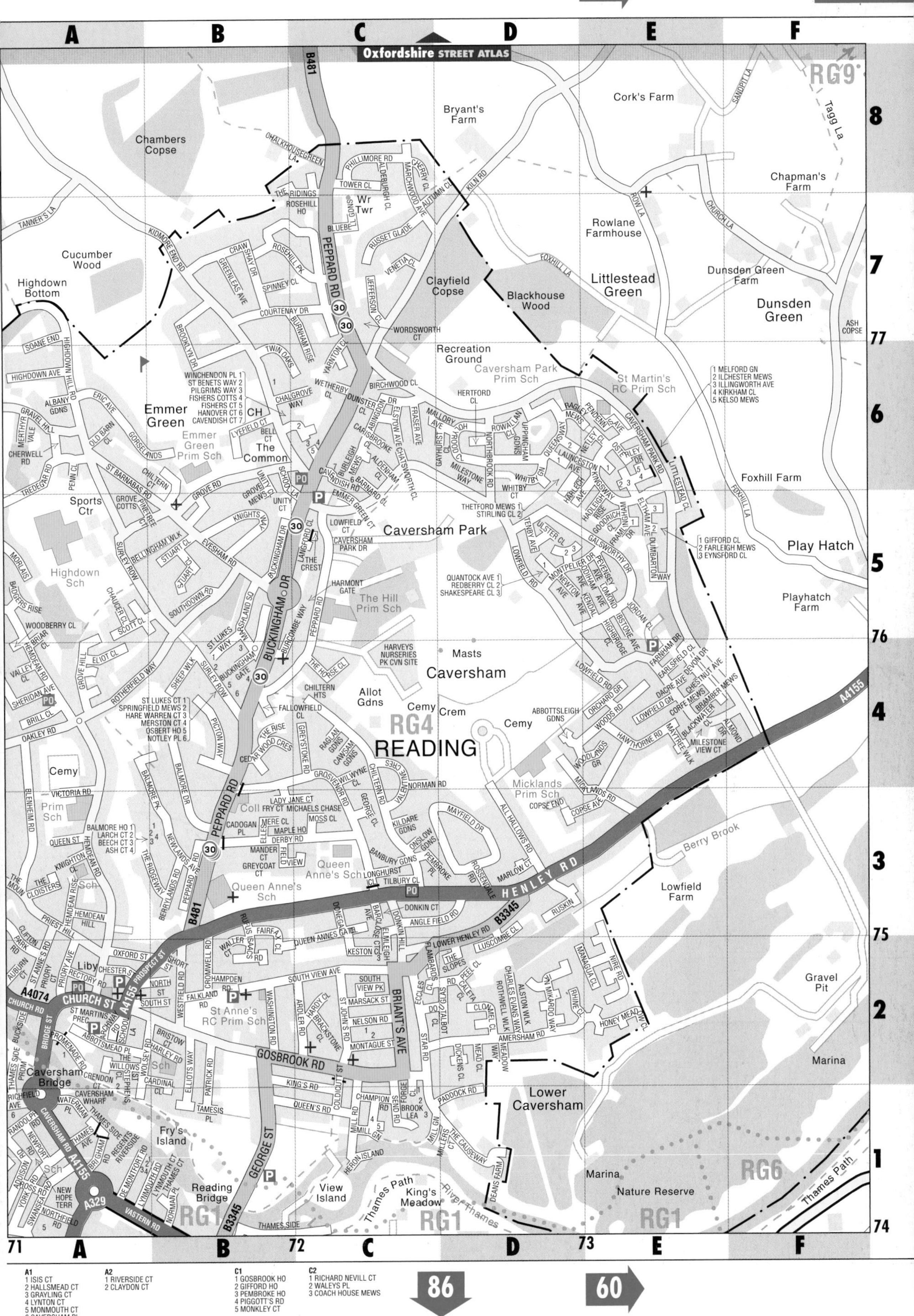

A1	A2	C1	C2
1 ISIS CT	1 RIVERSIDE CT	1 GOSBROOK HO	1 RICHARD NEVILL CT
2 HALLSMEAD CT	2 CLAYDON CT	2 GIFFORD HO	2 WALEYS PL
3 GRAYLING CT		3 PEMBROKE HO	3 COACH HOUSE MEWS
4 LYNTON CT		4 PIGGOTT'S RD	
5 MONMOUTH CT		5 MONKLEY CT	
6 CAVERSHAM PL			

86

60

59 35

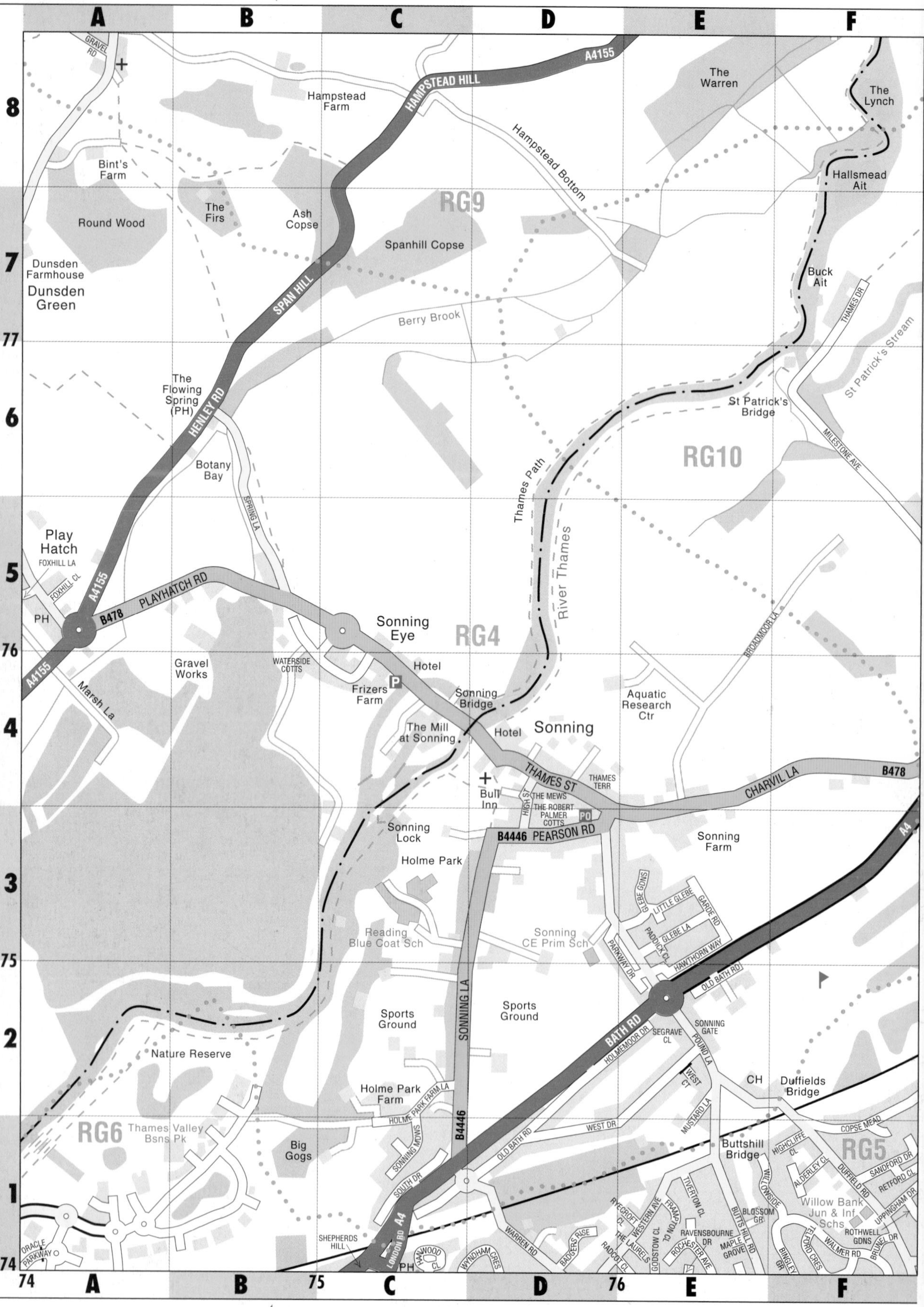

A B C D E F

8 7 77 6 5 76 4 3 75 2 1 74

The Warren
The Lynch
Hampstead Farm
HAMPSTEAD HILL
A4155
Hampstead Bottom
Bint's Farm
Hallsmead Ait
The Firs
Ash Copse
RG9
Round Wood
Spanhill Copse
Dunsden Farmhouse
Dunsden Green
SPAN HILL
Buck Ait
Berry Brook
THAMES DR
St Patrick's Stream
The Flowing Spring (PH)
HENLEY RD
St Patrick's Bridge
MILESTONE AVE
Botany Bay
Thames Path
RG10
SPRING LA
River Thames
Play Hatch
FOXHILL LA
FOXHILL CL
A4155
PLAYHATCH RD
B478
PH
Sonning Eye
RG4
BROADMOOR LA
Hotel
Gravel Works
WATERSIDE COTTS
Marsh La
Frizers Farm
Sonning Bridge
Aquatic Research Ctr
The Mill at Sonning
Hotel
Sonning
THAMES ST
THAMES TERR
CHARVIL LA
B478
Bull Inn
HIGH ST
THE MEWS
THE ROBERT PALMER COTTS
PO
Sonning Lock
B4446 PEARSON RD
Sonning Farm
A4
Holme Park
GLEBE GDNS
LITTLE GLEBE
GARDE RD
Reading Blue Coat Sch
Sonning CE Prim Sch
GLEBE LA
PADDICK CL
HAWTHORN WAY
PARKWAY DR
OLD BATH RD
Sports Ground
SONNING LA
Sports Ground
BATH RD
SEGRAVE CL
SONNING GATE
HOLMEMOOR DR
POUND LA
Nature Reserve
WEST CT
CH
Duffields Bridge
Holme Park Farm
HOLME PARK FARM LA
MUSTARD LA
RG6
Thames Valley Bsns Pk
WEST DR
COPSE MEAD
Big Gogs
SONNING MEWS
B4446
OLD BATH RD
Buttshill Bridge
HIGHCLIFFE CL
RG5
ALDERLEY CL
DUFFIELD RD
SANDFORD DR
RETFORD CL
SOUTH DR
WILLOWSIDE
TIVERTON CL
Willow Bank Jun & Inf Schs
UPPINGHAM DR
RYECROFT CL
WESTERN AVE
FRAMPTON CL
BLOSSOM GR
ROTHWELL GDNS
A4
THE LAURELS
RAVENSBOURNE DR
BUTTS HILL RD
WALMER RD
BRUNEL DR
SHEPHERDS HILL
LONDON RD
HAYWOOD CL
PH
WYNDHAM CRES
WARREN RD
BADGERS RISE
RADCOT CL
GODSTOW CL
ROCHESTER AVE
MAPLE GROVE
BINGLEY GR
TELFORD CRES
ORACLE PARKWAY

74 A B 75 C D 76 E F

59 87

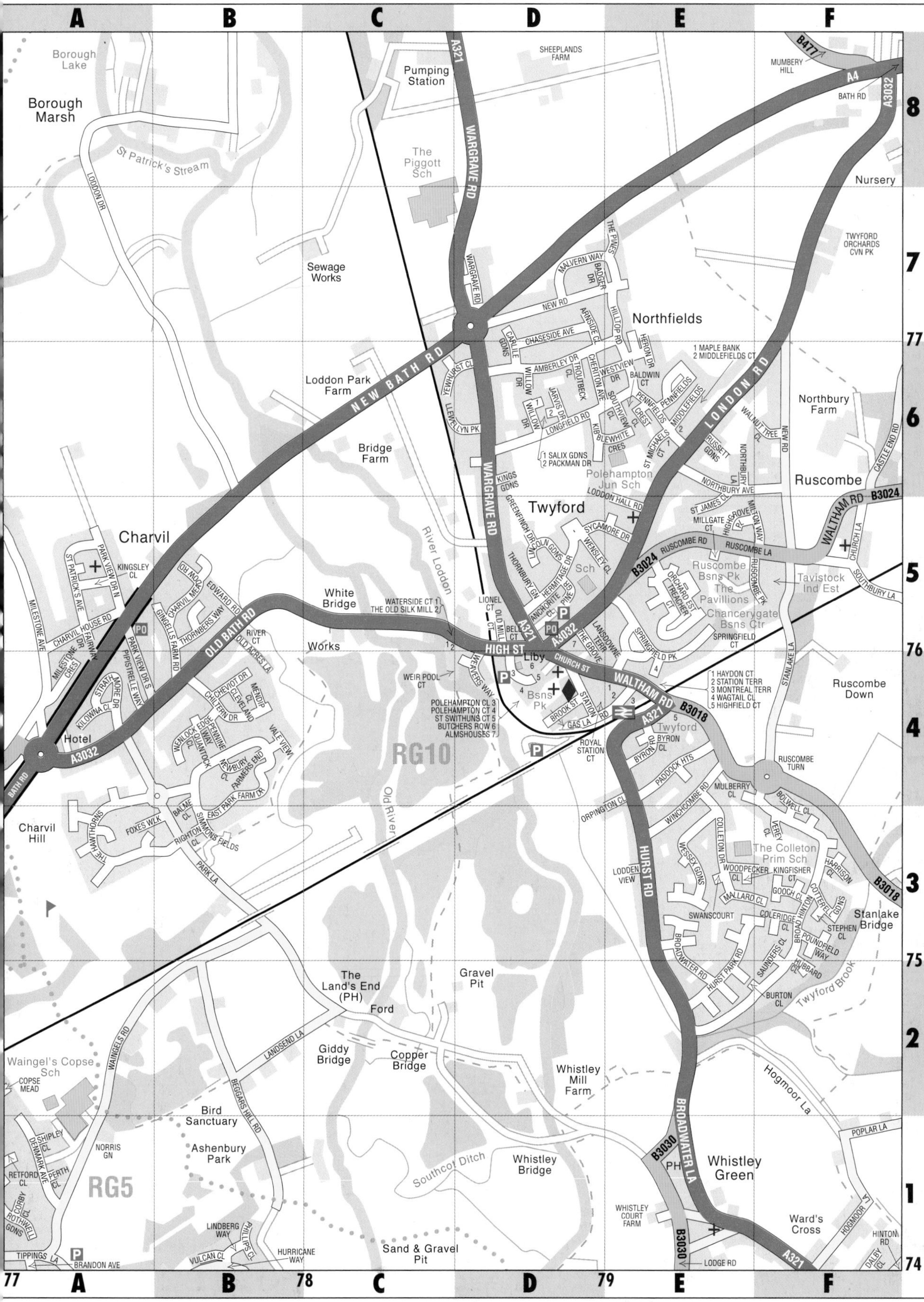

A B C D E F

8 7 77 6 5 76 4 3 75 2 1 74

Borough Lake
Borough Marsh
St Patrick's Stream
LODDON DR
Pumping Station
SHEEPLANDS FARM
A321
WARGRAVE RD
The Piggott Sch
Sewage Works
B477
MUMBERY HILL
A4
BATH RD
A3032
Nursery
TWYFORD ORCHARDS CVN PK
THE PINES
MALVERN WAY
BADGER DR
NEW RD
Northfields
ARNSIDE CL
HILLTOP RD
CARLILE GDNS
CHASESIDE AVE
HERON DR
1 MAPLE BANK
2 MIDDLEFIELDS CT
Loddon Park Farm
NEW BATH RD
YEWHURST CL
AMBERLEY DR
WILLOW DR
TROUTBECK CL
CHERITON AVE
WESTVIEW DR
BALDWIN CT
PENNFIELDS
MIDDLEFIELDS
LONDON RD
Northbury Farm
LLEWELLYN PK
JARVIS DR
LONGFIELD RD
SOUTHVIEW CL
CREST
KIBBLEWHITE CRES
ST MICHAELS CT
WALNUT TREE CL
NEW RD
RUSSETT GDNS
NORTHBURY LA
CASTLE END RD
Bridge Farm
1 SALIX GDNS
2 PACKMAN DR
Polehampton Jun Sch
KINGS GDNS
NORTHBURY AVE
Ruscombe
Twyford
LODDON HALL RD
ST JAMES CL
HIGHGROVE PL
MILTON WAY
WALTHAM RD
B3024
Charvil
River Loddon
GREENFINCH DR
MILLGATE CT
SYCAMORE DR
RUSCOMBE RD
RUSCOMBE LA
CHURCH LA
PARK VIEW DR N
ST PATRICK'S AVE
KINGSLEY CL
PARK VIEW DR S
CHARVIL MEADOW RD
EDWARD RD
LINCOLN GDNS
WENSLEY CL
Sch
Ruscombe Bsns Pk
Tavistock Ind Est
SOUTHBURY LA
THORNBURY GN
HERMITAGE DR
ANCHORITE CL
PINE CT
ORCHARD EST
TREACHER CT
RUSCOMBE PK
The Pavillions
White Bridge
WATERSIDE CT 1
THE OLD SILK MILL 2
LIONEL CT
OLD MILL CT
BELL CT
Chancerygate Bsns Ctr
SPRINGFIELD CT
CHARVIL HOUSE RD
FAIRWAY DR
GINGELLS FARM RD
THORNBERS WAY
OLD BATH RD
RIVER CT
OLD ACRES LA
PO
Works
HIGH ST
Liby
CHURCH ST
THE GROVE
LANSDOWNE TERR
SPRINGFIELD PK
MILESTONE AVE
MILESTONE CRES
STRATHMORE DR
PIPISTRELLE WAY
CHEVIOT DR
CLEVELAND
MENDIP CL
WEIR POOL CT
WEAVERS WAY
Bsns Pk
STATION RD
BROOK ST
GAS LA
1 HAYDON CT
2 STATION TERR
3 MONTREAL TERR
4 WAGTAIL CL
5 HIGHFIELD CT
STANLAKE LA
Ruscombe Down
KILOWNA CL
CHILTERN DR
WENLOCK EDGE
PENNINE WAY
QUANTOCK CL
VALE VIEW
POLEHAMPTON CL 3
POLEHAMPTON CT 4
ST SWITHUNS CT 5
BUTCHERS ROW 6
ALMSHOUSES 7
B3018
Twyford
BYRON RD
BYRON CL
Hotel
A3032
RG10
ROYAL STATION CT
PADDOCK HTS
RUSCOMBE TURN
NEWBURY CL
FARMERS END
EAST PARK FARM DR
MULBERRY CL
BOLWELL CL
BATH RD
ORPINGTON CL
WINCHCOMBE RD
Charvil Hill
THE HAWTHORNS
FOXES WLK
BALME CL
SIMMONS FIELDS
RIGHTON CL
Old River
HURST RD
COLLETON DR
VERITY CL
The Colleton Prim Sch
HARRISON CL
PARK LA
WESSEX GDNS
LODDEN VIEW
WOODPECKER CL
KINGFISHER CT
MALLARD CL
GOOCH CL
COTTERELL GDNS
B3018
SWANSCOURT
COLERIDGE CL
BROAD HINTON
STEPHEN CL
Stanlake Bridge
POUNDFIELD WAY
BROADWATER RD
HURST PARK RD
SAUNDERS CL
HUBBARD
The Land's End (PH)
Gravel Pit
Ford
BURTON CL
Twyford Brook
Waingel's Copse Sch
WAINGELS RD
LANDSEND LA
Giddy Bridge
Copper Bridge
Whistley Mill Farm
Hogmoor La
COPSE MEAD
BEGGARS HILL RD
Bird Sanctuary
BROADWATER LA
SHIPLEY CL
DENMARK AVE
NORRIS GN
Ashenbury Park
B3030
POPLAR LA
Southcot Ditch
Whistley Bridge
Whistley Green
PH
PERTH CL
RETFORD CL
RG5
CORBY CL
ROTHWELL GDNS
WHISTLEY COURT FARM
Ward's Cross
HOGMOOR LA
LINDBERG WAY
PHILLIPS CL
Sand & Gravel Pit
HINTON RD
B3030
TIPPINGS LA
BRANDON AVE
VULCAN CL
HURRICANE WAY
LODGE RD
A321
DALBY CL

77 A B 78 C D 79 E F

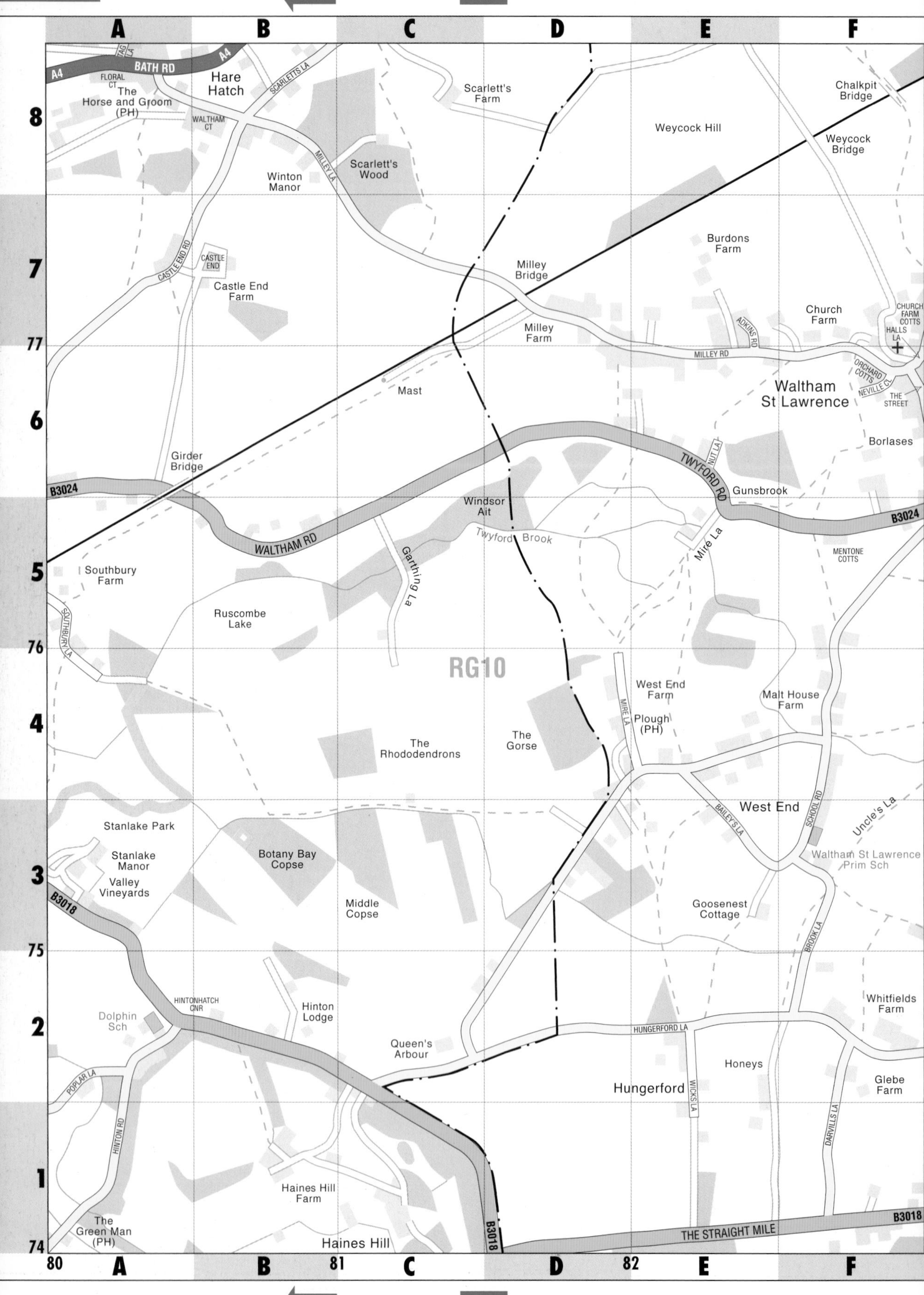

61
37
A
B
C
D
E
F
8
7
77
6
5
76
4
3
75
2
1
74
80
81
82
A4
BATH RD
FLORAL CT
The Horse and Groom (PH)
Hare Hatch
SCARLETTS LA
WALTHAM CT
Scarlett's Farm
Chalkpit Bridge
Weycock Hill
Weycock Bridge
Winton Manor
MILLEY LA
Scarlett's Wood
Burdons Farm
CASTLE END RD
CASTLE END
Castle End Farm
Milley Bridge
Church Farm
CHURCH FARM COTTS
HALLS LA
Milley Farm
ADKINS RD
MILLEY RD
ORCHARD COTTS
NEVILLE CL
THE STREET
Mast
Waltham St Lawrence
Borlases
NUT LA
Girder Bridge
TWYFORD RD
Gunsbrook
B3024
Windsor Ait
Twyford Brook
WALTHAM RD
Mire La
MENTONE COTTS
Southbury Farm
Garthing La
Ruscombe Lake
SOUTHBURY LA
RG10
West End Farm
Malt House Farm
MIRE LA
Plough (PH)
The Rhododendrons
The Gorse
BAILEY'S LA
West End
SCHOOL RD
Uncle's La
Stanlake Park
Stanlake Manor
Botany Bay Copse
Waltham St Lawrence Prim Sch
Valley Vineyards
B3018
Middle Copse
Goosenest Cottage
BROOK LA
Dolphin Sch
HINTONHATCH CNR
Hinton Lodge
Whitfields Farm
Queen's Arbour
HUNGERFORD LA
Honeys
POPLAR LA
Hungerford
Glebe Farm
WICKS LA
DARVILLS LA
HINTON RD
Haines Hill Farm
The Green Man (PH)
Haines Hill
THE STRAIGHT MILE
61
89

A B C D E F

8 7 77 6 5 76 4 3 75 2 1 74

Airfield
Sewage Works
Grove Pk
CHURCH VIEW
VICARAGE GDNS
BUTCHERS LA
CHERRY GARDEN LA
WALTHAM RD
White Waltham CE Sch
Shottesbrooke Park
White Waltham
Waltham Place
INNINGS LA
The Beehive (PH)
Shottesbrooke Park
BRAEMAR
WALGROVE GDNS
Halls Farm
HALLS LA
Burringham Wood
South Wood
BROADMOOR RD
PUNDLES LA
SL6
LITTLEFIELD GN
Littlefield Green
B3024
THE STREET
PH
Marsh Down
Refuse Tip
Cvn Pk
POOL LA
DOWNFIELD LA
Great Wood
M4
Smewins Farm
SMEWINS RD
DOWNFIELD RD
RG10
Crockford's Bridge
Pond Wood
Pondwood Farm
Uncle's La
Twyford Brook
Crockford's Copse
Long Wood
The Cut
Beenham's Farm
CALLIN'S LA
MARE LA
Old Malt House (Hill Farm)
Beenham's Heath
Pope's Farm
The Royal Oak (PH)
Great Martins
Little Hazes
HUNGERFORD LA
OAK COTT
Great Hazes
Manor Farm
RG42
HOWE LA
Buck Farm
Furze Ground
Shurlock Row
The Plantation
The White Hart (PH)
Yate's Farm
Mare La
Mast
Spinningwheel La
Benhams Copse
Jolly Farmer (PH)
THE STRAIGHT MILE
B3018
M4
WESTLEY MILL

83 A B 84 C D 85 E F

63
39

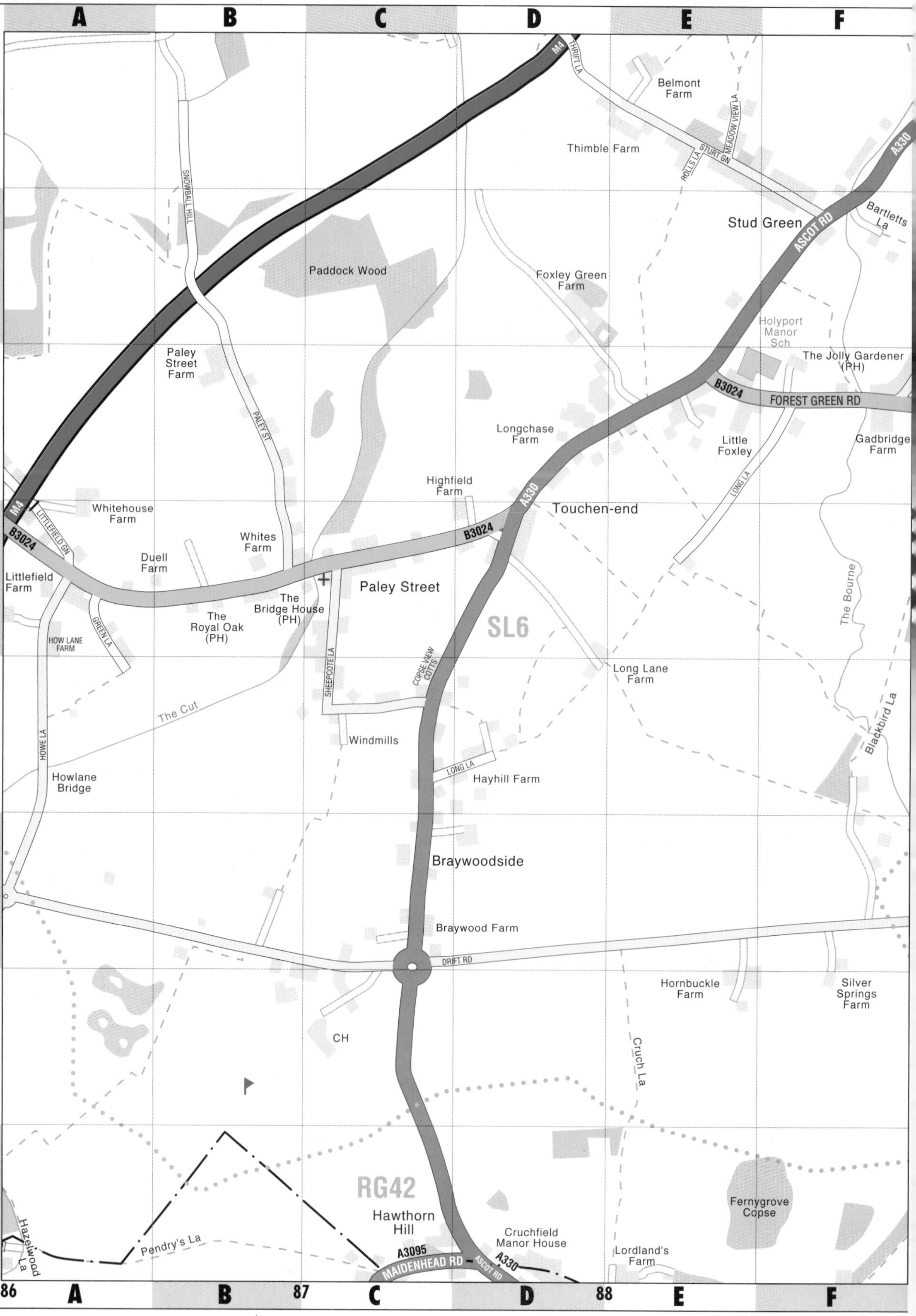

A B C D E F

8 7 77 6 5 76 4 3 75 2 1 74

M4
Thrift La
Belmont Farm
Meadow View La
Sturt Gn
Rolls La
Thimble Farm
A330
Snowball Hill
Stud Green
Ascot Rd
Bartletts La
Paddock Wood
Foxley Green Farm
Holyport Manor Sch
Paley Street Farm
The Jolly Gardener (PH)
B3024
Forest Green Rd
Paley St
Longchase Farm
Little Foxley
Gadbridge Farm
Highfield Farm
Long La
Whitehouse Farm
Littlefield Gn
Touchen-end
Whites Farm
Duell Farm
Littlefield Farm
Paley Street
The Bridge House (PH)
The Royal Oak (PH)
SL6
The Bourne
How Lane Farm
Green La
Copse View Cotts
Sheepcote La
Long Lane Farm
The Cut
Windmills
Blackbird La
Howe La
Howlane Bridge
Hayhill Farm
Braywoodside
Braywood Farm
Drift Rd
Hornbuckle Farm
Silver Springs Farm
CH
Cruch La
RG42
Fernygrove Copse
Hazelwood La
Hawthorn Hill
Cruchfield Manor House
Pendry's La
A3095
Maidenhead Rd
Ascot Rd
Lordland's Farm

86 87 88

63
91

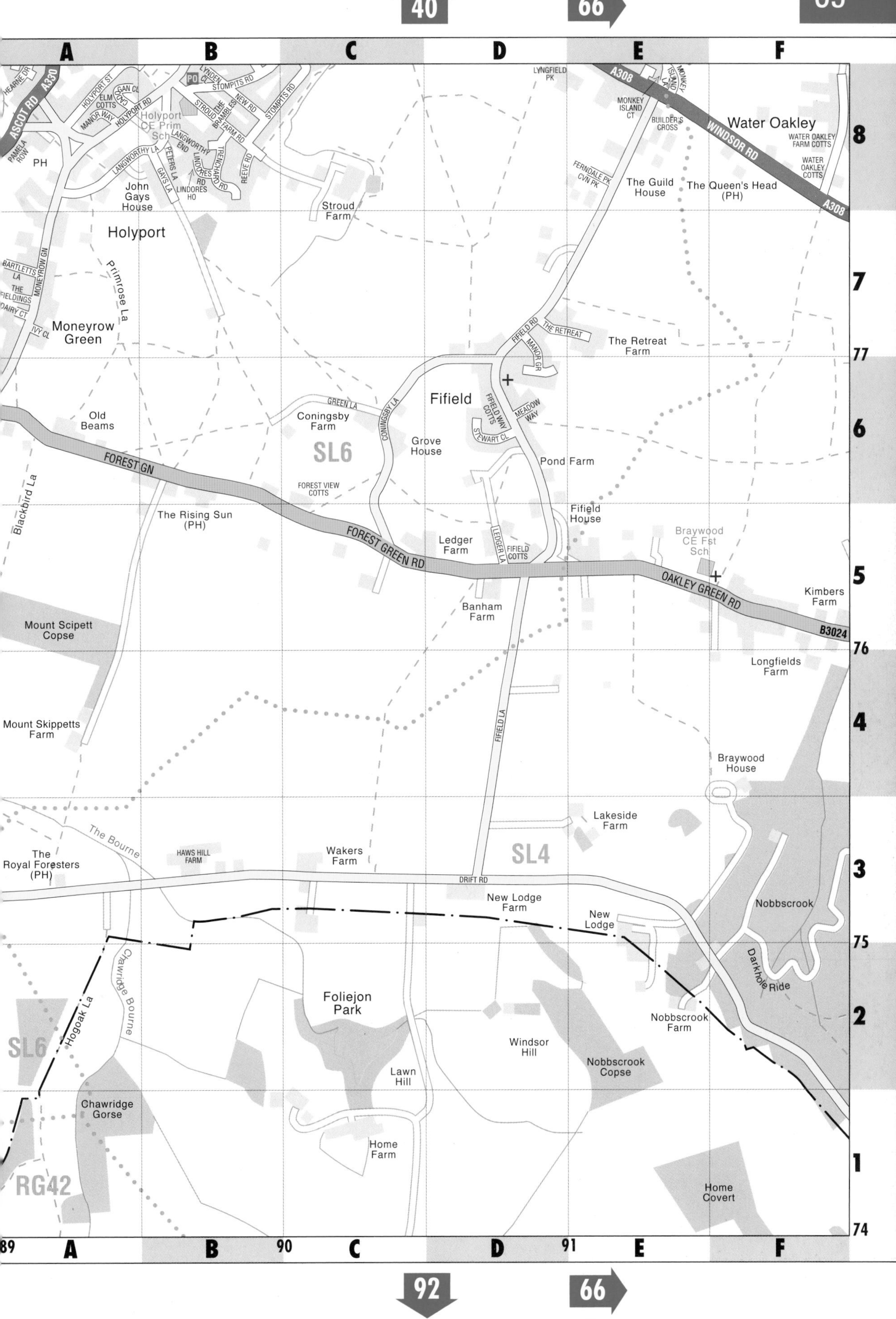
40
66
A
B
C
D
E
F
HEARNE DR
A330
ASCOT RD
PAMELA ROW
PH
HOLYPORT ST
ELM COTTS
MANOR WAY
GAN CL
HOLYPORT RD
Holyport CE Prim Sch
LYNDEN CL
STOMPITS RD
NEW RD
STROUD
THE BRAMBLES
FARM RD
LANGWORTHY END
LANGWORTHY LA
PETERS LA
GAYS LA
LINDORES RD
LINDORES HO
TRENCHARD RD
REEVE RD
John Gays House
Holyport
Stroud Farm
LYNGFIELD PK
A308
MONKEY ISLAND LA
MONKEY ISLAND CT
BUILDER'S CROSS
Water Oakley
WINDSOR RD
WATER OAKLEY FARM COTTS
WATER OAKLEY COTTS
FERNDALE PK CVN PK
The Guild House
The Queen's Head (PH)
BARTLETTS LA
THE FIELDINGS
DAIRY CT
MONEYROW GN
IVY CL
Primrose La
Moneyrow Green
FIFIELD RD
THE RETREAT
MANOR GR
The Retreat Farm
Old Beams
GREEN LA
Coningsby Farm
CONINGSBY LA
Fifield
FIFIELD WAY COTTS
MEADOW WAY
STEWART CL
Grove House
SL6
FOREST GN
Pond Farm
Blackbird La
FOREST VIEW COTTS
The Rising Sun (PH)
Fifield House
FOREST GREEN RD
Ledger Farm
LEDGER LA
FIFIELD COTTS
Braywood CE Fst Sch
OAKLEY GREEN RD
Kimbers Farm
B3024
Mount Scipett Copse
Banham Farm
Longfields Farm
Mount Skippetts Farm
FIFIELD LA
Braywood House
Lakeside Farm
The Bourne
HAWS HILL FARM
Wakers Farm
SL4
The Royal Foresters (PH)
DRIFT RD
New Lodge Farm
New Lodge
Nobbscrook
Darkhole Ride
Chawridge Bourne
Hogoak La
Foliejon Park
Nobbscrook Farm
SL6
Windsor Hill
Lawn Hill
Nobbscrook Copse
Chawridge Gorse
Home Farm
RG42
Home Covert
8
7
77
6
5
76
4
3
75
2
1
74
89
90
91

65 41

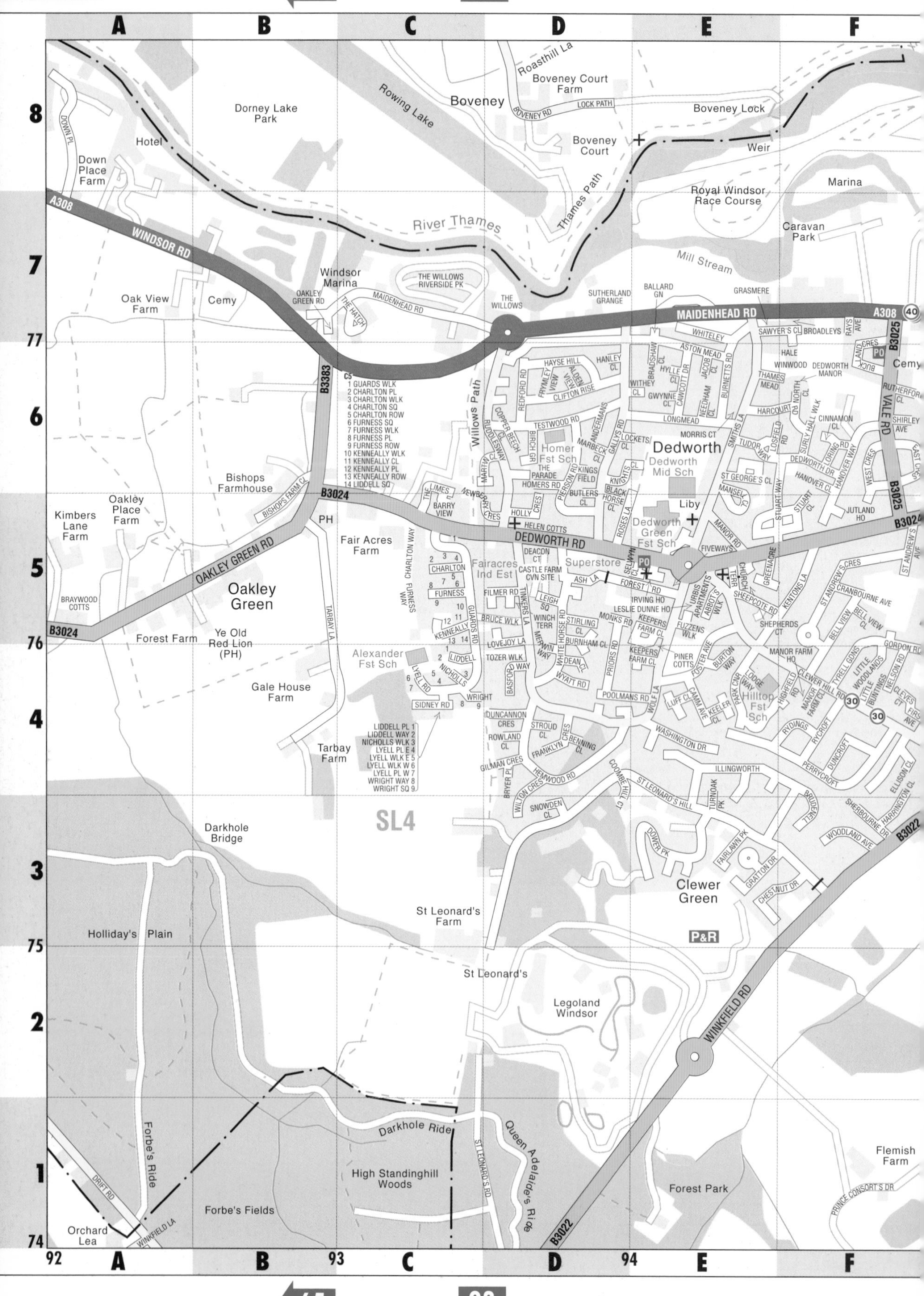

A
B
C
D
E
F
8
7
77
6
5
76
4
3
75
2
1
74
92
93
94
Roasthill La
Boveney Court Farm
Boveney
Rowing Lake
Dorney Lake Park
LOCK PATH
BOVENEY RD
Boveney Lock
Boveney Court
Weir
Thames Path
DOWN PL
Hotel
Down Place Farm
Royal Windsor Race Course
Marina
A308
WINDSOR RD
River Thames
Caravan Park
Mill Stream
Windsor Marina
Oak View Farm
Cemy
OAKLEY GREEN RD
THE HATCH
THE WILLOWS RIVERSIDE PK
MAIDENHEAD RD
THE WILLOWS
SUTHERLAND GRANGE
BALLARD GN
GRASMERE
MAIDENHEAD RD
A308
40
B3025
B3383
WHITELEY
SAWYER'S CL
BROADLEYS
HAYSE HILL
HANLEY CL
ASTON MEAD
HALE
WINWOOD
DEDWORTH MANOR
PO
Cemy
C5
1 GUARDS WLK
2 CHARLTON PL
3 CHARLTON WLK
4 CHARLTON SQ
5 CHARLTON ROW
6 FURNESS SQ
7 FURNESS WLK
8 FURNESS PL
9 FURNESS ROW
10 KENNEALLY WLK
11 KENNEALLY CL
12 KENNEALLY PL
13 KENNEALLY ROW
14 LIDDELL SQ
CLIFTON RISE
WITHEY CL
GWYNNE CL
THAMES MEAD
RUTHERFORD CL
VALE RD
Willows Path
TESTWOOD RD
LONGMEAD
HARCOURT RD
CINNAMON CL
SHIRLEY AVE
Homer Fst Sch
MORRIS CT
Dedworth
Dedworth Mid Sch
Bishops Farmhouse
BISHOPS FARM CL
THE PARADE
HOMERS RD
BUTLERS CL
ST GEORGE'S CL
HANOVER CL
Oakley Place Farm
Kimbers Lane Farm
B3024
BARRY VIEW
HOLLY CRES
Liby
JUTLAND HO
B3024
PH
Fair Acres Farm
HELEN COTTS
DEDWORTH RD
Dedworth Green Fst Sch
FIVEWAYS
Fairacres Ind Est
DEACON CT
CASTLE FARM CVN SITE
Superstore
PO
ASH LA
FOREST RD
CHARLTON
FURNESS
Oakley Green
BRAYWOOD COTTS
FILMER RD
IRVING HO
LESLIE DUNNE HO
SHEEPCOTE RD
CRANBOURNE AVE
B3024
Forest Farm
Ye Old Red Lion (PH)
TARBAY LA
KENNEALLY
BRUCE WLK
LOVEJOY LA
MONKS RD
STIRLING CL
BURNHAM CL
KEEPERS FARM CL
FUZZENS WLK
SHEPHERDS CT
MANOR FARM HO
Alexander Fst Sch
LIDDELL
TOZER WLK
PINER COTTS
GORDON RD
Gale House Farm
SIDNEY RD
WRIGHT
WYATT RD
POOLMANS RD
Hilltop Fst Sch
CLEWER HILL RD
30
30
LIDDELL PL 1
LIDDELL WAY 2
NICHOLLS WLK 3
LYELL PL E 4
LYELL WLK E 5
LYELL WLK W 6
LYELL PL W 7
WRIGHT WAY 8
WRIGHT SQ 9
Tarbay Farm
DUNCANNON CRES
ROWLAND CL
STROUD CL
FRANKLYN CRES
BENNING CL
WASHINGTON DR
RYDINGS
RYCROFT
DUNCROFT
PERRYCROFT
GILMAN CRES
HEMWOOD RD
ILLINGWORTH
ST LEONARD'S HILL
SNOWDEN CL
SL4
Darkhole Bridge
DOWER PK
FAIRLAWN PK
GRATTON DR
CHESTNUT DR
WOODLAND AVE
SHERBOURNE DR
B3022
Clewer Green
Holliday's Plain
St Leonard's Farm
P&R
St Leonard's
Legoland Windsor
WINKFIELD RD
Darkhole Ride
Queen Adelaide's Ride
ST LEONARD'S RD
Forbe's Ride
High Standinghill Woods
Forest Park
Flemish Farm
PRINCE CONSORT'S DR
DRIFT RD
Forbe's Fields
Orchard Lea
WINKFIELD LA
B3022

65 93

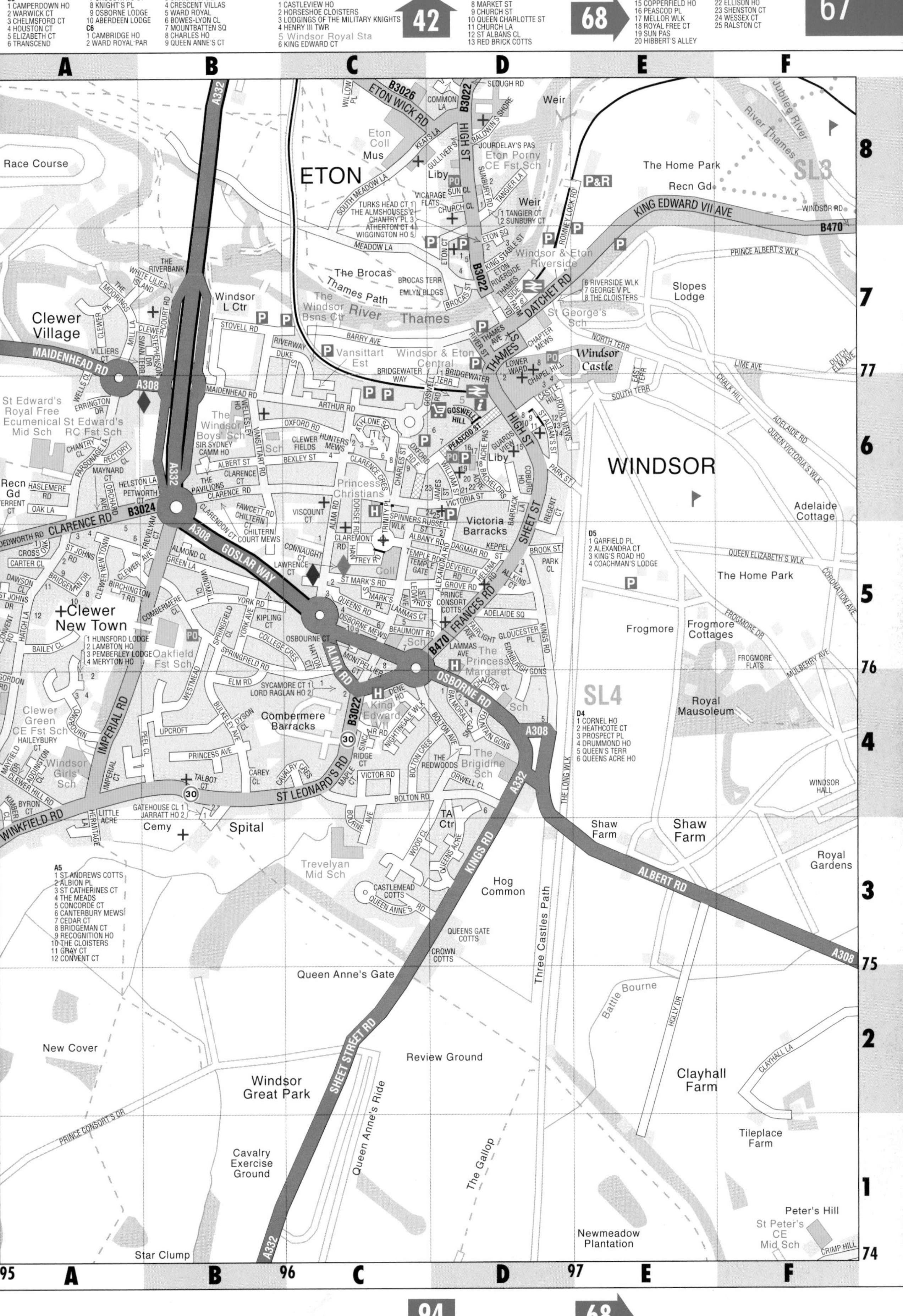
C5
1 CAMPERDOWN HO
2 WARWICK CT
3 CHELMSFORD CT
4 HOUSTON CT
5 ELIZABETH CT
6 TRANSCEND
7 CROSSWAYS CT
8 KNIGHT'S PL
9 OSBORNE LODGE
10 ABERDEEN LODGE
C6
1 CAMBRIDGE HO
2 WARD ROYAL PAR
3 CHRISTIAN SQ
4 CRESCENT VILLAS
5 WARD ROYAL
6 BOWES-LYON CL
7 MOUNTBATTEN SQ
8 CHARLES HO
9 QUEEN ANNE'S CT
D6
1 CASTLEVIEW HO
2 HORSESHOE CLOISTERS
3 LODGINGS OF THE MILITARY KNIGHTS
4 HENRY III TWR
5 Windsor Royal Sta
6 KING EDWARD CT
42
7 AMBERLEY PL
8 MARKET ST
9 CHURCH ST
10 QUEEN CHARLOTTE ST
11 CHURCH LA
12 ST ALBANS CL
13 RED BRICK COTTS
68
14 BURFORD HO
15 COPPERFIELD HO
16 PEASCOD PL
17 MELLOR WLK
18 ROYAL FREE CT
19 SUN PAS
20 HIBBERT'S ALLEY
21 CHARIOTT'S PL
22 ELLISON HO
23 SHENSTON CT
24 WESSEX CT
25 RALSTON CT
A B C D E F
8 7 77 6 5 76 4 3 75 2 1 74
ETON
Eton Coll Mus
Race Course
Weir
The Home Park
Recn Gd
SL3
KING EDWARD VII AVE
B470
WINDSOR RD
PRINCE ALBERT'S WLK
The Brocas
Thames Path
River Thames
The Windsor Bsns Ctr
Windsor & Eton Riverside
Windsor L Ctr
Clewer Village
MAIDENHEAD RD
A308
A332
Vansittart Est
Windsor & Eton Central
Windsor Castle
St George's Sch
Slopes Lodge
St Edward's Royal Free Ecumenical Mid Sch
St Edward's RC Fst Sch
The Windsor Boys' Sch
WINDSOR
Recn Gd
CLARENCE RD
B3024
Princess Christians
Victoria Barracks
SHEET ST
Adelaide Cottage
D5
1 GARFIELD PL
2 ALEXANDRA CT
3 KING'S ROAD HO
4 COACHMAN'S LODGE
The Home Park
GOSLAR WAY
Clewer New Town
1 HUNSFORD LODGE
2 LAMBTON HO
3 PEMBERLEY LODGE
4 MERYTON HO
Oakfield Fst Sch
Frogmore
Frogmore Cottages
FRANCES RD
B470
The Princess Margaret
OSBORNE RD
SL4
Royal Mausoleum
D4
1 CORNEL HO
2 HEATHCOTE CT
3 PROSPECT PL
4 DRUMMOND HO
5 QUEEN'S TERR
6 QUEENS ACRE HO
Clewer Green CE Fst Sch
Combermere Barracks
King Edward VII
IMPERIAL RD
Windsor Girls' Sch
The Brigidine Sch
ST LEONARD'S RD
WINKFIELD RD
Cemy
Spital
TA Ctr
Shaw Farm
Shaw Farm
Royal Gardens
Trevelyan Mid Sch
Hog Common
ALBERT RD
A5
1 ST ANDREWS COTTS
2 ALBION PL
3 ST CATHERINES CT
4 THE MEADS
5 CONCORDE CT
6 CANTERBURY MEWS
7 CEDAR CT
8 BRIDGEMAN CT
9 RECOGNITION HO
10 THE CLOISTERS
11 GRAY CT
12 CONVENT CT
KINGS RD
Three Castles Path
A308
Queen Anne's Gate
Battle Bourne
HOLLY DR
New Cover
Review Ground
SHEET STREET RD
Clayhall Farm
Windsor Great Park
PRINCE CONSORT'S DR
Queen Anne's Ride
The Gallop
Tileplace Farm
Cavalry Exercise Ground
Peter's Hill
St Peter's CE Mid Sch
Star Clump
Newmeadow Plantation
CRIMP HILL
95 96 97
94
68

67
43

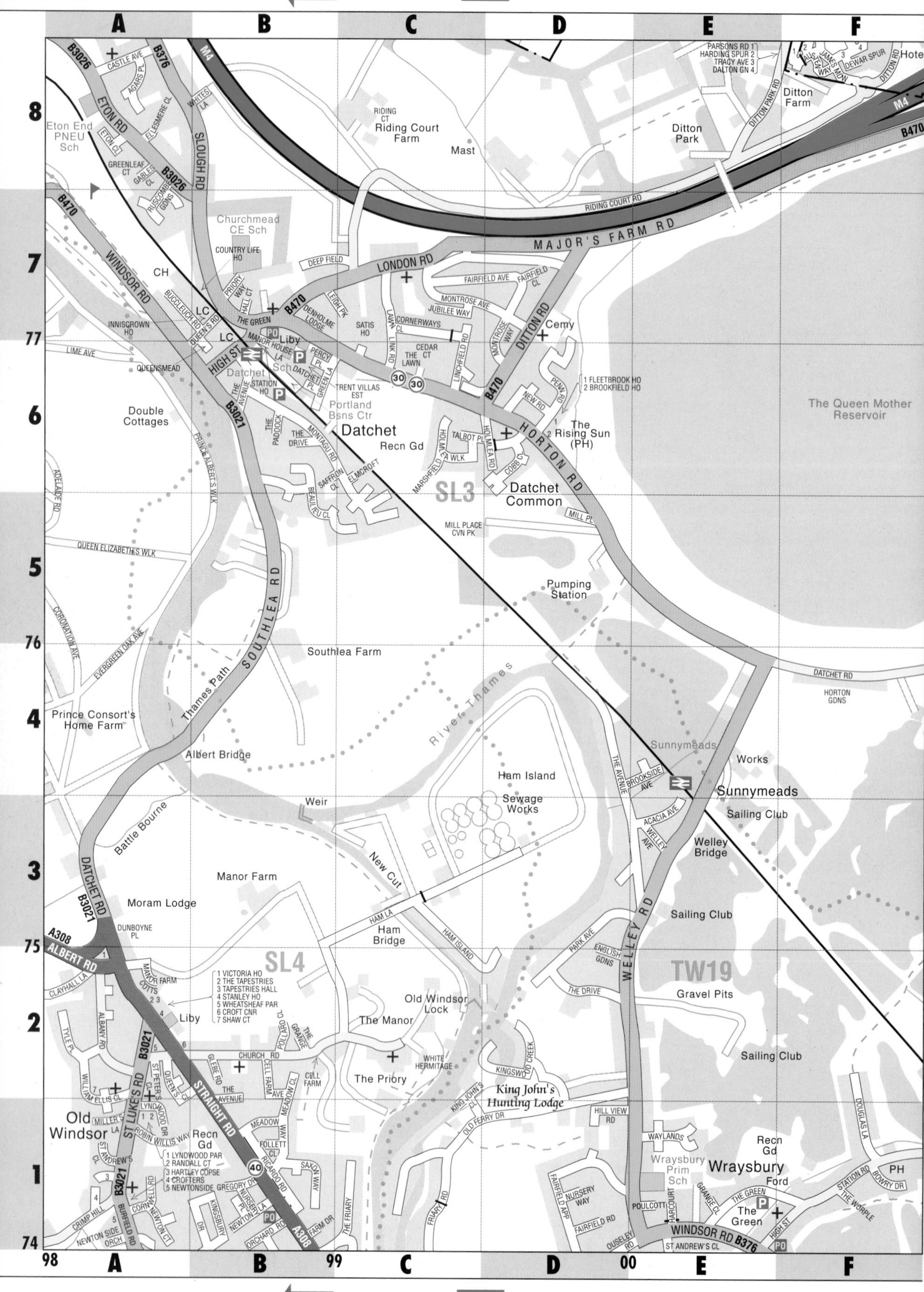

Eton End PNEU Sch
Churchmead CE Sch
Riding Court Farm
Mast
Ditton Park
Ditton Farm
Datchet
Recn Gd
Datchet Common
The Rising Sun (PH)
Cemy
The Queen Mother Reservoir
Double Cottages
Portland Bsns Ctr
Pumping Station
Southlea Farm
Prince Consort's Home Farm
Albert Bridge
Thames Path
River Thames
Ham Island
Sewage Works
Weir
New Cut
Battle Bourne
Manor Farm
Moram Lodge
Ham Bridge
Old Windsor Lock
The Manor
The Priory
King John's Hunting Lodge
Old Windsor
Recn Gd
Sunnymeads
Works
Sailing Club
Welley Bridge
Gravel Pits
Wraysbury
Wraysbury Prim Sch
Ford
The Green
SL3
SL4
TW19
M4
B470
B3026
B376
B3021
A308
B376
MAJOR'S FARM RD
LONDON RD
HORTON RD
DITTON RD
WINDSOR RD
SOUTHLEA RD
DATCHET RD
ALBERT RD
STRAIGHT RD
ST LUKE'S RD
WELLEY RD
WINDSOR RD
DATCHET RD
HIGH ST
SLOUGH RD
ETON RD
1 VICTORIA HO
2 THE TAPESTRIES
3 TAPESTRIES HALL
4 STANLEY HO
5 WHEATSHEAF PAR
6 CROFT CNR
7 SHAW CT
1 LYNDWOOD PAR
2 RANDALL CT
3 HARTLEY COPSE
4 CROFTERS
5 NEWTONSIDE
1 FLEETBROOK HO
2 BROOKFIELD HO
PARSONS RD 1
HARDING SPUR 2
TRACY AVE 3
DALTON GN 4
A B C D E F
8 7 77 6 5 76 4 3 75 2 1 74
98 99 00

67
95

44
70

Brands Hill
Colnbrook
Poyle
Horton
Wraysbury
Stanwell Moor
Stanwell Manor
Gravel Pit
The Crown (PH)
Brook Farm
The Greyhound (PH)
Lakeside Est
Colnbrook CE Prim Sch
Pippins Sch
Coln Trad Est
Argonaut Pk
Riverside Pk
Poyle Lodge
The Poyle Tech Ctr
McKay Trad Est
Britannia Ind Est
Polygon Bsns Ctr
Trident Ind Est
Viscount Ind Est
Polye 14 Trad Est
Skyway 14 Trad Est
Polye Pk
Horton Lodge
Rectory
Ashgood Farm
Berkyn Manor Farm
The Five Bells (PH)
Horton Trad Est
Horton Depot
Wraysbury Resr
King George VI Resr
Sailing Club
Lower Mill Farm
Mildridge Farmhouse
Manor Farm
Colne Brook
Wraysbury River
River Colne
COLNBROOK BY-PASS
LONDON RD
A4
M4
M25
A3113
AIRPORT WAY
B470
SL0
SL3
TW19
HORTON RD
STANWELL RD
COPPERMILL RD
STATION RD
DATCHET RD
1 SEVERN CRES
2 DART CL
3 CHERWELL CL
4 DISRAELI CT
5 CLARENCE CT
MARKET PL 1
BELMONT COTTS 2
MORELAND CL 3
BROOKSIDE 4
HONEYSUCKLE CT 5
THE WEINT 6
FESTIVAL COTTS 7
WHEELWRIGHTS PL 8
SHERWOOD CT 9
GARDEN COTTS 10
ST ANDREWS CT 11
HAMPTON HO 12
THE FAIRMEAD 13
ABINGTON 14
KING JOHN'S PALACE 15
OLD PALACE CT 16
CLAREMONT 17
HEATHACRE 1
CAVENDISH CT 2
ELGIN HO 3
BATH ROAD COTTS 4
5 RODDELL CT
6 COLNBROOK CT
A B C D E F
8 7 6 5 4 3 2 1
77 76 75 74
02 03

96
70

D1
1 CROFTERS CL
2 BAKERS CT
3 SPIRE VIEW
4 THE GRANGE
5 CRESSWELL CT

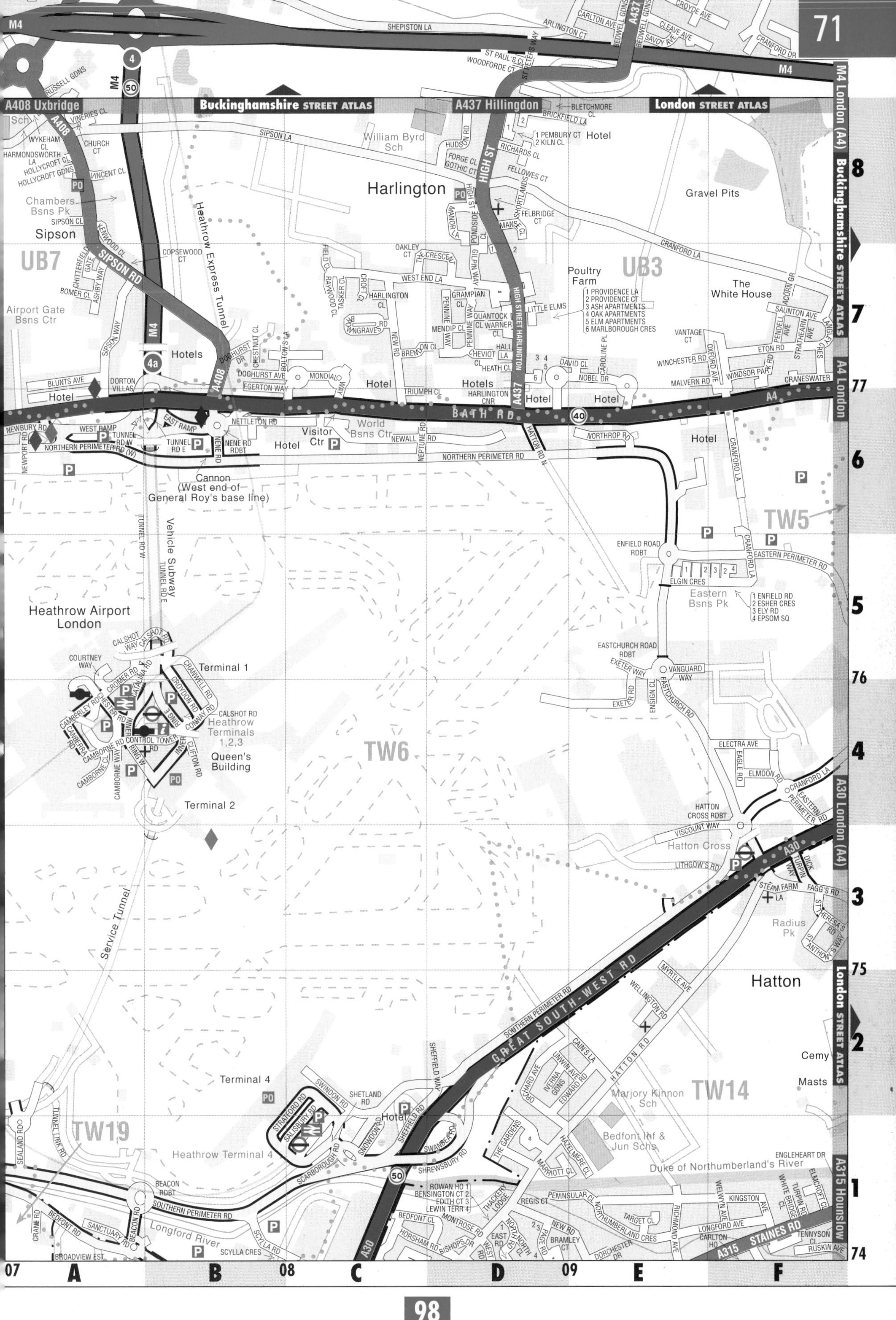

M4
SHEPISTON LA
ARLINGTON CT
CARLTON AVE
BEDWELL GDNS
A437
CROYDE AVE
CLEAVE AVE
SAVOY AVE
CRANFORD DR
ST PAUL'S CL
WOODFORDE CT
ST PETERS WAY
RUSSELL GDNS
A408 Uxbridge
Buckinghamshire STREET ATLAS
A437 Hillingdon
London STREET ATLAS
M4 London (A4)
Buckinghamshire STREET ATLAS
BLETCHMORE CL
BRICKFIELD LA
VINERIES CL
WYKEHAM CL
HARMONDSWORTH LA
HOLLYCROFT CL
HOLLYCROFT GDNS
CHURCH CT
VINCENT CL
SIPSON LA
William Byrd Sch
HUDSON RD
FORGE CL
GOTHIC CT
HIGH ST
1 PEMBURY CT
2 KILN CL
Hotel
RICHARDS CL
FELLOWES CT
Harlington
Gravel Pits
Chambers Bsns Pk
SIPSON CL
Sipson
UB7
SIPSON RD
COPSEWOOD CT
Heathrow Express Tunnel
MANOR LA
POND SIDE
SHORTLANDS
FELBRIDGE CT
MANSE CL
CRANFORD LA
OAKLEY CT
THE CRESCENT
WEST END LA
Poultry Farm
UB3
The White House
CHITTERFIELD GATE
ASHBY WAY
BOMER CL
HARLINGTON CL
GRAMPIAN CL
1 PROVIDENCE LA
2 PROVIDENCE CT
3 ASH APARTMENTS
4 OAK APARTMENTS
5 ELM APARTMENTS
6 MARLBOROUGH CRES
LITTLE ELMS
HIGH STREET HARLINGTON
SAUNTON AVE
Airport Gate Bsns Ctr
SIPSON WAY
MENDIP CL
PENNINE WAY
QUANTOCK CL
WARNER CL
VANTAGE CT
PENDELL AVE
STRATHEARN AVE
LANGLEY CRES
WINCHESTER RD
OXFORD AVE
ETON RD
Hotels
DOGHURST DR
CHESTNUT CL
BOLTON'S LA
BRENDON CL
CHEVIOT CL
HEATH CL
DAVID CL
CAROLINE PL
NOBEL DR
WINDSOR PARK RD
CRANESWATER
BLUNTS AVE
DORTON VILLAS
DOGHURST AVE
EGERTON WAY
MONDIAL WAY
Hotel
TRIUMPH CL
HARLINGTON CNR
MALVERN RD
A4 London
A4
BATH RD
WEST RAMP
EAST RAMP
NEWBURY RD
TUNNEL RD W
NETTLETON RD
Visitor Ctr
World Bsns Ctr
NEWALL RD
NEPTUNE RD
NORTHROP RD
HATTON RD N
CRANFORD LA
NORTHERN PERIMETER RD (W)
NEWPORT RD
TUNNEL RD E
NENE RD
NENE RD RDBT
NORTHERN PERIMETER RD
Cannon (West end of General Roy's base line)
TW5
TUNNEL RD W
Vehicle Subway
ENFIELD ROAD RDBT
EASTERN PERIMETER RD
ELGIN CRES
Eastern Bsns Pk
1 ENFIELD RD
2 ESHER CRES
3 ELY RD
4 EPSOM SQ
Heathrow Airport London
CALSHOT WAY
CALSHOT RD
EASTCHURCH ROAD RDBT
COURTNEY WAY
Terminal 1
EXETER WAY
VANGUARD WAY
CROMER RD
CRANWELL RD
CROYDON RD
CAMBERLEY RD
ENSIGN CL
EASTCHURCH RD
EXETER RD
CALSHOT RD
Heathrow Terminals 1,2,3
CONWAY RD
INNER RING W
CONTROL TOWER RD
INNER RING E
CLIFTON RD
ELECTRA AVE
Queen's Building
EAGLE RD
TW6
CAMBORNE RD
CAMBORNE CL
ELMDON RD
CRANFORD LA
EASTERN PERIMETER RD
Terminal 2
HATTON CROSS RDBT
VISCOUNT WAY
Hatton Cross
A30 London (A4)
LITHGOW'S RD
A30
DICK TURPIN WAY
STEAM FARM LA
FAGG'S RD
ST THERESA'S RD
ST ANTHONY'S WAY
Radius Pk
Service Tunnel
MYRTLE AVE
Hatton
London STREET ATLAS
WELLINGTON RD
SOUTHERN PERIMETER RD
GREAT SOUTH-WEST RD
SHEFFIELD WAY
CAIN'S LA
HATTON RD
Cemy
UNWIN AVE
IVERNA GDNS
EDWARD RD
ORCHARD AVE
Masts
Terminal 4
SWINDON RD
SHETLAND RD
Marjory Kinnon Sch
TW14
STRATFORD RD
SALISBURY RD
Hotel
SHEFFIELD RD
THE GARDENS
SEALAND RD
TUNNEL LINK RD
TW19
SNOWDON RD
SWANSEA RD
HAZELMERE CL
Bedfont Inf & Jun Schs
Heathrow Terminal 4
SCARBOROUGH RD
SHREWSBURY RD
MARRIOTT CL
ENGLEHEART DR
Duke of Northumberland's River
BEACON RDBT
ROWAN HO 1
BENSINGTON CT 2
EDITH CT 3
LEWIN TERR 4
THACKERY LODGE
PENINSULAR CL
KINGSTON AVE
WELWYN AVE
WHITE BRIDGE CL
TURPIN RD
ELMCROFT CL
A315 Hounslow
SOUTHERN PERIMETER RD
REGIS CT
NORTHUMBERLAND CRES
TARGET CL
RICHMOND AVE
CRANE RD
BEDFONT RD
SANCTUARY RD
BEACON RD
Longford River
SCYLLA RD
BEDFONT CL
MONTROSE RD
EAST RD
NORTH RD
NEW RD
LONGFORD AVE
STAINES RD
TENNYSON CL
RUSKIN AVE
HORSHAM RD
BISHOPS DR
WEST RD
PAGE RD
BRAMLEY CT
DORCHESTER DR
CARLTON HO
A315
BROADVIEW EST
SCYLLA CRES
A30
8
7
77
6
5
76
4
3
75
2
1
74
07
A
B
08
C
D
09
E
F

98

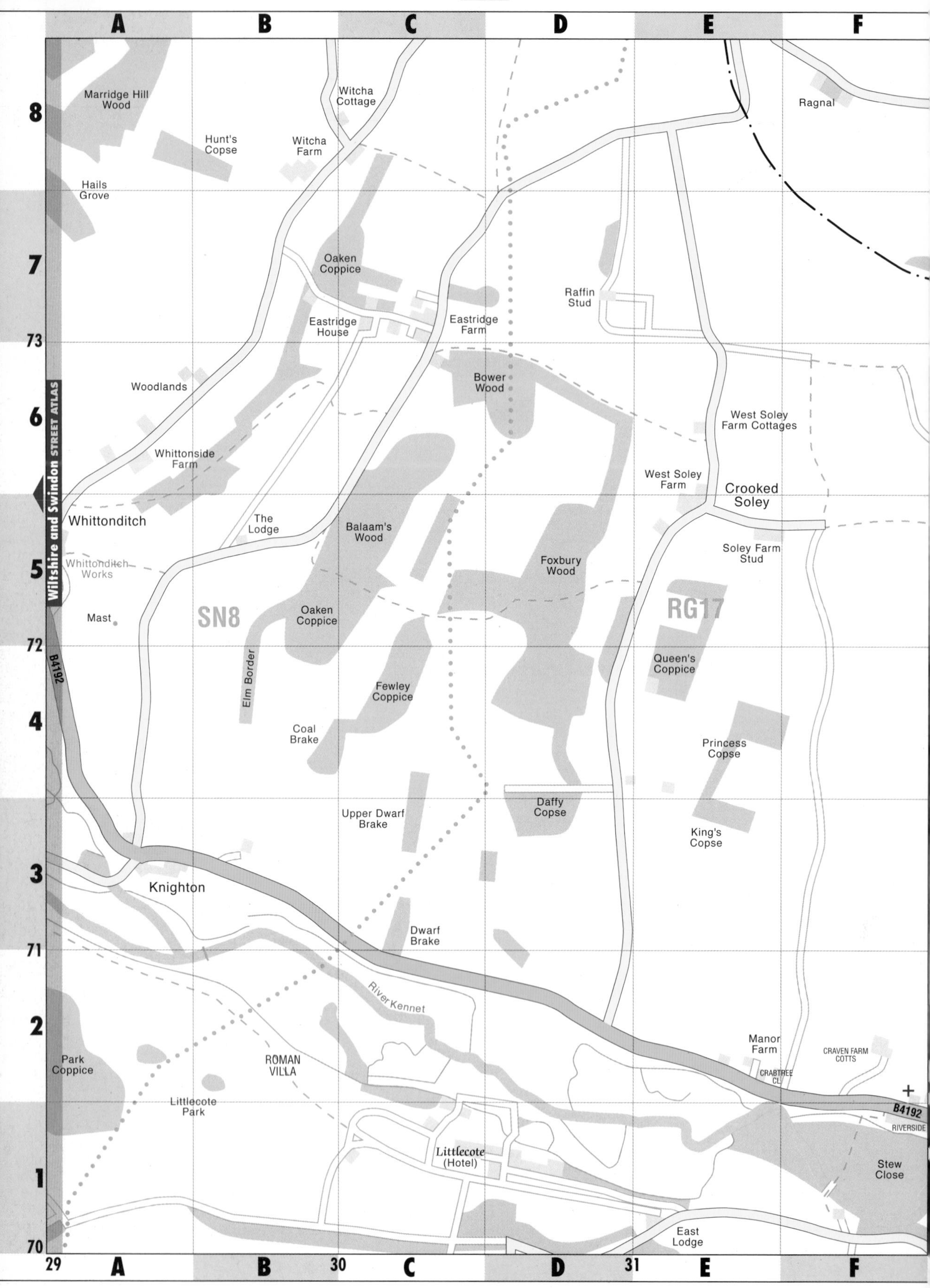

45
A
B
C
D
E
F
8
7
73
6
5
72
4
3
71
2
1
70
29
30
31
99
Marridge Hill Wood
Hunt's Copse
Witcha Cottage
Witcha Farm
Ragnal
Hails Grove
Oaken Coppice
Raffin Stud
Eastridge House
Eastridge Farm
Woodlands
Bower Wood
West Soley Farm Cottages
Whittonside Farm
West Soley Farm
Crooked Soley
Whittonditch
The Lodge
Balaam's Wood
Soley Farm Stud
Whittonditch Works
Foxbury Wood
Mast
SN8
Oaken Coppice
RG17
B4192
Queen's Coppice
Elm Border
Fewley Coppice
Coal Brake
Princess Copse
Upper Dwarf Brake
Daffy Copse
King's Copse
Knighton
Dwarf Brake
River Kennet
Manor Farm
CRAVEN FARM COTTS
Park Coppice
ROMAN VILLA
CRABTREE CL
Littlecote Park
B4192
RIVERSIDE
Littlecote (Hotel)
Stew Close
East Lodge
Wiltshire and Swindon STREET ATLAS

46

74

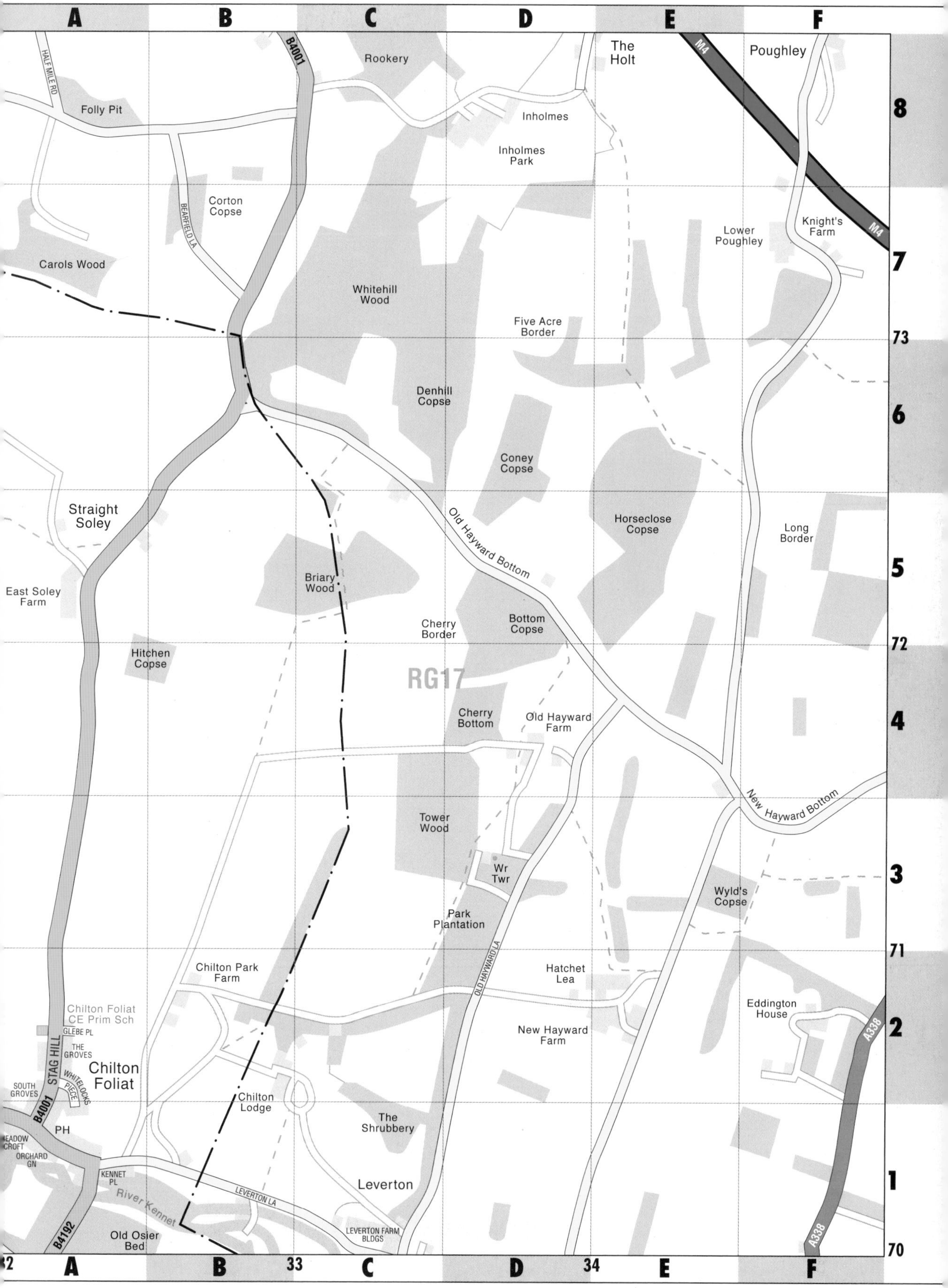

A B C D E F

8 7 73 6 5 72 4 3 71 2 1 70

HALF MILE RD
B4001
Rookery
The Holt
M4
Poughley
Folly Pit
Inholmes
Inholmes Park
Corton Copse
BEARFIELD LA
Carols Wood
Lower Poughley
Knight's Farm
M4
Whitehill Wood
Five Acre Border
Denhill Copse
Coney Copse
Straight Soley
Old Hayward Bottom
Horseclose Copse
Long Border
East Soley Farm
Briary Wood
Cherry Border
Bottom Copse
Hitchen Copse
RG17
Cherry Bottom
Old Hayward Farm
New Hayward Bottom
Tower Wood
Wr Twr
Wyld's Copse
Park Plantation
OLD HAYWARD LA
Chilton Park Farm
Hatchet Lea
Eddington House
Chilton Foliat CE Prim Sch
GLEBE PL
THE GROVES
STAG HILL
New Hayward Farm
A338
Chilton Foliat
WHITELOCKS PIECE
SOUTH GROVES
B4001
Chilton Lodge
The Shrubbery
PH
MEADOW CROFT
ORCHARD GN
KENNET PL
River Kennet
LEVERTON LA
Leverton
B4192
Old Osier Bed
LEVERTON FARM BLDGS
A338

32 A B 33 C D 34 E F

100
74

73 47

A B C D E F

8
Somercourt
B4000
ERMIN ST
Fisher's Farm
A338

7
Tommylands Copse
The Pheasant Inn (PH)
B4000
ERMIN ST
B4000
Shefford Woodlands
Templars Farm
BARN COTTS
ERMIN ST
M4
73
A338
14

6
Newtown Lodge Farm
Breach Copse
BAYDON RD
Lovelocks
B4000
North Hidden Farm

5
Norbin's Wood
M4
North Hidden Cottages
72
RG17

4
Wickfield Copse
Windingwood La
Lower Farm
Jeffrey's Border
The Tally-ho (PH)
RADLEY BOTTOM
Hungerford Newtown

3
Little Hidden Farm
Windingwood Bottom
71
North Denford Farm
A338

2
Winding Wood
Dunkin's Copse
Three Gate Copse
Heath Hanger La
Heath Hanger Copse
Stibbs Wood
Radley Farm

1
The Hassock
Great Hidden Farm
70

35 A B 36 C D 37 E F

73 101

48
76

A
B
C
D
E
F
Daldridge Barn
Weston
WALNUT TREE COTTS
Mill
Weston Farm
The Rookery
River Lambourn
Lambourn Valley Way
Royal Ground Border
Welford Park Gardens
Welford Park
Wickfield Farm
Oakhanger House
HOME FARM
Blindman's Border
Scroggin's Copse
Highwood Copse
Queen's Plantation
Mantclose Copse
Buck's Copse
M4
ERMIN ST
RG20
Tullock Farm
WHITE GATES
MANT CL
Wickham
WELFORD RD
Newground Border
BAYDON RD
ST SWITHINS CL
PH
Welford & Wickham CE Prim Sch
Wickham Green
RG17
Grey's Copse
Windingwood La
Mast
Resr
Long Border
Wickham Rails
New Copse
CHURCH HILL
Wormstall
Wormstall Wood
LIP LA
Lip La
Orpenham Farm
B4000
Clapton
Harrod's Border
Harrod's Barn
Clapton Farm
Lower Farm
8
7
73
6
5
72
4
3
71
2
1
70
38
39
40

102
76

75
49

Bradleywood Farm
Grove Corner
Welford Farm
Welford
M4
Tullock Bottom
Easton Farm
Westbrook Farm
Easton
River Lambourn
Knapps Farm
Borough Copse
SWEDISH HOS
Showells
ROOD HILL
Westbrook
RG20
EASTON HILL
SHEPHERD'S HILL
SCHOOL LA
Boxford Farm
WINTERBOURNE RD
Sole Border
Boxford
PH
SOUTHFIELDS
Sole Farm
High Street Farm
Woodmansfield Cottages
Hoar Hill
HIGH ST
Moorbridge Farm
Sole Plantation
Ownham Old Farm
Upper Farm
Ownham
B4000
Ownham Lower Farm
COOMBESBURY LA
Coombesbury Farm
ERMIN ST
Ownham Plantation
William's Copse
Jannaways
Hunt's Green
A
B
C
D
E
F
8
7
73
6
5
72
4
3
71
2
1
70
41
42
43

75
103

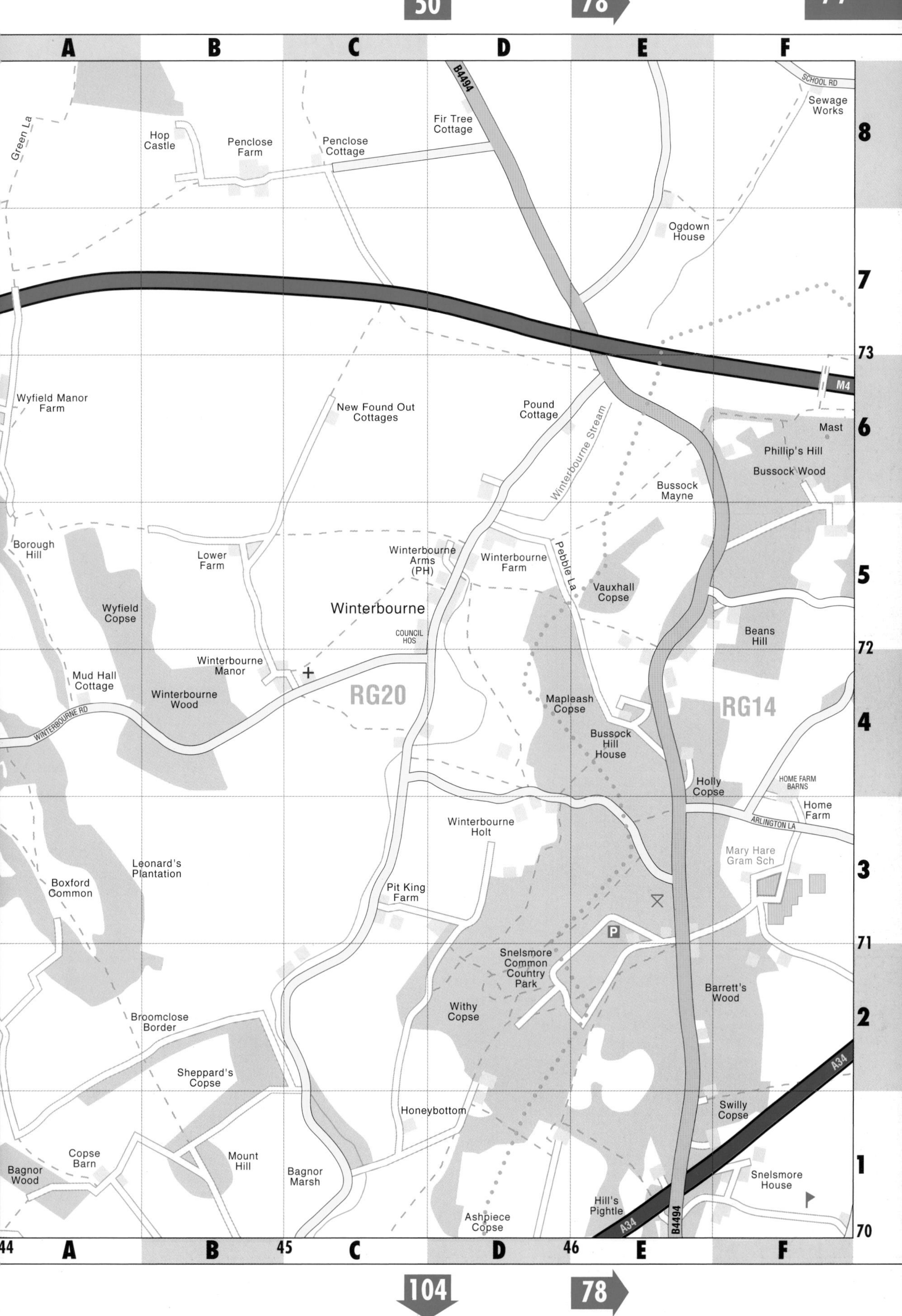
A B C D E F
8 7 73 6 5 72 4 3 71 2 1 70
44 45 46
Green La
Hop Castle
Penclose Farm
Penclose Cottage
Fir Tree Cottage
B4494
School Rd
Sewage Works
Ogdown House
M4
Wyfield Manor Farm
New Found Out Cottages
Pound Cottage
Winterbourne Stream
Mast
Phillip's Hill
Bussock Wood
Bussock Mayne
Borough Hill
Lower Farm
Winterbourne Arms (PH)
Winterbourne Farm
Pebble La
Vauxhall Copse
Wyfield Copse
Winterbourne
Council Hos
Beans Hill
Winterbourne Manor
Mud Hall Cottage
Winterbourne Wood
Winterbourne Rd
RG20
Mapleash Copse
RG14
Bussock Hill House
Holly Copse
Home Farm Barns
Home Farm
Arlington La
Winterbourne Holt
Leonard's Plantation
Mary Hare Gram Sch
Boxford Common
Pit King Farm
P
Snelsmore Common Country Park
Barrett's Wood
Withy Copse
Broomclose Border
A34
Sheppard's Copse
Honeybottom
Swilly Copse
Copse Barn
Mount Hill
Bagnor Wood
Bagnor Marsh
Snelsmore House
Hill's Pightle
Ashpiece Copse

77
51

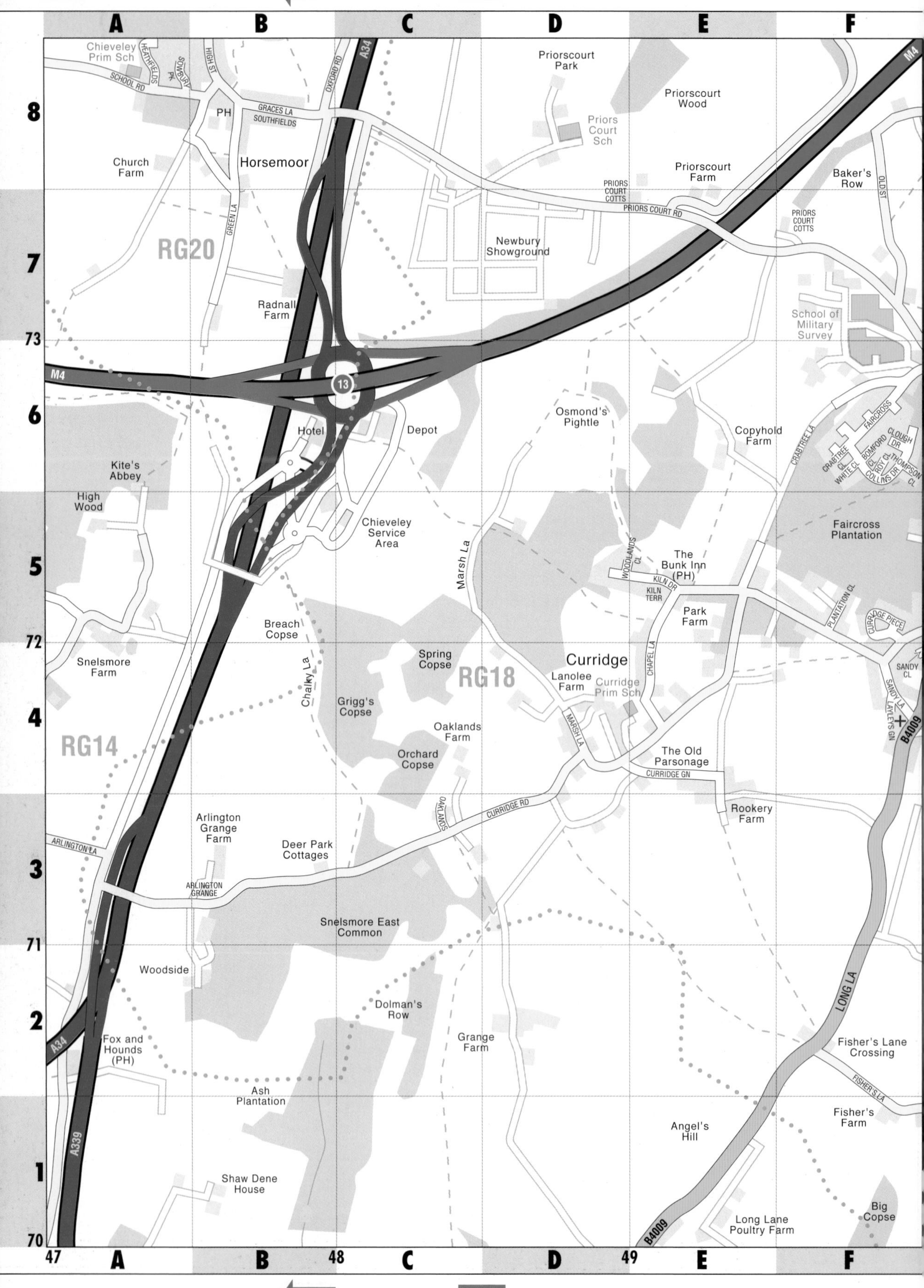
Chieveley Prim Sch
School Rd
Heathfields
High St
Graces La
Southfields
Oxford Rd
A34
PH
Horsemoor
Church Farm
RG20
Green La
Radnall Farm
Priorscourt Park
Priors Court Sch
Priorscourt Wood
Priorscourt Farm
Priors Court Cotts
Priors Court Rd
Newbury Showground
M4
Baker's Row
Old St
Priors Court Cotts
School of Military Survey
13
Hotel
Depot
Osmond's Pightle
Copyhold Farm
Kite's Abbey
High Wood
Chieveley Service Area
Faircross Plantation
Marsh La
Woodlands Cl
The Bunk Inn (PH)
Kiln Dr
Kiln Terr
Park Farm
Plantation Cl
Breach Copse
Spring Copse
Snelsmore Farm
RG18
Curridge
Lanolee Farm
Curridge Prim Sch
Chapel La
Sandy Cl
Sandy La
Chalky La
Grigg's Copse
RG14
Oaklands Farm
Orchard Copse
The Old Parsonage
Curridge Gn
B4009
Curridge Rd
Oaklands
Rookery Farm
Arlington Grange Farm
Arlington La
Deer Park Cottages
Arlington Grange
Snelsmore East Common
Woodside
Dolman's Row
Long La
Grange Farm
Fisher's Lane Crossing
Fox and Hounds (PH)
Fisher's La
Ash Plantation
Fisher's Farm
Angel's Hill
A339
Shaw Dene House
Big Copse
Long Lane Poultry Farm
A B C D E F
8 7 73 6 5 72 4 3 71 2 1 70
47 48 49

77
105

A B C D E F

M4

Oare
Hermitage Prim Sch
MANOR LA
B4009
HAMPSTEAD NORREYS RD
LEA VIEW
COLYER CL
ORCHARD CL
WYTHE CL
PINEWOOD CRES
BRICK WLK
SANDSTONE GR
STRETCH DR
FLETTON LINK
CLAY WLK
ROWLOCK GDNS
Chalkpit Piece
Birch Cottage
Rook's Copse
EVERINGTON LA
Kiln Farm
Little Hungerford
Windmill Farm
CHAPEL LA
Common Firs
8
Roebuck Wood
Spring Copse
Hermitage
DEACONS LA
POND LA
YATTENDON RD
Cuckoo Pits
Box Wood
DINES WAY
KILN CL
RIDGEWAY CL
Parsons Piece
Well La
Poundpit Piece
Box Cottage
7
PO
73
THE OLD NURSERY
PRIORS COURT RD
DOCTORS LA
NEWBURY RD
BRIANTS PIECE
New Plantation
States Hill Wood
Wellhouse Farm
CRABTREE LA
PH
CHARLOTTE CL
LIPSCOMB CL
LITTLE SAFFRON
WOODSIDE DR
WELLHOUSE LA
Long Grove
Pheasant Hill Wood
6
HERMITAGE GN
Allen's Allotment
Wellhouse
LONG LA
Faircross Farm
Grimsbury Castle
THE BARN
Fifield Farm
MARLSTON RD
Grimsbury Wood
Fairfield Farm
MARLSTON COTTS
5
Adams Lane Copse
Round Hill Wood
CURRIDGE RD
Grimsbury Bank
72
SANDY CL
Red Shute Ind Est
SAWMILL RD
SLANTING HILL
RG18
Gravelly Pightles
Boar's Hole Farm
Brockhurst & Marlston House Schs
The Common
Longlane
RED SHUTE HILL
Fence La
4
West Wood
Fence Wood
Money's Allotment
Hangings Copse
Downe House Sch
3
WILLIS CL
Bushnell's Copse
Bucklebury Alley
Stonecroft Copse
71
Westrop Green
Nothing Hill
DROVE LA
Hunters Hill Wood
Cold Ash Farm
Cold Ash Common
HERMITAGE RD
Sermons Copse
Westrop Wood
2
Oaken Copse
Westrop Hill
SEWELL CL
GORSE COTTAGE DR
WOODSIDE
ANNADALE
RG7
FISHER'S LA
Malthouse Wood
Westrop Farm
Henwicklands Copse
THIRTOVER
Holly Farm House
1
ST MARY'S HO
Thirtover
ASHMORE GREEN RD
COLD ASH HILL
THE RIDGE
Prim Sch
Salt's Copse
70

50 A B 51 C D 52 E F

79
53

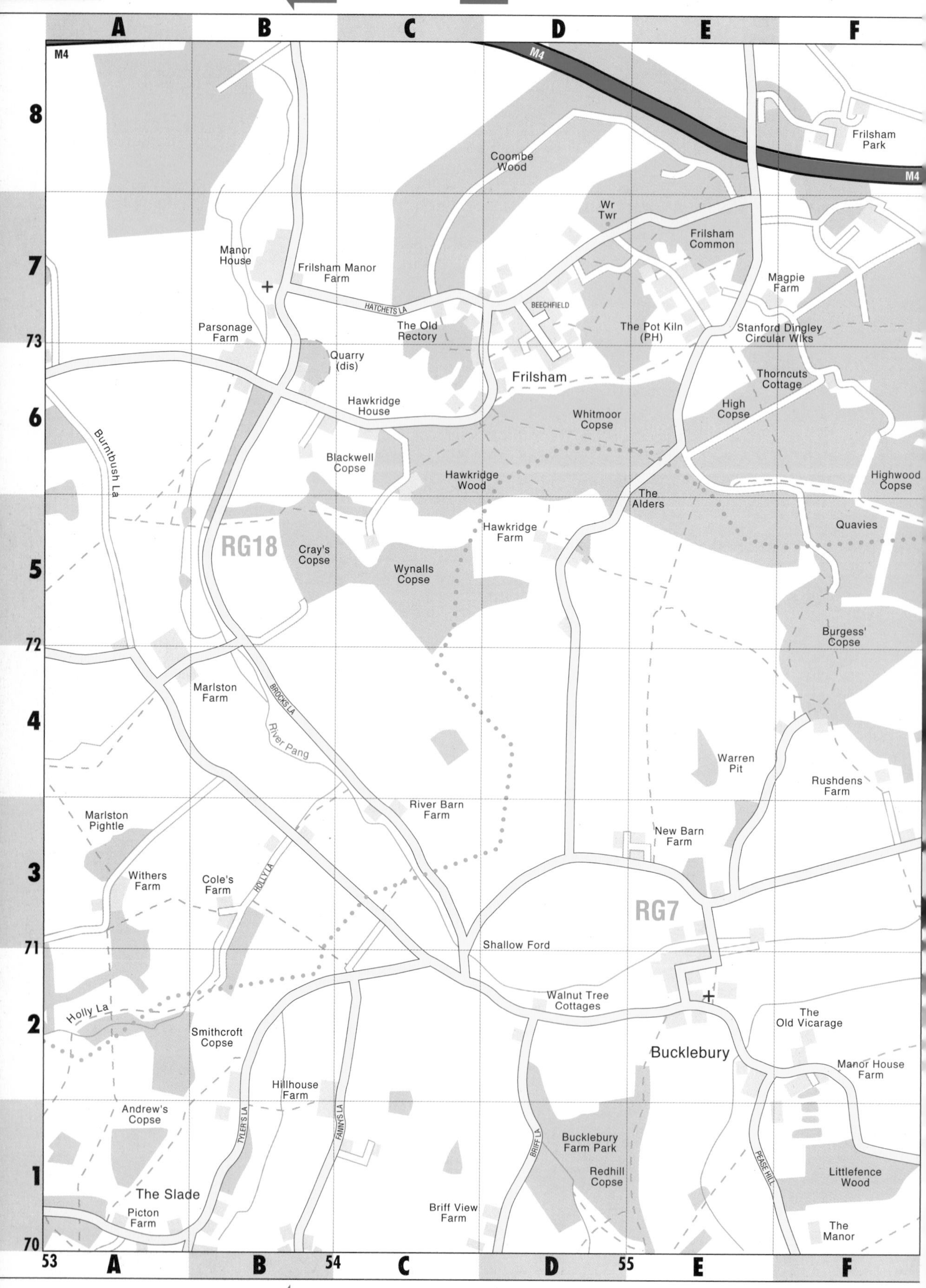
A
B
C
D
E
F
M4
8
Frilsham Park
Coombe Wood
Wr Twr
Frilsham Common
7
Manor House
Frilsham Manor Farm
HATCHETS LA
BEECHFIELD
Magpie Farm
Parsonage Farm
The Old Rectory
The Pot Kiln (PH)
Stanford Dingley Circular Wlks
73
Quarry (dis)
Frilsham
Thorncuts Cottage
Hawkridge House
Whitmoor Copse
High Copse
6
Burntbush La
Blackwell Copse
Hawkridge Wood
Highwood Copse
The Alders
Hawkridge Farm
Quavies
RG18
Cray's Copse
5
Wynalls Copse
Burgess' Copse
72
Marlston Farm
BROCKS LA
River Pang
4
Warren Pit
Rushdens Farm
Marlston Pightle
River Barn Farm
New Barn Farm
3
Withers Farm
Cole's Farm
HOLLY LA
RG7
71
Shallow Ford
Walnut Tree Cottages
Holly La
2
Smithcroft Copse
The Old Vicarage
Bucklebury
Manor House Farm
Hillhouse Farm
Andrew's Copse
TYLER'S LA
FANNYS LA
BRIFF LA
Bucklebury Farm Park
PEASE HILL
1
Redhill Copse
Littlefence Wood
The Slade
Picton Farm
Briff View Farm
The Manor
70
53
54
55

79
107

A B C D E F

Chalkangles Copse
Tanner's Copse
Birchlands Copse
Lambden's Bottom
RG8
Beard's Hill
M4
8
Gravel Copse
New Fields
Stone Copse
Broomhill Copse
The Gravels
Coxland Cottages
Timber Copse
RG18
7
Collier's Copse
Owlpit Copse
SCRATCHFACE LA
Cook's Copse
73
Oxley's Shaw
Hangers Copse
Miram's Copse
Quill Copse
Mazelands Farm
Round Copse
Mazelands Copse
6
Rushall Farm
Long Copse
Bradfield House
House Leas
New Common
Rushall Manor Farm
Rushall Copse
5
Mounthill Copse
Manor Farm
Nightingale's Green
Frogmoor Farm
BACK LA
72
Pangfield Farm
MEADOWLANDS
RG7
Severals Farm
4
Manor Farm
Bradfield Hall
Stanford Dingley
The Bull (PH)
River Pang
Kimberhead Farm
Rotten Row
Bradfield Farm
ROTTEN ROW HILL
Jewell's Farm
The Old Boot Inn (PH)
Jennetshill Wood
3
CASEY CT
Jennetts Hill
BISHOPS RD
GREEN LA
JENNETTS CL
Jewell's Spring
Tutts Clump
71
Clay Hill
COCK LA
2
King's Copse
The Travellers Rest (PH)
HUNGERFORD LA
Bushnells Green
Hillfoot Farm
Acres Farm
1
HILLFOOT
SOUTH END RD
Nine Elms
St Crispins Farm
70

56 A B 57 C D 58 E F

108
82

81
55

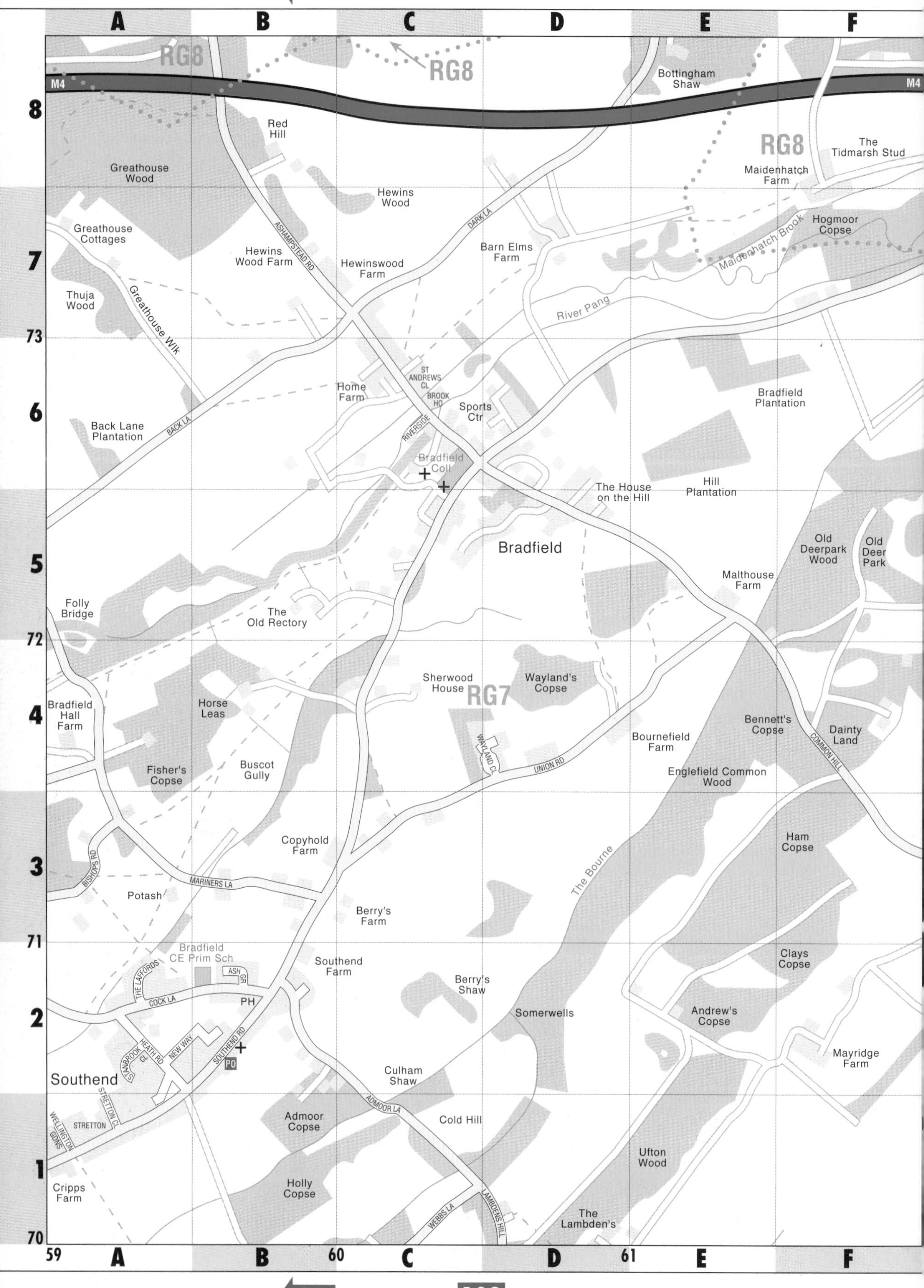
A
B
C
D
E
F
RG8
RG8
M4
M4
Bottingham Shaw
8
Red Hill
RG8
The Tidmarsh Stud
Maidenhatch Farm
Greathouse Wood
Hewins Wood
Greathouse Cottages
DARK LA
ASHAMPSTEAD RD
Hogmoor Copse
Barn Elms Farm
Maidenhatch Brook
7
Hewins Wood Farm
Hewinswood Farm
Thuja Wood
Greathouse Wlk
River Pang
73
ST ANDREWS CL
Home Farm
BROOK HO
Bradfield Plantation
6
Sports Ctr
Back Lane Plantation
BACK LA
RIVERSIDE
Bradfield Coll
The House on the Hill
Hill Plantation
Bradfield
Old Deerpark Wood
Old Deer Park
5
Malthouse Farm
Folly Bridge
The Old Rectory
72
Sherwood House
RG7
Wayland's Copse
Bradfield Hall Farm
Horse Leas
4
Bennett's Copse
Bournefield Farm
Dainty Land
WAYLAND CL
COMMON HILL
UNION RD
Fisher's Copse
Buscot Gully
Englefield Common Wood
Ham Copse
Copyhold Farm
3
BISHOPS RD
The Bourne
MARINERS LA
Potash
Berry's Farm
71
Bradfield CE Prim Sch
Southend Farm
Clays Copse
ASH GR
THE LAFFORDS
Berry's Shaw
COCK LA
PH
2
Somerwells
Andrew's Copse
HEATH RD
NEW WAY
SOUTHEND RD
STANBROOK CL
PO
Mayridge Farm
Southend
Culham Shaw
STRETTON CL
ADMOOR LA
WELLINGTON GDNS
STRETTON
Admoor Copse
Cold Hill
1
Ufton Wood
Cripps Farm
Holly Copse
WEBBS LA
LAMBDENS HILL
The Lambden's
70
59
A
B
60
C
D
61
E
F

56
84
A
B
C
D
E
F
8
7
73
6
5
72
4
3
71
2
1
70
62
63
64
Flobrigham's Copse
River Pang
Hogmoor Bridge
Withy Eyot
RG8
Moor Copse
RG31
Alder Copse
Wigley Copse
Horsemoor Wood
The Bourne
Chalkpit Farm
Horns Copse
CHALKPIT COTTS
Malpas Farm
Pond Farm
Malpas
Sluice Copse
NUNHIDE LA
Nunhide Farm
Dovecot
Beech Hill Wood
PH
Blossomsend Copse
North Street
Englefield Est Yd
Englefield
THE STREET
ST MARK'S CL
PO
North Street Farm
RG31
Englefield CE Prim Sch
Englefield House
Works
RG7
CH
Wickcroft Farm
WHITEHART CL
KATHLEEN SANDERS CT
CHESTNUT CL
Theale
ENGLEFIELD RD
BLOSSOM AVE
THE CRESCENT
ORCHARD CL
BLOSSOM LA
WOODFIELD WAY
ELLERTON CL
ALDERFIELD CL
ROTHERFIELD CL
MORTON PL
WORSLEY PL
SWALLOWFIELD GDNS
PLAY PLATT
THE COURTYARD
ANDREWS CL
CROWN LA
BREWERY CT
HIGH ST
ANGEL CT
LEONARD CT
ELIZABETH CT
JAMES BUTCHER DR
PINCENTS LA
12
M4
A4
Englefield Park (Deer Park)
Cranemoor Lake
DEADMAN'S LA
Recn Ctr
Theale CE Prim Sch
PH
CLOISTER MEWS
LAMBFIELDS
Liby
CHURCH ST
TRINITY CT
Theale Green Com Sch
WATERSIDE DR
Arlington Bsns Pk
Commerce Pk
Wigmore Wood
PARKER'S CNR
SPRING GDNS
ROUNDHEAD RD
MEADOW WAY
MYTON WLK
MULBERRY WAY
MUSWELL CL
BLATCH'S CL
CAVALIER CL
VOLUNTEER RD
Chilton Ent Ctr
Tech Ctr
EXETER WAY
ELY RD
BRUNEL RD
Kennet Weir Bsns Pk
THE GREEN
ST IVES CL
THE GREEN
STONELEIGH CT
ROCKLEY CT
A340
The Markham Ctr Trad Est
Theale
STATION RD
ARROWHEAD RD
A4
Haywards Farm House
Kennet and Avon Canal
BOSTOCK LA
Gravel Pit Cottages
BATH RD
WIGMORE LA
Mill
Swing Bridge
Draper's Osier Bed Stream
River Kennet
HANGER RD
MOULDEN WAY
A4
Milehouse Cottages
A
B
C
D
E
F
110
84

83
57

D8
1 APPLESHAW CT
2 ELIZABETH CT
3 SOVEREIGN PK

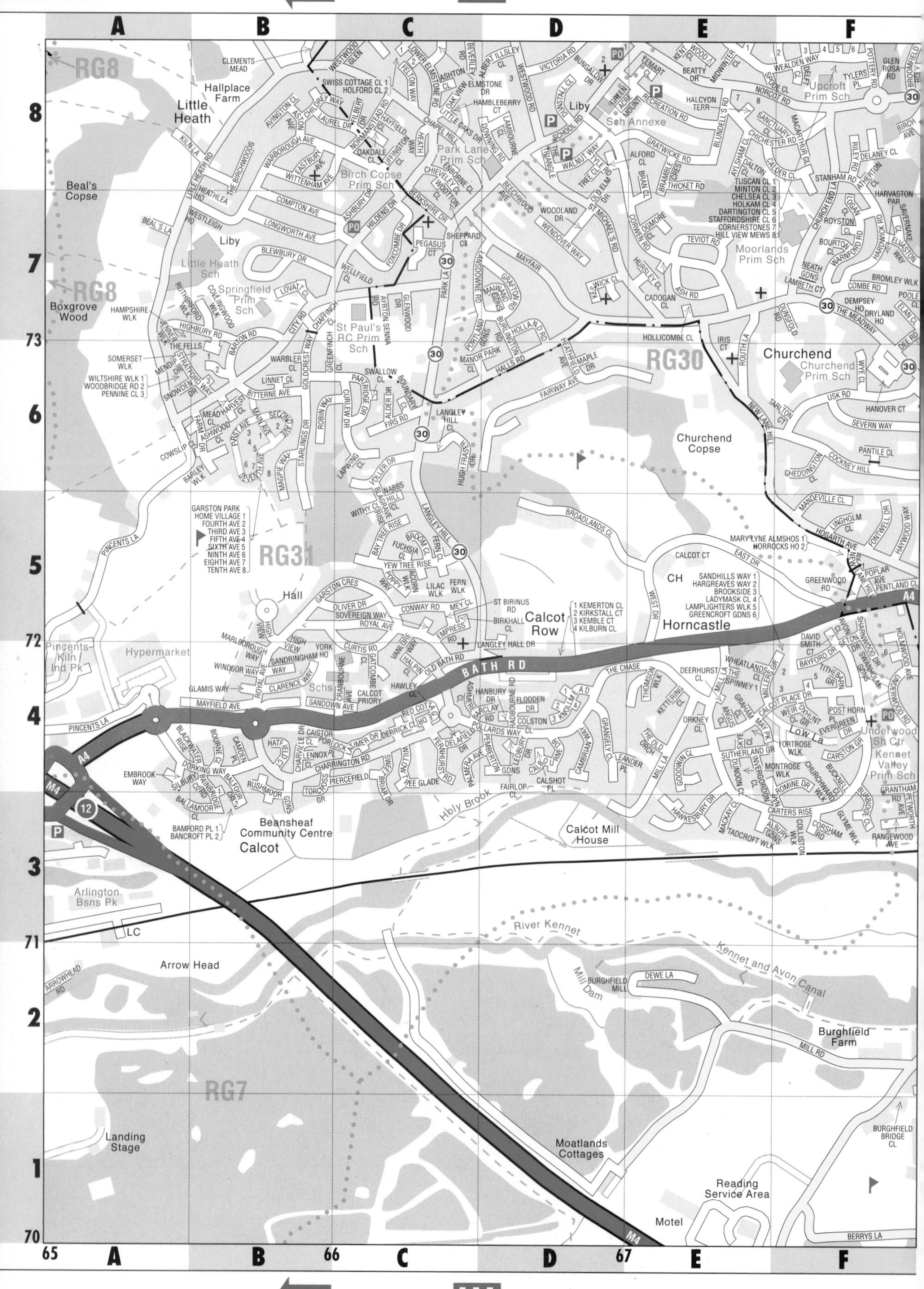

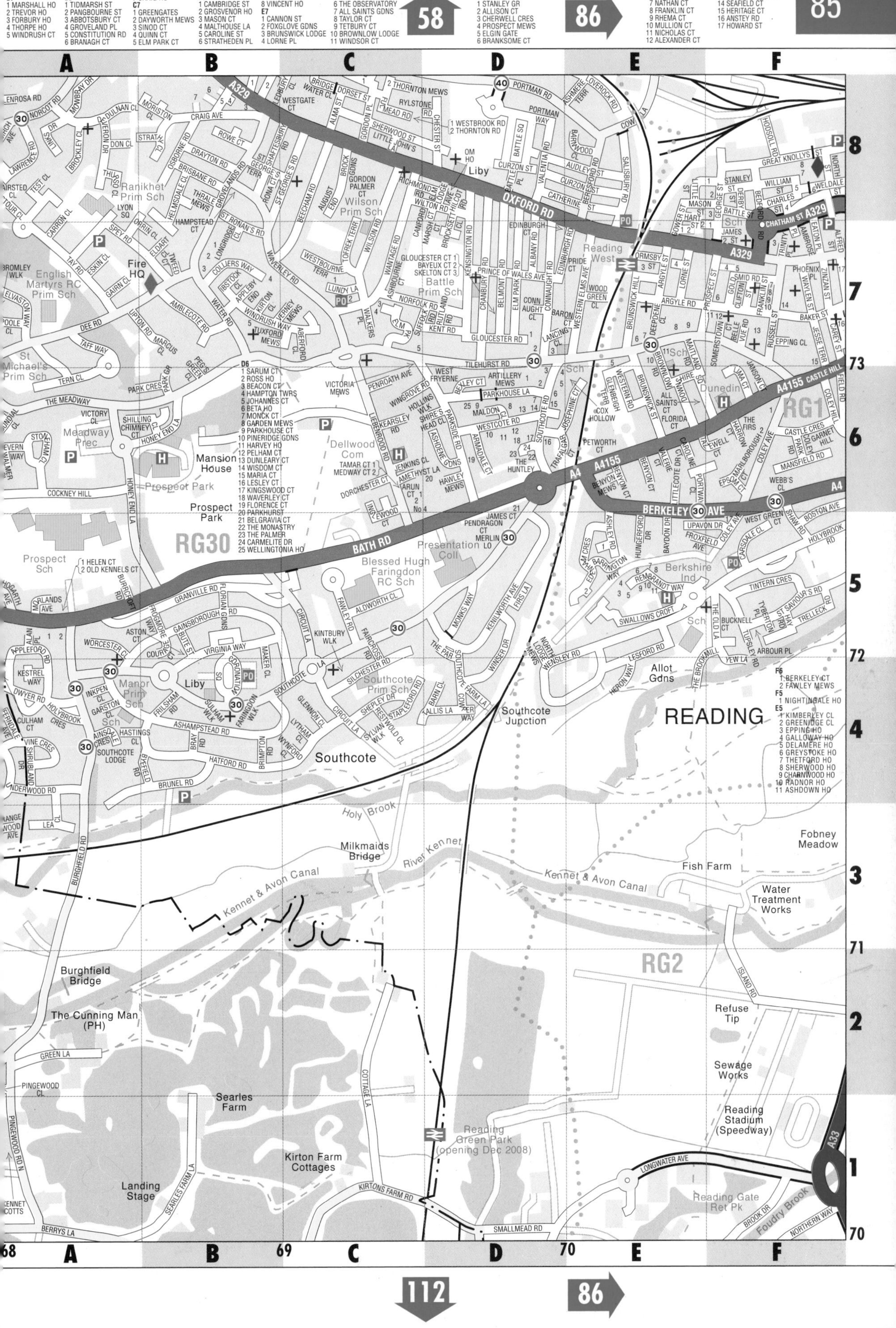

B7
1 MARSHALL HO
2 TREVOR HO
3 FORBURY HO
4 THORPE HO
5 WINDRUSH CT
B8
1 TIDMARSH ST
2 PANGBOURNE ST
3 ABBOTSBURY CT
4 GROVELAND PL
5 CONSTITUTION RD
6 BRANAGH CT
7 CRAIG HO
C7
1 GREENGATES
2 DAYWORTH MEWS
3 SINOD CT
4 QUINN CT
5 ELM PARK CT
F8
1 CAMBRIDGE ST
2 GROSVENOR HO
3 MASON CT
4 MALTHOUSE LA
5 CAROLINE ST
6 STRATHEDEN PL
7 BURFORD CT
8 VINCENT HO
E7
1 CANNON ST
2 FOXGLOVE GDNS
3 BRUNSWICK LODGE
4 LORNE PL
5 BELLEVUE TERR
6 THE OBSERVATORY
7 ALL SAINTS GDNS
8 TAYLOR CT
9 TETBURY CT
10 BROWNLOW LODGE
11 WINDSOR CT
58
F7
1 STANLEY GR
2 ALLISON CT
3 CHERWELL CRES
4 PROSPECT MEWS
5 ELGIN GATE
6 BRANKSOME CT
86
F7
7 NATHAN CT
8 FRANKLIN CT
9 RHEMA CT
10 MULLION CT
11 NICHOLAS CT
12 ALEXANDER CT
13 CHANCERY MEWS
14 SEAFIELD CT
15 HERITAGE CT
16 ANSTEY RD
17 HOWARD ST
A B C D E F
8 7 73 6 5 72 4 3 71 2 1 70
68 69 70
OXFORD RD
A329
BATH RD
A4
A4155
BERKELEY AVE
CASTLE HILL
TILEHURST RD
RG30
RG1
RG2
READING
Reading West
Southcote
Southcote Junction
Prospect Park
Mansion House
Fire HQ
Ranikhet Prim Sch
English Martyrs RC Prim Sch
St Michael's Prim Sch
Wilson Prim Sch
Battle Prim Sch
Presentation Coll
Blessed Hugh Faringdon RC Sch
Southcote Prim Sch
Manor Prim Sch
Berkshire Ind
Dunedin
Allot Gdns
Holy Brook
Milkmaids Bridge
River Kennet
Kennet & Avon Canal
Fish Farm
Fobney Meadow
Water Treatment Works
Burghfield Bridge
The Cunning Man (PH)
Searles Farm
Kirton Farm Cottages
Landing Stage
Reading Green Park (opening Dec 2008)
Refuse Tip
Sewage Works
Reading Stadium (Speedway)
Reading Gate Ret Pk
Foudry Brook
A33
LONGWATER AVE
SMALLMEAD RD
BURGHFIELD RD
PINGEWOOD RD N
D6
1 SARUM CT
2 ROSS HO
3 BEACON CT
4 HAMPTON TWRS
5 JOHANNES CT
6 BETA HO
7 MONCK CT
8 GARDEN MEWS
9 PARKHOUSE CT
10 PINERIDGE GDNS
11 HARVEY HO
12 PELHAM CT
13 DUNLEARY CT
14 WISDOM CT
15 MARIA CT
16 LESLEY CT
17 KINGSWOOD CT
18 WAVERLEY CT
19 FLORENCE CT
20 PARKHURST
21 BELGRAVIA CT
22 THE MONASTRY
23 THE PALMER
24 CARMELITE DR
25 WELLINGTONIA HO
F6
1 BERKELEY CT
2 FAWLEY MEWS
F5
1 NIGHTINGALE HO
E5
1 KIMBERLEY CL
2 GREENIDGE CL
3 EPPING HO
4 GALLOWAY HO
5 DELAMERE HO
6 GREYSTOKE HO
7 THETFORD HO
8 SHERWOOD HO
9 CHARNWOOD HO
10 RADNOR HO
11 ASHDOWN HO
112
86

B7
1 THE ARCADE
2 MARKET WAY
3 ABBEY POINT
4 MINISTER CT
5 YIELD HALL LA
6 THORN LA
7 IL-LIBRO CT
8 DUKESBRIDGE CT
9 HIGHBRIDGE WHARF
10 MAYFLOWER CT
11 KINGS REACH CT
12 CRANE WHARF

85

B7
13 OYSTER WHARF
14 CHAPEL CT
15 COMPASS HO
16 MARIE DAVIS CT
17 THE CHAMBERS
18 SOUTHERN CT

C7
1 THE PLUMMERY
2 SELBORNE CT
3 ST JAMES WHARF
4 KING' OAK CT
5 OSPREY CT
6 GRANTLEY HTS

59

7 ROYAL CT
8 HARRY TEE CT
9 KENNET SIDE
10 MORRISS CT
11 ALEXANDRA HO
12 SHEPTON HO
13 SIDMOUTH CT
14 BARKHAM MEWS
15 ELDON LODGE
16 CONQUEST CT
17 HENRYS CT
18 PADLEY CT
19 THE DELL
20 TYRREL CT

D7
1 WEIRSIDE CT
2 MANDELA CT
3 VICTORIA WAY
4 SYDENHAM HO
5 RUPERT WLK
6 ICARUS CT
7 RUPERT SQ
8 KINGSGATE PL
9 ST STEPHENS CT
10 SAXON CT
11 HAVEN CT
12 CROSSWAY POINT
13 TOWN PL
14 EDWARD PL
15 CHARLES PL
16 ALDERNEY CT
17 CARNOUSTIE CT
18 GLENEAGLES CT
19 TURNBERRY CT
20 GULLANE CT
21 TROON CT
22 ST ANDREWS CT
23 PRESTWICK CT
24 JOHN BALLIOL CT
25 HENLEY CT
26 APPLETON HO
27 WEAVERS CT

A6
1 BLENHEIM TERR
2 CHERITON CT
3 WILLOW ST
4 AVOCET CT
5 SIMMONDS MALTHOUSE
6 NEW BRIGHT ST
7 ASANTEWA HO
8 BEAR WHARF
9 GARNET HILL
10 CHURCH TERR
11 ST SAVIOUR'S TERR
12 CRANFORD MEWS
13 RODNEY CT
14 WOODVILLE CT
15 BUNYAN CT
16 BELFORD CT
17 CAPITAL POINT
18 RIVER RD
19 PHOEBE CT
20 TEMPLE PL
21 LOWER BROOK ST
22 HUNTERS WHARF
23 FOUNDRY PL

A7
1 THE PICTURE HO
2 BODY RD
3 CASTLE GATE
4 WATERSIDE GDNS
5 SWAN PL

85

A7
6 MALTINGS PL

A8
1 THE CHATHAM
2 BELLMAN CT
3 LION CT
4 ALASTAIR NICHOLAS CT
5 JEFFREY PL
6 MALCOLM PL
7 MONTROSE HO

113

A8
8 FRIARS WLK
9 MERCHANTS PL
10 PROJECTION W
11 PROJECTION E
12 ICON HO

B5
1 MELLOR WLK
2 AVELEY WLK
3 ELIZABETH WLK
4 SPRING TERR
5 KINVER WLK
6 BLYTH WLK
7 WESTERHAM WLK
8 TAYNTON WLK
9 JACK PRICE CT

B6
1 ST GILES CT
2 CENTURION CL
3 SOLENT CT
4 HAMBLE CT
5 DOROTHY ST
6 LETCOMBE CT
7 HOME CT
8 NELSON MEWS
9 ELIZABETH MEWS
10 BEDIVERE CT
11 BLENHEIM CT
12 THE FACULTY
13 THOMPSONS YD
14 SHERMAN PL
15 INDIGO APARTMENTS
16 PRIORS CT
17 PLATINUM APARTMENTS
18 RIMAUD HO
19 AVELEY HO
20 ILIFFE CL
21 HIEATT CL
22 BASILDON HO
23 QUADRANT CT
24 NELSON TERR
25 SILVER SCREEN FLATS
26 STIRLING HO
27 WINDSOR SQ

A6
1 BRIGHTON PL
2 FULCHER ROW
3 AMHURST MEWS
4 GARDNERS PL

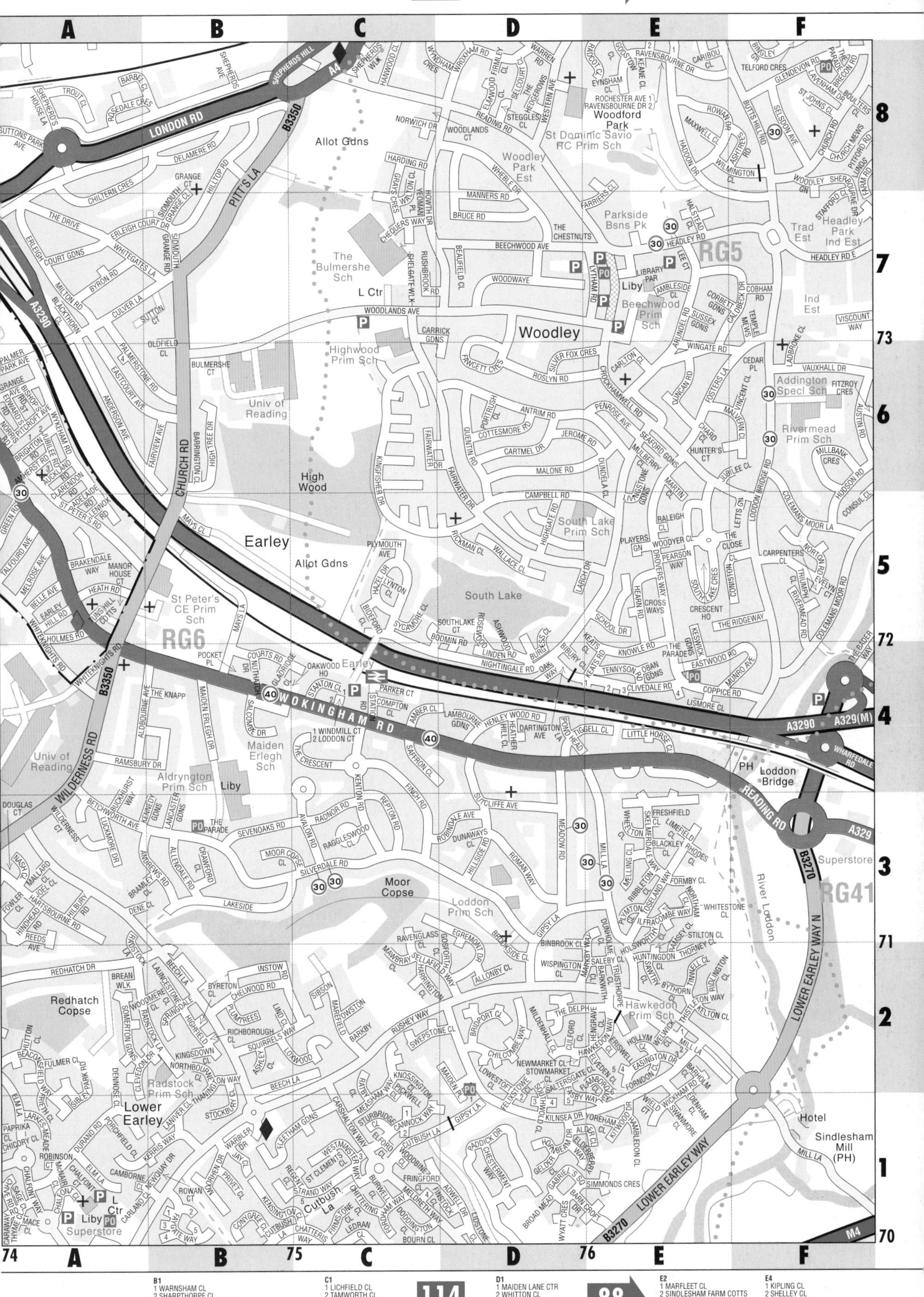

B1
1 WARNSHAM CL
2 SHARPTHORPE CL
3 BERSTEAD CL
4 WATERSFIELD CL
5 RUSTINGTON CL

C1
1 LICHFIELD CL
2 TAMWORTH CL
3 ST MARTINS CL
4 DRIFTWAY CL
5 LIBERTY OF EARLEY HO

D1
1 MAIDEN LANE CTR
2 WHITTON CL
3 LEISTON CL
4 HARWICH CL
5 BROMPTON CL

E2
1 MARFLEET CL
2 SINDLESHAM FARM COTTS
3 SETTRINGTON CL
4 SKEFFLING CL
5 FLAMBOROUGH PATH
6 BURNISTON CL

E4
1 KIPLING CL
2 SHELLEY CL
3 BURNS CL
4 BOSWORTH GDNS

87
61

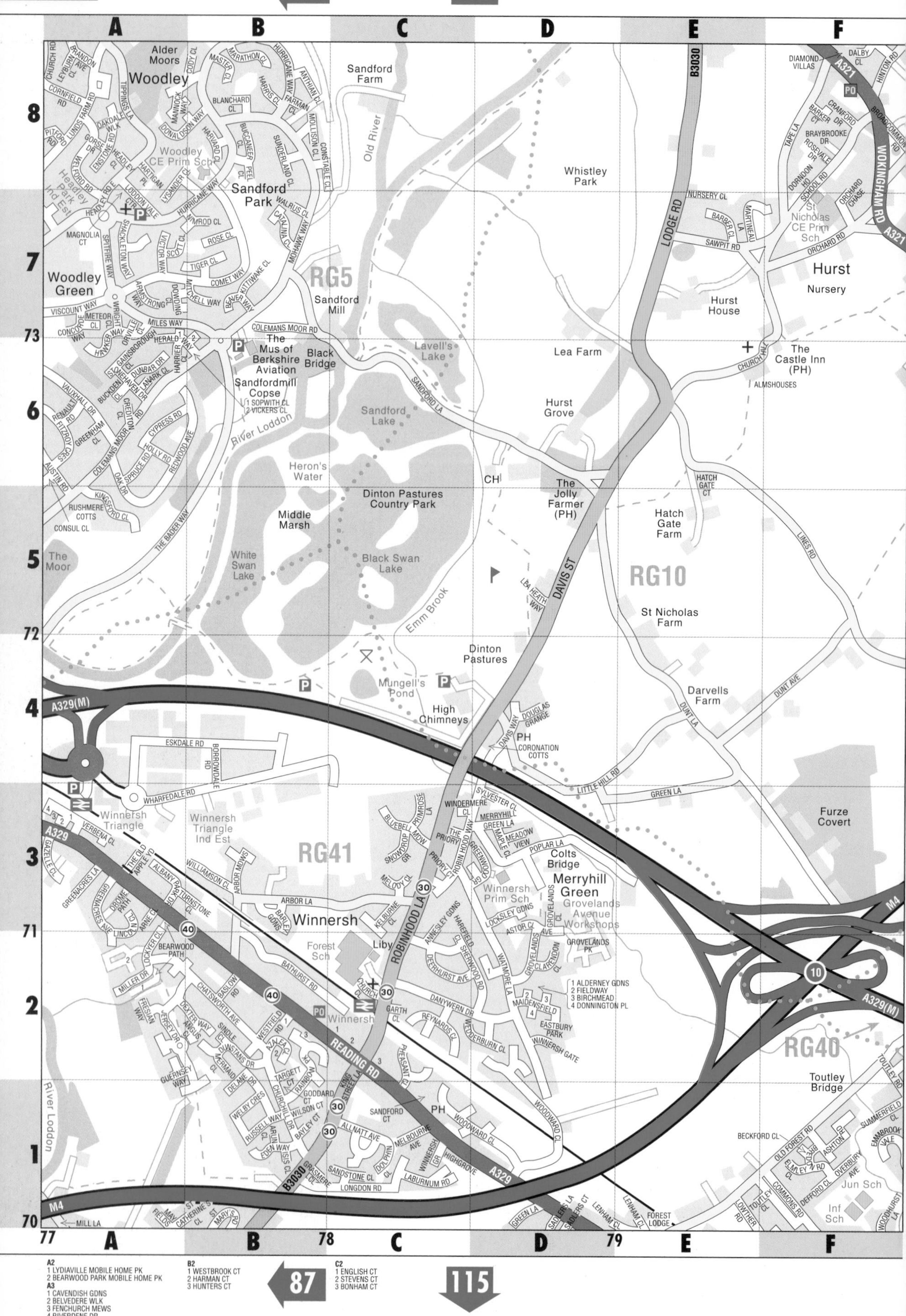

A2
1 LYDIAVILLE MOBILE HOME PK
2 BEARWOOD PARK MOBILE HOME PK
A3
1 CAVENDISH GDNS
2 BELVEDERE WLK
3 FENCHURCH MEWS
4 RIVERDENE DR

B2
1 WESTBROOK CT
2 HARMAN CT
3 HUNTERS CT

C2
1 ENGLISH CT
2 STEVENS CT
3 BONHAM CT

87
115

A
B
C
D
E
F
8
7
73
6
5
72
4
3
71
2
1
70
80
81
82
B3018
Hurst Lodge
Surrells Wood
Charity Wood
Park Farm
Bushy Lees
BROADCOMMON LA
BONHOMIE CT
BEECH CT
Grange Farm
BROADCOMMON RD
RG10
WOKINGHAM RD
M4
Buckland Farm
ISLANDSTONE LA
Broad Common
THE STRAIGHT MILE
Warren Copse
Birch Plantation
Penn Bushes
NELSON'S LA
Grange Farm
Oakley Farm
Pound Lane Farm
POUND LA
North Ockett Wood
The Mount Farm
Churchmans Farm
LINES RD
Beech Wood
Straight Mile Stud
Warren Farm
Pond Wood
Bill Hill Park
RG40
MAIDENHEAD RD
Tippen's Wood
Harp Farm
Ashridge Wood
Targetts Farm
B3034
FOREST RD
FOREST RD
B3034
Bill Hill
Pike's Farm
Ashridge Manor
ASHRIDGE MANOR FARM
The Bullfinch (PH)
OLD FOREST RD
Ashridgewood House
Ashridgewood Farm
Toutley Works
The Metro Ctr
TWYFORD RD
Rushton's Farm
WARREN HOUSE RD
BRIMBLECOMBE CL
RG41
TOUTLEY RD
AMBROOK VALE
FULLBROOK CL
Bell Farm
A321
BELL FOUNDRY LA
Ashridge Water Reclamation Plant
A329 (M)
Pebblestone Copse

89
63

A B C D E F

8
7
73
6
5
72
4
3
71
2
1
70

Baldasarre Farm
RG10
B3018
M4
Bear Farm
SPINNINGWHEEL LA
Gardener's Copse
Felix Farm
WESTLEY MILL
Picked Point
Brooklands Farm
TWYFORD RD
Oak Tree Farm
HOWE LA
Kiln Copse
M4
Binfield Lodge
Cokeley Bridge
BOTTLE LA
Allanbay Park
Seven Acres
The Cut
Billingbear Farm
RG42
White Gables
Billingbear Stables
Billingbear
BILLINGBEAR LA
Hill Farm
Hawland's Copse
CHURCH HILL
Billingbear Park
Hazelwood House
The Old Sch
RYEHURST LA
RG40
Billingbear House
Jack o'Newbury (PH)
Cemy
CHURCH LA
CARTER'S HILL
Sewage Works
Cartershill Plantation
Caswalls
WONDESFORD DALE
SYMONDSON MEWS
TERRACE RD N
Ryehurst Farm
CABBAGE HILL LA
HAZELWOOD LA
KETCHER GN
P
WICK'S GN
STEVENSON DR
MINCHIN GN
THE PATHWAY
1 CARPENTER MEWS
2 ELFORD CT
WINCH CL
POUND PL
TILEHURST LA
COOTE CL
ARTHURSTONE BIRCHES
B3018
B3034
Cabbage Hill
Wiltshire Farm
BINFIELD HO
EAGLEHURST COTTS
RED ROSE
PH
CHASE GDNS
ROSEDALE
ROSE HILL
MINORU PL
YORK RD
BROOKE PL
PITCH PL
KNOX GN
THORP CL
HILLCREST
TORLEVEN HTS
The Cut
Marchfield House
ALBEN RD
B3018
Binfield Manor
The Grange
GREEN LA
FOREST RD
B3034
P
EMMETS NEST
HILLSIDE DR
PITTS CL
CHENEY CL
Liby
PO
EMMETS PK
Binfield
Wood La
Grange Cottages
HORSNAPE GDNS
FISHER GN
CASWALL CL
WYTHEMEDE
1 OAKMEDE PL
2 HADDENHURST CT
3 FLORENTINA CT
4 COURTNEY PL
TEMPLE PARK RDBT
ROUGHGROVE COPSE
Binfield CE Prim Sch
CRESSEX CL
AVON CT
NASH PK
BENETFELD RD
TERRACE RD S
BINFIELD RD
Foxley Farm
RANDAL MEAD
SAVORY WLK
WIGGETT GR
ANGEL PL
CH
FRAMPTON BRIDGE RDBT
BLATCHLEY HO
UNDERWOOD CT
BLAMIRE DR
WILSTRODE AVE
Tinkers Copse
WILMOT CL
FOXLEY LA
ELLIOTT CT
ROEBUCK ESTATE
CHAPEL LA
Temple Park
TEMPLE WAY
MATTHEWS CHASE
B3018
BINFIELD RD
Swain's Copse
Whitehouse Farm
CHAPEL TERR
Newbold Coll
DUNFORD PL
MUNDAY CT
POLTONS LA
Jock's Copse
3 WALLCROFT CL
4 APSEY CT
WOODIES CL
WOOD LA
SAMIAN PL
CULVER CFT
BLOUNT CRES
CROCKFORD PL
COPPICE GN
MURRELL HILL LA
ST MARK'S RD
CRISP GDNS
WEBB CL
HALLBROOKE GDNS
DELLER ST
JOCK'S LA
FERNHILL CL
WEYCROFTS
ENGLEMERE RD
Long Copse
POPESWOOD RD
Newbold Sch
WOODHOUSE ST 1
HITHERHOOKS HILL 2
LAMMAS MEAD
PARK LA
MILL GN
WILWOOD RD
PRIESTWOOD AVE
Sch
EASTBURY CT
MOORDALE AVE

83 A B 84 C D 85 E F

89
117

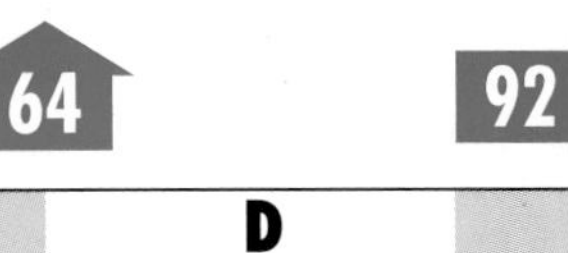

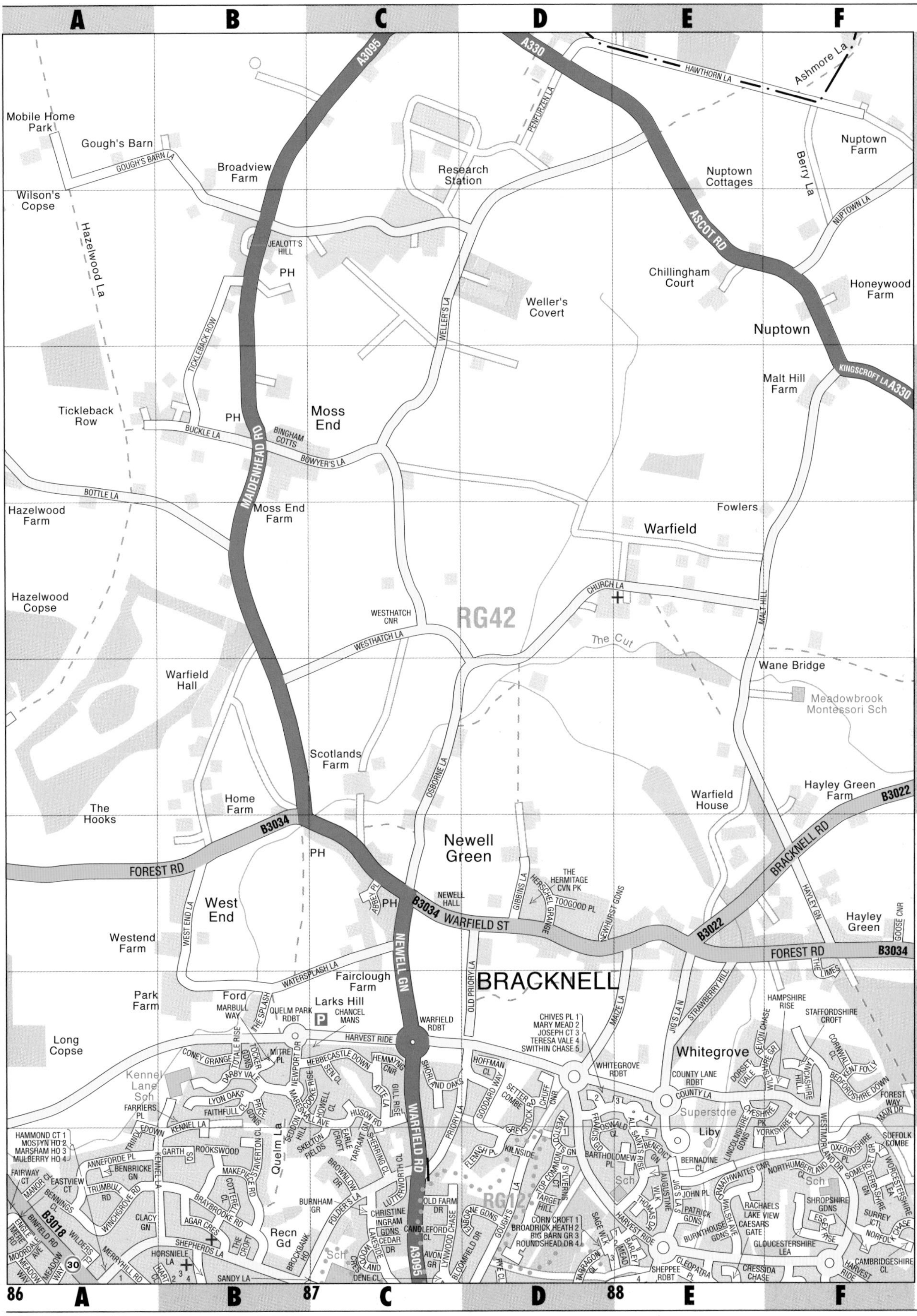

64
92

A
B
C
D
E
F
8
7
73
6
5
72
4
3
71
2
1
70
86
87
88
Mobile Home Park
Gough's Barn
GOUGH'S BARN LA
Broadview Farm
Wilson's Copse
Hazelwood La
A3095
A330
HAWTHORN LA
Ashmore La
PENFURZEN LA
Research Station
Nuptown Farm
Nuptown Cottages
Berry La
NUPTOWN LA
ASCOT RD
JEALOTT'S HILL
PH
Chillingham Court
Honeywood Farm
Weller's Covert
WELLER'S LA
Nuptown
TICKLEBACK ROW
KINGSCROFT LA
Malt Hill Farm
Tickleback Row
Moss End
BUCKLE LA
MAIDENHEAD RD
BINGHAM COTTS
BOWYER'S LA
BOTTLE LA
Hazelwood Farm
Moss End Farm
Fowlers
Warfield
CHURCH LA
Hazelwood Copse
WESTHATCH CNR
RG42
MALT HILL
WESTHATCH LA
The Cut
Wane Bridge
Warfield Hall
Meadowbrook Montessori Sch
Scotlands Farm
OSBORNE LA
Hayley Green Farm
Warfield House
The Hooks
Home Farm
B3034
B3022
Newell Green
FOREST RD
BRACKNELL RD
THE HERMITAGE CVN PK
GIBBINS LA
HERSCHEL GRANGE
TOOGOOD PL
NEWHURST GDNS
West End
ABBEY PL
NEWELL HALL
WARFIELD ST
HAYLEY GN
Hayley Green
GOOSE CNR
Westend Farm
WEST END LA
NEWELL GN
OLD PRIORY LA
THE LIMES
Fairclough Farm
WATERSPLASH LA
BRACKNELL
MAIZE LA
JIG'S LA N
STRAWBERRY HILL
HAMPSHIRE RISE
STAFFORDSHIRE CROFT
Park Farm
Ford
MARBULL WAY
QUELM PARK RDBT
Larks Hill
CHANCEL MANS
WARFIELD RDBT
CHIVES PL 1
MARY MEAD 2
JOSEPH CT 3
TERESA VALE 4
SWITHIN CHASE 5
Whitegrove
Long Copse
HARVEST RIDE
Kennel Lane Sch
WHITEGROVE RDBT
COUNTY LANE RDBT
COUNTY LA
Superstore
Liby
Sch
HAMMOND CT 1
MOSTYN HO 2
MARSHAM HO 3
MULBERRY HO 4
KENNEL LA
Quelm La
WARFIELD RD
RG12
Recn Gd
CORN CROFT 1
BROADRICK HEATH 2
BIG BARN GR 3
ROUNDSHEAD DR 4
B3018
BINFIELD RD
SANDY LA
SHEPPEE RDBT
CLEOPATRA PL
CRESSIDA CHASE
CAMBRIDGESHIRE CL

118
92

91
65

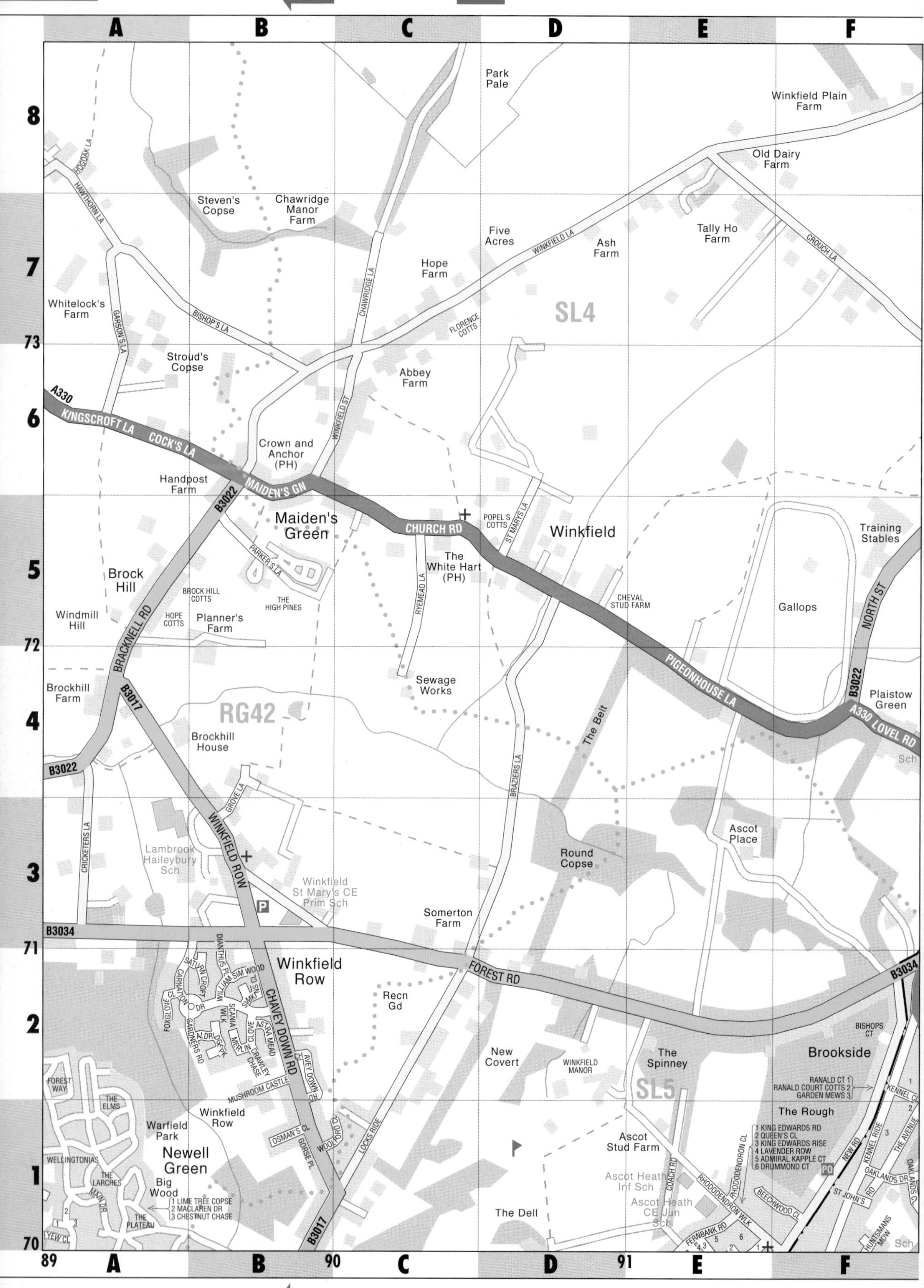
A B C D E F
8 7 73 6 5 72 4 3 71 2 1 70
Park Pale
Winkfield Plain Farm
Old Dairy Farm
Steven's Copse
Chawridge Manor Farm
Five Acres
Ash Farm
Tally Ho Farm
Hope Farm
Whitelock's Farm
SL4
Stroud's Copse
Abbey Farm
Crown and Anchor (PH)
Handpost Farm
Maiden's Green
Winkfield
Training Stables
Brock Hill
The White Hart (PH)
Windmill Hill
Planner's Farm
Gallops
Brockhill Farm
Sewage Works
Plaistow Green
RG42
Brockhill House
The Belt
Ascot Place
Lambrook Haileybury Sch
Round Copse
Winkfield St Mary's CE Prim Sch
Somerton Farm
Winkfield Row
Recn Gd
New Covert
The Spinney
Brookside
SL5
The Rough
Warfield Park
Winkfield Row
Newell Green
Big Wood
Ascot Stud Farm
Ascot Heath Inf Sch
Ascot Heath CE Jun Sch
The Dell
A330
KINGSCROFT LA
COCK'S LA
MAIDEN'S GN
CHURCH RD
PIGEONHOUSE LA
A330 LOVEL RD
B3022
BRACKNELL RD
B3017
WINKFIELD ROW
B3034
FOREST RD
CHAVEY DOWN RD
WINKFIELD LA
CROUCH LA
CHAWRIDGE LA
WINKFIELD ST
BISHOP'S LA
GARSON'S LA
HAWTHORN LA
HOBOAK LA
FLORENCE COTTS
POPEL'S COTTS
ST MARYS LA
RYEMEAD LA
PARKER'S LA
BROCK HILL COTTS
HOPE COTTS
THE HIGH PINES
CHEVAL STUD FARM
NORTH ST
BRAZIERS LA
GROVE LA
CRICKETERS LA
LOCKS RIDE
WINKFIELD MANOR
COACH RD
RHODODENDRON RD
RHODODENDRON WLK
BEECHWOOD CL
FERNBANK RD
BISHOPS CT
RANALD CT 1
RANALD COURT COTTS 2
GARDEN MEWS 3
1 KING EDWARDS RD
2 QUEEN'S CL
3 KING EDWARDS RISE
4 LAVENDER ROW
5 ADMIRAL KAPPLE CT
6 DRUMMOND CT
KENNEL CL
KENNEL RIDE
THE AVENUE
NEW RD
OAKLANDS DR
ST JOHN'S RD
HUNTSMANS MDW
Sch
PO
1 LIME TREE COPSE
2 MACLAREN DR
3 CHESTNUT CHASE
FOREST WAY
THE ELMS
WELLINGTONIAS
THE LARCHES
MAIN DR
THE PLATEAU
YEW CL
MUSHROOM CASTLE
OSMAN'S CL
GORSE PL
WOOD CL
CHAVEY DOWN
DIANTHUS PL
SATURN CROFT
WILLIAM SIM WOOD
CARNATION DR
FOXGLOVE CL
GARDENERS RD
SCANIA WLK
ASTRA MEAD
CRAWLEY CHASE
89 90 91

91
119

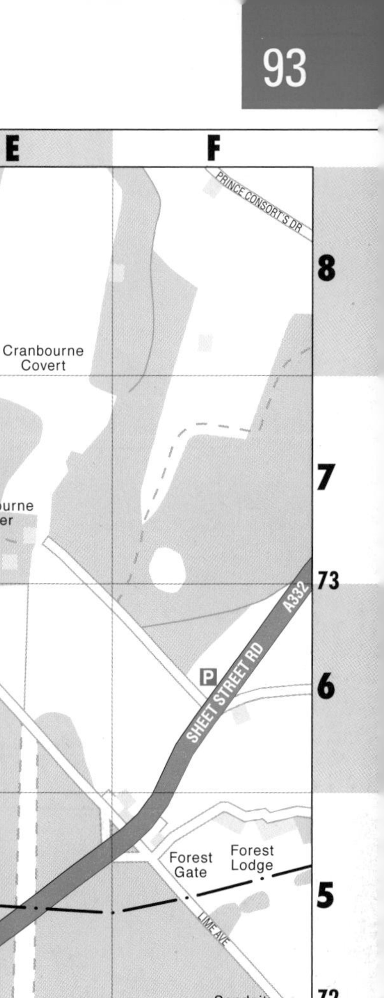

66
94
A 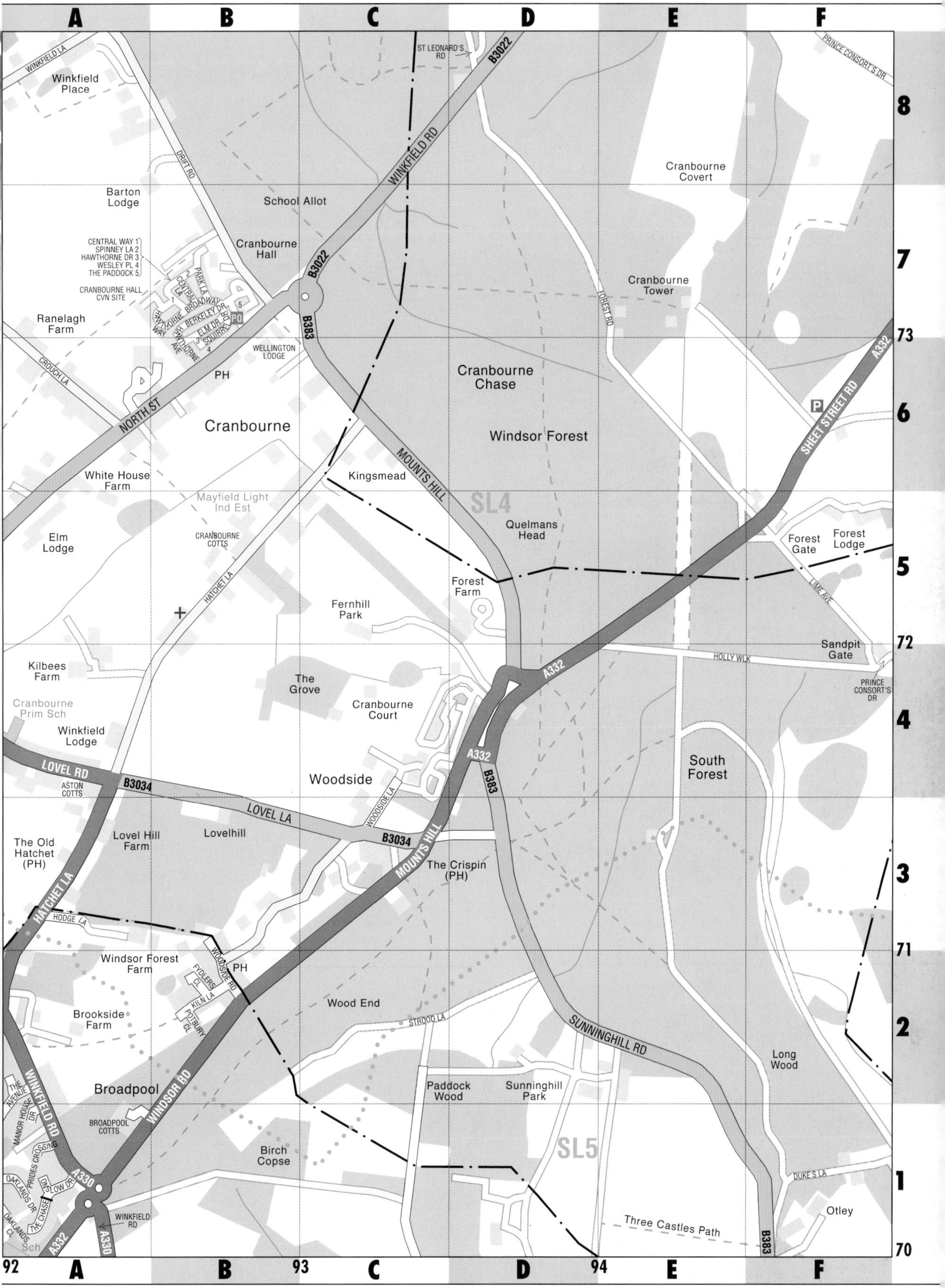
B
C
D
E
F
WINKFIELD LA
Winkfield Place
ST LEONARD'S RD
B3022
PRINCE CONSORT'S DR
DRIFT RD
WINKFIELD RD
Cranbourne Covert
Barton Lodge
School Allot
Cranbourne Hall
CENTRAL WAY 1
SPINNEY LA 2
HAWTHORNE DR 3
WESLEY PL 4
THE PADDOCK 5
CRANBOURNE HALL CVN SITE
Cranbourne Tower
FOREST RD
Ranelagh Farm
B383
WELLINGTON LODGE
Cranbourne Chase
A332
CROUCH LA
PH
NORTH ST
Cranbourne
Windsor Forest
SHEET STREET RD
White House Farm
Kingsmead
MOUNTS HILL
Mayfield Light Ind Est
SL4
Elm Lodge
CRANBOURNE COTTS
Quelmans Head
Forest Gate
Forest Lodge
Forest Farm
HATCHET LA
LIME AVE
Fernhill Park
Sandpit Gate
HOLLY WLK
Kilbees Farm
The Grove
Cranbourne Court
PRINCE CONSORT'S DR
Cranbourne Prim Sch
Winkfield Lodge
South Forest
LOVEL RD
ASTON COTTS
B3034
Woodside
LOVEL LA
WOODSIDE LA
The Old Hatchet (PH)
Lovel Hill Farm
Lovelhill
The Crispin (PH)
HATCHET LA
HODGE LA
Windsor Forest Farm
WOODSIDE RD
FYDLERS CL
KILN LA
POTBURY CL
PH
Wood End
STROOD LA
Brookside Farm
SUNNINGHILL RD
Long Wood
THE AVENUE
MANOR HOUSE DR
Broadpool
WINDSOR RD
Paddock Wood
Sunninghill Park
BROADPOOL COTTS
PRIDES CROSSING
Birch Copse
SL5
OAKLANDS DR
LONGLOW DR
THE CHASE
A330
DUKE'S LA
WINKFIELD RD
Otley
Three Castles Path
OAKLANDS CL
Sch
8
7
73
6
5
72
4
3
71
2
1
70
92
93
94
120

93
67

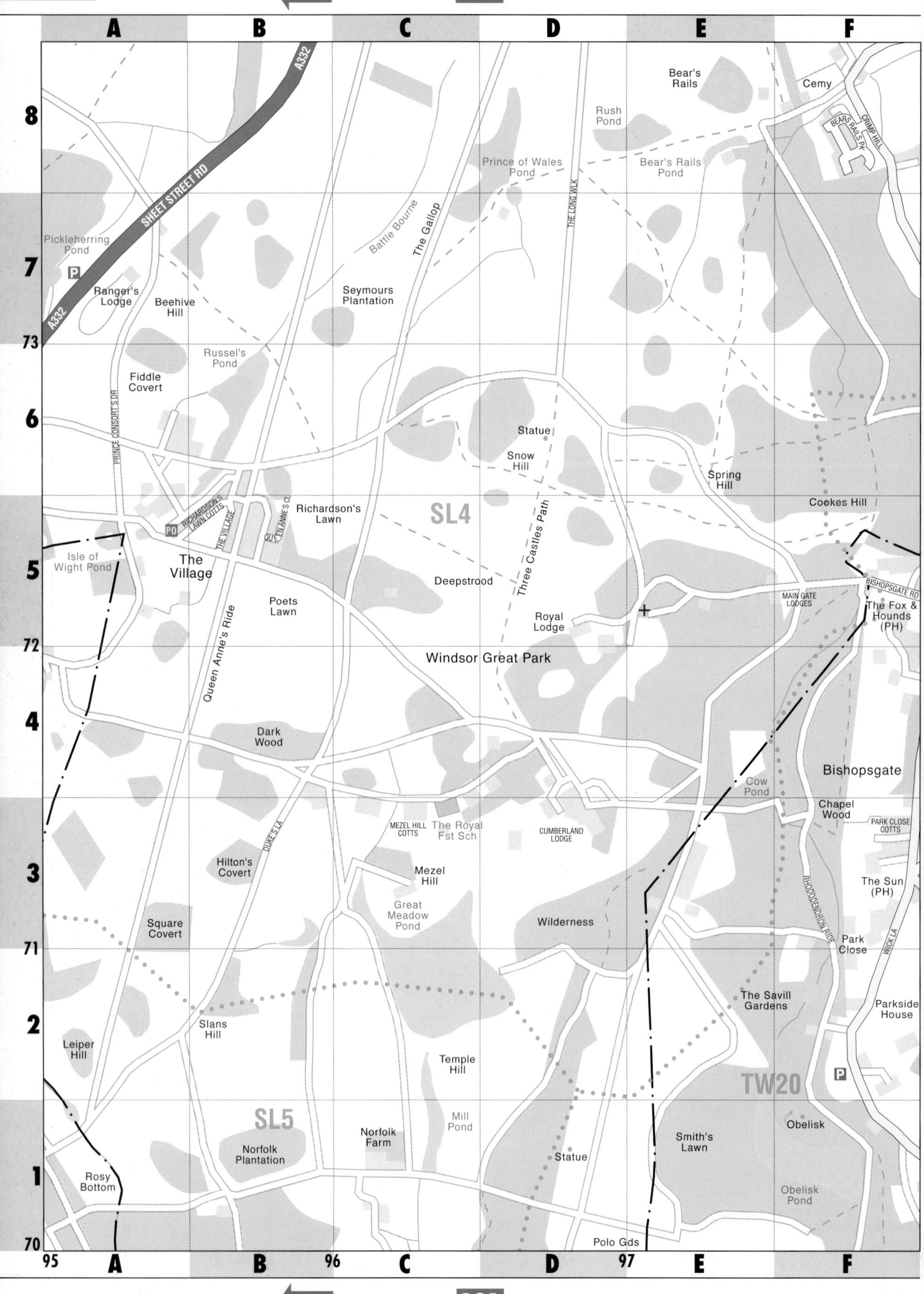
A
B
C
D
E
F
8
7
73
6
5
72
4
3
71
2
1
70
95
96
97
A332
SHEET STREET RD
Pickleherring Pond
P
Ranger's Lodge
Beehive Hill
Russel's Pond
Fiddle Covert
PRINCE CONSORT'S DR
Battle Bourne
The Gallop
Seymours Plantation
Prince of Wales Pond
THE LONG WLK
Rush Pond
Bear's Rails
Bear's Rails Pond
Cemy
BEARS RAILS PK
CRIMP HILL
Statue
Snow Hill
Spring Hill
Cookes Hill
Richardson's Lawn
RICHARDSON'S LAWN COTTS
PO
THE VILLAGE
QUEEN ANNE'S CL
SL4
Three Castles Path
Isle of Wight Pond
The Village
Deepstrood
Poets Lawn
Royal Lodge
BISHOPSGATE RD
MAIN GATE LODGES
The Fox & Hounds (PH)
Queen Anne's Ride
Windsor Great Park
Dark Wood
Bishopsgate
Cow Pond
Chapel Wood
PARK CLOSE COTTS
MEZEL HILL COTTS
The Royal Fst Sch
CUMBERLAND LODGE
DUKE'S LA
Hilton's Covert
Mezel Hill
Great Meadow Pond
Wilderness
RHODODENDRON RIDE
The Sun (PH)
Square Covert
Park Close
WICK LA
The Savill Gardens
Parkside House
Slans Hill
Leiper Hill
Temple Hill
TW20
Mill Pond
SL5
Norfolk Farm
Norfolk Plantation
Statue
Smith's Lawn
Obelisk
Rosy Bottom
Obelisk Pond
Polo Gds

93
121

68
96

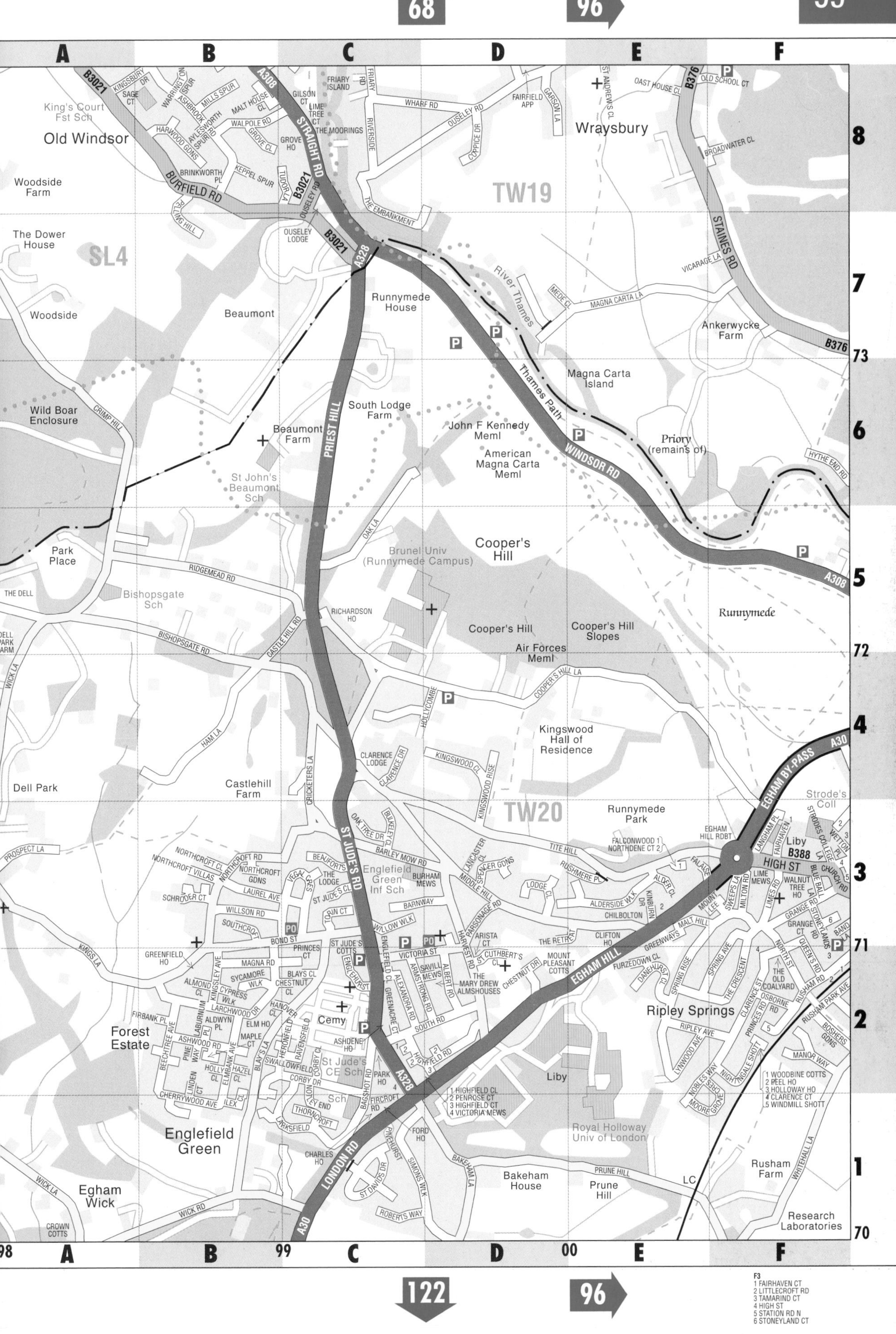
A
B
C
D
E
F
8
7
6
5
4
3
2
1
73
72
71
70
98
99
00
Old Windsor
King's Court Fst Sch
Woodside Farm
The Dower House
SL4
Woodside
Wild Boar Enclosure
Park Place
THE DELL
DELL PARK FARM
Dell Park
Beaumont
Beaumont Farm
St John's Beaumont Sch
Bishopsgate Sch
Castlehill Farm
Forest Estate
Englefield Green
Egham Wick
CROWN COTTS
Runnymede House
South Lodge Farm
John F Kennedy Meml
American Magna Carta Meml
Cooper's Hill
Brunel Univ (Runnymede Campus)
RICHARDSON HO
Cooper's Hill
Cooper's Hill Slopes
Air Forces Meml
Kingswood Hall of Residence
TW20
Runnymede Park
Englefield Green Inf Sch
Cemy
St Jude's CE Sch
Sch
Liby
Royal Holloway Univ of London
Bakeham House
Prune Hill
Ripley Springs
Rusham Farm
Research Laboratories
Wraysbury
TW19
River Thames
Thames Path
Magna Carta Island
Ankerwycke Farm
Priory (remains of)
Runnymede
Strode's Coll
EGHAM HILL RDBT
FALCONWOOD 1
NORTHDENE CT 2
B3021
A308
A328
A30
B376
B388
STRAIGHT RD
BURFIELD RD
PRIEST HILL
ST JUDE'S RD
WINDSOR RD
STAINES RD
EGHAM BY-PASS
EGHAM HILL
LONDON RD
HIGH ST
RIDGEMEAD RD
BISHOPSGATE RD
CASTLE HILL RD
CRIMP HILL
HAM LA
WICK LA
WICK RD
PROSPECT LA
KINGS LA
NORTHCROFT RD
NORTHCROFT CL
NORTHCROFT VILLAS
NORTHCROFT GDNS
LAUREL AVE
SCHRODER CT
WILLSON RD
SOUTHCROFT
BOND ST
GREENFIELD HO
MAGNA RD
SYCAMORE WLK
CYPRESS WLK
ALMOND CL
KINGSLEY AVE
LARCHWOOD DR
ALDWYN PL
ELM HO
MAPLE CT
ASHWOOD RD
FIRBANK PL
BEECHTREE AVE
PINE WAY
LINDEN CT
HOLLY CL
HAZEL CL
ELMBANK AVE
ILEX CL
CHERRYWOOD AVE
BLAY'S LA
HERONFIELD
RAVENSFIELD
SWALLOWFIELD
CORBY CL
CORBY DR
LYON CL
HEY END
THORNCROFT
LARKSFIELD
CHARLES HO
CRICKETERS LA
CLARENCE LODGE
CLARENCE DR
KINGSWOOD CL
KINGSWOOD RISE
OAK TREE DR
BULKELEY CL
BARLEY MOW RD
BEAUFORTS
THE LODGE
VEGAL CRES
ST JUDE'S CL
TORIN CT
WILLOW WLK
PRINCES CT
BLAYS CL
CHESTNUT CL
HANOVER CL
ST JUDE'S COTTS
ENGLEHURST
ASHDENE HO
PARK HO
BAGSHOT RD
FIRCROFT RD
PINEHURST
ST DAVIDS DR
SIMONS WLK
ROBERTS WAY
FORD HO
BAKEHAM LA
PRUNE HILL
LC
BURHAM MEWS
BARNWAY
ENGLEFIELD CL
GREENACRE CT
ALEXANDRA RD
ARMSTRONG RD
SAVILL MEWS
VICTORIA ST
ALBERT RD
SOUTH RD
HIGHFIELD RD
HARVEST RD
PARSONAGE RD
ARISTA CT
ST CUTHBERT'S CL
THE MARY DREW ALMSHOUSES
CHESTNUT DR
MOUNT PLEASANT COTTS
THE RETREAT
CLIFTON HO
FURZEDOWN CL
GREENWAYS
DANEHURST CL
LANCASTER CL
SPENCER GDNS
MIDDLE HILL
LODGE CL
TITE HILL
RUSHMERE PL
ALDERSIDE WLK
CHILBOLTON
KINBURN DR
ALDER CL
FALAISE
MOUNT LEE
SWEEPS LA
MILTON RD
LIME MEWS
WALNUT TREE HO
LIMES RD
MALT HILL
SPRING RISE
SPRING AVE
THE CRESCENT
CLARENCE ST
NORTH ST
THE OLD COALYARD
OSBORNE RD
PRINCES RD
QUEENS RD
RUSHAM RD
RUSHAM PARK AVE
BOSHERS GDNS
MANOR WAY
RIPLEY AVE
LYNWOOD AVE
NOBLES WAY
MOORE GROVE CRES
NIGHTINGALE SHOTT
WHITEHALL LA
GRANGE RD
GRANGE CT
STONEYLAND RD
BLUE BALL LA
CHURCH RD
LANGHAM PL
FAIRHAVEN
STRODES COLLEGE LA
WETTON PL
HOLLYCOMBE
COOPER'S HILL LA
OAK LA
KINGSBURY DR
SAGE CT
WARRINGTON SPUR
ASHBROOK RD
MILLS SPUR
HARWOOD GDNS
AYLESWORTH SPUR
MALT HOUSE CL
WALPOLE RD
GROVE CL
BRINKWORTH PL
KEPPEL SPUR
PELLING HILL
TUDOR LA
OUSELEY RD
OUSELEY LODGE
GROVE HO
GILSON CT
LIME TREE CT
THE MOORINGS
FRIARY ISLAND
FRIARY RD
RIVERSIDE
WHARF RD
COPPICE DR
FAIRFIELD APP
GARSON LA
ST ANDREWS CL
OAST HOUSE CL
OLD SCHOOL CT
BROADWATER CL
VICARAGE LA
MEDE CL
MAGNA CARTA LA
THE EMBANKMENT
HYTHE END RD
1 HIGHFIELD CL
2 PENROSE CT
3 HIGHFIELD CT
4 VICTORIA MEWS
1 WOODBINE COTTS
2 PEEL HO
3 HOLLOWAY HO
4 CLARENCE CT
5 WINDMILL SHOTT
F3
1 FAIRHAVEN CT
2 LITTLECROFT RD
3 TAMARIND CT
4 HIGH ST
5 STATION RD N
6 STONEYLAND CT

122
96

95
69

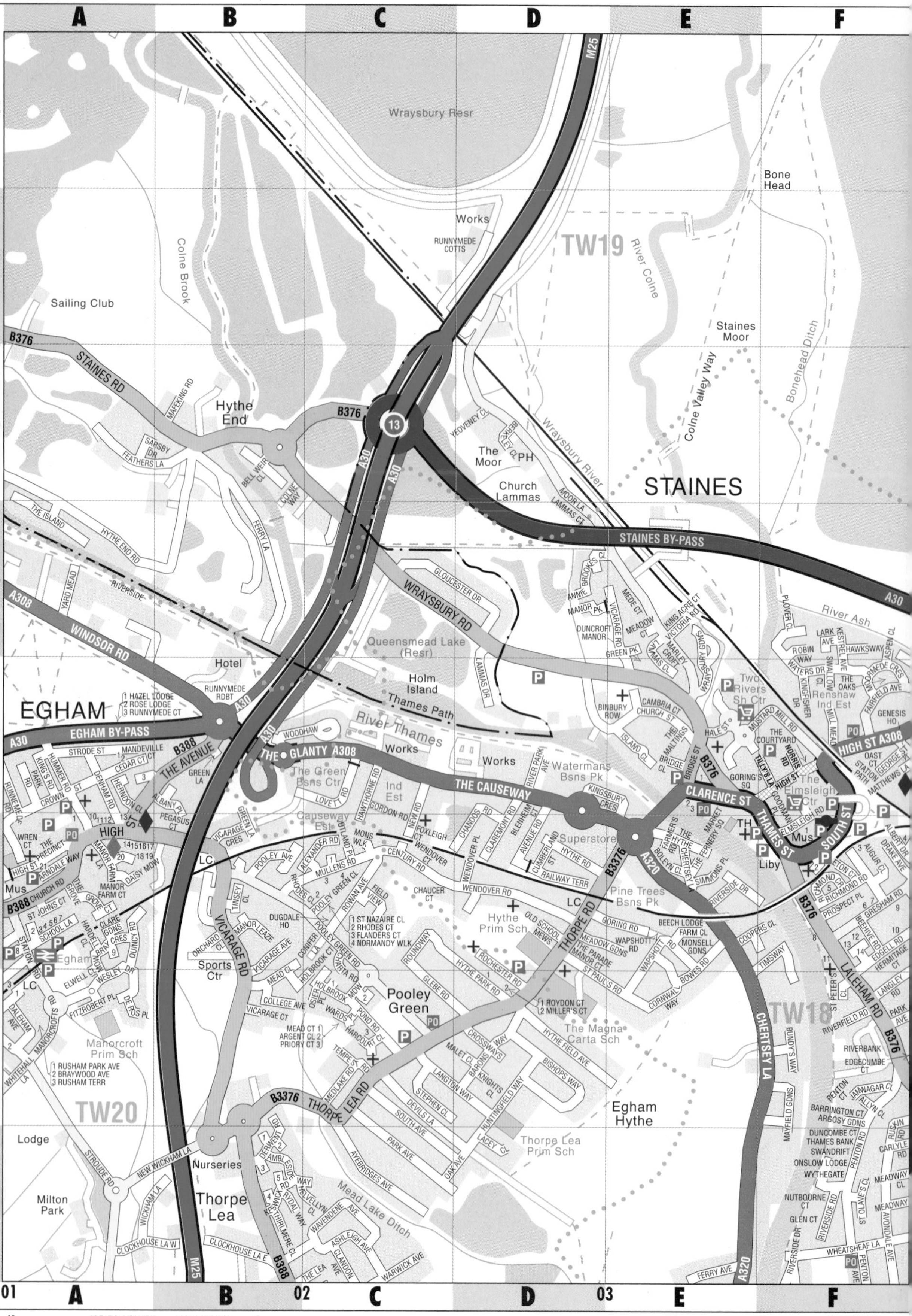

A B C D E F

Wraysbury Resr

Works

RUNNYMEDE COTTS

TW19

River Colne

Bone Head

Colne Brook

Sailing Club

B376

STAINES RD

Hythe End

Staines Moor

Colne Valley Way

Bonehead Ditch

The Moor

Church Lammas

Wraysbury River

STAINES

STAINES BY-PASS

A30

WRAYSBURY RD

Queensmead Lake (Resr)

Holm Island

Thames Path

River Thames

Hotel

EGHAM

EGHAM BY-PASS

RUNNYMEDE RDBT

1 HAZEL LODGE
2 ROSE LODGE
3 RUNNYMEDE CT

WINDSOR RD

A308

THE GLANTY A308

THE CAUSEWAY

Watermans Bsns Pk

Two Rivers Sh Ctr

Renshaw Ind Est

HIGH ST A308

CLARENCE ST

THAMES ST

SOUTH ST

Superstore

Pine Trees Bsns Pk

Hythe Prim Sch

1 ST NAZAIRE CL
2 RHODES CT
3 FLANDERS CT
4 NORMANDY WLK

Pooley Green

1 ROYDON CT
2 MILLER'S CT

The Magna Carta Sch

MEAD CT 1
ARGENT CL 2
PRIORY CT 3

Manorcroft Prim Sch

1 RUSHAM PARK AVE
2 BRAYWOOD AVE
3 RUSHAM TERR

TW20

TW18

CHERTSEY LA

LALEHAM RD

Egham Hythe

Thorpe Lea Prim Sch

Mead Lake Ditch

Nurseries

Thorpe Lea

Lodge

Milton Park

Sports Ctr

01 A B 02 C D 03 E F

A3
1 ST CATHERINES PL
2 NICHOLSON WLK
3 REGENTS HO
4 WINDSOR HO
5 SAVILLE HO
6 ETON HO
7 ASCOT HO
8 HERITAGE CT
9 CADDY CL
10 THE OLD BAKERY
11 WILLOWBROOK CT
12 HENLEY CT
13 RUNNYMEDE HO
14 TOWER CT
15 CHANCERY CT
16 GALLERY CT
17 CHAPTER CT
18 TUDOR CT
19 STEEPLE CT
20 MANOR FARM
21 TUDOR CT

B1
1 WINDERMERE CL
2 CONISTON WAY
3 BORROWDALE CL
4 BUTTERMERE WAY
5 GRASMERE CL

95
123

E4
1 ALDOUS HO
2 THAMES EDGE CT
3 COLNEBRIDGE CL

F3
1 FRIENDS WLK
2 WESTBROOK RD
3 BRACKLEY HO
4 MANSFIELD HO
5 CRESCENT CT
6 ABBEY LODGE
7 LAZARE CT
8 REGATTA HO
9 BOSSINGTON CT
10 TROSTON CT
11 IFFLEY CT
12 LAUDERDALE HO
13 AMBER CT
14 THE CYGNETS

70 98

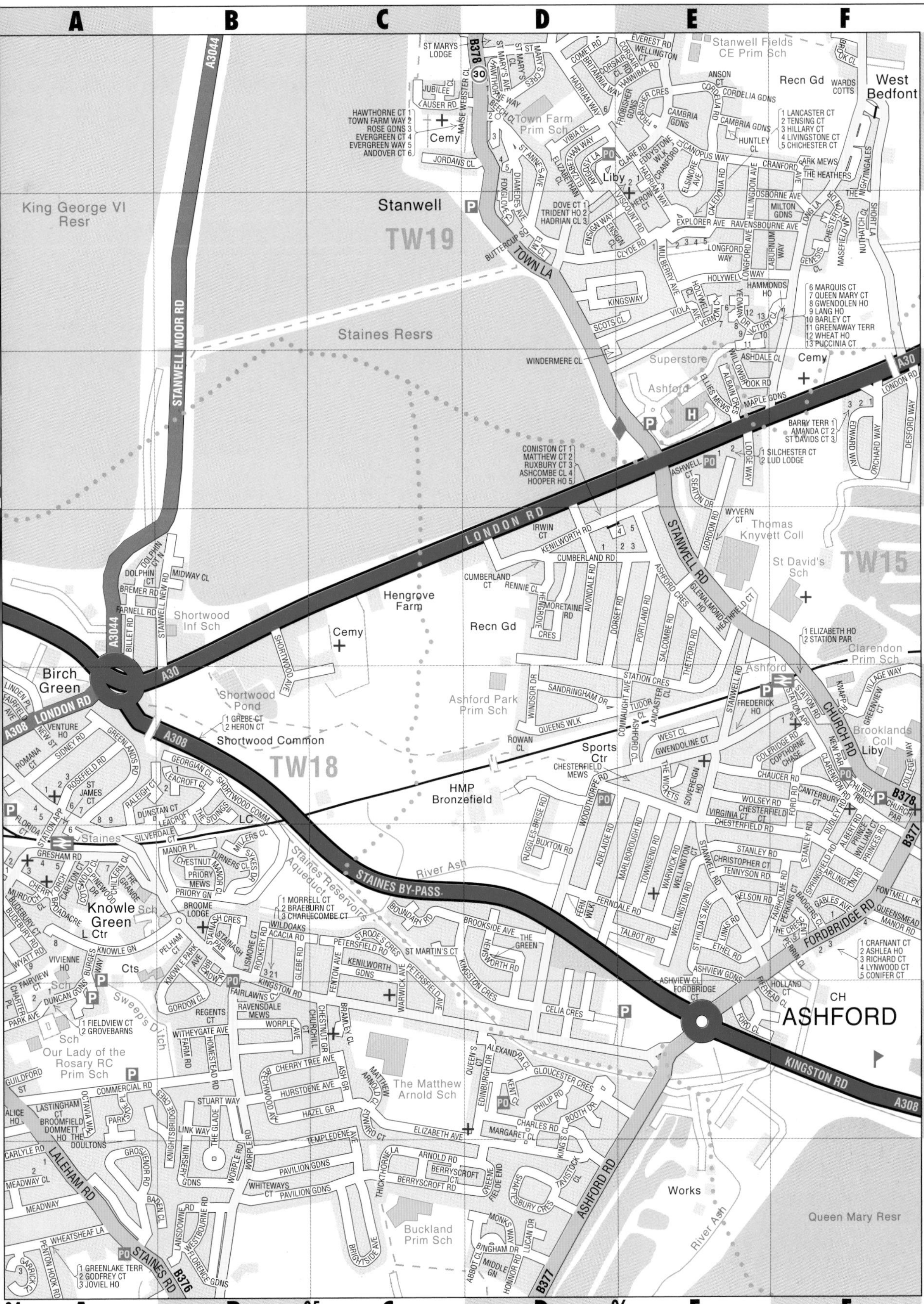

Stanwell

TW19

King George VI Resr

Staines Resrs

West Bedfont

TW15

TW18

Birch Green

Knowle Green

Hengrove Farm

HMP Bronzefield

Shortwood Common

Ashford

ASHFORD

Queen Mary Resr

Stanwell Fields CE Prim Sch

Town Farm Prim Sch

Thomas Knyvett Coll

St David's Sch

Clarendon Prim Sch

Brooklands Coll

Ashford Park Prim Sch

Shortwood Inf Sch

Shortwood Pond

The Matthew Arnold Sch

Buckland Prim Sch

Our Lady of the Rosary RC Prim Sch

STANWELL MOOR RD

LONDON RD

STAINES BY-PASS

KINGSTON RD

STANWELL RD

CHURCH RD

ASHFORD RD

STAINES RD

LALEHAM RD

TOWN LA

HAWTHORNE CT 1
TOWN FARM WAY 2
ROSE GDNS 3
EVERGREEN CT 4
EVERGREEN WAY 5
ANDOVER CT 6

DOVE CT 1
TRIDENT HO 2
HADRIAN CL 3

1 LANCASTER CT
2 TENSING CT
3 HILLARY CT
4 LIVINGSTONE CT
5 CHICHESTER CT

6 MARQUIS CT
7 QUEEN MARY CT
8 GWENDOLEN HO
9 LANG HO
10 BARLEY CT
11 GREENAWAY TERR
12 WHEAT HO
13 PUCCINIA CT

BARRY TERR 1
AMANDA CT 2
ST DAVIDS CT 3

1 SILCHESTER CT
2 LUD LODGE

CONISTON CT 1
MATTHEW CT 2
RUXBURY CT 3
ASHCOMBE CL 4
HOOPER HO 5

1 ELIZABETH HO
2 STATION PAR

1 GREBE CT
2 HERON CT

1 MORRELL CT
2 BRAEBURN CT
3 CHARLECOMBE CT

1 CRAFNANT CT
2 ASHLEA HO
3 RICHARD CT
4 LYNWOOD CT
5 CONIFER CT

1 FIELDVIEW CT
2 GROVEBARNS

1 GREENLAKE TERR
2 GODFREY CT
3 JOVIEL HO

A3
1 ALBERT DR
2 BEACH'S HO
3 GRESHAM CT
4 FRIENDSHIP HO
5 PHOENIX PL
6 PULLMANS PL
7 GRANGE CT
8 THE BEECHES
9 WORCESTER CT

A4
1 BUCKINGHAM CT
2 ST CATHERINES CT
3 DAVID CT
4 NORMAN CT
5 CLAYDON CT
6 MAYNARD CT
7 GREENLANDS CT
8 DORCHESTER CT
9 JUBILEE CT

124 98

97
71

F5
1 THE HERMITAGE
2 SPRING CNR
3 QUEENS PARK GDNS
4 CROMWELL LODGE
5 RUBY CT
6 OCHRE CT
7 SIENNA CT
8 FUSCIA CT
9 INDIGO CT
10 VIRIDIAN CT
11 TOPAZ CT
12 AZURE CT
13 VERMILLION CT

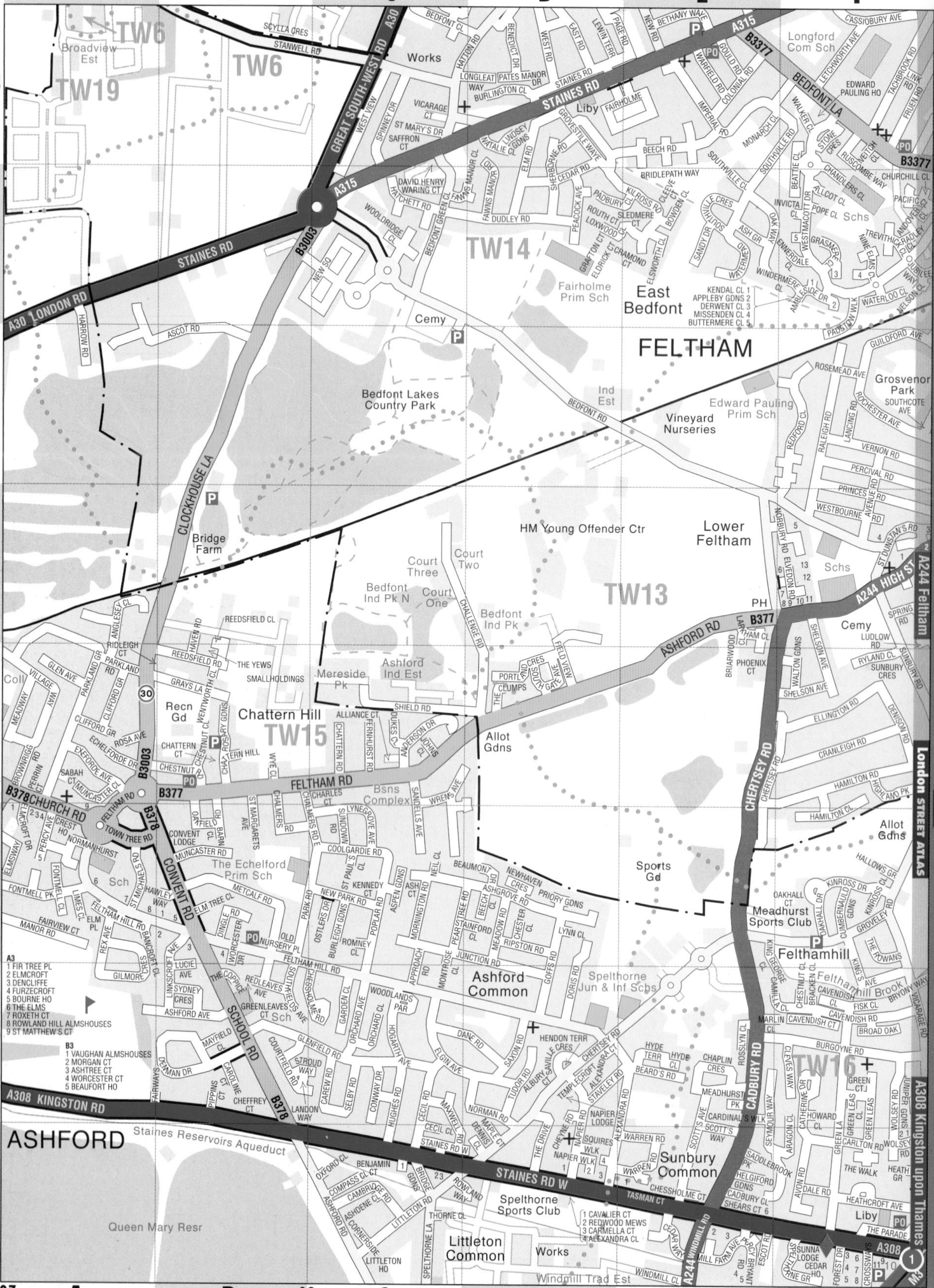

A B C D E F

8 7 73 6 5 72 4 3 71 2 1 70

Broadview Est
TW6
TW19
Works
Longford Com Sch
Edward Pauling Ho
Liby
TW14
Fairholme Prim Sch
East Bedfont
KENDAL CL 1
APPLEBY GDNS 2
DERWENT CL 3
MISSENDEN CL 4
BUTTERMERE CL 5
Cemy
FELTHAM
Bedfont Lakes Country Park
Ind Est
Edward Pauling Prim Sch
Vineyard Nurseries
Grosvenor Park
Bridge Farm
HM Young Offender Ctr
Lower Feltham
Court Two
Court Three
Court One
Bedfont Ind Pk N
Bedfont Ind Pk
TW13
Mereside Pk
Ashford Ind Est
Chattern Hill
TW15
Recn Gd
Allot Gdns
Bsns Complex
The Echelford Prim Sch
Sports Gd
Meadhurst Sports Club
Felthamhill
Ashford Common
Spelthorne Jun & Inf Schs
Feltham Hill Brook
TW16
Sunbury Common
Spelthorne Sports Club
Littleton Common
Works
Windmill Trad Est
ASHFORD
Staines Reservoirs Aqueduct
Queen Mary Resr

A3
1 FIR TREE PL
2 ELMCROFT
3 DENCLIFFE
4 FURZECROFT
5 BOURNE HO
6 THE ELMS
7 ROXETH CT
8 ROWLAND HILL ALMSHOUSES
9 ST MATTHEW'S CT

B3
1 VAUGHAN ALMSHOUSES
2 MORGAN CT
3 ASHTREE CT
4 WORCESTER CT
5 BEAUFORT HO

1 CAVALIER CT
2 REDWOOD MEWS
3 CARMELLA CT
4 ALEXANDRA CL

London STREET ATLAS

07 A B 08 C D 09 E F

97
125

C1
1 HAWTHORN CT
2 VICOUNT CT
3 BLACKTHORNE CT

E1
1 CHARMILE CT
2 WILLOW CT
3 CASTLE CL
4 KILLIGREW HO
5 GRANTHAM HO
6 PRINCE ALBERT CT

F1
1 BISHOPS CT
2 WOLSEY CT
3 ASH LODGE
4 LIME LODGE
5 OAK LODGE
6 ELM CT
7 WILLOW LODGE
8 SYCAMORE LODGE
9 PRISCILLA HO
10 Sunbury Cross Ctr
11 ISOBEL HO

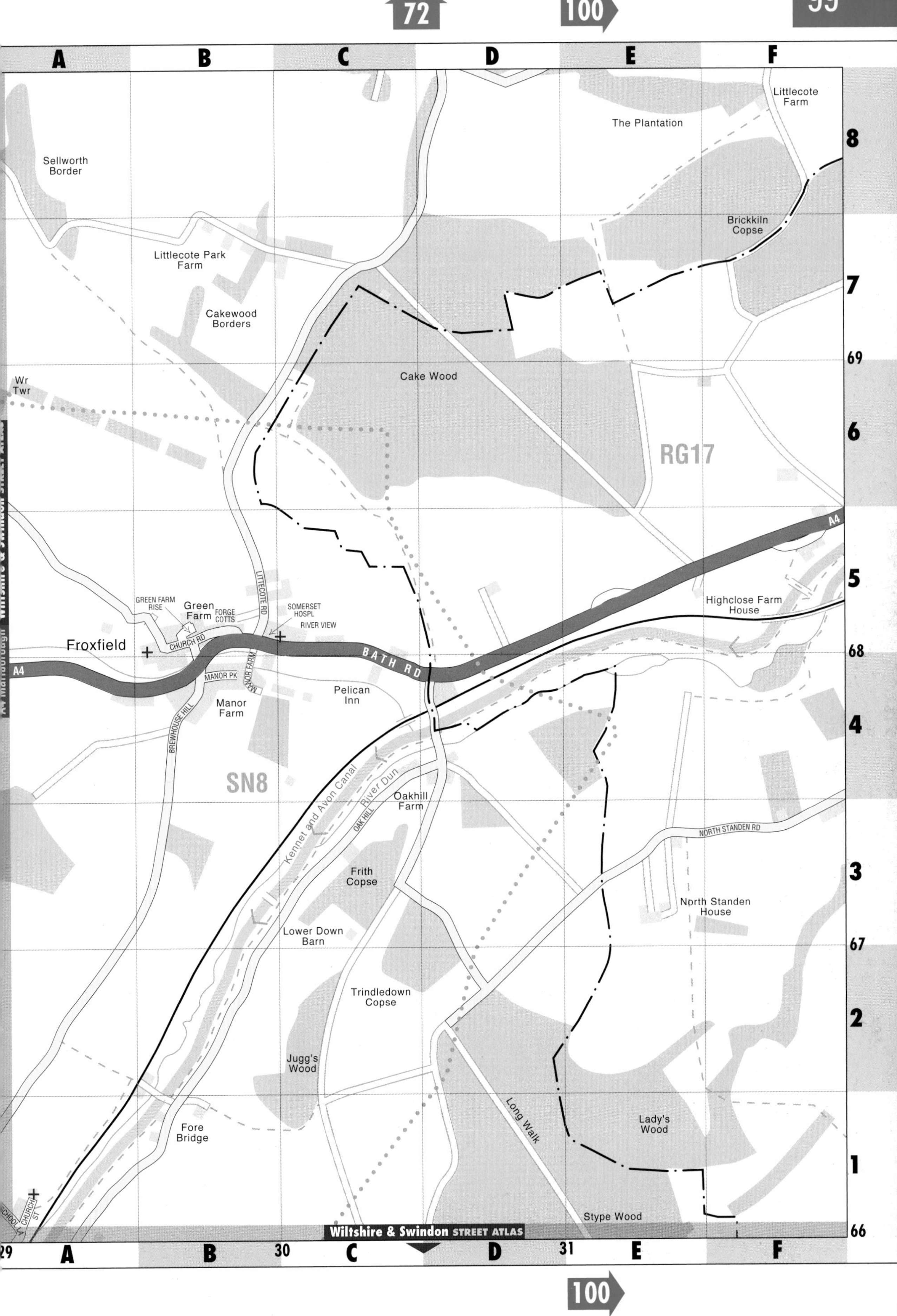
A
B
C
D
E
F
Littlecote Farm
The Plantation
Sellworth Border
Brickkiln Copse
Littlecote Park Farm
Cakewood Borders
Wr Twr
Cake Wood
RG17
A4
LITTLECOTE RD
GREEN FARM RISE
Green Farm
FORGE COTTS
SOMERSET HOSPL
RIVER VIEW
Highclose Farm House
Froxfield
CHURCH RD
BATH RD
MANOR PK
MANOR FARM
Pelican Inn
Manor Farm
BREWHOUSE HILL
SN8
Kennet and Avon Canal
River Dun
OAK HILL
Oakhill Farm
NORTH STANDEN RD
Frith Copse
North Standen House
Lower Down Barn
Trindledown Copse
Jugg's Wood
Long Walk
Lady's Wood
Fore Bridge
SCHOOL LA
CHURCH ST
Stype Wood
8
7
69
6
5
68
4
3
67
2
1
66
29
30
31

99
73
126
A B C D E F
8 7 69 6 5 68 4 2 3 67 2 1 66
32 33 34
Leverton
LEVERTON COTTS
LEVERTON LA
GIPSY LA
Furze Hill
River Kennet
UPPER EDDINGTON
Eddington
EDDINGTON HILL
WANTAGE RD
Folly Farm
Cemy
MIDDLETONS CL
SWANGATE
CYGNET WAY
TEALGATE
HERONSGATE
CHARNHAM PK
CHARNHAM LA
Kennet Ent Ctr
KENNET WAY
FOUNDRY HO
THE LAURELS
HAMBLIN MDW
OXFORD ST
KENNET CT
COTTRELL CL
MEADOWVIEW CT
CHAPEL
WEST VIEW CT
L Ctr
B4192
STRONGROVE HILL
CHARNHAM ST
BATH RD
A4
A338
CHARNHAM CT
Eddington Bridge
Hotel
CHURCH CROFT 1
CHAPEL HO 2
NEWTON'S MEWS 3
CHURCH LA 4
River Dun
BEARWATER
CANAL WLK
THE FORGE
BRIDGE ST
Hopgrass Farm
Kennet & Avon Canal
PO
PARSONAGE LA
ST LAWRENCE SQ
Liby
EVERLAND RD
Hungerford
LC
MARSHGATE APARTMENTS
MARSH LA
Marsh Gate
CHURCH ST
WILLIAMS CT
STATION RD
Station Yard Ind Est
TH
CROWN MEWS
OAKES CT
HONEY FIELDS
PROSPECT RD
CROFT RD
POUND PIECE
PRETMANS CL
WILTSHIRE CL
WESSEX CL
SOMERSET CL
SMITHAM BRIDGE RD
CHERRY GR
SHALBOURNE CL
PARK ST
NORTHVIEW
PORT DOWN
DOWN VIEW
1 RAMSBURY TERR
2 FIRGROVE CT
3 CROFTON HO
Berkshire Trout Farm
Down Gate
CHILTON WAY
WEATHERVANE COTTS
CHANTRY MEAD
MOORES PL
CHURCH WAY
REGENT CL
ATHERTON RD
HIGH ST
UPLANDS
HOMEFIELD WAY
Hungerford Trad Est
FAIRVIEW RD
MACKLIN CL
RAMSBURY DR
Hungerford Prim Sch
SOUTH VIEW
D5
1 ALDBOURNE CL
2 NORTHVIEW HTS
3 BARNARD'S CT
4 SALISBURY ROW
5 FAIRFIELDS
6 PRIORY PL
7 MARLBOROUGH CT
8 THE OLD GRANARY
BORNE VALE
SAWDEN CL
WESTBROOK CL
ATHERTON CRES
MORLEY PL
TARRANT'S HILL
CLARK'S GDNS
LEWINGTON MEWS
NORTH STANDEN RD
RG17
PRIORY RD
ORCHARD PARK CL
HILLSIDE RD
PRIORY CL
HUNGERFORD
SARUM WAY
Hungerford Town FC
Hungerford Port Down
Hungerford Common
LANCASTER SQ
BULPIT LA
PRIORY AVE
LANCASTER CL
YORK RD
BEACH SQ
CHESTNUT WLK
COLDHARBOUR RD
PARK WAY
KENNEDY MDW
DE MONTFORT GR
Inkpen Gate
LIGUEL CL
PRIORY RD
PLATT CT
COMBE VIEW
SALISBURY RD
L Ctr
Heart Clump
John O'Gaunt Com Tech Coll
INKPEN RD
Beacon Farm
Sanham Green
Cold Harbour
Standen Manor
Hornhill
FARM COTTS
Standen Farm

74
102

A
B
C
D
E
F
Heath Hanger Copse
Oaken Copse
Hawkshill Clump
DENFORD LA
Furze Ground
Paddock Plantation
RADLEY BOTTOM
Radley Bottom Cottages
Denford Park
DARK LA
Five Acre Plantation
Four Acre Plantation
Denford Lodge
Denford Manor
Denford Mill
Denford Gate
A4
Avington Manor
Avington
River Kennet
Kintbury Gate
Home Farm
RG17
Kennet and Avon Canal
Park Farm Dairy
PARK COTTS
Foxley Covert
Withybed Copse
WITHYBED LA
HUNGERFORD LA
INGLEWOOD RD
HIGH ST
Kintbury Farm
Little Templeton
Templeton
Inglewood Health Hydro
WALLINGTONS RD
Inglewood Spinney
Templeton Stud
INKPEN RD
South Wood
Inglewood Farm
Winterly La
8
7
69
6
5
68
4
3
67
2
1
66
36
37

127
102

101
75

A B C D E F

8 7 69 6 5 68 4 3 67 2 1 66

Clapton Farm
Lower Farm
LIP LA
Rowland's Copse
Hoe Benham
Elcot Farm
Elcot
Highcroft Copse
Field's Copse
Elcot Park Hotel
Pound's Border
HOE BENHAM LA
Bottom Barn
Halfway Manor Farm
The Halfway Inn (PH)
Halfway Farm
A4
Lodges
HALFWAY FARM COTTS
Halfway
BOARD LA
Little Wawcott
RG17
Wawcott
RG20
Richen's Cottage
Wawcott Farm
WAWCOTT FARM COTTS
River Kennet
Barton Court
Barton Holt
The Wilderness
Kintbury
LC
P
PH
Dreweat Lock
Sewage Works
Kennet and Avon Canal
Shepherd's Bridge
Irish Hill Copse
KINTBURY MILL
MILL BANK
Kintbury Park Farm
Irish Hill
CHURCH ST
FORGE CL
STATION RD
THE CROFT
PO
KINTBURY SQ
Kintbury St Mary's CE Prim Sch
HIGH ST
NEWBURY ST
ELIZABETH GDNS
TITCOMBE WAY
NOTREES
BARN CL
IRISH HILL RD
WALLINGTONS RD
HOP GDNS
MORRISH GR
GAINSBOROUGH AVE
HOLT RD
HAROLD RD
SEVERALS
GREAT
GLADSTONE CL
KENNET RD
BURTONS HILL
THE PENTLANDS
Irish Hill Cottages
LAWRENCE MEAD
LONG CL
CRAVEN WAY
THE HAVEN
ASHTON PL
INKPEN RD
BRADLEY CL
DUNN CRES
CRAVEN CL
QUEENS WAY
THE CRESCENT
Peartree Cottage
Kintbury
Illwills Border
THE GREEN
LAYLAND'S GN
OLD LA
Barrymore Lodge
Dongall's Wood
Hamstead Holt Farm
Horn Copse
Hankin's La
BLANDYS HILL

38 A B 39 C D 40 E F

101
128

76
104
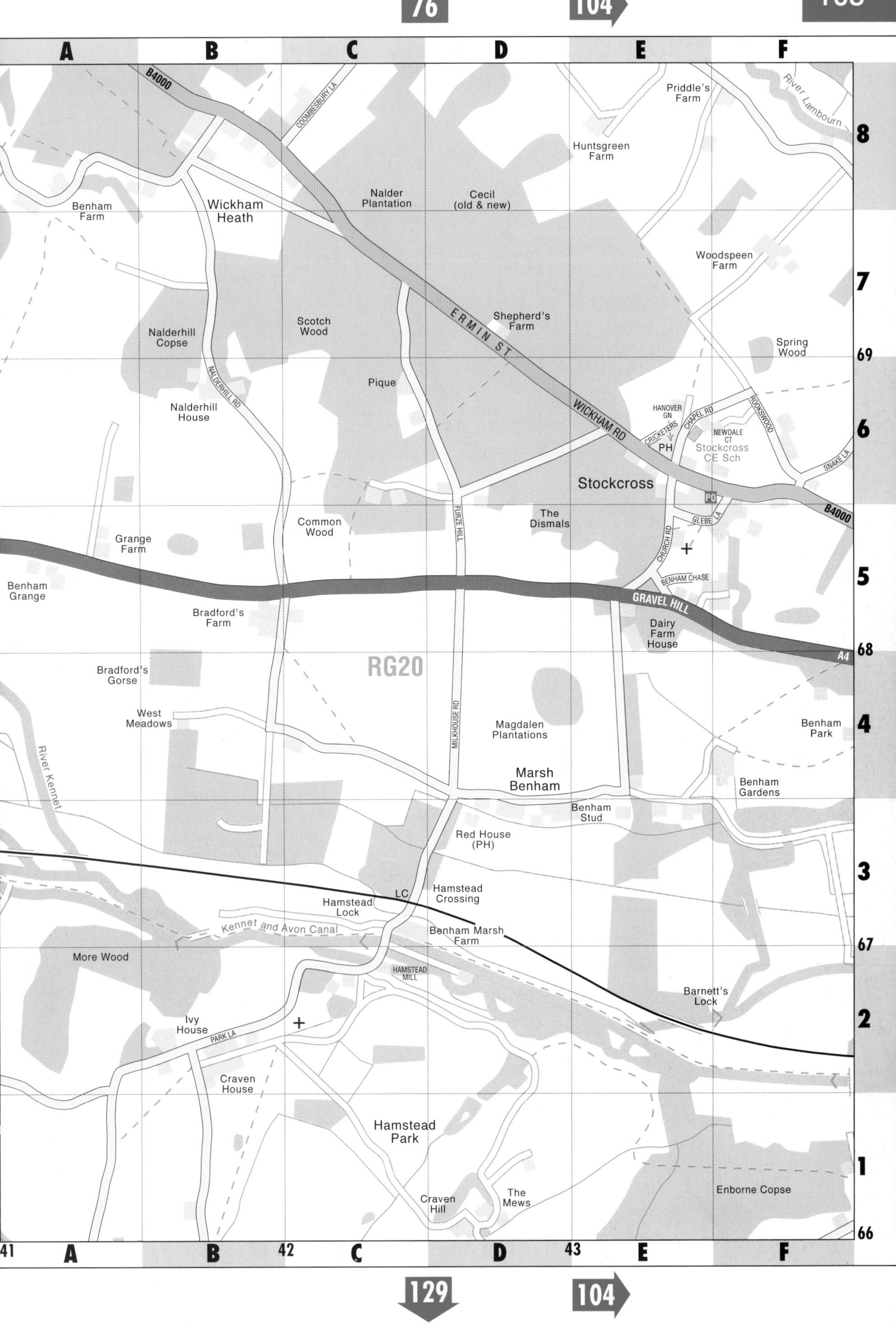

129
104

103 77

F4
1 BRUNEL CT
2 OLD COLLEGE RD
3 TELFORD CT
4 McKENZIE CT
5 ORMONDE GDNS
6 BRINDLEY CT
7 SMEATON CT
8 STEPHENSON CT
9 MALT CT
10 CORPORATION COTTS

A B C D E F

8
Whitefield Farm
Packer's Copse
Castle Farm
Hotel
Donnington Holt
Nothing Hill
Winterbourne Stream
Newton's La
A34
B4494

7
Woodspeen
Bagnor
The Blackbird (PH)
Bagnor Bridge
Castle Wood
Donnington Castle
Donnington
The Chase
Whitefields Cotts
Link View
Hillcrest Cotts
Donnington Lodge

69
Snake La
Lower Woodspeen Ct
Donnington Grove Hotel
The Castle Sch

6
Foley Farm
Five Bells (PH)
Belmont Cotts
Dairy Farm
River Lambourn
Groombridge Pl
Abberbury Cl
Castle La
Donnington Elms
Shop La
Hunts Cotts
Aldwych Cotts
Sunnyside
Donnington Hospl
Love La
Yew Gate
The Priory
Donnington Pk
Oxford Rd

5
Hotel
CH
B4000
Ermin St
Deanwood Farm
Deanwood Ho
Whittle Copse
Lambourn Rd
The Sydings
Speen
Cromwell Terr
Grove Rd
Sylvester Cl
Groveland Rd
Lewendon Rd
Cowslade
Kersey Cres
Chaucer Cres
Charmwood Cl
Lockett's Bridge
RG14
Station Rd
Winterton Dr
Manor Pl
Larch Cl
Penn Rd
Sutton Rd
Coster Cl
De Montfort Rd
Brummell Rd
Talbot Cl
Burchell Rd
Digby Rd
Donnington Sq
Penrose Cl
Benett Gdns
Castle Gr
Lisle Cl
Cherry Cl

68
RG20
A4
Kimbers Dr
Marshalls Ct
Majendie Cl
Pound La
Newbold Rd
Caunter Rd
Battle Cl
Coxeter Rd
Bath Rd
Prim Sch
Rennie Ct
Amberley Cl
St Leger Ct
Herewood Cl
Linden Cl

4
Benham Park
East Lodge
Speen House
Elmore Abbey
Church La
Speen La
Speen Pl
Speen Lodge Ct
Speen Hill Cl
Western Ave
Superstore
Sch
Angel Ct
Pelican La
Old Bath Rd
Maplespeen Ct
Oxford St
Elmfield Gdns
Hill Rd
Croft La
Posting House Mews 1
Wilson Valkenburg Ho 2
Back Lodge
Goldwell Park
Jesmond Dene
Goldwell Dr
Leys Gdns
Strawberry Hill
Pelican Ho
Moor La
Fitzgerald Ct
Freeman Ct

3
Kinghams
Speen Moor Plantations
NEWBURY
North Croft
Cleveland Gr
Saffron Cl
Crawford Pl
Cansfield End
Regents Ct
Bewicks Reach
Northcroft Terr
Northcroft La
Dolton Mews
Town Mills
River Kennet
Kennet & Avon Canal
Dysons Cl
Russell Ct
Butson Cl
Russell Rd
West Mills
Mallard Ct
Kimber's Yd
Lincoln Ct
Oddfellows Rd

67
Lipscombe Cl
The Mews
Chalford Rd
Gloucester Rd
Blenheim Rd
Berkeley Rd
Garland Ct
Kennet Rd
Enborne Bridge
Guyer's Lock
Puffers Way 1
Braunfels Wlk 2
Western End 3
Westfield Way 4
Greenways Ho 5
Wentworth Lodge 6
Clifton Rd
Grosvenor Lawn
The Rectory
Giles Cl
Craven Rd
West Fields
Rockingham Rd
St David's Rd
St Nicholas Rd
Bartholomew St

2
Parsons Cl
Green La
St George's Ave
St Michael's Rd
Bonemill La
Enborne House
Bagnols Way
Pound St
Enborne Gr
Remembrance Rd
Arthur Rd
Rosemary Terr
Westgate Ct
West Gate Rd
Enborne Pl
Enborne Rd
Oak Dr
Rectory Cl
Argyle Rd
Derby Rd
Kew Cotts
Shrewsbury Terr
Astley Cl
Sunderland Gdns
Benham Bridge

1
Gate Lodge
Enborne Gate
Enborne Gate Farm
Oaken Hedges
Skinners Green La
Kingsbridge Rd
Salcombe Rd
Floreat Gdns
Mayfair Dr
Buckingham Rd
Fifth Rd
Harvest Gn
St Bartholomew's Sch
City
A343 Andover Rd
PO
Willow Cl
Old Newtown Rd
Newtown Rd
Paddock Rd
Highfield Rd
Wendan Rd
Erleigh Dene
Sch
Oaken Gr
Valley Rd

66
Borne Copse
The Hanging

44 A B 45 C D 46 E F

103 130

E1
1 THOMAS ASKEW HO
2 CURNOCK CT

F1
1 HAMPTON RD
2 CARNARVON PL
3 ST JOHN'S GDNS
4 THURLOW GRANGE
5 MALVERN CT
6 STONEMASONS CT

F2
1 JOHN KIMBER'S ALMSHOUSES
2 MULBERRY CT
3 CYPRESS HO
4 BECKET HO
5 FISHER HO
6 CAMPION HO
7 IMPERIAL CT
8 EIGHT BELLS
9 BARTHOLOMEW CT
10 BOWDOWN CT
11 KYFTLE COURT FLAT
12 BARNES TERR
13 LOWER RAYMOND ALMSHOUSES
14 UPPER RAYMOND ALMSHOUSES
15 FELTRE PL
16 TRINITY CT
17 ROCKINGHAM GATE
18 ROCKINGHAM HO
19 THE MALTINGS
20 HELEN CT
21 MAIDENHEAD HO

105
78
106
131
A4
1 CORPORATION COTTS
2 ANGEL CT
3 WESTBOURNE TERR
4 LYNTON CT
5 SPEENHAMLAND CT
6 ST MARY'S CT
7 BEECH CT
8 ST MARY'S PL
9 CONISTON CT
10 CHESTNUT CT
11 ASH CT
12 THE PENTANGLE
13 THE BROADWAY
14 THE OLD POLICE HO
B4
1 ST JOSEPHS CT
2 NORTH VIEW GDNS
3 SOUTH VIEW GDNS
4 KENNET PL
5 NEWPORT CL
D4
1 ELMS HO
2 ARBOUR HO
3 OVERBECKS
4 OWLETTS GR
High Wood
Brickkiln Wood
Red Farm House
Craven Farm
Dymond Farm
Easton Copse
Shaw Farm
Weaver's Wood
Mast
Sun in the Wood (PH)
Mousefield Farm
Highwood Farm
Stone Copse
Ivy Cottages
RG14
RG18
Messenger's Copse
Yate's Copse
Sett Copse
Cemy
Shaw
Clay Hill
Coley Farm
Hartgrove Farm
Henwick Manor
1 DESBOROUGH CL
2 ELY GR
3 EDGEHILL CL
4 INGOLDSBY COPSE
Trinity Sch
Castle Ind Pk
Turnpike Ind Est
LOWER HENWICK FARM
Nursery
West Berkshire Com
Fir Tree Prim Sch
WESTERN AVE
LONDON RD
BENHAM HILL
BATH RD
SHAW HILL
LONG LA
River Lambourn
Newbury Bsns Pk
Swan Inn (PH)
Victoria Park
Riverpark Ind Est
Ind Est
Superstore
Ham Lock
Hambridge Farm
Ham Bridge
River Kennet
Newbury L Ctr
RG19
Lower Way Farm
Kennet & Avon Canal
Football Ground
Liby
Cts
MILL LA
Bone Lane Ind Est
Ham Marsh
Kingfisher Court Ind Est
Horizon West Ind Est
Trad Est
The Galloway Ctr
Vo-Tec Ctr
HAMBRIDGE RD
KINGS RD
Sterling Ind Est
Raceview Bsns Ctr
Newbury Racecourse
Denvale Trade Pk
Hambridge Bsns Ctr
Bull's Lock
FB
Superstore
East Fields
Newbury
Newbury Race Course
C1
1 PLUMPTON RD
2 LINGFIELD RD
3 STARTING GATES
4 THE BAXENDALES
5 GOODWOOD WAY
6 CHARLOTTOWN
7 CORMORANT WOOD
Stroud Green
Young Copse
RG19
LOWER FARM CT
A1
1 KENNET CT
2 HILARY HO
3 QUEENS CT
4 BUTTERFIELD HO
A2
1 FAIR CLOSE HO
2 LINK HO
3 SHEFFORD LODGE
4 ASHRIDGE CT
5 WINCHESTER HO
6 DISCOVERY CT
7 ILCHESTER CT
8 MADEIRA PL
9 INCH'S YD
10 THE OLD LIBRARY
11 FOUNTAIN GDNS
12 The Kennet Ctr
A3
1 ALBERT RD
2 WEAVERS WLK
3 CROMWELL PL
4 PEMBROKE RD
5 BOLTON PL
6 TOWN MILLS
7 MANSION HOUSE ST
8 MARKET PL
9 THE ARCADE
10 ARCADE MEWS
B2
1 HECTORS WAY
2 GORDON CT
3 ROMANO CT
4 BRAMBLE CT
5 LAUNDRY CT
6 VICTORIA GR
7 AUDREY NEEDHAM HO
8 REGAL CT
B2
9 ALEXANDER CT
B3
1 THORNYCROFT CL
2 ATLANTEAN CT
3 DOYEN CT
4 REGENTS CT

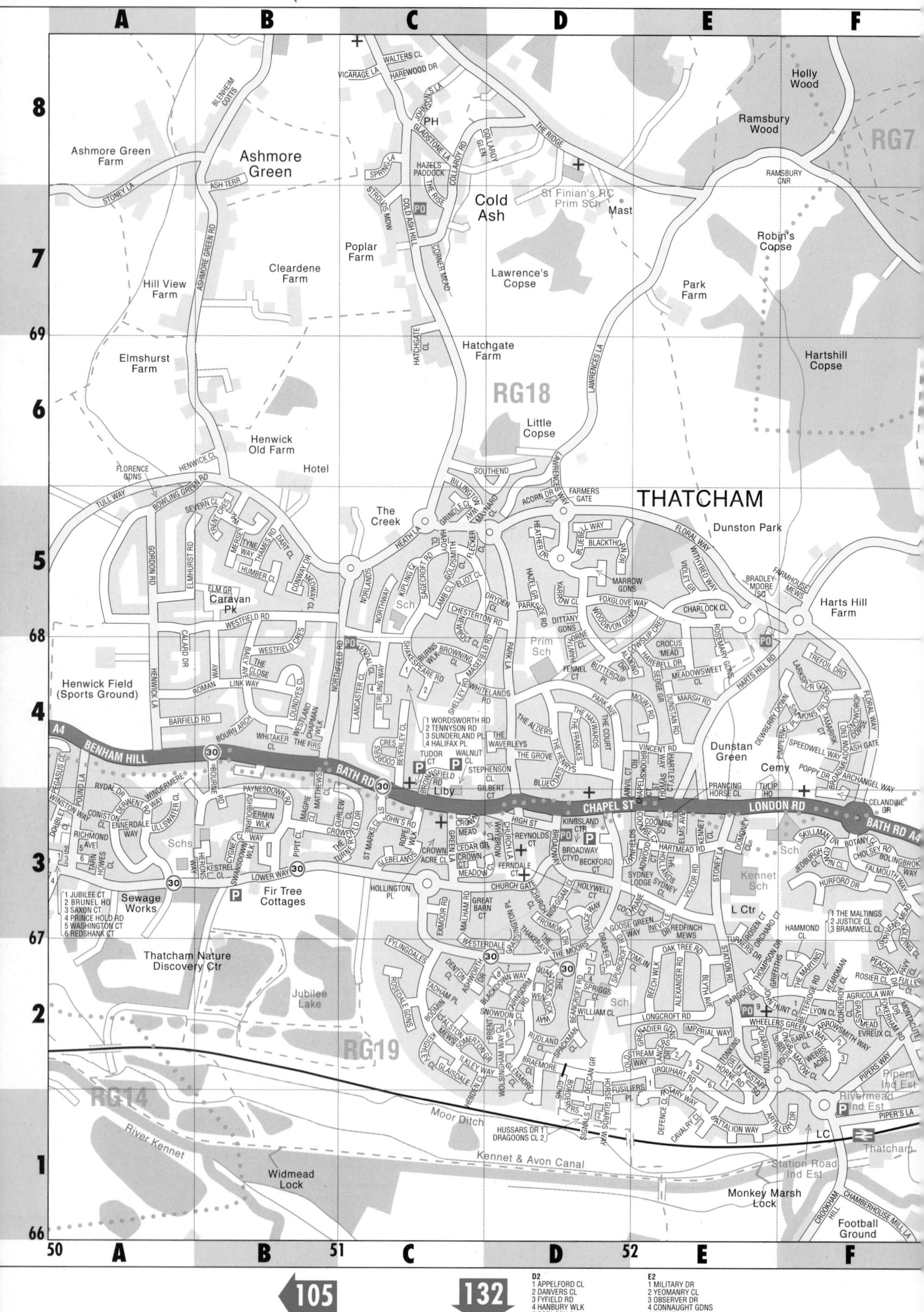

D2
1 APPELFORD CL
2 DANVERS CL
3 FYFIELD RD
4 HANBURY WLK
5 PORLOCK CL
6 BOWES RD
7 NEVIL CT
8 PENTLAND PL

E2
1 MILITARY DR
2 YEOMANRY CL
3 OBSERVER DR
4 CONNAUGHT GDNS
5 INFANTRY DR
6 PADDISON CT
7 DICKSON GLADE
8 MALTHOUSE CL
9 BURDWOOD CTR

A B C D E F

8 7 69 6 5 68 4 3 67 2 1 66

The Slade
Hopgood's Farm
Winchcombe Farm
Sewage Works
Vanners
Woodground Shaw
Lodge Copse
FANNYS LA
Briff Farm
BRIFF LA
Sadgrove Farm
PEASE HILL
Upper Common
Miles's Green
Workhouse Gn
Osgood's Gully
Turner's Green
Cemy
BURDENS HEATH
ROUNDFIELD
LITTLE LA
Bucklebury Common
Upper Bucklebury
MORTONS LA
PH
PO
Burden's Heath Plantation
BROAD LA
Tomlins
CARBINSWOOD LA
HARTS HILL RD
WOODSIDE CL
BLACKLANDS RD
BERRYS RD
LONG GR
Wimble's Wood
RG7
Hart's Hill
Bucklebury CE Prim Sch
Bucklebury Grange
Hockett Wood
Upper Hartshill Farm
Big Gully
Midgham Wood
Blacklands Copse
Wootten's
Long Grove Copse
Kent's Down Gully
Webb's Farm
King's Farm
RG18
Siege Cross Farm
Ouzel Gully
BIRDS LA
Colthrop Manor
SCHOOL HILL
GODDARD DR
COX'S LA
Nursery Copse
Midgham
ASHMAN RD
FRED WAY
CROPPER CL
MUNKLE MARSH
CHURCH HILL
POFFLEY PL
BOSCAWEN WAY
Crem
Meadowside
PIPERS WAY
ENTERPRISE WAY
Berkshire Bsns Ctr
Hotel
Hotel
BERKSHIRE DR
BATH RD
PIPERS CT
Ind Est
COLTHROP LA
COLTHROP WAY
Ind Est
Coach and Horses (PH)
RG19
FULLER CL
AYLESFORD WAY
DAYTONA DR
MILL LA
GABLES WAY
Midgham Marsh
A4
Colthrop Mill
Colthrop
LC
COLTHROP LA
Colthrop Bsns Pk
Kennet and Avon Canal
BRIMPTON RD
Midgham Bridge
LC
COLTHROP COTTS
Midgham Lock
River Kennet
River Kennet

53 A B 54 C D 55 E F

133 108

107
81

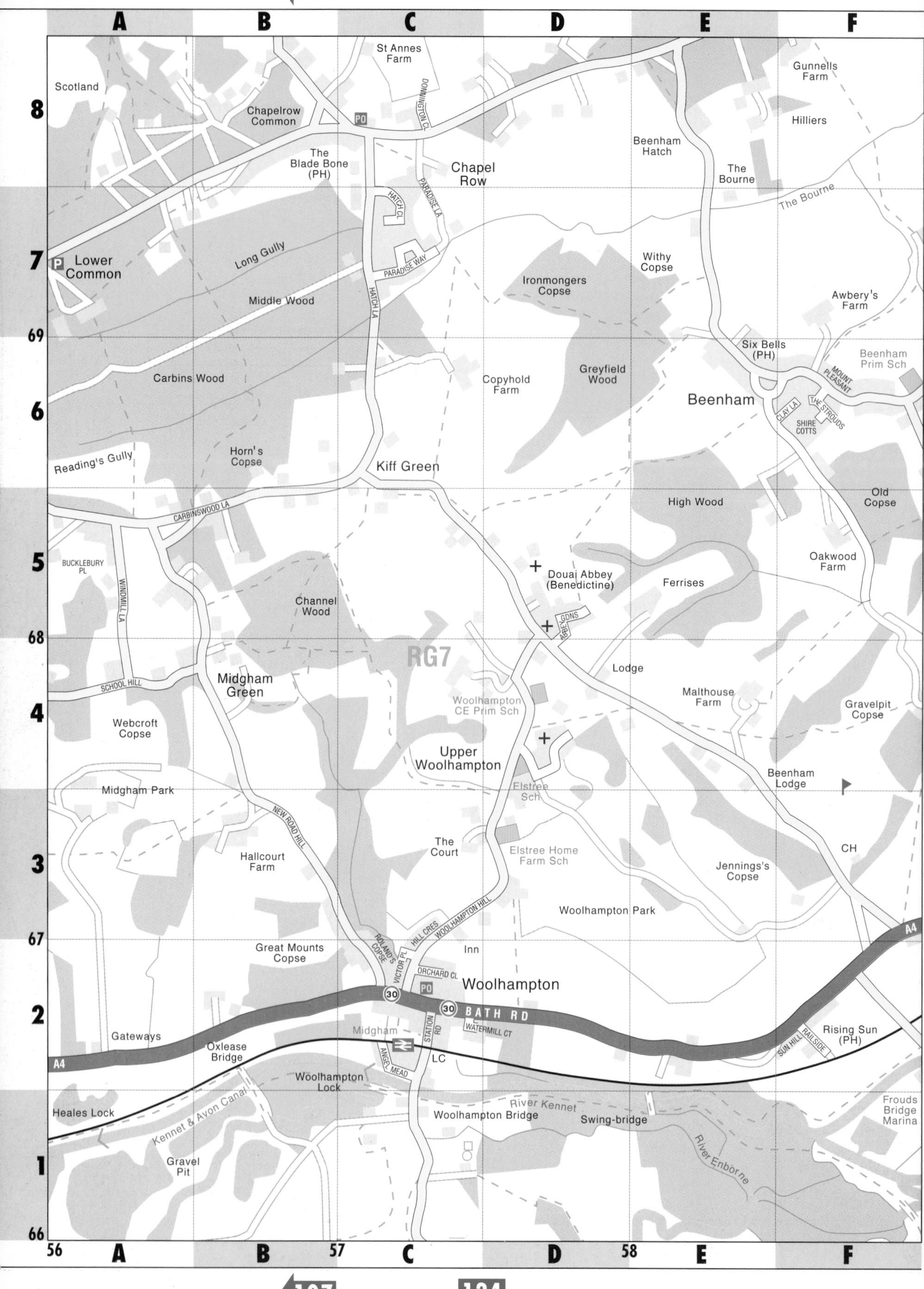

107
134

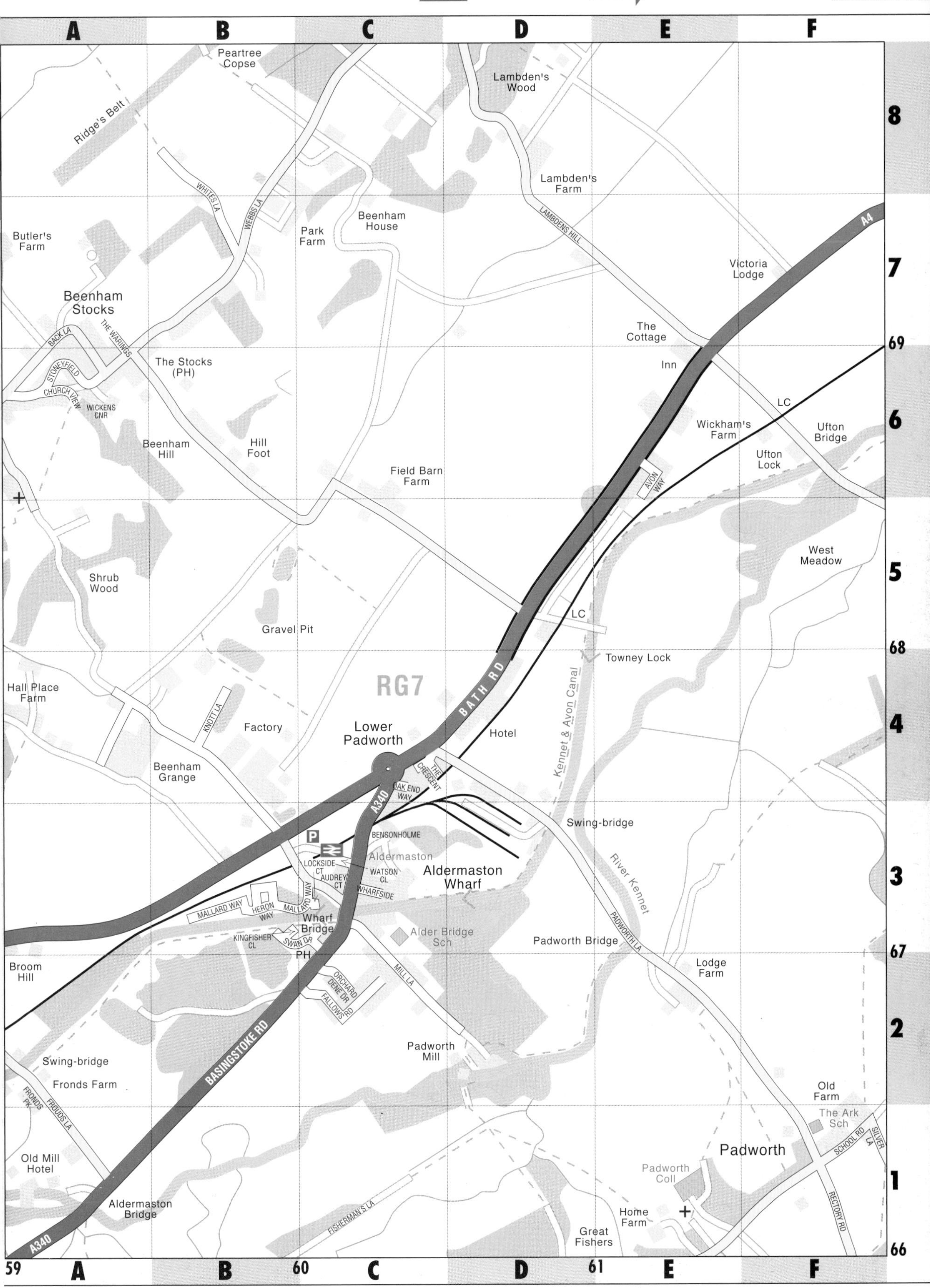
A
B
C
D
E
F
Peartree Copse
Lambden's Wood
Ridge's Belt
Lambden's Farm
WHITES LA
WEBBS LA
Butler's Farm
Park Farm
Beenham House
LAMBDENS HILL
A4
Victoria Lodge
Beenham Stocks
BACK LA
THE WARINGS
The Cottage
STONEYFIELD
The Stocks (PH)
Inn
CHURCH VIEW
WICKENS CNR
LC
Wickham's Farm
Ufton Bridge
Ufton Lock
Beenham Hill
Hill Foot
Field Barn Farm
AVON WAY
West Meadow
Shrub Wood
LC
Gravel Pit
Towney Lock
Hall Place Farm
RG7
BATH RD
Kennet & Avon Canal
KNOTT LA
Factory
Lower Padworth
Hotel
Beenham Grange
THE CRESCENT
OAK END WAY
A340
Swing-bridge
BENSONHOLME
Aldermaston
LOCKSIDE CT
AUDREY CT
WATSON CL
Aldermaston Wharf
River Kennet
WHARFSIDE
MALLARD WAY
HERON WAY
MALLARD WAY
Wharf Bridge
Alder Bridge Sch
KINGFISHER CL
SWAN DR
Padworth Bridge
PADWORTH LA
PH
Broom Hill
MILL LA
Lodge Farm
ORCHARD
DENE DR
FALLOWS RD
BASINGSTOKE RD
Padworth Mill
Swing-bridge
Fronds Farm
FRONDS PK
FRONDS LA
Old Farm
The Ark Sch
SCHOOL RD
SILVER LA
Padworth
Old Mill Hotel
Padworth Coll
Aldermaston Bridge
RECTORY RD
Home Farm
FISHERMAN'S LA
A340
Great Fishers
8
7
69
6
5
68
4
3
67
2
1
66
59
60
61

109
83

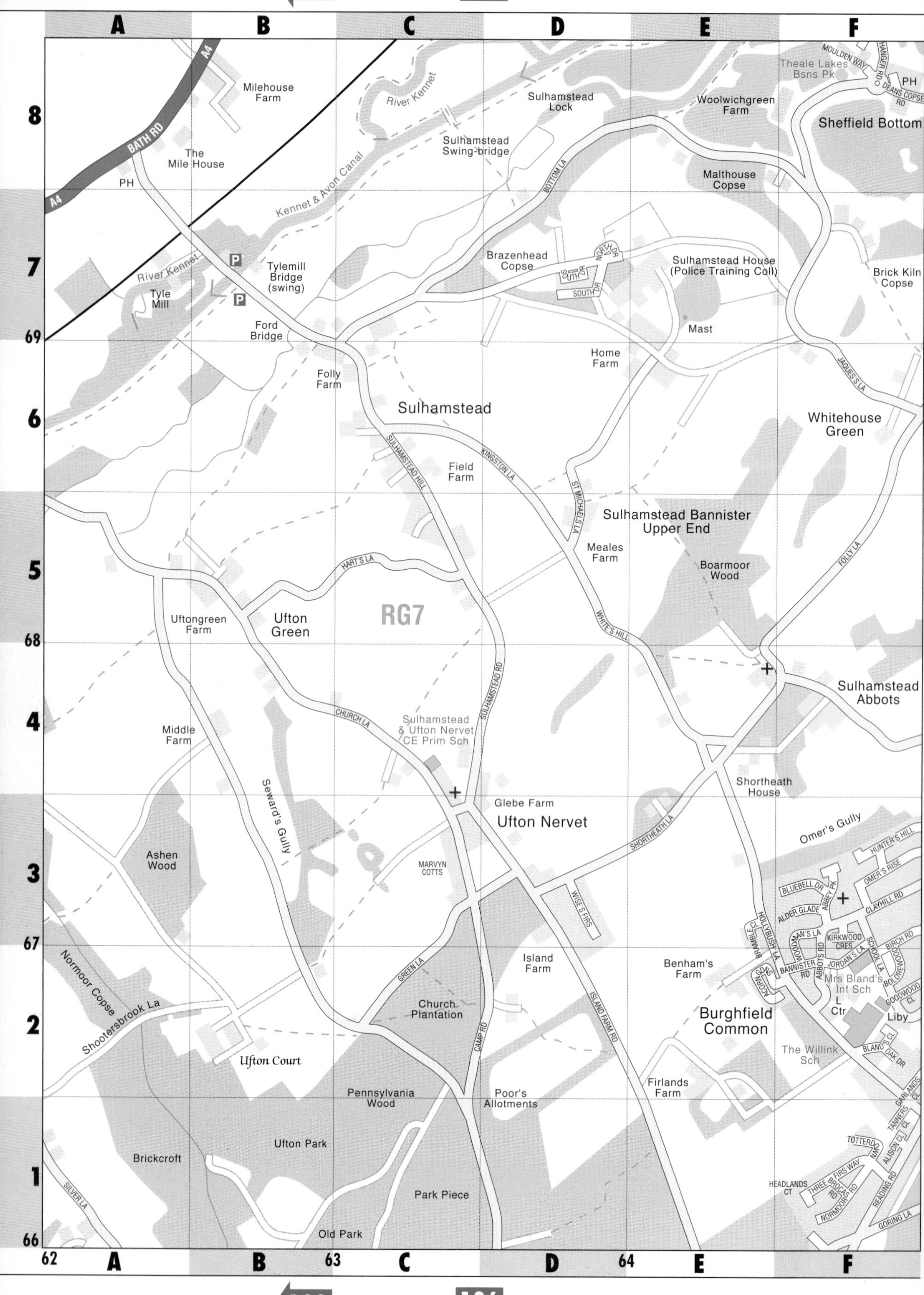

109
136

84
112

137
112

111 85

111 138

C8
1 DENBURY GDNS
2 PENTRIDGE HO
3 PURBECK HO
4 ABBOTSBURY HO
5 ROSSINGTON PL
86
114

A B C D E F
8 7 69 6 5 68 4 3 67 2 1 66
71 72 73

113
87

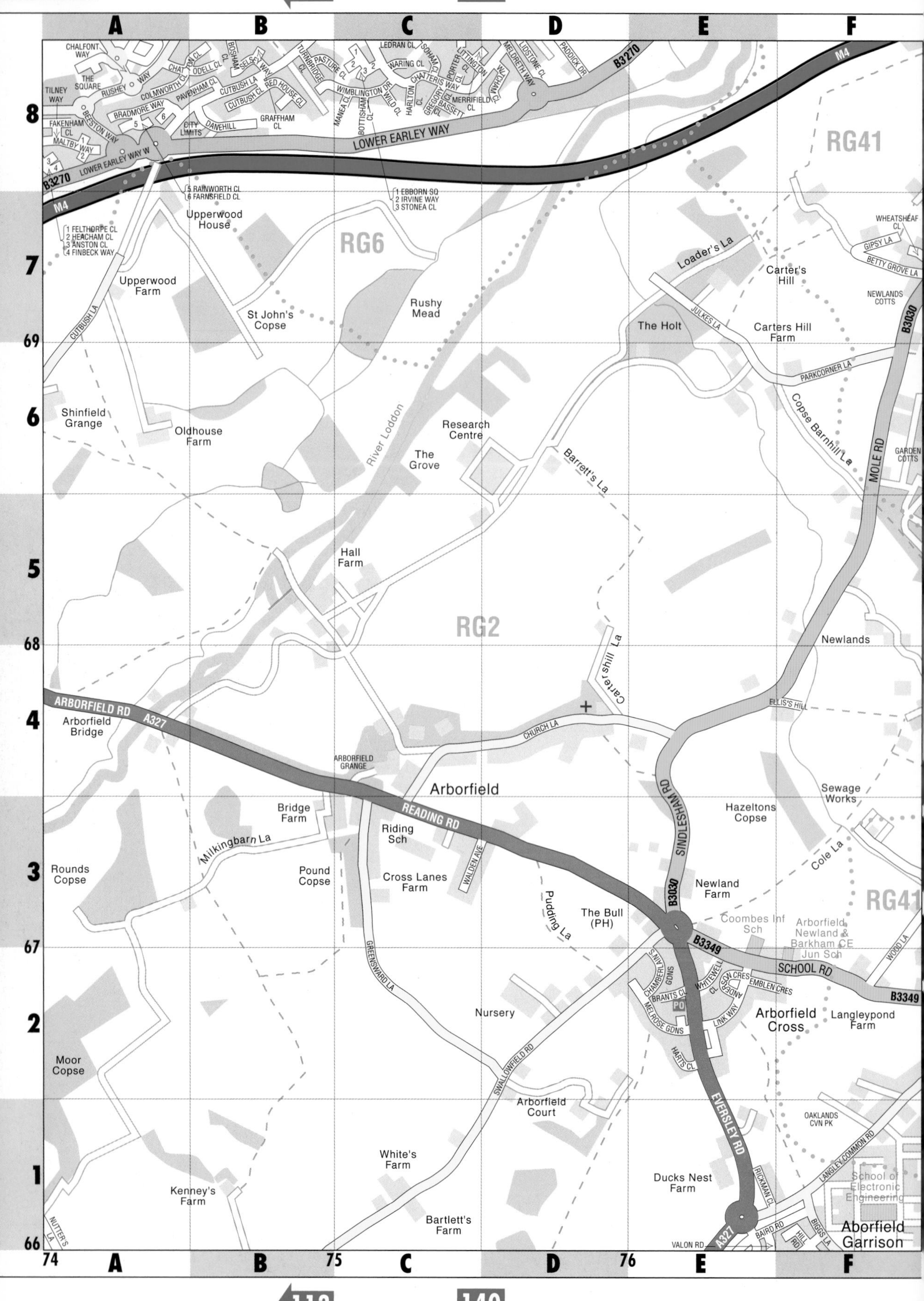

113
140

88
116

141
116

115 89

C6
1 WOODSTOCK
2 MEACHEN CT
3 WALNUT CT
4 ROSE CT
5 MULBERRY CT
6 BUCKINGHAM CT
7 BROAD ST WLK
8 ROSE GDNS

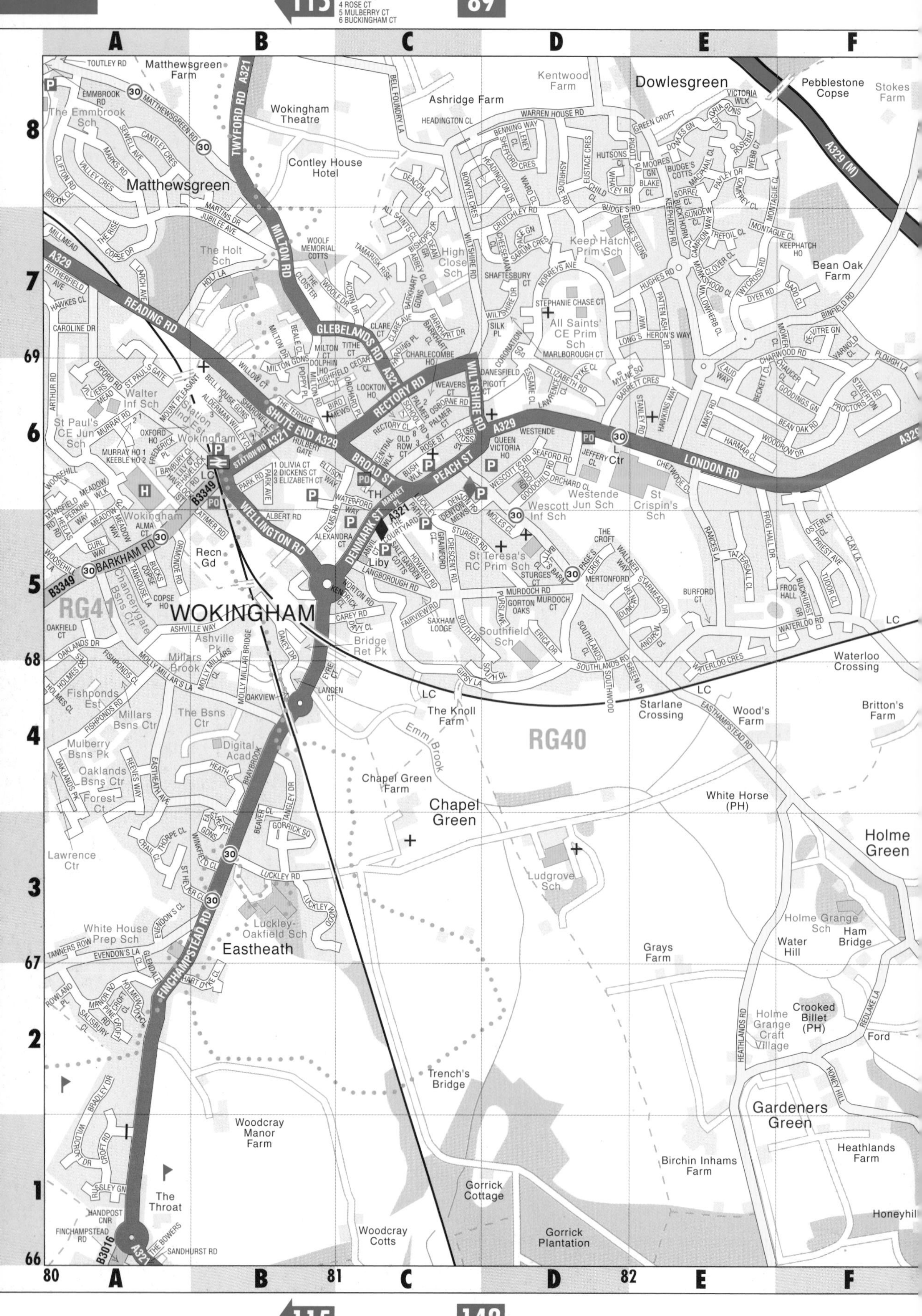

115 142

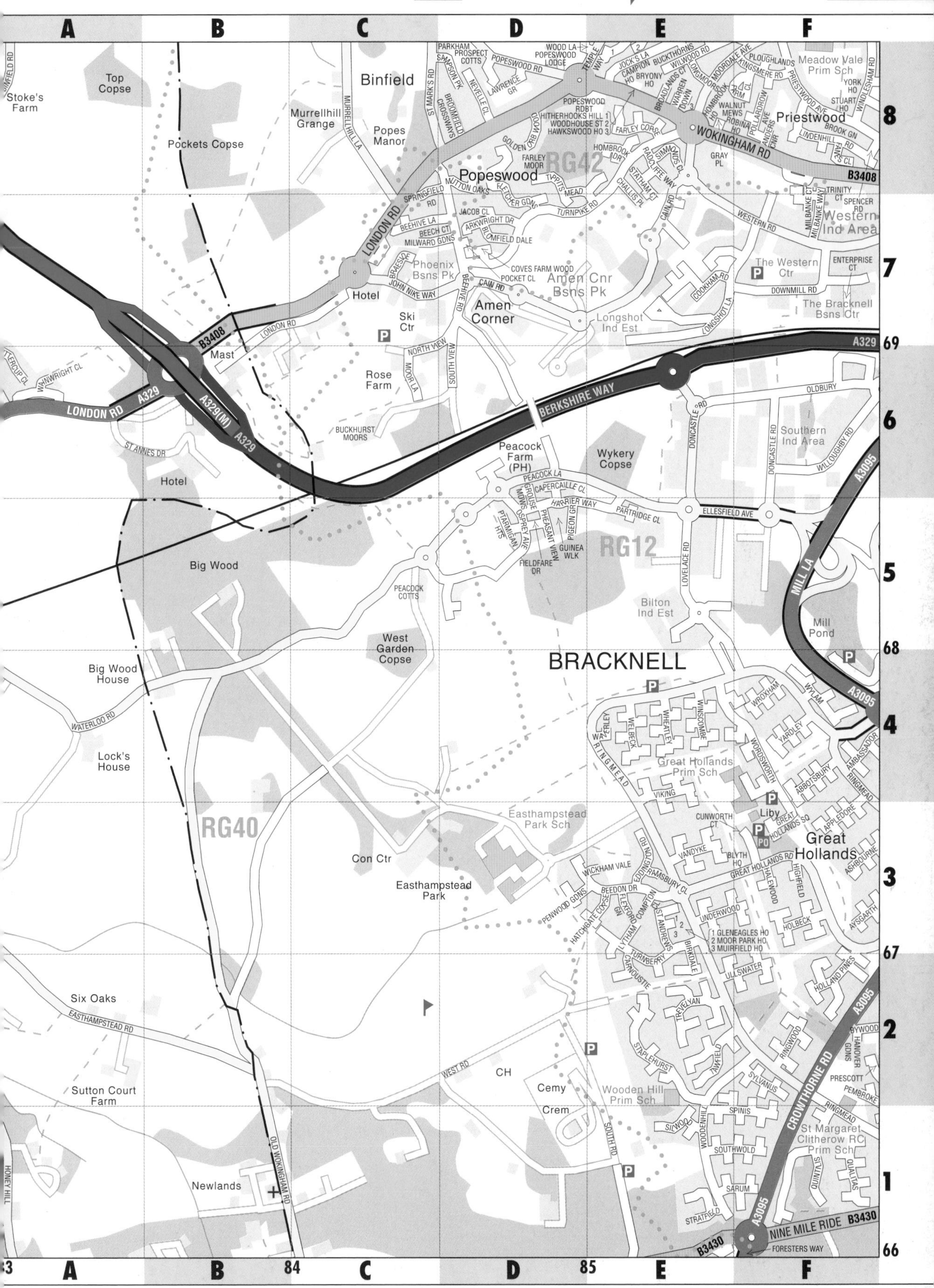
A
B
C
D
E
F
Binfield
Stoke's Farm
Top Copse
Pockets Copse
Murrellhill Grange
Popes Manor
Popeswood
RG42
Priestwood
Meadow Vale Prim Sch
WOKINGHAM RD
LONDON RD
B3408
Western Ind Area
Phoenix Bsns Pk
Amen Cnr Bsns Pk
Amen Corner
Hotel
Ski Ctr
Mast
The Western Ctr
The Bracknell Bsns Ctr
Longshot Ind Est
A329
A329(M)
BERKSHIRE WAY
Rose Farm
Southern Ind Area
Peacock Farm (PH)
Wykery Copse
Hotel
Big Wood
RG12
ELLESFIELD AVE
Bilton Ind Est
Mill Pond
West Garden Copse
BRACKNELL
Big Wood House
WATERLOO RD
Lock's House
Great Hollands Prim Sch
RG40
Easthampstead Park Sch
Great Hollands
Con Ctr
Easthampstead Park
Six Oaks
EASTHAMPSTEAD RD
Sutton Court Farm
CH
Cemy
Crem
Wooden Hill Prim Sch
WEST RD
CROWTHORNE RD
A3095
St Margaret Clitherow RC Prim Sch
Newlands
OLD WOKINGHAM RD
NINE MILE RIDE
B3430
FORESTERS WAY
8
7
69
6
5
68
4
3
67
2
1
66
83
84
85

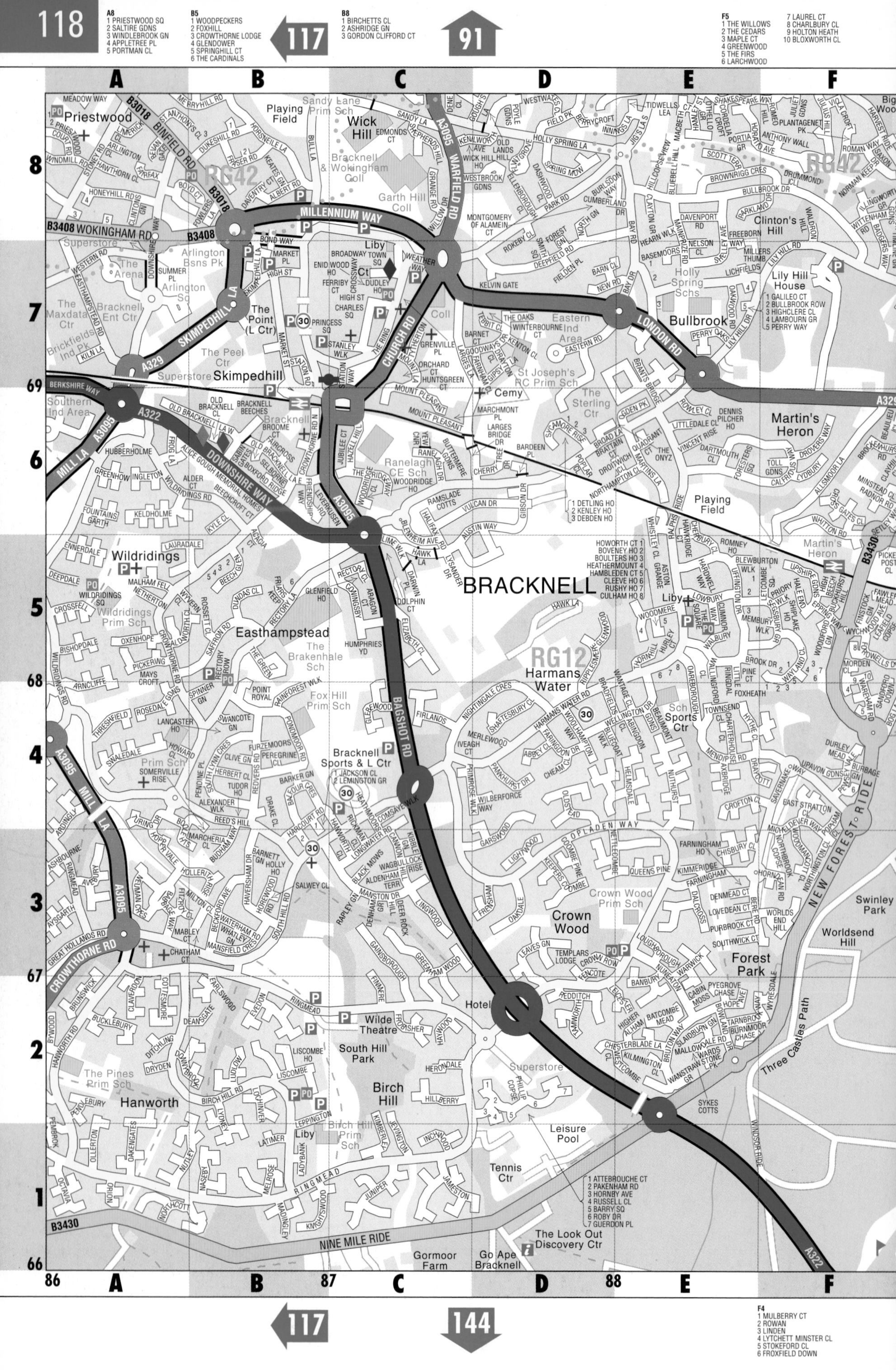
A8
1 PRIESTWOOD SQ
2 SALTIRE GDNS
3 WINDLEBROOK GN
4 APPLETREE PL
5 PORTMAN CL
B5
1 WOODPECKERS
2 FOXHILL
3 CROWTHORNE LODGE
4 GLENDOWER
5 SPRINGHILL CT
6 THE CARDINALS
117
B8
1 BIRCHETTS CL
2 ASHRIDGE GN
3 GORDON CLIFFORD CT
91
F5
1 THE WILLOWS
2 THE CEDARS
3 MAPLE CT
4 GREENWOOD
5 THE FIRS
6 LARCHWOOD
7 LAUREL CT
8 CHARLBURY CL
9 HOLTON HEATH
10 BLOXWORTH CL
A B C D E F
8 7 69 6 5 68 4 3 67 2 1 66
86 87 88
Priestwood
Playing Field
Sandy Lane Prim Sch
Wick Hill
Bracknell & Wokingham Coll
Garth Hill Coll
RG42
MILLENNIUM WAY
WARFIELD RD
B3408 WOKINGHAM RD
B3018 BINFIELD RD
Superstore
The Arena
Arlington Bsns Pk
Arlington Sq
The Maxdata Ctr
Bracknell Ent Ctr
Brickfields Ind Pk
The Point (L Ctr)
The Peel Ctr
Superstore
Skimpedhill
SKIMPEDHILL LA
A329
Liby
Ct
Coll
Clinton's Hill
Holly Spring Schs
Lily Hill House
1 GALILEO CT
2 BULLBROOK ROW
3 HIGHCLERE CL
4 LAMBOURN GR
5 PERRY WAY
Bullbrook
LONDON RD
KELVIN GATE
Eastern Ind Area
St Joseph's RC Prim Sch
Cemy
The Sterling Ctr
Martin's Heron
Southern Ind Area
BERKSHIRE WAY
A322
DOWNSHIRE WAY
MILL LA
A3095
Bracknell
Ranelagh CE Sch
Playing Field
1 DETLING HO
2 KENLEY HO
3 DEBDEN HO
HOWORTH CT 1
BOVENEY HO 2
BOULTERS HO 3
HEATHERMOUNT 4
HAMBLEDEN CT 5
CLEEVE HO 6
RUSHY HO 7
CULHAM HO 8
Martin's Heron
B3430
Wildridings
Wildridings Prim Sch
Easthampstead
The Brakenhale Sch
BRACKNELL
RG12
Harmans Water
Fox Hill Prim Sch
Sch Sports Ctr
BAGSHOT RD
Bracknell Sports & L Ctr
1 JACKSON CL
2 LEMINGTON GR
Prim Sch
OPLADEN WAY
Crown Wood Prim Sch
Crown Wood
NEW FOREST RIDE
Swinley Park
Worldsend Hill
Forest Park
CROWTHORNE RD
Hotel
Wilde Theatre
South Hill Park
Birch Hill
Birch Hill Prim Sch
Liby
Superstore
Leisure Pool
Tennis Ctr
Three Castles Path
The Pines Prim Sch
Hanworth
1 ATTEBROUCHE CT
2 PAKENHAM RD
3 HORNBY AVE
4 RUSSELL CL
5 BARRY SQ
6 ROBY DR
7 GUERDON PL
B3430
NINE MILE RIDE
The Look Out Discovery Ctr
Gormoor Farm
Go Ape Bracknell
A322
117
144
F4
1 MULBERRY CT
2 ROWAN
3 LINDEN
4 LYTCHETT MINSTER CL
5 STOKEFORD CL
6 FROXFIELD DOWN

92
120

145
120

119
93

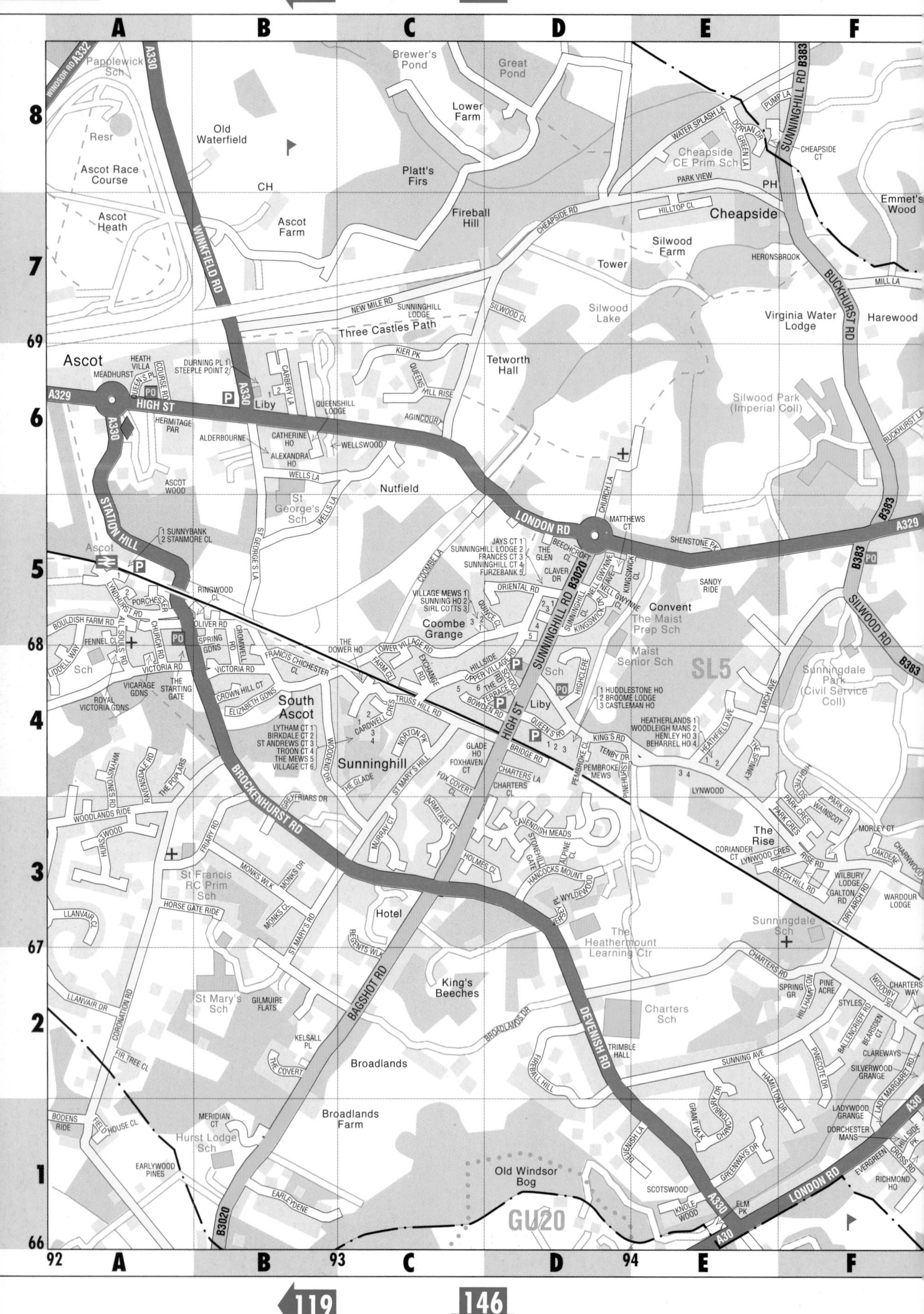

119
146

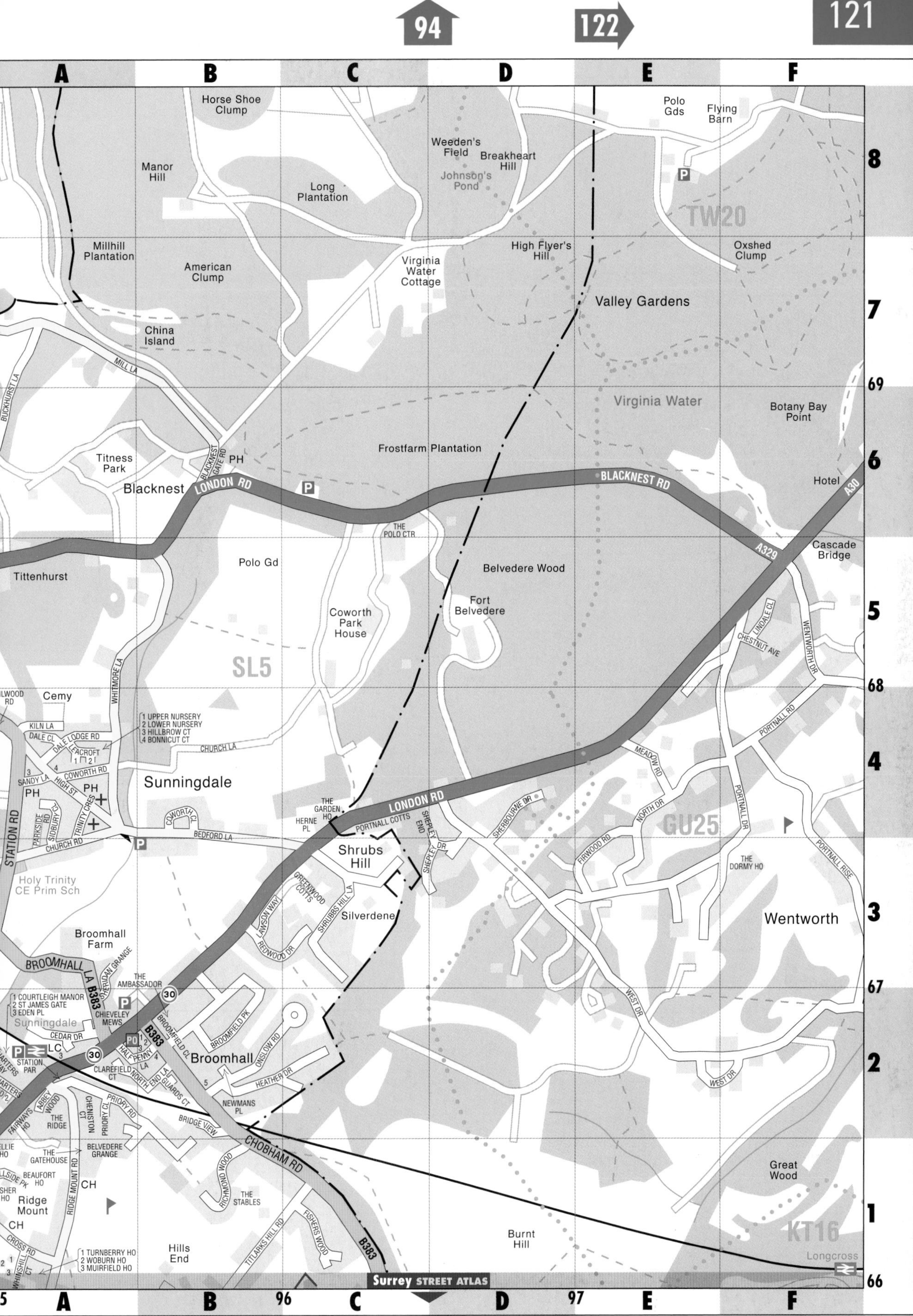

B2
1 BROOMHALL BLDGS
2 HALFPENNY CT
3 FARTHING CT
4 SOVEREIGN CT
5 ROBINWOOD

121
95

Egham Wick Plantations
Wick Pond
Totem Pole
ACS Egham Int Sch
Woodlee Hall
Callow Hill
Virginia Water Plantations
Great Wood
Whitehall Farm
Stroude
The Dell
The Clockcase
Merlewood
Stroude Farm
Virginia Water
General's Copse
St Ann's Heath
Home Farm
Broom Hill
Wentworth Golf Club
GU25
The Bourne
Waterloo Bridge
Harpesford
Trumps Green
Knowle Hill
Westwood
Beech Wood
Knowle Grove
Trumps Farm
Lyne Place Manor
Longcross Bridge
Hersham Copse
Works
TW20
KT16
LONDON RD
CHRISTCHURCH RD
SANDHILLS LA
M3 Camberley
Surrey STREET ATLAS

121

96
124

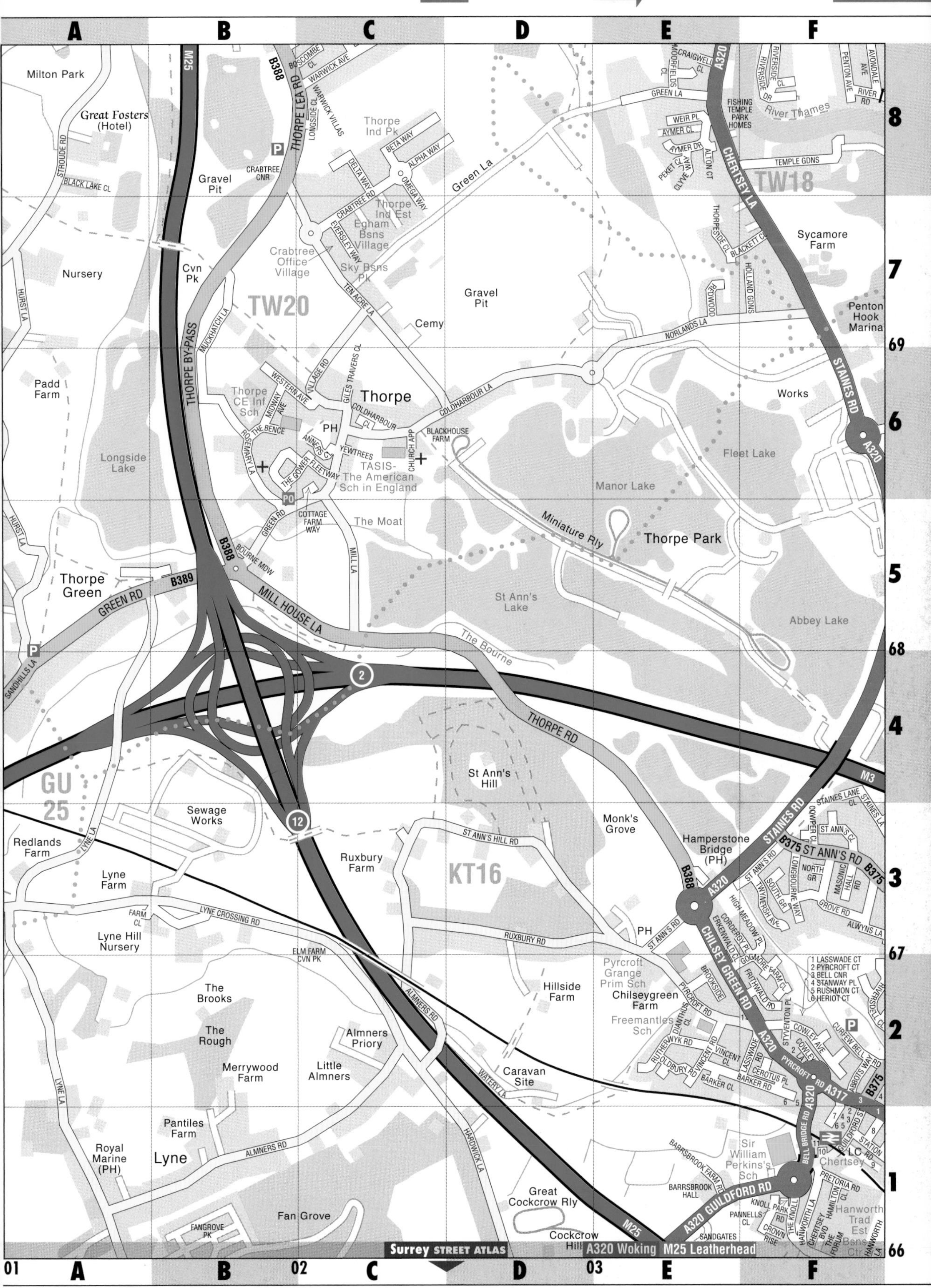

124

F1
1 EASTWORTH RD
2 LIBERTY HO
3 CHARLES HO
4 FOX HO
5 REGENCY HO
6 FOX CT
7 FOX LANE N
8 CHARLES ST
9 DOWNSIDE
10 FOX LANE S
11 FLORAL HO

A1
1 HOLLY CT
2 CAVENDISH CT
3 BLAKES CT
4 NELSON CT
5 COLLINGWOOD CT
6 LABURNUM CT
7 REGENCY PL
8 PAINESFIELD DR

A2
1 FOUNDRY MEWS
2 BEOMONDS ROW
3 WHITE HART ROW
4 GALSWORTHY RD
5 BEOMONDS
6 CHERTSEY WLK
7 BURWOOD PAR
8 PRIORY MEWS

98

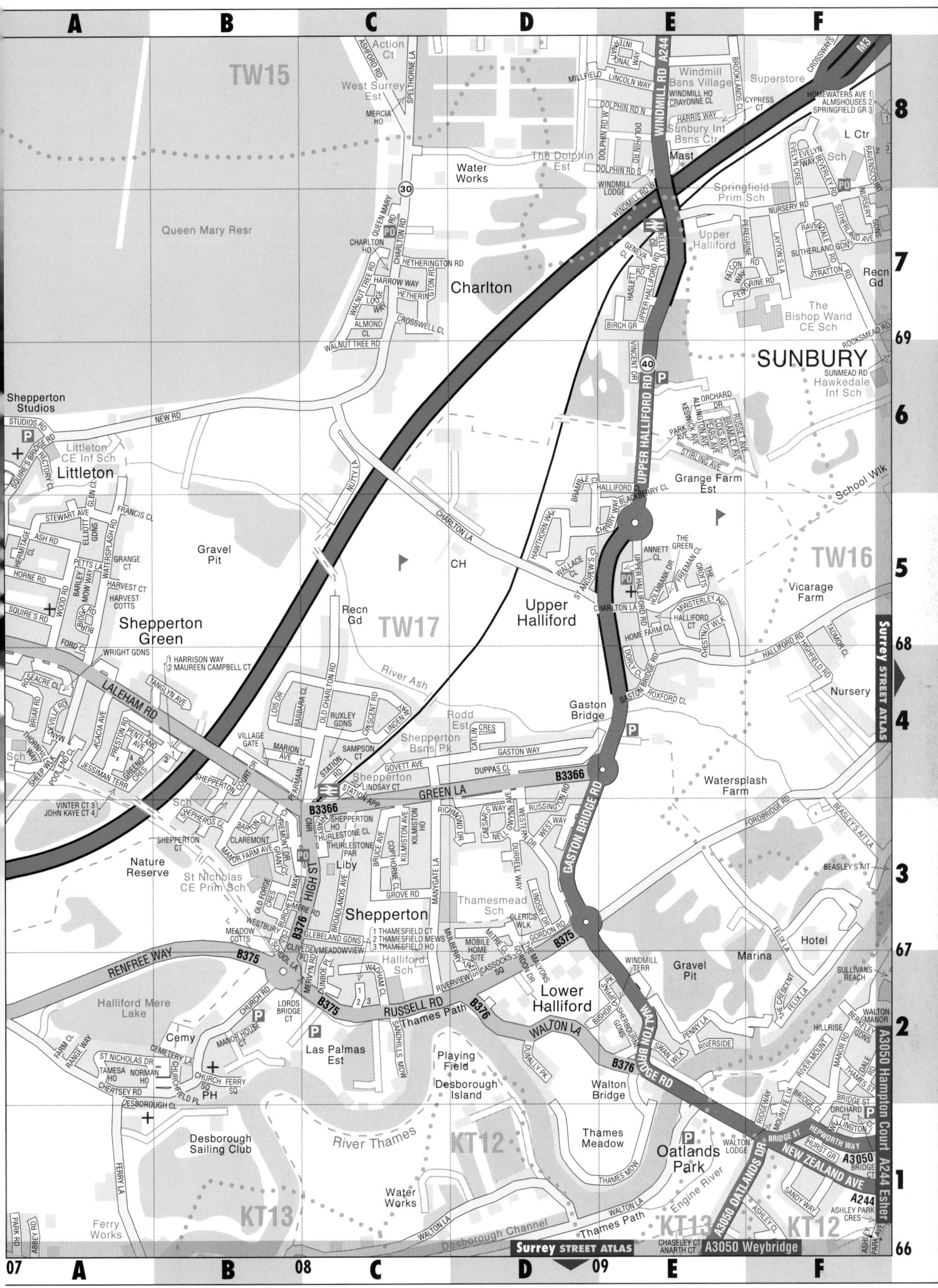
A
B
C
D
E
F
8
7
69
6
5
68
4
3
67
2
1
66
07
08
09
TW15
TW16
TW17
KT12
KT13
Queen Mary Resr
Action Ct
West Surrey Est
Mercia Ho
Ashford Rd
Spelthorne La
Windmill Rd A244
Windmill Bsns Village
Superstore
Sunbury Int Bsns Ctr
The Dolphin Est
Water Works
Mast
Springfield Prim Sch
Upper Halliford
Charlton
The Bishop Wand CE Sch
Recn Gd
SUNBURY
Hawkedale Inf Sch
Shepperton Studios
New Rd
Littleton CE Inf Sch
Littleton
Gravel Pit
Upper Halliford Rd
Grange Farm Est
School Wlk
Charlton La
CH
Upper Halliford
Vicarage Farm
Shepperton Green
Laleham Rd
River Ash
Gaston Bridge
Rodd Est
Shepperton Bsns Pk
Nursery
Gaston Way
Green La
B3366
Watersplash Farm
Gaston Bridge Rd
High St
B376
Liby
Shepperton
Nature Reserve
St Nicholas CE Prim Sch
Thamesmead Sch
Fordbridge Rd
Hotel
Marina
Gravel Pit
Renfree Way
B375
Halliford Mere Lake
Halliford Sch
Russell Rd
Lower Halliford
Walton Bridge Rd
Thames Path
Walton La
Cemy
Las Palmas Est
Playing Field
Desborough Island
Walton Bridge
Desborough Sailing Club
River Thames
Thames Meadow
Oatlands Park
Water Works
Ferry Works
Desborough Channel
Engine River
A3050 Oatlands Dr
New Zealand Ave
A3050 Hampton Court A244 Esher
A3050 Weybridge
Surrey STREET ATLAS
M3

100

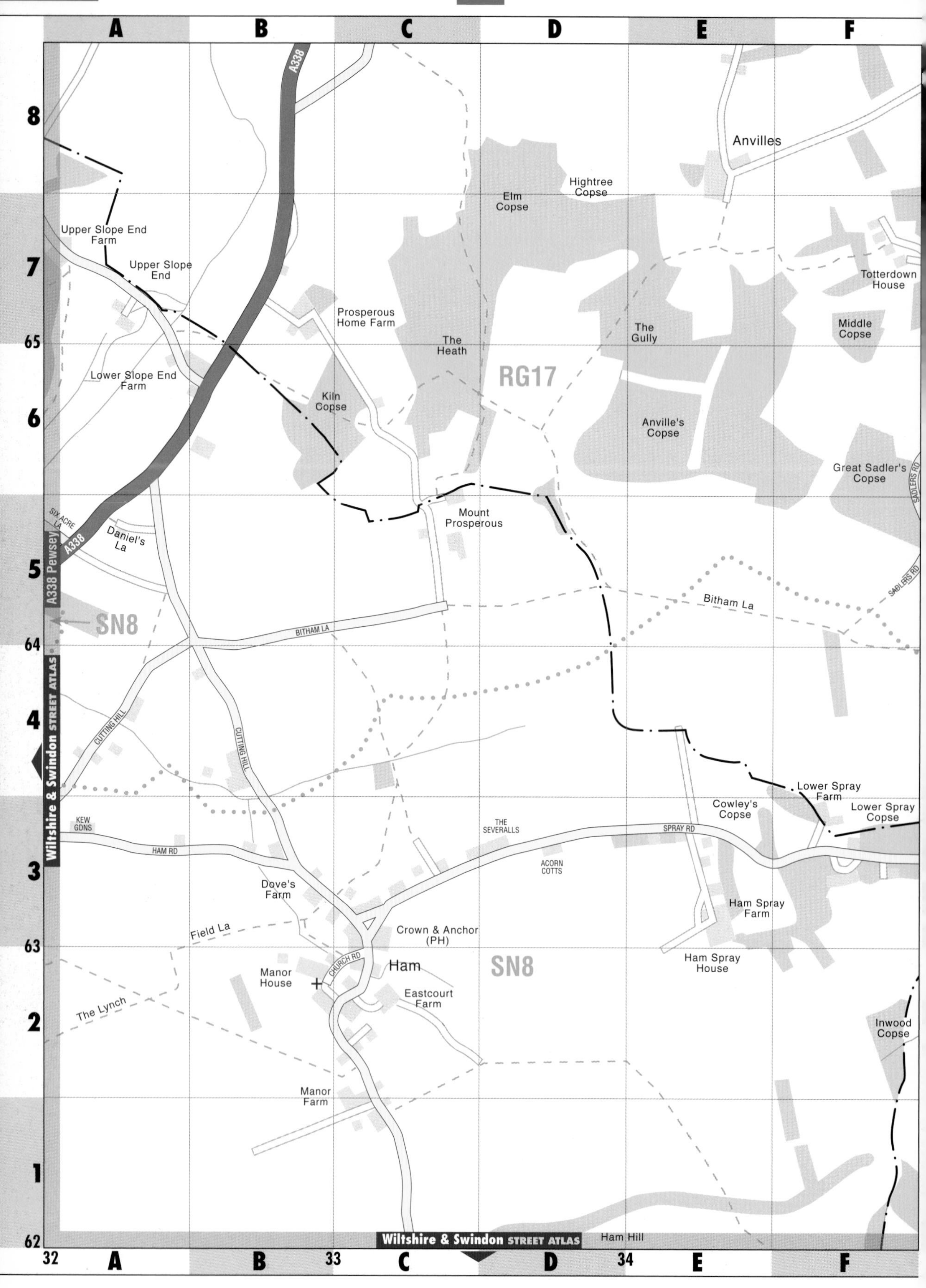
A
B
C
D
E
F
8
7
65
6
5
64
4
3
63
2
1
62
32
33
34
A338
Anvilles
Hightree Copse
Elm Copse
Upper Slope End Farm
Upper Slope End
Totterdown House
Prosperous Home Farm
The Gully
Middle Copse
The Heath
RG17
Lower Slope End Farm
Kiln Copse
Anville's Copse
Great Sadler's Copse
SADLERS RD
SIX ACRE LA
Mount Prosperous
Daniel's La
A338 Pewsey
SN8
Bitham La
BITHAM LA
CUTTING HILL
Lower Spray Farm
Cowley's Copse
Lower Spray Copse
KEW GDNS
THE SEVERALLS
SPRAY RD
HAM RD
ACORN COTTS
Dove's Farm
Ham Spray Farm
Field La
Crown & Anchor (PH)
Ham Spray House
CHURCH RD
Ham
Manor House
Eastcourt Farm
The Lynch
Inwood Copse
Manor Farm
Ham Hill

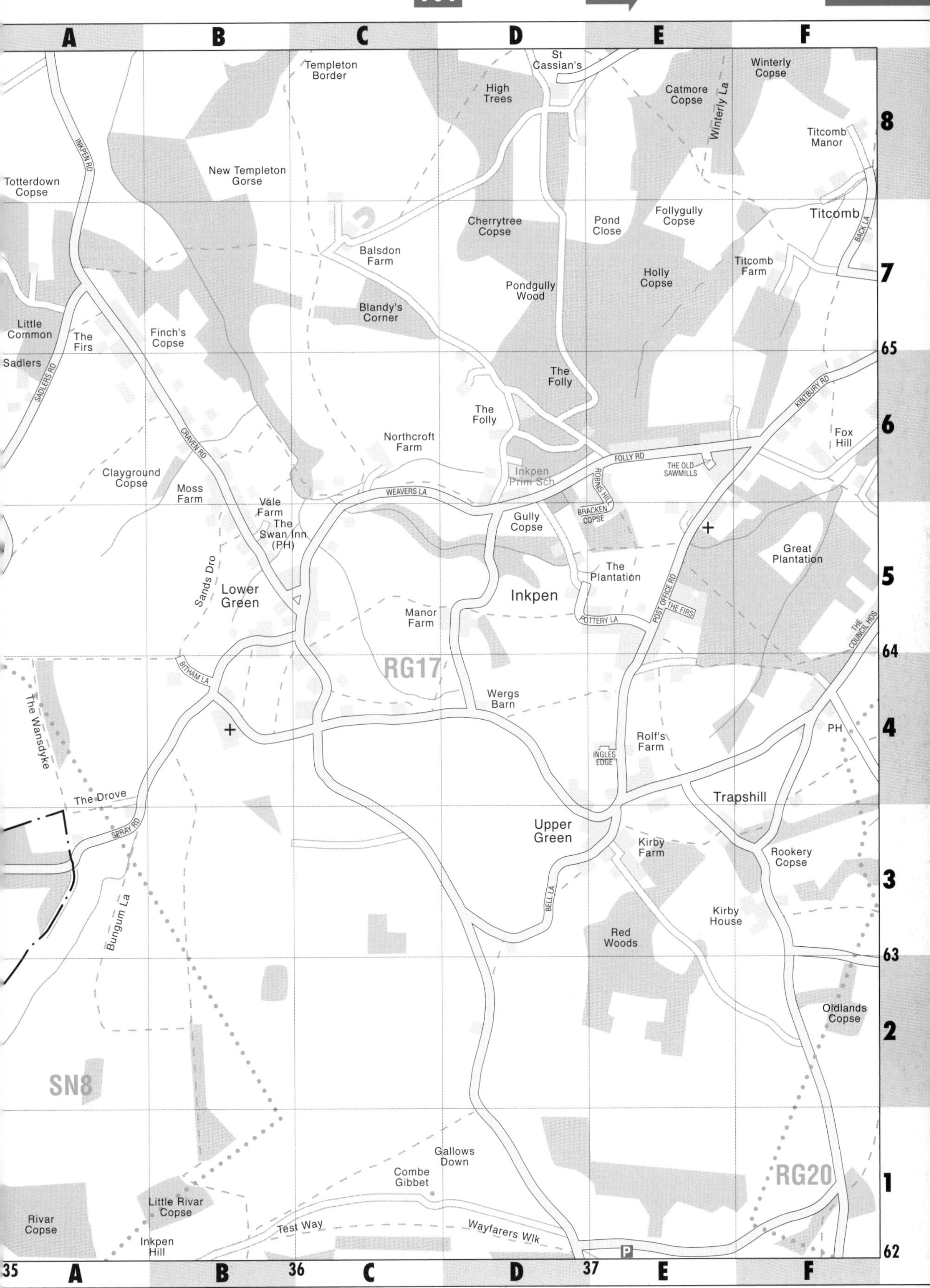
A
B
C
D
E
F
Templeton Border
St Cassian's
High Trees
Catmore Copse
Winterly La
Winterly Copse
Titcomb Manor
8
INKPEN RD
New Templeton Gorse
Totterdown Copse
Cherrytree Copse
Pond Close
Follygully Copse
Titcomb
BACK LA
Balsdon Farm
Holly Copse
Titcomb Farm
7
Pondgully Wood
Blandy's Corner
Little Common
The Firs
Finch's Copse
Sadlers
SADLERS RD
65
The Folly
KINTBURY RD
The Folly
6
Fox Hill
CRAVEN RD
Northcroft Farm
FOLLY RD
THE OLD SAWMILLS
Clayground Copse
Inkpen Prim Sch
ROBINS HILL
Moss Farm
WEAVERS LA
Vale Farm
BRACKEN COPSE
Gully Copse
The Swan Inn (PH)
Great Plantation
Sands Dro
The Plantation
5
Lower Green
Inkpen
POST OFFICE RD
THE FIRS
Manor Farm
POTTERY LA
THE COUNCIL HOS
64
BITHAM LA
RG17
Wergs Barn
The Wansdyke
Rolf's Farm
PH
4
INGLES EDGE
The Drove
Trapshill
SPRAY RD
Upper Green
Kirby Farm
Rookery Copse
3
BELL LA
Bungum La
Kirby House
Red Woods
63
Oldlands Copse
2
SN8
Gallows Down
Combe Gibbet
RG20
1
Little Rivar Copse
Rivar Copse
Test Way
Wayfarers Wlk
Inkpen Hill
62
35
36
37

127
102

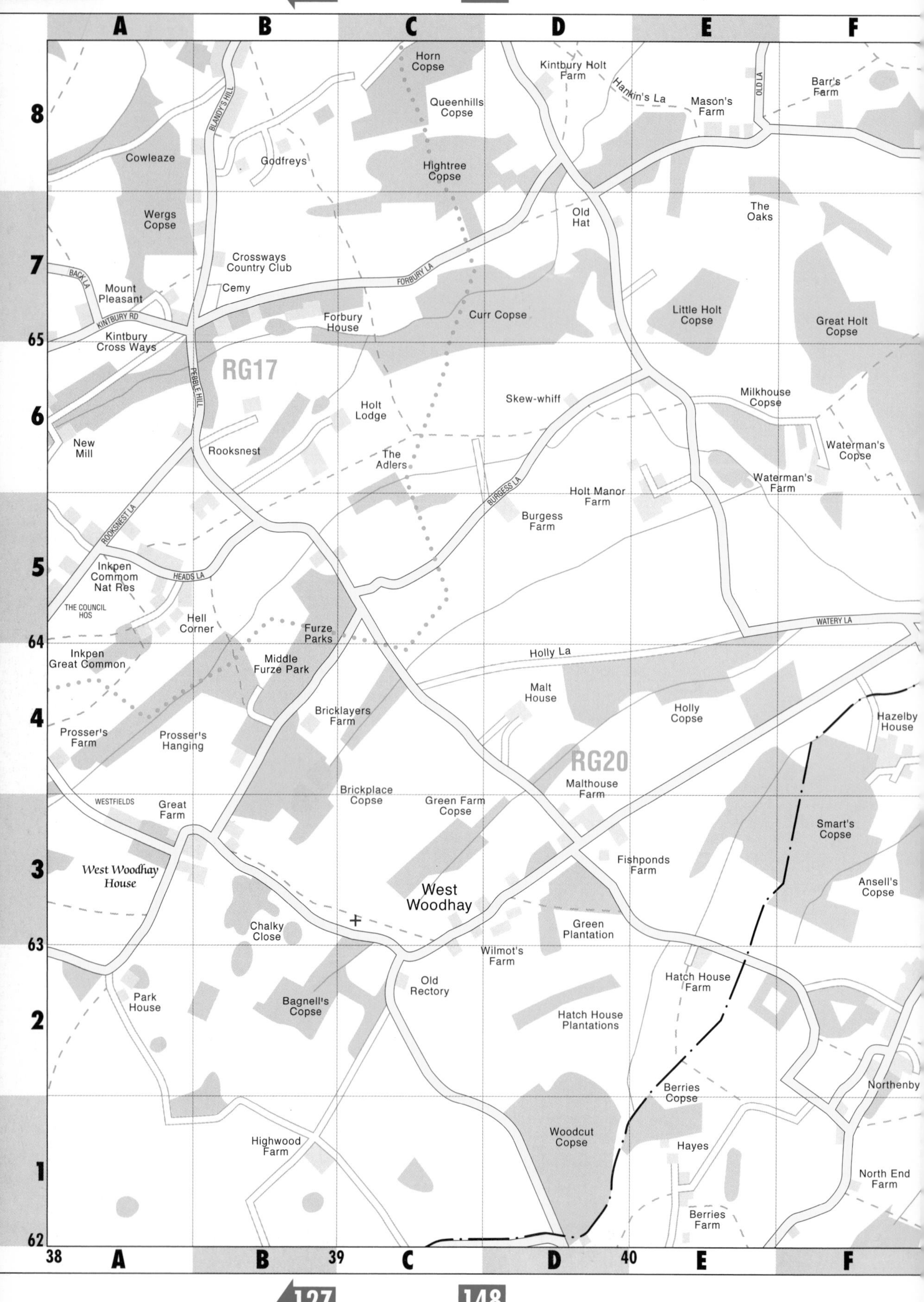

127
148

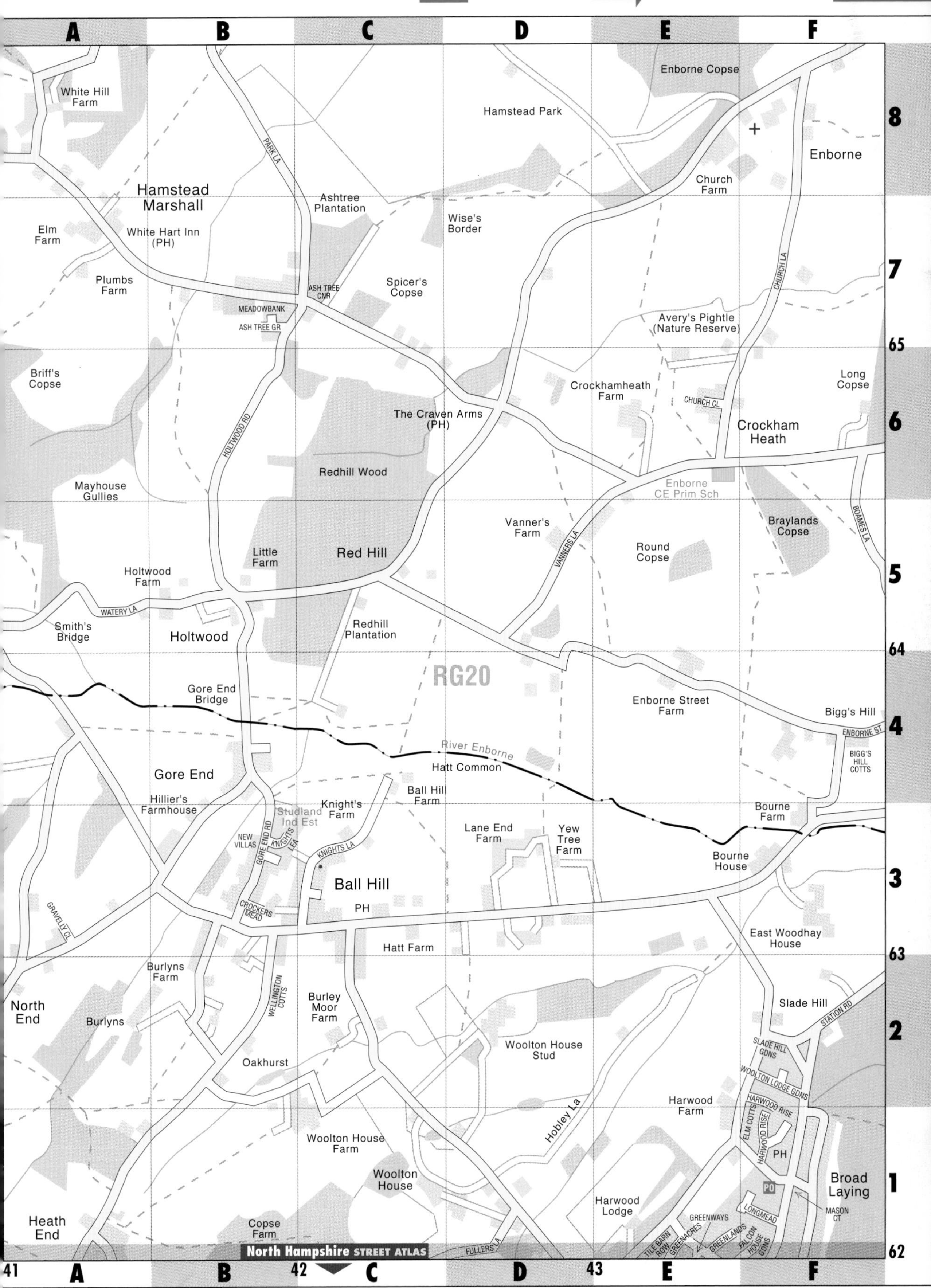
A
B
C
D
E
F
8
7
65
6
5
64
4
3
63
2
1
62
41
42
43
White Hill Farm
Hamstead Park
Enborne Copse
Enborne
Church Farm
Hamstead Marshall
Ashtree Plantation
Elm Farm
White Hart Inn (PH)
Wise's Border
Plumbs Farm
Spicer's Copse
PARK LA
ASH TREE CNR
MEADOWBANK
ASH TREE GR
CHURCH LA
Avery's Pightle (Nature Reserve)
Briff's Copse
Crockhamheath Farm
Long Copse
CHURCH CL
Crockham Heath
The Craven Arms (PH)
HOLTWOOD RD
Redhill Wood
Enborne CE Prim Sch
Mayhouse Gullies
Vanner's Farm
Braylands Copse
BOAMES LA
Round Copse
VANNERS LA
Little Farm
Red Hill
Holtwood Farm
WATERY LA
Smith's Bridge
Holtwood
Redhill Plantation
RG20
Gore End Bridge
Enborne Street Farm
Bigg's Hill
ENBORNE ST
BIGG'S HILL COTTS
River Enborne
Hatt Common
Gore End
Hillier's Farmhouse
Ball Hill Farm
Knight's Farm
Studland Ind Est
Bourne Farm
NEW VILLAS
GORE END RD
KNIGHTS LEA
KNIGHTS LA
Lane End Farm
Yew Tree Farm
Bourne House
Ball Hill
PH
GRAVELLY CL
CROCKERS MEAD
Hatt Farm
East Woodhay House
Burlyns Farm
WELLINGTON COTTS
North End
Burlyns
Burley Moor Farm
Slade Hill
STATION RD
Woolton House Stud
SLADE HILL GDNS
Oakhurst
WOOLTON LODGE GDNS
Harwood Farm
HARWOOD RISE
ELM COTTS
Hobley La
Woolton House Farm
PH
Woolton House
Broad Laying
PO
Harwood Lodge
MASON CT
LONGMEAD
Heath End
Copse Farm
GREENWAYS
TILE BARN ROW
GREENACRES
GREENLANDS
FALCON HOUSE GDNS
FULLERS LA

129
104

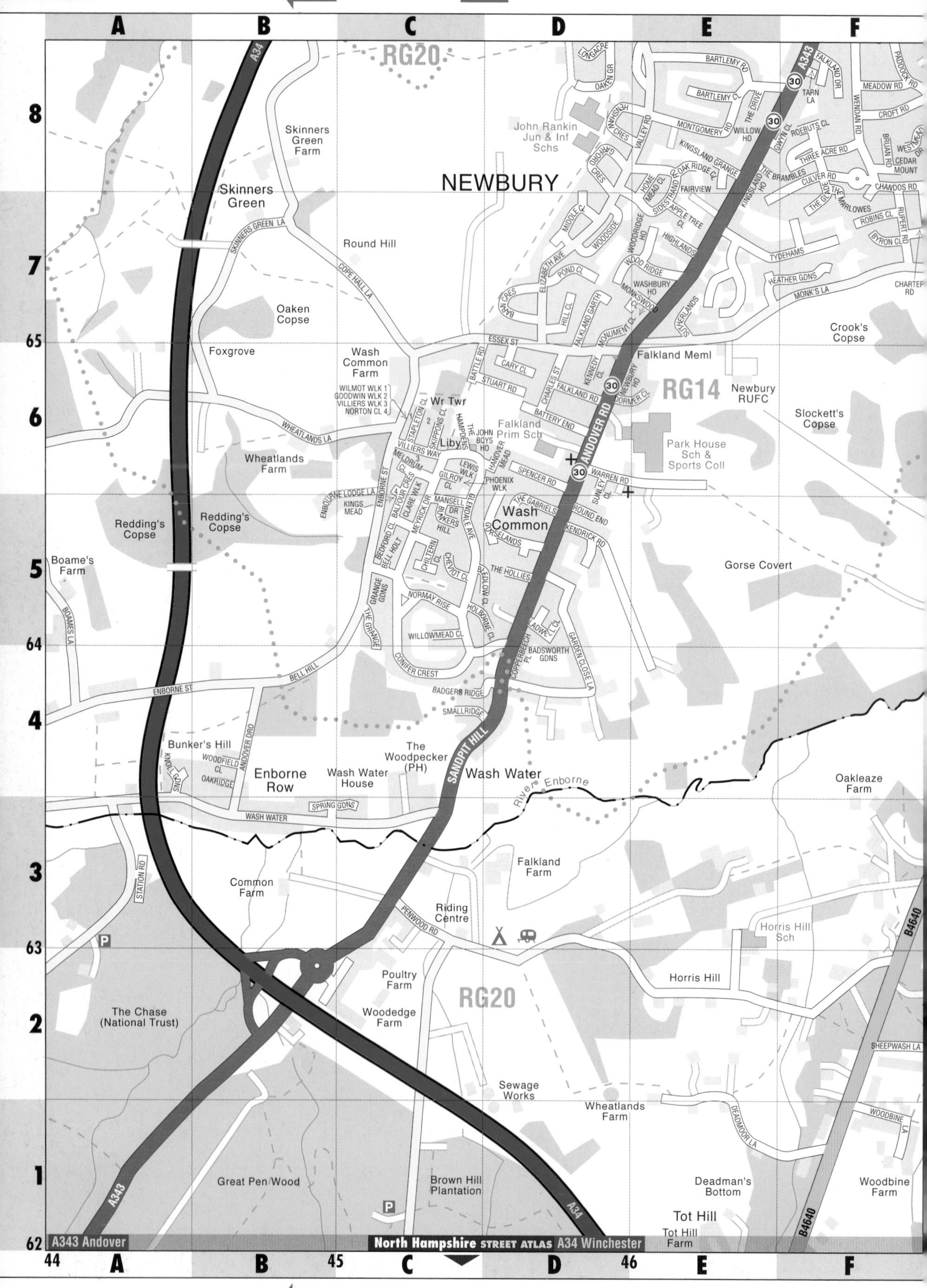
NEWBURY
RG20
RG14
Skinners Green Farm
Skinners Green
Skinners Green La
Round Hill
Cope Hall La
Oaken Copse
Foxgrove
Wash Common Farm
Wheatlands La
Wheatlands Farm
Redding's Copse
Boame's Farm
Boames La
Enborne St
Bell Hill
Bunker's Hill
Woodfield Cl
Oakridge
Knoll Gdns
Andover Dro
Enborne Row
Wash Water House
The Woodpecker (PH)
Wash Water
Spring Gdns
River Enborne
Sandpit Hill
Station Rd
Common Farm
Falkland Farm
Riding Centre
Penwood Rd
Poultry Farm
Woodedge Farm
The Chase (National Trust)
Sewage Works
Wheatlands Farm
Great Pen Wood
Brown Hill Plantation
Horris Hill Sch
Horris Hill
Deadmoor La
Deadman's Bottom
Tot Hill
Tot Hill Farm
Woodbine La
Woodbine Farm
Sheepwash La
Oakleaze Farm
Gorse Covert
Slockett's Copse
Newbury RUFC
Crook's Copse
Park House Sch & Sports Coll
Falkland Meml
Falkland Prim Sch
John Rankin Jun & Inf Schs
Wr Twr
Liby
Wash Common
Andover Rd
Essex St
Battle Rd
Cary Cl
Stuart Rd
Charles St
Falkland Rd
Kennedy Cl
Newbury Ho
Dormer Cl
Battery End
Warren Rd
Sunley Cl
Spencer Rd
Phoenix Wlk
Hanover Mead
Lewis Wlk
Gilroy Cl
John Boys Ho
The Hampdens
Skippons Cl
Stapleton Cl
Villiers Way
Meldrum Cl
Wilmot Wlk 1
Goodwin Wlk 2
Villiers Wlk 3
Norton Cl 4
Enborne Lodge La
Kings Mead
Balfour Cres
Clare Wlk
Meyrick Dr
Mansell Dr
Blakers Hill
Glendale Ave
Bedford Cl
Bell Holt
Chiltern Cl
Cheviot Cl
Bedlow Cl
Holborne Cl
Normay Rise
Grange Gdns
The Grange
Willowmead Cl
Conifer Crest
Badgers Ridge
Smallridge
Copperbeech Pl
Badsworth Gdns
Ladwell Cl
Garden Close La
The Hollies
Gorselands
The Gabriels
Round End
Kendrick Rd
Bartlemy Rd
Bartlemy Cl
Longacre
Oaken Gr
Henshaw Cres
Garford Cres
Valley Rd
Montgomery Rd
Kingsland Grange
Oak Ridge Cl
Home Mead Cl
Sidestrand Rd
Fairview
Apple Tree Cl
Highlands
Middle Cl
Woodside
Woodridge Ho
Wood Ridge
Washbury Ho
Monkswood Cl
Monument Cl
Falkland Garth
Hill Cl
Pond Cl
Elizabeth Ave
Baron Cres
Sutherlands
The Drive
Willow Ho
Gwyn Cl
Kingsland Ho
The Brambles
Tarn La
Falkland Dr
Paddock Rd
Meadow Rd
Wendan Rd
Croft Rd
Roebuts Cl
Three Acre Rd
Briuan Rd
Westmead Dr
Cedar Mount
Culver Rd
The Glade
The Marlowes
Chandos Rd
Robins Cl
Rupert Rd
Byron Cl
Tydehams
Heather Gdns
Monk's La
Charter Rd
A34
A343
B4640
44
45
46
62
63
64
65
A343 Andover
A34 Winchester

129

105
132

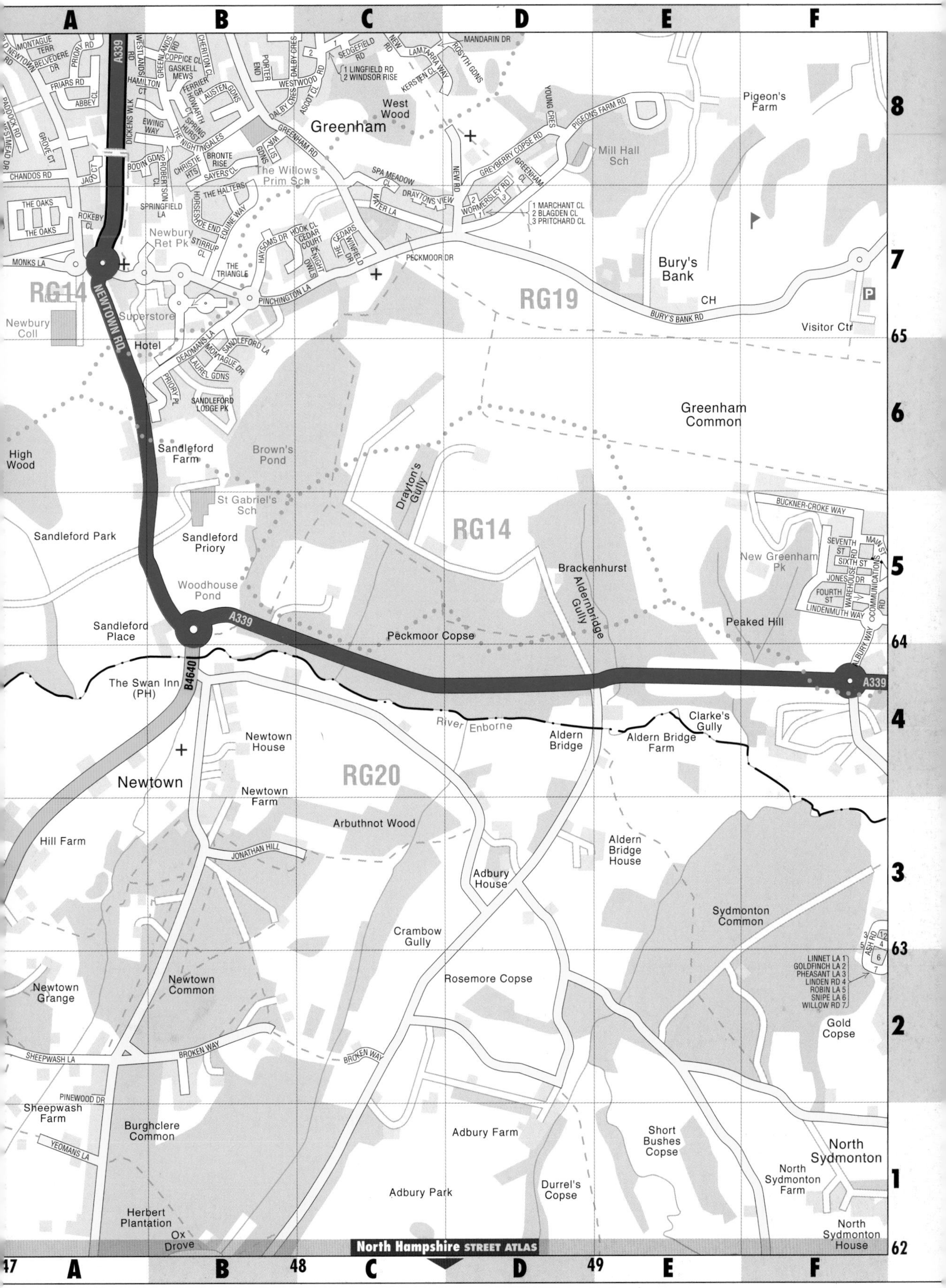

A B C D E F

8
MONTAGUE TERR
NEWTOWN RD
BELVEDERE DR
PRIORY RD
FRIARS RD
ABBEY CL
PADDOCK RD
MEADOW RD
GROVE CT
CHANDOS RD
JAG CT
A339
WESTLANDS RD
DICKENS WLK
HAMILTON CT
GREENLANDS RD
COPPICE CL
GASKELL MEWS
CHERITON CL
FERRIER GR
HOWARTH CT
AUSTEN GDNS
EWING WAY
SPRING HURST
THE NIGHTINGALES
BODIN GDNS
ROBERTSON CL
CHRISTIE HTS
BRONTE RISE
SAYERS CL
PORTER END
DALBY CRES
WESTWOOD RD
ASCOT CL
SEDGEFIELD RD
1 LINGFIELD RD
2 WINDSOR RISE
NEW RD
LAMTARRA WAY
KERSTEN CL
MANDARIN DR
ROSYTH GDNS
West Wood
Greenham
GREENHAM RD
YOUNG CRES
PIGEONS FARM RD
Pigeon's Farm
Mill Hall Sch
GREYBERRY COPSE RD
GREENHAM CL
WORMERSLEY RD
1 MARCHANT CL
2 BLAGDEN CL
3 PRITCHARD CL
The Willows Prim Sch
SPA MEADOW CL
DRAYTONS VIEW
WATER LA
THE HALTERS
7
THE OAKS
ROKEBY CL
SPRINGFIELD LA
HORSESHOE END
EQUINE WAY
Newbury Ret Pk
STIRRUP CL
HAYSOMS DR
HOOK CL
CEDAR COURT PK
OWLS
KNIGHT
THE CEDARS
WINFIELD DR
PECKMOOR DR
MONKS LA
THE TRIANGLE
PINCHINGTON LA
RG14
RG19
Bury's Bank
CH
BURY'S BANK RD
Newbury Coll
Superstore
NEWTOWN RD
Hotel
DEADMANS LA
MONTAGUE DR
SANDLEFORD LA
LAUREL GDNS
PRIORY PL
SANDLEFORD LODGE PK
Visitor Ctr
65
6
Greenham Common
High Wood
Sandleford Farm
Brown's Pond
St Gabriel's Sch
Drayton's Gully
RG14
BUCKNER-CROKE WAY
Sandleford Park
Sandleford Priory
SEVENTH ST
MAIN ST
SIXTH ST
New Greenham Pk
JONES RD
WAREHOUSE RD
COMMUNICATIONS RD
FOURTH ST
LINDENMUTH WAY
5
Brackenhurst
Aldernbridge Gully
Woodhouse Pond
Peaked Hill
Sandleford Place
A339
Peckmoor Copse
64
ALBURY WAY
B4640
The Swan Inn (PH)
A339
River Enborne
Clarke's Gully
4
Newtown House
Aldern Bridge
Aldern Bridge Farm
RG20
Newtown
Newtown Farm
Arbuthnot Wood
Hill Farm
JONATHAN HILL
Aldern Bridge House
3
Adbury House
Sydmonton Common
Crambow Gully
ASH RD
63
LINNET LA 1
GOLDFINCH LA 2
PHEASANT LA 3
LINDEN RD 4
ROBIN LA 5
SNIPE LA 6
WILLOW RD 7
Newtown Grange
Newtown Common
Rosemore Copse
Gold Copse
2
SHEEPWASH LA
BROKEN WAY
BROKEN WAY
PINEWOOD DR
Sheepwash Farm
Burghclere Common
Adbury Farm
Short Bushes Copse
North Sydmonton
YEOMANS LA
Durrel's Copse
North Sydmonton Farm
1
Adbury Park
Herbert Plantation
North Sydmonton House
Ox Drove
62

47 A B 48 C D 49 E F

132

A
B
C
D
E
F
8
7
65
6
5
64
4
3
63
2
1
62
50
51
52
Football Ground
CHAMBERHOUSE MILL LA
Bowdown Farm
Cakeball Copse
Sayer's Copse
River Kennet
Chamberhouse Farm
Avenell's Cottages
Highfield Copse
Conduit Copse
Bowdown House
Ashen Copse
Longlane Gully
Great Wood
The Round House
Nature Reserve
BURY'S BANK RD
Crookham House
Thornford Hights
CROOKHAM HILL
Greenham Common
OLD THORNFORD RD
CROOKHAM COMMON RD
P
RG19
New Greenham Pk
1 Liberty Ho
2 Galaxy Ho
3 New Horizon Ho
4 Unity Ho
ENGINEER'S RD
MINISTRY RD
THIRD ST E
WOFFORD WAY
LINDENMUTH WAY
MAIN ST
FIRST ST
WEBER RD
THE SQUARE
Goldfinch Bottom
Crookham Common
George's Farm
Foxhold Farm
Boar's Gully
Head's Hill
Head's Hill Farm
Foxhold House
THORNFORD RD
South Lands
Ford
A339
Martindale Farm
Long Copse
River Enborne
George's Wood
Ppg Sta
Knight's Bridge
The Oven
Folly Farm
Knightsbridge Farm
Sewage Works
Bishop's Green
BLACKBIRD LA
KNIGHTSBRIDGE DR
Knightsbridge House
ASH RD
BEECH RD
Bishop's Green Farm
THORNFIELD
MILLGREEN LA
EAGLE RD
Bishop's Green Farm
Upper Knightsbridge Farm
Forge Farm
Mill Green
Holly Bush Farm
HOLLY BUSH
ASHFORD HILL RD
PO
ROOKSFIELD
Cherry Tree Farm
RG20
Headley
Pitts Farm
ST PETERS CL
Hill View Farm
HYDE LA
Longcross Farm
Nursery
COMMON RD
The Harrow (PH)
Fuces Farm
North Ecchinswell Farm
Headley Stud
Headley House
BEENHAMPLACE RD
GALLEY LA
A339 Basingstoke
North Hampshire STREET ATLAS
A
B
C
D
E
F

107
134

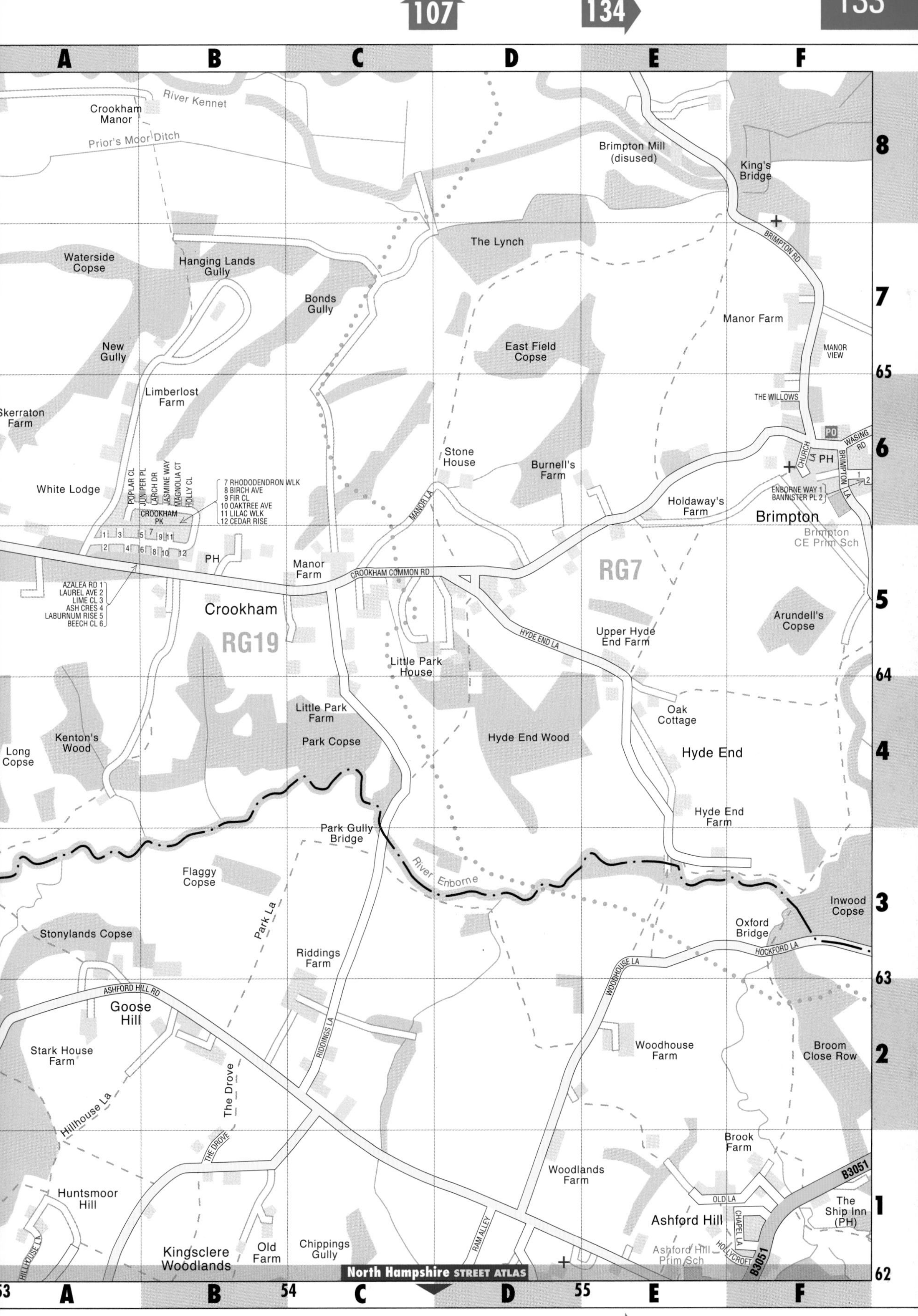
A
B
C
D
E
F
River Kennet
Crookham Manor
Prior's Moor Ditch
Brimpton Mill (disused)
King's Bridge
8
The Lynch
BRIMPTON RD
Waterside Copse
Hanging Lands Gully
Bonds Gully
7
Manor Farm
New Gully
East Field Copse
MANOR VIEW
65
Limberlost Farm
THE WILLOWS
Skerraton Farm
PO
WASING RD
6
Stone House
Burnell's Farm
CHURCH LA
PH
BRIMPTON LA
White Lodge
POPLAR CL
JUNIPER PL
LARCH DR
JASMINE WAY
MAGNOLIA CT
HOLLY CL
7 RHODODENDRON WLK
8 BIRCH AVE
9 FIR CL
10 OAKTREE AVE
11 LILAC WLK
12 CEDAR RISE
CROOKHAM PK
MANOR LA
Holdaway's Farm
ENBORNE WAY 1
BANNISTER PL 2
Brimpton
Brimpton CE Prim Sch
PH
Manor Farm
CROOKHAM COMMON RD
RG7
AZALEA RD 1
LAUREL AVE 2
LIME CL 3
ASH CRES 4
LABURNUM RISE 5
BEECH CL 6
Crookham
RG19
HYDE END LA
Upper Hyde End Farm
Arundell's Copse
5
Little Park House
64
Little Park Farm
Oak Cottage
Long Copse
Kenton's Wood
Park Copse
Hyde End Wood
Hyde End
4
Park Gully Bridge
Hyde End Farm
Flaggy Copse
River Enborne
Inwood Copse
3
Park La
Oxford Bridge
Stonylands Copse
Riddings Farm
HOCKFORD LA
WOODHOUSE LA
63
ASHFORD HILL RD
Goose Hill
RIDDINGS LA
Woodhouse Farm
Broom Close Row
Stark House Farm
2
The Drove
Hillhouse La
THE DROVE
Brook Farm
B3051
Huntsmoor Hill
Woodlands Farm
OLD LA
The Ship Inn (PH)
1
CHAPEL LA
Ashford Hill
RAM ALLEY
HILLHOUSE LA
Kingsclere Woodlands
Old Farm
Chippings Gully
Ashford Hill Prim Sch
HOLLYCROFT
B3051
North Hampshire STREET ATLAS
62
53
54
55

134

133
108

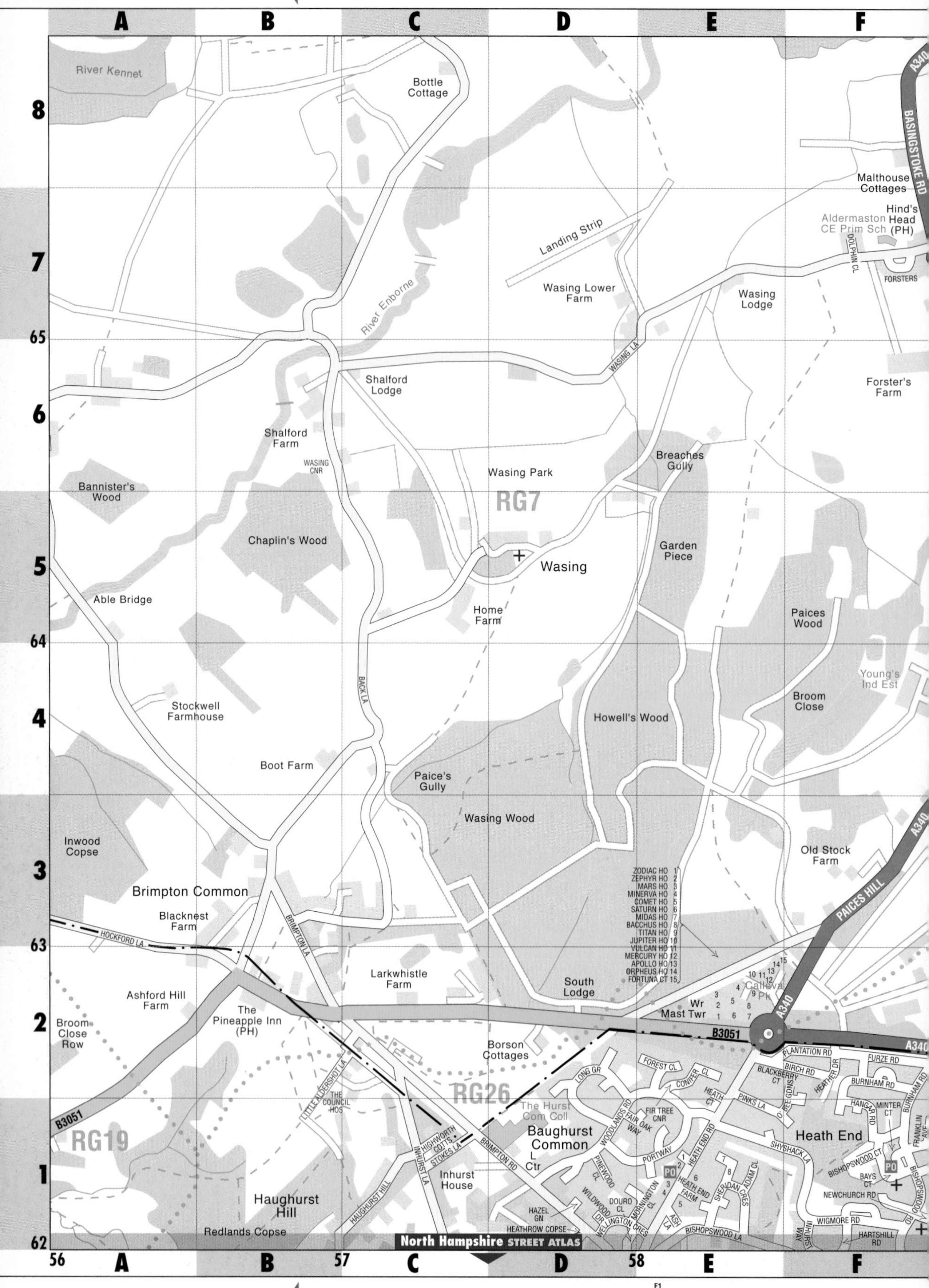

133

E1
1 HEATHLAND
2 THE OLD FORGE
3 BEECH COPSE
4 OAKLANDS
5 HEATH HO
6 LANDSEER CT
7 HEPPLEWHITE CL
8 CHIPPENDALE CL

A B C D E F

Aqua Vitae Copse
Fisherman's Cottage
Sawmill
Upper Lodge Farm
Upper Church Farm
The Old Rectory
FISHERMAN'S LA
Padworth Gully
RECTORY RD
Aldermaston
Church Farm
Cedars Sch
Springhill Farm
Wrays Farm
THE STREET
Hatch Farm House
CONGREVE CL
CHURCH RD
SPRING LA
FORSTERS FARM CT
The Manor House
Portland House
The Birches
REDLANE HILL
COURT FARM
RAGHILL
Wr Twr
Raghill Farm
PAICES HILL
Harbourhill Copse
Aldermaston Park
Black Pightle
Old Warren
READING RD
RED LA
RG7
CHAPEL LA
A340
WELSHMAN'S RD
PINELANDS MOBILE HOME PK
Little Heath
Berkshire Bsns Pk
Depot
Decoy Pond
SOKE RD
Aldermaston Soke
Upper Moor's Gully
THIRD AVE
SECOND AVE
FIRST AVE
RAVENSWING PK
Soke Pig Farm
The Falcon (PH)
KESTRELS MEAD
FALCON FIELDS
WINKWORTH LA
MITCHELL CL
WHITEHOUSE FARM
VERICA GDNS
PEMBERE CL
ALDERMASTON RD
PELICAN RD
ALMSWOOD RD
WAKEFORD CT
PRIORS RD
PAMBER RD
FRANKLIN CT
BRACKENWOOD DR
Tadley
SILCHESTER RD
PH
PO
WAKEFORD CL
THE BURROWS
SARUM RD
BOND CL
SMALLWOOD DR
SPENCER CL
KNOLLYS RD
MEON CL
CL
WESSEX CT
RG26
CHURCH RD
OAKFIELD RD
SPRINGFIELD RD
CLAPPSGATE
ERSKINE CL
FRANKLIN AVE
A340 MULFORDS HILL
Tadley Horizon
STROUD CL
JUBILEE CL
Pamber Heath
Burnham Copse Prim Sch
BISHOPS CL
TURBARY GDNS
HONEYBOTTOM RD
Liby
Brick Kiln Ind Est
BROAD HALFPENNY LA
TADLEY COMMON RD
ILEX CL
IMPSTONE RD
ROMANS GATE
NEWTOWN
GLENDALE RD
THE PARADE
ODETTE GDNS
ANDERSON GDNS
Tadley Common
PAMBER HEATH RD
CHURCH RD
VALLEY WAY
NEWCHURCH RD
OAK TREE CL
HILLCREST
THE GLEN
SEARING WAY
SOUTHDOWN RD
BLAKE'S LA
SYMPSON RD
ARNEWOOD AVE
WESTLYN RD
EASTLYN RD
BEAVERS CL
HUNTSMOOR RD
SILVERDALE RD
MOUNT PLEASANT
HEATH RD
BURNEY BIT
WOODCOTT HO
STANFIELD
A340 Basingstoke
North Hampshire STREET ATLAS

8
7
65
6
5
64
4
3
63
2
1
62

59 A B 60 C D 61 E F

135
110

A
B
C
D
E
F
8
7
65
6
5
64
4
3
63
2
1
62
Oval Pond
Ufton Park
Brent's Gully
Cowpond Piece
FOUR HOUSES CORNER
ISLAND FARM RD
Caravan Site
Mast
Wr Twr
Five Oaken
LONGMOOR LA
Roundoak Piece
CAMP RD
Gibbet Piece
SILVER LA
The Croft
MAY'S LA
PADWORTH RD
Holden's Firs
The Round Oak (PH)
Fifty Acre Piece
COLLEGE PIECE
RECTORY RD
BAUGHURST RD
BLOCK COTTS
Padworth Common
RAMPTONS LA
Hundred Acre Piece
Pond Bay
Pickling Yard Plantation
STEPHENS FIRS
VICTORIA RD
BRIARLEA RD
GROVES LEA
PINE DR
ST CATHERINE'S HILL
SWEETZER'S PIECE
BIRCHLAND CL
RAVENSWORTH RD
FIRS END
STEPHENS CL
STEPHENS RD
LEIGH FIELD
CROFT RD
GLENAPP GRANGE
Stockwell's Piece
Chaplin's Copse
LANESWOOD
BIRCH LA
FAIRFIELD PK
WEST END RD
Burnt Common
Budd's Firs
Turner's Arms (PH)
STANMORE GDNS
DRURY LA
LOVES WOOD
CHAPEL RD
ROWLAND'S CL
RG7
Summerlug
WELSHMAN'S RD
THE BRIDGES
CHURCH RD
West End Farm
TURK'S LA
Simms's Copse
SIMMS FARM LA
Fox Hill
Lovegrove's Farm
BACK LA
Mortimer West End
Simms Stud Farm
Benyon's Inclosure
Red Lion (PH)
West End Brook
Alders Slade
Nine Acre Copse
Simms's Plantation
Hungry Hill
Pond Farm
Stone Hill
Catthaw Lands Copse
WALL LA
Kiln Yard Copse
SOKE RD
Catthawlands Farm
PAMBER RD
KINGS RD
The Drove
Silchester CE Prim Sch
SCHOOL LA
Calleva Mus
CALLEVA ATREBATUM ROMAN TOWN (remains of)
Manor Farm
CLAPPERS FARM RD
PAMBER RD
BRAMLEY RD
Silchester Common
Calleva Arms (PH)
Silchester
CHURCH LA
LITTLE LONDON RD
Silchester Hall
DUKES RIDE
ROMANS FIELD
WHISTLERS LA
62
63
64
THE CRESCENT

135

111
138

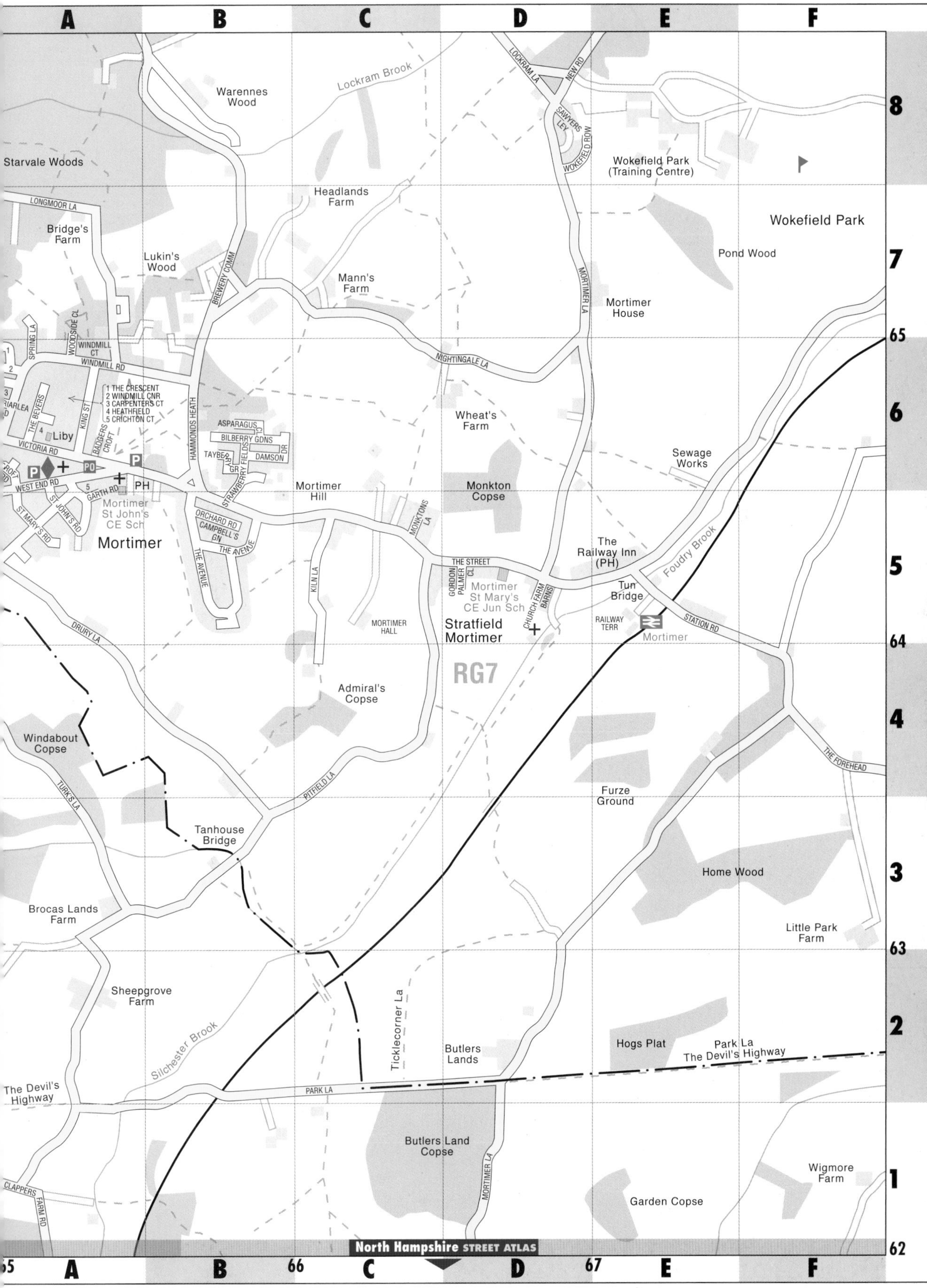

A B C D E F
8 7 6 5 4 3 2 1
65 64 63 62
66 67
Lockram Brook
Warennes Wood
Starvale Woods
LOCKRAM LA
NEW RD
SAWYERS LEY
WOKEFIELD ROW
Wokefield Park (Training Centre)
Wokefield Park
Pond Wood
Headlands Farm
LONGMOOR LA
Bridge's Farm
Lukin's Wood
BREWERY COMM
Mann's Farm
MORTIMER LA
Mortimer House
WOODSIDE CL
SPRING LA
WINDMILL CT
WINDMILL RD
NIGHTINGALE LA
1 THE CRESCENT
2 WINDMILL CNR
3 CARPENTERS CT
4 HEATHFIELD
5 CRICHTON CT
THE BEVERS
KING ST
HAMMONDS HEATH
ASPARAGUS
BILBERRY GDNS
DAMSON
TAYBERRY GR
STRAWBERRY FIELDS
Liby
BADGERS CROFT
VICTORIA RD
Wheat's Farm
Sewage Works
PO
PH
WEST END RD
GARTH RD
ST JOHN'S RD
ST MARY'S RD
Mortimer St John's CE Sch
Mortimer
Mortimer Hill
Monkton Copse
MONKTONS LA
ORCHARD RD
CAMPBELL'S GN
THE AVENUE
KILN LA
THE STREET
GORDON PALMER CL
Mortimer St Mary's CE Jun Sch
CHURCH FARM BARNS
The Railway Inn (PH)
Tun Bridge
Foudry Brook
RAILWAY TERR
STATION RD
Mortimer
MORTIMER HALL
Stratfield Mortimer
RG7
DRURY LA
Admiral's Copse
Windabout Copse
TURK'S LA
PITFIELD LA
THE FOREHEAD
Furze Ground
Tanhouse Bridge
Home Wood
Brocas Lands Farm
Little Park Farm
Sheepgrove Farm
Silchester Brook
Ticklecorner La
Butlers Lands
Hogs Plat
Park La
The Devil's Highway
The Devil's Highway
PARK LA
Butlers Land Copse
MORTIMER LA
Wigmore Farm
Garden Copse
CLAPPERS FARM RD

137
112

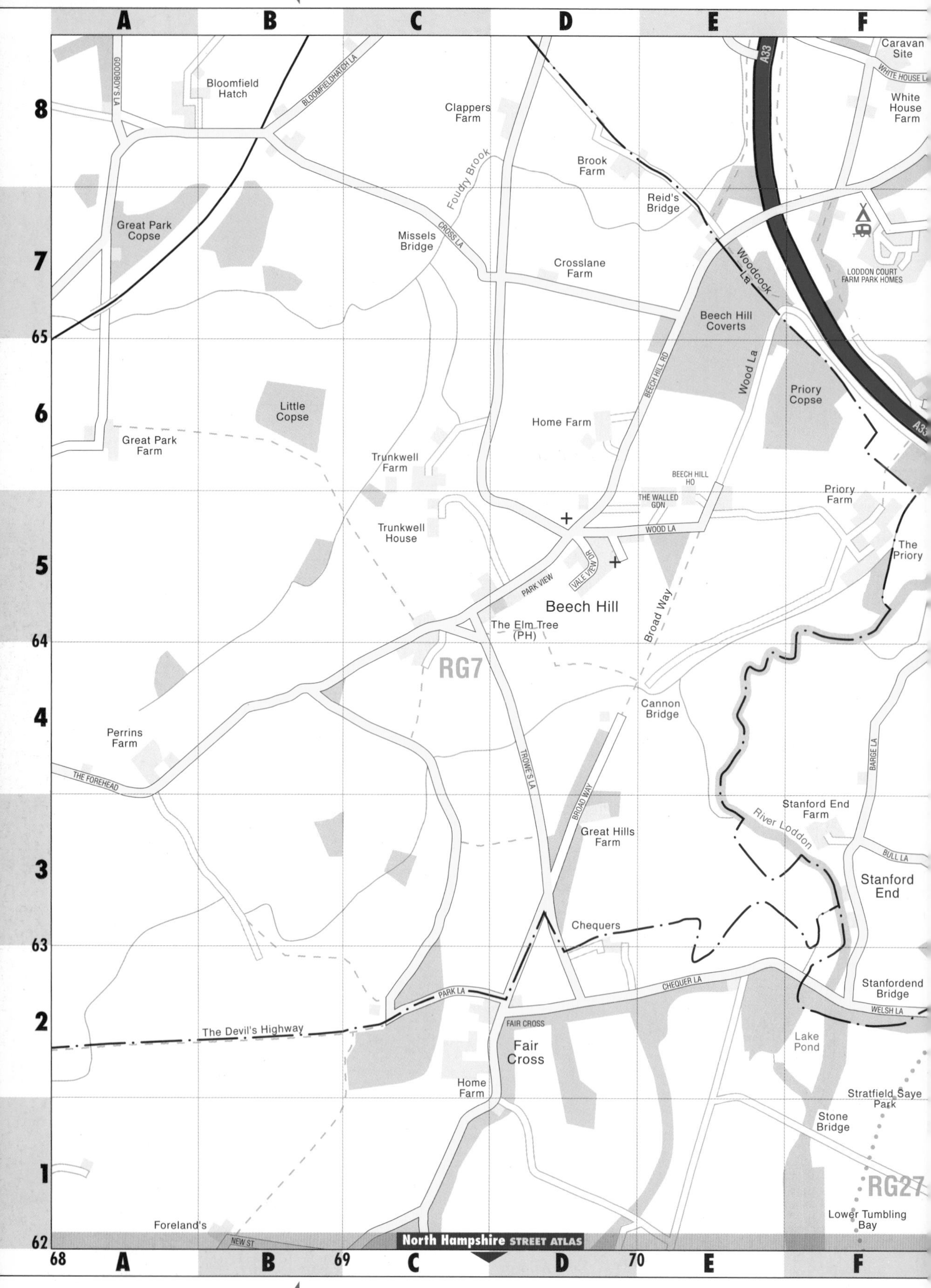
A
B
C
D
E
F
8
7
65
6
5
64
4
3
63
2
1
62
68
69
70
Bloomfield Hatch
GOODBOY'S LA
BLOOMFIELDHATCH LA
Clappers Farm
Brook Farm
Reid's Bridge
Caravan Site
WHITE HOUSE LA
White House Farm
A33
Foudry Brook
Missels Bridge
CROSS LA
Great Park Copse
Crosslane Farm
Woodcock La
LODDON COURT FARM PARK HOMES
Beech Hill Coverts
Wood La
BEECH HILL RD
Priory Copse
Little Copse
Home Farm
Great Park Farm
Trunkwell Farm
BEECH HILL HO
THE WALLED GDN
Priory Farm
Trunkwell House
WOOD LA
The Priory
VALE VIEW DR
PARK VIEW
Broad Way
Beech Hill
The Elm Tree (PH)
RG7
Cannon Bridge
Perrins Farm
BARGE LA
THE FOREHEAD
TROWE'S LA
BROAD WAY
Stanford End Farm
River Loddon
Great Hills Farm
BULL LA
Stanford End
Chequers
CHEQUER LA
PARK LA
Stanfordend Bridge
WELSH LA
The Devil's Highway
FAIR CROSS
Fair Cross
Lake Pond
Home Farm
Stratfield Saye Park
Stone Bridge
RG27
Lower Tumbling Bay
Foreland's
NEW ST

137

A
B
C
D
E
F
RG2
Great Wood
8
BEECH HILL RD
BEATY RISE
BENHAM DR
BRYANT CRES
B3349
Heron Ind Est
BACK LA
Lambs Lane Prim Sch
Sheepbridge Court Farm
River Loddon
SWALLOWFIELD PK
Lambs Farm Bsns Pk
Loddon Court Farm
LAMB'S LA
Hotel
Sheep Bridge
7
SWALLOWFIELD ST
65
Cuckoo Pen
HORNBEAMS
Loddon Court
Wyvols Court
VILLA PL
THE STREET
PH
PO
CURLY'S WAY
KINGSBRIDGE HILL
King's Bridge
FOXBOROUGH
THE NAYLORS
Brookside Bsns Ctr
Brookside Nursery
George & Dragon (PH)
6
Swallowfield
Salter's Bridge
CHURCH RD
Rowe's Farm
Handpost Farm
Blackwater River
BARGE LA
CHARLTON LA
BASINGSTOKE RD
NUTBEAN LA
5
Cemy
TROWE'S LA
The Broadwater
RG7
Goddard's Farm
64
Taylor's La
Springalls Farm
Wheelers Farm
SPRING LA
Yew Tree Farm
Riseley Farm
4
PART LA
Collins Copse
Highgrove Copse
Glasspool Farm
JUBILEE COTTS
Riseley Gorse Farm
SCHOOL RD
SCHOOL LA
Riseley Bsns Pk
St Leger's Copse
THE OLD RISELEY STORES
HALPIN HO
PH
BENHAM LA
Walnut Tree Farm
3
BULL LA
Newbarn Farm
Spring Barn
YEOSFIELD
CHAPEL LA
KENT COTTS
Riseley
63
NORTON RD
PORTWAY
SUN LA
RG27
WELSH LA
P
Ham's Wood
P
River Whitewater
2
B3349
Park Corner
RG27
Birchen Copse
BASINGSTOKE RD
Pound Copse
ODIHAM RD
Wellington Country Park
Riseley Mill
Top Hill Copse
Mill Wood
1
A33
B3349
62
A33 Basingstoke
71
72
73

139
114

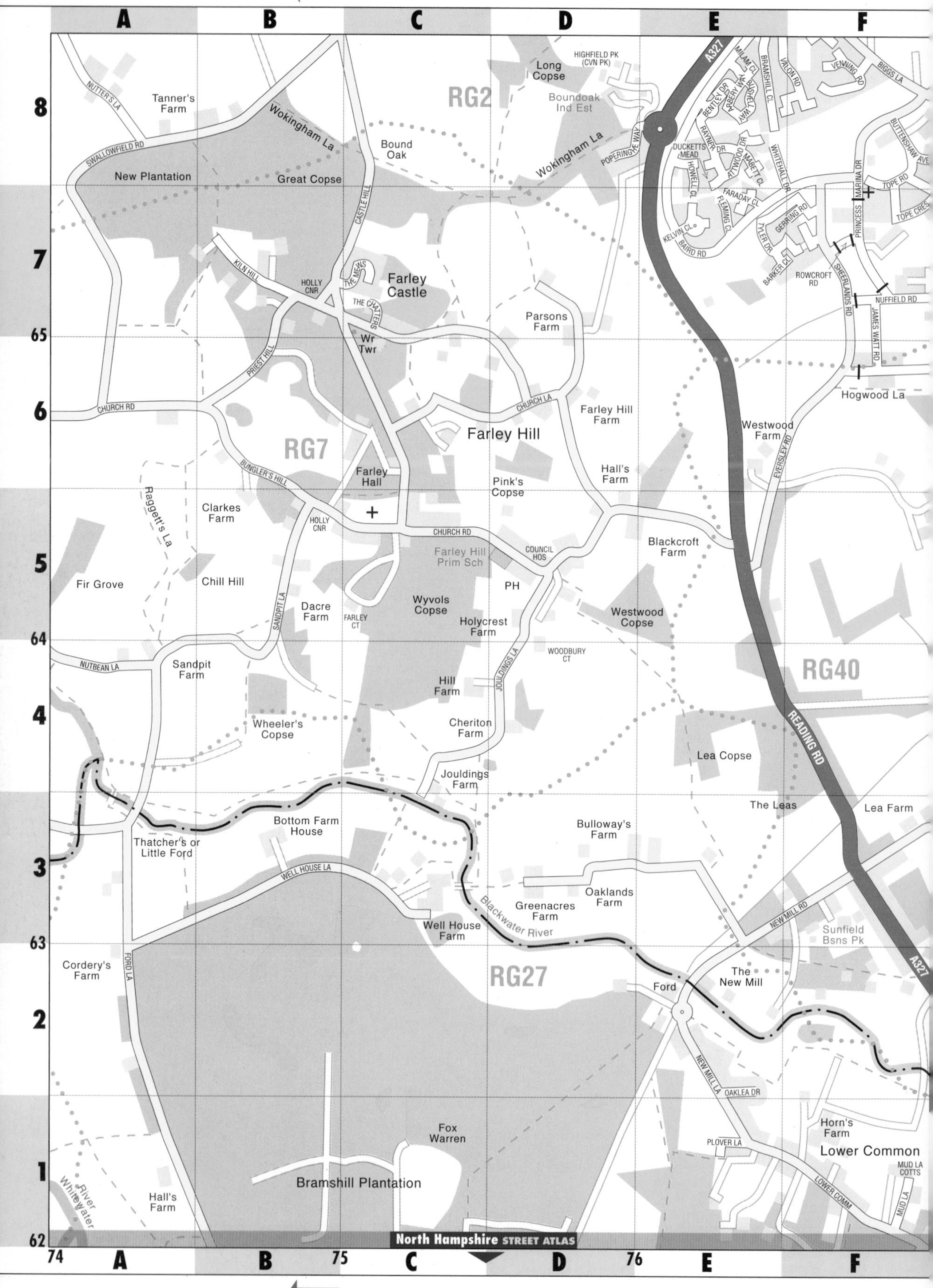
A
B
C
D
E
F
8
7
65
6
5
64
4
3
63
2
1
62
74
75
76
RG2
RG7
RG40
RG27
A327
Tanner's Farm
New Plantation
Great Copse
Wokingham La
Bound Oak
Long Copse
HIGHFIELD PK (CVN PK)
Boundoak Ind Est
POPERINGHE WAY
Farley Castle
THE MEWS
THE CHATERS
HOLLY CNR
KILN HILL
CASTLE HILL
PRIEST HILL
Wr Twr
Parsons Farm
CHURCH LA
CHURCH RD
SWALLOWFIELD RD
NUTTER'S LA
Farley Hill
Farley Hill Farm
Hall's Farm
Pink's Copse
Farley Hall
BUNGLER'S HILL
Raggett's La
Clarkes Farm
Chill Hill
Fir Grove
Farley Hill Prim Sch
COUNCIL HOS
PH
Blackcroft Farm
Westwood Copse
Westwood Farm
EVERSLEY RD
Wyvols Copse
Holycrest Farm
Dacre Farm
FARLEY CT
SANDPIT LA
NUTBEAN LA
Sandpit Farm
WOODBURY CT
JOULDINGS LA
Hill Farm
Cheriton Farm
Wheeler's Copse
Jouldings Farm
Lea Copse
READING RD
The Leas
Lea Farm
Bottom Farm House
Thatcher's or Little Ford
Bulloway's Farm
WELL HOUSE LA
Blackwater River
Greenacres Farm
Oaklands Farm
Well House Farm
NEW MILL RD
Sunfield Bsns Pk
Cordery's Farm
FORD LA
Ford
The New Mill
NEW MILL LA
OAKLEA DR
PLOVER LA
Horn's Farm
Lower Common
MUD LA COTTS
MUD LA
LOWER COMM
Fox Warren
Bramshill Plantation
Hall's Farm
River Whitewater
Hogwood La
ROWCROFT RD
SHEERLANDS RD
NUFFIELD RD
JAMES WATT RD
PRINCESS MARINA DR
TOPE RD
TOPE CRES
BUTTENSHAW AVE
BIGGS LA
VENNING RD
VALON RD
BRAMSHILL CL
WHITEHALL DR
MILLAN CL
BENTLEY DR
ABBEY WAY
BUSHELL WAY
RAYNER DR
DUCKETTS MEAD
HOWELL CL
ATTWOOD DR
MABETT CL
FARADAY CL
FLEMING CL
KELVIN CL
BAIRD RD
TYLER DR
GERRING RD
BARKER CL

139

A B C D E F

JAMES WATT RD
NUFFIELD RD
ISAAC NEWTON RD
REME Mus of Technology
PRINCESS MARINA DR
Rifle Range
Model Farm
GILBERT WAY
FIR COTTAGE RD
SPRINGDALE
CHARLTON CL
WAVERLEY WAY
DODSELLS WELL
THE LEA
BURCHETT COPPICE
ELGARTH DR
THOMAS LA
BIGGS LA
BUTTENSHAW AVE
BUTTENSHAW CL
COMMONFIELD LA
Rook's Nest Farm
GARRETT RD
ST JAMES RD
WOODSIDE CL
BARKHAM RIDE
ROYCROFT LA
NASH GROVE LA
McCARTHY WAY
THE SPINNEY
BURNT OAK
MORNINGTON AVE
JERRYMOOR HILL
8
Windmill Farm
PARSONS CL
STEPHENSON RD
RG2
Arborfield Garrison
DITCHFIELD LA
MOORS CT
30
COLUMBIA CT
MARYLAND
OREGON WLK
VERMONT WOODS
CAROLINA PL
MOOR CL
COPSE WAY
HEATHER CL
California Country Park
WILLOWDALE
CHALLENOR CL
WILD BRIAR
RADICAL RIDE
TICKENOR DR
B3016
Long Moor Bog
Moor Farm
Longmoor Lake
CHIVERS DR
WATKINS CL
GORSE RIDE N
DRAKE CL
ARNETT AVE
FINCHAMPSTEAD RD
7
Long Moor
CALIFORNIA CVN PK
BUCHANAN DR
COCKAYNE CT
BIRCH RD
WINDSOR RIDE
SUMMIT CL
WHITWORTH RD
Gorse Ride Inf & Jun Schs
WHITTLE CL
FIRS CL
ORBIT CL
DART CL
65
Longmoor Farm
FERNBANK
MANOR PARK DR
BRIARWOOD
GIBBS CL
GORSE RIDE S
BILLING AVE
VICARAGE CL
BANK SIDE
WIMBUSHES
CHURCH HAMS
HAZELBANK
REDGAUNTLET
MASDAR GDNS
KELSEY AVE
LONGMOOR CL
B3430
WICK HILL LA
Coleshill Farm
ROOKERY CT
WELLER DR
MARINO WAY
CHAPEL LODGE
AVERY CL
6
Falcon Bsns Pk
IVANHOE RD
HOGWOOD LA
ROBINSON CRUSOE PK
NINE MILE RIDE
THE DITTONS
WARREN CL
Kestrel Bldgs
ROWANWOOD
Hogwood Ind Est
Greenacres
Nine Mile Ride Prim Sch
Hogwood Farm Ind Est
Nine Mile Ride Ind
WARREN LA
PARK LA
Wheatlands Farm
Warren Lodge
Furze Hill
5
Shepperlands Copse
RG40
WHITE HORSE LA
Ridge Farm
Larchwood Farm
PH
Church Farm
WICK HILL LA
64
CHURCH LA
West Court
Manor House
NORTH CT
Wheatlands Manor
4
CHURCH LA
B3016
B3348
Park Farm
JUBILEE RD
Rectory Farm
East Court
3
Finchampstead CE Prim Sch
Manor Farm
B3348
THE VILLAGE
ROMAN MILESTONE
Banisters Farm
Agates Meadow
PO
PH
LIDDELL CL
CORFIELD CL
LONGWATER LA
MANOR BARNS LA
63
FLEET HILL
CRICKET HILL
BURNMOOR MDW
WOOD MOOR
LOWER SANDHURST RD
2
READING RD
THE RISE
B3348
Fleet Copse
Finchampstead
LONGWATER RD
Longwater La
FLEET LA
The Tally Ho (PH)
Eversley Bridge
Fleethill Farm
EVERSLEY ST A327
BONNY'S YD
1
Eversley
Long Water
Finchampstead Bridge
Blackwater River
RG27
WARBROOK LA
B3016
62

141
116

141
149

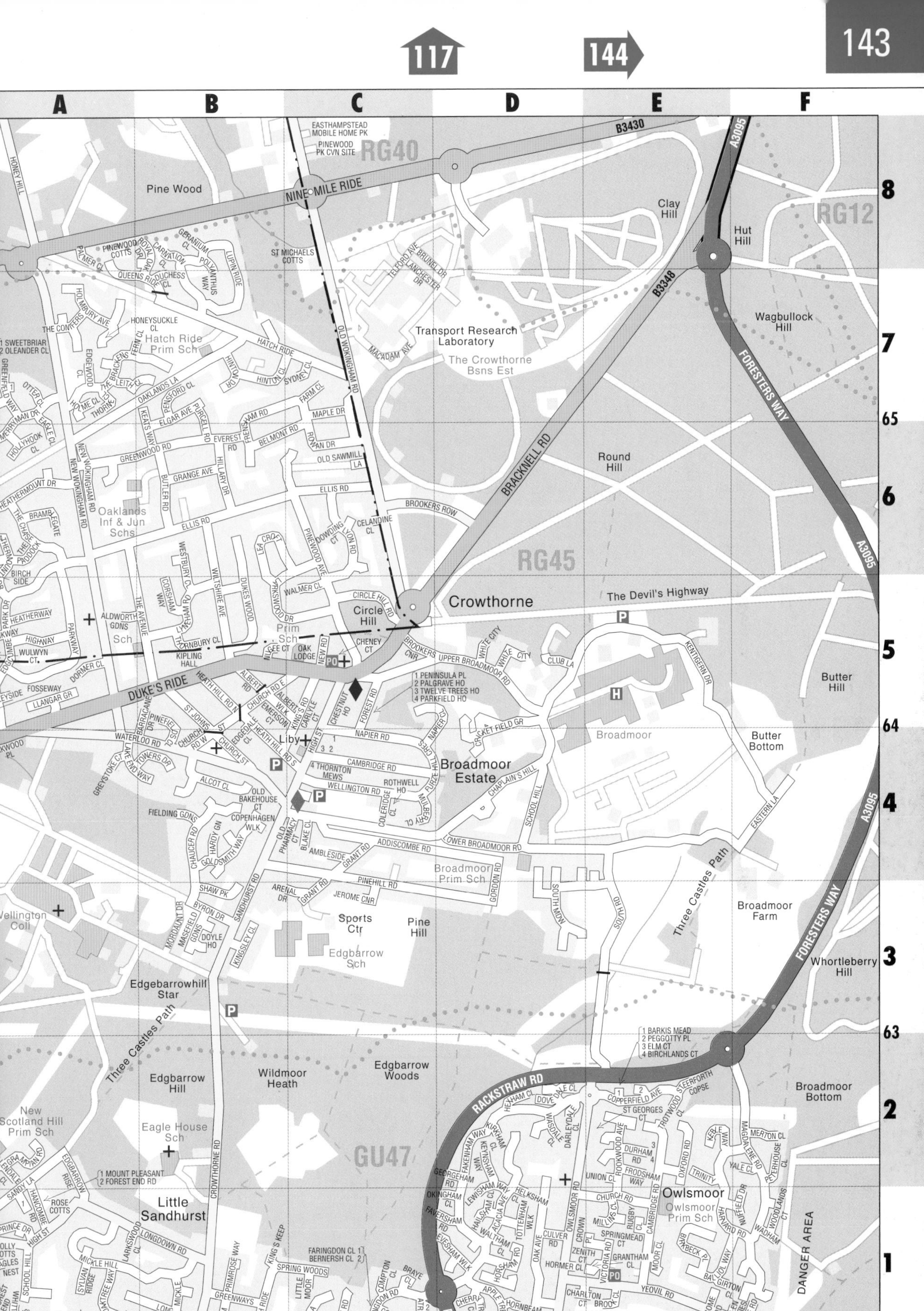
Pine Wood
NINE MILE RIDE
RG40
B3430
EASTHAMPSTEAD MOBILE HOME PK
PINEWOOD PK CVN SITE
Clay Hill
Hut Hill
RG12
A3095
B3348
Wagbullock Hill
Transport Research Laboratory
The Crowthorne Bsns Est
FORESTERS WAY
Hatch Ride Prim Sch
HATCH RIDE
OLD WOKINGHAM RD
Round Hill
BRACKNELL RD
Oaklands Inf & Jun Schs
RG45
Crowthorne
The Devil's Highway
Circle Hill
Prim Sch
DUKE'S RIDE
Butter Hill
Broadmoor
Butter Bottom
Broadmoor Estate
Liby
Broadmoor Prim Sch
Three Castles Path
Broadmoor Farm
Wellington Coll
Sports Ctr
Pine Hill
Edgbarrow Sch
Whortleberry Hill
Edgebarrowhill Star
Wildmoor Heath
Edgbarrow Woods
Edgbarrow Hill
RACKSTRAW RD
Broadmoor Bottom
New Scotland Hill Prim Sch
Eagle House Sch
GU47
Little Sandhurst
Owlsmoor
Owlsmoor Prim Sch
DANGER AREA
Sandhurst Sch
A B C D E F
8 7 6 5 4 3 2 1
65 64 63 62
83 84 85

143 118

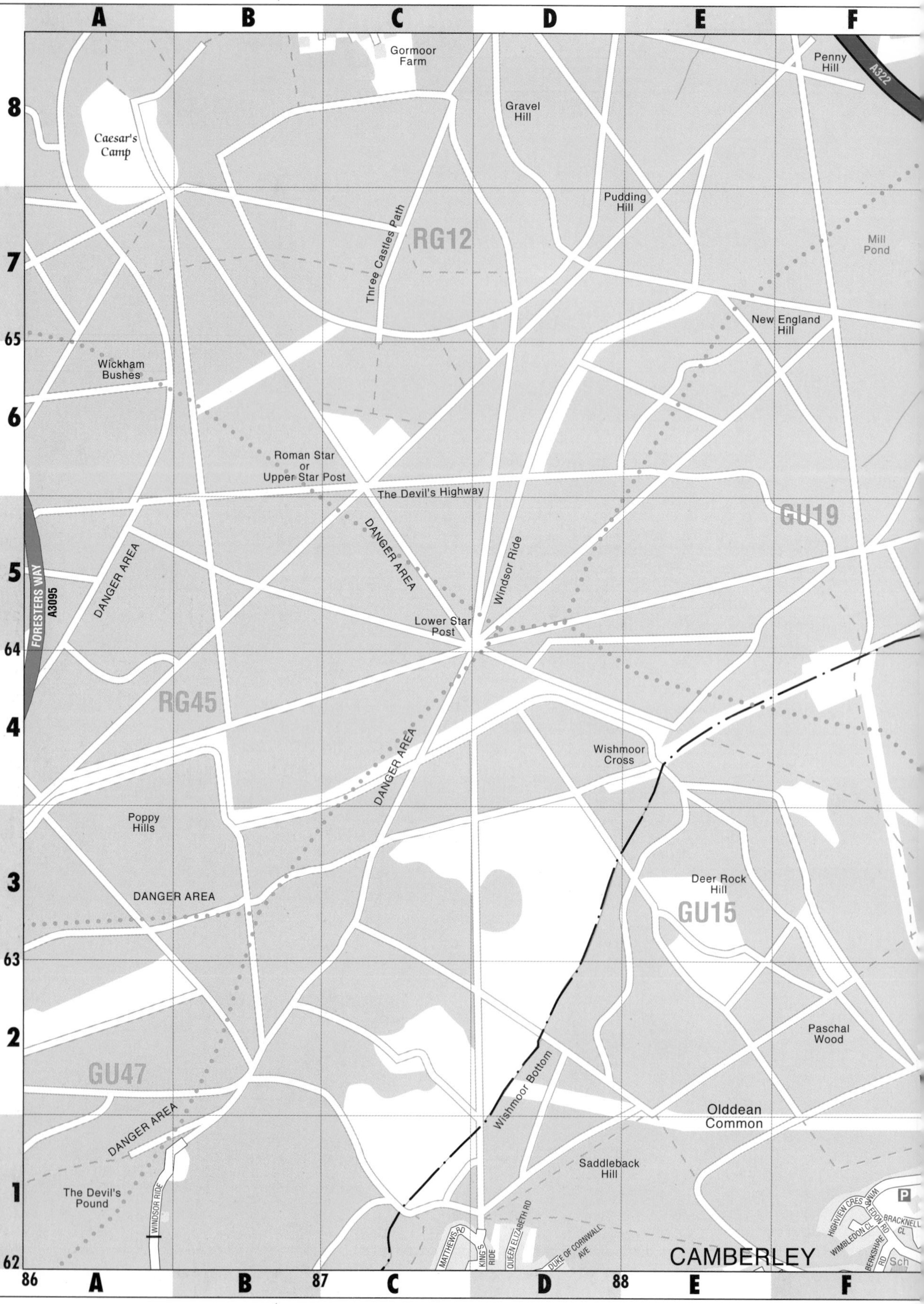

143 151

A B C D E F

8 7 65 6 5 64 4 3 63 2 1 62

RG12
Thornhill Allotment
CH
A332
SL5
SWINLEY RD
A322
Dukeshill Allotment
Fern Hill
Winklands Allotment
GU20
Red Cottage
Broom Covert
Rapley Farm
Fan Covert
HOLLYBUSH TK
DUKES COVERT
BRACKNELL RD
DUKE'S HILL
Longacres Nursery
HALLGROVE BOTTOM
Cuckoo Pen
Rapley Lake
Lake Cottage
The Orangery
Laundry Cottage
A30
Hall Grove Farm Ind Est
Bagshot Park
The Cricketers (Hotel)
Surrey Hill
Cobblers Hole
GROVE END
Freemantle Cottage
GU19
HOME FARM
CH
Queen's Wood
Windle Brook
LORY RIDGE
ANDERSON PL
Bagshot
STATION RD
1 FAULKNER PL
2 HEWLETT PL
3 GLOUCESTER GDNS
4 CHEWTER CL
Ford
VICARAGE RD
TALBOT PL
HART DENE CT
FREEMANTLE RD
GLOUCESTER RD
Bagshot Heath
TANNERS YD
HALF MOON ST
B3029
BRIDGE RD
PARKERS CT
WARDLE CL
KEPPLE PL
Park Lodge
PARK VIEW
PARK ST
HIGH ST
THE SQUARE
DUVAL PL
BELL PL
Gloucester Br
NEW RD
Bagshot
Liby
PO
WAVERLEY RD
PROVIDENCE HO
GUILDFORD RD
CONNAUGHT RD
CHURCH RD
MILL CL
MILL FIELD
ST ANNES GLADE
CEDAR CT
CEDAR CL
HEATH RD
GREEN FARM RD
Nurseries
SWIFT LA
WELLESLEY CL
PINEWOOD GDNS
COLLEGE RIDE
HEYWOOD DR
HIGGS LA
LONDON RD
SCHOOL LA
ST MARY'S GDNS
HAMILTON CL
BAGSHOT GN
MANOR WAY
5 HEATH FLATS
6 MEADE CT
STONEHILL HO
YAVERLAND DR
LOWER MILL FIELD
CHANTRY RD
LAMBOURNE DR
Bagshot Inf Sch
BROOK RD
GREEN LA
REGENT CT
ELIZABETH AVE
BROOMSQUIRES RD
GUILDFORD RD
CHAPEL LA
FRY LA
STABLE CROFT
WAGGONERS HOLLOW
Connaught Jun Sch
WESTON GR
BUTLER RD
KEMP CT
M3
Mast
Hotel
Penny Hill
JENKINS' HILL
1 ROWAN CT
2 JENKINS CT
SHEPHERDS CHASE
SUFFOLK CL
SHIRE CL
WHITMOOR RD
HOULTON CT
LAIRD CT
GU15
Pine Ridge Inf Sch
Nurseries
WEBB CL
HODGES CL
PRINCES WAY
ALBERT RD
VICTORIA CT
BRACKNELL RD
ESHER RD
MAULTWAY N
MITCHAM RD
WALLINGTON RD
SURBITON RD
KINGSTON RD
SUTTON RD
CARSHALTON RD
LUPIN CL
SOUTHWICK
ARTHUR CL
Hammond's Pond
Lightwater Country Park
GU18
Sports Ctr
Coll
WYCHWOOD PL

89 A B 90 C D 91 E F

145
120

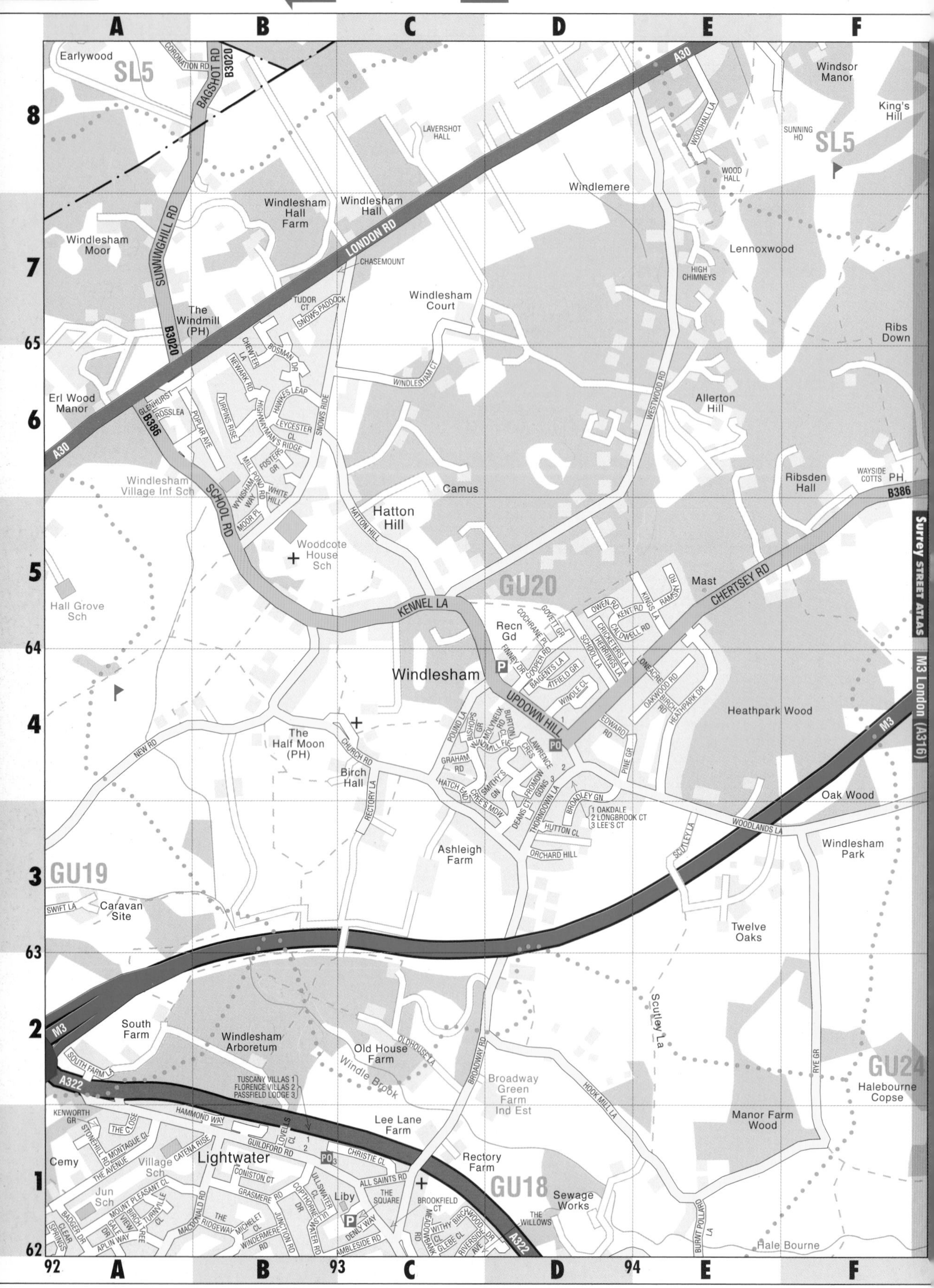

145
153

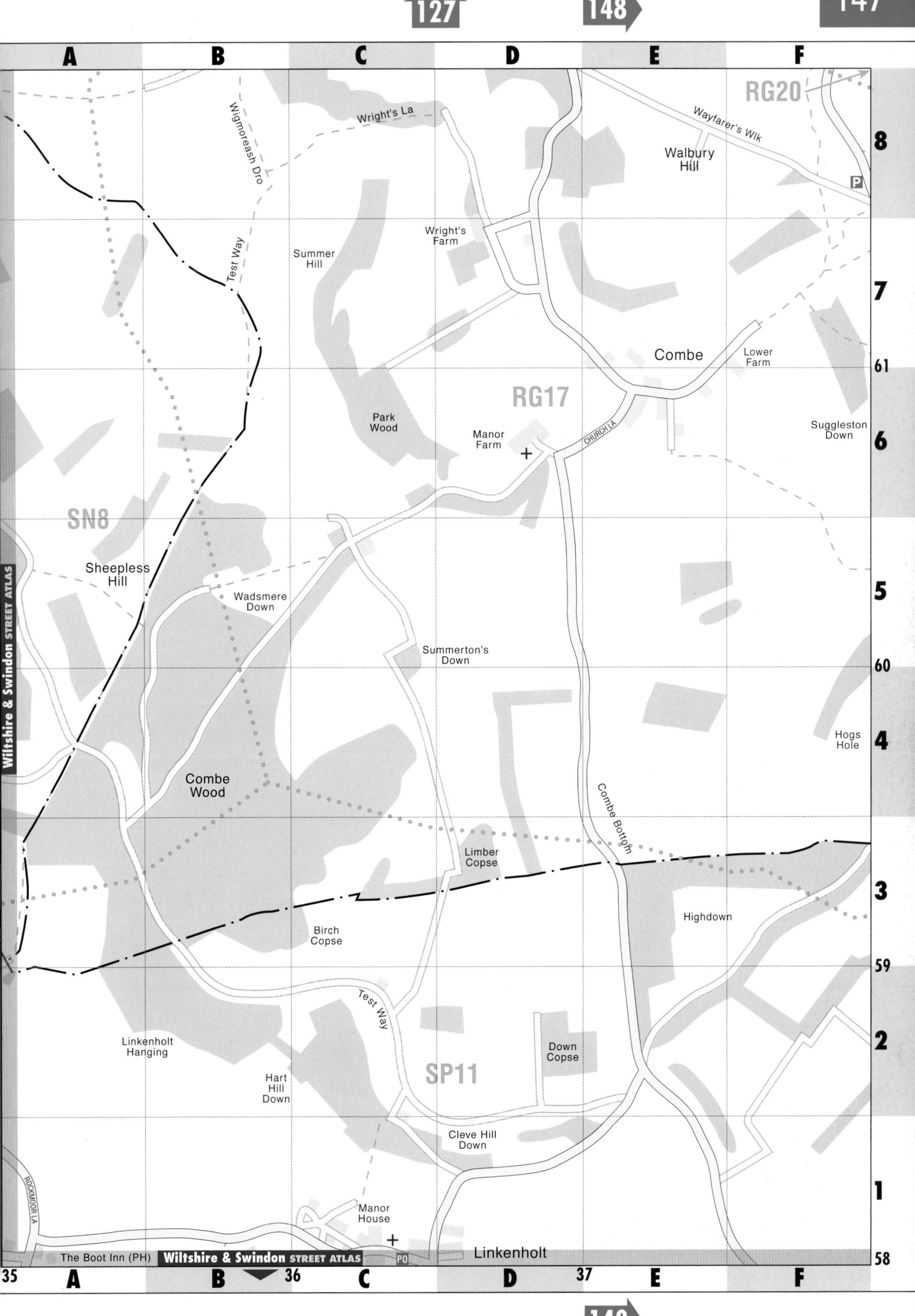
A
B
C
D
E
F
RG20
Wright's La
Wigmoreash Dro
Wayfarer's Wlk
Walbury Hill
8
Wright's Farm
Summer Hill
Test Way
7
Combe
Lower Farm
61
RG17
Park Wood
Manor Farm
CHURCH LA
Suggleston Down
6
SN8
Sheepless Hill
Wadsmere Down
5
Summerton's Down
60
Hogs Hole
4
Combe Wood
Combe Bottom
Limber Copse
3
Highdown
Birch Copse
59
Test Way
2
Linkenholt Hanging
Down Copse
Hart Hill Down
SP11
Cleve Hill Down
1
ROCKMOOR LA
Manor House
The Boot Inn (PH)
PO
Linkenholt
58
35
36
37

147
128

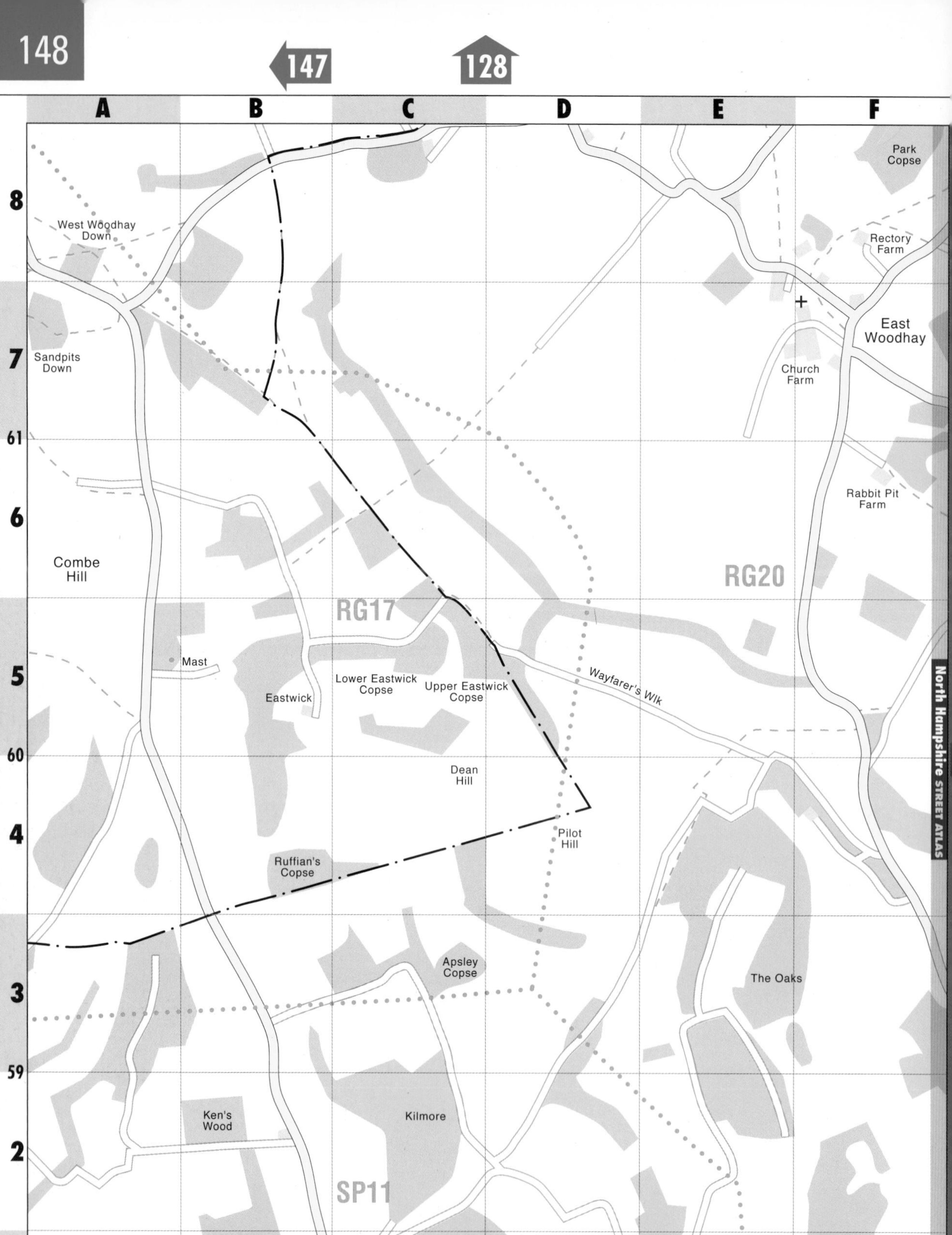
A
B
C
D
E
F
8
7
61
6
5
60
4
3
59
2
1
58
38
39
40
Park Copse
West Woodhay Down
Rectory Farm
East Woodhay
Sandpits Down
Church Farm
Rabbit Pit Farm
Combe Hill
RG20
RG17
Mast
Lower Eastwick Copse
Upper Eastwick Copse
Eastwick
Wayfarer's Wlk
Dean Hill
Pilot Hill
Ruffian's Copse
Apsley Copse
The Oaks
Ken's Wood
Kilmore
SP11
Roe Wood
Hitchen
Iron's Hill
ARTHUR'S LA
Faccombe
Faccombe Manor
Pump House
Curzon Street Farm
Robin's Croft Copse
Privet Copse
North Hampshire STREET ATLAS

147

142
150

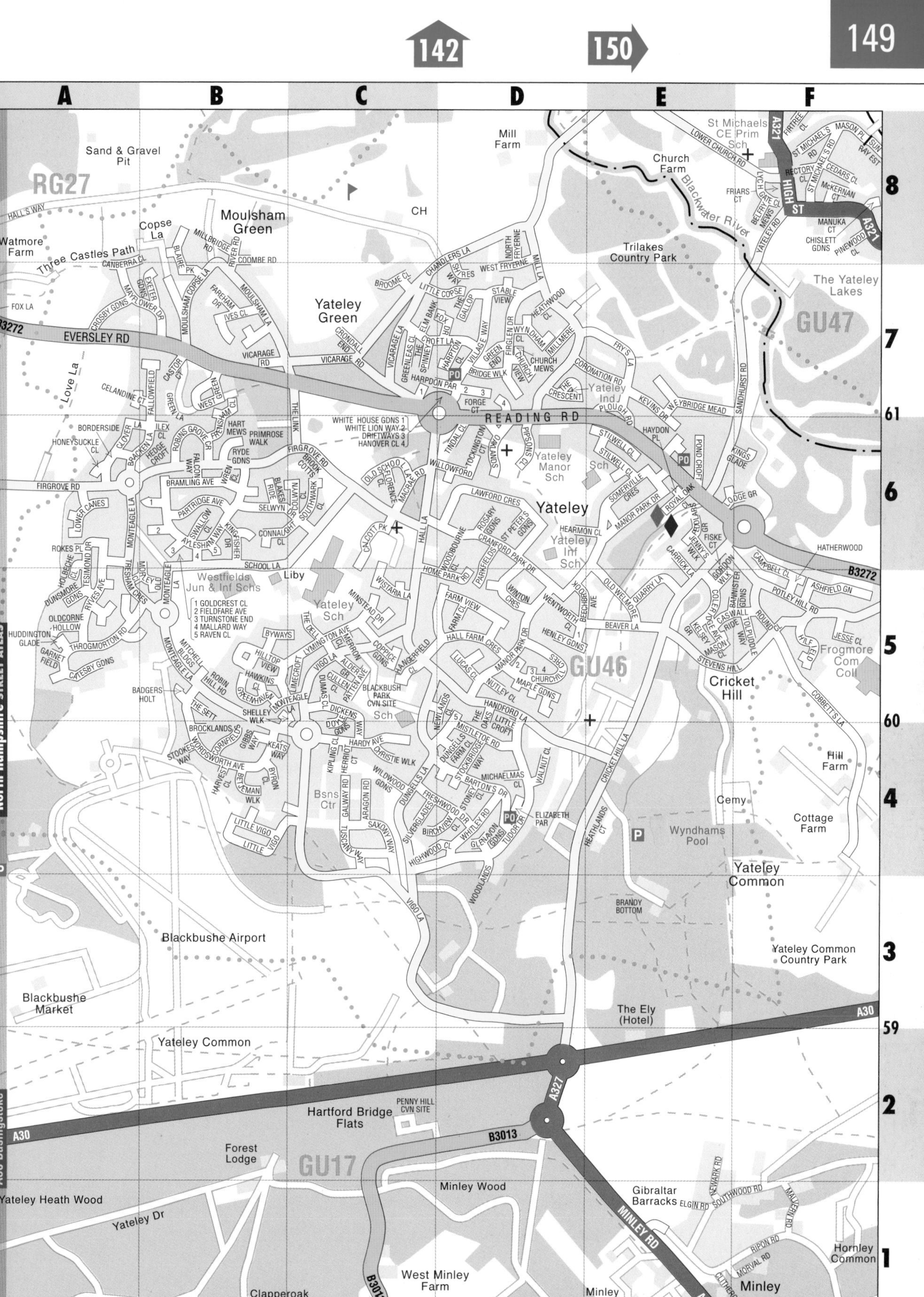

A B 81 C D 82 E F

D5
1 DENHAM DR
2 LOWER MOOR
3 BARNFIELD
4 HOLLY ACRE
5 BROCKENHURST DR

150

B7
1 GOTHIC CT
2 BROADWAY HO
3 FARRIER PL
4 SADLER CNR
149

143

D8
1 MULBERRY CL
2 MAY CL
3 SHRIVENHAM CL
4 CENTURION CL
5 CHAFFINCH CL
6 TARBAT CT
7 ROCKFIELD WAY
8 BALINTORE CT

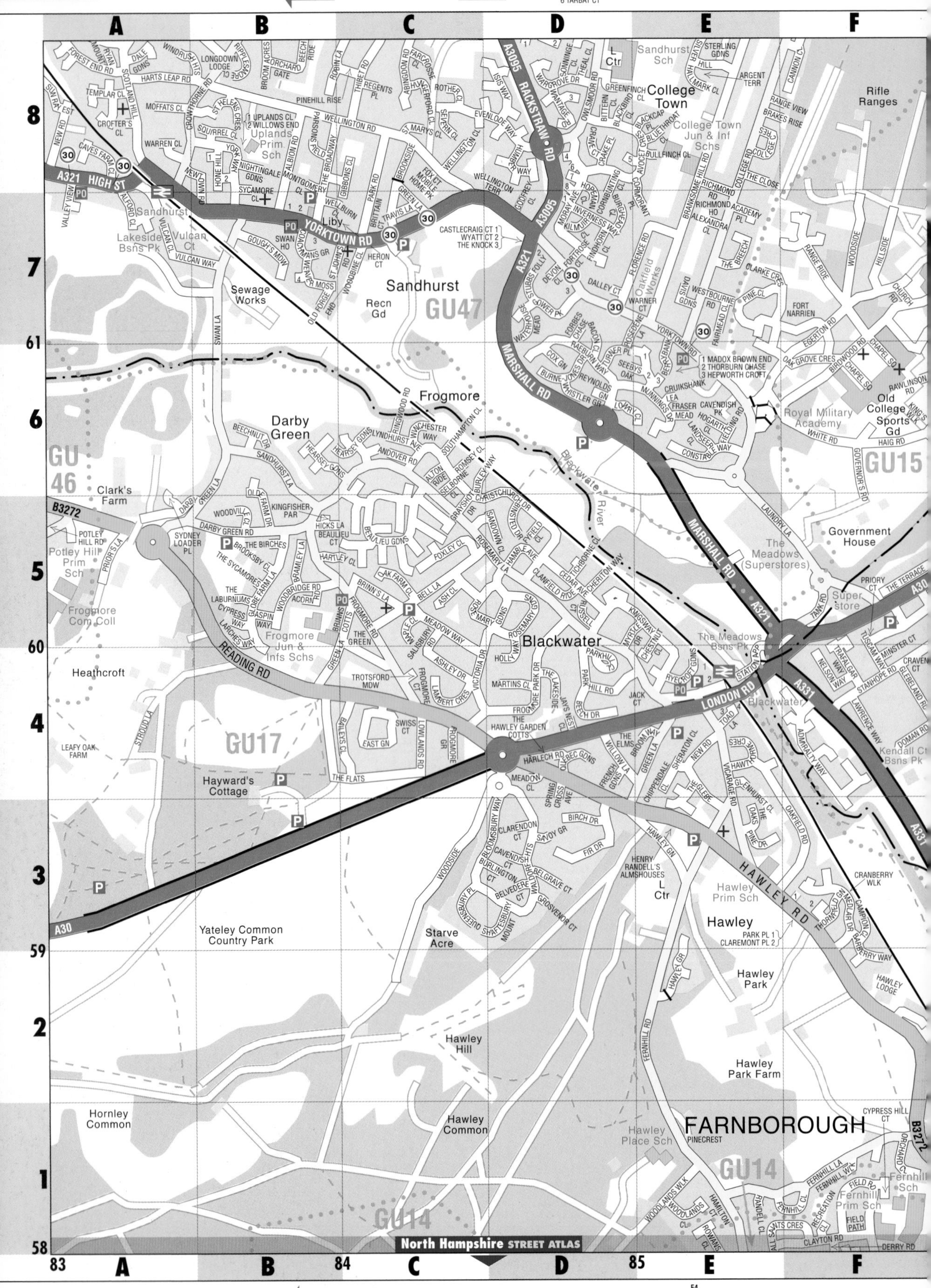

149

E4
1 White Hart Ind Est
2 WHITE HART HO
3 SWAN CT
4 MEADOW HO

144

152

D5
1 CAMBERLEY TOWERS
2 KATHERINE CT
3 STRATHMORE CT
4 BENTLEY CT

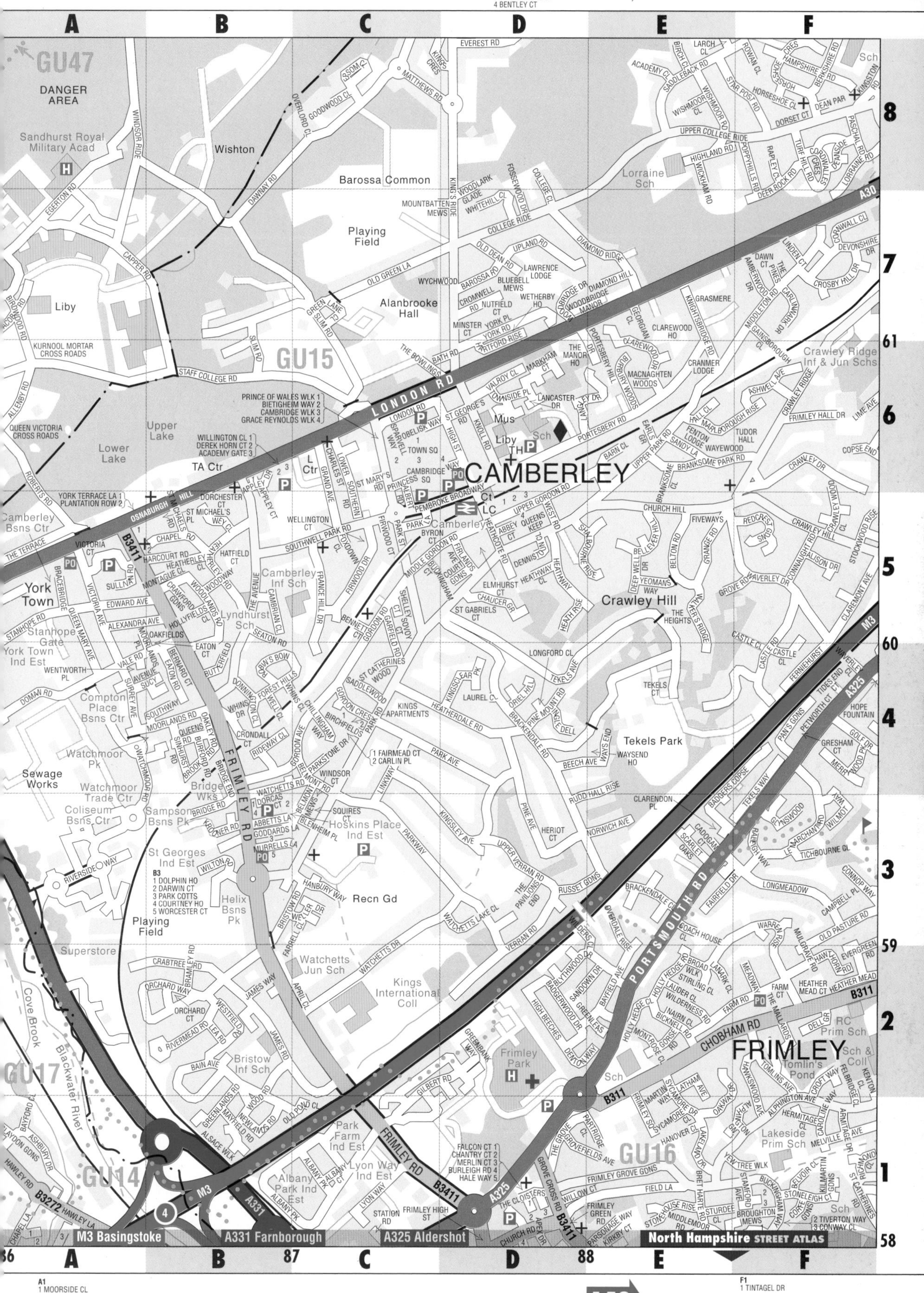

A1
1 MOORSIDE CL
2 MALLARD PL
3 BROOKSIDE PK

F1
1 TINTAGEL DR

152

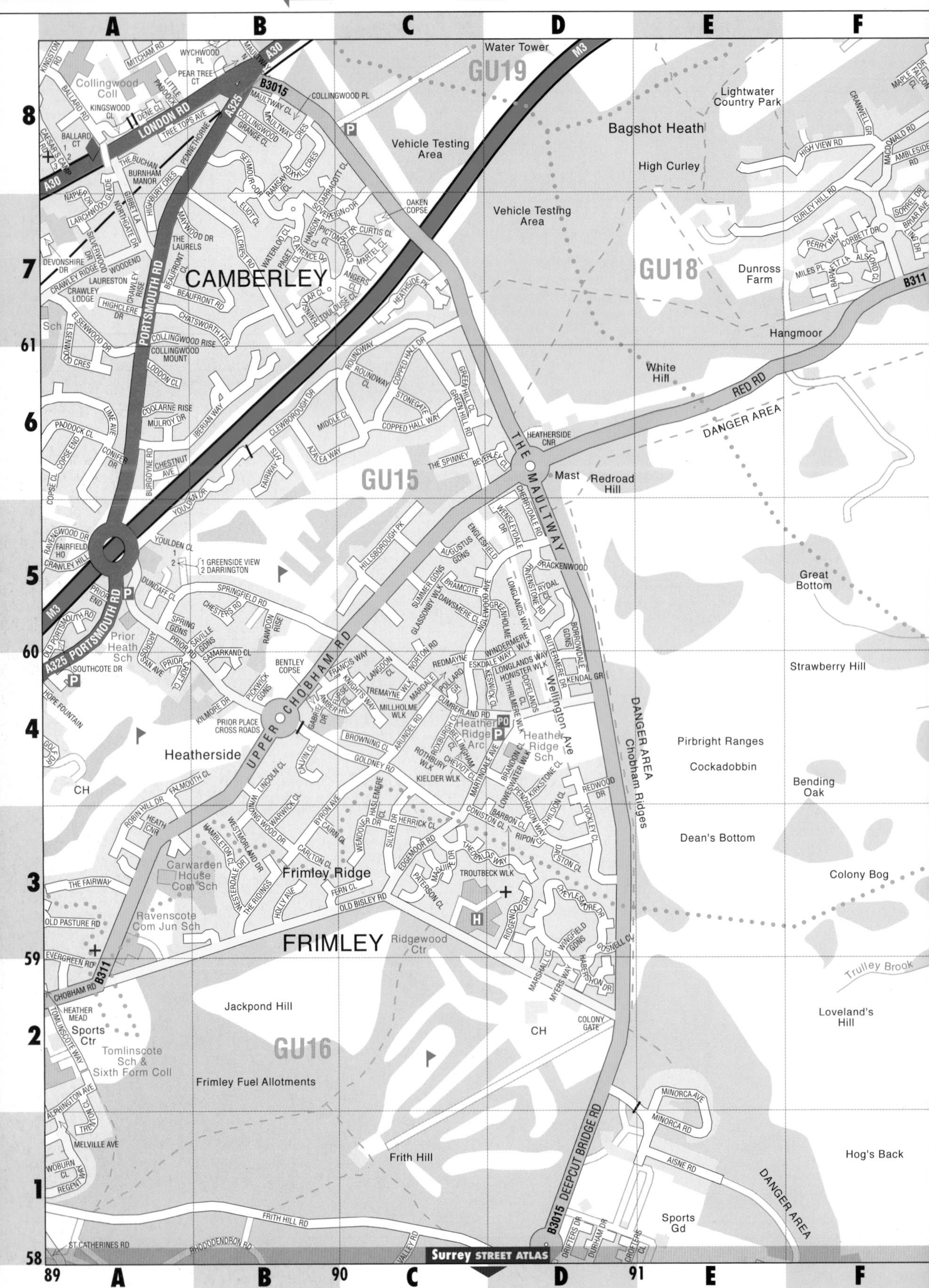
CAMBERLEY
FRIMLEY
Heatherside
Frimley Ridge
GU15
GU16
GU18
GU19
Bagshot Heath
Lightwater Country Park
High Curley
Vehicle Testing Area
Vehicle Testing Area
Water Tower
Dunross Farm
Hangmoor
White Hill
RED RD
DANGER AREA
HEATHERSIDE CNR
Mast
Redroad Hill
THE MAULTWAY
UPPER CHOBHAM RD
PORTSMOUTH RD
LONDON RD
Great Bottom
Strawberry Hill
Pirbright Ranges
Cockadobbin
Bending Oak
Dean's Bottom
Colony Bog
DANGER AREA Chobham Ridges
Trulley Brook
Loveland's Hill
Hog's Back
Sports Gd
DEEPCUT BRIDGE RD
MINORCA AVE
MINORCA RD
AISNE RD
Frith Hill
Frimley Fuel Allotments
Jackpond Hill
Ridgewood Ctr
COLONY GATE
Carwarden House Com Sch
Ravenscote Com Jun Sch
Tomlinscote Sch & Sixth Form Coll
Sports Ctr
Prior Heath Sch
Heather Ridge Arc
Heather Ridge Sch
Collingwood Coll
FRITH HILL RD
CHOBHAM RD
OLD BISLEY RD
Wellington Ave
1 GREENSIDE VIEW
2 DARRINGTON
PRIOR PLACE CROSS ROADS
BENTLEY COPSE
OAKEN COPSE

146

A
B
C
D
E
F
8
7
61
6
5
60
4
3
59
2
1
58
92
93
94
Lightwater
MAPLE DR
MACDONALD RD
FOX COVERT
RIDGEWAY CL
RYDAL PL
AMBLESIDE RD
OAKLEIGH
DEER LEAP
OSBORNE DR
BRIAR AVE
ORCHARD
BLUEBELL RISE
BROOMFIELD
SPRUCE DR
GORSE BANK
BLACKTHORN DR
BURDOCK CL
NORTHFIELD
THE
LOWFIELD CL
SHRUBLANDS DR
MYRTLE CL
LIGHTWATER MDW
KESWICK DR
DERWENT RD
LIGHTWATER RD
COLVILLE GDNS
RIVERSIDE AVE
WYCHELM RD
PARNHAM AVE
SPRINGFIELD
HERONSCOURT
GUILDFORD RD
MARSHWOOD RD
BLACKSTROUD LA W
SUNDEW CL
BLACKSTROUD LA E
BLACKSTROUD LANE
Turf Hill
A322
Brooklands Farm
Hookstone Farm
HOOKSTONE LA
Halebourne Farm
A319 Chertsey
A319
CH
WINDLESHAM RD
COLDHARBOUR LA
BAGSHOT RD
RED RD
The Folly
B311
A319
A322
COUNCIL COTTS
CHURCH RD
TRINGHAM COTTS
STREETS HEATH
FAIRFIELD LA
BENNER LA
DANGER AREA
GU18
New England
Sandpit Hill
Gordon's Sch
GUILDFORD RD
Grayspot Hill
Cuckoo Hill
TANGLEWOOD RIDE
STREETS HEATH
OLDACRE
MALTHOUSE LA
BOLDING HOUSE LA
HIGH ST
PO
MEADOW WAY
MEADOW COTTS
COMMONFIELDS
DANGER AREA
BIRCH LA
ASHLEY WAY
CUCKOO VALE
BROAD ST
ORCHARD CL
CUCKOO LA
REVESBY CL
BRENTMOOR RD
PH
WESTSIDE
FENNISCOMBE CT
OAKRIDGE
HOLLYBANK
West End
SEFTON CL
ROSEWOOD WAY
PRUNUS CL
RUBUS CL
KERRIA WAY
VIBURNUM CT
CAMELLIA CT
GARDNER DR
FIELD END
Westend Common
HOLLY RIDGE
BURNET CL
ABELIA CL
RUGOSA RD
BERGENIA CT
FUCHSIA WAY
DAMASK CL
ERICA CL
ACER DR
FELLOW GN
FELLOW GREEN RD
HOOK LA
BIRCH PLATT
ROUNCE LA
Pirbright Ranges
Donkey Town
Rounce Farm
FENNS LA
Fenns Farm
MAHONIA CL
Hagthorn Bog
Dog Hill
KINGS RD 1
SEARLWOOD CT 2
WILLOW GN 3
Trulley Brook
PRIEST LA
Lucas Green
GU24
Nurseries
Surrey STREET ATLAS
LUCAS GREEN RD
FORD RD
Strawberry Bottom
Brock Hill
THE TIMBER YD
Works
White Cott Farm
Lucas Green Farm
Hall
SCHOOL CL 1
CHURCH LA 2
GUILDFORD RD
Straight Oak
Peatmoor Pond
LUCAS GN
P
A322
Nursery
PO
GU15
Round Butt
Bayfield
SHAFTESBURY RD
ARETHUSA WAY
A322 Guildford
Bisley
COTTESLOE CL
Colony Bog
DANGER AREA
Furze Farm
Bullhousen Farm
MAINSTONE CL
SOUTH RD
DANGER AREA
HM Prison
Pirbright Common
Bisley Common
Miles Green
GU16
Bisley Ranges
QUEENS RD
Polledoak Slade
DANGER AREA
Chaseley
Mainstone Bottom
GU21
DANGER AREA
Hog Lees
Staffordlake
STAFFORD LAKE
Surrey STREET ATLAS

Index

Place name May be abbreviated on the map	**Church Rd** [6] Beckenham BR2.........**53** C6
Location number Present when a number indicates the place's position in a crowded area of mapping	
Locality, town or village Shown when more than one place has the same name	
Postcode district District for the indexed place	
Page and grid square Page number and grid reference for the standard mapping	

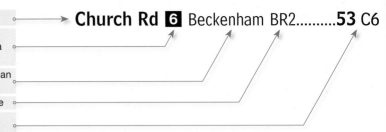

Cities, towns and villages are listed in CAPITAL LETTERS

Public and commercial buildings are highlighted in magenta **Places of interest** are highlighted in blue with a star★

Abbreviations used in the index

Acad	**Academy**	Comm	**Common**	Gd	**Ground**	L	**Leisure**	Prom	**Promenade**
App	**Approach**	Cott	**Cottage**	Gdn	**Garden**	La	**Lane**	Rd	**Road**
Arc	**Arcade**	Cres	**Crescent**	Gn	**Green**	Liby	**Library**	Recn	**Recreation**
Ave	**Avenue**	Cswy	**Causeway**	Gr	**Grove**	Mdw	**Meadow**	Ret	**Retail**
Bglw	**Bungalow**	Ct	**Court**	H	**Hall**	Meml	**Memorial**	Sh	**Shopping**
Bldg	**Building**	Ctr	**Centre**	Ho	**House**	Mkt	**Market**	Sq	**Square**
Bsns, Bus	**Business**	Ctry	**Country**	Hospl	**Hospital**	Mus	**Museum**	St	**Street**
Bvd	**Boulevard**	Cty	**County**	HQ	**Headquarters**	Orch	**Orchard**	Sta	**Station**
Cath	**Cathedral**	Dr	**Drive**	Hts	**Heights**	Pal	**Palace**	Terr	**Terrace**
Cir	**Circus**	Dro	**Drove**	Ind	**Industrial**	Par	**Parade**	TH	**Town Hall**
Cl	**Close**	Ed	**Education**	Inst	**Institute**	Pas	**Passage**	Univ	**University**
Cnr	**Corner**	Emb	**Embankment**	Int	**International**	Pk	**Park**	Wk, Wlk	**Walk**
Coll	**College**	Est	**Estate**	Intc	**Interchange**	Pl	**Place**	Wr	**Water**
Com	**Community**	Ex	**Exhibition**	Junc	**Junction**	Prec	**Precinct**	Yd	**Yard**

Index of towns, villages, streets, hospitals, industrial estates, railway stations, schools, shopping centres, universities and places of interest

Aba–ALD

A

Abattoirs Rd RG1 86 A8
Abberbury Cl RG14 104 E6
Abbetts La GU15 151 B3
Abbey Cl
Bracknell RG12 118 D4
Newbury RG14 131 A8
Slough SL1 41 E6
Wokingham RG40 116 C7
Abbey Cotts SL7 17 B4
Abbey Ct
Camberley GU15 151 D5
Chertsey KT16 124 B2
Laleham TW18 124 C5
Abbey Dr TW18 124 C5
Abbeyfields Pk KT16 124 C2
Abbey Gate SL6 41 A7
Abbey Gdns
Chertsey KT16 124 A3
Woolhampton RG7 108 D5
Abbey Gn KT16 124 A3
Abbey Jun Sch The RG1 86 C5
Abbey Lodge [6] TW18 96 F3
Abbey Mdws KT16 124 C2
Abbey Mead SL8 2 F5
Abbey Mews TW18 124 C5
Abbey Pk RG7 110 F3
Abbey Pl
Chertsey KT16 124 A6
Newell Green RG42 91 C3
Abbey Point [3] RG1 86 B7
Abbey Rd
Bourne End SL8 2 F5
Chertsey KT16 124 B2
Lower Halliford TW17 125 A1
Virginia Water GU25 122 D5
Abbey River Cotts KT16 124 C3
Abbey School The RG1 86 C6
Abbey Sq RG1 86 B7
Abbey St RG1 86 B7
Abbey Way SL7 18 D6
Abbey Wood SL5 121 A2
Abbot Cl TW18 97 D1
ABBOTSBROOK 2 F3
Abbotsbury RG12 117 F4
Abbotsbury Ct [3] RG30 85 B8
Abbotsbury Ho [4] RG2 113 C8
Abbots Dr GU25 122 C5
Abbots Mead OX10 14 A8
Abbotsmead Pl RG4 59 A2
Abbots Rd
Burghfield Common RG7 110 F2
Newbury RG14 105 A1
Abbots Way KT16 123 F2
Abbot's Wlk
Reading RG1 86 B8
Windsor SL4 66 E5
Abbottsleigh Gdns RG4 59 D4
Abbotts Way SL1 41 D6
Abelia Cl GU24 153 E6
Abell Gdns SL6 19 B1
Aberaman RG4 58 F6
Aberdeen Ave SL1 42 A6
Aberdeen Lodge [10] SL4 67 C5
Aberford Cl RG30 85 C7
Abex Rd RG14 105 C3
Abingdon Cl RG12 118 E4
Abingdon Dr RG4 59 C6
Abingdon Rd
East Ilsley RG20 30 E7
Sandhurst GU47 143 C1
Abingdon Wlk SL6 19 E3
Abington SL3 69 D6
Abney Court Dr SL8 3 A2
Abrahams Rd RG9 15 C3
Acacia RG9 15 D2
Acacia Ave
Littleton TW17 125 A4
Sandhurst GU47 143 D1
Wraysbury TW19 68 E3
Acacia Ct RG12 118 B6
Acacia Mews UB7 70 D8
Acacia Rd
Reading RG1 86 C6
Staines TW18 97 B3
Academy Cl GU15 151 E8
Academy Gate GU15 151 B6
Academy Pl GU47 150 E7
Accommodation La UB7 70 C8
Acer Cl RG42 119 A8
Acer Dr GU24 153 F6
Ackrells Mead GU47 142 F1
Acorn Cl SL3 44 B1
Acorn Cotts SN8 126 D3
Acorn Dr
Thatcham RG18 106 D5
Wokingham RG40 116 C7
Acorn Gdns RG7 110 E2
Acorn Gr UB3 71 F7
Acorn Rd GU17 150 B5
Acorn Wlk RG31 84 C5
Acre Bsns Pk RG2 113 B8
Acre Pas SL4 67 D6
Acre Rd RG2 113 A8
Acre The SL7 1 F2
ACS Egham Int Sch
TW20 122 C7
Action Ct TW15 125 C8
Adam Cl
Slough SL1 42 A5
Tadley RG26 134 E1
Adam Ct RG9 15 E2
Adams Way RG6 86 F2
Addington Cl SL4 67 A4
Addington Ho RG1 86 E6
Addington Rd RG1 86 D6
Addington Specl Sch RG5 87 F6
Addiscombe Chase RG31 57 B3
Addiscombe Rd RG45 143 C4
Addison Cl SL0 44 E6
Addison Ct SL6 20 B1
Addison Rd RG1 59 A1
Adelaide Cl SL1 42 A4
Adelaide Rd
Reading RG6 87 A6
Staines TW15 97 D3
Windsor SL4 67 F6
Adelaide Sq SL4 67 D5
Adelphi Gdns SL1 42 E4
Adey's Cl RG14 105 B1
Adkins Rd RG10 62 E7
Admiral Kapple Ct SL5 92 E1
Admirals Ct RG2 86 A5
Admiralty Way GU15 150 F4
Admoor La RG7 82 C1
Adrians Wlk SL2 42 F5
Adwell Dr RG6 87 D1
Adwell Sq RG9 15 D2
Adwood Ct RG19 106 E3
Aerial Bsns Pk RG17 45 E3
Agar Cres RG42 91 B1
Agars Pl SL3 68 A8
Agate Cl RG41 115 E7
Aggisters La RG41 115 C3
Agincourt SL5 120 C6
Agincourt Cl RG41 115 E6
Agricola Way RG19 106 F2
Agua Ho KT16 124 C2
Ainsdale Cres RG30 85 A4
Aintree RG17 25 B2
Aintree Cl
Newbury RG14 105 C1
Poyle SL3 69 E6
Air Forces Meml★ TW20 95 D4
Airport Gate Bsns Ctr
UB7 71 A7
Airport Way TW19 70 A3
Aisne Rd GU16 152 E1
Ajax Ave SL1 42 B6
Alandale Cl RG2 113 D8
Alan Pl RG30 85 A5
Alan Way SL3 43 E7
Alastair Nicholas Ct [4]
RG1 86 A8
Albain Cres TW15 97 E6
Albany Ct GU16 151 C1
Albany Gdns RG4 59 A6
Albany Park Dr RG41 88 A3
Albany Park Ind Est
GU15 151 C1
Albany Pk
Frimley GU15 151 C1
Poyle SL3 69 D7
Albany Pl TW20 96 B4
Albany Rd
Old Windsor SL4 68 A2
Reading RG30 85 D7
Windsor SL4 67 D5
Alben Rd RG42 90 C3
Albert Ave KT16 124 A6
Albert Cl [3] SL1 42 F3
Albert Dr [1] TW18 97 A3
Albert Illsley Cl RG31 84 D8
Albert Pl SL4 42 A1
Albert Rd
Ashford TW15 97 F3
Bagshot GU19 145 E1
Bracknell RG42 118 B8
Camberley GU15 151 C5
Caversham RG4 58 F4
Crowthorne RG45 143 B5
Englefield Green TW20 95 D2
Henley-on-T RG9 15 E1
[1] Newbury RG14 105 A3
Windsor SL4 67 E3
Wokingham RG40 116 B5
Albert St
Maidenhead SL6 39 F7
Slough SL1 42 F3
Windsor SL4 67 B6
Albert Wlk RG45 143 B5
Albion Cl SL2 43 A5
Albion Cotts SL6 19 C7
Albion Pl [2] SL4 67 A5
Albion Rd GU47 150 B8
Albury Cl RG30 58 C1
Albury Ct TW15 98 D2
Albury Gdns RG31 84 E3
Albury Way RG19 131 F4
Alcot Cl RG45 143 B4
Aldborough Spur SL1 42 E7
Aldbourne Ave RG6 87 A4
Aldbourne Cl [1] RG17 100 D5
Aldbourne Rd SL1 41 B8
Aldeburgh Cl RG4 59 C8
Aldebury Rd SL6 19 F2
Aldenham Cl RG4 59 C6
Aldenham Terr RG12 118 C3
Alden View SL4 66 D6
Alderbourne SL5 120 B6
Alderbourne La SL3 23 E8
Alder Bridge Sch RG7 109 C3
Alderbrook Cl RG45 142 E4
Alderbury Rd SL3 43 F4
Alderbury Rd W SL3 43 F4
Alder Cl
Englefield Green TW20 95 E3
Lower Earley RG6 87 D1
Newbury RG14 105 D4
Slough SL1 41 F5
Alder Ct RG12 118 B6
Alder Dr RG31 84 C6
Alderfield Cl RG7 83 F4
Alder Glade RG7 110 F3
Alder Gr GU46 149 C5
Alderley Cl RG5 60 F1
Alderman Willey Cl
RG41 116 B6
ALDERMASTON 135 A7
Aldermaston CE Prim Sch
RG7 134 F7
Aldermaston Rd RG26 135 A2
ALDERMASTON SOKE 135 F3
Aldermaston Sta RG7 109 C3
ALDERMASTON
WHARF 109 D3
Alder Mews RG41 115 B8
Alderney Ct [16] RG1 86 D7
Alderney Gdns RG41 88 D2
Alderside Wlk TW20 95 E3
Alders The RG18 106 D4
Aldin Ave N SL1 43 A4
Aldin Ave S SL1 43 A4
Aldous Ho [1] TW18 96 E4
Aldridge Pk RG42 92 B2
Aldridge Rd SL2 22 A1
Aldryngton Prim Sch RG6 87 B4
Aldwick Dr SL6 39 D6
ALDWORTH 32 F3

Aldworth Cl
Bracknell RG12 . . . 118 A5
Reading RG30 . . . 85 C5
Aldworth Gdns RG45 . . . 143 A5
Aldworth Rd
Compton RG20 . . . 31 F4
Upper Basildon RG8 . . . 55 A5
Aldwych Cotts RG14 . . . 104 F6
Aldwyn Pl TW20 . . . 95 B2
Alexander Ct
9 Newbury RG14 . . . 105 B2
12 Reading RG1 . . . 85 F7
Alexander Fst Sch SL4 . . . 66 C4
Alexander Rd
Egham TW20 . . . 96 C3
Thatcham RG19 . . . 106 E2
Alexander Wlk RG12 . . . 118 B4
Alexandra Ave GU15 . . . 151 A5
Alexandra Cl
Ashford TW15 . . . 98 D1
Sandhurst GU47 . . . 150 E7
Staines TW18 . . . 97 D2
Alexandra Ct
Ashford TW15 . . . 98 D2
2 Windsor SL4 . . . 67 D5
Wokingham RG40 . . . 116 C5
Alexandra Ho
Ascot SL5 . . . 120 B6
11 Reading RG1 . . . 86 C7
Alexandra Rd
Ashford TW15 . . . 98 E2
Englefield Green TW20 . . . 95 C2
Maidenhead SL6 . . . 39 D8
Reading RG1 . . . 86 D6
Slough SL1 . . . 42 D3
Windsor SL4 . . . 67 D5
Alford Cl
Reading RG30 . . . 84 D8
Sandhurst GU47 . . . 150 A7
Alfred Ct 3 SL8 . . . 3 B3
Alfred Davis Ct SL7 . . . 1 D3
Alfred Sutton Prim Sch
RG1 . . . 86 F6
Alice Gough Memorial
Homes RG12 . . . 118 B6
Alice Ho TW18 . . . 97 A2
Alice La SL1 . . . 21 B1
Alison Cl RG7 . . . 110 F1
Alison Dr GU15 . . . 151 F5
Allanson Rd SL7 . . . 1 F3
Allcot Cl TW14 . . . 98 F7
Allcroft Rd RG1 . . . 86 C5
Allenby Rd
Maidenhead SL6 . . . 39 B7
Sandhurst GU15 . . . 151 A6
Allendale Cl GU47 . . . 143 A2
Allendale Rd RG6 . . . 87 B3
Allerds Rd SL2 . . . 22 A4
Alleyns La SL6 . . . 19 D8
Allfrey Gr RG7 . . . 113 A1
All Hallows Rd RG4 . . . 59 D3
Allhusen Gdns SL3 . . . 23 E8
Alliance Ct TW15 . . . 98 C4
Allington Ave TW17 . . . 125 E6
Allington Ct SL2 . . . 42 F6
Allison Ct 2 RG1 . . . 85 F7
Allison Gdns RG8 . . . 57 C5
Allison Ho RG9 . . . 35 E8
Allkins Ct SL4 . . . 67 D5
Allnatt Ave RG41 . . . 88 C1
Allonby Cl RG6 . . . 87 D2
All Saints Ave SL6 . . . 39 D7
All Saints CE Inf Sch RG1 . 85 E7
All Saints CE Jun Sch SL6 39 C6
All Saints' CE Prim Sch
RG40 . . . 116 D7
All Saints Cl RG40 . . . 116 C7
All Saints Cres GU14 . . . 150 E1
All Saints Ct RG1 . . . 85 E6
All Saints Gdns 7 RG1 . . . 85 E7
All Saints Rd GU18 . . . 146 C1
All Saints Rise RG42 . . . 91 E1
Allsmoor La RG12 . . . 118 F6
All Souls Cotts SL3 . . . 43 E8
All Souls' Rd SL5 . . . 120 A5
Allyn Cl TW18 . . . 96 F2
Alma Ct
Burnham SL1 . . . 21 C2
Eton SL4 . . . 41 F2
Wokingham RG41 . . . 116 A5
Alma Rd
Eton SL4 . . . 41 F2
Windsor SL4 . . . 67 C5
Alma St RG30 . . . 85 C8
Almners Rd
Chertsey KT16 . . . 123 C2
Lyne KT16 . . . 123 B1
Almond Ave RG14 . . . 105 A5
Almond Cl
Charlton TW17 . . . 125 C7
Englefield Green TW20 . . . 95 B2
Windsor SL4 . . . 67 B5
Wokingham RG41 . . . 115 C4
Almond Dr
Caversham RG4 . . . 59 F4
Chieveley RG20 . . . 51 C5
Thatcham RG18 . . . 106 D4
Almond Rd SL1 . . . 21 C2
Almons Way SL2 . . . 43 B8
Almshouses
Hurst RG10 . . . 88 E6
Reading RG1 . . . 86 A7
Slough SL3 . . . 43 E4
Sunbury TW16 . . . 125 F8
Twyford RG10 . . . 61 D5
Almshouses The SL4 . . . 67 D7
Almswood Rd RG26 . . . 135 A2
Alpha Ho 4 RG1 . . . 86 C6
Alpha St N 6 SL1 . . . 43 A4
Alpha St S SL1 . . . 42 F3
Alpha Way TW20 . . . 123 C8
Alphington Ave GU16 . . . 151 F1
Alphington Gn GU16 . . . 151 F1
Alphington Rd RG2 . . . 113 B8
Alpine Cl
Ascot SL5 . . . 120 D3
Maidenhead SL6 . . . 40 A6
Alpine St RG1 . . . 86 B6
Alsace Wlk GU15 . . . 151 B1
Alsford Cl GU18 . . . 152 F7
Alston Gdns SL6 . . . 39 E7
Alston Mews RG19 . . . 106 C2
Alston Wlk RG4 . . . 59 D2
ALTMORE . . . 38 E4
Altmore SL6 . . . 38 E4
Altona Way SL1 . . . 42 B7
Alton Ct TW18 . . . 123 E8
Alton Ride GU17 . . . 150 C6
Altwood Bailey SL6 . . . 39 B5
Altwood CE Sec Sch SL6 . 39 B5
Altwood Cl
Maidenhead SL6 . . . 39 B5
Slough SL1 . . . 41 E8
Altwood Dr SL6 . . . 39 B5
Altwood Rd SL6 . . . 39 B5
Alvista Ave SL6 . . . 41 B7
Alwyn Inf Sch SL6 . . . 39 C8
Alwyn Rd SL6 . . . 39 B8
Alwyns Cl KT16 . . . 124 A3
Alwyns La KT16 . . . 124 A3
Alyson Ct 2 SL6 . . . 19 F1
Amanda Ct
Ashford TW15 . . . 97 F6
Slough SL3 . . . 43 D3
Ambarrow Cres GU47 . . . 142 F1
Ambarrow La GU47 . . . 142 E2
Ambassador RG12 . . . 117 F4
Ambassador The SL5 . . . 121 B2
Amber Cl RG6 . . . 87 C4
Amber Ct 13 TW18 . . . 96 F3
Amber Hill GU15 . . . 152 B4
Amberley Cl RG14 . . . 104 F4
Amberley Ct SL6 . . . 20 C3
Amberley Dr RG10 . . . 61 D6
Amberley Gdns RG41 . . . 115 E8
Amberley Pl 7 SL4 . . . 67 D6
Amberley Rd SL2 . . . 41 E8
Amberwood Dr GU15 . . . 151 F7
Amblecote Rd RG30 . . . 85 B7
Ambleside RG45 . . . 143 C4
Ambleside Cl RG5 . . . 87 E7
Ambleside Dr TW14 . . . 98 F7
Ambleside Rd GU18 . . . 153 B8
Ambleside Way TW20 . . . 96 B1
Ambrook Rd RG2 . . . 113 B8
Ambrose Pl RG1 . . . 85 F7
Ambury Rd RG8 . . . 32 E4
AMEN CORNER . . . 117 D7
Amen Corner Bsns Pk
RG12 . . . 117 D7
Amerden Cl SL6 . . . 40 D7
Amerden La SL6 . . . 40 D7
Amerden Priory Cvn Pk
SL6 . . . 40 E4
Amerden Way SL1 . . . 42 A4
American Magna Carta
Meml* TW20 . . . 95 D6
Amersham Rd RG4 . . . 59 D2
Amethyst Cl RG41 . . . 115 D7
Amethyst La RG30 . . . 85 C6
Amherst Rd RG6 . . . 87 A6
Amhurst Mews 3 RG6 . . . 87 A6
Amity Rd RG1 . . . 86 E7
Amity St RG1 . . . 86 E8
Ammanford RG4 . . . 58 F5
Amners Farm RG30 . . . 111 F7
Amners Farm Rd RG30 . . . 112 A7
Ampere Rd RG14 . . . 105 B3
Anarth Ct KT13 . . . 125 E1
Ancaster Dr SL5 . . . 119 E8
Ancastle Gn RG9 . . . 15 D2
Anchor Ct SL6 . . . 19 F7
Anchorite Cl RG10 . . . 61 D5
Andermans SL4 . . . 66 D6
Anders Cnr RG42 . . . 117 F8
Anderson Ave RG6 . . . 87 A6
Anderson Cres RG2 . . . 114 E2
Anderson Dr TW15 . . . 98 C4
Anderson Gdns RG26 . . . 135 B1
Anderson Pl GU19 . . . 145 E4
Andover Cl
East Bedfont TW14 . . . 98 F7
Reading RG31 . . . 57 D1
Andover Ct TW19 . . . 97 D8
Andover Dro RG20 . . . 130 B4
Andover Rd
Blackwater GU17 . . . 150 C6
Newbury RG14 . . . 130 D6
Andrew Cl RG40 . . . 116 E5
Andrews Cl RG7 . . . 83 E3
Andrews Rd RG6 . . . 87 B3
Andrews Reach SL8 . . . 3 A2
Andrews Way SL7 . . . 1 D8
Angel Ct
Newbury RG14 . . . 104 F4
Theale RG7 . . . 83 E3
Angel Mead RG7 . . . 108 C2
Angel Pl RG42 . . . 90 C2
Angers Cl GU15 . . . 152 C7
Angle Field Rd RG4 . . . 59 C3
Anglers Way RG1 . . . 86 D7
Anglesey Cl TW15 . . . 98 A5
Angus Cl
Reading RG31 . . . 84 E4
Winnersh RG41 . . . 88 B2
Annadale RG18 . . . 79 C1
Anne Cl SL6 . . . 19 E2
Anneforde Pl RG42 . . . 91 A1
Anners Cl TW20 . . . 123 C6
Annesley Gdns RG41 . . . 88 C2
Annett Cl TW17 . . . 125 E5
Annie Brookes Cl TW18 . . 96 D5
Anscult Rd SL2 . . . 22 A2
Ansell Rd GU16 . . . 151 E1
Anslow Pl SL1 . . . 41 C8
Anson Cres RG2 . . . 113 D8
Anson Ct TW19 . . . 97 E8
Anson Wlk RG2 . . . 113 D8
Anstey Pl RG7 . . . 111 A3
Anstey Rd 16 RG1 . . . 85 F7
Anston Cl RG6 . . . 114 A8
Antares Cl RG41 . . . 115 F6
Anthian Cl RG5 . . . 88 B8
Anthony Wall RG42 . . . 118 F8
Anthony Way SL1 . . . 41 D6
Antrim Rd RG5 . . . 87 D6
Anvil Cl RG7 . . . 113 A1
Anvil Ct
4 Slough SL3 . . . 44 A2
Thatcham RG18 . . . 106 D3
Wokingham RG40 . . . 116 C5
ANVILLES . . . 126 E8
Apex Dr GU16 . . . 151 D1
Aphelion Way RG2 . . . 113 E7
Aplin Way GU18 . . . 146 A1
Apollo Ho RG7 . . . 134 E2
Appelford Cl RG19 . . . 106 D2
Appleby End RG30 . . . 85 B7
Appleby Gdns TW14 . . . 98 F7
Apple Cl
Purley on T RG31 . . . 57 B4
Wokingham RG41 . . . 115 F5
Applecroft SL6 . . . 39 C3
Appledore RG12 . . . 117 F3
Appleford Rd RG30 . . . 85 A5
Appleshaw Ct 1 RG31 . . . 84 D8
Appleton Ho 26 RG1 . . . 86 D7
Apple Tree Cl RG14 . . . 130 E7
Appletree La
Shinfield RG7 . . . 113 B2
Slough SL3 . . . 43 C3
Appletree Pl 4 RG42 . . . 118 A8
Apple Tree Way GU47 . . . 143 D1
Appley Ct GU15 . . . 151 B6
Appley Dr GU15 . . . 151 B6
Approach Rd
Ashford TW15 . . . 98 C2
Taplow SL6 . . . 40 E7
April Cl GU15 . . . 151 C2
Apsey Ct RG42 . . . 90 E1
Apsley Cotts SL6 . . . 19 E7
Apsley Ho SL1 . . . 43 A4
Aquila Cl RG41 . . . 115 E6
Araby Cnr TW17 . . . 125 C3
Aragon Cl TW16 . . . 98 F1
Aragon Ct
Bracknell RG12 . . . 118 C5
Maidenhead SL6 . . . 39 E5
Aragon Rd GU46 . . . 149 C4
Arbery Way RG2 . . . 140 E8
ARBORFIELD . . . 114 C4
Arborfield Cl SL1 . . . 42 E3
ARBORFIELD CROSS . . . 114 F2
ARBORFIELD
GARRISON . . . 114 F1
Arborfield Grange RG2 . . 114 C4
Arborfield, Newland &
Barkham CE Jun Sch
RG2 . . . 114 F2
Arborfield Rd RG2 . . . 113 F4
Arbor La RG41 . . . 88 B3
Arbor Mdws RG41 . . . 88 B3
Arbour Cl RG1 . . . 85 F5
Arbour Ho 2 RG14 . . . 105 D4
Arbour Vale Sch SL2 . . . 22 B2
Arcade Mews 10 RG14 . . . 105 A3
Arcade The
Goring RG8 . . . 34 C6
9 Newbury RG14 . . . 105 A3
1 Reading RG1 . . . 86 B7
Archangel Way RG18 . . . 106 F4
Archer Cl SL6 . . . 39 D8
Archway Rd RG4 . . . 59 A2
Arden Cl RG12 . . . 119 A7
Ardingly RG12 . . . 118 A4
Ardler Rd RG4 . . . 59 C2
Ardrossan Ave GU15 . . . 152 A5
Ardrossan Cl SL2 . . . 22 C1
Ardwell Cl RG45 . . . 142 E5
Arenal Dr RG45 . . . 143 C3
Arena The RG12 . . . 118 A7
Arethusa Way GU24 . . . 153 F3
Argent Cl TW20 . . . 96 C2
Argent Terr GU47 . . . 150 E8
Argonaut Pk SL3 . . . 69 F6
Argosy Gdns TW18 . . . 96 F2
Argosy La TW19 . . . 97 D8
Argyle Rd
Newbury RG14 . . . 104 F2
Reading RG1 . . . 85 E7
Argyle St RG1 . . . 85 E7
Argyll Ave SL1 . . . 42 A6
Aries Ho HP10 . . . 3 A8
Arista Ct TW20 . . . 95 D2
Arkle Ave RG19 . . . 105 F3
Arkley Ct SL6 . . . 40 C1
Ark Sch The RG7 . . . 109 F1
Arkwright Dr RG42 . . . 117 D7
Arkwright Rd
Poyle SL3 . . . 69 E5
Reading RG2 . . . 86 B3
Arlington Bsns Pk
Bracknell RG12 . . . 118 B7
Theale RG7 . . . 83 F3
Arlington Cl
Bracknell RG42 . . . 118 A8
Maidenhead SL6 . . . 39 A8
Arlington Grange RG18 . . . 78 B3
Arlington La RG14 . . . 77 F3
Arlington Rd TW15 . . . 97 F3
Arlington Sq RG12 . . . 118 A7
Armadale Ct RG30 . . . 85 D6
Armitage Ct SL5 . . . 120 C3
Armitage Dr GU16 . . . 151 F1
Armour Hill RG31 . . . 57 D1
Armour Lodge RG31 . . . 57 D1
Armour Rd RG31 . . . 57 D1
Armour Wlk RG31 . . . 57 D1
Armstrong Ho SL2 . . . 43 C7
Armstrong Rd TW20 . . . 95 C2
Armstrong Way RG5 . . . 88 A7
Arncliffe RG12 . . . 118 A4
Arndale Way TW20 . . . 96 A3
Arne Cl RG41 . . . 88 A3
Arnett Ave RG40 . . . 141 F7
Arnewood Ave RG26 . . . 135 D1
Arnhem Rd RG14 . . . 105 B3
Arnold Rd TW18 . . . 97 C1
Arnside Cl RG10 . . . 61 D7
Arnwood RG41 . . . 115 E8
Arrowhead Rd RG7 . . . 83 F2
Arrowsmith Way RG19 . . 106 E1
Artemis Ho RG14 . . . 105 B4
Arthur Cl GU19 . . . 145 E1
Arthur Pl RG1 . . . 86 D7
Arthur Rd
Newbury RG14 . . . 104 E2
Slough SL1 . . . 42 D4
Windsor SL4 . . . 67 C6
Wokingham RG41 . . . 116 A6
Arthur's La SP11 . . . 148 C1
Arthurstone Birches
RG42 . . . 90 D3
Artillery Dr RG19 . . . 106 E1
Artillery Mews RG30 . . . 85 D6
Arun Cl RG41 . . . 88 B1
Arun Ct RG30 . . . 85 C6
Arundel Cl SL6 . . . 39 A8
Arundel Ct SL3 . . . 43 D2
Arundel Rd
Frimley GU15 . . . 152 C4
Woodley RG5 . . . 87 E7
Asantewa Ho 7 RG1 . . . 86 A6
ASCOT . . . 120 A6
Ascot Cl RG14 . . . 131 C8
Ascot Heath CE Jun Sch
SL5 . . . 92 E1
Ascot Heath Inf Sch SL5 . . 92 E1
Ascot Ho 7 TW20 . . . 96 A3
Ascot Pl SL5 . . . 119 F7
Ascot Race Course SL5 . . 119 F6
Ascot Rd
East Bedfont TW14 . . . 98 B6
Holyport SL6 . . . 65 A8
Newell Green RG42 . . . 91 E8
Ascot Sta SL5 . . . 120 A5
Ascott Way RG14 . . . 105 D4
Ascot Twrs SL5 . . . 119 F7
Ascot Wood SL5 . . . 120 A6
ASHAMPSTEAD . . . 54 A6
Ashampstead Rd
Bradfield RG7 . . . 82 B7
Reading RG30 . . . 85 B4
Upper Basildon RG8 . . . 55 A5
Ash Apartments UB3 . . . 71 D7
Ashbourne RG12 . . . 117 F3
Ashbourne Ct RG30 . . . 85 C7
Ashbourne Gr SL6 . . . 39 C3
Ashbourne Ho 5 SL1 . . . 42 E4
Ashbourne Way RG19 . . . 106 B3
Ashbrook Mews OX11 . . . 11 F8
Ashbrook Rd SL4 . . . 95 B8
Ashburton Rd RG2 . . . 86 C2
Ashbury Dr
Farnborough GU17 . . . 151 A1
Reading RG31 . . . 84 C7
Ashby Ct RG2 . . . 113 B7
Ashby Way UB7 . . . 71 A7
Ash Cl
Blackwater GU17 . . . 150 C5
Brightwalton RG20 . . . 28 D3
Slough SL3 . . . 44 B3
Ashcombe Cl TW15 . . . 97 E5
Ash Copse RG4 . . . 59 F7
Ash Cres RG19 . . . 133 A5
Ashcroft Cl RG4 . . . 58 E5
Ashcroft Ct SL1 . . . 21 B3
Ashcroft Rd SL6 . . . 39 C8
Ash Ct
Ashford TW15 . . . 98 C3
Caversham RG4 . . . 59 B3
11 Newbury RG14 . . . 105 A4
Ashdale Cl TW15 . . . 97 E6
Ashdale Pk RG40 . . . 142 D6
Ashdene Cl TW15 . . . 98 C1
Ashdene Gdns RG30 . . . 85 D6
Ashdene Ho TW20 . . . 95 C2
Ashdown SL6 . . . 20 B3
Ashdown Cl RG12 . . . 119 A7
Ashdown Ho 11 RG1 . . . 85 E5
Ashen Cross SL0 . . . 44 B8
Ashenden Wlk SL2 . . . 22 D8
Asher Dr SL5 . . . 119 C8
Ashes The RG7 . . . 113 B2
Ashfield Gn GU46 . . . 149 F5
Ashfield's Farm Ind Est
RG20 . . . 51 D1
ASHFORD . . . 97 F2
Ashford Ave TW15 . . . 98 B2
Ashford Bsns Complex
TW15 . . . 98 C4
Ashford CE Prim Sch
TW15 . . . 98 B2
Ashford Cl TW15 . . . 97 E4
ASHFORD COMMON . . . 98 D2
Ashford Cres TW15 . . . 97 E5
ASHFORD HILL . . . 133 E1
Ashford Hill Prim Sch
RG19 . . . 133 E1
Ashford Hill Rd RG19 . . . 132 F2
Ashford Hospl TW15 . . . 97 E6
Ashford Ind Est TW15 . . . 98 C4
Ashford La SL4 . . . 41 B4
Ashford Park Prim Sch
TW15 . . . 97 D4
Ashford Rd
Feltham TW13, TW15 . . . 98 E4
Littleton TW15 . . . 98 C1
Staines TW18 . . . 124 D8
Ashford Sta TW15 . . . 97 F4
Ash Gate RG18 . . . 106 F4
Ash Gn RG2 . . . 113 D8
Ash Gr
East Bedfont TW14 . . . 98 E7
Southend RG7 . . . 82 B2
Staines TW18 . . . 97 C2
Stoke Poges SL2 . . . 22 F5
Ashgrove Ct SL6 . . . 39 C6
Ashgrove Rd TW15 . . . 98 D3
Ashington Ho SL6 . . . 39 E6
Ash La
Burghfield Common RG7 . . 111 A4
Tadley RG26 . . . 134 E1
Windsor SL4 . . . 66 D5
Ashlea Ho TW15 . . . 97 F3
Ashleigh Ave TW20 . . . 96 C1
Ashley HP10 . . . 3 E7
Ashley Cl
Earley RG6 . . . 87 B2
Oatlands Park KT12, KT13 . 125 F1
Ashley Ct SL6 . . . 40 B7
Ashley Dr GU17 . . . 150 C4
Ashley Hill Pl RG10 . . . 36 F7
Ashley Park Ave KT12 . . . 125 F1
Ashley Park Cres KT12 . . 125 F1
Ashley Pk SL6 . . . 20 B2
Ashley Rd RG1 . . . 85 E5
Ashley Way GU24 . . . 153 D6
Ash Lodge 3 TW16 . . . 98 F1
Ashman Rd RG19 . . . 107 A3
Ashmere Cl RG31 . . . 84 C4
Ashmere Terr RG30 . . . 85 E8
ASHMORE GREEN . . . 106 B8
Ashmore Green Rd RG18 106 B7
Ashmore Rd RG2 . . . 86 C1
Ash Rd
Littleton TW17 . . . 125 A5
Reading RG30 . . . 84 E7
Ashridge Ct 4 RG14 . . . 105 A2
Ashridge Gn 2 RG42 . . . 118 B8
Ashridge Manor Farm
RG40 . . . 89 B2
Ashridge Rd RG40 . . . 116 D8
Ash Terr RG18 . . . 106 B8
Ashton Cl RG31 . . . 84 C8
Ashton Pl
Kintbury RG17 . . . 102 B2
Maidenhead SL6 . . . 39 A6
Ashton Rd
Newbury RG14 . . . 105 B2
Wokingham RG41 . . . 88 F1
Ash Tree Cnr RG20 . . . 129 C7
Ashtree Ct 3 TW15 . . . 98 B3
Ash Tree Gr RG20 . . . 129 B7
Ashtrees Rd RG5 . . . 87 F8
Ashurst Dr TW17 . . . 124 E5
Ashview Cl TW15 . . . 97 E3
Ashview Gdns TW15 . . . 97 E3
Ashville Pk RG41 . . . 116 B5
Ashville Way RG41 . . . 116 A5
Ash Way RG41 . . . 115 D3
Ashwell Ave GU15 . . . 151 F6
Ashwell Ct TW15 . . . 97 E6
Ashwood RG5 . . . 87 D4
Ashwood Cl RG31 . . . 84 B6
Ashwood Dr RG14 . . . 105 D4
Ashwood Rd TW20 . . . 95 B2
Ashworth Dr RG19 . . . 106 C2
Askew Dr RG7 . . . 113 B3
Asparagus Cl RG7 . . . 137 B6
Aspects Ct SL1 . . . 42 E4
Aspen Cl
Slough SL2 . . . 42 B8
Staines TW18 . . . 96 F5
Aspen Ct GU25 . . . 122 E5
Aspen Gdns TW15 . . . 98 C3
Aspin Way GU17 . . . 150 B5
Astleham Rd TW17 . . . 124 E6
Astley Cl
Newbury RG14 . . . 104 D2
Wokingham RG41 . . . 115 F7
ASTON . . . 16 C5
Aston Ave RG31 . . . 84 B8
Aston Cl RG8 . . . 56 D5
Aston Cotts SL4 . . . 93 A4
Aston Ct RG30 . . . 85 B5
Aston Ferry La RG9 . . . 16 D5
Aston Grange RG12 . . . 118 E5
Aston La RG9 . . . 16 C3
Aston Mead SL4 . . . 66 E6
Aston St OX11 . . . 12 F8
ASTON TIRROLD . . . 12 E8
Astonville SL2 . . . 22 C8
Astor Cl
Maidenhead SL6 . . . 40 B6
Winnersh RG41 . . . 88 D3

Astra Mead RG42 92 B2
Atfield Gr GU20 146 D4
Atherton Cl
  Reading RG30 84 F8
  Stanwell TW19 70 D1
Atherton Cres RG17 100 D5
Atherton Ct SL4 67 D7
Atherton Pl RG17 25 B3
Atherton Rd RG17 100 D5
Athlone Cl SL6 19 E1
Athlone Sq SL4 67 C6
Atlantean Ct 2 RG14 105 B3
Atrebatti Rd GU47 143 C1
Attebrouche Ct RG12 118 D2
Atte La RG42 91 C2
Atterbury Gdns RG4 58 E4
Attwood Dr RG2 140 E8
Auburn Ct RG4 59 A2
Auckland Cl SL6 40 B8
Auckland Rd RG6 87 A6
Auclum Cl RG7 111 B2
Auclum La RG7 111 B2
Audley Cl RG14 105 D5
Audley Dr SL6 39 B6
Audley St RG30 85 E8
Audley Way SL5 119 D6
Audrey Ct RG7 109 C3
Audrey Needham Ho 7 RG14 105 B2
Augur Cl TW18 96 F3
August End
  Reading RG30 85 C8
  Slough SL3 43 E7
Augustine Cl SL3 69 E4
Augustine Wlk RG42 91 E1
Augustus Gdns GU15 152 C5
Austen Gdns RG14 131 B8
Austen Way SL3 68 F8
Austin Rd RG5 87 F6
Austinsgate SL6 38 F8
Austin Way RG12 118 D6
Australia Ave SL6 39 F8
Australia Rd SL1 43 B4
Auton Pl RG9 35 D8
Autumn Cl
  Caversham RG4 59 C7
  Slough SL1 41 F5
Autumn Wlk
  Maidenhead SL6 39 A5
  Wargrave RG10 36 D2
Avalon Rd
  Bourne End SL8 3 B5
  Earley RG6 87 C3
Avebury
  Bracknell RG12 118 A3
  Slough SL1 42 A6
Avebury Sq RG1 86 D5
Aveley Ho 19 RG1 86 B6
Aveley Wlk 2 RG1 86 B5
Avenue Dr SL3 23 F1
Avenue Ho RG4 58 D3
Avenue Hts RG2 86 C4
Avenue Rd
  Egham TW18 96 D3
  Feltham TW13 98 F5
  Maidenhead SL6 40 B5
Avenue Sch The RG2 86 C4
Avenue Sucy GU15 151 B4
Avenue The
  Bourne End SL8 2 F4
  Camberley GU15 151 B5
  Crowthorne RG45 143 B5
  Datchet SL3 68 B6
  Egham TW20 96 B4
  Farnham Common SL2 22 B8
  Lightwater GU18 146 A1
  Maidenhead SL6 20 C3
  Mortimer RG7 137 B5
  North Ascot SL5 92 F1
  Old Windsor SL4 68 B2
  Staines TW18 124 B8
  Wraysbury TW19 68 D4
Averil Ct SL6 41 C7
Avery Cl RG40 141 F6
AVINGTON 101 E5
Avington Cl RG31 84 B8
Avocet Cres GU47 150 E8
Avocet Ct 4 RG1 86 A6
Avon Cl
  Reading RG31 84 F5
  Slough SL1 41 E6
Avon Ct RG42 90 C2
Avondale SL6 19 C1
Avondale Ave TW18 96 F1
Avondale Rd TW15 97 D5
Avon Gr RG12 91 C1
Avonmoor SL6 40 B8
Avon Pl RG1 86 D8
Avon Rd TW16 98 F1
Avonway RG14 105 D4
Avon Way RG7 109 E6
Axbridge RG12 118 E4
Axbridge Rd RG2 86 C2
Axis Pk SL3 44 B1
Ayebridges Ave TW20 96 C1
Aylesbury Cres SL1 42 D7
Aylesford Way RG19 107 A2
Aylesham Way GU46 149 B6
Aylesworth Ave SL2 22 B2
Aylesworth Spur SL4 95 B8
Aylsham Cl RG30 84 E8
Aymer Cl TW18 123 E8
Aymer Dr TW18 123 E8
Ayrton Senna Rd RG31 84 C7
Aysgarth RG12 118 A3
Aysgarth Pk SL6 40 B1
Azalea Cl RG41 88 B2
Azalea Rd RG19 133 A5
Azalea Way
  Frimley GU15 152 B6
  Slough SL3 43 E7
Azure Ct 12 TW13 98 F5

B

Babbage Way RG12 118 A3
Babbington Rd RG2 113 D6
Bacchus Ho RG7 134 E2
Bachelors Acre SL4 67 D6
Back La
  Beenham RG7 109 A7
  Brimpton RG7 134 C4
  Kintbury RG17 127 F7
  Shinfield RG7 139 A8
  Silchester RG7 136 D4
  Stanford Dingley RG7 81 E4
Backsideans RG10 36 D2
Back St RG17 47 C6
Bacon Cl GU47 150 D6
Baden Cl TW18 97 B1
Bader Gdns SL1 42 A4
Bader Way The RG5 88 A5
Badgebury Rise SL7 1 C7
Badgemore Com Sch RG9 15 D2
Badgemore La RG9 15 D3
Badger Cl SL6 39 D4
Badger Dr
  Lightwater GU18 146 A1
  Twyford RG10 61 D7
Badgers Cl TW15 97 F3
Badgers Copse GU15 151 E4
Badgers Croft RG7 137 A6
Badgers Glade RG7 111 A2
Badgers Hill GU25 122 C4
Badgers Holt GU46 149 B5
Badgers Ridge RG20 130 C4
Badgers Rise
  Caversham RG4 59 A5
  Woodley RG5 60 D1
Badgers Sett RG45 142 F5
Badgers Way
  Bracknell RG12 118 F7
  Marlow Bottom SL7 1 D7
Badgers Wlk RG9 36 A3
Badgers Wood SL2 22 C7
Badgerwood Dr GU16 151 D2
Bad Godesberg Way SL6 39 F7
Badminton Rd SL6 39 B6
Badsworth Gdns RG14 130 D4
Bagnols Way RG14 104 E2
BAGSHOT 145 D3
Bagshot Gn GU19 145 E3
Bagshot Inf Sch GU19 145 E2
Bagshot Rd
  Ascot SL5 120 C2
  Bracknell RG12 118 C4
  Englefield Green TW20 95 C2
Bagshot Sta GU19 145 E4
Baigents La GU20 146 D4
Bailey Cl
  Maidenhead SL6 39 F7
  Windsor SL4 67 A5
Bailey Ho 9 SL8 3 A4
Baileys Cl GU17 150 C4
Bailey's La RG10 62 E3
Baily Ave RG18 106 B4
Bain Ave GU15 151 B2
Bainbridge Rd RG31 84 B4
Bainhurst Cotts SL6 38 B5
Baird Cl SL1 42 B4
Baird Rd RG2 140 E7
Bakeham La TW20 95 D1
Bakehouse Ct SL5 119 B8
Bakers Ct 2 TW19 70 D1
Bakers La SL6 38 F8
Bakers Orch HP10 3 E5
Bakers Row SL6 38 F8
Baker St
  Aston Tirrold OX11 12 F8
  Reading RG1 85 F7
Baldwin Ct RG10 61 E6
Baldwin Pl SL6 39 C7
Baldwin Rd SL1 21 C2
Baldwin's Shore SL4 67 D8
Balfour Cres
  Bracknell RG12 118 B4
  Newbury RG14 130 C6
Balfour Dr RG31 84 B4
Balfour Pl SL7 1 C4
Balintore Ct 8 GU47 150 D8
Ballamoor Cl RG31 84 B3
Ballard Ct GU15 152 A8
Ballard Gn SL4 66 E7
Ballard Rd GU15 152 A8
Ballencrieff Rd SL5 120 F2
BALL HILL 129 C3
Balliol Rd RG4 58 D3
Balliol Way GU47 143 E1
Ball Pit Rd RG20 30 B5
Balme Cl RG10 61 B4
Balmoral SL6 19 B1
Balmoral Cl SL1 41 E7
Balmoral Gdns SL4 67 D4
Balmoral Grange TW18 124 B7
Balmore Dr RG4 59 B4
Balmore Ho RG4 59 B3
Balmore Pk RG4 59 B3
Bamburgh Cl RG2 86 C3
Bamford Pl RG31 84 B4
Banbury RG12 118 E2
Banbury Ave SL1 41 F8
Banbury Cl RG41 116 A6
Banbury Gdns RG4 59 C3
Bancroft Cl TW15 98 A3
Bancroft Pl RG31 84 B3
Bangors Cl SL0 44 F7
Bangors Rd S SL0 44 E8
Bank Apartments SL7 1 D3
Bank Side RG40 141 F6
Bankside Cl RG2 86 D2
Banks Spur SL1 42 B4
Bannard Rd SL6 39 A5
Bannister Cl SL3 43 E4
Bannister Gdns GU46 149 F5
Bannister Pl RG7 133 F6
Bannister Rd RG7 110 F2
Barbara Cl TW17 125 B4
Barbara's Mdw RG31 57 B2
Barbel Cl RG6 87 B8
Barber Cl RG10 88 E7
Barberry Way GU17 150 F2
Barbicus Ct 1 SL6 40 B8
Barbon Cl GU15 152 D3
Barbrook Cl RG31 57 D3
Barchester Rd SL3 43 F4
Barclay Rd RG31 84 D4
Barclose Ave RG4 59 C3
Bardeen Pl RG12 118 D6
Bardney Cl SL6 39 D3
Bardolph's Cl RG4 58 D8
Bardown RG20 51 B2
Barefoot Cl RG31 57 B1
Barfield Rd RG18 106 A4
Barge La RG7 139 A5
Bargeman Rd SL6 39 E5
Barholm Cl RG6 87 E2
Barkby RG6 87 C2
Barker Cl
  Arborfield Garrison RG2 140 E7
  Chertsey KT16 123 E2
Barker Ct RG10 88 F8
Barker Gn RG12 118 B4
Barker Rd KT16 123 F2
Barkers Mdw SL5 119 D8
BARKHAM 115 C2
Barkham Manor RG41 115 C3
Barkham Mews 14 RG1 86 C7
Barkham Rd
  Barkham RG41 115 D3
  Wokingham RG41 116 A5
Barkham Ride RG40 141 E8
Barkham St RG40 115 C2
Barkhart Cl RG40 116 C7
Barkhart Dr RG40 116 C7
Barkhart Gdns RG40 116 C7
Barkis Mead GU47 143 E2
Barkwith Cl RG6 87 E2
Barley Cl RG19 106 F2
Barley Ct TW19 97 E7
Barley Fields HP10 3 E8
Barley Gdns RG41 88 B3
Barley Mead
  Bracknell RG42 91 E1
  Maidenhead SL6 39 A5
Barley Mow Rd TW20 95 C3
Barley Mow Way TW17 125 A5
Barley Way 3 SL7 1 D1
Barley Wlk RG31 84 A5
Barnard Cl RG4 59 C6
Barnard's Ct 3 RG17 100 D5
Barnards Hill SL7 1 C2
Barn Cl
  Ashford TW15 98 B3
  Bracknell RG12 118 D7
  Camberley GU15 151 E6
  Farnham Common SL2 22 B8
  Kintbury RG17 102 B2
  Maidenhead SL6 19 F2
  Reading RG30 85 D4
Barn Cotts RG17 74 D7
Barn Cres RG14 130 D7
Barn Croft Dr RG6 87 D1
Barn Dr SL6 39 A4
Barnes Terr 12 RG14 104 F2
Barnes Way SL0 44 F6
Barnet Ct RG12 118 C7
Barnett Gn RG12 118 B3
Barnett La GU18 152 F7
Barn Farm SL7 1 D3
Barnfield
  Iver SL0 44 E7
  Slough SL1 41 D5
  3 Yateley GU46 149 D5
Barnfield Cl SL6 19 F5
Barnhill Cl SL7 1 D4
Barnhill Gdns SL7 1 D4
Barnhill Rd SL7 1 D4
Barn La RG9 15 C4
Barn Owl Way RG7 111 B3
Barnsdale Rd RG2 86 D3
Barn The RG18 79 F5
Barnway TW20 95 C3
Barnwood Cl RG30 85 E8
Baroma Way RG9 15 E2
Baron Ct RG30 85 E7
Barons Ct 1 SL7 1 E2
Baronsmead RG9 15 D2
Barons Way TW20 96 D2
Barossa Rd GU15 151 D7
Barracane Dr RG45 143 B5
Barrack La SL4 67 D6
Barracks La RG7 113 B1
Barrett Cres RG40 116 E6
Barrett Ct RG1 58 F1
Barrington Cl RG6 87 B6
Barrington Ct TW18 96 F2
Barrington Ho RG2 113 B7
Barrington Way RG1 85 E5
Barrow Lodge SL2 22 C1
Barrsbrook Farm Rd KT16 123 E1
Barrsbrook Hall KT16 123 E1
Barr's Rd SL6 41 B7
Barry Ave SL4 67 C7
Barry Pl RG1 86 A8
Barry Sq RG12 118 D2
Barry Terr TW15 97 F6
Barry View SL4 66 C5
Bartelotts Rd SL2 21 E1
Bartholemew St RG14 105 A2
Bartholemew Ct 9 RG14 104 F2
Bartholomew Pl RG42 91 E1
Bartlemy Cl RG14 130 E8
Bartlemy Rd RG14 130 E8
Bartletts La SL6 65 A7
Barton Cl TW17 125 B3
Barton Copse RG20 51 B2
Barton Rd
  Reading RG31 84 B7
  Slough SL3 43 F4
Barton's Dr GU46 149 D4
Barwell Cl RG45 142 F4
Basemoors RG12 118 E7
Basford Way SL4 66 D4
Basil Cl RG6 86 F1
Basildon CE Prim Sch RG8 55 A6
Basildon Ho 22 RG1 86 B6
Basildon Pk* RG8 34 D1
Basingstoke Rd
  Aldermaston RG7 109 B2
  Reading RG2 86 B3
  Riseley RG7 139 B1
  Shinfield RG7 113 B3
  Swallowfield RG7 139 B5
  Three Mile Cross RG7 113 A5
Baskerville La RG9 36 A3
Baslow Rd RG41 88 B2
Basmore La RG9 36 B4
Bassett Cl RG6 114 C8
Bassett Rd OX12 6 F8
Bassett Way SL2 21 E1
Bass Mead SL6 19 F5
Batcombe Mead RG12 118 E2
Bates Cl SL3 43 E7
Bath Ct SL6 39 C6
Bath Rd
  Camberley GU15 151 D6
  Colthrop RG7, RG19 107 D2
  Froxfield SN8, RG17 99 C4
  Harlington TW6, UB7, TW5 71 D6
  Harmondsworth TW6, UB7 70 E6
  Hungerford RG17 100 F6
  Knowl Hill RG10, SL6 37 D2
  Littlewick Green SL6 38 C5
  Maidenhead SL6 39 C6
  Newbury RG18 105 F4
  Padworth RG7 109 D4
  Poyle SL3, UB7, TW6 69 E6
  Reading RG30, RG31, RG1 85 C5
  Slough, Cippenham SL1, SL6 41 D6
  Slough SL1, SL6 41 D6
  Sonning RG4 60 E2
  Speen RG20 104 D4
  Thatcham RG18 106 C4
  Woolhampton RG7 108 D2
Bath Road Cotts SL3 69 E6
Bathurst Cl SL0 44 F4
Bathurst Rd RG41 88 B2
Bathurst Wlk SL0 44 F4
Battalion Way RG19 106 E1
Battery End RG14 130 D6
Battle Cl RG14 104 D4
Battlemead Cl SL6 20 C3
Battle Pl RG30 85 D8
Battle Prim Sch RG30 85 D7
Battle Rd
  Goring RG8 34 F7
  Newbury RG14 130 C6
Battle Sq RG30 85 D8
Battle St RG1 85 F8
Batty's Barn Cl RG40 116 D5
BAUGHURST COMMON 134 D1
Baughurst Rd RG7 136 A6
Baxendales The 4 RG14 105 C1
Baxter Cl SL1 42 E3
Baybrook SL6 19 F6
Bay Cl RG6 86 F1
Baydon Dr RG1 85 E5
Baydon Ho 6 RG17 25 B2
Baydon Rd
  Lambourn RG17 24 E1
  Lambourn RG17 45 A7
  Shefford Woodlands RG17 74 E7
  Wickham RG20 75 B4
Bay Dr RG12 118 E7
Bayeux Ct RG30 85 D7
Bayfield Ave GU16 151 E2
Bayford Cl GU17 151 A1
Bayford Dr RG31 84 F4
Bayley Cres SL1 41 A8
Bayley Ct RG41 88 B1
Baylis Bsns Ctr SL1 42 D6
Baylis Court Sch SL1, SL2 42 D8
Baylis Par SL1 42 E7
Baylis Rd SL1 42 E6
Bayliss Rd RG10 36 D1
Bay Rd RG12 118 E8
Bays Ct RG26 134 F1
Bays Farm Ct UB7 70 C6
Bay Tree Ct SL1 21 C2
Bay Tree Rise RG31 84 C5
Beach's Ho 2 TW18 97 A3
Beacon Ct
  Colnbrook SL3 69 C7
  3 Reading RG30 85 D6
Beacon Rd TW6 71 A1
Beacon Rdbt TW6 71 B1
Beaconsfield Cotts SL8 3 B2
Beaconsfield Rd SL2 22 C6
Beaconsfield Way RG6 87 A2
Beacontree Plaza RG2 86 B2
Beale Cl RG40 116 B7
Beale Park Wildlife Pk*
  Lower Basildon RG8 34 F1
  Pangbourne RG8 55 F8
Beales Farm Rd RG17 25 B2
Beal's La RG31 84 A7
Beancroft Rd RG19 106 D2
Bean Oak Rd RG40 116 F6
Beard's Rd TW15 98 E2
Bearfield La RG17 73 B7
Bear La
  Newbury RG14 105 A3
  Wargrave RG10 37 B3
Bearsden Ct SL5 120 F2
Bears Rail Pk SL4 94 F8
Bears Rails Pk SL4 94 F8
Bearwater RG17 100 D6
Bear Wharf 8 RG1 86 A6
Bearwood Coll RG41 115 B7
Bearwood Park Mobile Home Pk 2 RG41 88 A2
Bearwood Path RG41 88 A2
Bearwood Prim Sch RG41 115 B8
Bearwood Rd RG41 115 C6
Beasley's Ait TW16 125 F3
Beasley's Ait La TW16 125 F3
Beattie Cl TW14 98 F7
Beatty Dr RG30 84 E8
Beatty Rise RG7 139 A8
Beauchamp Ct SL1 42 E6
Beauchief Cl RG6 113 F8
Beaufield Cl RG5 87 D7
Beaufort Cl SL7 1 E2
Beaufort Gdns
  Marlow SL7 1 E2
  North Ascot SL5 119 E8
Beaufort Ho
  5 Ashford TW15 98 B3
  Sunningdale SL5 121 A1
Beaufort Pl SL6 40 D4
Beauforts TW20 95 C3
Beaufront Cl GU15 152 A7
Beaufront Rd GU15 152 B7
Beaulieu Cl
  Bracknell RG12 119 A6
  Datchet SL3 68 B5
Beaulieu Ct GU17 150 B5
Beaulieu Gdns GU17 150 C5
Beaumaris Ct SL1 42 C8
Beaumont Cl SL6 39 A3
Beaumont Ct
  Ascot SL5 119 F5
  Slough SL3 43 D7
Beaumont Dr TW15 98 D3
Beaumont Gdns RG12 118 E4
Beaumont Rd
  Slough SL2 42 D8
  Windsor SL4 67 C5
Beaumont Rise SL7 1 E2
Beaver Cl RG41 116 B3
Beaver La GU46 149 E5
Beavers Cl RG26 135 A1
Beaver Way RG5 88 B7
Beck Ct RG1 86 C6
Becket Ho 4 RG14 104 F2
Beckett Chase 7 SL3 43 F1
Beckett Cl RG40 116 E6
Beckford Ave RG12 118 B3
Beckford Cl RG41 88 F1
Beckford Ct RG19 106 D3
Beckfords RG8 55 A5
Beckingham Pl RG7 113 B2
Beckings Way HP10 3 C7
Beckwell Rd SL1 42 C4
Bede Wlk RG2 86 C3
Bedfont Cl TW14 71 C1
Bedfont Court Est TW19 70 B4
Bedfont Ct TW19 70 B4
Bedfont Green Cl TW14 98 C7
Bedfont Ind Pk TW15 98 D5
Bedfont Ind Pk N TW15 98 C5
Bedfont Inf Sch TW14 71 E1
Bedfont Jun Sch TW14 71 E1
Bedfont La TW14 98 F8
Bedfont Lakes Ctry Pk* TW14 98 C6
Bedfont Rd
  Feltham TW14, TW13 98 D6
  Stanwell TW19 70 F1
Bedford Ave SL1 42 A7
Bedford Cl
  Maidenhead SL6 39 A3
  Newbury RG14 130 C5
Bedford Dr SL2 22 B6
Bedford Gdns RG41 115 F7
Bedford La SL5 121 B4
Bedford Rd RG1 85 F8
Bedfordshire Down RG42 91 F2
Bedfordshire Way RG41 115 E6
Bedivere Ct 10 RG1 86 B6
Bedwins La SL6 19 B6
Beech RG9 15 D2
Beecham Rd RG30 85 C8
Beech Ave GU15 151 D4
Beechbrook Ave GU46 149 D5
Beech Cl
  Ashford TW15 98 D3
  Brimpton RG19 133 B5
  Burghfield RG30 111 B4
  Hampstead Norreys RG18 53 A5
  Maidenhead SL6 39 B8

Beech Cl *continued*
Stanwell TW19 97 D8
Beech Copse 3 RG26 134 E1
Beechcroft RG18 53 A5
Beechcroft Cl SL5 120 D5
Beechcroft Ct RG12 118 B6
Beech Ct
Bracknell RG42 117 D7
Burnham SL1 21 C2
Caversham RG4 59 B3
Hurst RG10 89 A7
2 Marlow SL7 1 E2
7 Newbury RG14 105 A4
Beech Dr GU17 150 D4
Beeches Dr SL2 22 B7
Beeches Rd SL2 22 B7
Beeches The
Goring RG8 34 B5
Reading RG31 57 D3
Slough SL2 21 F2
8 Staines TW18 97 A3
Beechfield RG18 80 D7
Beechfield Pl SL6 39 C4
Beech Glen RG12 118 B5
BEECH HILL 138 D5
Beech Hill Ho RG7 138 E6
Beech Hill Rd
Beech Hill RG7 138 E6
Spencers Wood RG7 113 A1
Sunningdale SL5 120 F3
Beechingstoke 4 SL7 1 F3
Beech La
Earley RG6 87 B2
South Stoke RG8 14 F1
Beech Lodge TW18 96 E3
Beechmont Ave GU25 122 D4
Beechnut Cl RG41 115 F5
Beechnut Dr GU17 150 B6
Beech Rd
East Bedfont TW14 98 E8
Newtown RG20 132 A3
Purley on T RG8 57 B5
Reading RG2 86 E2
Slough SL3 43 E4
Tokers Green RG4 58 D7
Beech Ride GU47 143 B1
Beechtree Ave
Englefield Green TW20 95 B2
Marlow Bottom SL7 1 D5
Beech Tree Ct TW18 124 B7
Beech Tree La TW18 124 B7
Beech Wlk RG19 106 E2
Beechwood Ave
Reading RG31 84 D8
Staines TW18 97 B2
Woodley RG5 87 D7
Beechwood Cl SL5 92 F1
Beechwood Dr
Maidenhead SL6 39 A6
Marlow SL7 18 B8
Beechwood Gdns SL1 42 E4
Beechwood Prim Sch RG5 87 E7
Beechwood Rd
Slough SL2 42 D8
Wentworth GU25 122 B1
Beechwood Sch SL2 22 B2
BEEDON 51 D7
Beedon CE Prim Sch RG20 51 D8
Beedon Dr RG12 117 E3
Beehive La RG12 117 C7
Beehive Rd
Bracknell RG12, RG42 117 D7
Staines TW18 96 F3
BEENHAM 108 E6
Beenhamplace Rd RG19 132 D1
Beenham Prim Sch RG7 108 F6
BEENHAM'S HEATH 63 C3
BEENHAM STOCKS 109 A7
Beeston Way RG6 114 A8
Beggars Hill Rd RG10 61 B1
Beharrel Ho SL5 120 E4
Beighton Cl RG6 113 F8
Belfast Ave SL1 42 D7
Belford Ct 16 RG1 86 A6
Belfry Mews GU47 149 F8
Belgrave Ct GU17 150 D3
Belgrave Par SL1 42 E6
Belgrave Rd SL1 42 F6
Belgravia Ct 21 RG30 85 D6
Bell Bridge Rd KT16 123 F1
Bell Bsns Ctr SL6 39 F6
Bell Cl SL2 43 B8
Bell Cnr KT16 123 F2
Bell Ct
Caversham RG4 59 B6
Hurley SL6 17 F3
Twyford RG10 61 D5
Belle Ave RG6 87 A5
Belleisle RG8 57 B5
Belleme Mews RG8 34 B6
Bellever Hill GU15 151 E5
Belle Vue Cl TW18 124 A8
Belle Vue Rd
Henley-on-T RG9 35 D8
Reading RG1 85 F7
Bellevue Terr 5 RG1 85 E7
Bell Foundry La RG40 116 C8
Bell Hill RG14, RG20 130 B4
Bell Holt RG14 130 C5
Bell House Gdns RG41 116 B6
Bellingham Cl GU15 152 C4
Bellingham Wlk RG4 59 A5
Bell La
Aldworth RG8 32 F4
Blackwater GU17 150 C5
Eton SL4 41 F2
Bell La *continued*
Henley-on-T RG9 15 E3
Inkpen RG17 127 D3
Bellman Ct 2 RG1 86 A8
Bell Pl GU19 145 F3
Bellsfield Ct SL4 41 F2
Bells Hill SL2 23 A4
Bells Hill Gn SL2 23 A5
Bells La SL3 69 B4
Bell St
Henley-on-T RG9 15 E2
Maidenhead SL6 39 F6
Bell Street Mews RG9 15 E2
Bellswood La SL0 44 B8
Bell View SL4 66 F5
Bell View Cl SL4 66 F5
Bell Weir Cl TW19 96 B6
Belmont SL2 42 A8
Belmont Cotts
Colnbrook SL3 69 C7
Speen RG20 104 C6
Belmont Cres SL6 39 D8
Belmont Dr SL6 39 D8
Belmont Mews GU15 151 C3
Belmont Park Ave SL6 39 D8
Belmont Park Rd SL6 39 D8
Belmont Rd
Camberley GU15 151 C4
Crowthorne RG45 143 B6
Maidenhead SL6 39 D8
Reading RG30 85 D7
Belmont Vale SL6 39 D8
Belsize Grange KT16 124 C2
Belton Rd GU15 151 E5
Belvedere Ct GU17 150 D3
Belvedere Dr RG14 131 A8
Belvedere Grange SL5 121 A1
Belvedere Mans SL1 42 D4
Belvedere Wlk 2 RG41 88 A3
Belvoir Cl GU16 151 F1
Bembridge Ct
Crowthorne RG45 142 E4
12 Slough SL1 42 F4
Bembridge Pl RG1 86 C7
Benbricke Gn RG42 91 A1
Bence The TW20 123 B6
Bencombe Rd SL7 1 E5
Benedict Dr TW14 98 D8
Benedict Gn RG42 91 E1
Benen-Stock Rd TW19 70 A2
Benetfeld Rd RG42 90 B2
Benett Cl RG14 104 F5
Benett Gdns RG14 104 F5
Benham Chase RG20 103 E5
Benham Dr RG7 139 A8
Benham Hill
Newbury RG18 105 F4
Thatcham RG18 106 A4
Benham La RG7 139 D3
Benhams La RG9 15 E8
Benjamin Ct TW15 98 C1
Bennet Ct RG2 86 A1
Bennet Rd RG2 86 A1
Bennett Ct GU15 151 C5
Bennetts Cl SL1 42 A5
Bennett's Hill RG7, RG30 111 C7
Benning Cl SL4 66 D4
Bennings Cl RG42 91 A1
Benning Way RG40 116 D8
Bensington Ct TW14 71 D1
Benson Cl
Reading RG2 86 D3
Slough SL2 43 A5
Bensonholme RG7 109 C3
Benson Rd RG45 142 F5
Bentley Copse GU15 152 B4
Bentley Ct
4 Camberley GU15 151 D5
Maidenhead SL6 39 D4
Bentley Dr RG2 140 E8
Bentley Pk SL2 21 D3
Bentley Rd SL1 42 A5
Benyon Ct RG1 85 E6
Benyon Mews RG1 85 E6
Beomonds 5 KT16 124 A2
Beomonds Row 2 KT16 124 A2
Bere Court Rd RG8 56 B4
Bere Rd RG12 118 E3
Beresford Ave SL2 43 C6
Beresford Rd RG30 85 E8
Bergenia Ct GU24 153 E6
Berkeley Ave RG1 85 E6
Berkeley Cl TW19 96 D6
Berkeley Ct 1 RG1 85 F6
Berkeley Dr SL4 93 B7
Berkeley Gdns KT12 125 F2
Berkeley Mews
Marlow SL7 1 F2
Slough SL1 41 E7
Berkeley Rd RG14 104 F2
Berkley Cl SL6 39 A8
Berkshire Ave SL1 42 B7
Berkshire Bsns Ctr RG19 107 A2
Berkshire Bsns Pk RG7 135 E4
Berkshire Coll of Agriculture SL6 18 A1
Berkshire Coll of Agriculture (Hall Place) SL6 38 A8
Berkshire Dr
Reading RG31 84 C7
Thatcham RG19 107 A2
Berkshire Ind Hospl RG1 85 E5
Berkshire Lodge 1 SL6 39 F6
Berkshire Rd
Camberley GU15 151 F8
Henley-on-T RG9 35 D8
Berkshire Way RG12 117 D6
Bernadine Cl RG42 91 E1
Bernard Ct GU15 151 B4
Berners Cl SL1 41 E6
Bernersh Cl GU47 143 C1
Berries Rd SL6 20 A8
Berrybank GU47 150 E6
Berrycroft RG12 118 D8
Berryfield SL2 43 C7
Berry Hill SL6 40 D7
Berry Hill Ct SL6 40 D8
Berrylands Rd RG4 59 B3
Berryscroft Ct TW18 97 C1
Berryscroft Rd TW18 97 C1
Berrys La RG30 85 A1
Berrys Rd RG7 107 C5
Berstead Cl 3 RG6 87 B1
Berwick Ave SL1 42 B6
Berwick Cl SL7 1 D3
Berwick La SL7 1 C3
Berwick Rd SL7 1 C3
Berwyn Ho RG2 113 C7
Beryl Cl RG41 115 E7
Bessel's Way OX11 12 B8
Bessemer Cl 3 SL3 43 F1
Bestobell Rd SL1 42 C7
Beswick Gdns RG12 118 F8
Beta Ho 6 RG30 85 D6
Betam Rd RG1 86 D7
Beta Way TW20 123 C8
Betchworth Ave RG6 87 A3
Bethany Waye TW14 98 E8
Bethesda Cl RG8 55 A6
Bethesda St RG8 55 A7
Betjeman Wlk GU46 149 B4
Betteridge Rd RG19 106 F2
Bettoney Vere SL6 40 C4
Betty Grove La RG41 114 F7
Bevan Gate RG42 118 A8
Beverley Cl
Frimley GU15 152 D6
Marlow SL7 1 B2
Thatcham RG18 106 C4
Beverley Ct SL1 43 B4
Beverley Gdns
Maidenhead SL6 19 B1
Wargrave RG10 36 E1
Beverley Rd
Reading RG31 57 C1
Sunbury TW16 125 F8
Bevers The RG7 137 A6
Bewicks Reach RG14 104 F3
Bexley Ct RG30 85 D6
Bexley St SL4 67 C6
Bibury Cl RG5 87 D4
Bicknell Rd GU16 151 E2
Biddles Cl SL1 41 E5
Bideford Cl RG5 87 C5
Bideford Spur SL2 22 B2
Bietigheim Way GU15 151 C6
Big Barn Gr RG42 91 D1
Bigbury Gdns RG2 86 C3
Bigfrith La SL6 19 B6
Bigg's Hill Cotts RG20 129 F4
Biggs La RG2, RG40 141 A8
Big La RG17 25 B3
Bilberry Gdns RG7 137 B6
Billet La SL0, SL3 44 B7
Billet Rd TW18, TW19 97 A5
BILL HILL 89 B2
Billing Ave RG40 141 F6
BILLINGBEAR 90 B6
Billingbear La RG42 90 B5
Billington Way RG18 106 C5
Bilton Ind Est RG12 117 E5
Binbrook Cl RG6 87 D2
Binbury Row TW18 96 E4
BINFIELD 90 D2
Binfield CE Prim Sch RG42 90 C2
BINFIELD HEATH 35 A2
Binfield Ho RG42 90 C3
Binfield Rd
Bracknell, Priestwood RG42 118 A8
Wokingham RG40 116 F7
Bingham Cotts RG42 91 B6
Bingham Dr TW18 97 D1
Bingham Rd SL1 41 A8
Binghams The SL6 40 B3
Bingley Gr RG5 60 F1
Binsted Dr GU17 150 D5
Birch Ave
Brimpton RG19 133 B5
Reading RG30 85 A8
Birch Cl GU15 151 E8
Birch Copse Prim Sch RG31 84 C8
Birch Ct RG45 142 F6
Birch Dr GU17 150 D3
Birches The
Blackwater GU17 150 B5
Goring RG8 34 B6
Birchetts Cl 1 RG42 118 B8
Birchfields GU15 151 C4
Birch Gn RG2 113 D8
Birch Gr
Slough SL2 42 B8
Upper Halliford TW17 125 E7
Windsor SL4 66 D6
BIRCH GREEN 97 A4
BIRCH HILL 118 C2
Birch Hill Prim Sch RG12 118 B1
Birch Hill Rd RG12 118 B2
Birchington Rd SL4 67 A5
Birch La
Mortimer RG7 136 E5
West End GU24 153 D7
Winkfield RG12, SL5 119 B8
Birchland Cl RG7 136 E6
Birchlands Ct GU47 143 E2
Birchmead RG41 88 D2
Birch Platt GU24 153 D6
Birch Rd
Burghfield Common RG7 111 A3
Tadley RG26 134 F2
Windlesham GU20 146 E4
Wokingham RG40 142 A7
Birch Side RG45 143 A6
Birch Tree View GU18 146 A1
Birchview Cl GU46 149 D4
Birchwood Cl RG4 59 C6
Birchwood Dr GU18 146 C1
Birchwood Rd RG14 105 D4
Birchwoods The RG31 84 B8
Birdhill Ave RG2 86 D2
Bird Mews RG40 116 B6
Birds La RG7 107 E4
Birdwood Rd
Maidenhead SL6 39 B7
Sandhurst GU15 150 F6
Birkbeck Pl GU47 143 E1
Birkdale RG12 117 E2
Birkdale Ct SL5 120 C4
Birkhall Cl RG31 84 C5
Birley Rd SL1 42 D7
Biscuit Way RG2 112 F8
BISHAM 18 E7
Bisham Abbey National Sports Ctr SL7 18 D7
Bisham CE Prim Sch SL7 18 D7
Bisham Ct
Bisham SL7 18 E6
11 Slough SL1 42 F4
Bisham Gn SL7 18 E6
Bisham Rd SL7 18 E8
Bishop Ct SL6 39 D6
Bishop Ctr The SL6 40 F7
Bishopdale RG12 118 A5
Bishop Duppas Pk TW17 125 E2
Bishops Cl RG26 135 A1
Bishops Ct
1 Ashford TW16 98 F1
North Ascot SL5 92 F2
Bishops Dr
East Bedfont TW14 71 D1
Wokingham RG40 116 C7
Bishops Farm Cl SL4 66 B6
BISHOPSGATE 94 F4
Bishops Gate SL6 40 F7
Bishopsgate Rd TW20 95 B5
Bishopsgate Sch TW20 95 A5
Bishops Gr GU20 146 C4
BISHOPS GREEN 132 A3
BISHOP'S GREEN 132 A3
Bishop's La SL4 92 B7
Bishops Orch SL2 22 B2
Bishops Rd
Slough SL1 43 A4
Stanford Dingley RG7 81 F3
Bishop's Rd RG6 87 A6
Bishops Way TW20 96 D2
Bishops Wlk HP10 3 E5
Bishopswood Ct RG26 134 F1
Bishopswood La RG26 134 E1
Bishopswood Rd RG26 134 F1
Bishop Wand CE Sch The TW16 125 F7
BISLEY 153 F3
Bispham Ct 2 RG1 86 C6
Bissley Dr SL6 39 A3
Bitham La
Ham RG17 126 B5
Inkpen RG17 127 B4
Bitham Rd OX12 8 C7
Bittern Cl GU47 150 D8
Bitterne Ave RG31 84 B6
Bix Hill RG9 15 A6
Bix La SL6 38 F8
Blackamoor La SL6 40 A8
Blackberry Cl TW17 125 E5
Blackberry Ct RG26 134 E2
Blackbird Cl
Burghfield Common RG7 111 B3
Sandhurst GU47 150 D8
Blackbird La RG20 132 A3
Black Boy La SL6 17 C3
Blackburn Trad Est TW19 70 F1
Blackbush Bsns Ctr GU46 149 C4
Blackbush Park Cvn Site GU46 149 C5
Black Butt Cotts SL6 20 B7
Blackcap Pl GU47 150 E8
Blackdown Way RG19 106 D2
Blackett Cl TW18 123 F7
Black Horse Cl SL4 66 D5
Blackhouse Farm TW20 123 C6
Black Lake Cl TW20 123 A8
Blacklands Rd RG7 107 C5
Blackley Cl RG6 87 E3
Black Mdws RG12 118 C3
Blackmoor Cl SL5 119 D7
Blackmoor Wood SL5 119 D7
BLACKNEST 121 B6
Blacknest Gate Rd SL5 121 B6
Blacknest Rd GU25, SL5 121 E6
Black Park Ctry Pk & Visitor Ctr* SL3 23 F3
Black Park Rd SL3 23 E4
Blackpond La SL2 22 B4
Blacksmith Row SL3 44 A2
Blacksmiths Ct UB7 70 B6
Blacksmiths La KT16 124 A2
Blacksmith's La TW18 124 C6
Blackstroud La E GU18, GU24 153 E8
Blackstroud La W GU18 153 D8
Blackthorn Cl
Earley RG6 87 A7
Purley on T RG31 57 B1
Blackthorn Dell SL3 43 C3
Blackthorn Dr
Lightwater GU18 153 B7
Thatcham RG18 106 D5
Blackthorne Cres SL3 69 E5
Blackthorne Ct 3 TW15 98 C1
Blackthorne Rd SL3 69 E4
BLACKWATER 150 D5
Blackwater Cl
Caversham RG4 59 E4
Shinfield RG7 113 B1
Blackwater Rise RG31 84 B4
Blackwater Sta GU17 150 E4
Blackwater View RG40 142 B2
Blaenant RG4 58 F5
Blaenavon RG4 58 F5
Blagden Cl RG19 131 D7
Blagdon Rd RG2 86 D2
Blagrave Farm La RG4 58 D5
Blagrave La RG4 58 D4
Blagrave Rise RG31 84 C6
Blagrave St RG1 86 B8
Blagrove Dr RG41 115 F4
Blagrove La RG41 115 F3
Blaire Pk GU46 149 B8
Blair Rd SL1 42 E5
Blake Cl
Crowthorne RG45 143 C4
Wokingham RG40 116 E8
Blakeney Ct SL6 19 F1
Blakeney Fields RG17 48 B4
Blakes Cotts
Reading RG1 86 C7
Wargrave RG10 37 B1
Blakes Ct 3 KT16 124 A1
Blakes La RG10 37 B2
Blake's La RG26 135 C1
Blakes Rd RG10 36 F3
Blakes Ride GU46 149 B6
Blamire Dr RG42 90 F2
Blanchard Cl RG5 88 B8
Blandford Cl SL3 43 D3
Blandford Dr RG41 115 E4
Blandford Ho SL6 39 C8
Blandford Rd RG2 113 C8
Blandford Rd N SL3 43 D3
Blandford Rd S SL3 43 D3
Bland's Cl RG7 110 F2
Blands Ct RG7 111 A2
Blandy Rd RG9 35 D7
Blandys Hill RG17 128 B8
Blandy's La RG8 55 B6
Blane's La SL5 119 C3
Blatchley Ho RG42 90 C2
Blatch's Cl RG7 83 D3
Blays Cl TW20 95 C2
Blay's La TW20 95 B2
Bledlow Cl RG14 130 D5
Blenheim Ave RG12 118 C5
Blenheim Cl
Slough SL3 43 F5
Wokingham RG41 115 E6
Blenheim Cotts RG18 106 B8
Blenheim Ct
Egham TW18 96 D4
11 Reading RG1 86 B6
Blenheim Gdns RG1 86 E6
Blenheim Pl GU15 151 C3
Blenheim Rd
Caversham RG4 59 A3
Maidenhead SL6 39 B8
Newbury RG14 104 F2
Reading RG1 86 E6
Slough SL3 43 D2
Blenheim Terr 1 RG1 86 A6
Blessed Hugh Faringdon RC Sch RG30 85 C5
Bletchmore Cl UB3 71 D8
Blewburton Wlk RG12 118 E5
BLEWBURY 12 B8
Blewbury Dr RG31 84 B7
Blewbury Hill OX11 12 B8
Blinco La SL3 43 E7
Blind La
Bourne End HP10, SL8 3 B6
Lambourn RG17 25 B2
Block A SL2 23 B1
Block B SL2 23 B1
Block C SL2 23 B1
Block Cotts RG7 136 B6
Block D SL2 23 B1
Block F SL2 23 C1
Blomfield Dale RG42 117 D7
Blondell Cl UB7 70 D8
Bloomfield Dr RG12 91 C1
Bloomfieldhatch La RG7 138 B8
Bloomfield Rd SL6 39 A5
Bloomsbury Way GU17 150 D3
Blossom Ave RG7 83 E4
Blossom Gr RG5 60 E1
Blossom La RG7 83 E4
Blossom Rd RG4 58 F3
Blossoms The RG20 51 C4
Blount Cres RG42 90 E1
Bloxworth Cl 10 RG12 118 F5
Blue Ball La TW20 95 F3
Bluebell Dr RG7 110 F3
Bluebell Gdns RG4 59 C7
Bluebell Hill RG12 118 E8
Bluebell Mdw RG41 88 C3
Bluebell Mews GU15 151 D7

Bluebell Rise GU18 . . . . . . 153 B8
Bluebell Way RG18 . . . . . . 106 D5
Bluecoats RG18 . . . . 106 D4
Bluecoat Wlk RG12 . . . . . . 118 D4
Bluethroat Cl GU47 . . . . . 150 E8
Blumfield Cres SL1 . . . . . . 41 E8
Blumfield Ct SL1 . . . . 21 D1
Blundell's Rd RG30 . . . . . . 84 E8
Blunden Dr SL3 . . . . 44 C2
Blunts Ave UB7 . . . . 71 A7
Blyth Ave RG19 . . . . 106 E2
Blythe Cl SL0 . . . . 44 F7
Blythe Ho SL1 . . . . 41 D5
Blythewood La SL5 . . . . . . 119 E7
Blyth Ho RG12 . . . . 117 F3
Blyth Wlk 6 RG1 . . . . 86 B5
Blythwood Dr GU16 . . . . . 151 D2
Boadicea Cl SL1 . . . . 41 E5
Boames La RG20 . . . . 129 F5
Board La RG20 . . . . 102 F5
Boarlands Cl SL1 . . . . 41 F6
Boathouse Reach RG9 . . . . 15 E1
Bobgreen Ct RG2 . . . . 113 C6
Bobmore La SL7 . . . . 1 F3
Bockhampton Rd RG17 . . . 25 C1
Bockmer La SL7 . . . . 17 B7
Bodens Ride SL5 . . . . 119 F1
Bodin Gdns RG14 . . . . 131 B8
Bodmin Ave SL2 . . . . 42 A8
Bodmin Cl RG19 . . . . 106 C2
Bodmin Rd RG5 . . . . 87 C5
Body Rd 2 RG1 . . . . 86 A7
Bog La RG12 . . . . 119 A5
Boham's Rd OX11 . . . . 11 D6
Bolding House La GU24 . 153 F7
Boldrewood RG7 . . . . 110 F2
Bold's Ct SL2 . . . . 23 A5
Boleyn Cl TW18 . . . . 96 E3
Bolingbroke Way RG19 . . 106 F3
Bolney La RG9 . . . . 36 A5
Bolney Rd RG9 . . . . 36 B5
Bolney Trevor Dr RG9 . . . . 36 A4
Bolton Ave SL4 . . . . 67 D4
Bolton Cres SL4 . . . . 67 C4
Bolton Pl 5 RG14 . . . . 105 A3
Bolton Rd SL4 . . . . 67 C4
Bolton Row RG20 . . . . 50 D7
Boltons La RG42 . . . . 90 F1
Bolton's La TW6, UB7 . . . . . 71 B7
Bolwell Cl RG10 . . . . 61 F4
Bomer Cl UB7 . . . . 71 A7
Bomford Cl RG18 . . . . 78 F6
Bond Cl RG26 . . . . 135 A1
Bond St TW20 . . . . 95 C3
Bond Way RG12 . . . . 118 B8
Bone La RG14 . . . . 105 C3
Bone Lane Ind Est RG14 105 C3
Bonemill La RG20 . . . . 104 D2
Bones La RG9 . . . . 35 A3
Bonham Ct 3 RG41 . . . . . . 88 C2
Bonhomie Ct RG10 . . . . 89 A7
Bonnicut Ct SL5 . . . . 121 A4
Bonny's Yd RG27 . . . . 141 A1
Boole Hts RG12 . . . . 118 A4
Boot End RG2 . . . . 112 F8
Booth Dr
Finchampstead RG40 . . . . . 115 E1
Staines TW18 . . . . 97 D2
Borderers Gdns RG19 . . . 106 D1
Borderside
Slough SL2 . . . . 43 A7
Yateley GU46 . . . . 149 A6
Borrowdale Cl 3 TW20 . . 96 B1
Borrowdale Gdns GU15 . . 152 D4
Borrowdale Rd RG41 . . . . . 88 B4
Boscawen Way RG19 . . . . 107 A3
Boscombe Cl TW20 . . . . . 123 C8
Bosham Cl RG6 . . . . 114 B8
Boshers Gdns TW20 . . . . . . 95 F2
Bosman Dr GU20 . . . . 146 B6
Bossington Ct 9 TW18 . . . 96 F3
Bostock La RG7 . . . . 83 A2
Boston Ave RG1 . . . . 85 F6
Boston Dr SL8 . . . . 3 B3
Boston Gr SL1 . . . . 42 C7
Boston Rd RG9 . . . . 35 E8
Bosworth Ct SL1 . . . . 41 C6
Bosworth Gdns
Earley RG5 . . . . 87 E4
4 Woodley RG5 . . . . 87 E4
Botany Cl RG19 . . . . 106 F3
Botham Dr SL1 . . . . 42 E3
BOTHAMPSTEAD 52 B4
Bothy The RG10 . . . . 36 D2
Botmoor Way RG20 . . . . . . 48 F7
Bottisham Cl RG6 . . . . 114 C8
Bottle La
Knowl Hill SL6 . . . . 38 A2
Newell Green RG42 . . . . . . 91 A6
Bottom La RG7 . . . . 110 D8
Bottom Waltons Cvn Site
SL2 . . . . 21 F3
Boughton Ho RG9 . . . . 35 D8
Bouldish Farm Rd SL5 . . . 120 A5
Boulters Cl
Maidenhead SL6 . . . . 20 C1
Slough SL1 . . . . 42 A4
Woodley RG5 . . . . 87 F8
Boulters Ct SL6 . . . . 20 C1
Boulters Gdns SL6 . . . . 20 C1
Boulters Ho RG12 . . . . 118 E5
Boulters La SL6 . . . . 20 C1
Boulton Rd RG2 . . . . 86 A3
Boult St RG1 . . . . 86 C7
Boults Wlk RG2 . . . . 86 B5
Boundary Cl RG31 . . . . 84 C6
Boundary La RG4 . . . . 58 E3
Boundary Pl HP10 . . . . 3 D8
Boundary Rd
Newbury RG14 . . . . 105 B2
Staines TW15 . . . . 97 C3
Taplow SL1, SL6 . . . . 40 F8
Wooburn Green HP10 . . . . . 3 D8
Boundoak Ind Est RG2 . . 140 D8
Bourn Arch RG18 . . . . 106 B4
Bourn Cl RG6 . . . . 87 C1
Bourne Ave
Chertsey KT16 . . . . 124 A6
Reading RG2 . . . . 86 B4
Windsor SL4 . . . . 67 C3
Bourne Cl
Bourne End SL8 . . . . 3 B5
Reading RG31 . . . . 84 B4
BOURNE END 3 B2
Bourne End Bsns Pk 1
SL8 . . . . 3 B3
Bourne End Rd SL6, SL8 . . . 20 E8
Bourne End Sta SL8 . . . . 3 A3
Bourne Ho 5 TW15 . . . . . . 98 A3
Bourne Mdw TW20 . . . . . . 123 B5
Bourne Rd
Pangbourne RG8 . . . . 56 E5
Slough SL1 . . . . 42 D4
Thatcham RG18, RG19 . . . 106 B4
Wentworth GU25 . . . . 122 D4
Bourneside GU25 . . . . 122 A2
Bourne-Stevens Cl RG1 . . 86 B7
Bourne Vale RG17 . . . . 100 C5
Bourton Cl RG30 . . . . 84 F7
Bouverie Way SL3 . . . . 43 E2
BOVENEY 66 C8
Boveney Cl SL1 . . . . 42 A4
Boveney Ho RG12 . . . . 118 E5
Boveney New Rd SL4 . . . . . 41 E2
Boveney Rd SL4 . . . . 41 C1
BOVINGDON GREEN 1 A3
Bovingdon Hts SL7 . . . . 1 B2
Bowden Cl TW14 . . . . 98 E7
Bowden Rd SL5 . . . . 120 D4
Bowdown Ct 10 RG14 . . . . 104 F2
Bower Ct SL1 . . . . 41 F6
Bowers The RG40 . . . . 116 A1
Bower Way SL1 . . . . 41 E6
Bowes-Lyon Cl 6 SL4 . . . . 67 C6
Bowes Rd
Egham TW18 . . . . 96 E2
6 Thatcham RG19 . . . . . . 106 D2
Bowfell Cl RG31 . . . . 57 C2
Bowland Dr RG12 . . . . 118 E2
Bowling Ct RG9 . . . . 15 D3
Bowling Green Farmhouse
RG8 . . . . 57 B5
Bowling Green La RG8 . . . 57 B5
Bowling Green Rd RG18 . 106 B6
Bowlings The GU15 . . . . . 151 C6
Bowman Ct RG45 . . . . 142 F4
Bowmans Cl SL1 . . . . 21 B3
Bowry Dr TW19 . . . . 68 F1
Bowyer Cres RG40 . . . . . . 116 C8
Bowyer Dr SL1 . . . . 41 E6
Bowyer's La RG42 . . . . 91 C6
Bowyer Wlk SL5 . . . . 119 E8
BOXFORD 76 D3
Boxford Ridge RG12 . . . . . 118 B6
Boyd Ct RG42 . . . . 118 A8
Boyndon Rd SL6 . . . . 39 D7
Boyne Hill CE Inf Sch SL6 39 D6
BOYN HILL 39 D6
Boyn Hill Ave SL6 . . . . 39 D6
Boyn Hill Cl SL6 . . . . 39 D6
Boyn Hill Rd SL6 . . . . 39 D6
Boyn Valley Ind Est SL6 . . . 39 E6
Boyn Valley Rd SL6 . . . . . . 39 D5
Bracebridge GU15 . . . . . . 151 A5
Bracken Bank SL5 . . . . . . 119 C8
Bracken Cl
Ashford TW16 . . . . 98 F2
Farnham Common SL2 . . . . 22 D8
Purley on T RG31 . . . . 57 C1
Bracken Copse RG17 . . . . 127 E5
Brackendale Cl GU15 . . . . 151 E3
Brackendale Rd GU15 . . . 151 D4
Brackendale Way RG6 . . . . 87 A5
Brackenforde SL3 . . . . 43 C4
Bracken La GU46 . . . . 149 B6
Bracken Rd SL6 . . . . 39 C4
Brackens The RG45 . . . . . 143 A7
Bracken Way
Burghfield Common RG7 . . 111 A2
Flackwell Heath HP10 . . . . . . 3 B7
Brackenwood GU15 . . . . . 152 D5
Brackenwood Dr RG26 . . 135 A1
Brackley Ho 3 TW18 . . . . . 96 F3
BRACKNELL 118 D5
Bracknell Beeches RG12 118 B6
Bracknell Bsns Ctr The
RG12 . . . . 117 F7
Bracknell Cl GU15 . . . . . . 144 F1
Bracknell Enterprise Ctr
RG12 . . . . 118 A7
Bracknell Rd
Bagshot GU19 . . . . 145 E6
Camberley GU15 . . . . 145 A1
Crowthorne RG45 . . . . 143 D6
Winkfield RG42 . . . . 92 A5
Bracknell Sta RG12 . . . . . . 118 B6
Bracknell & Wokingham Coll
Bracknell RG12 . . . . 118 C7
Bracknell, Wick Hill RG12 . 118 C8
Brackstone Cl RG4 . . . . 59 C2
Bradbury Gdns SL3 . . . . . . 23 D8
Bradcutts La SL6 . . . . 19 E8
Bradenham La SL7 . . . . 18 C5
BRADFIELD 82 D5
Bradfield CE Prim Sch
RG7 . . . . 82 B2
Bradfield Coll RG7 . . . . 82 C6
Bradfields RG12 . . . . 118 D4
Bradford Rd SL1 . . . . 42 A7
Brading Way RG8 . . . . 57 D5
Bradley Cl RG17 . . . . 102 B1
Bradley Dr RG40 . . . . 116 A2
Bradley-Moore Sq RG18 . 106 E5
Bradley Rd SL1 . . . . 42 E6
Bradmore Way RG6 . . . . . 114 A8
Bradshaw Cl SL4 . . . . 66 E6
Bradwell Rd RG31 . . . . 57 C3
Braeburn Ct TW18 . . . . 97 B3
Braemar SL6 . . . . 63 D7
Braemar Ct 3 SL7 . . . . 1 D2
Braemar Gdns SL1 . . . . 42 A4
Braemore Cl RG19 . . . . . . 106 D2
Braeside RG12 . . . . 117 C7
Brakenhale Sch The
RG12 . . . . 118 B5
Brakes Rise GU47 . . . . 150 E8
Bramber Ct SL1 . . . . 42 A5
Bramber Mews RG4 . . . . . . 59 E4
Bramble Cl
Burghfield Common RG7 . . 110 E3
Upper Halliford TW17 . . . . 125 D6
Bramble Cres RG30 . . . . . . 84 E8
Bramble Ct 4 RG14 . . . . . 105 B2
Brambledown TW18 . . . . . 124 B8
Bramble Dr SL6 . . . . 39 A4
Bramblegate RG45 . . . . . . 143 A6
Brambles The
Crowthorne RG45 . . . . 142 D6
Holyport SL6 . . . . 65 B8
Newbury RG14 . . . . 130 E8
Bramblings RG4 . . . . 58 E6
Bramcote GU15 . . . . 152 C5
Bramley Ave TW17 . . . . . . 125 E6
Bramley Chase SL6 . . . . 39 C4
Bramley Cl
Chertsey KT16 . . . . 124 B1
Earley RG6 . . . . 87 B3
Maidenhead SL6 . . . . 39 C3
Staines TW18 . . . . 97 C2
Bramley Ct
Crowthorne RG45 . . . . 142 D5
East Bedfont TW14 . . . . 71 D1
Bramley Gr RG45 . . . . 142 D5
Bramley La GU17 . . . . 150 B5
Bramley Rd
Camberley GU15 . . . . 151 B2
Silchester RG7 . . . . 136 B1
Bramling Ave GU46 . . . . . 149 B6
Brammas Cl SL1 . . . . 42 C3
Brampton Chase RG9 . . . . 36 A4
Brampton Ct SL6 . . . . 40 B8
Bramshaw Rd RG30 . . . . . . 58 A1
Bramshill Cl RG2 . . . . 140 E8
Bramwell Cl RG19 . . . . . . 106 F2
Branagh Ct 6 RG30 . . . . . . 85 B8
Branch End RG14 . . . . 105 C5
Bran Cl RG30 . . . . 84 E8
Brandon Ave RG5 . . . . 88 A8
Brandon Cl GU15 . . . . 152 D4
BRANDS HILL 69 A8
Brands Rd SL3 . . . . 69 B8
Brandy Bottom GU46 . . . . 149 E3
Branksome Cl GU15 . . . . . 151 E6
Branksome Ct 6 RG1 . . . . . 85 F7
Branksome Hill Rd GU47 150 E8
Branksome Park Rd
GU15 . . . . 151 E6
Brants Bridge RG12 . . . . . 118 E7
Brants Cl RG2 . . . . 114 E2
Brattain Ct RG12 . . . . 118 D6
Braunfels Wlk RG14 . . . . . 104 E2
Bravington Cl TW17 . . . . . 124 F4
BRAY 40 D3
Braybank SL6 . . . . 40 D4
Braybrook RG41 . . . . 116 B4
Braybrooke Dr RG10 . . . . . 88 F8
Braybrooke Gdns RG10 . . . 36 D1
Braybrooke Rd
Bracknell RG42 . . . . 91 B1
Wargrave RG10 . . . . 36 D1
Bray Cl SL6 . . . . 40 C3
Bray Ct SL6 . . . . 40 C2
Braye Cl GU47 . . . . 143 C1
Brayfield Rd SL6 . . . . 40 C4
Brayford Rd RG2 . . . . 113 C8
Bray Rd
Maidenhead SL6 . . . . 40 B5
Reading RG30 . . . . 85 B4
BRAY WICK 40 B3
Braywick Park & Nature Ctr*
SL6 . . . . 40 B3
Braywick Rd SL6 . . . . 40 A4
Braywood Ave TW20 . . . . . 96 A2
Braywood CE Fst Sch SL4 65 E5
Braywood Cotts SL4 . . . . . . 66 A5
BRAYWOODSIDE 64 D3
Braziers La RG42, SL4 . . . . 92 D4
Breach Sq RG17 . . . . 100 D4
Breadcroft La SL6 . . . . 38 E3
Breadcroft Rd SL6 . . . . 38 F3
Bream Cl SL7 . . . . 18 C8
Brean Wlk RG6 . . . . 87 A2
Brechin Ct 3 RG1 . . . . 86 C6
Brecon Ct SL1 . . . . 42 C4
Brecon Rd RG5 . . . . 87 F8
Bredon Rd RG41 . . . . 88 F1
Bredward Cl SL1 . . . . 21 B2
Breech The GU47 . . . . 150 E7
Breedons Hill RG8 . . . . 56 C5
Breezes The SL6 . . . . 39 E4
Bremer Rd TW18 . . . . 97 A5
Brendon Cl
Harlington UB7 . . . . 71 C7
Reading RG30 . . . . 57 E1
Brent Cl RG19 . . . . 106 D2
Brent Gdns RG2 . . . . 86 B3
Brentmoor Rd GU24 . . . . . 153 D6
Brent Rd SL8 . . . . 3 A4
Brerewood RG6 . . . . 86 F2
Bret Harte Rd GU16 . . . . . 151 E1
Brewery Comm RG7 . . . . . 137 B7
Brewery Ct RG7 . . . . 83 E3
Brewhouse Hill SN8 . . . . . . 99 B4
Brew Twr 4 SL7 . . . . 1 D1
Briant's Ave RG4 . . . . 59 C2
Briants Piece RG18 . . . . . . 79 B6
Briar Ave GU18 . . . . 153 A8
Briar Cl
Burnham SL6 . . . . 41 B7
Caversham RG4 . . . . 59 A5
Briar Dene SL6 . . . . 19 C1
Briar Glen SL6 . . . . 19 E6
Briarlea Rd RG7 . . . . 136 F6
Briar Rd TW17 . . . . 125 A4
Briars Cl RG8 . . . . 56 E5
Briars The SL3 . . . . 43 F1
Briar Way SL2 . . . . 42 B8
Briarwood RG40 . . . . 141 E6
Briarwood Cl TW13 . . . . . . 98 E5
Brickfield La
Burnham SL1 . . . . 21 B4
Harlington UB3 . . . . 71 D8
Brickfields Ind Pk RG12 . 118 A7
Brick Kiln Ind Est RG26 . . 135 C1
Brick Wlk RG18 . . . . 79 C8
Bridge Ave
Cookham Rise SL6 . . . . 19 E6
Maidenhead SL6 . . . . 40 A7
Bridge Cl
Lower Halliford KT12 . . . . 125 F1
Slough SL1 . . . . 41 F6
Staines TW18 . . . . 96 E4
Bridge Cotts RG41 . . . . . . 115 B2
Bridge Ct
Chertsey KT16 . . . . 124 C2
5 Maidenhead SL6 . . . . 40 A7
Oatlands Park KT12 . . . . . 125 F1
Taplow SL6 . . . . 40 C7
Bridge End GU15 . . . . 151 B4
Bridge Gdns TW15 . . . . 98 C1
Bridge Ho KT16 . . . . 124 C2
Bridge La GU25 . . . . 122 F3
Bridgeman Ct 8 SL4 . . . . . . 67 A5
Bridgeman Dr SL4 . . . . 67 A5
Bridge Rd
Ascot SL5 . . . . 120 D4
Bagshot GU19 . . . . 145 E3
Camberley GU15 . . . . 151 B3
Chertsey KT16 . . . . 124 B2
Maidenhead SL6 . . . . 40 B7
Bridge Ret Pk RG40 . . . . . 116 B5
Bridges Cl RG41 . . . . 115 F7
Bridge St
Caversham RG4 . . . . 59 A2
Colnbrook SL3 . . . . 69 D7
Hungerford RG17 . . . . 100 D6
Maidenhead SL6 . . . . 40 A7
Newbury RG14 . . . . 105 A3
Oatlands Park KT12 . . . . . . 125 F2
Reading RG1 . . . . 86 A7
Staines TW18 . . . . 96 E4
Bridges The RG7 . . . . 136 C5
Bridgestone Dr SL8 . . . . 3 C3
Bridge View
Maidenhead SL6 . . . . 40 C7
Sunningdale SL5 . . . . 121 B2
Bridgewater Cl RG30 . . . . . 58 C1
Bridgewater Ct SL3 . . . . . . 44 A2
Bridgewater Terr SL4 . . . . . 67 D6
Bridgewater Way SL4 . . . . 67 D6
Bridge Wharf KT16 . . . . . . 124 C2
Bridge Wlk GU46 . . . . 149 D7
Bridge Works GU15 . . . . . 151 B3
Bridle Cl SL6 . . . . 19 E1
Bridlepath Way TW14 . . . . 98 E7
Bridle Rd SL6 . . . . 19 E1
Bridlington Spur SL1 . . . . . 42 B4
Bridport Cl RG6 . . . . 87 D2
Bridport Way SL2 . . . . 22 B1
Brierley Pl RG31 . . . . 57 C4
Briff La RG7 . . . . 107 C7
Brigham Rd RG1 . . . . 59 A1
Brighton Pl 1 RG6 . . . . 87 A6
Brighton Rd RG6 . . . . 87 A6
Brighton Spur SL2 . . . . 22 B1
Brightside Ave TW18 . . . . . 97 C1
BRIGHTWALTON 28 E3
Brightwalton CE Prim Sch
RG20 . . . . 28 D3
Brightwalton Gn RG20 . . . . 28 D2
BRIGHTWALTON GREEN . . . 28 D2
BRIGHTWALTON HOLT 49 F8
Brigidine Sch The SL4 . . . . 67 D4
Brill Cl
Caversham RG4 . . . . 59 A4
Maidenhead SL6 . . . . 39 D3
Marlow SL7 . . . . 1 C2
Brill Ho SL6 . . . . 39 C3
Brimblecombe Cl RG41 . . . 89 A1
BRIMPTON 133 F6
Brimpton CE Prim Sch
RG7 . . . . 133 F6
BRIMPTON COMMON 134 A3
Brimpton La
Brimpton Common RG7 . . . 134 B3
Brimpton RG7 . . . . 133 F6
Brimpton Rd
Brimpton RG7 . . . . 133 F7
Reading RG30 . . . . 85 B4
Brimpton Rd *continued*
Tadley RG26 . . . . 134 D1
Brindley Ct 6 RG14 . . . . . 104 F4
Brinkhurst SL7 . . . . 1 D2
Brinkworth Pl SL4 . . . . 95 B8
Brinns Cotts GU17 . . . . . . 150 C5
Brinn's La GU17 . . . . 150 C5
Briony Ho RG2 . . . . 113 B7
Brisbane Rd RG30 . . . . 85 B8
Bristol Cl TW19 . . . . 70 E1
Bristol Ct 10 TW19 . . . . 70 E1
Bristol Way SL1 . . . . 42 F5
Bristow Ct
Caversham RG4 . . . . 59 B2
Marlow SL7 . . . . 2 A3
Bristow Inf Sch GU15 . . . 151 B2
Bristow Rd GU15 . . . . 151 B3
Britannia Ind Est SL3 . . . . . 69 E5
Britannia Way TW19 . . . . . 97 D8
Brittain Ct GU47 . . . . 150 C7
Britten Rd RG2 . . . . 86 B5
BRITWELL 21 F1
Britwell Rd SL1 . . . . 21 D2
Brixham Rd RG2 . . . . 86 B2
Broadacre TW18 . . . . 97 A3
Broadcommon La RG10 . . 89 C7
Broadcommon Rd RG10 . . 89 B7
Broad Halfpenny La
RG26 . . . . 135 C1
Broad Hinton RG10 . . . . . . 61 F3
Broad La
Bracknell RG12 . . . . 118 D6
Upper Bucklebury RG7 . . . 107 C6
Wooburn Green HP10 . . . . . 3 F5
Broadlands Ave TW17 . . . 125 C3
Broadlands Cl RG31 . . . . . . 84 D5
Broadlands Ct RG42 . . . . . 117 E8
Broadlands Dr SL5 . . . . . . 120 D2
BROAD LAYING 129 F1
Broadley Gn GU20 . . . . . . 146 D4
Broadleys SL4 . . . . 66 F7
Broadmark Rd SL2 . . . . 43 B6
Broad Mead RG6 . . . . 87 D1
Broadmeadow End RG18 106 F4
BROADMOOR ESTATE 143 D4
Broadmoor Hospl RG45 . 143 E5
Broadmoor La RG4, RG10 . 60 E5
Broadmoor Prim Sch
RG45 . . . . 143 D4
Broadmoor Rd RG10, SL6 . 63 B6
Broad Oak
Ashford TW16 . . . . 98 F2
Slough SL2 . . . . 22 C1
Broad Oak Ct SL2 . . . . 22 C1
Broad Platts SL3 . . . . 43 D3
BROADPOOL 93 A2
Broadpool Cotts SL5 . . . . . 93 A1
Broadrick Heath RG42 . . . . 91 E1
Broad St Wlk 7 RG40 . . . 116 C6
Broad St
East Ilsley RG20 . . . . 30 E7
Reading RG1 . . . . 86 A7
West End GU24 . . . . 153 D6
Wokingham RG40 . . . . 116 C6
Broad Street Mall RG1 . . . 86 A7
Broadview Est TW19 . . . . . 98 A8
Broadwater Cl TW19 . . . . . 95 E8
Broadwater La RG10 . . . . . 61 E1
Broadwater Pk SL6 . . . . . . 40 E1
Broadwater Rd RG10 . . . . . 61 E2
Broadway
Bracknell RG12 . . . . 118 C7
Maidenhead SL6 . . . . 39 F7
Staines TW18 . . . . 97 B3
Thatcham RG19 . . . . 106 D3
Winkfield SL4 . . . . 93 B7
Broad Way RG7 . . . . 138 D3
Broadway Ctyd RG19 . . . . 106 D3
Broadway Green Farm Ind
Est GU18 . . . . 146 D2
Broadway Ho 2 GU47 . . . . 150 B7
Broadway Mall 6 SL6 . . . . 39 F7
Broadway Rd GU18, GU20 146 C2
Broadway The
Farnham Common SL2 . . . . . 22 C6
Laleham TW18 . . . . 124 C7
Lambourn RG17 . . . . 25 B3
13 Newbury RG14 . . . . 105 A4
Sandhurst GU47 . . . . 150 B8
Broad Wlk GU16 . . . . 151 E2
Brocas Rd RG7 . . . . 110 F1
Brocas St SL4 . . . . 67 D7
Brocas Terr SL4 . . . . 67 D7
Brockbank Ho RG42 . . . . . . 91 B1
Brockenhurst Dr 5
GU46 . . . . 149 D5
Brockenhurst Rd
Ascot SL5 . . . . 120 B3
Bracknell RG12 . . . . 119 A6
Brock Gdns RG30 . . . . 85 C8
BROCK HILL 92 A5
Brock Hill Cotts RG42 . . . . 92 A5
Brockhurst & Marlston
House Schs RG18 . . . . 79 F4
Brock La SL6 . . . . 39 F7
Brocklands GU46 . . . . 149 B4
Brock Lane Mall 7 SL6 . . . 39 F7
Brockley Cl RG30 . . . . 85 A8
Brocksett Cl RG30 . . . . 85 D7
Brocks La RG7, RG18 . . . . . 80 B4
Brocks Way RG9 . . . . 36 A4
Brockton Ct SL6 . . . . 39 F6
Brock Way GU25 . . . . 122 C5
Broken Furlong SL4 . . . . 42 B1
Broken Way RG20 . . . . 131 B2
Bromley Wlk RG30 . . . . 84 F7
Brompton Cl 5 RG6 . . . . . . 87 D1
Brompton Dr SL6 . . . . 19 C2

Bromycroft Rd SL2 22 A2
Bronte Cl SL1 42 E4
Bronte Rise RG14 131 B8
Brookbank HP10 3 D3
Brook Cl
Sandhurst GU47 143 E1
Stanwell TW19 97 F8
Wokingham RG41 116 A8
Brook Cotts GU46 149 C6
Brook Cres SL1 41 E7
Brookdene Cl SL6 19 F2
Brook Dr
Bracknell RG12 118 E5
Reading RG30 112 E8
Brooke Furmston Pl SL7 1 E3
Brooke Pl RG42 90 D3
Brookers Cnr RG45 143 C5
Brooker's Hill RG2 113 D6
Brookers Row RG45 143 C6
Brookfield Ct GU18 146 C1
Brookfield Ho SL3 68 D6
Brookfield Rd HP10 3 D3
Brookfields Sch RG31 57 C3
Brook Gn RG42 117 F8
Brook Ho
Bradfield RG7 82 C7
Newbury RG14 105 A3
Slough SL1 42 D3
Brookhouse Dr SL8 3 C3
Brook La RG10 62 F3
Brooklands Cl TW16 125 E8
Brooklands Coll Ashford Campus TW15 97 F4
Brook Lea RG4 59 C1
Brooklyn Dr RG4 59 B6
Brookmill The RG1 85 F5
Brook Path SL1 41 F6
Brook Rd
Bagshot GU19 145 E2
Camberley GU15 151 B4
Brook St W RG1 86 A6
Brooksby Cl GU17 150 B5
Brooksby Rd RG31 57 D2
BROOKSIDE 92 F2
Brookside
Chertsey KT16 123 E2
Colnbrook SL3 69 C7
Reading RG31 84 F4
Sandhurst GU47 150 C8
Slough SL3 43 E7
Wokingham RG41 115 F7
Brookside Ave
Staines TW15 97 D3
Wraysbury TW19 68 E4
Brookside Bsns Ctr RG7 139 D6
Brookside Cl RG6 87 D2
Brookside Nursery RG7 139 D6
Brookside Pk 3 GU14 151 A1
Brookside Wlk RG7 111 A4
Brooks Rd RG18 106 E4
Brook St
Twyford RG10 61 D4
Windsor SL4 67 D5
Brookway RG14 105 E2
Brookway Trad Est RG14 105 E2
Broom Acres GU47 143 B1
Broom Cl RG31 84 C5
Broome Cl GU46 149 C7
Broome Ct RG12 118 B6
Broome Lodge
Ascot SL5 120 D4
Staines TW18 97 B3
Broomfield
Bracknell RG42 117 D8
Staines TW18 97 A2
Broom Field GU18 153 A7
Broomfield Cl SL5 121 B2
Broomfield Gate SL2 22 B1
Broomfield Pk SL5 121 B2
Broomfield Rd RG30 84 F8
Broom Gr RG41 115 D4
BROOMHALL 121 B2
Broomhall Bldgs 1 SL5 121 B2
Broomhall La SL5 121 A3
Broom Hill
Cookham Rise SL6 19 E6
Stoke Poges SL2 23 A5
Broom Ho SL3 43 F2
Broomsquires Rd GU19 145 F2
Broom Way GU17 150 E4
Broughton Cl RG30 58 C1
Broughton Mews GU16 151 F1
Brownfield Gdns (Cvn Pk) SL6 39 E5
Browngraves Rd UB7 71 C7
Browning Cl
Frimley GU15 152 C4
Thatcham RG18 106 C4
Brownlow Dr RG42 91 C1
Brownlow Lodge 10 RG1 85 E7
Brownlow Rd RG1 85 E7
Brownrigg Cres RG12 118 E8
Brownrigg Rd TW15 98 A4
Browns Ct SL1 41 E6
Brownsfield Rd RG18 106 C4
Bruan Rd RG14 130 F8
Bruce Ave TW17 125 C3
Bruce Cl SL1 42 A5
Bruce Rd RG5 87 D7
Bruce Wlk SL4 66 D5
Brucewood Par SL7 1 E5
Brudenell SL4 66 F3
Brummell Rd RG14 104 E5
Brunel Cl SL6 39 E5
Brunel Ct 1 RG14 104 F4
Brunel Ctr SL6 39 D5
Brunel Dr
Crowthorne RG45 143 C8
Brunel Dr *continued*
Woodley RG5 60 F1
Brunel Ho RG19 106 A3
Brunel Rd
Maidenhead SL6 39 D5
Reading RG30 85 B4
Theale RG7 83 F2
Brunel Ret Pk RG2 86 A3
Brunel Univ (Runnymede Campus) TW20 95 C5
Brunel Way SL1 42 F5
Brunswick RG12 118 A2
Brunswick Hill RG1 85 E7
Brunswick Lodge 3 RG1 85 E7
Brunswick St RG1 85 E6
Bruton Way RG12 118 E2
Bryant Ave SL2 42 E8
Bryant Cres RG7 113 A1
Bryant Pl RG8 57 B5
Bryants La RG18 53 E1
Brybur Cl RG2 113 D8
Bryer Pl SL4 66 D4
Bryher The SL6 39 A7
Bryony Ho RG42 117 E8
Bryony Way TW16 98 F2
Buccaneer Cl RG5 88 B8
Buccleuch Rd SL3 68 A7
Buchanan Dr RG40 141 E7
Buchan The GU15 152 A8
Buckden Cl RG5 88 A6
Buckfield Ct SL0 44 F4
Buckham Hill RG17, RG20 48 D6
Buckhurst Gr RG40 116 F5
Buckhurst Hill RG12 118 F5
Buckhurst La SL5 121 A6
Buckhurst Moors RG12 117 C6
Buckhurst Rd SL5 120 F7
Buckhurst Way RG6 87 A3
Buckingham Ave SL1 42 B7
Buckingham Ave E SL1 42 C7
Buckingham Ct
Camberley GU15 151 C5
1 Staines TW18 97 A4
6 Wokingham RG40 116 C6
Buckingham Dr RG4 59 B5
Buckingham Gate
Caversham RG4 59 B4
Medmenham SL7 17 D7
Buckingham Gdns 4 SL1 42 F4
Buckingham Ho 4 SL6 39 F6
Buckingham Rd RG14 104 F1
Buckingham Way GU16 151 F1
Buckland Ave SL2 43 B3
Buckland Cres SL4 66 F6
Buckland Gate SL3 23 B2
Buckland Prim Sch TW18 97 C1
Buckland Rd RG2 86 B3
BUCKLEBURY 80 E2
Bucklebury RG12 118 A2
Bucklebury CE Prim Sch RG7 107 C5
Bucklebury Cl SL6 40 C1
Bucklebury Farm Pk★ RG7 80 D1
Bucklebury Pl RG7 108 A5
Buckle La RG42 91 B6
Bucknell Ave RG8 56 E5
Bucknell Cl RG31 84 F4
Bucknell Ct RG1 85 F5
Buckner-Croke Way RG19 131 F5
Bucks Copse RG41 116 A5
Buckside RG4 59 A2
Buckthorn Cl RG40 116 E7
Buckthorns RG42 117 E8
Budebury Ct TW18 97 A3
Budebury Rd TW18 97 A3
Budge's Cotts RG40 116 E8
Budge's Gdns RG40 116 E7
Budge's Rd RG40 116 D7
Budham Way RG12 118 B3
Buffins SL6 20 E2
Builder's Cross SL6 65 E8
Bulkeley Ave SL4 67 B4
Bulkeley Cl TW20 95 C3
BULLBROOK 118 E7
Bullbrook Dr RG12 118 F8
Bullbrook Row RG12 118 E7
Bullfinch Cl GU47 150 E8
Bull La
Bracknell RG42 118 B8
Riseley RG7 139 A3
Bull Mdw The RG8 33 F6
Bulmershe Ct RG6 87 B6
Bulmershe Rd RG1 86 F6
Bulmershe Sch The RG5 87 C7
Bulpit La RG17 100 D4
Bulstrode Pl SL1 42 F3
Bunby Rd SL2 22 F5
Bunces Cl SL4 42 B1
Bunces La RG7 111 A2
Bundy's Way TW18 96 F2
Bungalow Dr RG31 84 D8
Bungler's Hill RG7 140 B6
Bunkers Hill RG14 130 C5
Bunten Meade SL1 42 B5
Bunyan Ct 15 RG1 86 A6
Burbage Gn RG12 118 F4
Burbidge Cl RG31 84 F3
Burbidge Rd TW17 125 A5
Burbury Woods GU15 151 E6
Burchell Rd RG14 104 E5
Burchett Coppice RG40 141 F8
BURCHETT'S GREEN 38 C8
Burchett's Green CE Inf Sch SL6 38 B7
Burchetts Green La SL6 38 C6
Burchett's Green Rd SL6 38 B7
Burchetts Way TW17 125 B3
Burcombe Way RG4 59 B4
Burcot Gdns SL6 19 E3
Burdens Heath RG7 107 A6
Burdett Ct RG2 86 D3
Burdock Cl
Burghfield Common RG7 111 B2
Lightwater GU18 153 B8
Burdwood Ctr 9 RG19 106 E2
Burfield Rd SL4 95 B8
Burford Cl SL7 1 C5
Burford Ct
7 Reading RG1 85 F8
Wokingham RG40 116 E5
Burford Gdns SL1 41 C8
Burford Ho 14 SL4 67 D6
Burford Rd GU15 151 B4
Burford's RG17 47 C6
Burford Sch SL7 1 C5
Burgess Cl RG5 87 D4
Burgess La RG17, RG20 128 D6
Burges Way TW18 97 A3
Burgett Rd SL1 42 B3
Burghead Cl GU47 150 D7
BURGHFIELD 111 C6
Burghfield Bridge Cl RG30 84 F1
BURGHFIELD COMMON 110 E2
Burghfield Mill RG30 84 D2
Burghfield Rd RG30 85 A3
Burghfield St Mary's CE Prim Sch RG30 111 C6
Burgoyne Rd
Ashford TW16 98 F2
Camberley GU15 152 A6
Burham Mews TW20 95 D3
Burleigh Gdns TW15 98 C3
Burleigh La SL5 119 E8
Burleigh Mews RG4 59 C6
Burleigh Rd
Frimley GU16 151 D1
North Ascot SL5 119 E7
Burley Orch KT16 124 A3
Burley Way GU17 150 C6
Burlingham Cl RG2 113 C6
Burlings The SL5 119 F7
Burlington Ave SL1 42 E4
Burlington Cl TW14 98 D8
Burlington Ct
Blackwater GU17 150 D3
1 Slough SL1 42 E4
Burlington Rd
Burnham SL1 21 B1
Reading RG30 84 D7
2 Slough SL1 42 E4
Burlsdon Way RG12 118 E8
Burne-Jones Dr GU47 150 D6
Burnet Cl GU24 153 E6
Burnetts Rd SL4 66 E6
Burney Bit RG26 135 E1
BURNHAM 21 C3
Burnham Beeches National Nature Reserve★ SL2 22 A7
Burnham Cl
Bourne End SL8 3 A4
Windsor SL4 66 D5
Burnham Copse Prim Sch RG26 135 A1
Burnham Ct SL6 39 F8
Burnham Gr RG42 91 C1
Burnham Gram Sch SL1 21 D1
Burnham Hts SL1 41 C7
Burnham La SL1 41 E7
Burnham Manor GU15 152 A8
Burnham Rd RG26 134 F2
Burnham Rise RG4 59 C7
Burnham Sta SL1 41 D7
Burnham Upper Sch SL1 41 B8
Burniston Cl 6 RG6 87 E2
Burnmoor Chase RG12 118 E2
Burnmoor Mdw RG27 141 E2
Burns Cl 3 RG5 87 E4
Burns Wlk RG18 106 C4
BURNT HILL 54 B1
Burnthouse Gdns RG42 91 E1
Burnthouse La RG7, RG30 112 B6
Burnt Oak
Cookham Rise SL6 19 F7
Finchampstead RG40 141 F8
Burnt Pollard La GU24 146 E1
Burn Wlk SL1 21 B2
Burrcroft Rd RG30 85 A5
Burrell Rd RG20 31 E4
Burrells The KT16 124 B1
Burroughs Cres SL8 3 A4
BURROUGHS GROVE 1 F7
Burroway Rd SL3 44 B3
Burrows The RG26 135 A1
Burton Cl
Twyford RG10 61 E2
Windlesham GU20 146 D4
Burtons Hill RG17 102 B2
Burton Way SL4 66 E4
Burway Cres KT16 124 A5
Burwell Cl RG6 87 C1
Burwood Par 7 KT16 124 A2
Bury La RG20 10 A2
BURY'S BANK 131 E7
Bury's Bank Rd RG19 132 C6
Bushell Way RG2 140 E8
Bush Rd TW17 124 F4
Bush Wlk RG40 116 C6
Business Ctr The RG41 116 B4
Business Village The SL2 43 B5
Butchers La SL6 63 D8
Butchers Row RG10 61 D4
Bute St RG30 85 B5
Butler Ct 5 SL7 1 F3
Butler Rd
Bagshot GU19 145 F2
Crowthorne RG45 143 B6
Butlers Cl SL4 66 D6
Butson Cl RG14 104 E3
Buttenshaw Ave RG2 141 A8
Buttenshaw Cl RG2 141 A8
Buttercup Cl RG40 117 A6
Buttercup Pl RG18 106 D4
Buttercup Sq TW19 97 D7
Butterfield
Camberley GU15 151 B4
Wooburn HP10 3 D4
Butterfield Ho 4 RG14 105 A1
Butter Market RG1 86 B7
Buttermere Ave SL1 41 C8
Buttermere Cl TW14 98 F7
Buttermere Dr GU15 152 D4
Buttermere Gdns RG12 118 C6
Buttermere Way 4 TW20 96 B1
Buttersteep Rise GU20, SL5 119 C1
Buttsfield Rd RG20 48 F8
Butts Furlong RG20 28 D3
Butts Hill Rd RG5 87 F8
Buxton Ave RG4 58 F4
Buxton Rd TW15 97 D3
Bybend Cl SL2 22 B4
Byefield Rd RG30 85 B4
Byeways Cl RG10 37 E3
Byland Dr SL6 40 B1
Byreton Cl RG6 87 B2
Byron Ave GU15 152 B3
Byron Cl
6 Marlow SL7 1 F3
Newbury RG14 130 F7
Twyford RG10 61 E4
Yateley GU46 149 B4
Byron Ct
Camberley GU15 151 C5
Windsor SL4 67 A4
Byron Dr RG45 143 B3
Byron Ho SL3 44 B1
Byron Rd
Earley RG6 87 A7
Twyford RG10 61 E4
Bythorn Cl RG6 87 E2
Byways
Burnham SL1 41 A8
Yateley GU46 149 B5
Bywood RG12 118 A2
Byworth Cl RG2 113 B7

C

Cabbage Hill La RG42 90 E4
Cabin Moss RG12 118 E2
Cabrera Ave GU25 122 D3
Cabrera Cl GU25 122 D3
Cadbury Cl TW16 98 E1
Cadbury Rd TW16 98 E2
Caddy Cl 9 TW20 96 A3
Cadogan Cl
Holyport SL6 65 A8
Reading RG30 84 E7
Cadogan Ct GU15 151 E3
Cadogan Pl RG4 59 B3
Cadugan Pl RG1 86 D6
Cadwell Dr SL6 39 D3
Caesar's Camp Rd GU15 152 A8
Caesar's Cl 3 GU15 152 A8
Caesars Ct 2 GU15 152 A8
Caesars Gate RG42 91 E1
Caesar's Way TW17 125 D3
Cages Wood Dr SL2 22 B8
Cain Rd RG12 117 D7
Cain's La TW14 71 E2
Cairn Cl GU15 152 B3
Cairngorm Pl SL2 22 D1
Cairngorm Rd RG19 106 D2
Caistor Cl RG31 84 B4
Calard Dr RG18 106 A5
Calbourne Dr RG31 84 D4
Calbroke Rd SL2 21 F2
CALCOT 84 B3
Calcot Ct RG31 84 E5
Calcot Inf Sch RG31 84 C4
Calcot Jun Sch RG31 84 C4
Calcot Place Dr RG31 84 F4
Calcot Priory RG31 84 C4
CALCOT ROW 84 D5
Calcott Pk GU46 149 C6
Caldbeck Dr RG5 87 F7
Calder Cl
Maidenhead SL6 19 E1
Reading RG30 84 F8
Calder Ct
Maidenhead SL6 19 D1
1 Slough SL3 43 F1
Calder Way SL3 69 E4
Caldicott Sch SL2 22 B5
Caldwell Rd GU20 146 D5
Caledonia Rd TW19 97 E7
Caleta Cl RG4 59 D2
Calfridus Way RG12 118 F6
California Ctry Pk★ RG2 141 C7
California Cvn Pk RG40 141 D7
Callaway SL6 39 E5
Calleva Atrebatum Roman Town★ RG7 136 D1
Calleva Mus★ RG7 136 B1
Calleva Pk RG7 134 E2
Callington Rd RG2 86 C1
Callin's La RG10 63 B3
Callis Farm Cl TW19 70 E1
Callow Hill GU25 122 C7
Calshot Pl RG31 84 D4
Calshot Rd
Harlington TW6 71 B4
Harlington TW6 71 B5
Calshot Way TW6 71 A5
Calvin Cl GU15 152 B4
CAMBERLEY 151 D6
Camberley Bsns Ctr GU15 151 A5
Camberley Inf Sch GU15 151 C5
Camberley Rd TW6 71 A4
Camberley Sta GU15 151 D5
Camberley Towers 1 GU15 151 D5
Camborne Cl
Earley RG6 87 A1
Harmondsworth TW6 71 A4
Camborne Rd TW6 71 A4
Camborne Way TW6 71 A4
Cambria Ct
Slough SL3 43 C4
Staines TW18 96 E4
Cambria Gdns TW19 97 E8
Cambrian Cl GU15 151 B5
Cambrian Way
Reading RG31 84 D4
Wokingham RG40 142 A8
Cambridge Ave
Burnham SL1 21 B3
Slough SL1 42 A7
Cambridge Cl UB7 70 D8
Cambridge Ho 1 SL4 67 C6
Cambridge Rd
Crowthorne RG45 143 C4
Littleton TW15 98 C1
Marlow SL7 1 D2
Sandhurst GU47 143 E1
Cambridgeshire Cl
Bracknell RG42 91 F1
Wokingham RG41 115 E6
Cambridge Sq GU15 151 C6
Cambridge St 1 RG1 85 F8
Cambridge Wlk GU15 151 C6
Camden Pl
Bourne End SL8 3 A3
Reading RG31 84 B4
Camden Rd SL6 19 D1
Camelford Cl RG2 86 B1
Camellia Ct GU24 153 F6
Camellia Way RG41 115 D7
Camfield Ct SL6 39 A8
Camilla Cl TW16 98 F2
Camley Gdns SL6 39 A8
Camley Park Dr SL6 38 F8
Camm Ave SL4 66 E4
Campbell Cl GU46 149 F6
Campbell Pl GU16 151 F3
Campbell Rd RG5 87 D6
Campbell's Gn RG7 137 B5
Camperdown SL6 20 B1
Camperdown Ho 1 SL4 67 C5
Campion Cl GU17 150 F3
Campion Ho
Bracknell RG42 117 E8
6 Newbury RG14 104 F2
Campion Way RG40 116 E7
Camp Rd RG7 110 D2
Canada Rd SL1 43 B4
Canal View Rd RG14 105 D3
Canal Way RG1 86 D7
Canal Wharf SL3 44 A4
Canal Wlk
Hungerford RG17 100 D6
Newbury RG14 105 A3
Canberra Cl GU46 149 A7
Canberra Rd TW6 71 A4
Candleford Cl RG12 91 C1
Candover Cl UB7 70 D7
Canford Ct RG30 85 D8
Canhurst La RG10 37 D3
Cannock Cl SL6 40 B6
Cannock Way RG6 87 C1
Cannon Cl GU47 150 F8
Cannon Court Rd SL6 19 D3
Cannondown Rd SL6 19 E5
Cannon Gate SL2 43 C6
Cannon Hill RG12 118 C3
Cannon Hill Cl SL6 40 C2
Cannon La SL6 38 F3
Cannon Mews SL5 119 B8
Cannon St 1 RG1 85 E7
Cannon (West end of General Roy's base line)★ TW6 71 B6
Canon Hill Dr SL6 40 B3
Canon Hill Way SL6 40 B3
Canopus Way TW19 97 E8
Cansfield End RG14 104 F3
Canterbury Ave SL2 22 C1
Canterbury Ct TW15 97 F4
Canterbury Mews 6 SL4 67 A5
Canterbury Rd RG2 86 C3
Cantley Cres RG41 116 A8
Capercaille Cl RG12 117 D6
Cape Villas SL0 44 E7
Capital Point 17 RG1 86 A6
Capper Rd GU15 151 A7
Capricorn Ho HP10 3 A8
Captains Gorse RG8 54 F6
Caraway Rd RG6 87 A1
Carbery La SL5 120 B6
Carbinswood La RG7 108 B5
Cardiff Mews RG4 58 F1
Cardiff Rd RG1 58 F1
Cardigan Cl SL1 41 F6
Cardigan Gdns RG1 86 E5

Cardigan Rd RG1 86 E6
Cardinal Cl RG4 59 B2
Cardinals The 6 RG12 118 B5
Cardinals Wlk SL6 41 C7
Cardinal's Wlk TW16 98 E2
Cardwell Cres SL5 120 C4
Carew Cl RG31 57 B4
Carew Rd TW15 98 C2
Carey Cl SL4 67 B4
Carey Rd RG40 116 C5
Carey St RG1 85 F7
Cariad Ct RG8 34 B7
Caribou Cl RG5 87 E8
Carisbrooke Cl
Caversham RG4 59 C6
Maidenhead SL6 39 C6
Carisbrooke Ct SL1 42 F6
Carland Cl RG6 87 A1
Carlesgill Pl RG9 35 E7
Carlile Gdns RG10 61 D6
Carlin Pl GU15 151 C4
Carlinwark Dr GU15 151 F7
Carlisle Rd
Reading RG31 57 E3
Slough SL1 42 D6
Carlton Cl
Frimley GU15 152 B3
Woodley RG5 87 E6
Carlton Ct TW18 97 A3
Carlton Ho
Feltham TW14 71 F1
Stanwell TW19 70 D2
Carlton Rd
Ashford TW16 98 F1
Caversham RG4 58 E5
Slough SL2 43 B6
Carlyle Ct RG45 143 C5
Carlyle Rd TW18 97 A1
Carmarthen Rd SL1 42 E6
Carmel Ct SL7 1 B1
Carmelite Dr 24 RG30 85 D6
Carmella Ct TW15 98 D1
Carnarvon Pl 2 RG14 104 F1
Carnarvon Rd RG1 86 E6
Carnation Cl
Crowthorne RG45 143 B8
Shinfield RG2 113 E6
Carnation Dr RG42 92 B2
Carnegie Rd RG14 105 A2
Carnoustie RG12 117 E2
Carnoustie Ct 17 RG1 86 D7
Carolina Pl RG40 141 E7
Caroline Ct
Ashford TW15 98 B2
Marlow SL7 1 E3
Reading RG1 85 E6
Caroline Dr RG41 116 A7
Caroline Pl UB3 71 E7
Caroline St 5 RG1 85 F8
Caroline Way GU16 151 F1
Carousel Ct RG2 86 C2
Carpenter Mews RG42 90 D3
Carpenters Cl RG5 87 F5
Carpenters Ct RG7 137 A6
Carrick Gdns RG5 87 D7
Carrick La GU46 149 E6
Carrington Ave HP10 3 A8
Carrington Jun Sch HP10 3 A8
Carrington Rd SL1 42 E6
Carroll Cres SL5 119 F5
Carron Cl RG30 85 A7
Carsdale Cl RG1 85 F5
Carshalton Rd GU15 145 A1
Carshalton Way RG6 87 C1
Carston Gr RG31 84 F4
Carter Cl SL4 67 A5
Carter's Hill RG40, RG42 90 A4
Carters Rise RG31 84 F3
Cartmel Dr RG5 87 D6
Carwarden House Com Sch
GU15 152 A3
Cary Cl RG14 130 D6
Casey Ct RG7 81 D3
Cassia Dr RG6 86 F1
Cassiobury Ave TW14 98 F8
Cassocks Sq TW17 125 D2
Castle Ave SL3 68 A8
Castle Cl
Camberley GU15 151 F4
3 Charlton TW16 98 E1
Castlecraig Ct GU47 150 D7
Castle Cres RG1 85 F6
Castle Ct SL6 39 D7
Castle Dr SL6 39 D7
Castle End RG10 62 B7
Castle End Rd RG10 62 A7
Castle Farm Cvn Site SL4 66 D5
Castle Gate 3 RG1 86 A7
Castle Gr RG14 104 F5
Castle Hill
Farley Hill RG2, RG7 140 C7
Maidenhead SL6 39 E7
Reading RG1 85 F6
Windsor SL4 67 D6
Castle Hill Rd TW20 95 C5
Castle Hill Terr SL6 39 E7
Castle Ind Pk RG14 105 C5
Castle La RG14 104 E6
Castle Lodge SL6 39 F7
Castleman Ho SL5 120 D4
Castlemead Cotts SL4 67 C3
Castle Mews SL6 39 E7
Castle Rd GU15 151 F4
Castle Sch The RG14 104 F6
Castle St
Reading RG1 86 A7
Slough SL1 42 F3
Castleton Ct SL7 1 E2
Castleview Ho 1 SL4 67 D6
Castleview Prim Sch SL3 43 D2
Castleview Rd SL3 43 C2
Castor Ct GU46 149 B7
Caswall Cl RG42 90 C2
Caswall Ride GU46 149 F5
Catalina Cl RG5 88 B7
Catalina Rd TW6 71 A4
Catcliffe Way RG6 113 F8
Catena Rise GU18 146 B1
Catesby Gdns GU46 149 A5
Catherine Dr TW16 98 F2
Catherine Ho SL5 120 B6
Catherine Rd RG14 105 A2
Catherine St RG30 85 E8
Catlin Cres TW17 125 D4
CATMORE 29 C5
Catmore Rd RG20 29 C7
Caunter Rd RG14 104 D4
Causeway Est TW20 96 C4
Causeway The
Bray SL6 40 C4
Caversham RG4 59 D1
Egham TW18 96 D4
Marlow SL7 1 E1
Causmans Way RG31 57 C2
Cavalier Cl
Newbury RG14 105 C5
Theale RG7 83 D2
Cavalier Ct TW15 98 D1
Cavalry Cl RG19 106 E1
Cavalry Cres SL4 67 C4
Cavendish Cl
Ashford TW16 98 F2
Burnham SL6 41 A7
Cavendish Ct
Ashford TW16 98 F2
Blackwater GU17 150 D3
Caversham RG4 59 C6
2 Chertsey KT16 124 A1
Newbury RG14 105 E5
Poyle SL3 69 E6
Cavendish Gdns 1 RG41 88 A3
Cavendish Meads SL5 120 D3
Cavendish Pk GU47 150 E6
Cavendish Rd
Ashford TW16 98 F2
Caversham RG4 59 C6
CAVERSHAM 59 D4
CAVERSHAM HEIGHTS 58 F3
CAVERSHAM PARK 59 C5
Caversham Park Dr RG4 59 C5
Caversham Park Prim Sch
RG4 59 D6
Caversham Park Rd RG4 59 E6
Caversham Pl 6 RG1 59 A1
Caversham Prim Sch RG4 59 A3
Caversham Rd RG1 59 A1
Caversham Wharf RG1 59 A1
Caves Farm Cl GU47 150 A8
Cawcott Dr SL4 66 E6
Cawsam Gdns RG4 59 C4
Caxton Cl RG30 58 C1
Caxton Ct RG9 15 E1
Cecil Aldin Dr RG31 57 C5
Cecil Cl TW15 98 C1
Cecil Rd
Ashford TW15 98 C2
Iver SL0 44 E7
Cecil Way SL2 21 F1
Cedar RG9 15 D2
Cedar Ave GU17 150 D5
Cedar Chase SL6 20 D1
Cedar Cl
Bagshot GU19 145 E3
Laleham TW18 124 C6
Wokingham RG40 116 C6
Cedar Court Pk RG19 131 C7
Cedar Ct
Bagshot GU19 145 E3
Datchet SL3 68 C6
Egham TW20 96 A4
Maidenhead SL6 39 D7
Marlow SL7 1 E2
7 Windsor SL4 67 A5
Cedar Dr
Bracknell RG42 91 C1
Cookham SL6 20 A7
Marlow Bottom SL7 1 C7
Pangbourne RG8 56 C4
Sunningdale SL5 121 A2
Cedar Gr RG19 106 C3
Cedar Ho
Ashford TW16 98 F1
Maidenhead SL6 19 D1
Cedar Mount RG14 130 F8
Cedar Pl RG5 87 F6
Cedar Rd
East Bedfont TW14 98 D7
Reading RG2 86 E1
Cedar Rise RG19 133 B5
Cedars Cl GU47 149 F8
Cedars Ho SL6 40 A7
Cedars Rd SL6 40 A7
Cedars Sch RG7 135 A7
Cedars The
2 Bracknell RG12 118 F5
Greenham RG19 131 C7
Reading RG31 57 D2
Slough SL2 21 F2
Cedar Way
Charlton TW16 98 E1
Slough SL3 43 E2
Cedar Wood Cres RG4 59 B4
Celandine Cl RG45 143 C6
Celandine Ct GU46 149 B7
Celandine Gr RG18 106 F3
Celia Cres TW15 97 D2
Cell Farm SL4 68 B2
Cell Farm Ave SL4 68 B2
Celsea Pl OX10 14 A8
Cemetery La TW17 125 B2
Centenary Bsns Pk RG9 15 E1
Central Dr SL1 41 F6
Central Est SL6 39 E8
Central La SL4 93 B7
Central Way SL4 93 B7
Central Wlk RG40 116 C6
Centre The SL2 22 C6
Centrika SL1 42 E5
Centurion Cl
2 Reading RG1 86 B6
4 Sandhurst GU47 150 D8
Century Cl RG10 37 E4
Century Dr RG7 113 C1
Century Rd TW18, TW20 96 C3
Cerotus Pl KT16 123 F2
Chackfield Dr RG41 115 D8
CHADDLEWORTH 49 B8
Chaddleworth St Andrews CE
Prim Sch RG20 49 B7
Chaffinch Cl
Reading RG31 84 B7
5 Sandhurst GU47 150 D8
Wokingham RG41 115 E5
Chagford Rd RG2 86 B1
Chainhill Rd Ox12 8 A7
Chain St RG1 86 A7
Chalcott SL1 42 E3
Chalcraft Cl RG9 35 C8
Chalfont Cl RG6 87 A1
Chalfont Ct RG6 87 A1
Chalfont Way RG6 87 A1
Chalford Flats HP10 3 F6
Chalford Rd RG14 104 E2
Chalgrove Cl SL6 40 B6
Chalgrove Way RG4 59 B6
Chalk Hill
Aston Tirrold OX11 12 F8
Shiplake RG9 35 C6
Windsor SL4 67 F6
Chalkhousegreen La RG4 59 C8
Chalklands SL8 3 A4
Chalkpit Cotts RG7 83 C6
Chalkpit La SL7 1 B2
Chalk Pit La SL1 21 B4
Chalkpits The HP10 3 E6
Chalkstream Way HP10 3 E7
Challenge Rd TW15 98 D5
Challenor Cl RG40 141 F7
Challis Pl RG42 117 E8
Challow Ct SL6 19 D1
Chalmers Rd TW15 98 B3
Chalmers Rd E TW15 98 C3
CHALVEY 42 C3
Chalvey Gdns SL1 42 E4
Chalvey Gr SL1 42 B4
Chalvey Pk SL1 42 E4
Chalvey Rd E SL1 42 E4
Chalvey Rd W SL1 42 D4
Chamberhouse Mill La
RG19 106 F1
Chamberlain's Gdns RG2 114 E2
Chambers Bsns Pk UB7 71 A8
Chambers The 17 RG1 86 B7
Champion Rd RG4 59 C1
Champney Cl SL3 69 A4
Chancellor's Way The RG2,
RG6 86 E4
Chancel Mans RG42 91 C2
Chancery Ct 15 TW20 96 A3
Chancerygate Bsns Ctr
Slough SL3 43 E4
Twyford RG10 61 E5
Wokingham RG41 116 A5
Chancery Mews 13 RG1 85 F7
Chanctonbury Dr SL5 120 E1
Chandlers Cl TW14 98 F8
Chandlers La GU46 149 D8
Chandlers Quay SL6 40 C8
Chandos Mall 8 SL1 42 F4
Chandos Rd
Egham TW18 96 D3
Newbury RG14 131 A8
Chantry Cl SL4 67 A6
Chantry Ct GU16 151 D1
Chantry Mead RG17 100 C5
Chantry Pl SL4 67 D7
Chantry Rd
Bagshot GU19 145 D2
Chertsey KT16 124 C2
Chapel Arches 4 SL6 40 A7
Chapel Cl RG8 14 C3
Chapel Cotts SL2 23 B5
Chapel Ct
Chieveley RG20 51 D6
Hungerford RG17 100 D6
Maidenhead SL6 39 D4
14 Reading RG1 86 B7
Thatcham RG18 106 E3
CHAPEL GREEN 116 C3
Chapel Hill
Reading RG31 84 C8
Windsor SL4 67 D6
Chapel Ho RG17 100 D6
Chapel La
Ashampstead RG8 54 B7
Bagshot GU19 145 D2
Binfield RG42 90 C1
Blewbury OX11 12 A8
Curridge RG18 78 E4
Farnborough GU14 151 A1
Chapel La *continued*
Headley RG19 133 F1
Hermitage RG18 79 C8
Lambourn RG17 25 B3
Riseley RG7 139 C3
Shinfield RG7 113 B2
Silchester RG7 135 F5
Stoke Poges SL2 23 B5
Yattendon RG18 53 E1
Chapel Lodge RG40 141 F6
Chapel Rd
Camberley GU15 151 B5
Flackwell Heath HP10 3 A8
Silchester RG7 136 C5
Stockcross RG20 103 E6
CHAPEL ROW 108 C8
Chapels Cl SL1 41 E5
Chapel Sq
Sandhurst GU15 150 F6
Virginia Water GU25 122 E5
Chapel St
Marlow SL7 1 E2
Slough SL1 42 F4
Thatcham RG18, RG19 106 D3
Chapel Terr RG42 90 C1
Chaplain's Hill RG45 143 D4
Chaplin Cres TW16 98 E2
Chaplin Mews 10 SL3 43 F1
Chapman La HP10, SL8 3 A6
Chapman Wlk RG18 106 B4
Chapter Ct 17 TW20 96 A3
Chapter Mews SL4 67 D7
Chard Cl RG5 87 E6
Charfield Ct RG1 86 E7
Chargers Paddock Cvn Pk
SL7 18 A5
Chariott's Pl 21 SL4 67 D6
Charlbury Cl 8 RG12 118 F5
Charlcot Mews SL1 41 E6
Charlecombe Ct TW18 97 B3
Charlecombe Ho RG40 116 C6
Charles Ct TW15 98 C4
Charles Evans Way RG4 59 D2
Charles Gdns SL2 43 A7
Charles Ho
3 Chertsey KT16 123 F1
Englefield Green TW20 95 C1
Henley-on-T RG9 15 E3
8 Windsor SL4 67 C6
Charles Pl 15 RG1 86 D7
Charles Rd
Cholsey OX10 14 A8
Staines TW18 97 D2
Charles Sq RG12 118 C7
Charles St
8 Chertsey KT16 123 F1
Newbury RG14 130 D6
Reading RG1 85 F8
Windsor SL4 67 C6
Charlock Cl RG18 106 E5
Charlotte Ave SL2 42 F6
Charlotte Cl RG18 79 A6
Charlotte Lodge SL6 40 B8
Charlotte Way 8 SL7 1 E2
Charlottown 6 RG14 105 C1
CHARLTON 125 D7
Charlton SL4 66 C5
Charlton Cl
Finchampstead RG40 141 F8
Slough SL1 42 B4
Charlton Ct GU47 143 D1
Charlton Ho TW17 125 C7
Charlton La
Swallowfield RG7 139 C5
Upper Halliford TW17 125 D5
Charlton Pl
Newbury RG14 105 A4
2 Windsor SL4 66 C5
Charlton Rd TW17 125 C7
Charlton Row 5 SL4 66 C5
Charlton Sq 4 SL4 66 C5
Charlton Way SL4 66 C5
Charlton Wlk 3 SL4 66 C5
Charlville Dr RG31 84 B4
Charmile Ct 1 TW16 98 E1
Charmwood Cl RG14 104 F5
Charndon Cl RG2 86 B5
Charnham Ct RG17 100 E6
Charnham La RG17 100 D6
Charnham Pk RG17 100 D7
Charnham St RG17 100 D6
Charnwood SL5 120 F3
Charnwood Ct RG2 86 B2
Charnwood Ho 9 RG1 85 E5
Charrington Rd RG31 84 C4
Charta Rd TW20 96 C3
Charter Cl SL1 42 F3
Charterhouse Cl RG12 118 E4
Charter Pl TW18 97 A2
Charter Rd
Newbury RG14 130 F7
Slough SL1 41 E6
Charters Cl SL5 120 D4
Charters La SL5 120 D4
Charters Rd SL5 120 E2
Charters Sch SL5 120 D2
Charters Way SL5 120 F2
CHARVIL 61 A5
Charvil House Rd RG10 61 A5
Charvil La RG4 60 F4
Charvil Meadow Rd RG10 61 B5
Charwood Rd RG40 116 F7
Chase Gdns RG42 90 C3
Chaseley Ct KT13 125 E1
Chasemount GU20 146 C7
Chaseside Ave RG10 61 D7
Chaseside Gdns KT16 124 B2
Chase The
Ascot SL5 93 A1
Crowthorne RG45 143 A6
Maidenhead SL6 19 C3
Marlow SL7 2 A3
Newbury RG14 104 F7
Reading RG31 84 D4
Chatfield SL2 42 A8
Chatham Ct
Bracknell RG12 118 B3
3 Slough SL1 43 A3
Chatham St RG1 85 F8
Chatham The 1 RG1 86 A8
Chatsworth Ave RG41 88 B2
Chatsworth Cl
Caversham RG4 59 C6
Maidenhead SL6 39 C5
Chatsworth Hts GU15 152 B7
Chatteris Way RG6 114 C8
Chattern Ct TW15 98 B4
CHATTERN HILL 98 B4
Chattern Hill TW15 98 B4
Chattern Rd TW15 98 C4
Chatters The RG7 140 C7
Chatton Cl RG6 114 A8
Chaucer Cl
Caversham RG4 59 A5
Windsor SL4 67 D4
Wokingham RG40 116 F6
Chaucer Cres RG14 104 E5
Chaucer Ct TW20 96 C2
Chaucer Gr GU15 151 D5
Chaucer Rd
Ashford TW15 97 F4
Crowthorne RG45 143 B4
Chaucer Way
Slough SL1 42 F5
Wokingham RG41 115 E5
Chauntry Cl SL6 40 C6
Chauntry Rd SL6 40 B6
CHAVEY DOWN 119 A8
Chavey Down Rd RG42 92 B2
Chawridge La SL4 92 C7
Chazey Cl RG4 58 C8
CHAZEY HEATH 58 C7
Chazey Rd RG4 58 D3
Cheam Cl RG12 118 D4
CHEAPSIDE 120 E7
Cheapside RG1 86 A7
Cheapside CE Prim Sch
SL5 120 E8
Cheapside Ct SL5 120 E8
Cheapside Rd SL5 120 D7
Cheap St
Compton RG20 31 E5
Newbury RG14 105 A2
Cheddington Cl RG30 84 F6
Cheeseman Cl RG40 116 D7
Cheffrey Ct TW15 98 B2
Chelford Way RG4 58 F4
Chelmsford Ct 3 SL4 67 C5
Chelsea Cl RG30 84 F8
Chelwood Dr GU47 142 F1
Chelwood Rd RG6 87 B2
Cheney Cl RG42 90 D2
Cheney Ct RG45 143 C5
Cheniston Ct SL5 121 A2
Cheniston Gr SL6 38 F7
Chepstow Rd RG31 57 D2
Chequer La RG7 138 E2
Chequers Bridge Cotts
SL0 44 C4
Chequers Orch SL0 44 F7
Chequers Way RG5 87 C7
Cherbury Cl RG12 118 E5
Cherington Gate SL6 19 B1
Cherington Way SL5 119 E7
Cheriton Ave RG10 61 D6
Cheriton Cl RG14 131 B8
Cheriton Ct 2 RG1 86 A6
Cheriton Way GU17 150 D5
Cherries The SL2 43 B7
Cherry Ave SL3 43 D4
Cherry Cl
Caversham RG4 59 C8
Flackwell Heath HP10 3 B7
Newbury RG14 104 F4
Cherry Cnr HP10 3 B8
Cherrydale Rd GU15 152 D5
Cherry Garden La
Littlewick Green SL6 38 E4
White Waltham SL6 63 E8
Cherry Gr
Hungerford RG17 100 C5
Reading RG2 86 E2
Cherry Orch
Great Shefford RG17 48 B4
Staines TW18 97 A3
Stoke Poges SL2 23 A5
Cherry Rise HP10 3 B7
Cherry Tree Ave TW18 97 B2
Cherry Tree Cl
Chieveley RG20 51 C4
Sandhurst GU47 143 D1
Cherry Tree Dr RG12 118 D6
Cherry Tree Gr RG41 115 D4
Cherry Tree Ho 9 SL7 1 D2
Cherry Tree La SL3 23 F6
Cherry Tree Rd SL2 22 C5
Cherry Way
Horton SL3 69 C4
Upper Halliford TW17 125 E5
Cherrywood Ave TW20 95 B1
Cherrywood Gdns HP10 3 B8
CHERTSEY 124 B2
Chertsey Bridge Rd
KT16 124 D2
Chertsey Bvd KT16 123 F1

Chertsey La TW18 ... 96 F2
Chertsey Mus★ KT15 ... 124 A3
Chertsey Rd
Ashford TW15, TW16 ... 98 D2
Feltham TW13, TW16 ... 98 E4
Lower Halliford TW17 ... 125 A2
Shepperton TW17 ... 124 F2
Windlesham GU20 ... 146 E5
Chertsey Sta KT16 ... 123 F1
Chertsey Wlk 6 KT16 ... 124 A2
Chervil Way RG7 ... 111 B2
Cherwell Cl
Brands Hill SL3 ... 69 B8
Maidenhead SL6 ... 40 A8
Cherwell Cres 3 RG1 ... 85 F7
Cherwell Rd
Bourne End SL8 ... 3 B4
Caversham RG4 ... 59 A6
Cheseridge Rd RG20 ... 31 C4
Cheshire Ct SL1 ... 43 B4
Cheshire Pk RG42 ... 91 E2
Chessholme Ct TW16 ... 98 E1
Chessholme Rd TW15 ... 98 C2
Chesterblade La RG12 ... 118 E2
Chester Cl
Ashford TW15 ... 98 D3
Newbury RG14 ... 105 C1
Chesterfield Ct TW15 ... 97 E4
Chesterfield Mews TW15 ... 97 E4
Chesterfield Rd
Ashford TW15 ... 97 E3
Newbury RG14 ... 105 A1
Chesterman St RG1 ... 86 B6
Chesterment Way RG6 ... 87 D1
Chester Rd
Harlington TW6 ... 71 A4
Slough SL1 ... 42 D7
Chesters Rd GU15 ... 152 B5
Chester St
Caversham RG4 ... 59 A2
Reading RG30 ... 85 D8
Chesterton Dr TW19 ... 97 F7
Chesterton Rd RG18 ... 106 C5
Chestnut Ave
Camberley GU15 ... 152 A6
Caversham RG4 ... 59 E4
Slough SL3 ... 43 E4
Wentworth GU25 ... 121 F5
Wokingham RG41 ... 115 E7
Chestnut Chase RG42 ... 92 A1
Chestnut Cl
Ashford, Chattern Hill TW15 ... 98 B4
Ashford, Felthamhill TW16 ... 98 F2
Blackwater GU17 ... 150 E4
Englefield Green TW20 ... 95 C2
Fawley OX12 ... 27 C7
Harlington UB7 ... 71 B7
Maidenhead SL6 ... 20 B1
Medmenham SL7 ... 17 D7
Theale RG7 ... 83 E4
Chestnut Cotts RG8 ... 34 A6
Chestnut Cres
Newbury RG14 ... 105 A4
Shinfield RG2 ... 113 F4
Chestnut Ct
10 Newbury RG14 ... 105 A4
Wokingham RG41 ... 115 E7
Chestnut Dr
Burghfield RG30 ... 111 B4
Englefield Green TW20 ... 95 D2
Windsor SL4 ... 66 F3
Chestnut Gr
Purley on T RG8 ... 57 D5
Staines TW18 ... 97 C2
Chestnut Ho RG45 ... 143 C5
Chestnut La RG17 ... 25 E4
Chestnut Manor Cl TW18 ... 97 B3
Chestnut Pk SL6 ... 40 E3
Chestnut Rd TW15 ... 98 B4
Chestnuts The
Lower Shiplake RG9 ... 36 A3
Woodley RG5 ... 87 D7
Chestnut Wlk
Hungerford RG17 ... 100 D4
Upper Halliford TW17 ... 125 E5
Chetwode Cl RG40 ... 116 E6
Cheval Stud Farm SL4 ... 92 D5
Cheveley Gdns SL1 ... 21 C3
Cheviot Cl
Frimley GU15 ... 152 C4
Harlington UB3 ... 71 D7
Maidenhead SL6 ... 40 B6
Newbury RG14 ... 130 C5
Cheviot Dr RG10 ... 61 B4
Cheviot Rd
Sandhurst GU47 ... 142 F2
Slough SL3 ... 44 A1
Chewter Cl GU19 ... 145 F3
Chewter La GU20 ... 146 B6
Cheylesmore Dr GU16 ... 152 D3
Cheyne Rd TW15 ... 98 D2
Chichester Ct
Slough SL1 ... 43 B4
Stanwell TW19 ... 97 E7
Chichester Rd RG30 ... 84 E8
Chicory Cl RG6 ... 86 F1
CHIEVELEY ... 51 B1
Chieveley Cl RG31 ... 84 C8
Chieveley Mews SL5 ... 121 A2
Chieveley Prim Sch RG20 ... 78 A8
Chilbolton TW20 ... 95 E3
Chilcombe Way RG6 ... 87 D2
Child Cl RG40 ... 116 D8
Childrey Way RG31 ... 84 B8
Child St RG17 ... 25 A3
Chillingham Way GU15 ... 151 C4
Chilsey Green Rd KT16 ... 123 E2
Chiltern Cl
Henley-on-T RG9 ... 35 B8
Newbury RG14 ... 130 C5
Staines TW18 ... 97 A3
Chiltern Coll The RG4 ... 59 B3
Chiltern Court Mews SL4 ... 67 B6
Chiltern Cres RG6 ... 87 A8
Chiltern Ct
Caversham RG4 ... 59 B6
Windsor SL4 ... 67 B6
Chiltern Dr RG10 ... 61 B4
Chiltern Gn HP10 ... 3 A8
Chiltern Hts RG4 ... 59 C4
Chiltern Manor RG10 ... 36 D2
Chiltern Rd
Burnham SL1 ... 41 B8
Caversham RG4 ... 59 C4
Maidenhead SL6 ... 40 B6
Marlow SL7 ... 1 C2
Sandhurst GU47 ... 142 F1
Chilterns Cl HP10 ... 3 B7
Chilterns End Cl RG9 ... 35 C8
Chilterns Pk SL8 ... 3 B5
Chiltern View RG8 ... 57 D5
Chiltern Wlk RG8 ... 56 D5
CHILTON ... 10 E8
Chilton Ct SL6 ... 41 C7
Chilton Cty Prim Sch OX11 ... 10 C8
Chilton Ent Ctr RG7 ... 83 E3
CHILTON FOLIAT ... 73 A2
Chilton Foliat CE Prim Sch RG17 ... 73 A2
Chilton Way RG17 ... 100 C5
Chilwick Rd SL2 ... 21 F1
Chimney Ct RG30 ... 85 A6
Chimney La HP10 ... 3 E8
Chineham Ct RG2 ... 86 B1
Chippendale Cl
Blackwater GU17 ... 150 E4
8 Tadley RG26 ... 134 E1
Chippenham Cl RG6 ... 113 F8
Chisbury Cl RG12 ... 118 E3
Chislett Gdns GU47 ... 149 F8
Chiswick Lodge 4 SL7 ... 1 D2
Chitterfield Gate UB7 ... 71 A7
Chittering Cl RG6 ... 87 C1
Chive Rd RG6 ... 87 A1
Chivers Dr RG40 ... 141 E7
Chives Pl RG42 ... 91 D1
Chobham La GU25 ... 122 B1
Chobham Rd GU16 ... 152 A2
Choke La SL6 ... 19 B4
Cholmeley Pl RG1 ... 86 E7
Cholmeley Rd RG1 ... 86 E8
Cholmeley Terr RG1 ... 86 E7
CHOLSEY ... 14 A8
Cholsey Rd RG19 ... 106 E3
Choseley Cl RG10 ... 37 E4
Choseley Rd RG10 ... 37 E4
Chrislaine Cl TW19 ... 70 D1
Christ Church CE Inf Sch GU25 ... 122 B6
Christchurch Cotts GU25 ... 122 B6
Christchurch Ct 4 RG1 ... 86 C5
Christchurch Dr GU47 ... 150 D6
Christchurch Gdns RG2 ... 86 C5
Christchurch Rd
Reading RG2 ... 86 C5
Virginia Water GU25 ... 122 C5
Christian Smith Ho SL6 ... 39 A1
Christian Sq 3 SL4 ... 67 C6
Christie Cl GU18 ... 146 C1
Christie Hts RG14 ... 131 B8
Christie Wlk GU46 ... 149 C4
Christine Ingram Gdns RG42 ... 91 C1
Christopher Ct
Ashford TW15 ... 97 E3
Newbury RG14 ... 105 B2
Christopher Ho SL2 ... 22 C7
Christ the King RC Prim Sch RG2 ... 113 C8
Chrysanthemum Dr RG2 ... 113 E6
Chudleigh Gdns RG2 ... 86 C2
Chuff Cnr RG42 ... 91 D2
Church App TW20 ... 123 C6
Church Cl
Eton SL4 ... 67 D8
Hamstead Marshall RG20 ... 129 E6
Laleham TW18 ... 124 C6
Lambourn RG17 ... 25 B2
Maidenhead SL6 ... 39 D6
Thatcham RG19 ... 106 D3
Winnersh RG41 ... 88 C2
Church Cotts SL6 ... 20 E2
Church Croft RG17 ... 100 D6
Church Ct UB7 ... 71 A8
Church Dr SL6 ... 40 C4
CHURCHEND ... 84 F6
Church End La RG30 ... 84 F7
Churchend Prim Sch RG30 ... 84 F6
Church Farm Barns
Compton RG20 ... 31 F4
Mortimer RG7 ... 137 D5
Church Farm Cotts RG10 ... 62 F7
Churchfield Mews SL2 ... 43 B7
Churchfield Pl TW17 ... 125 B2
Church Gate RG19 ... 106 D3
Church Gr SL3 ... 43 C8
Church Hams RG40 ... 141 D6
Church Hill
Binfield RG42 ... 90 C5
Camberley GU15 ... 151 E5
Chilton OX11 ... 10 D8
East Ilsley RG20 ... 30 E6
Hurst RG10 ... 88 E6
Church Hill *continued*
Midgham RG7 ... 107 E3
Wickham RG20 ... 75 C3
Churchill Cl
East Bedfont TW14 ... 98 F7
Flackwell Heath HP10 ... 3 B7
Reading RG2 ... 86 B2
Churchill Cres GU46 ... 149 D5
Churchill Ct TW18 ... 97 C2
Churchill Dr
Marlow SL7 ... 1 F4
Winnersh RG41 ... 88 B1
Churchill Rd
North Ascot SL5 ... 119 F7
Slough SL3 ... 43 F2
Church La
Arborfield RG2 ... 114 D4
Ascot SL5 ... 120 D5
Ashampstead RG8 ... 54 A6
Barkham RG40 ... 115 C1
Binfield RG42 ... 90 E4
Bisham SL7 ... 18 D7
Bisley GU24 ... 153 F4
Bray SL6 ... 40 C4
Brimpton RG7 ... 133 F6
Burghfield Common RG30 ... 111 E6
Caversham RG4 ... 59 E7
Chieveley RG20 ... 51 B1
Combe RG17 ... 147 E6
Farley Hill RG7 ... 140 D6
Finchampstead RG40 ... 141 E4
Hamstead Marshall RG20 ... 129 F7
Hungerford RG17 ... 100 D6
Newbury RG14 ... 104 D4
Newell Green RG42 ... 91 D5
Shinfield RG2 ... 113 C5
Shiplake RG9 ... 35 F1
Silchester RG7 ... 136 E1
Slough SL2, SL3 ... 43 C8
Stoke Poges SL2 ... 22 F2
Sunningdale SL5 ... 121 B4
Thatcham RG19 ... 106 D3
Twyford RG10 ... 61 F5
Ufton Nervet RG7 ... 110 C4
11 Windsor SL4 ... 67 D6
Yattendon RG18 ... 53 E1
Churchmead CE Sch SL3 ... 68 B7
Church Mews
Purley on T RG8 ... 57 D5
Woodley RG5 ... 87 F8
Yateley GU46 ... 149 D7
Church Par TW15 ... 97 F4
Church Path SL6 ... 40 C4
Church Rd
Aldermaston RG7 ... 135 B7
Ascot SL5 ... 120 A5
Ashford TW15 ... 97 F4
Bagshot GU19 ... 145 D3
Blewbury OX11 ... 12 A8
Bracknell RG12 ... 118 C7
Caversham RG4 ... 59 A2
Cookham Dean SL6 ... 19 B6
Egham TW20 ... 96 A3
Farley Hill RG7 ... 140 C5
Farnham Royal SL2 ... 22 C2
Frimley GU16 ... 151 D1
Froxfield SN8 ... 99 B5
Ham SN8 ... 126 C2
Little Marlow SL7 ... 2 C5
Lower Halliford TW17 ... 125 B2
Maidenhead SL6 ... 40 B5
Newbury RG14 ... 105 B5
Old Windsor SL4 ... 68 B2
Pamber Heath RG26 ... 135 E1
3 Pangbourne RG8 ... 56 C6
Sandhurst GU15 ... 150 F7
Sandhurst, Little Sandhurst GU47 ... 142 F1
Sandhurst, Owlsmoor GU47 ... 143 E1
Silchester RG7 ... 136 C5
Stockcross RG20 ... 103 E5
Sunningdale SL5 ... 121 A3
Swallowfield RG7 ... 139 E6
West End GU24 ... 153 F7
Windlesham GU20 ... 146 C4
Winkfield, Chavey Down SL5 ... 119 B8
Winkfield SL4 ... 92 C5
Church Rd E RG45 ... 143 B5
Church Rd W RG45 ... 143 B4
Church Row SL3 ... 23 D8
Church Side RG20 ... 30 E6
Church Sq TW17 ... 125 B2
Church St
Burnham SL1 ... 21 C1
Caversham RG4 ... 59 A2
Crowthorne RG45 ... 143 B4
Froxfield SN8 ... 99 A1
Great Shefford RG17 ... 48 A3
Hampstead Norreys RG18 ... 52 F5
Henley-on-T RG9 ... 15 D1
Hungerford RG17 ... 100 D6
Kintbury RG17 ... 102 A2
Reading RG1 ... 86 B6
Slough SL1 ... 42 D4
Slough, Upton Park SL1 ... 42 F4
Staines TW18 ... 96 E4
Theale RG7 ... 83 D3
Twyford RG10 ... 61 D4
Wargrave RG10 ... 36 C2
9 Windsor SL4 ... 67 D6
Church Terr
10 Reading RG1 ... 86 A6
Windsor SL4 ... 66 E5
Church View
Beenham RG7 ... 109 A6
8 Slough SL1 ... 43 A3
Church View *continued*
White Waltham SL6 ... 63 E8
Yateley GU46 ... 149 D7
Church Views SL6 ... 39 F8
Churchward Wlk RG31 ... 84 F4
Churchway RG20 ... 10 B1
Church Way RG17 ... 100 D5
Church Wlk KT16 ... 124 A3
Churn Rd RG20 ... 31 D5
Cinnamon Cl
Earley RG6 ... 86 F1
Windsor SL4 ... 66 F6
Cintra Ave RG2 ... 86 C5
Cintra Cl RG1 ... 86 D5
CIPPENHAM ... 41 F4
Cippenham Cl SL1 ... 41 F6
Cippenham Inf Sch SL1 ... 41 D6
Cippenham Jun Sch SL1 ... 41 E6
Cippenham La SL1 ... 42 B5
Circle Hill Rd RG45 ... 143 C5
Circuit La RG30 ... 85 C5
Cirrus Dr RG2 ... 113 D7
Cissbury SL5 ... 119 F7
CITY ... 104 F1
City Gate RG1 ... 86 B6
City Limits RG6 ... 114 B8
City Rd RG31 ... 84 B7
Clacy Gn RG42 ... 91 A1
Claires Court Sch-Ridgeway SL6 ... 38 E5
Claires Court Sch (Senior Boys) SL6 ... 20 B1
Claires Court Schs-The College & Sixth Form SL6 ... 39 E7
Clairmore Gdns RG31 ... 57 C4
Clandon Ave TW20 ... 96 C1
Clanfield Cres RG31 ... 57 C2
Clanfield Ride GU17 ... 150 D5
Clappers Farm Rd RG7 ... 136 F1
Clappers Mdw SL6 ... 20 C1
Clappsgate Rd RG26 ... 135 E1
CLAPTON ... 75 A1
Clapton App HP10 ... 3 D8
Clare Ave RG40 ... 116 C7
Clare Ct RG40 ... 116 C7
Clare Dr SL2 ... 22 B8
Clarefield Cl SL6 ... 19 B1
Clarefield Ct SL5 ... 121 A2
Clarefield Dr SL6 ... 19 A1
Clarefield Rd SL6 ... 19 B1
Clare Gdns TW20 ... 96 A3
Claremont
Poyle SL3 ... 69 D6
Shepperton TW17 ... 125 B3
Claremont Ave GU15 ... 151 F5
Claremont Cres RG14 ... 105 D4
Claremont Dr TW17 ... 125 B3
Claremont Gdns SL7 ... 1 E2
Claremont Pl GU17 ... 150 F3
Claremont Rd
Egham TW18 ... 96 D3
Marlow SL7 ... 1 E2
Windsor SL4 ... 67 C5
Clarence Cres SL4 ... 67 C6
Clarence Ct
Brands Hill SL3 ... 69 B8
Egham TW20 ... 95 F2
Maidenhead SL6 ... 39 E8
Windsor SL4 ... 67 B6
Clarence Dr
Camberley GU15 ... 152 B7
Englefield Green TW20 ... 95 C4
Clarence Lodge TW20 ... 95 C4
Clarence Rd
Henley-on-T RG9 ... 15 D2
Windsor SL4 ... 67 B6
Clarence St
Egham TW20 ... 95 F2
Staines TW18 ... 96 E4
Clarence Way RG31 ... 84 B4
Clarendon Cl RG41 ... 88 D2
Clarendon Copse SL6 ... 39 D6
Clarendon Ct
Blackwater GU17 ... 150 D3
Slough SL2 ... 43 B6
Windsor SL4 ... 67 B6
Clarendon Gdns RG14 ... 105 A4
Clarendon Pl GU15 ... 151 E3
Clarendon Prim Sch TW15 ... 97 F4
Clarendon Rd
Ashford TW15 ... 97 F4
Reading RG6 ... 87 A6
Clarendon Rise RG31 ... 57 B4
Clare Rd
Maidenhead SL6 ... 39 D6
Slough SL6 ... 41 C7
Stanwell TW19 ... 97 E8
Clares Green Rd RG7 ... 113 B3
Clareways SL5 ... 120 F2
Clare Wlk RG14 ... 130 C5
Clarewood Dr GU15 ... 151 E6
Clarewood Ho GU15 ... 151 E7
Clarke Cres GU15 ... 150 E7
Clark's Gdns RG17 ... 100 D5
Classics The RG17 ... 25 B1
Claverdon RG12 ... 118 A2
Claver Dr SL5 ... 120 D5
Clay Cl
Flackwell Heath HP10 ... 3 B8
Purley on T RG31 ... 57 B1
Clay Cnr KT15 ... 124 B1
Claycots Sch SL2 ... 22 A2
Claydon Ct
2 Caversham RG4 ... 59 A2
5 Staines TW18 ... 97 A4
Claydon Gdns GU17 ... 151 A1
CLAYHALL FARM ... 67 E2
Clayhall La SL4 ... 67 F2
Clayhill Cl RG12 ... 119 A6
Clay Hill Cres RG14 ... 105 D5
Clayhill Rd RG7, RG30 ... 111 B4
Clay La
Beenham RG7 ... 108 F6
Wokingham RG40 ... 116 F5
Clayton Ct SL3 ... 44 A3
Clayton Gr RG12 ... 118 E8
Clayton Rd GU14 ... 150 F1
Claytons Mdw SL8 ... 3 B3
Claytons Prim Sch SL8 ... 3 A5
Clayton Wlk RG2 ... 86 C4
Clay Wlk RG18 ... 79 C8
Cleares Pasture SL1 ... 21 B2
Clearsprings GU18 ... 153 A8
CLEEVE ... 34 D7
Cleeve Ct
East Bedfont TW14 ... 98 E7
Streatley RG8 ... 34 B7
Cleeve Down RG8 ... 34 D7
Cleeve Ho RG12 ... 118 E5
Cleeve Park Cotts RG8 ... 34 D8
Cleeve Rd RG8 ... 34 B7
Clements Cl
Slough SL1 ... 43 B4
Spencers Wood RG7 ... 113 A1
Clements Mead RG31 ... 57 B1
Clements Rd RG9 ... 15 C3
Clent Rd RG2 ... 86 B4
Cleopatra Pl RG42 ... 91 E1
Clerewater Pl RG19 ... 105 F3
Clerics Wlk TW17 ... 125 D3
Clevedon Dr RG6 ... 87 A2
Clevedon Rd RG31 ... 57 E3
Clevehurst Cl SL2 ... 23 A6
Cleveland RG10 ... 61 B4
Cleveland Cl
Maidenhead SL6 ... 40 B6
Wooburn Green HP10 ... 3 E8
Cleveland Dr TW18 ... 124 B8
Cleveland Gr RG14 ... 104 F3
Cleveland Pk TW19 ... 70 E1
Clevemede RG8 ... 34 C7
Clevemede Ho RG8 ... 34 C7
Cleves Ct SL4 ... 66 F4
Cleves Way TW16 ... 98 F2
Clewborough Dr GU15 ... 152 B6
Clewborough House Sch GU16 ... 151 F1
Clewer Ave SL4 ... 67 A5
Clewer Court Rd SL4 ... 67 B7
Clewer Fields SL4 ... 67 C6
CLEWER GREEN ... 66 E3
Clewer Green CE Fst Sch SL4 ... 67 A4
Clewer Hill Rd SL4 ... 66 F4
CLEWER NEW TOWN ... 67 A5
Clewer New Town SL4 ... 67 A5
Clewer Pk SL4 ... 67 A7
CLEWER VILLAGE ... 67 A7
Clifford Gr TW15 ... 98 A4
Cliffords Way SL8 ... 3 B5
Clifton Cl SL6 ... 40 A4
Clifton Ct 8 TW19 ... 70 E1
Clifton Ho TW20 ... 95 E3
Clifton Lodge
Eton SL4 ... 42 A1
3 Slough SL1 ... 43 A4
Clifton Park Rd RG4 ... 59 A2
Clifton Rd
Harlington TW6 ... 71 B4
Newbury RG14 ... 104 E2
Slough SL1 ... 43 B4
Wokingham RG41 ... 116 A8
Clifton Rise
Wargrave RG10 ... 36 E1
Windsor SL4 ... 66 D6
Clifton St RG1 ... 85 F7
Clintons Gn RG42 ... 118 A8
Clitheroe Rd GU17 ... 149 E1
Clive Ct SL1 ... 42 D4
Clivedale Rd RG5 ... 87 E4
Cliveden★ SL6 ... 20 E7
Cliveden Mead SL6 ... 20 C2
Cliveden Pl TW17 ... 125 C3
Cliveden Rd SL6 ... 20 E4
Clive Gn RG12 ... 118 B4
Clivemont Rd SL6 ... 39 F8
Clockhouse La
Ashford TW14, TW15 ... 98 B5
East Bedfont TW14, TW15 ... 98 B5
Clockhouse La E TW20 ... 96 B1
Clockhouse La W TW20 ... 96 A1
Cloister Mews RG7 ... 83 E3
Cloisters The
Caversham RG4 ... 59 A3
Eton SL4 ... 67 D7
Frimley GU16 ... 151 D1
Slough SL1 ... 42 D4
10 Windsor SL4 ... 67 A5
Cloister The RG40 ... 116 B7
Clonmel Cl RG4 ... 59 D2
Clonmel Way SL1 ... 21 B2
Close End RG17 ... 25 B2
Close The
Aston Tirrold OX11 ... 12 F8
Bourne End SL8 ... 3 A6
Burghfield Common RG7 ... 111 A3
Burnham SL1 ... 41 D6
Great Shefford RG17 ... 48 A3
Hampstead Norreys RG18 ... 52 F5
Henley-on-T RG9 ... 35 D8
Lightwater GU18 ... 146 A1

Close The *continued*
North Ascot SL5 119 D7
Sandhurst GU47 150 E8
Thatcham RG18 106 B4
Virginia Water GU25 122 D4
Woodley RG5 87 E5
Clough Dr RG18 78 F6
Clove Cl RG6 86 F1
Clover Cl RG40 116 E7
Clover La GU46 149 A6
Club La RG45 143 D5
Clumps The TW15 98 D4
Clyde Rd TW19 97 E7
Clyve Way TW18 123 E8
Coach Ho The HP10 3 E6
Coach House Cl GU16 151 E3
Coach House Ct RG8 56 E5
Coach House Mews 3 RG4 59 C2
Coachman's Ct RG14 105 A3
Coachmans Gr GU47 150 B7
Coachman's Lodge 4 SL4 67 D5
Coach Rd SL5 92 E1
Coach Ride SL7 1 D4
Coalmans Way SL1, SL6 41 A8
Coalport Way RG30 57 E1
Coaters La HP10 3 E7
Cobb Cl SL3 68 D6
Cobbett's La GU46 149 F5
Cobblers Cl SL2 22 B3
Cobham Cl SL1 41 F5
Cobham Ho RG2 113 E4
Cobham Rd RG5 87 F7
Coburg Ho SL4 67 D6
Cochrane Cl RG19 106 E3
Cochrane Pl GU20 146 D5
Cock-A-Dobby GU47 143 A1
Cockayne Ct RG40 141 F7
Cockett Rd SL3 43 E3
Cock La RG7 82 A2
Cockney Hill RG30 84 F6
COCKPOLE GREEN 36 F8
Cock's La RG42 92 A6
Cody Cl RG5 88 B8
Coe Spur SL1 42 B3
Coftards SL2 43 C7
Cokers Ct 3 SL8 3 A4
Colby Gdns SL6 39 F8
COLD ASH 106 C7
Cold Ash Hill RG18 106 C7
Cold Ash St Mark's CE Prim Sch RG18 79 C1
Cold Grove Cotts SL6 20 E2
COLD HARBOUR
Hungerford 100 F2
Maidenhead 38 A3
Coldharbour Cl
Henley-on-T RG9 35 C8
Thorpe TW20 123 C6
Coldharbour La
Thorpe TW20 123 D6
West End GU24 153 F8
Coldharbour Rd
Chilton OX12 9 A7
Hungerford RG17 100 D4
Coldicutt St RG4 59 C1
Coldmoorholme La SL8 2 E4
Coldstream Way RG19 106 E2
Colemans Moor La RG5 87 F5
Colemans Moor Rd RG5 88 A6
Colenorton Cres SL4 41 E2
Coleridge Ave GU46 149 E5
Coleridge Cl
Crowthorne RG45 143 C4
Twyford RG10 61 F3
Coleridge Cres SL3 69 E6
Coleridge Rd TW15 97 F4
COLEY 86 A6
Coley Ave RG1 85 F6
Coley Hill RG1 85 F6
Coley Park Rd RG1 85 F6
Coley Pl RG1 86 A6
Coley Prim Sch RG1 86 A6
Colin Way SL1 42 B3
Coliseum Bsns Ctr GU15 151 A3
Collaroy Glen RG18 106 C7
Collaroy Rd RG18 106 C8
College Ave
Egham TW20 96 B2
Maidenhead SL6 39 E7
Slough SL1 42 E3
College Cl GU15 151 D7
College Cres
Sandhurst GU47 150 E8
Windsor SL4 67 B5
College Glen SL6 39 D7
College Ho 5 RG17 25 B2
College Piece RG7 136 F6
College Rd
Maidenhead SL6 39 E7
Reading RG6 86 F6
Sandhurst GU47 150 E8
Slough SL1 41 F5
College Ride
Bagshot GU19 145 C2
Camberley GU15 151 D7
College Rise SL6 39 D7
COLLEGE TOWN 150 E8
College Town Inf Sch GU47 150 E8
College Town Jun Sch GU47 150 E8
College Way
Ashford TW15 97 F4
College Way *continued*
East Garston RG17 47 D6
Colleton Dr RG10 61 E3
Colleton Prim Sch The RG10 61 E3
Collier Cl SL6 19 F1
Colliers Way RG30 85 B7
Collingwood Coll GU15 152 A8
Collingwood Ct 5 KT16 124 A1
Collingwood Grange Cl GU15 152 B8
Collingwood Mount GU15 152 A7
Collingwood Pl GU15 152 B8
Collingwood Rise GU15 152 A7
Collingwood Wlk RG31 84 B7
Collins Cl RG14 105 C4
Collins Dr RG18 78 F6
Collinswood Rd SL2 22 C8
Collis St RG2 86 B5
Colliston Wlk RG31 84 F3
Collum Green Rd SL2 23 A8
Colmworth Cl RG6 114 A8
COLNBROOK 69 D7
Colnbrook By-Pass
Colnbrook SL3, UB7 69 D7
Harmondsworth UB7 70 C7
Colnbrook CE Prim Sch SL3 69 D7
Colnbrook Ct SL3 69 F6
Coln Cl SL6 39 F8
Colndale Rd SL3 69 E5
Colne Bank SL3, TW19 69 C4
Colnebridge Cl 3 TW18 96 E4
Colne Orch SL0 44 F6
Colne Reach TW19 69 F2
Colne Way TW19 96 B6
Coln Trad Est SL3 69 F6
Colonel's La KT16 124 A3
Colonial Rd
East Bedfont TW14 98 E8
Slough SL1 43 A4
Colonnade 1 SL6 40 A7
Colonnade The RG31 57 C2
Colony Gate GU16 152 D2
Colston Cl RG31 84 D4
COLTHROP 107 B2
Colthrop Bsns Pk RG19 107 A1
Colthrop Cotts RG19 107 B1
Colthrop La RG19 107 B2
Colthrop Way RG19 107 B2
Coltsfoot Cl RG7 111 B3
Columbia Ct RG40 141 E8
Colville Gdns GU18 153 C8
Colwyn Cl GU46 149 C6
Colyer Cl RG18 79 C8
Colyton Way RG8 57 D5
COMBE 147 E7
Combe Rd RG30 84 E7
Combermere Cl SL4 67 B5
Combe View RG17 100 D4
Comet Ho RG7 134 E2
Comet Rd TW19 97 D8
Comet Way RG5 88 B7
Comfrey Cl RG40 116 E8
Commerce Pk RG7 83 E3
Commercial Rd
Reading RG2 86 A1
Staines TW18 97 A2
Commonfield La RG40 141 B8
Commonfields GU24 153 F6
Common Hill RG7 82 F4
Common La
Brightwalton RG20 28 D5
Eton SL4 42 D1
Common Rd
Dorney SL4 41 D2
Eton SL4 42 A2
Flackwell Heath HP10 3 B8
Headley RG19 132 F1
Slough SL3 44 A1
Commons Rd RG41 88 F1
Common The HP10 3 B8
Common Wood SL2 22 C8
Communications Rd RG19 131 F5
Compass Cl TW15 98 C1
Compass Ho 15 RG1 86 B7
COMPTON 31 E4
Compton Ave RG31 84 B7
Compton CE Prim Sch RG20 31 E4
Compton Cl
Bracknell RG12 117 E3
Earley RG6 87 C4
Sandhurst GU47 143 C1
Compton Ct SL1 41 E7
Compton Dr SL6 39 A8
Compton Manor RG20 31 D4
Compton Place Bsns Ctr GU15 151 A4
Comsaye Wlk RG12 118 C4
Concorde Ct 5 SL4 67 A5
Concorde Rd SL6 39 D4
Concorde Way
Slough SL1 42 C4
Woodley RG5 88 A7
Condor Cl RG31 57 C3
Condor Rd TW18 124 C6
Conduit La SL3 43 E1
Conegar Ct SL1 42 E5
Coney Grange RG42 91 B2
Congreve Cl RG7 135 A7
Conifer Cl RG26 134 E2
Conifer Crest RG14 130 C4
Conifer Ct TW15 97 F3
Conifer Dr
Camberley GU15 152 A6
Conifer Dr *continued*
Purley on T RG31 57 B2
Conifer La TW20 96 C3
Conifers The
Crowthorne RG45 143 A7
Maidenhead SL6 39 A8
Coningham Rd RG2 113 C6
Coningsby RG12 118 C5
Coningsby Cl SL6 39 D3
Coningsby La SL6 65 C6
Conisboro Ave RG4 58 E5
Conisboro Way RG4 58 E5
Coniston Cl
Frimley GU15 152 C3
Thatcham RG19 106 A3
Woodley RG5 87 F5
Coniston Cres SL1 41 C8
Coniston Ct
Ashford TW15 97 D5
Lightwater GU18 146 B1
9 Newbury RG14 105 A4
Coniston Dr RG30 57 F2
Coniston Way 2 TW20 96 B1
Conkers SL6 40 B8
Connaught Ave TW15 97 E4
Connaught Cl
Crowthorne RG45 142 F3
Maidenhead SL6 19 E1
Reading RG30 85 D7
Yateley GU46 149 B6
Connaught Ct SL4 67 C5
Connaught Gdns 4 RG19 106 E2
Connaught Jun Sch GU19 145 E2
Connaught Rd
Bagshot GU19 145 C3
Camberley GU15 151 F5
Newbury RG14 105 B3
Reading RG30 85 D7
Slough SL1 43 B4
Connection The RG14 105 A6
Conniston Cl SL7 1 B2
Connolly Ct GU25 122 E5
Connop Way GU16 151 F3
Conought Ho RG9 15 E3
Conquest Ct 16 RG1 86 C7
Consort Dr GU15 152 C7
Constable Cl RG5 88 B8
Constable Way GU47 150 E6
Constitution Rd 5 RG30 85 B8
Consul Cl RG5 88 A6
Control Tower Rd TW6 71 B4
Convent Ct 12 SL4 67 A5
Convent Lodge TW15 98 B3
Convent Rd
Ashford TW15 98 B3
Windsor SL4 67 A5
Conway Cl GU16 151 F1
Conway Dr
Ashford TW15 98 C2
Thatcham RG18 106 B5
Conway Rd
Burnham SL6 41 B7
Harlington TW6 71 B4
Reading RG31 84 C5
Conygree Cl RG6 87 B1
Cooke Rise RG42 91 B2
COOKHAM 20 B7
Cookham Cl GU47 143 C1
COOKHAM DEAN 19 B7
Cookham Dean Bottom SL6 19 C8
Cookham Dean CE Prim Sch SL6 19 B7
Cookham Lodge 13 SL6 39 F6
Cookham Montessori Sch SL6 19 F7
Cookham Rd
Bracknell RG12 117 E7
Maidenhead SL6 19 F1
COOKHAM RISE 19 E6
Cookham Rise Prim Sch SL6 19 E6
Cookham Sta SL6 19 F7
Coolarne Rise GU15 152 A6
Coolgardie Rd TW15 98 C3
Coombe Cotts RG8 33 F6
Coombe Ct RG19 106 E3
Coombe Hill Ct SL4 66 D4
Coombe La SL5 120 C5
Coombe Pine RG12 118 D3
Coombe Rd
Compton RG20 31 F2
Yateley GU46 149 B7
Coombesbury La RG20 76 D1
Coombes Inf Sch RG2 114 E3
Coombes La RG41 115 C4
Coombe Sq RG19 106 E3
Coombe The RG8 33 F6
Cooper Cl RG2 113 C7
Cooper Rd
Henley-on-T RG9 15 D3
Windlesham GU20 146 D4
Coopers Cl TW18 96 E3
Coopers Cres RG18 106 C4
COOPER'S HILL 95 D5
Cooper's Hill La TW20 95 D4
Cooper Way SL1 42 B3
Coote Cl RG42 90 D3
Cope Ct SL6 39 C7
Cope Hall La RG14 130 C7
Copelands Cl GU15 152 D4
Copenhagen Cl RG2 113 C7
Copenhagen Wlk RG45 143 B4
Copped Hall Dr GU15 152 C6
Copped Hall Way GU15 152 C6
Copperage Rd OX12 9 A2
Copper Beech RG42 119 A8
Copper Beech Cl SL4 66 D6
Copperbeech Pl RG14 130 D4
Copperdale Cl RG6 86 F3
Copperfield Ave GU47 143 E2
Copperfield Ho 15 SL4 67 D6
Copperfields RG4 58 F3
Copperfield Terr SL2 43 B6
Coppermill Rd TW19 69 B2
Coppice Cl RG14 131 B8
Coppice Dr TW19 95 D8
Coppice Gdns
Crowthorne RG45 142 F5
Yateley GU46 149 C5
Coppice Gn RG42 90 F1
Coppice Rd RG5 87 E4
Coppice The TW15 98 B2
Coppins La SL0 44 F8
Copse Ave RG4 59 E3
Copse Cl
Camberley GU15 152 A6
Marlow SL7 1 C2
Purley on T RG31 57 D3
Slough SL1 41 F5
Copse Dr RG41 116 A7
Copse End
Camberley GU15 152 A6
Caversham RG4 59 D3
Copse Ho RG41 116 A5
Copse Mead RG5 60 F2
Copse The RG10 36 E3
Copse View Cotts SL6 64 C4
Copse Way RG40 141 E7
Copsewood Ct UB7 71 A7
Copthall Ho SL6 40 A7
Copthorn Cl SL6 39 A4
Copthorne Chase TW15 97 F4
Copthorne Cl TW17 125 C3
Copthorne Dr GU18 146 B1
Corbett Dr GU18 152 F7
Corbett Gdns RG5 87 F7
Corbridge Rd RG2 86 C4
Corby Cl
Englefield Green TW20 95 C2
Woodley RG5 61 A1
Corby Dr TW20 95 C2
Cordelia Croft RG42 118 E8
Cordelia Gdns TW19 97 E8
Cordelia Rd TW19 97 E8
Corderoy Cl RG19 106 F2
Corderoy Pl KT16 123 F3
Cordwalles Cres GU15 151 F8
Cordwalles Jun Sch GU15 151 F8
Cordwallis Est 1 SL6 39 F8
Cordwallis Pk SL6 39 E8
Cordwallis Rd SL6 39 F8
Cordwallis St SL6 39 E8
CORES END 3 D4
Cores End Rd SL8 3 B3
Corfe Gdns
Frimley GU16 151 F1
Slough SL1 42 A6
Corfe Mews RG4 59 E4
Corfe Pl SL6 39 C7
Corfield Cl RG40 141 E3
Corfield Gn RG41 115 F8
Coriander Ct SL5 120 E3
Coriander Way RG6 86 F1
Corinne Cl RG2 86 B1
Cormorant Pl GU47 150 E7
Cormorant Wood 7 RG14 105 C1
Cornbunting Cl GU47 150 D8
Corn Croft RG42 91 E1
Cornel Ho 1 SL4 67 D4
Corner Mead RG18 106 C7
Cornerside TW15 98 C1
Cornerstones RG30 84 E8
Cornerways SL3 68 C7
Cornfield Rd RG5 88 A8
Cornfields GU46 149 B4
Cornflower Cl RG41 115 D7
Cornwall Ave SL2 22 C1
Cornwall Cl
Bracknell RG42 91 F2
Camberley GU15 151 F7
Eton SL4 41 E1
Maidenhead SL6 19 E2
Purley on T RG31 57 B4
Wokingham RG41 115 E6
Cornwall Lodge 11 SL6 39 F6
Cornwall Way TW18 96 E2
Cornwell Rd SL4 68 A1
Cornwood Gdns RG2 86 C3
Coronation Ave
Slough SL3 43 E7
Windsor SL4 67 F5
Coronation Cotts RG10 88 D4
Coronation Rd
Ascot SL5 120 A2
Littlewick Green SL6 38 B5
Yateley GU46 149 E7
Coronation Sq
Reading RG30 85 B4
Wokingham RG40 116 D7
Corporation Cotts 1 RG14 105 A4
Corrie Gdns GU25 122 C2
Corsair Cl TW19 97 E8
Corsair Rd TW19 97 E8
Corsham Rd RG31 84 F3
Corsham Way RG45 143 B5
Corwen Rd RG30 84 E7
Coster Cl RG14 104 D5
Costers Cotts SL8 3 B2
Cotswold Cl
Maidenhead SL6 40 B6
Cotswold Cl *continued*
Slough SL1 42 B3
Staines TW18 97 A3
Cotswold Rd GU47 142 F1
Cotswold Way RG31 57 C2
Cottage Farm Way TW20 123 C6
Cottage La RG30 85 C2
Cottages The RG2 86 C4
Cotterell Cl RG42 91 B1
Cotterell Gdns RG10 61 F3
Cottesbrooke Cl SL3 69 D6
Cottesloe Cl GU24 153 F3
Cottesmore RG12 118 A2
Cottesmore Rd RG5 87 D6
Cottrell Cl RG17 100 E6
Coulson Way SL1 41 B7
Council Cotts GU24 153 F7
Council Hos
Eastbury RG17 46 F6
Farley Hill RG7 140 D5
Shiplake RG9 35 B2
Sindlesham RG41 115 A7
Three Mile Cross RG7 113 A5
Winterbourne RG20 77 C5
Council Hos The
Inkpen RG17 127 F5
Tadley RG26 134 B1
Country Life Ho SL3 68 B7
County La RG42 91 E2
County Lane Rdbt RG42 91 E2
Courage Ct RG30 85 B5
Courage Shire Horse Ctr* SL6 38 E5
Course Rd SL5 120 A6
Court Cl SL6 40 C2
Court Cres SL1 42 D7
Court Dr SL6 20 C3
Courtenay Dr RG4 59 B7
Court Farm RG7 135 D6
Court Farm Cl SL1 42 B5
Court Farm Ind Est TW19 70 F1
Courtfield Dr SL6 39 C6
Courtfield Rd TW15 98 B2
Court Garden L Complex SL7 1 D1
Court Gdns
Camberley GU15 151 D5
Goring RG8 34 C7
Court Hill Rd OX12 7 C7
Courthouse Jun Sch SL6 39 B8
Courthouse Rd SL6 39 C8
Court La
Burnham SL1 21 D2
Dorney SL4 41 B3
Courtlands 14 SL6 39 F6
Courtlands Ave SL3 43 D2
Courtlands Hill RG8 56 C4
Courtlands Rd RG14 105 B1
Courtleigh Manor SL5 121 A2
Courtney Ho 4 GU15 151 B3
Courtney Pl RG42 90 C2
Courtney Way TW6 71 A5
Court One TW15 98 C5
Court Rd SL6 20 C3
Courts Rd RG6 87 B4
Court The RG18 106 D4
Court Three TW15 98 C5
Court Two TW15 98 C5
Courtyard The
12 Bourne End SL8 3 B3
Henley-on-T RG9 15 E3
7 Marlow SL7 1 D2
Marlow SL7 1 E2
Staines TW18 96 F4
Theale RG7 83 E3
Wokingham RG40 116 C5
Coventry Rd RG1 86 E8
Coverdale Way SL2 21 E1
Covert The SL5 120 B2
Coves Farm Wood RG42 117 D7
Cow La
East Ilsley RG20 30 F7
Moulsford OX10 13 F3
Reading RG1, RG30 85 E8
Cowley Ave KT16 123 F2
Cowley La KT16 123 F2
Coworth Cl SL5 121 B4
Coworth Rd SL5 121 A4
Cowper Cl KT16 123 F3
Cowper Rd SL2 22 A1
Cowper Way RG30 85 D4
Cowslade RG14 104 D5
Cowslip Cl RG31 84 A6
Cowslip Cres RG18 106 E5
Coxborrow Cl SL6 19 E7
Coxeter Rd RG14 104 E4
Cox Gn GU47 150 D6
COX GREEN 39 C3
Cox Green La SL6 39 C3
Cox Green Rd SL6 39 D3
Cox Green Sch SL6 39 A4
Cox Hollow RG30 85 E6
Coxs Ave TW17 125 E6
Cox's La RG7 107 D3
Crabtree Cl
Chilton Foliat RG17 72 E2
Hermitage RG18 78 F6
Crabtree Cnr TW20 123 B8
Crabtree La RG18 78 F6
Crabtree Office Village TW20 123 C7
Crabtree Rd
Camberley GU15 151 B2
Thorpe TW20 123 C7
Cradock Rd RG2 86 B4
Crafnant Ct TW15 97 F3
Crafts End OX11 10 E8

Craig Ave RG30 85 B8
Craig Ho 7 RG30 85 B8
Craigwell Cl TW18 123 E8
Crail Cl RG41 116 A3
Crake Pl GU47 150 D8
Cramond Ct TW14 98 E7
Cranberry Wlk GU17 150 F3
CRANBOURNE 93 B6
Cranbourne Ave
Reading RG31 84 C4
Windsor SL4 66 F5
Cranbourne Cl SL1 42 C5
Cranbourne Cotts SL4 93 B5
Cranbourne Gdns RG30 58 A2
Cranbourne Hall Cvn Site SL4 93 B7
Cranbourne Prim Sch SL5 93 A4
Cranbourne Rd SL1 42 C5
Cranbourne Twrs SL5 119 D8
Cranbrook Dr SL6 19 C1
Cranbury Rd RG30 85 D7
Crane Ct GU47 150 D8
Crane Rd TW6, TW19 71 A1
Craneswater UB3 71 F7
Crane Wharf 12 RG1 86 B7
Cranford Ave TW19 97 F8
Cranford Cl TW19 97 E8
Cranford Dr RG10 88 F8
Cranford House Sch OX10 13 F5
Cranford La
Harlington TW6 71 F6
Harlington UB3 71 E7
Hatton TW6 71 F4
Hatton TW6 71 F5
Cranford Mews 12 RG1 86 A6
Cranford Park Dr GU46 149 D6
Cranleigh Rd TW13 98 F4
Cranmer Cl RG31 57 B3
Cranmer Lodge GU15 151 E6
Cranwell Gr
Lightwater GU18 152 F8
Littleton TW17 124 F5
Cranwell Rd TW6 71 B5
Craufurd Ct SL6 39 E8
Craufurd Rise SL6 39 E8
Craven Cl RG17 102 B1
Craven Ct GU15 150 F4
Craven Dene RG14 105 B4
Craven Farm Cotts RG17 72 F2
Craven Rd
Inkpen RG17 127 B6
Newbury RG14 104 F2
Reading RG1 86 D6
Craven Way RG17 102 B2
Crawford Cl RG6 87 B3
Crawford Gdns GU15 151 B5
Crawford Pl RG14 104 F3
Crawley Chase RG42 92 B2
Crawley Dr GU15 151 F6
CRAWLEY HILL 151 E5
Crawley Hill GU15 151 F5
Crawley Lodge GU15 152 A7
Crawley Ridge GU15 151 F6
Crawley Ridge Inf Sch GU15 151 F6
Crawley Ridge Jun Sch GU15 151 F7
Crawley Rise GU15 152 A7
Crawley Wood Cl GU15 151 F5
Crawshay Dr RG4 59 B7
Crawshays SL6 40 C8
Crayle St SL2 22 B2
Crayonne Cl TW16 125 E8
CRAZIES HILL 36 F6
Crazies Hill CE Prim Sch RG10 36 F6
Crecy Cl RG41 115 E6
Creden Cl SL6 19 D1
Crediton Cl RG5 88 A6
Cree's Mdw GU20 146 D3
Creighton Ct RG2 86 D4
Cremyll Rd RG1 58 F1
Crendon Ct RG4 59 A2
Crescent Ct 5 TW18 96 F3
Crescent Dale SL6 39 F6
Crescent Dr SL6 39 E7
Crescent Ho RG5 87 E5
Crescent Rd
Reading, Tilehurst RG31 57 D1
Reading, Whiteknights RG1 86 F6
Shepperton TW17 125 C4
Wokingham RG40 116 C5
Crescent The
Aldermaston Wharf RG7 109 C4
Ashford TW15 97 F3
Chertsey KT16 124 A6
Earley RG6 87 C4
Egham TW20 95 F2
Harlington UB7 71 D7
Kintbury RG17 102 A1
Knowl Hill RG10 37 A6
Lower Halliford TW17 125 F2
Lower Shiplake RG9 36 B4
Maidenhead SL6 39 E7
Mortimer RG7 137 A6
Slough SL1 42 E4
Theale RG7 83 E4
Yateley GU46 149 D7
Crescent Villas 4 SL4 67 C6
Cressex Cl RG42 90 C2
Cressida Chase RG42 91 E1
Cressingham Rd RG2 86 D2
Cressington Ct 2 SL8 3 A4
Cressington Pl SL8 3 A4
Cress Rd SL1 42 B4
Cresswell Cl RG2 113 C6
Cresswell Ct 5 TW19 70 D1
Cresswell Rd RG14 105 D4
Cresswells Mead SL6 40 C1
Crest Cl RG10 61 E6
Crest Ho TW15 98 A3
Crest The RG4 59 C5
Creswell Row SL7 1 D2
Crichton Ct RG7 137 A6
Cricketers RG20 103 E6
Cricketers La
Englefield Green TW20 95 C4
Windlesham GU20 146 D4
Winkfield RG42 92 A3
Cricket Field Gr RG45 143 D4
CRICKET HILL 149 E5
Cricket Hill RG40 141 F2
Cricket Hill La GU17, GU46 149 E4
Cricklewood Cott OX11 12 A8
Crimp Hill SL4, TW20 95 A6
Crisp Gdns RG42 90 E1
Crispin Cl RG4 58 D5
Crispin Way SL2 22 D8
Crisp Rd RG9 15 C3
Crocker Cl SL5 119 F8
Crockers Mead RG20 129 B3
Crockford Pl RG42 90 F1
CROCKHAM HEATH 129 F6
Crockhamwell Rd RG5 87 E6
Crocus Mead RG18 106 E4
Crocus Way RG41 115 D7
Croft Cl
Harlington UB7 71 C7
Wokingham RG41 116 A2
Croft Cnr SL4 68 A2
Crofters SL4 68 A1
Crofters Cl
Frimley GU16 152 D1
1 Stanwell TW19 70 D1
Crofter's Cl GU47 150 A8
Crofthill Rd SL2 22 B1
Croft Ho SL0 44 E7
Croft La
Newbury RG14 104 E4
Yateley GU46 149 D7
Crofton Cl RG12 118 E4
Crofton Ho RG17 100 E5
Croft Rd
Goring RG8 34 C5
Hungerford RG17 100 D6
Mortimer RG7 136 F6
Newbury RG14 130 F8
Shinfield RG7 113 C2
Wokingham RG40 116 A1
Crofts The TW17 125 E5
Croft The
Bracknell RG42 91 B1
Kintbury RG17 102 A2
Maidenhead SL6 39 C5
Marlow SL7 2 A3
Wokingham RG40 116 D5
Croft Way GU16 151 F2
Cromer Cl RG31 57 C1
Cromer Ct SL1 42 E7
Cromer Rd TW6 71 A5
Cromwell Cl RG9 35 E8
Cromwell Dr SL1 42 E8
Cromwell Gdns SL7 1 E2
Cromwell Lodge 4 TW13 98 F5
Cromwell Pl 3 RG14 105 A3
Cromwell Rd
Ascot SL5 120 B4
Camberley GU15 151 D7
Caversham RG4 59 B2
Henley-on-T RG9 35 E8
Maidenhead SL6 39 D7
Marlow SL7 1 E2
Newbury RG14 105 C5
Cromwell Terr RG14 104 D5
Crondall Ct GU15 151 B4
Crondall End GU46 149 C7
CROOKED SOLEY 72 E6
CROOKHAM 133 B5
Crookham Common Rd RG7, RG19 133 C5
Crookham Hill
Crookham RG19 132 E6
Thatcham RG19 106 F1
Crookham Pk RG19 133 B6
Cropper Cl RG19 107 A3
Crosby Gdns GU46 149 A7
Crosby Hill Dr GU15 151 F7
Crosfields Cl 113 E8
Crosfields Sch RG2 113 E8
Crossfell RG12 118 A5
Cross Gates Cl RG12 118 F6
Cross Keys Rd RG8 14 C4
Cross La RG7 138 C7
Crossland Ho GU25 122 E5
Crossland Rd RG1 86 B7
Cross Oak SL4 67 A5
Cross Rd SL5 121 A1
Cross St
Reading RG1 86 B8
Wokingham RG40 116 C6
Crossway RG12 118 C7
Crossway Point
12 Reading RG1 86 D7
5 Reading RG1 86 E7
Crossways
Ashford TW16 98 F1
Bracknell RG42 117 D8
Egham TW20 96 D2
Woodley RG5 87 E5
Crossways Ct 7 SL4 67 C5
Crosswell Cl TW17 125 C7
Crosthwaite Way SL1 41 D8
Crouch La SL4 92 F7
Crowfield Dr RG19 106 C3
Crowle Rd RG17 25 A2
Crown Acre Cl RG19 106 C3
Crown Cl SL3 69 C7
Crown Colonnade 3 RG1 86 E7
Crown Cotts
Bracknell SL5 119 C4
Englefield Green TW20 95 A1
Windsor SL4 67 D3
Crown Ct RG19 106 C3
Crown Hill Ct SL5 120 B4
Crown La
Farnham Royal SL2 22 A4
Maidenhead SL6 40 A7
Marlow SL7 1 D2
Theale RG7 83 E3
Wentworth GU25 122 D3
Crown Mdw SL3 69 B7
Crown Mead RG18, RG19 106 C3
Crown Mews RG17 100 D5
Crown Pl
Marlow SL7 1 D2
Reading RG1 86 C6
Sandhurst GU47 143 E1
Crown Rd
Marlow SL7 1 D2
Wentworth GU25 122 C3
Crown Rise KT16 123 F1
Crown Row RG12 118 D3
Crown St
Egham TW20 96 A4
Reading RG1 86 B6
CROWN WOOD 118 D3
Crown Wood Prim Sch RG12 118 E3
Crow Piece La SL2 21 F4
Crowsley Rd RG9 36 A3
CROWTHORNE 143 D5
Crowthorne Bsns Est The RG45 143 D7
Crowthorne CE Prim Sch RG45 143 C5
Crowthorne Lodge 3 RG12 118 B5
Crowthorne Rd
Bracknell, Easthampstead RG12 118 A5
Bracknell RG40, RG12 117 F2
Sandhurst GU47 143 B2
Crowthorne Rd N RG12 118 B6
Crowthorne Sta RG45 142 E4
Croxley Rise SL6 39 D6
Croydon Rd TW6 71 B4
Cruikshank Lea GU47 150 E6
Crummock Cl SL1 41 C7
Crutchley Rd RG40 116 D7
Cuba Cotts SL6 20 B3
Cuckoo La GU24 153 D6
Cuckoo Vale GU24 153 D6
Culford Cl RG6 87 D2
Culham Ct RG30 85 A4
Culham Dr SL6 19 E2
Culham Ho RG12 118 E5
Cullen Cl GU46 149 C5
Cullern's Pass 18 SL6 39 F6
Culley Way SL6 39 A4
Culloden Way RG41 115 E6
Culver Croft RG42 90 E1
Culver La RG6 87 A7
Culver Rd
Newbury RG14 130 F8
Reading RG6 86 F6
Sandhurst GU47 143 D1
Cumberland Ave SL2 22 C1
Cumberland Ct TW15 97 D5
Cumberland Dr RG12 118 E8
Cumberland Lodge SL4 94 D3
Cumberland Rd
Ashford TW15 97 D5
Frimley GU15 152 C4
Reading RG1 86 E7
Cumberland St TW18 96 D3
Cumberland Villa 6 RG1 86 E7
Cumberland Way RG41 115 D6
Cumbernauld Gdns TW16 98 F3
Cumbrae Cl SL2 43 A5
Cumbria Cl SL6 39 C4
Cumnor Way RG12 118 E5
Cunworth Ct RG12 117 F3
Curfew Bell Rd KT16 123 F2
Curlew Cl RG19 106 C3
Curlew Dr RG31 84 C6
Curley Hill Rd GU18 152 F7
Curling Way RG14 105 C4
Curls La SL6 39 E4
Curls Rd SL6 39 D4
Curl Way RG41 116 A5
Curly's Way RG7 139 D6
Curnock Ct 2 RG14 104 E1
CURRIDGE 78 D4
Curridge Gn RG18 78 E4
Curridge Piece RG18 78 F5
Curridge Prim Sch RG18 78 D4
Curridge Rd RG18 78 D4
Curriers La SL1 21 D7
Curtis Cl GU15 152 C7
Curtis Rd RG31 84 C4
Curzon Mall 7 SL1 42 F4
Curzon St RG30 85 E8
Cutbush Cl RG6 114 B8
Cutbush La
Earley RG6 87 C1
Lower Earley RG6 114 B8
Shinfield RG2 113 F6
Cutting Hill SN8, RG17 126 A4
Cuttings The RG18 52 F5
Cwmcarn RG4 58 F6
Cygnet Cl RG19 106 B3
Cygnet Ho SL6 20 C1
Cygnets The 14 TW18 96 F3
Cygnet Way RG17 100 D7
Cypress Cl RG40 142 A8
Cypress Ct
Charlton TW16 125 E8
Virginia Water GU25 122 F5
Cypress Hill Ct GU14 150 F1
Cypress Ho
3 Newbury RG14 104 F2
Slough SL3 44 B1
Cypress Rd RG5 88 A6
Cypress Way GU17 150 B5
Cypress Wlk TW20 95 B2
Cyril Vokins Rd RG14 105 E2

D

Daceberry Ct RG9 16 C2
Dacre Ave RG4 59 E4
Dagmar Rd SL4 67 D5
Dair House Sch SL2 22 C4
Dairy Ct SL6 65 A7
Dairy La RG9 16 B8
Daisy Mdw TW20 96 A3
Dalby Cl RG10 88 F8
Dalby Cres RG14 131 B8
Dalby Gdns SL6 19 F1
Dalcross RG12 118 E3
Dale Cl SL5 121 A4
Dale Ct SL1 42 C4
Dale Gdns GU47 150 A8
Daleham Ave TW20 96 A2
Dale Lodge Rd SL5 121 A4
Dale Rd
Ashford TW16 98 F1
Oatlands Park KT12 125 F2
Reading RG2 86 B5
Dalley Ct GU47 150 D7
Dalston Cl GU15 152 D3
Dalton Cl RG30 84 E8
Dalton Gn
Datchet SL3 68 F8
14 Slough SL3 43 F1
Damask Cl GU24 153 E6
Damer Gdns RG9 35 E8
Damson Dr RG7 137 B6
Damson Gr SL1 42 C4
Dandridge Cl SL3 43 D2
Dandridge Dr SL8 3 C3
Danehill RG6 114 B8
Danehurst Cl TW20 95 E2
Dane Rd TW15 98 D2
Danes Ct SL6 39 D7
Danesfield RG40 116 D6
Danesfield Sch SL7 17 E7
Danes Gdns SL6 19 F6
Danvers Cl 2 RG19 106 D2
Danywern Dr RG41 88 C2
DARBY GREEN 150 B6
Darby Green La GU17 150 B6
Darby Green Rd GU17 150 B5
Darby La RG8 55 B5
Darby Vale RG42 91 B2
Darell Rd RG4 58 F3
Dark La
Bradfield RG7 82 C7
Purley on T RG31 57 B2
Wargrave RG10 36 D2
Wickham RG17 101 A7
Darleydale Cl GU47 143 D2
Darling's La SL6 18 E1
Darracott Cl GU15 152 B8
Darrell Cl SL3 43 F2
Darrngton GU15 152 A5
Dart Cl
Brands Hill SL3 69 B8
Finchampstead RG40 141 F6
Thatcham RG18 106 B5
Dartington Ave RG5 87 D4
Dartington Cl RG30 84 F8
Dartmouth Cl RG12 118 E6
Dartmouth Ct 2 SL1 42 F3
Dartmouth Terr 1 RG1 86 C6
Darvills La RG10 62 F1
Darvill's La SL1 42 D4
Darwall Dr SL5 119 D7
Darwin Cl RG2 86 A1
Darwin Ct 2 GU15 151 B3
Darwin Pl RG12 118 C5
Darwin Rd SL3 43 F4
Dashwood Cl
Bracknell RG12 118 D8
Slough SL3 43 C2
DATCHET 68 C6
DATCHET COMMON 68 D6
Datchet Pl SL3 68 B6
Datchet Rd
Horton SL3 68 F4
Old Windsor SL4 68 A3
Slough SL3 42 F2
Windsor SL4 67 D7
Datchet St Mary's CE Prim Sch SL3 68 B6
Datchet Sta SL3 68 B6
Dauntless Rd RG7 111 B3
Davenport Rd RG12 118 E8
Daventry Cl SL3 69 F6
Daventry Ct RG42 118 B8
David Cl UB3 71 E7
David Ct 3 TW18 97 A4
David Henry Waring Ct TW14 98 C7
David Rd SL3 69 F5
David Smith Ct RG31 84 F5
Davidson Rd 8 SL3 43 F1
Davis Cl SL7 1 E1
Davis Gdns GU47 150 E7
Davis St RG10 88 D5
Davis Way RG10 88 D4
Davy Cl RG40 116 C5
Dawes East Rd SL1 21 C2
Dawes Moor Cl SL2 43 C7
Dawley Ride SL3 69 E6
Dawlish Rd RG2 86 C2
Dawnay Cl SL5 119 F8
Dawnay Rd GU15 151 B7
Dawn Ct GU15 151 F7
Dawn Redwood Cl SL3 69 A4
Daws Ct SL0 44 F7
Dawsmere Cl GU15 152 C5
Dawson Cl SL4 67 A5
Daytona Dr RG19 107 B2
Dayworth Mews 2 RG30 85 C7
Deacon Cl RG40 116 C8
Deacon Ct SL4 66 D5
Deaconfield RG8 14 C3
Deacons La RG18 79 C7
Deacon Way RG30 58 A2
Deadmans La RG14, RG19 131 B6
Deadman's La RG7 83 D3
Deadmoor La RG20 130 E1
Deal Ave SL1 41 F7
Dean Cl SL4 66 D4
Dean Ct KT16 124 A3
Deanfield Ave RG9 15 D1
Deanfield Cl SL7 1 D3
Deanfield Rd RG9 15 D1
Dean Gr RG40 116 C7
Dean Ho RG1 86 D6
Dean La SL6 19 C8
Dean Par GU15 151 F8
Deans Cl SL2 23 B4
Deans Copse Rd RG7, RG30 111 C8
Deans Ct GU20 146 D4
Deans Farm RG4 59 D1
Deansfield Cl SL6 19 D2
Deansgate RG12 118 B2
Deansgate Rd RG1 86 B6
Deanside GU15 151 F8
Dean St SL7 1 D2
Dean View SL6 19 E6
Deanwood Farm RG20 104 B5
Deanwood Ho RG20 104 B5
Deardon Way RG2 113 D5
Debden Ho RG12 118 D6
De Beauvoir Rd RG1 86 E6
Deccan Gr RG19 106 D2
Decies Way SL2 23 A4
Dedmere Ct SL7 1 F2
Dedmere Rd SL7 1 F2
Dedmere Rise SL7 1 E2
DEDWORTH 66 E6
Dedworth Dr SL4 66 F6
Dedworth Green Fst Sch SL4 66 E5
Dedworth Manor SL4 66 F6
Dedworth Mid Sch SL4 66 E6
Dedworth Rd SL4 66 D5
Deena Cl SL1 41 E6
Deepdale RG12 118 A5
Deepdene Cl RG1 85 E7
Deep Field SL3 68 B7
Deepfield Rd RG12 118 D7
Deep Well Dr GU15 151 E5
Dee Rd RG30 85 A7
Deerhurst Ave RG41 88 C2
Deerhurst Cl RG31 84 E4
Deer Leap GU18 153 A8
Deer Rock Hill RG12 118 C3
Deer Rock Rd GU15 151 F8
Deerswood SL6 20 B1
Defence Cl RG19 106 E1
Defford Cl RG41 88 F1
De Havilland Way TW19 70 E1
Delafield Dr RG31 84 C4
Delaford Cl SL0 44 F7
Delamere Ho 5 RG1 85 E5
Delamere Rd RG6 87 B8
Delane Dr RG41 88 B1
Delaney Cl RG30 84 F8
Delft Cl RG30 84 F8
Dellars Hill SL6 38 A7
Dell Cl SL2 22 C7
Deller St RG42 90 F1
Dell Gr GU16 151 F2
Dell Park Farm TW20 95 A5
Dell Rd
Finchampstead RG40 142 A3
Purley on T RG31 57 C2
Dell The
Englefield Green TW20 95 A5
Maidenhead SL6 38 F2
19 Reading RG1 86 C7
Yateley GU46 149 C5
Dellwood Com Hospl RG30 85 C6
Dellwood Pk RG4 58 F4
Delph The RG6 87 D2
Delta Ct SL6 39 F6
Delta Way TW20 123 C8
De Montfort Gr RG17 100 D4
De Montfort Rd
Newbury RG14 104 E5
Reading RG1 59 A1
Dempsey Ho RG30 84 F7
Denbeigh Pl RG1 58 F1
Denbury Gdns 1 RG2 113 C8
Denby Way RG30 57 F1
Dencliffe 3 TW15 98 A3
Dene Cl
Bracknell RG42 91 C1

Dene Cl *continued*
Camberley GU15 . . . . 152 A8
Earley RG6. . . . . 87 A3
Denefield Gdns RG31. . . . . 57 B2
Denefield Sch RG31. . . . . . 57 B3
Dene Ho SL4 . . . . 67 C4
Dene Hollow OX11 . . . . 10 E8
Dene Way RG14. . . . . 105 A5
Denford La RG17. . . . . 101 C8
Denham Cl SL6 . . . . 39 C6
Denham Dr 1 GU46. . . . . 149 D5
Denham Gr RG12 . . . . 118 C3
Denham Rd TW20. . . . . 96 A4
Denholme Lodge SL3 . . . . 68 B7
Denison Rd TW13 . . . . 98 F4
Denly Way GU18 . . . . 146 C1
Denman Dr TW15 . . . . 98 B2
Denmark Ave RG5 . . . . 61 A1
Denmark Rd
Newbury RG14. . . . . 105 A3
Reading RG1 . . . . 86 D6
Denmark St
Maidenhead SL6 . . . . 39 E8
Wokingham RG40 . . . . 116 C5
Denmead Ct RG12 . . . . . . 118 E3
Dennis Cl TW15. . . . . 98 D1
Dennisford Rd RG20 . . . . . 31 A6
Dennis Pilcher Ho RG12. 118 E6
Dennistoun Cl GU15. . . . . 151 D5
Dennis Way SL1 . . . . 41 D6
Dennose Cl RG6 . . . . 87 A1
Denny Rd SL3. . . . . 43 F2
Denton Cl RG19. . . . . 106 C2
Denton Ct
Marlow SL7 . . . . 1 F3
Reading RG2 . . . . 86 D3
Denton Mews RG40 . . . . . 116 C6
Denton Rd RG40 . . . . 116 C6
Denton Way GU16. . . . . . . 151 D2
Denvale Trade Pk RG14. . 105 D2
Derby Cl RG17 . . . . 25 A2
Derby Rd
Caversham RG4. . . . . 59 B3
Newbury RG14. . . . . 104 F1
Derbyshire Gn RG42. . . . . . . 91 F1
Derby St RG1 . . . . 85 F8
Derek Horn Ct GU15 . . . . 151 B6
Derek Rd SL6. . . . . 40 C8
Deri Dene Cl 2 TW19 . . . . 70 E1
De Ros Pl TW20. . . . . 96 A2
Derrick Cl RG31. . . . . 84 C4
Derry Rd GU14. . . . . 150 F1
Derwent Ave RG30 . . . . 57 E2
Derwent Cl
East Bedfont TW14 . . . . 98 F7
Wokingham RG41 . . . . 115 E6
Derwent Dr
Burnham SL1. . . . . 41 C8
Maidenhead SL6 . . . . 39 D8
Derwent Rd
Lightwater GU18 . . . . 153 B8
Thatcham RG19 . . . . 106 A3
Thorpe Lea TW20. . . . . 96 B1
Desborough Cl
Lower Halliford TW17 . . . . 125 A2
Newbury RG14. . . . . 105 E5
Desborough Cotts SL6 . . . 20 E2
Desborough Cres SL6. . . . 39 C5
Desborough Sch SL6. . . . . 39 E5
Deseronto Wharf Ind Est
SL3 . . . . 43 E4
Desford Way TW15. . . . . . . 97 F6
Detling Ho RG12 . . . . 118 D6
Devenish La GU20, SL5 . . . 120 D1
Devenish Rd GU20, SL5 . . 120 D2
Devereux Rd SL4. . . . . 67 D5
Deverills Way SL3. . . . . 44 C2
Deveron Dr RG30 . . . . 85 A8
Devil's Highway The
RG45 . . . . 142 F5
Devils La TW20 . . . . 96 C2
De-Vitre Gn RG40. . . . . . . 116 F7
Devitt Cl RG2 . . . . 86 F1
Devon Ave SL1. . . . . 42 C7
Devon Chase RG42. . . . . . . 91 E2
Devon Cl
Sandhurst GU47 . . . . 150 D7
Wokingham RG41 . . . . 115 E6
Devon Dr RG4 . . . . 59 E4
Devonshire Cl SL2 . . . . 22 B3
Devonshire Dr GU15 . . . . 151 F7
Devonshire Gdns RG31. . . 57 B3
Devonshire Gn SL2. . . . . . . 22 B3
Devonshire Lodge 10 SL6. 39 F6
Devonshire Pk RG2 . . . . 86 E2
Dewar Spur SL3 . . . . 68 F8
Dewberry Down RG18 . . . 106 F4
Dewe La RG30 . . . . 84 E2
Dexter Way RG41 . . . . 88 B2
Dhoon Rise SL6. . . . . 39 F6
Diamedes Ave TW19 . . . . . . 97 D7
Diamond Cotts RG10 . . . . . 37 C6
Diamond Hill GU15. . . . . . 151 E7
Diamond Rd SL1. . . . . 43 B4
Diamond Ridge GU15 . . . 151 E7
Diamond Villas RG10. . . . . 88 F8
Diamond Way RG41 . . . . . 115 E7
Diana Cl
Slough SL3. . . . . 43 E7
Spencers Wood RG7 . . . . . 113 A1
Dianthus Cl KT16 . . . . 123 E2
Dianthus Pl RG42 . . . . 92 B2
Dibleys OX11 . . . . 12 A8
Dickens Cl RG4 . . . . 59 D2
Dickens Ct RG41. . . . . 116 B6
Dickens Pl SL3. . . . . 69 E6
Dickens Way GU46 . . . . . . 149 C5
Dickens Wlk RG14 . . . . . . 131 A8
Dickson Glade 7 RG19. . 106 E2
Dick Turpin Way TW14 . . . 71 F3
Diddenham Cotts RG7. . . 112 D2
Diddenham Ct RG7. . . . . . 112 D2
Dido Rd OX11. . . . . 9 F8
Dieppe Cl RG41 . . . . 115 E6
Digby Rd RG14. . . . . 104 E4
Digital Acad RG41 . . . . . . 116 B4
Dines Way RG18 . . . . 79 C7
Dingle Rd TW15 . . . . 98 B3
Dinton Pastures Ctry Pk★
RG10. . . . . 88 C5
Discovery Ct 6 RG14. . . . 105 A2
Disraeli Ct SL3. . . . . 69 B8
Ditchfield La RG40 . . . . . . 141 E8
Ditchling RG12 . . . . 118 A2
Dittany Gdns RG18 . . . . . . 106 D5
Ditton Park Cvn Site 2
SL3. 43 F1
Ditton Park Rd SL3. . . . . . . 68 E8
Ditton Rd
Datchet SL3. . . . . 68 D7
Slough SL3. . . . . 68 F8
Dittons The RG40 . . . . 141 F6
Dobson's La RG9. . . . . 15 C8
Dockett Eddy La TW17 . . 124 F1
Dockett Moorings KT16 . 124 F1
Doctors La RG18 . . . . 79 A6
Doddington Cl RG6 . . . . . . 87 C1
Doddsfield Rd SL2 . . . . 22 A2
Dodsells Well RG40 . . . . . 141 F8
Doghurst Ave UB7 . . . . 71 B7
Doghurst Dr UB7 . . . . 71 B7
Dogkennel La OX12 . . . . . . 27 C4
Dog La RG8. . . . . 54 A6
Doles Hill RG41 . . . . 115 D4
Doles La RG41 . . . . 115 E3
Dolman Rd RG14. . . . . 105 A4
Dolphin Cl
Aldermaston RG7 . . . . 134 F7
Winnersh RG41 . . . . 88 C1
Dolphin Ct
Bracknell RG12 . . . . 118 C5
Slough SL1. . . . . 43 B4
Stanwell TW19. . . . . 97 A5
Dolphin Ct N TW19. . . . . . . 97 A5
Dolphin Est The TW16 . . . 125 D8
Dolphin Ho
1 Camberley GU15 . . . . . 151 B3
Wokingham RG40 . . . . 116 B6
Dolphin Rd
Charlton TW16. . . . . 125 E8
Slough SL1. . . . . 43 B4
Dolphin Rd N TW16 . . . . . 125 E8
Dolphin Rd S TW16 . . . . . 125 E8
Dolphin Rd W TW16. . . . . 125 E8
Dolphin Sch RG10 . . . . 62 A2
Dolton Mews RG14. . . . . . 104 F3
Doman Rd GU15 . . . . 151 A4
Dommett Ho TW18. . . . . . . 97 A2
Domoney Cl RG19. . . . . . . 106 E3
Donaldson Way RG5 . . . . . 88 B8
Doncastle Rd RG12. . . . . . 117 E6
Don Cl RG30 . . . . 85 A8
Donegal Cl RG4. . . . . 59 C3
Donkey La SL8. . . . . 3 A3
DONKEY TOWN 153 D6
Donkin Ct RG4. . . . . 59 C3
Donkin Hill RG4. . . . . 59 C3
DONNINGTON. 104 F7
Donnington Castle★
RG14. . . . . 104 E7
Donnington Cl
Bucklebury RG7 . . . . 108 C8
Camberley GU15 . . . . 151 B4
Donnington Elms RG14. . 104 F6
Donnington Gdns
Maidenhead SL6 . . . . 19 F1
Reading RG1 . . . . 86 E6
Donnington Hospl RG14. 104 F6
Donnington Lodge RG14 104 F7
Donnington Pk RG14. . . . . 104 F6
Donnington Pl RG41 . . . . . 88 D2
Donnington Rd RG1. . . . . . 86 D6
Donnington Sq RG14. . . . . 104 F5
Donnybrook RG12. . . . . . 118 A2
Dorcas Ct GU15. . . . . 151 B3
Dorchester Cl SL6 . . . . 19 B1
Dorchester Ct
Camberley GU15 . . . . 151 B5
Reading RG30 . . . . 85 C6
8 Staines TW18. . . . . 97 A4
Dorchester Dr TW14 . . . . . 71 E1
Dorchester Mans SL5 . . . 120 F1
Dorian Dr SL5 . . . . 120 E8
Doris Rd TW15. . . . . 98 D2
Dorking Way RG31. . . . . . . 84 B4
Dorly Cl TW17 . . . . 125 E4
Dormer Cl
Crowthorne RG45 . . . . 143 A5
Newbury RG14. . . . . 130 E6
Dormy Ho The GU25 . . . . 121 F3
Dorndon Ho RG10. . . . . 88 F8
Dornels SL2 . . . . 43 C7
DORNEY 41 C3
Dorney Court★ SL4 . . . . . . 41 B3
DORNEY REACH 40 F3
Dorney Reach Rd SL6 . . . . 40 F3
Dorney Sch SL6. . . . . 40 F3
Dorney Wood Rd SL1 . . . . 21 D6
Dorneywood Way RG14 . 105 D4
Dorothy St 5 RG1 . . . . 86 B6
Dorset Ct GU15 . . . . 151 F8
Dorset Lodge 9 SL6 . . . . . 39 F6
Dorset Rd
Ashford TW15 . . . . 97 D5
Windsor SL4 . . . . 67 C6
Dorset St RG30 . . . . 85 C8
Dorset Vale RG42 . . . . 91 E2
Dorset Way RG41 . . . . 115 E5
Dorton Villas UB7. . . . . 71 A6
Doublet Cl RG19 . . . . 106 A3
Douglas Ct
Earley RG6. . . . . 87 A3
Marlow SL7 . . . . 2 A3
Douglas Grange RG10. . . . 88 D4
Douglas La TW19 . . . . 68 F1
Douglas Rd
Caversham RG4. . . . . 59 D2
Slough SL2. . . . . 42 D8
Stanwell TW19. . . . . 70 D1
Doultons The TW18 . . . . . . 97 A2
Douro Cl RG26. . . . . 134 D1
Dove Cl RG6 . . . . 113 F8
Dovecote Rd RG2 . . . . 113 B7
Dove Ct TW19 . . . . 97 E8
Dovedale Cl
Caversham RG4. . . . . 58 F3
Sandhurst GU47 . . . . 143 D2
Dove House Cres SL2 . . . . 21 E2
Dover Rd SL1. . . . . 41 F7
Dover St RG1 . . . . 86 A6
Doveton Way RG14. . . . . . 105 B4
Dowding Cl RG5 . . . . 88 A7
Dowding Ct RG45 . . . . 143 C6
Dower Ho The SL5 . . . . . . 120 C4
Dower Pk SL4 . . . . 66 E3
Dowles Gn RG40 . . . . 116 E8
DOWLESGREEN 116 E8
Downe House Sch RG18. . 79 A3
DOWNEND 51 A3
Downend La RG20 . . . . 51 B2
Downfield La SL6 . . . . 63 C5
Downfield Rd RG10 . . . . . . 63 A4
Downham Ct RG2. . . . . 86 E1
Downing Path SL2 . . . . 21 E1
Downing Rd RG31. . . . . 84 D8
Downlands RG17. . . . . 47 C6
Downmill Rd RG12 . . . . . . 117 F7
Down Pl SL4. . . . . 66 A8
Downs Cl RG17 . . . . 46 F7
Downshire Cl RG17 . . . . . . 48 B4
Downshire Sq RG1. . . . . . . 85 E6
Downshire Way
Bracknell, Priestwood RG12,
RG42. . . . . 118 A7
Bracknell RG12 . . . . 118 B6
Downside
9 Chertsey KT16 . . . . 123 F1
Chilton OX11 . . . . 10 C8
Downs Rd
Aldworth RG20 . . . . 32 A4
Slough SL3. . . . . 43 D4
Downs Sch The RG20. . . . . 31 D4
Downs View OX11. . . . . 12 F8
Downs Way
Chilton OX11 . . . . 9 F8
Purley on T RG31. . . . . 57 C2
Downsway Prim Sch
RG31. . . . . 57 C3
Down View RG17. . . . . . . 100 E5
Doyen Ct 3 RG14. . . . . . . 105 B3
Doyle Gdns GU46 . . . . 149 C4
Doyle Ho RG45. . . . . 143 B3
Dragoons Cl RG19 . . . . . . 106 D1
Drain Hill RG17 . . . . 25 A4
Drake Ave
Slough SL3. . . . . 43 D2
Staines TW18. . . . . 96 F3
Drake Cl
Bracknell RG12 . . . . 118 B4
Finchampstead RG40. . . . . 141 E7
Drake Way RG2. . . . . 86 A2
Draper Cl RG19 . . . . 106 D2
Draycott RG12 . . . . 118 E4
Drayhorse Dr GU19 . . . . . 145 E2
Draymans La 5 SL7. . . . . . . 1 D1
Drayton Cl RG12 . . . . 118 D7
Drayton Rd RG30. . . . . 85 B8
Draytons View RG19 . . . . 131 C7
Dresden Way RG30. . . . . . . 57 F1
Drewett Cl RG2 . . . . 113 C6
Drew Mdw SL2 . . . . 22 C8
Drey Ho RG41. . . . . 115 F7
Drifters Dr GU16 . . . . 152 D1
Drift Rd SL4, SL6 . . . . 65 D3
Drift Way SL3. . . . . 69 C7
Driftway Cl 4 RG6. . . . . . . 87 C1
Driftways GU46 . . . . 149 D7
Drill Hall Rd KT16. . . . . . . 124 A2
Drive The
Ashford TW15 . . . . 98 D1
Bourne End SL8. . . . . 2 F4
Datchet SL3. . . . . 68 B6
Earley RG6. . . . . 87 A7
Newbury RG14. . . . . 130 E8
Slough SL3. . . . . 43 E4
Virginia Water GU25 . . . . 122 F4
Wraysbury TW19. . . . . 68 D2
Droitwich Cl RG12 . . . . . . 118 E6
Drome Path RG41. . . . . 88 A3
Dropmore Rd SL1. . . . . 21 C5
Drove La RG18. . . . . 79 C2
Drovers Way
Bracknell RG12 . . . . 118 F6
Woodley RG5. . . . . 87 E5
Drove The RG19 . . . . 133 B1
Druce Way RG19. . . . . 106 D3
Druce Wood SL5. . . . . 119 E8
Drummond Cl RG12. . . . . 118 F8
Drummond Ct SL5 . . . . 92 E1
Drummond Ho 4 SL4. . . . 67 D4
Drury La RG7 . . . . 137 A5
Dry Arch Rd SL5 . . . . 120 F3
Dryden RG12 . . . . 118 A2
Dryden Cl RG18 . . . . 106 D5
Dryland Ho RG30. . . . . 84 F7
Duchess Cl RG45. . . . . 143 B7
Duchess St SL1 . . . . 41 E5
Ducketts Mead
Arborfield Garrison RG2 . . 140 E8
Reading RG2 . . . . 113 E7
Dudley Cl RG31 . . . . 57 E1
Dudley Ct SL1 . . . . 43 A3
Dudley Ho RG12 . . . . 118 C7
Dudley Mews RG31 . . . . . . 57 E1
Dudley Pl TW19. . . . . 70 F1
Dudley Rd
Ashford TW15 . . . . 97 F4
East Bedfont TW14 . . . . 98 D7
Duffield La SL2 . . . . 22 F6
Duffield Pk SL2. . . . . 23 A2
Duffield Rd RG5 . . . . 60 F1
Dugdale Ho TW20. . . . . 96 C3
Duke Of Cornwall Ave
GU15 . . . . 144 D1
Dukesbridge Ct 8 RG1. . . 86 B7
Dukes Cl TW15 . . . . 98 C4
Dukes Covert GU19 . . . . . 145 E6
Dukes Dr SL1, SL2 . . . . 22 A8
Duke's Hill GU19. . . . . 145 E5
Dukeshill Rd RG42 . . . . . . 118 B8
Duke's La
Old Windsor SL4, SL5 . . . . . 94 B3
Winkfield SL5. . . . . 93 F1
Dukes Mdw SL8. . . . . 3 B3
Dukes Pl
Marlow SL7 . . . . 1 D2
Slough SL1. . . . . 42 F6
Dukes Ride RG7 . . . . 136 B1
Duke's Ride RG45. . . . . . . 143 B5
Duke St
Eton SL4. . . . . 67 C7
Henley-on-T RG9 . . . . 15 E2
Reading RG1 . . . . 86 B7
Dukes Wood RG45 . . . . . . 143 B5
Dulnan Cl RG30. . . . . 85 A8
Dulverton Gdns RG2 . . . . . 86 C2
Dumas Cl GU46 . . . . 149 C5
Dumbarton Way RG4. . . . . 59 E5
Dunally Pk TW17. . . . . 125 D2
Dunaways Cl RG6 . . . . 87 D3
Dunbar Cl SL2 . . . . 43 A6
Dunbar Dr RG5 . . . . 88 A6
Dunboe Pl TW17 . . . . 125 C2
Dunboyne Pl SL4 . . . . 68 A3
Duncan Dr RG40 . . . . 116 E5
Duncan Gdns
Purley on T RG8. . . . . 57 C4
Staines TW18. . . . . 97 A2
Duncannon Cres SL4. . . . . 66 D4
Duncan Rd RG5 . . . . 87 E6
Duncansby Ho SL1 . . . . 43 A4
Duncombe Ct TW18 . . . . . . 96 F1
Duncroft SL4 . . . . 66 F4
Duncroft Manor TW18. . . . 96 E4
Dundaff Cl GU15 . . . . 152 A5
Dundas Cl RG12. . . . . 118 B5
Dundee Rd SL1 . . . . 42 A8
Dundela Cl RG5. . . . . 87 E6
Dunedin Hospl RG1 . . . . . . 85 F6
Dunford Pl RG42. . . . . 90 E1
Dungells Farm Cl GU46. . 149 D4
Dungells La GU46 . . . . 149 C4
Dungrovehill La SL6 . . . . . 18 D3
Dunholme Cl RG6. . . . . 87 E2
Dunholme End SL6. . . . . . . 39 D3
Dunkirk Cl RG41 . . . . 115 E6
Dunleary Ct 13 RG30 . . . . 85 D6
Dunluce Gdns RG8 . . . . 56 E5
Dunn Cres RG17 . . . . 102 B1
Dunnock Way RG10 . . . . . . 36 E3
Dunoon Cl RG31 . . . . 84 E4
DUNSDEN GREEN 59 F7
Dunsfold Rd RG30. . . . . 84 F7
Dunsmore Gdns GU46 . . . 149 A5
Dunstable Ho 3 SL7 . . . . . . 1 E1
Dunstall Cl RG31 . . . . 84 D8
Dunstan Ct TW18 . . . . 97 A4
Dunstan Rd RG18 . . . . 106 E4
Dunstans Dr RG41 . . . . 88 B2
Dunster Cl RG4 . . . . 59 C6
Dunster Gdns SL1. . . . . 42 A6
Dunt Ave RG10. . . . . 88 F4
Dunt La RG10. . . . . 88 E4
Dunwood Ct SL6. . . . . 39 C5
Duppas Cl TW17 . . . . 125 D4
Dupre Cl SL1 . . . . 41 E4
Du Pre Wlk HP10 . . . . 3 D4
Durand Rd RG6 . . . . 87 A1
Durant Way RG31 . . . . 57 D3
Durham Ave SL1 . . . . 42 A7
Durham Cl
Reading RG2 . . . . 113 C8
Wokingham RG41 . . . . 115 E6
Durham Dr GU16. . . . . 152 D1
Durham Rd GU47 . . . . 143 E2
Durley Mead RG12 . . . . . . 118 F4
Durning Pl SL5 . . . . 120 B6
Durrell Way TW17 . . . . . . 125 D3
Dutch Barn Cl TW19. . . . . . 70 D1
Dutton Way SL0 . . . . 44 E7
Duvall Ct SL1. . . . . 43 A3
Duval Pl GU19 . . . . 145 E3
Dwyer Rd RG30 . . . . 85 A4
Dyer Rd RG40. . . . . 116 E7
Dyer Straits OX12. . . . . 9 F8
Dyson Cl SL4 . . . . 67 B4
Dysons Cl RG14. . . . . 104 E3
Dysonswood La RG4 . . . . . 58 E8

E

Eagle Cl
Crowthorne RG45 . . . . 143 A7
Wokingham RG41 . . . . 115 F5
Eagle House Sch GU47 . . 143 B2
Eaglehurst Cotts RG42 . . . 90 C3
Eagle Rd
Hatton TW6 . . . . 71 F4
Newtown RG20 . . . . 132 A2
Eagles Nest GU47 . . . . 143 A1
Earle Croft RG42. . . . . 91 C1
EARLEY 87 B5
Earleydene SL5 . . . . 120 B1
Earley Hill Rd RG6 . . . . 87 A5
Earley Pl RG1. . . . . 86 B7
Earley Sta RG6. . . . . 87 C4
Earlsfield SL6. . . . . 40 C2
Earlsfield Cl RG4. . . . . 59 E4
Earls Gr GU15. . . . . 151 E6
Earls La SL1 . . . . 41 F5
Earlswood RG12 . . . . 118 B2
Easby Way RG6 . . . . 87 D1
Easington Dr RG6. . . . . 87 E2
EAST BEDFONT 98 E7
East Berkshire Coll
Slough SL3. . . . . 44 A3
Windsor SL4 . . . . 67 C5
Eastbourne Rd SL1. . . . . . . 42 A7
Eastbridge SL2 . . . . 43 B5
EAST BURNHAM. 22 A4
East Burnham Cotts SL2. . 22 A4
East Burnham La SL2 . . . . 22 A4
EASTBURY 46 F7
Eastbury Ave RG31. . . . . . . 84 B8
Eastbury Ct RG42 . . . . 90 F1
Eastbury Pk RG41. . . . . 88 D2
Eastbury Shute RG17. . . . . 46 E2
Eastchurch Rd TW6 . . . . . . 71 E4
Eastchurch Rd Rdbt TW6. 71 E5
Eastcliff RG4 . . . . 58 E3
Eastcourt Ave RG6 . . . . 87 A6
East Cres SL4. . . . . 66 F6
Eastcroft SL2 . . . . 22 B1
East Dr
Reading RG31 . . . . 84 E5
Stoke Poges SL2 . . . . 22 E2
Wentworth GU25. . . . . 122 B3
Eastern Ave
Chertsey KT16. . . . . 124 A6
Reading RG1 . . . . 86 E6
Eastern Bsns Pk TW6 . . . . 71 E5
Eastern Dr SL8. . . . . 3 C4
Eastern Ind Area RG12 . . 118 D7
Eastern La RG45 . . . . 143 F4
Eastern Perimeter Rd
Hatton TW6 . . . . 71 F4
Hatton TW14, TW6. . . . . 71 F5
Eastern Rd RG12. . . . . 118 D7
Eastfield OX11. . . . . 12 A8
Eastfield Cl 4 SL1 . . . . 43 A3
Eastfield La RG8 . . . . 56 D7
Eastfield Rd SL1 . . . . 41 A8
EAST FIELDS. 105 B2
EAST GARSTON 47 D6
EAST GARSTON
WOODLANDS. 47 B3
Eastgate Ct 7 RG1. . . . . . . 86 E7
East Gn GU17. . . . . 150 C4
EASTHAMPSTEAD 118 B5
Easthampstead Mobile Home
Pk RG40 . . . . 143 C8
Easthampstead Park Sch
RG12. . . . . 117 D3
Easthampstead Rd
Bracknell RG12 . . . . 118 A7
Wokingham RG40 . . . . 116 E4
EASTHEATH 116 B3
Eastheath Ave RG41. . . . . 116 A4
Eastheath Gdns RG41 . . . 116 B3
EAST ILSLEY. 30 F6
East La RG20 . . . . 51 B1
Eastleigh Rd TW6. . . . . 71 F4
Eastlyn Rd RG26 . . . . 135 E1
EASTON. 76 C5
Easton Hill RG20. . . . . 76 A4
East Paddock SL6. . . . . 18 F6
East Park Farm Dr RG10. . 61 B4
East Ramp TW6. . . . . 71 B6
East Rd
East Bedfont TW14 . . . . 98 D8
Maidenhead SL6 . . . . 39 E7
East Ridge SL8. . . . . 3 B4
East St RG1. . . . . 86 B7
East Stratton Cl RG12 . . . 118 F4
East Terr SL4. . . . . 67 E6
Eastview Cl RG10 . . . . 36 E2
Eastview Ct RG42 . . . . 91 A1
Eastview Rd RG10. . . . . 36 E2
Eastwood Ct 1 SL7 . . . . 1 F3
EAST WOODHAY 148 F7
Eastwood Rd RG5. . . . . 87 E4
Eastworth Rd KT16. . . . . . 124 A1
Eaton Ct GU15 . . . . 151 B4
Eaton Pl RG1 . . . . 85 F7
Eaton Rd GU15. . . . . 151 B4
Ebborn Sq RG6 . . . . 114 C8
Ebsworth Cl SL6 . . . . 20 C3
Eccles Cl RG4. . . . . 59 C2
Echelforde Dr TW15. . . . . . 98 A4
Echelford Prim Sch The
TW15 . . . . 98 B3
EDDINGTON 100 E7
Eddington Hill RG17. . . . . 100 F7
Eddington Rd RG12 . . . . . 117 E3
Eddystone Wlk TW19. . . . . 97 E8
Eden Cl SL3 . . . . 44 A1

Edenhall Cl RG31 57 D3
Edenham Cl RG6 87 E2
Edenham Cres RG1 85 E5
Eden Pl SL5 121 A2
Eden Way RG41 88 B1
Edgar Milward Cl RG30 58 A1
Edgar Wallace Pl SL8 3 B5
Edgbarrow Rise GU47 143 A2
Edgbarrow Sch RG45 143 C3
Edgcumbe Park Dr RG45 143 A5
Edgecombe La RG14 105 C5
Edgecumbe Ct TW18 96 F2
Edgedale Cl RG45 143 B4
Edgehill Cl RG14 105 E5
Edgehill St RG1 86 B5
Edgell Cl GU25 122 F6
Edgell Rd TW18 96 F3
Edgemoor Rd GU16 152 C3
Edgewood Cl RG45 143 A7
Edinburgh Ave SL1 42 B7
Edinburgh Ct RG30 85 D7
Edinburgh Dr TW18 97 D2
Edinburgh Gdns SL4 67 D5
Edinburgh Ho SL1 42 F4
Edinburgh Rd
Maidenhead SL6 19 E2
Marlow SL7 1 E3
Reading RG30 85 E7
Edith Ct TW14 71 D1
Edith Rd SL6 39 A7
Edmonds Ct RG12 118 C8
Edmunds Way SL2 43 B7
Edneys Hill RG41 115 D2
Edward Ave GU15 151 A5
Edward Ct TW18 97 C2
Edward Pauling Ho TW14 98 F8
Edward Pauling Prim Sch TW13 98 E6
Edward Pl 14 RG1 86 D7
Edward Rd
Hatton TW14 71 E2
Twyford RG10 61 B5
Windlesham GU20 146 D4
Edwards Ct SL1 42 E4
Edwards Hill RG17 25 B2
Edward Way TW15 97 F6
Edwin Cl RG19 106 F3
Eeklo Pl RG14 105 A1
Egerton Rd
Reading RG2 86 E1
Sandhurst GU15 150 F7
Sandhurst GU15 151 A7
Slough SL2 21 E1
Egerton Way UB7 71 B7
EGHAM 96 A4
Egham Bsns Village TW20 123 C7
Egham By-Pass TW20 96 A4
Egham Hill TW20 95 E2
Egham Hill Rdbt TW20 95 F3
EGHAM HYTHE 96 E2
Egham Mus* TW20 96 A3
Eghams Ct 4 SL8 3 B3
Eghams Gn SL8 3 B3
Egham Sta TW20 96 A3
EGHAM WICK 95 A1
Egremont Dr RG6 87 D3
Egremont Gdns SL1 42 A5
EGYPT
Farnham Common 22 B8
Leckhampstead 50 A5
Egypt La SL2 22 B8
Eight Acres SL1 21 B1
Eight Bells 8 RG14 104 F2
Eighth Ave RG31 84 B6
Eisenhower Ave RG20 49 A4
Elan Cl RG30 84 F7
Elbow Mdw SL3 69 F6
ELCOT 102 D8
Eldart Cl RG30 85 B7
Elderberry Way RG6 87 D1
Elder Cl RG31 57 C1
Elderfield Cres OX11 10 D8
Elderfield Rd SL2 22 F6
Eldon Lodge 15 RG1 86 C7
Eldon Pl RG1 86 C7
Eldon Rd RG1 86 C7
Eldon Sq RG1 86 D7
Eldon St RG1 86 D7
Eldon Terr RG1 86 D7
Eldrick Ct TW14 98 D7
Electra Ave TW6 71 F4
Elford Cl RG6 87 C1
Elford Ct RG42 90 D3
Elgar Ave RG45 143 B7
Elgar Rd RG2 86 A5
Elgar Rd S RG2 86 B4
Elgarth Dr RG40 141 F8
Elgin Ave TW15 98 C2
Elgin Cres TW6 71 E5
Elgin Gate 5 RG1 85 F7
Elgin Ho SL3 69 E6
Elgin Rd GU17 149 E1
ELING 52 E3
Eliot Cl
Camberley GU15 152 B7
Caversham RG4 59 A4
Thatcham RG18 106 C5
Eliot Dr SL7 1 F4
Elizabethan Cl TW19 97 D8
Elizabethan Way TW19 97 D8
Elizabeth Ave
Bagshot GU19 145 F2
Newbury RG14 130 D7
Staines TW18 97 C2
Elizabeth Cl
Bracknell RG12 118 C5
Cookham Rise SL6 19 F7
Elizabeth Cl *continued*
Henley-on-T RG9 35 B8
Elizabeth Ct
2 Reading RG31 84 D8
1 Slough SL1 43 A4
Theale RG7 83 F3
Wargrave RG10 36 E2
5 Windsor SL4 67 C5
Wokingham RG41 116 B6
Elizabeth Gdns
Ascot SL5 120 B4
Kintbury RG17 102 B2
Elizabeth Ho TW15 97 F4
Elizabeth Mews 9 RG1 86 B6
Elizabeth Par GU46 149 D4
Elizabeth Rd
Henley-on-T RG9 35 B8
Marlow SL7 1 E3
Wokingham RG40 116 D6
Elizabeth Rout Cl RG7 113 C2
Elizabeth Way SL2 22 F4
Elizabeth Wlk 3 RG1 86 B5
Ellenborough Cl RG12 118 D8
Ellerton Cl RG7 83 E4
Ellesfield Ave RG12 117 E5
Ellesmere Cl
Caversham RG4 59 B3
Datchet SL3 68 A8
Ellies Mews TW15 97 E6
Elliman Ave SL2 42 F6
Ellington Ct SL6 40 C7
Ellington Gdns SL6 40 C7
Ellington Pk SL6 19 E1
Ellington Prim Sch SL6 19 F1
Ellington Rd
Feltham TW13 98 F4
Taplow SL6 40 C7
Elliot Rise SL5 119 D7
Elliots Way RG4 59 B2
Elliott Ct RG42 90 C1
Elliott Gdns TW17 125 A5
Ellis Ave SL1 42 E4
Ellison Cl SL4 66 F4
Ellison Ho 22 SL4 67 D6
Ellison Way RG40 116 B6
Ellis Rd RG45 143 B6
Ellis's Hill RG2 114 F4
Elm Apartments UB3 71 D7
Elmar Gn SL2 22 A2
Elm Bank GU46 149 C7
Elmbank Ave TW20 95 B2
Elm Cl
Farnham Common SL2 22 C6
Stanwell TW19 97 D7
Elm Cotts
Ball Hill RG20 129 F1
Holyport SL6 65 A8
Elmcroft
2 Ashford TW15 98 A3
Goring RG8 34 C5
Elm Croft SL3 68 C6
Elmcroft Cl TW14 71 F1
Elmcroft Dr TW15 98 A3
Elm Ct
6 Ashford TW16 98 F1
Henley-on-T RG9 35 D7
Sandhurst GU47 143 E2
Elmdon Rd TW6 71 F4
Elm Dr
Burghfield RG30 111 B5
Winkfield SL4 93 B7
Elm Farm Cvn Pk KT16 123 C3
Elmfield Gdns RG14 104 E4
Elm Gr
Maidenhead SL6 39 E7
Thatcham RG18 106 B5
Elm Ho TW20 95 B2
Elmhurst Ct
Camberley GU15 151 D5
Slough SL3 44 A3
Elmhurst Rd
Goring RG8 34 C7
Reading RG1 86 D5
Slough SL3 44 A3
Thatcham RG18 106 A5
Elm La
Bourne End SL8 2 F5
Earley RG6 86 F2
Elmleigh Ct RG4 59 C3
Elmley Cl RG41 88 F1
Elm Lodge Ave RG30 85 D8
Elm Park Ct 5 RG30 85 C7
Elm Park Rd RG30 85 D7
Elm Pk
Reading RG30 85 C7
Sunningdale SL5 120 E1
Elm Pl TW15 98 A3
Elm Rd
Earley RG2 & RG6 86 F2
East Bedfont TW14 98 D8
Tokers Green RG4 58 D7
Windsor SL4 67 B4
Elms Ave RG19 106 E3
Elms Dr SL8 3 C3
Elms Ho 1 RG14 105 D4
Elmshott La SL1 41 E6
Elmsleigh Ctr The TW18 96 F4
Elmsleigh Rd TW18 96 F3
Elmslie Ct 4 SL6 39 E7
Elms Rd RG40 116 B5
Elms The
6 Ashford TW15 98 A3
Blackwater GU17 150 D4
Newell Green RG42 92 A1
Elmstone Dr RG31 57 C1
Elmsway TW15 98 A3
Elm Tree Cl TW15 98 B3
Elmwood SL6 20 B4
Elmwood Cl RG5 87 D8
Elmwood Rd SL2 43 B6
Elsenwood Cres GU15 152 A6
Elsenwood Dr GU15 152 A7
Elsinore Ave TW19 97 E8
Elsley Rd RG31 57 E3
Elstow Ave RG4 59 C6
Elstree Cl RG31 57 D2
Elstree Home Farm Sch RG7 108 D3
Elstree Sch RG7 108 D4
Elsworth Cl TW14 98 E7
Eltham Ave
Caversham RG4 59 E5
Slough SL1 41 E4
Elton Dr SL6 39 D8
Elvaston Way RG30 85 A7
Elveden Cl RG6 87 E2
Elvedon Rd TW13 98 F5
Elvendon Rd RG8 34 D7
Elwell Cl TW20 96 A2
Ely Ave SL1 42 C8
Ely Gr RG14 105 E5
Elyham RG8 57 B5
Ely Rd
Hatton TW6 71 F5
Theale RG7 83 F3
Embankment The TW19 95 C7
Ember Rd SL3 44 B3
Emblen Cres RG2 114 E2
Embrook Way RG31 84 A4
Emerald Cl RG41 115 E7
Emerald Ct SL1 42 E4
Emerson Ct
Crowthorne RG45 143 B5
Wooburn Green HP10 3 E6
Emery Acres RG8 55 A6
Emery Down Cl RG12 119 A6
Emilia Cl SL6 19 F1
Emlyn Bldgs SL4 67 D7
Emma La RG10 36 E2
EMMBROOK 115 F8
Emmbrook Ct RG2 86 E2
Emmbrook Gate RG41 115 F8
Emmbrook Inf Sch RG41 88 F1
Emmbrook Jun Sch RG41 88 F1
Emmbrook Rd RG41 115 F8
Emmbrook Sch The RG41 116 A8
Emmbrook Vale RG41 89 A1
Emm Cl RG41 115 F8
EMMER GREEN 59 B6
Emmer Green Ct RG4 59 C5
Emmer Green Prim Sch RG4 59 B6
Emmets Nest RG42 90 C2
Emmets Pk RG42 90 D2
Emmview Cl RG41 115 F7
Empress Rd RG31 84 C5
Empstead Ct RG9 15 D2
Empstead Works RG9 15 D1
Enborne CE Prim Sch RG20 129 E6
Enborne Cl RG31 84 C8
Enborne Gate RG14 104 D1
Enborne Gdns RG12 91 D1
Enborne Gr RG14 104 E2
Enborne Lodge La RG14 130 C6
Enborne Pl RG14 104 E2
Enborne Rd RG14 104 D1
ENBORNE ROW 130 B4
Enborne St RG14 130 C6
Enborne Way RG7 133 F6
Endfield Pl SL6 39 A6
Enfield Rd TW6 71 E5
Enfield Road Rdbt TW6 71 E5
Engineer's Rd RG19 132 A5
ENGLEFIELD 83 B5
Englefield CE Prim Sch RG7 83 B4
Englefield Cl TW20 95 C2
Englefield Est Yd RG7 83 B5
ENGLEFIELD GREEN 95 B1
Englefield Green Inf Sch TW20 95 C3
Englefield Rd RG7 83 D4
Engleheart Dr TW14 71 F1
Englehurst TW20 95 C2
Englemere Pk SL5 119 D5
Englemere Pond Nature Trail* SL5 119 C6
Englemere Rd RG42 90 F1
Englesfield GU15 152 D5
English Ct 1 RG41 88 C2
English Gdns TW19 68 D2
English Martyrs RC Prim Sch RG30 85 A7
Enid Wood Ho RG12 118 C7
Ennerdale RG12 118 A5
Ennerdale Cl TW14 98 F7
Ennerdale Cres SL1 41 C8
Ennerdale Rd RG2 86 D3
Ennerdale Way RG19 106 A3
Ensign Cl
Harlington TW6 71 E4
Stanwell TW19 97 D7
Ensign Way TW19 97 D7
Enstone Rd RG5 88 A8
Enterprise Ct RG12 117 F7
Enterprise Way RG19 107 A2
EP Collier Prim Sch RG1 59 A1
Epping Cl RG1 85 F7
Epping Ho 3 RG1 85 E5
Epping Way RG12 118 F5
Epsom Cl GU15 151 C8
Epsom Cres RG14 105 B1
Epsom Ct RG1 85 F6
Epsom Sq TW6 71 F5
Equine Way RG14 131 B7
Erica Cl
Slough SL1 41 E6
West End GU24 153 E6
Erica Dr RG40 116 D5
Eric Ave RG4 59 A6
Eriswell Cl RG6 87 E2
Erkenwald Cl KT16 123 E3
Erleigh Court Dr RG6 87 B7
Erleigh Court Gdns RG6 87 A7
Erleigh Dene RG14 104 F1
Erleigh Rd RG1 86 D6
Ermin St
Lambourn RG17 45 E5
Shefford Woodlands RG17 74 C7
Stockcross RG20 103 D7
Wickham RG17 75 A5
Woodlands St M RG17 46 D2
Ermin Wlk RG19 106 B3
Errington Dr SL4 67 A6
Erskine Cl RG26 135 F1
Escot Rd TW16 98 E1
Esher Cres
Harlington TW6 71 E5
Hatton TW6 71 F5
Esher Rd GU15 145 A1
Eskdale Gdns SL6 40 B2
Eskdale Rd RG41 88 B4
Eskdale Way GU15 152 D4
Eskin Cl RG30 85 A7
Essame Cl RG40 116 D6
Essex Ave SL2 42 C8
Essex Cotts RG7 111 B3
Essex Pl RG17 25 B3
Essex Rise RG42 91 F1
Essex St
Newbury RG14 130 D7
Reading RG2 86 B5
Ethel Rd TW15 97 E3
ETON 67 C8
Eton Cl SL3 68 A8
Eton Coll SL4 67 C8
Eton Coll Mus* SL4 67 C8
Eton Ct
Eton SL4 67 D7
Staines TW18 96 F3
Eton End PNEU Sch SL3 68 A8
Eton Ho 6 TW20 96 A3
Eton Pl SL7 1 D2
Eton Porny CE Fst Sch SL4 67 D8
Eton Rd
Datchet SL3 68 A8
Harlington UB3 71 F7
Eton Riverside SL4 67 D7
Eton Sq SL4 67 D7
ETON WICK 41 E1
Eton Wick CE Fst Sch SL4 42 A1
Eton Wick Rd SL4 42 B1
Eton Wlk 1 SL1 42 E3
European Weather Ctr RG2 113 D7
Eustace Cres RG40 116 D8
Evedon RG12 118 B2
Evelyn Cres TW16 125 F8
Evelyn Ct RG5 87 F5
Evelyn Way TW16 125 F8
Evendon's Cl RG41 116 A3
Evendon's La RG41 115 E2
Evenlode SL6 40 A8
Evenlode Rd SL8 3 B4
Evenlode Way GU47 150 D8
Everard Ave SL1 42 E4
Everest Rd
Camberley GU15 151 D8
Crowthorne RG45 143 B6
Stanwell TW19 97 E8
Evergreen SL5 120 F1
Evergreen Ct TW19 97 D8
Evergreen Dr RG31 84 F4
Evergreen Oak Ave SL4 68 A4
Evergreen Rd GU16 152 A3
Evergreen Way
Stanwell TW19 97 D8
Wokingham RG41 115 F5
Everington La RG18 53 C1
Everland Rd RG17 100 D6
EVERSLEY 141 B1
Eversley Rd
Arborfield Cross RG2 114 E2
Arborfield Garrison RG2, RG40 140 E6
Yateley GU46 149 A7
Eversley St RG27 141 A1
Eversley Way TW20 123 C7
Evesham Pl RG41 115 F8
Evesham Rd RG4 59 B5
Evesham Wlk GU47 143 D1
Evreham Rd SL0 44 E7
Evreux Cl RG19 106 F2
Ewing Way RG14 131 B8
Exbourne Rd RG2 113 C8
Exchange Rd SL5 120 C4
Exeforde Ave TW15 98 A4
Exeter Ct RG2 113 B8
Exeter Gdns GU46 149 B7
Exeter Rd TW6 71 E4
Exeter Way
Harlington TW6 71 E5
Theale RG7 83 F3
Exmoor Rd RG19 106 C3
Explorer Ave TW19 97 E7
Express Way RG14 105 E2
Exwick Sq RG2 113 D8
Eynsford Cl RG4 59 E5
Eynsham Cl RG5 87 E8
Eyre Ct RG40 116 B4
Eyre Gn SL2 22 A2

F

FACCOMBE 148 B1
Faculty The 12 RG1 86 B6
Fagg's Rd TW14 71 F3
Fairacre SL6 39 C6
Fairacres Ind Est SL4 66 D5
Fair Close Ho 1 RG14 105 A2
Faircroft SL2 22 B1
FAIR CROSS 138 D2
Faircross
Bracknell RG12 118 B6
Hermitage RG18 78 F6
Fair Cross RG7 138 D2
Faircross Rd RG30 85 C5
Fairfax RG42 118 A8
Fairfax Cl RG4 59 B3
Fairfax Pl RG14 105 E5
Fairfield RG20 31 D4
Fairfield App TW19 68 D1
Fairfield Ave
Datchet SL3 68 D7
Staines TW18 96 F4
Fairfield Cl
Bourne End SL8 3 A4
Datchet SL3 68 D7
Fairfield Dr GU16 151 E3
Fairfield Ho GU15 152 A5
Fairfield La
Farnham Royal SL2 22 B3
West End GU24 153 F7
Fairfield Pk RG7 136 F5
Fairfield Rd
Burnham SL1 21 C2
Goring RG8 34 D7
Wraysbury TW19 68 D1
Fairfields
Chertsey KT15 124 B1
5 Hungerford RG17 100 D5
Fairford Rd
Maidenhead SL6 39 F8
Purley on T RG31 57 C2
Fairhaven TW20 95 F3
Fairhaven Ct 1 TW20 95 F3
Fairholme TW14 98 E8
Fairholme Prim Sch TW14 98 D7
Fairholme Rd TW15 97 F3
Fairlawn Gn RG2 86 F1
Fairlawn Pk SL4 66 E3
Fairlawns Cl TW18 97 B2
Fairlea SL6 39 B3
Fairlie Rd SL1 42 A8
Fairlight Ave SL4 67 D5
Fairlop Cl RG31 84 D4
Fairmead Cl GU47 150 E7
Fairmead Ct GU15 151 C4
Fairmead Rd RG2 113 E5
Fairmead The SL3 69 D7
Fair Mile RG9 15 C4
Fairmile Ct RG9 15 D3
Fair Oak Way RG26 134 D1
Fairsted Cl RG30 85 A8
Fairview RG14 130 E8
Fairview Ave RG6 87 B6
Fairview Cotts GU25 122 D3
Fair View Cotts SL6 19 E7
Fairview Ct
Ashford TW15 98 A3
Staines TW18 97 A2
Fairview Dr TW17 124 F4
Fairview Est RG9 35 F8
Fairview Rd
Burnham SL6 41 A7
Hungerford RG17 100 D5
Slough SL2 21 F1
Wokingham RG40 116 C5
Fairwater Dr RG5 87 D6
Fairway
Chertsey KT16 124 B1
Maidenhead SL6 39 E5
Fairway Ave RG30 84 D6
Fairway Ct RG42 91 A1
Fairway Dr RG10 61 A5
Fairway Hts GU15 152 B6
Fairways TW15 98 B2
Fairways Ho SL5 121 A2
Fairway The
Burnham SL1 21 C3
Flackwell Heath HP10 3 C7
Frimley GU15 152 A3
Maidenhead SL6 39 B3
Faithfull Cl RG42 91 B2
Fakenham Cl RG6 114 A8
Fakenham Way GU47 143 D2
Falaise TW20 95 F3
Falcon Ave RG2 86 F1
Falcon Bsns Pk RG40 141 A6
Falcon Cl GU18 152 F8
Falcon Ct GU16 151 D1
Falcon Dr TW19 70 E1
Falcon Fields RG26 135 B2
Falcon House Gdns RG20 129 F1
Falcons Croft HP10 3 E8
Falcon Way
Sunbury TW16 125 E7
Wokingham RG41 115 F6
Yateley GU46 149 B6
Falconwood TW20 95 E3
Falkland Dr RG14 130 F8
Falkland Garth RG14 130 D7
Falkland Ho SL6 39 F8

Falkland Prim Sch RG14 130 D6
Falkland Rd
Caversham RG4 59 B2
Newbury RG14 130 D6
Fallowfield GU46 149 B7
Fallowfield Cl RG4 59 B4
Fallows Rd RG7 109 C2
Fallows The SL6 20 A1
Falmouth Cl GU15 152 A4
Falmouth Rd
Reading RG2 113 C7
Slough SL1 42 A7
Falmouth Way RG19 106 F3
Falstaff Ave RG6 86 F2
Fanes Cl RG42 117 F8
Fane Way SL6 39 D5
Fangrove Pk KT16 123 B1
Fannys La RG7 80 C1
Faraday Cl
Arborfield Garrison RG2 140 E7
Slough SL2 42 B8
Faraday Rd
Newbury RG14 105 B3
Slough SL2 42 B8
Farcrosse Cl GU47 150 C8
Fareham Dr GU46 149 B7
Faringdon Cl GU47 143 C1
Faringdon Dr RG12 118 D4
Faringdon Wlk RG30 85 B4
Farleigh Mews RG4 59 E5
FARLEY CASTLE 140 C7
Farley Copse RG42 117 E8
Farley Ct RG7 140 C5
FARLEY HILL 140 D6
Farley Hill Prim Sch RG7 140 D5
Farley Moor RG42 117 D8
Farley Villas KT16 124 B2
Farman Cl RG5 88 B8
Farm Cl
Ascot SL5 120 C4
Bracknell RG42 117 F8
Crowthorne RG45 143 C7
Egham TW18 96 E3
Holyport SL6 40 C1
Lower Halliford TW17 125 A2
Lyne KT16 123 A3
Maidenhead SL6 39 A7
Purley on T RG8 57 C5
Yateley GU46 149 D5
Farm Cotts RG17 100 A1
Farm Cres SL2 43 C8
Farm Ct GU16 151 F2
Farm Dr
Old Windsor SL4 68 B1
Reading RG31 84 B6
Farmers Cl
Maidenhead SL6 39 A4
Reading RG2 113 C6
Farmers End RG10 61 B4
Farmers Gate RG18 106 D5
Farmer's Rd TW18 96 E3
Farmers Way SL6 39 A4
Farmhouse Mews RG18 106 F5
Farmiloe Cl RG8 57 C4
Farm Lea HP10 3 F7
Farm Rd
Bourne End SL8 2 F4
Burnham SL6 41 A6
Frimley GU16 151 F2
Goring RG8 34 C6
Henley-on-T RG9 35 F8
Maidenhead SL6 39 A7
Staines TW18 97 B2
Farm View GU46 149 D5
Farm Way TW19 69 F1
Farm Yd SL4 67 D7
FARNBOROUGH
Camberley 150 E1
East Ilsley 8 E1
Farnburn Ave SL1 42 B8
Farnell Rd TW18 97 A5
Farnesdown Dr RG41 115 F8
Farnham Cl RG12 118 D7
FARNHAM COMMON 22 D6
Farnham Common Inf Sch SL2 22 B8
Farnham Common Jun Sch SL2 22 C8
Farnham Dr RG4 59 E4
Farnham La SL2 21 E2
FARNHAM PARK 22 C4
Farnham Park La SL2 22 C4
Farnham Rd SL1, SL2 42 C7
FARNHAM ROYAL 22 C3
Farningham RG12 118 E3
Farningham Ho RG12 118 E3
Farnsfield Cl RG6 114 A8
Farrell Cl GU15 151 C3
Farrier Ct 6 SL8 3 B3
Farrier Pl 3 GU47 150 B7
Farriers Cl RG5 87 E7
Farriers La RG20 30 E7
Farriers Pl RG42 91 B2
Farringdon Ct RG1 86 E6
Farrowdene Rd RG2 113 C8
Farthingales The SL6 40 B7
Farthing Ct 3 SL5 121 B2
Farthing Green La SL2 23 B4
Fatherson Rd RG1 86 D7
Faulkner Pl GU19 145 F4
Faversham Rd GU47 143 D1
Fawcett Cres RG5 87 D6
Fawcett Rd SL4 67 B6
Fawler Mead RG12 118 F5
FAWLEY
Hambleden 15 C8
Wantage 27 C7
Fawley Bottom La RG9 15 A8
Fawley Cl SL6 19 D2
Fawley Court House & Mus* RG9 15 F5
Fawley Mews 2 RG1 85 F6
Fawley Rd RG30 85 C5
Fawns Manor Cl TW14 98 C7
Fawns Manor Rd TW14 98 D7
Fawsley Cl SL3 69 E7
Faygate Way RG6 87 B1
Feathers La TW19 96 A6
Felbridge Cl GU16 151 F1
Felbridge Ct UB3 71 D8
Felix La TW17 125 F3
Felixstowe Cl RG6 87 D2
Fellowes Ct UB3 71 D8
Fellow Gn GU24 153 F6
Fellow Green Rd GU24 153 F6
Fellstead Ct SL6 39 C6
Fells The RG31 84 A6
Felstead Cl RG6 86 F3
FELTHAM 98 E6
FELTHAMHILL 98 F3
Feltham Hill Inf Sch TW13 98 F5
Feltham Hill Jun Sch TW13 98 F5
Feltham Hill Rd TW15 98 C2
Feltham Rd TW15 98 C4
Felthorpe Cl RG6 114 A8
Felton Way RG31 84 C8
Feltre Pl 15 RG14 104 F2
Fenchurch Mews 3 RG41 88 A3
Fencote RG12 118 D3
Fennel Cl
Ascot SL5 120 A5
Earley RG6 86 F1
Newbury RG14 105 D5
Fennel Ct RG18 106 D4
Fennscombe Ct GU24 153 F6
Fenns La GU24 153 E5
Fenton Ave TW18 97 C3
Fenton Lodge GU15 151 E6
FERN 2 E5
Fernbank RG40 141 D6
Fernbank Cres SL5 119 D8
Fernbank Pl SL5 119 D7
Fernbank Rd SL5 119 D8
Fernbrook Rd RG4 58 E5
Fern Cl
Crowthorne RG45 143 A7
Frimley GU16 152 C3
Reading RG31 84 C5
Fern Cotts SL7 2 E5
Ferndale Ave RG30 85 A4
Ferndale Cl RG31 57 E3
Ferndale Cres RG41 115 E8
Ferndale Ct RG19 106 D3
Ferndale Pk Cvn Pk SL6 65 E8
Ferndale Rd TW15 97 E3
Fern Dr SL6 41 B7
Ferne Cl RG8 34 C7
Fernery The TW18 96 E3
Fern Glen RG31 57 C1
Fernhill Cl
Bracknell RG42 90 F1
Farnborough GU17 150 F1
Fernhill La GU17 150 F1
Fernhill Prim Sch GU14 150 F1
Fernhill Rd GU14, GU17 150 E2
Fernhill Sch GU14 150 F1
Fernhill Wlk GU17 150 F1
Fernhurst Rd
Ashford TW15 98 C4
Reading RG31 84 C4
Ferniehurst GU15 151 F4
Fern La SL7 2 E5
Fernley Ct SL6 19 D1
Fern Wlk
Ashford TW15 97 D3
Reading RG31 84 C5
Ferrard Cl SL5 119 D8
Ferrers Cl SL1 41 E5
Ferriby Ct RG12 118 C7
Ferrier Gr RG14 131 B8
Ferry Ave TW18 96 E1
Ferry End SL6 40 C4
Ferry La
Bourne End SL8 3 B1
Chertsey KT16 124 A3
Cookham SL6 20 B7
Goring RG8 34 B6
Hambleden RG9 16 D6
Laleham TW18 124 C6
Lower Halliford TW17 125 A1
Medmenham SL7 17 B5
Moulsford OX10, RG8 14 B4
South Stoke RG8 14 A4
Wargrave RG10 36 C2
Wraysbury TW19 96 B5
Ferry Rd
Bray SL6 40 C4
South Stoke RG8 14 C4
Ferry Sq TW17 125 B2
Ferry Way OX10 14 B8
Ferry Works TW17 125 A1
Festival Cotts SL3 69 C7
Fettiplace RG17 48 B3
Fetty Pl SL6 39 D4
Fickling Ct RG2 86 C4
Fidler's La RG20 30 E7
Fidlers Wlk RG10 36 E2
Field Cl
Burghfield Common RG7 111 B2
Harlington UB7 71 C7
Field Ct RG17 25 C2
Field End
Wargrave RG10 36 F2
West End GU24 153 F6
Fielden Pl RG12 118 D7
Fieldfare Ave GU46 149 B6
Fieldfare Dr RG12 117 D5
Fieldhead Gdns SL8 3 A3
Field House Cl SL5 120 A1
Fieldhouse Ind Est SL7 1 F2
Fieldhouse La SL7 1 F2
Fieldhouse Way SL7 1 F2
Field Hurst SL3 43 F1
Fielding Gdns
Crowthorne RG45 143 B4
Slough SL3 43 C4
Fielding Rd
Maidenhead SL6 39 B8
Sandhurst GU47 150 E6
Fieldings The SL6 65 A7
Field La GU16 151 E1
Field Path GU14 150 F1
Field Pk RG12 118 D8
Field Rd
Farnborough GU14 150 F1
Peasemore RG20 50 D8
Reading RG1 86 A6
Fieldridge RG14 105 D5
Fields The SL1 42 D4
Field View
Caversham RG4 59 B3
Egham TW20 96 C3
Feltham TW13 98 D4
Fieldview Ct
Slough SL1 42 C8
Staines TW18 97 A2
Fieldway RG41 88 D2
Fifehead Cl TW15 97 E2
FIFIELD 65 D6
Fifield Cotts SL6 65 D5
Fifield La SL4, SL6 65 D4
Fifield Rd SL6 65 D7
Fifield Way Cotts SL6 65 D6
Fifth Ave RG31 84 B6
Fifth Rd RG14 104 E1
Filbert Dr RG31 84 C8
Filey Rd RG1 86 E7
Filey Spur SL1 42 B4
Filley Alley OX12 6 E7
Filmer Rd SL4 66 D5
Finbeck Way RG6 113 F8
Fincham End Dr RG45 142 F4
FINCHAMPSTEAD 141 E2
Finchampstead CE Prim Sch RG40 141 E3
Finchampstead Rd
Finchampstead RG40 141 F6
Wokingham RG41, RG40 116 B3
Finch Ct SL6 39 D5
Finch Rd RG6 87 C4
Finch Way RG7 111 B3
Findhorn Cl GU47 150 D7
Finlay Dr RG9 15 E2
Finlay Ho RG9 15 E3
Finmere RG12 118 C2
Finney Dr GU20 146 D4
Finstock Cl RG6 87 D1
Finstock Gn RG12 118 F5
Firbank Pl TW20 95 B2
Fir Cl RG19 133 B5
Fir Cottage Rd RG40 141 E8
Fircroft Cl
Reading RG31 57 C1
Stoke Poges SL2 23 A6
Fircroft Ct SL2 23 A6
Fircroft Rd TW20 95 C1
Fir Dr GU17 150 D3
Fireball Hill SL5 120 D2
Firfield SL6 40 B1
Firglen Dr GU46 149 D7
Firgrove Ct RG12 100 E5
Firgrove Rd RG27, GU46 149 C6
Firlands
Bracknell RG12 118 C4
North Ascot SL5 119 D6
Firlands Ave GU15 151 D5
Firmstone Cl RG6 87 C1
Firs Ave SL4 66 F4
Firs Cl RG40 141 F7
Firs Dr SL3 43 F5
Firs End RG7 136 E6
Fir's End RG7 111 A2
Firs La
Maidenhead SL6 38 F4
Reading RG30 85 D5
Firs Rd RG31 84 C6
First Ave
Marlow SL7 2 A2
Reading RG31 84 B6
Tadley RG7 135 D2
First Cres SL1 42 C8
Firs The
5 Bracknell RG12 118 F5
Inkpen RG17 127 E5
1 Maidenhead SL6 39 E7
Reading RG1 85 F6
Thatcham RG18 106 B4
First St RG19 132 A5
Fir Tree Ave SL2 22 F1
Firtree Cl GU47 142 F1
Fir Tree Cl SL5 120 A2
Fir Tree Cnr RG26 134 E2
Fir Tree Cotts RG20 10 B2
Fir Tree La RG14 105 E4
Fir Tree Paddock RG20 10 A2
Fir Tree Pl 1 TW15 98 A3
Fir Tree Prim Sch RG14 105 E4
Firview Cl SL7 1 F1
Firwood Ct GU15 151 C5
Firwood Dr GU15 151 C5
Firwood Rd GU25 121 E3
Fisher Gn RG42 90 B2
Fisher Ho
5 Newbury RG14 104 F2
Sunningdale SL5 121 A1
Fisherman Ho KT16 124 C1
Fisherman's La RG7 135 B8
Fishermans Retreat SL7 1 E1
Fisherman's Way SL8 3 B4
Fishers Cotts RG4 59 C6
Fishers Ct RG4 59 C6
Fisher's La RG18 79 A1
Fishers Wood SL5 121 C1
FISHERY 40 B6
Fishery Rd SL6 40 C5
Fishguard Spur SL1 43 B4
Fishing Temple Park Homes TW18 123 E8
Fishponds Cl RG41 116 A4
Fishponds Est RG41 116 A4
Fishponds Rd RG41 116 A4
Fisk Cl TW16 98 F2
Fiske Ct GU46 149 E6
Fitzgerald Ct RG14 104 F3
Fitzrobert Pl TW20 96 A2
Fitzroy Cl RG12 118 A3
Fitzroy Cres RG5 88 A6
Five Acre RG31 57 B1
Five Acres HP10 3 F7
Fiveways
Camberley GU15 151 E5
Windsor SL4 66 E5
Five Ways RG18 52 F6
FLACKWELL HEATH 3 A7
Flagstaff Sq RG19 106 E2
Flambards RG4 59 C2
Flamborough Cl RG6 87 E2
Flamborough Path 5 RG6 87 E2
Flamborough Spur SL1 42 A4
Flamingo Cl RG41 115 E5
Flanders Ct TW20 96 C3
Flats The GU17 150 C4
Flaxman Cl RG6 86 F2
Flecker Cl RG18 106 C5
Fleetbrook Ho SL3 68 D6
Fleet Cl RG41 115 E6
Fleetham Gdns RG6 87 C1
Fleet Hill RG40 141 C2
Fleet La RG40 141 B2
Fleetway TW20 123 C6
Fleetwood Cl RG14 105 D5
Fleetwood Ct 7 TW19 70 E1
Fleetwood Rd SL2 42 F6
Fleming Cl RG2 140 E7
Fleming Ct SL3 43 C3
Fleming Rd RG14 105 B3
Flemish Fields KT16 124 A2
Flemish Pl RG42 91 D1
Fletcher Gdns RG42 117 D7
Fletton Link RG18 79 C8
Flexford Gn RG12 117 E3
Flintgrove RG12 118 D8
Flintjack Pl RG17 25 A2
Flintlock Cl TW19 70 A3
Flodden Dr RG31 84 D4
Floral Ct RG10 62 A8
Floral Ho 11 KT16 123 F1
Floral Way RG18 106 E5
Floreat Gdns RG14 104 E1
Florence Ave SL6 40 A8
Florence Cl GU46 149 C6
Florence Cotts SL4 92 C7
Florence Ct 19 RG30 85 D6
Florence Gdns
Staines TW18 97 B1
Thatcham RG18 106 A5
Florence Rd GU47 150 E7
Florence Villas GU18 146 B1
Florence Wlk RG1 86 D7
Florentina Ct RG42 90 C2
Florian Gdns RG30 85 B5
Florida Ct
Reading RG1 85 E6
Staines TW18 97 A3
Flower's Hill RG8 56 C4
Flowers Piece RG8 54 B6
Fobney St RG1 86 A7
Fokerham Rd RG19 106 F2
Folder's La RG42 91 C1
Foliejohn Way SL6 38 F1
Folkestone Ct SL3 44 A1
Follett Cl SL4 68 B1
Folly La RG7, RG30 110 F5
Folly Orch RG41 115 F5
Folly Rd
Inkpen RG17 127 E6
Lambourn RG17 25 A3
Folly The RG14 105 B1
Fontmell Cl TW15 98 A3
Fontmell Pk TW15 98 A3
Fontwell Cl SL6 39 A8
Fontwell Dr RG30 84 F5
Fontwell Rd RG14 105 B1
Forbes Chase GU47 150 D7
Forbury Ho 3 RG30 85 B7
Forbury La RG17, RG20 128 C7
Forbury Rd RG1 86 C8
Forbury Ret Pk RG1 86 C8
Forbury The RG1 86 B8
Fordbridge Cl KT16 124 B1
Fordbridge Ct TW15 97 E2
Fordbridge Rd
Ashford TW15 97 F3
Upper Halliford TW16, TW17 125 F3
Ford Cl
Ashford TW15 97 E2
Littleton TW17 125 A4
Fordham Way RG6 87 C1
Ford Ho TW20 95 C1
Ford La RG7 140 A2
Ford Rd
Ashford TW15 97 F4
Bisley GU24 153 F4
Chertsey KT16 124 B1
Fordwater Rd KT16 124 B1
Fordwater Trad Est KT16 124 C1
Fordwells Dr RG12 118 F5
Forehead The RG7 137 F4
Forest Cl
Bracknell SL5 119 C6
Tadley RG26 134 E2
Forest Ct RG41 116 A4
Forest Dean RG2 113 C7
Forest Dr TW16 98 F1
Forest End GU47 143 A1
Forest End Rd GU47 150 A8
Foresters Sq RG12 118 E6
Foresters Way RG45 143 F1
FOREST ESTATE 95 B2
Forest Gn
Bracknell RG12 118 D7
Holyport SL6 65 A6
Forest Green Rd SL6 65 C5
Forest Hill RG30 57 F2
Forest Hills GU15 151 B4
Forest Lodge RG41 88 E1
FOREST PARK 118 E3
Forest Rd
Binfield RG42 90 D3
Crowthorne RG45 143 C5
Windsor, Dedworth SL4 66 E5
Windsor SL4 93 E7
Winkfield RG42, SL5 92 D2
Wokingham, Bill Hill RG40 89 A2
Forest Sch RG41 88 C2
Forest View Cotts SL6 65 C6
Forest Way RG42 92 A2
Forge Cl
Caversham RG4 59 C2
Harlington UB3 71 D8
Kintbury RG17 102 A2
Forge Cotts SN8 99 B5
Forge Ct GU46 149 D7
Forge Dr SL2 22 C6
Forge Hill RG18 53 A5
Forge The RG17 100 D6
Forlease Cl SL6 40 A6
Forlease Dr SL6 40 A6
Forlease Rd SL6 40 A6
Formby Cl
Earley RG6 87 E3
Slough SL3 44 C2
Forndon Cl RG6 87 E2
Forsete Pl RG1 86 E6
Forsters RG7 134 F7
Forsters Farm Ct RG7 135 A6
Forsters La OX12 6 E6
Forsythia Gdns SL3 43 E3
Fort Narrien GU15 150 F7
Fortrose Cl GU47 150 D7
Fortrose Wlk RG31 84 E4
Fortuna Ct RG7 134 E2
Forty Cross OX11 12 A8
FORTY GREEN 1 A1
Forty Green Dr SL7 1 B2
Forum The KT16 123 F1
Fosseway RG45 143 A5
Fossewood Dr GU15 151 D7
Foster Ave SL4 66 E4
Fosters Gr GU20 146 B6
Fosters La RG5 87 E6
Fosters Path SL2 21 F1
Fotherby Ct SL6 40 A6
Fotheringay Gdns SL1 42 A6
Foundation Pk SL6 38 F4
Foundry Ct
Chertsey KT16 124 A2
Slough SL2 42 F5
Foundry Ho RG17 100 E7
Foundry La SL3 69 B4
Foundry Mews 1 KT16 124 A2
Foundry Pl 23 RG1 86 A6
Fountain Gdns
11 Newbury RG14 105 A2
Windsor SL4 67 D4
Fountains Garth RG12 118 A6
Four Houses Corner RG7 136 E8
Fourth Ave
Marlow SL7 2 A2
Reading RG31 84 B6
Fourth St RG19 131 F5
Fowler Cl RG6 87 A3
Fowlers La RG42 118 B8
Foxborough RG7 139 D6
Foxborough Cl SL3 44 A1
Foxborough Ct SL6 39 E4
Foxborough Prim Sch SL3 44 A1
Foxbury RG17 25 B2
Fox Cl RG7 111 A3
Foxcombe Dr RG31 84 C7
Foxcote RG40 142 A7
Fox Court Mobile Home Pk GU47 150 C8
Fox Covert GU18 153 A8
Fox Covert Cl SL5 120 C4
Fox Ct 6 KT16 123 F1
Foxdown Cl GU15 151 C5
Fox Dr GU46 149 D7
Foxes Piece SL7 1 E2

Foxes Piece Sch SL7 1 E3
Foxes Wlk RG10 61 A3
Foxglove Cl
Stanwell TW19 97 D7
Winkfield RG42 92 A2
Wokingham RG41 115 D7
Foxglove Gdns 2 RG1 85 E7
Foxglove Way RG18 106 D5
Foxhaven Ct SL5 120 C4
Foxhays Rd RG2 113 D8
Foxheath RG12 118 E4
Foxherne SL3 43 C4
Foxhill 2 RG12 118 B5
Foxhill Cl RG4 60 A5
Foxhill Cres GU15 152 B8
Foxhill La RG4 59 D7
Fox Hill Prim Sch RG12 118 B4
Foxhill Rd RG1 86 E6
Fox Ho 4 KT16 123 F1
Foxhollow Dr SL2 22 C7
Foxhunter Way RG19 105 F3
Foxhunt Gr RG31 84 F4
Fox La RG27 149 A7
Fox Lane N 7 KT16 123 F1
Fox Lane S 10 KT16 123 F1
Foxleigh Ct TW18 96 C3
Foxley Cl GU17 150 C5
Foxley La RG42 90 C1
Fox Rd SL3 43 D2
Framewood Manor SL2 23 C6
Framewood Rd SL2, SL3 23 C6
Framlingham Dr RG4 59 E5
Frampton Bridge Rdbt
RG42 90 F2
Frampton Cl RG5 60 E1
France Hill Dr GU15 151 C5
Frances Ave SL6 20 C1
Frances Ct SL5 120 D5
Frances Rd SL4 67 D5
Frances The RG18 106 D4
Francis Baily Prim Sch
RG19 106 F3
Francis Chichester Cl
SL5 120 B4
Francis Cl TW17 125 A5
Francis Gdns RG42 91 D1
Francis St RG1 86 B6
Francis Way
Burnham SL1 41 D6
Frimley GU15 152 C4
Francomes Field RG17 25 C1
Franklin Ave
Slough SL2 42 B8
Tadley RG26 135 A1
Franklin Ct
8 Reading RG1 85 F7
Tadley RG26 135 A2
Franklin St RG1 85 F7
Frank Lunnon Cl SL8 3 C3
Franklyn Cres SL4 66 D4
Frank Sutton Way SL1 42 D6
Frantons The SL6 39 A7
Frascati Way SL6 39 F7
Fraser Ave RG4 59 C6
Fraser Mead GU47 150 E6
Fraser Rd RG42 118 B8
Fraunchies Ct SL1 42 E6
Frederick Ho TW15 97 E4
Frederick Pl RG41 116 A6
Freeborn Way RG12 118 E7
Freeman Cl TW17 125 E5
Freeman Ct RG14 104 F3
Freemans Cl
Hungerford RG17 100 C5
Stoke Poges SL2 23 A6
Freemantle Rd GU19 145 F4
Freemantles Sch KT16 123 E2
Free Prae Rd KT16 124 A1
Freesia Cl RG41 115 D7
French Gdns GU17 150 D4
Frenchum Gdns SL1 41 E6
Frensham RG12 118 D3
Frensham Cl GU46 149 B6
Frensham Gn RG2 86 F1
Frensham Rd RG45 143 B7
Frensham Wlk SL2 22 C7
Freshfield Cl RG6 87 E3
Freshfields La RG20 51 B2
Freshwater Rd RG1 86 E8
Freshwood Dr GU46 149 D4
Fresian Way RG41 88 A2
Friars Ct GU47 149 F8
Friars Keep RG12 118 B5
Friars Rd
Newbury RG14 131 A8
Virginia Water GU25 122 D5
Friar St RG1 86 A8
Friars Way KT16 124 A3
Friars Wlk 8 RG1 86 A8
Friary Island TW19 95 C8
Friary Rd
Ascot SL5 120 B3
Wraysbury TW19 68 C1
Friary The SL4 68 C1
Friday St RG9 15 E2
Friendship Ho 4 TW18 97 A3
Friendship Way RG12 118 B6
Friends Wlk 1 TW18 96 F3
Frieth Cl RG6 87 A1
Frieth Rd SL7 1 A3
FRILSHAM 80 D6
Frilsham Home Farm Bsns
Units RG18 53 F1
Frilsham Rd RG30 85 B4
FRIMLEY 151 F2
Frimley Cl RG5 87 D8
Frimley Green Rd GU16 151 D1
Frimley Grove Gdns
GU16 151 E1
Frimley Hall Dr GU15 151 F6
Frimley High St GU16 151 D1
Frimley Park Hospl
GU16 151 D2
Frimley Rd GU15, GU16 151 B3
FRIMLEY RIDGE 152 B3
Frimley Sq GU16 151 E1
Fringford Cl RG6 87 C1
Frithe The SL2 43 B7
Frith Hill Rd GU16 152 B1
Frithwald Rd KT16 123 F2
Frobisher RG12 118 C2
Frobisher Cres TW19 97 E8
Frobisher Gdns TW19 97 E8
Frodsham Way GU47 143 E2
Frog Hall RG40 116 F5
Frog Hall Dr RG40 116 E5
Frog La RG12 118 A6
Frogmill SL6 17 C3
Frogmill Ct SL6 17 C3
Frogmill Spinney SL6 17 C4
FROGMORE 150 C6
Frogmore Cl SL1 42 A4
Frogmore Com Coll
GU46 149 F5
Frogmore Ct
Blackwater GU17 150 C4
11 Maidenhead SL6 39 F7
Frogmore Dr SL4 67 F5
Frogmore Flats SL4 67 F5
Frogmore Gr GU17 150 C4
Frogmore Inf Sch GU17 150 B5
Frogmore Jun Sch GU17 150 B5
Frogmore Park Dr GU17 150 D4
Frogmore Rd GU17 150 C5
Frogmore Way RG30 85 B5
Fromer Rd HP10 3 D4
Fromont Dr RG19 106 D3
Fromow Gdns GU20 146 D4
Fronds Pk RG7 109 A2
Front St RG17 47 D6
Frouds Bridge Marina
RG7 108 F1
Frouds La RG7 109 A1
FROXFIELD 99 A5
Froxfield Ave RG1 85 F5
Froxfield Down 6 RG12 118 F4
Fruen Rd TW14 98 F8
Fry Ct RG4 59 B3
Fry La GU19 145 D2
Frymley View SL4 66 D6
Fry's La GU46 149 E7
Fuchsia Cl RG31 84 C5
Fuchsia Way GU24 153 E6
Fulcher Row 2 RG6 87 A6
Fullbrook Cl
Maidenhead SL6 40 A8
Wokingham RG41 89 A1
Fullbrook Cres RG31 57 D3
Fuller Cl RG19 106 F2
Fullers La RG20 129 D1
Fuller's La RG7 112 B4
Fullers Yd SL6 20 B2
Fulmead Rd RG30 85 C8
FULMER 23 C8
Fulmer Chase SL3 23 C8
Fulmer Cl RG6 87 A2
Fulmer Common Rd SL3 23 E6
Fulmer Inf Sch SL3 23 E8
Fulmer Rd SL3 23 E8
Fulmer Rise Est SL3 23 E6
Fulwood Ct TW19 70 F1
Funky Footprints Nature
Reserve* TW17 125 B3
Furlong Cl SL8 3 B3
Furlong Rd SL8 3 B3
Furness SL4 66 C5
Furness Pl 8 SL4 66 C5
Furness Row 9 SL4 66 C5
Furness Sq 6 SL4 66 C5
Furness Way SL4 66 C5
Furness Wlk 7 SL4 66 C5
Furnival Ave SL2 42 B8
Furnival Cl GU25 122 D3
Furrow Way SL6 39 A4
Furse Cl GU15 152 C4
Furzebank SL5 120 D5
Furzecroft 4 TW15 98 A3
Furzedown Cl TW20 95 E2
Furze Hill RG20 103 D5
Furze Hill Cres RG45 143 C4
Furzemoors RG12 118 B4
Furzen Cl SL2 22 A2
FURZE PLATT 19 D2
Furze Platt Bus Ctr Pk
SL6 19 D2
Furze Platt Halt SL6 19 E1
Furze Platt Inf Sch SL6 19 C1
Furze Platt Jun Sch SL6 19 C1
Furze Platt Rd SL6 19 B1
Furze Platt Senior Sch
SL6 19 C2
Furze Rd
Maidenhead SL6 19 D1
Tadley RG26 134 F2
Fuscia Ct 8 TW13 98 F5
Fushsia Gr RG2 113 E6
Fusiliers Pl RG19 106 D2
Fuzzens Wlk SL4 66 E5
Fydlers Cl SL4 93 B2
Fyfield Cl GU17 150 D5
Fyfield Rd 3 RG19 106 D2
Fylingdales RG19 106 C2

G

Gables Ave TW15 97 F3
Gables Cl
Datchet SL3 68 A8
Maidenhead SL6 40 B8
Gables Way RG19 107 C2
Gabriel Dr GU15 152 B4
Gabriel's Sq RG6 87 D1
Gabriels The RG14 130 D5
Gadd Cl RG40 116 F7
Gage Cl SL6 39 E4
Gainsborough
Bracknell RG12 118 C3
Cookham Rise SL6 19 F5
Gainsborough Ave RG17 102 B2
Gainsborough Cl
Camberley GU15 151 F7
Woodley RG5 88 A6
Gainsborough Cres RG9 35 C8
Gainsborough Dr
Maidenhead SL6 39 D3
North Ascot SL5 119 D7
Gainsborough Hill RG9 35 D8
Gainsborough Rd
Henley-on-T RG9 35 D8
Reading RG30 85 B5
Gairn Cl RG30 85 A7
Galahad Cl SL1 42 A4
Galaxy Ho RG19 132 A5
Gale Dr GU18 146 A1
Galileo Ct RG12 118 E7
Gallery Ct 16 TW20 96 A3
Galley La RG19 132 D1
Galleymead Rd SL3 69 F6
Gallops The
Chilton OX11 10 D8
East Ilsley RG20 30 E6
Gallop The GU46 149 D7
Galloway Chase SL2 43 A6
Galloway Ctr The RG14 105 E2
Galloway Ho 4 RG1 85 E5
Gallys Rd SL4 66 D6
Galsworthy Dr RG4 59 E5
Galsworthy Rd 4 KT16 124 A2
Galton Rd SL5 120 F3
Galvin Rd SL1 42 C6
Galway Rd GU46 149 C4
Garden Cl
Ashford TW15 98 C2
Maidenhead SL6 39 A5
Garden Close La RG14 130 D4
Garden Cotts
Arborfield RG41 114 F6
Colnbrook SL3 69 D7
GARDENERS GREEN 116 F2
Gardeners La RG8 55 C4
Garden Ho RG4 58 E3
Garden Ho The SL5 121 C4
Gardenia Dr GU24 153 F6
Garden Mews
North Ascot SL5 92 F1
8 Reading RG30 85 D6
Slough SL1 42 F5
Garden Mews The SL6 39 B7
Gardens The
Hatton TW14 71 D1
South Stoke RG8 14 C3
Garde Rd RG4 60 E3
Gardner Ho SL6 19 E1
Gardner Rd SL6 19 D2
Gardners Pl 4 RG6 87 A6
Gardners Rd RG42 92 A2
Garfield Pl 1 SL4 67 D5
Garfield Rd GU15 151 C5
Garford Cres RG14 130 D8
Garland Ct RG14 104 F2
Garland Jun Sch RG7 111 A3
Garlands Cl RG7 111 A2
Garner Ct TW19 70 D1
Garnet Cl SL1 42 A4
Garnet Ct SL7 1 C1
Garnet Field GU46 149 A5
Garnet Hill 9 RG1 86 A6
Garnet St RG1 86 A6
Garrard Rd SL2 21 F1
Garrard St RG1 86 A8
Garrett Rd RG40 141 E8
Garretts La SL6 19 F2
Garrick Cl TW18 97 A1
Garson La TW19 95 D8
Garson's La SL4 92 A7
Garston Cl RG30 85 A4
Garston Cres RG31 84 B5
Garston Gr RG40 115 F1
Garston Park Home Village
RG31 84 B6
Garswood RG12 118 D3
Garth Cl RG41 88 C2
Garth Hill Coll RG12 118 C8
Garthlands SL6 19 D2
Garth Rd RG7 137 A5
Garth Sq RG42 91 B1
Gascon's Gr SL2 22 A1
Gas House Hill RG17 25 C3
Gaskell Mews RG14 131 B8
Gaskells End RG4 58 D8
Gas La
Maidenhead SL6 40 B3
Twyford RG10 61 D4
Gaston Bridge Rd
Shepperton TW17 125 D3
Upper Halliford TW17 125 E4
Gaston Way TW17 125 D4
Gas Works Rd RG1 86 C7
Gatcombe Cl RG31 84 C4
Gatcombe Cres SL5 119 F8
Gatehampton Rd RG8 34 C5
Gatehouse Cl SL4 67 B4
Gatehouse The SL5 121 A1
Gate Lodge RG14 104 D1
Gatewick Cl SL1 42 E5
Gatward Ave SL6 39 A3
Gaveston Rd SL2 21 F2
Gayhurst Cl RG4 59 D6
Gays La SL6 65 B8
Gaywood Dr RG14 105 D4
Gazelle Cl RG41 88 A3
Geffers Ride SL5 119 E7
Gelder Cl RG6 87 D1
Genesis Cl TW19 97 F7
Genesis Ho TW18 96 F4
Geneva Cl TW17 125 E7
Geoffrey Field Inf Sch
RG2 113 C8
Geoffrey Field Jun Sch
RG2 113 C8
Geoffreyson Rd RG4 58 E5
George Cl
Caversham RG4 59 C3
Marlow SL7 1 F4
GEORGE GREEN 43 E7
George Green Dr SL3 43 F8
George Green Rd SL3 43 E7
Georgeham Rd GU47 143 D2
George Palmer Prim Sch
RG2 86 C4
Georges Dr HP10 3 C7
George St
Caversham RG4 59 B1
Reading RG1 85 F8
Staines TW18 96 F4
George V Pl SL4 67 D7
Georgian Cl
Camberley GU15 151 E7
Staines TW18 97 B4
Georgian Hts SL8 3 B5
Geranium Cl RG45 143 B8
Gerrards Cross Rd SL2 23 A7
Gerring Rd RG2 140 F7
Gervaise Cl SL1 41 F5
Gibbet La GU15 152 A7
Gibbins La RG42 91 D3
Gibbons Cl GU47 150 C8
Gibbs Cl RG40 141 E6
Gibbs Way GU46 149 B4
Gibraltar La SL6 2 C1
Gibson Ct 15 SL3 43 F1
Gibson Dr RG12 118 D6
Gibson Pl TW19 70 C1
Gidley La RG20 50 E2
Gifford Cl RG4 59 E5
Gifford Ho 2 RG4 59 C1
Gilbert Ct RG18 106 D3
Gilbert Rd GU15 151 C2
Gilbert Way
Finchampstead RG40 115 E1
6 Slough SL3 43 F1
Gilbey Wlk HP10 3 D4
Gilchrist Way SL6 38 B5
Giles Cl RG14 104 F2
Giles Travers Cl TW20 123 C6
Gillespie Ho GU25 122 E5
Gillette Way RG2 86 B2
Gilliat Rd SL1 42 E6
Gilliatt Cl SL0 44 E7
Gillott Ct SL6 39 F8
Gillotts Cl RG9 35 B8
Gillott's Hill RG9 35 C7
Gillott's La RG9 35 B7
Gillotts Sch RG9 35 B7
Gill Rise RG42 91 C2
Gilman Cres SL4 66 D4
Gilmore Cl SL3 43 C4
Gilmore Cres TW15 98 A2
Gilmuire Flats SL5 120 B2
Gilpin Way UB3 71 D7
Gilroy Cl RG14 130 C6
Gilson Ct SL4 95 C8
Gingells Farm Rd RG10 61 B5
Gipsy La
Bracknell RG12 118 D7
Earley RG6 87 D1
Hungerford RG17 100 E8
Lower Earley RG6 87 D3
Reading RG30 57 E1
Sindlesham RG41 114 F7
Wokingham RG40 116 C4
Girton Cl GU47 143 E1
Glade Ho
Ascot SL5 120 C4
4 Marlow SL7 1 E2
Glade Rd SL7 1 E2
Glade The
Ascot SL5 120 C4
Newbury RG14 130 F7
Purley on T RG8 57 C4
Staines TW18 97 B2
Gladridge Cl RG6 87 C4
Gladstone Cl RG17 102 B2
Gladstone Ind Est SL6 39 E8
Gladstone La RG18 106 C8
Gladstone Way SL1 42 A5
Glaisdale RG19 106 C2
Glamis Way RG31 84 B4
Glanmor Rd SL2 43 B6
Glanty The TW20 96 B4
Glassonby Wlk GU15 152 C5
Glebe Cl
Dorney SL6 40 F4
Lightwater GU18 146 C1
Moulsford OX10 13 F5
Glebe Cotts RG8 14 C3
Glebefields RG14 105 B5
Glebe Fields RG20 49 A7
Glebe Gdns RG4 60 E3
Glebe La
Sonning RG4 60 E3
Stockcross RG20 103 E5
Glebeland Gdns TW17 125 C3
Glebeland Rd GU15 150 F4
Glebelands RG19 106 C3
Glebelands Rd RG40 116 C7
Glebe Pl RG17 73 A2
Glebe Rd
Egham TW20 96 C2
Maidenhead SL6 40 B5
Old Windsor SL4 68 B2
Purley on T RG8 57 B5
Reading RG2 86 C5
Staines TW18 97 B3
Glebe Ride RG8 34 B6
Glebe The
Aldworth RG8 32 F3
Blackwater GU17 150 E4
Glebewood RG12 118 C4
Glenalmond Ho TW15 97 E5
Glenapp Grange RG7 136 F6
Glen Ave TW15 98 A4
Glenavon Gdns
Slough SL3 43 C3
Yateley GU46 149 D4
Glenbeigh Terr RG1 85 E6
Glen Cl TW17 125 A5
Glen Ct TW18 96 F1
Glendale Ave RG14 130 C5
Glendale Cl RG41 116 A3
Glendale Rd RG26 135 A1
Glendevon Rd RG5 87 F8
Glendower 4 RG12 118 B5
Gleneagles Cl TW19 70 D1
Gleneagles Ct 18 RG1 86 D7
Gleneagles Ho RG12 117 E3
Glenfield Ho RG12 118 C5
Glenfield Rd TW15 98 C2
Glenfields SL2 22 F4
Glenhurst GU20 146 A6
Glenhurst Cl GU17 150 E4
Glen Innes GU47 143 E1
Glenmore Cl RG19 106 D2
Glenn Miller Cl RG20 49 A5
Glennon Cl RG30 85 C4
Glenore SL6 20 A8
Glenrhondda RG4 58 F6
Glenridge Farm Cvn Site
GU25 122 B6
Glenrosa Rd RG30 85 A8
Glen The
Ascot SL5 120 D5
Pamber Heath RG26 135 E1
Slough SL3 43 C2
Glentworth Pl SL1 42 C5
Glenwood
Bracknell RG12 118 D5
Virginia Water GU25 122 C8
Glenwood Dr RG31 84 C7
Globe Farm La GU17 150 B5
Globeside Bsns Pk SL7 1 F2
Glory Cl HP10 3 F7
Glory Hill La HP9 3 F8
Glory Mill La HP10 3 E7
Gloucester Ave
Shinfield RG2 113 E5
Slough SL1 42 C8
Gloucester Cres TW18 97 D2
Gloucester Ct RG30 85 D7
Gloucester Dr TW18 96 D5
Gloucester Gdns GU19 145 E3
Gloucester Pl SL4 67 D5
Gloucester Rd
Bagshot GU19 145 E3
Maidenhead SL6 19 E2
Newbury RG14 104 E2
Reading RG30 85 D7
Gloucestershire Lea RG42 91 F1
Glyme Wlk RG31 84 F3
Glyncastle RG4 58 F5
Glynswood GU15 151 F3
Glynwood Ho 3 SL6 40 A7
Go Ape Bracknell*
RG12 118 D1
Goaters Rd SL5 119 C7
Goddard Cl
Littleton TW17 124 F6
Shinfield RG2 113 E5
Goddard Ct RG41 88 B1
Goddard Dr RG7 107 F3
GODDARD'S GREEN 111 D2
Goddards La GU15 151 B3
Goddard Way RG42 91 D2
Goddington Rd SL8 3 A5
Godfrey Cl GU47 150 D7
Godfrey Ct TW18 97 A1
Godolphin Inf Sch SL1 42 C7
Godolphin Jun Sch SL1 42 D7
Godolphin Rd SL1 42 D6
Godstow Cl RG5 87 E8
Goffs Rd TW15 98 D2
Gogmore Farm Cl KT16 123 F2
Gogmore La KT16 124 A2
Goldcrest Cl GU46 149 B6
Goldcrest Way RG31 84 B6
Gold Cup La SL5 119 D8
Golden Ball La SL6 19 A3
Golden Oak Cl SL2 22 C6
Golden Orb Wood RG42 117 D8
Goldfinch La RG20 131 F3
Golding Cl RG19 106 F3
Goldney Rd GU15 152 C4
Goldsmid Rd RG1 85 F7

Goldsmith Cl
Finchampstead RG40 115 E1
Thatcham RG18 106 C5
Goldsmith Way RG45 143 B4
Goldsworthy Way SL1 41 C7
Goldthorpe Gdns RG6 113 F8
Goldwell Dr RG14 104 F4
Golf Dr GU15 151 F4
Gooch Cl RG10 61 F3
Goodall Cl RG9 15 D1
Goodboy's La RG7 112 A1
Goodchild Rd RG40 116 D6
Goodings Gn RG40 116 F6
Goodings La RG17 47 B3
Goodliffe Gdns RG31 57 C4
Goodman Pk SL2 43 C5
Goodman Pl TW18 96 F4
Goodrich Cl RG4 59 E5
Goodways Dr RG12 118 D7
Goodwin Cl RG31 84 E4
Goodwin Mdws HP10 3 E6
Goodwin Rd SL2 21 F2
Goodwin Villas SL1 41 F5
Goodwin Wlk RG14 130 C6
Goodwood Cl
Burghfield Common RG7 111 A2
Camberley GU15 151 C8
Goodwood Rise SL7 1 C7
Goodwood Way 5 RG14 105 C1
Goose Cnr RG42 91 F3
Goosecroft La RG8 57 B5
Goose Gn
Farnham Royal SL2 22 B3
Lambourn RG17 25 B3
Goose Green Way RG19 106 D3
GOOSE HILL 133 A2
Goose La RG20 49 E5
Gordon Ave GU15 151 C4
Gordon Cl TW18 97 B2
Gordon Clifford Ct 3
RG42 118 B8
Gordon Cres
Camberley GU15 151 C4
Compton RG20 31 D4
Gordon Ct 2 RG14 105 B2
Gordon Dr TW17 125 D2
Gordon Palmer Cl RG7 137 D5
Gordon Palmer Ct RG30 85 C8
Gordon Pl RG30 85 C8
Gordon Rd
Ashford TW15 97 E5
Camberley GU15 151 C5
Crowthorne RG45 143 D3
Egham TW18 96 C4
Maidenhead SL6 39 D7
Newbury RG14 105 B2
Shepperton TW17 125 D3
Thatcham RG18 106 A5
Windsor SL4 66 F5
Gordon's Sch GU24 153 E7
Gordon Wlk GU46 149 F5
GORE END 129 B4
Gore End Rd RG20 129 B3
Gore Rd SL1 21 B2
Gore The SL1 21 A2
GORING 34 D6
Goring CE Prim Sch RG8 34 C7
Goring La RG7 111 A1
Goring Rd TW18 96 E3
Goring's Sq TW18 96 E4
Goring & Streatley Sta
RG8 34 C6
Gorrick Sq RG41 116 B3
Gorse Bank GU18 153 A8
Gorse Cottage Dr RG18 79 C1
Gorse Dr RG5 88 A8
Gorse Hill La GU25 122 D5
Gorse Hill Rd GU25 122 D5
Gorselands
Caversham RG4 59 B6
Newbury RG14 130 D5
Gorse Meade SL1 42 B5
Gorse Pl RG42 92 B1
Gorse Rd
Cookham Rise SL6 19 E6
Frimley GU16 151 E2
Gorse Ride Inf Sch RG40 141 E7
Gorse Ride Jun Sch
RG40 141 E7
Gorse Ride N RG40 141 E7
Gorse Ride S RG40 141 E6
Gorton Oaks RG40 116 D5
Gosbrook Ho 1 RG4 59 C1
Gosbrook Rd RG4 59 B2
Gosden Rd GU24 153 F6
Gosforth Cl RG6 87 D2
Goslar Way SL4 67 B5
Gosling Gn SL3 43 E3
Gosling Rd SL3 43 E3
Gosnell Cl GU16 152 D3
Gossmore Cl SL7 1 F1
Gossmore La SL7 1 F1
Gossmore Wlk SL7 1 F1
Goswell Hill SL4 67 D6
Goswell Rd SL4 67 D6
Gothic Ct
Harlington UB3 71 D8
1 Sandhurst GU47 150 B7
Gough's Barn La RG42 91 A8
Gough's La RG12 91 D1
Gough's Mdw GU47 150 B7
Gould Cl RG14 105 B3
Goulders Cotts RG10 36 F7
Gould Rd TW14 98 E8
Governor's Rd GU15 150 F6
Govett Ave TW17 125 C4
Govett Gr GU20 146 D5
Gower Pk GU47 150 D7
Gower St RG1 85 E8
Gower The TW20 123 C6
Gowings Gn SL1 41 E4
Grace Ct SL1 42 C5
Grace Reynolds Wlk
GU15 151 C6
Graces La RG20 78 B8
Graffham Cl RG6 114 B8
Grafton Cl
Maidenhead SL6 19 E2
Slough SL3 43 E7
Grafton Ct TW14 98 D7
Grafton Rd RG30 84 D7
Graham Cl
Blewbury OX11 12 A8
Maidenhead SL6 39 C5
Reading RG31 84 E4
Grahame Ave RG8 56 D5
Graham Rd
Cookham Rise SL6 19 E6
Windlesham GU20 146 C4
Grainford Ct RG40 116 C5
Grampian Cl UB3 71 D7
Grampian Rd GU47 143 A2
Grampian Way SL3 44 A1
Gramp's Hill OX12 6 E5
Granary The RG2 86 D4
Granby Ct RG1 86 E7
Granby End RG7 111 B3
Granby Gdns RG1 86 E7
Grand Ave GU15 151 C6
Grandison Ho RG9 15 E3
Grand Regency Hts SL5 119 E6
Grange Ave
Crowthorne RG45 143 B6
Reading RG6 87 A6
Grange Cl
Goring RG8 34 B6
Wraysbury TW19 68 E1
Grange Ct
Earley RG6 87 B8
Egham TW20 95 F3
Littleton TW17 125 A5
Newbury RG14 105 B2
7 Staines TW18 97 A3
Grange Dr HP10 3 D3
Grange Gdns
Farnham Common SL2 22 D7
Newbury RG14 130 C5
Grange La SL6 19 F8
Grangely Cl RG31 84 D4
Grange Pl TW18 124 C7
Grange Rd
Bracknell RG12 118 C8
Camberley GU15 151 E5
Cookham Rise SL6 19 F7
Egham TW20 95 F3
Henley-on-T RG9 15 E1
Grange The
Caversham RG4 58 D6
Newbury RG14 130 C5
Old Windsor SL4 68 B2
Staines TW18 97 A3
4 Stanwell TW19 70 D1
Virginia Water GU25 122 E5
Grange Way SL0 44 F7
Grangewood SL3 43 C8
Grant Ave SL1 42 E7
Grant Cl TW17 125 B3
Grantham Cl GU47 143 E1
Grantham Ho 5 TW16 98 E1
Grantham Rd RG30 84 F4
Granthams The RG17 25 B3
Grant Ho 6 SL8 3 A4
Grantley Hts 6 RG1 86 C7
Grant Rd RG45 143 C3
Grant Wlk SL5 120 E1
Granville Ave SL2 42 D8
Granville Rd RG30 85 B5
Grasholm Way SL3 44 C2
Grasmere
Camberley GU15 151 E7
Windsor SL4 66 E7
Grasmere Ave
Reading RG30 57 F2
Slough SL2 43 A6
Grasmere Cl
East Bedfont TW14 98 F7
5 Thorpe Lea TW20 96 B1
Winnersh RG41 88 B1
Grasmere Par SL2 43 B6
Grasmere Rd GU18 146 B1
Grass Hill RG4 58 E3
Grassington Pl RG19 106 D3
Grassmead RG19 106 F2
Grassy La SL6 39 E7
Grattan Ct SL7 2 A3
Gratton Dr SL4 66 E3
Gratton Rd RG2 113 C8
Gratwicke Rd RG30 84 E8
Gravel Hill
Caversham RG4 59 A6
Henley-on-T RG9 15 D2
Stockcross RG20 103 E5
Gravelly Cl RG20 129 A3
Gravel Rd RG9 35 A1
Graveney Dr RG4 58 E3
Gravett Cl RG9 35 C8
Gray Ct 11 SL4 67 A5
Grayling Cl SL7 18 C8
Grayling Ct 8 RG1 59 A1
Graylings Ho KT16 124 C1
Gray Pl RG42 117 E8
Grays Cres RG5 87 C7
Grayshot Dr GU17 150 C5
Grays La TW15 98 B4
Gray's Mon★ SL2 22 F2
Grays Park Rd SL2 23 A2
Grays Pl SL2 42 F5
Grays Rd SL1 42 F5
GRAZELEY 112 D2
GRAZELEY GREEN 112 A3
Grazeley Parochial CE Prim
Sch RG7 112 E2
Grazeley Rd RG7 113 A4
Great Auclum Pl RG7 111 B2
Great Barn Ct RG19 106 C3
Great Cockrow Rly★
KT16 123 D1
Great Hill Cres SL6 39 C6
GREAT HOLLANDS 117 F3
Great Hollands Prim Sch
RG12 117 F4
Great Hollands Rd RG12 117 F3
Great Hollands Sq RG12 117 F3
Great Knollys St RG1 85 F8
Great Lea RG7 113 A5
GREAT LEA COMMON 113 A5
Great Marlow Sch SL7 1 F4
Great Severals RG17 102 A2
GREAT SHEFFORD 48 B3
Great South-West Rd TW14,
TW6, TW4, TW5 71 D2
Grebe Ct TW18 97 B4
Greenacre SL4 66 E5
Greenacre Ct TW20 95 C2
Green Acre Mount RG30 84 D8
Greenacres RG20 129 E1
Greenacres Ave RG41 88 A3
Greenacres La RG41 88 A3
Greenaway Terr TW19 97 E7
Greenbank Way GU15 151 D2
Green Bsns Ctr The TW18 96 C4
Green Cl
Burnham SL6 41 A7
Maidenhead SL6 19 F1
Green Cres HP10 3 C7
Green Croft RG40 116 E8
Greencroft Gdns RG30 84 F4
Green Ct TW16 98 F2
Greendale Mews SL2 43 A6
Green Dr RG40 116 E4
Green Dragon La HP10 3 B7
Greene Fielde End TW18 97 D1
Green End GU46 149 D7
Greenend Cl RG7 113 B2
Green Farm Rd GU19 145 F3
Green Farm Rise SN8 99 B5
Greenfern Ave SL1 41 C7
Greenfield Ho TW20 95 B2
Greenfields SL6 40 A5
Greenfields Rd RG2 113 B8
Greenfield Way RG45 143 A7
Greenfinch Cl
Crowthorne RG45 142 F6
Reading RG31 84 B6
Sandhurst GU47 150 D8
Greenfinch Dr RG10 61 D5
Greengates 1 RG30 85 C7
GREENHAM 131 C8
Greenham Cl
Greenham RG19 131 D8
Woodley RG5 88 A6
GREENHAM COMMON 132 B6
Greenham Mill RG14 105 B3
Greenham Rd RG14 105 B1
Greenham Road Ret Pk
RG14 105 A2
Greenham Wood RG12 118 C3
Greenhaven GU46 149 B5
Green Hill Cl GU15 152 C6
Green Hill Rd GU15 152 C6
Greenholme GU15 152 D5
Greenhow RG12 118 A6
Greenidge Cl 2 RG1 85 E5
Green La
Ascot SL5 120 E8
Ashford TW16 98 F2
Bagshot GU19 145 F2
Binfield RG40 90 A3
Blackwater GU17 150 B4
Blackwater, Hawley GU17 150 E4
Burghfield Common RG30 85 A2
Burnham SL1 21 D4
Caversham RG9 35 A1
Chieveley RG20 78 B7
Datchet SL3 68 B6
Egham TW20 96 B3
Farnham Common SL2 22 B6
Fifield SL6 65 C6
Henley-on-T RG9 35 D8
Holyport SL6 64 A5
Hurst RG10 88 E3
Littlewick Green SL6 38 B5
Maidenhead SL6 40 A6
Newbury RG14 104 E2
Pangbourne RG8 56 C5
Sandhurst GU47 150 C7
Shepperton TW17 125 C4
Staines TW18 123 E8
Stanford Dingley RG7 81 F3
Thatcham RG19 106 C3
Ufton Nervet RG7 110 C2
Windsor SL4 67 B5
Wokingham RG41 88 D1
Yateley GU46 149 B7
Greenlake Terr TW18 97 A1
Greenlands
Ball Hill RG20 129 E1
Flackwell Heath HP10 3 B8
Greenlands Ct
2 Maidenhead SL6 39 B8
7 Staines TW18 97 A4
Greenlands Rd
Camberley GU15 151 B1
Newbury RG14 105 B1
Staines TW18 97 A4
Green Lane Cl GU15 151 C7
Green Lane Ct SL1 21 C2
Greenleaf Ct SL3 68 A8
Greenleas GU16 151 E2
Green Leas TW16 98 F2
Greenleas Ave RG4 59 B7
Greenleas Cl GU46 149 C7
Green Leas Cl TW16 98 F2
Green Leys SL6 19 F2
Greenock Rd SL1 42 A7
Greeno Cres TW17 125 A4
Green Pk TW18 96 E5
Green Pl HP10 3 C8
Green Rd
Reading RG6 87 A5
Virginia Water TW20 123 A5
Greenside
Bourne End SL8 3 A5
Crowthorne RG45 142 F5
Slough SL2 42 A8
Greenside View GU15 152 A5
Greensward La RG2 114 C2
Green The
Ashford TW18 97 D3
Blackwater GU17 150 C5
Bracknell RG12 118 B5
Burnham SL1 21 B1
Chieveley RG20 51 B2
Chilton OX11 10 E8
Crowthorne RG45 142 F6
Datchet SL3 68 B7
Kintbury RG17 102 B1
Slough SL1 42 D3
Theale RG7 83 C2
Theale RG7 83 D2
Upper Halliford TW17 125 E5
Wokingham RG41 115 E7
Wooburn Green HP10 3 E5
Wraysbury TW19 68 E1
Green Verges SL7 1 E3
Greenview Ct TW15 97 F4
Greenway SL1 21 B3
Greenway Dr TW18 124 D8
Greenways
Ball Hill RG20 129 E1
Egham TW20 95 E3
Lambourn RG17 25 B1
Pangbourne RG8 56 D5
Sandhurst GU47 143 B1
Greenways Dr
Maidenhead SL6 39 A8
Sunningdale SL5 120 E1
Greenways Ho RG14 104 E2
Greenway The
Fawley OX12 27 C7
Slough SL1 41 D5
Greenwich Rd RG2 113 E7
Greenwood
4 Bracknell RG12 118 F5
North Ascot SL5 119 C8
Greenwood Cotts SL5 121 C3
Greenwood Gr RG41 88 D3
Greenwood Rd
Crowthorne RG45 143 B6
Reading RG30 84 F5
Gregory Cl RG6 114 C8
Gregory Dr SL4 68 B1
Grenadier Gdns RG19 106 E2
Grenedier Cl RG2 113 E6
Grenfell Ave SL6 39 F6
Grenfell Pl SL6 39 F6
Grenfell Rd SL6 39 E6
Grenville Cl SL1 21 B3
Grenville Pl RG12 118 C7
Gresham Ct
Frimley GU15 151 F4
3 Staines TW18 97 A3
Gresham Rd
Slough SL1 42 A7
Staines TW18 97 A3
Gresham Way RG30 58 A2
Gresham Way Ind Est
RG30 58 A2
Greyberry Copse Rd
RG19 131 D8
Greycoat Ct RG4 59 B3
Greyfriars Dr SL5 120 B3
Greyfriars Rd RG1 86 A8
Greys Ct RG1 86 C7
Greys Hill RG9 15 D1
Greys Rd RG9 35 C8
Greystock Rd RG42 91 D2
Greystoke Ct RG45 143 A4
Greystoke Ho 6 RG1 85 E5
Greystoke Rd
Caversham RG4 59 C4
Slough SL2 41 F8
Griffin Cl
Maidenhead SL6 39 E5
Slough SL1 42 C4
Griffiths Cl RG19 106 F2
Grindle Cl RG18 106 C5
Gringer Hill SL6 39 E8
Groombridge Pl RG14 104 E6
Grosvenor Ct
Blackwater GU17 150 D3
Slough SL1 42 E7
Grosvenor Dr SL6 40 C8
Grosvenor Ho 2 RG1 85 F8
Grosvenor Lawn RG14 104 E2
Grosvenor Rd
Caversham RG4 59 C4
Staines TW18 97 A1
Grouse Mdws RG12 117 D6
Grovebarns TW18 97 A2
Grove Cl
Old Windsor SL4 95 B8
2 Slough SL1 43 A3
Wokingham RG40 142 E7
Grove Cotts
Caversham RG4 59 A5
Wokingham RG40 142 E7
Grove Cross Rd GU16 151 D1
Grove Ct
Egham TW20 96 A3
Maidenhead SL6 39 D7
Newbury RG14 131 A8
Grove End GU19 145 F5
Grovefields Ave GU16 151 D1
Grove Hill RG4 59 A4
Grove House SL4 95 C8
Grove La RG42 92 B4
Groveland Pl 4 RG30 85 B8
Groveland Rd RG14 104 E5
Grovelands Ave RG41 88 D2
Grovelands Avenue
Workshops RG41 88 D3
Grovelands Cl RG41 88 D3
Grovelands Pk RG41 88 D2
Grovelands Rd
Reading RG30 85 B8
Shinfield RG7 113 C2
Groveley Rd TW16 98 F3
Grove Mews RG4 59 B5
Grove Pk SL6 63 E8
Grove Prim Sch The
GU16 151 E2
Grove Rd
Burnham SL1 21 E4
Camberley GU15 151 F5
Caversham RG4 59 B6
Chertsey KT16 123 F3
Henley-on-T RG9 15 E1
Maidenhead SL6 39 F7
Newbury RG14 104 E5
Shepperton TW17 125 C3
South Stoke RG8 14 E2
Windsor SL4 67 D5
Groves Cl SL8 3 C3
Groves Lea RG7 136 F6
Groves The RG17 73 A2
Grovestile Waye TW14 98 D8
Groves Way SL6 19 E6
Grove The
Egham TW20 96 A3
Frimley GU16 151 D1
Medmenham SL7 17 E6
North Ascot SL5 119 C8
Reading RG1 86 C7
Slough SL1 43 A4
Thatcham RG18 106 D4
Twyford RG10 61 D5
Grubwood La SL6 19 A7
Guards Club Rd SL6 40 C7
Guards Ct SL5 121 B2
Guards Rd SL4 66 C5
Guards View SL4 67 D6
Guards Wlk 1 SL4 66 C5
Guerdon Pl RG12 118 D2
Guernsey Way RG41 88 A2
Guildford Ave TW13 98 F6
Guildford Rd
Bagshot GU19 145 E3
Bagshot GU19 145 F2
Bisley GU24 153 F4
Chertsey KT16 123 F1
Lightwater GU18, GU19 146 B1
West End GU24 153 F7
Guildford St
Chertsey KT16 124 A2
Staines TW18 97 A2
Guinea Wlk RG12 117 D5
Gullane Ct 20 RG1 86 D7
Gull Cl RG41 115 E4
Gulliver's SL4 67 D8
Gun St RG1 86 A7
Gunthorpe Rd SL7 2 A3
Gurney Cl RG4 58 D5
Gurney Dr RG4 58 D5
Gwendale SL6 19 C1
Gwendolen Ho TW19 97 E7
Gwendoline Ct TW15 97 E4
Gweneth Ct SL7 1 D3
Gwent Cl SL6 39 B4
Gwyn Cl RG14 130 E8
Gwynne Cl
Purley on T RG31 57 D3
Windsor SL4 66 E6
Gwyns Piece RG17 25 B3
Gypsy La
Marlow SL7 1 E4
Stoke Poges SL2 22 E8

H

Habershon Dr GU16 152 D2
Hackney Bottom RG18 53 A8
Haddenhurst Ct RG42 90 C2
Haddon Dr RG5 87 E8
Haddon Rd SL6 39 C5
Hadfield Rd TW19 70 D1
Hadleigh Rise RG4 59 E5
Hadley Ct SL3 69 E6
Hadlow Ct SL1 42 C5
Hadrian Cl TW19 97 E8
Hadrian Way TW19 97 D8
Hadrian Wlk E RG2 86 C4
Hadrian Wlk W RG2 86 C4
Hafod RG4 58 F6
Hag Hill La SL6 41 A7
Hag Hill Rise SL6 41 A7

Hagley Rd RG2 86 B4
Haig Dr SL1 42 B4
Haig Rd GU15 150 F6
Haileybury Ct SL4 67 A4
Hailey Ct SL6 39 F5
Hailey La RG20 29 F1
Hailsham Cl GU47 143 D1
HAINES HILL 62 C1
Halcyon Ct TW18 124 B7
Halcyon Terr RG30 84 E8
Haldane Rd RG4 58 F5
Hale SL4 66 F6
Hale End RG12 118 F5
Hale St TW18 96 E4
Hale Way GU16 151 D1
Halewood RG12 117 F3
Halfacre Cl RG7 113 B3
Half Mile Rd RG17 46 A1
Half Moon St GU19 145 E3
Halfpenny Ct [2] SL5 121 B2
Halfpenny La
Cholsey OX10 13 D5
Sunningdale SL5 121 A2
HALFWAY 102 F5
Halfway Farm Cotts RG20 102 E5
Halfway Hos SL6 19 E4
Halifax Cl SL6 39 A8
Halifax Pl RG18 106 C4
Halifax Rd
Bracknell RG12 118 C6
Maidenhead SL6 39 B8
Halifax Way SL6 39 A8
Halkingcroft SL3 43 C4
Hallbrooke Gdns RG42 90 E1
Hall Cl GU15 151 E6
Hall Ct SL3 68 B7
Halldore Hill SL6 19 E7
Halley Dr SL5 119 D7
Hall Farm Cres GU46 149 D5
Hallgrove Bottom GU19 145 F5
Hall Grove Farm Ind Est GU19 145 F5
Hall Grove Sch GU19 146 A5
Halliford Cl TW17 125 E6
Halliford Ct TW17 125 E5
Halliford Rd TW16, TW17 125 F5
Halliford Sch TW17 125 C2
Hall La
Harlington UB3 71 D7
Yateley GU46 149 C6
Hallmark Cl GU47 150 E8
Hallmark Ho SL1 21 C2
Hall Mdw SL1 21 C3
Hallows Gr TW16 98 F3
Hall Place La SL6 38 B7
Halls La
Earley RG2 86 E1
Waltham St L RG10 63 A7
Hallsmead Ct [2] RG1 59 A1
Halls Rd RG30 84 D6
Hall's Way RG27 149 A8
Halpin Cl RG31 84 C4
Halpin Ho RG7 139 C3
Halse Dr SL1, SL2 21 F7
Halstead Cl RG5 87 E7
Halters The RG14 131 B7
HAM 126 C2
Hamble Ave GU17 150 D5
Hambleberry Ct RG31 84 C8
Hamble Ct [4] RG1 86 B6
HAMBLEDEN 16 D8
Hambleden Ct RG12 118 E5
Hambleden Mill RG9 16 C7
Hambleden Rise RG9 16 D8
Hambleden Wlk SL6 19 E2
Hambledon Cl RG6 87 E1
Hambleton Cl GU16 152 B3
Hamblin Mdw RG17 100 E7
Hambridge Bsns Ctr RG14 105 E2
Hambridge La RG14 105 E2
Hambridge Rd RG14 105 D2
Hamfield Cotts SL6 19 E7
Hamilton Ave RG9 15 E1
Hamilton Cl
Ashford TW13 98 F3
Chertsey KT16 123 F1
Hamilton Cl GU19 145 E3
Hamilton Ct
Farnborough GU17 150 E1
Newbury RG14 131 B8
Hamilton Dr SL5 120 E2
Hamilton Gdns SL1 21 B2
Hamilton Pk SL6 39 A6
Hamilton Rd
Feltham TW13 98 F4
Reading RG1 86 E6
Slough SL1 42 A7
Wargrave RG10 36 E2
Hamilton Way SL2 22 C7
Ham Island SL4 68 C3
Ham La
Englefield Green TW20 95 B4
Old Windsor SL4 68 C3
Hamlet St RG42 118 E8
HAM MARSH 105 C3
Hammond Cl RG19 106 F2
Hammond Com Jun Sch GU18 146 A1
Hammond Ct RG42 91 A1
Hammond End SL2 22 B8
Hammonds Heath RG7 137 B6
Hammonds Ho TW19 97 F7
Hammond Way GU18 146 B1
Hampden Cl SL2 23 A2
Hampden Rd
Caversham RG4 59 B2
Hampden Rd *continued*
Maidenhead SL6 39 B8
Slough SL3 43 F3
Hampdens The RG14 130 C6
Hampshire Ave SL1 42 C8
Hampshire Lodge [8] SL6 39 F6
Hampshire Rd GU15 151 F8
Hampshire Rise RG42 91 F2
Hampshire Way RG41 115 D6
Hampshire Wlk RG31 84 A7
Hampstead Ct RG30 85 B7
Hampstead Hill RG9 60 C8
HAMPSTEAD NORREYS 52 F5
Hampstead Norreys CE Prim Sch RG18 52 F5
Hampstead Norreys Rd RG18 79 C8
Hampton Ho SL3 69 D7
Hampton Rd [1] RG14 104 F1
Hampton Twrs [4] RG30 85 D6
Ham Rd SN8 126 A3
HAMSTEAD MARSHALL 129 B7
Hamstead Mill RG20 103 C2
Hanbury Cl SL1 41 A8
Hanbury Dr RG31 84 D4
Hanbury Way GU15 151 C3
Hanbury Wlk [4] RG19 106 D2
Hancocks Mount SL5 120 D3
Hancombe Rd GU47 143 A1
Handford La GU46 149 D5
Handpost Cnr RG40 116 A1
Hangar Rd RG26 134 F1
Hangerfield Cl GU46 149 C5
Hanger Rd RG7 83 F1
Hangman's Stone La RG20 49 A5
Hanley Cl SL4 66 D6
Hannibal Rd TW19 97 E8
Hanningtons Way RG7 111 C3
Hanover Cl
Englefield Green TW20 95 B2
Frimley GU16 151 E1
Slough SL1 43 A3
Windsor SL4 66 F6
Yateley GU46 149 D7
Hanover Ct
Caversham RG4 59 C6
Reading RG30 84 F6
Hanover Gate SL1 42 A5
Hanover Gdns
Bracknell RG12 117 F2
Wargrave RG10 36 F3
Hanover Gn RG20 103 E6
Hanover Mead
Bray SL6 40 C3
Newbury RG14 130 D6
Hanover Pk SL5 119 F8
Hanover Way SL4 66 F6
Hanson Cl GU15 152 B7
Hanwood Cl RG5 87 C8
HANWORTH 118 A2
Hanworth Cl RG12 118 C3
Hanworth La KT16 123 F1
Hanworth Rd RG12 118 A2
Hanworth Trad Est KT16 123 F1
Harborough Cl SL1 41 D5
Harbury Ct RG14 105 B2
Harcourt TW19 68 E1
Harcourt Cl
Dorney SL6 40 F3
Egham TW20 96 C2
Henley-on-T RG9 15 C1
Harcourt Dr RG6 86 F3
Harcourt Rd
Bracknell RG12 118 B4
Camberley GU15 151 B5
Dorney SL6 40 F3
Windsor SL4 66 F6
Hardell Cl TW20 96 A3
Harding Pl RG40 116 C7
Harding Rd RG5 87 C8
Harding Spur SL3 68 F8
Hardwell Way RG12 118 E5
Hardwick Cl SL6 39 A8
Hardwick La KT16 123 D1
Hardwick Rd
Reading RG30 84 F7
Whitchurch-on-T RG8 56 D7
Hardy Ave GU46 149 C4
Hardy Cl
Caversham RG4 59 C2
Slough SL1 42 A5
Thatcham RG18 106 C5
Hardy Gn RG45 143 B4
Harebell Dr RG18 106 E4
Harefield Cl RG41 88 C2
Harefield Rd SL6 39 A7
HARE HATCH 62 B8
Hare Shoots SL6 39 E5
Hare Warren Ct RG4 59 B4
Harewood Dr RG18 106 C8
Harewood Pl SL1 43 A3
Hargrave Rd SL6 39 D8
Hargreaves Way RG31 84 F4
Harkness Rd SL1 41 B8
Harlech Ave RG4 59 D6
Harlech Rd GU17 150 D4
Harley Ct SL1 42 C4
Harleyford La SL7 18 B7
Harley Rd RG4 59 B2
HARLINGTON 71 C8
Harlington Cl UB7 71 C7
Harlington Cnr UB3 71 D6
Harlton Cl RG6 114 C8
Harman Ct [2] RG41 88 B2
HARMANS WATER 118 D5
Harmans Water Prim Sch RG12 118 E4
Harmans Water Rd RG12 118 D4
Harmar Cl RG40 116 E6
Harmer Mews SL6 40 B7
HARMONDSWORTH 70 E8
Harmondsworth La UB7 70 E8
Harmondsworth Moor Ctry Pk UB7 70 B7
Harmondsworth Prim Sch UB7 70 D7
Harmont Gate RG4 59 C5
Harness Cl RG2 113 B6
Harold Rd RG17 102 B2
Harpdon Par GU46 149 D7
HARPESFORD 122 C3
Harpesford Ave GU25 122 C4
HARPSDEN 35 D6
HARPSDEN BOTTOM 35 B6
Harpsden Rd RG9 35 E8
Harpsden Way RG9 35 E7
Harpton Cl GU46 149 D7
Harrier Cl RG5 88 A6
Harrier Way RG12 117 D5
Harrington Cl
Earley RG6 87 C2
Newbury RG14 105 E5
Windsor SL4 66 F3
Harris Arc RG1 86 B8
Harris Cl
Lambourn RG17 25 B3
Woodley RG5 88 B8
Harris Gdns SL1 42 C4
Harrison Cl RG10 61 F3
Harrison Way
Burnham SL1 41 D5
Shepperton TW17 125 B4
Harris Way TW16 125 E8
Harrogate Ct SL3 44 A1
Harrogate Rd RG4 58 E4
Harrow Bottom Rd GU25 122 F3
Harrow Cl SL6 19 E1
Harrow Ct RG1 85 F6
Harrow La SL6 19 E1
Harrow Mkt SL3 44 A3
Harrow Rd
Ashford TW15 98 A6
Slough SL3 43 F3
Harrow Way
Charlton TW17 125 C7
Sindlesham RG41 115 A8
Harry Tee Ct [8] RG1 86 C7
Hart Cl RG42 91 B1
Hart Dene Ct GU19 145 E3
Hart Dyke Cl RG41 116 B2
Hartford Rise GU15 151 D6
Hartigan Pl RG5 88 A8
Hartland Cl SL1 42 D5
Hartland Rd RG2 86 C1
Hartley Cl
Blackwater GU17 150 B5
Stoke Poges SL3 23 C4
Hartley Copse SL4 68 A1
Hartley Court Rd RG7 112 F6
Hartley Way RG18 106 E4
Hartmead Rd RG19 106 E3
Hart Mews GU46 149 B6
Hartsbourne Rd RG6 87 A3
Harts Cl RG2 114 E2
HART'S HILL 107 A5
Hartshill Rd RG26 134 F1
Harts Hill Rd RG18 106 F4
Hart's La RG7 110 C5
Harts Leap Cl GU47 143 B1
Harts Leap Rd GU47 150 A8
Hartslock Bridleway RG8 56 B8
Hartslock Ct RG8 56 C6
Hartslock View RG8 34 E2
Hartslock Way RG31 57 C2
Hart St
Henley-on-T RG9 15 E2
Reading RG1 85 E8
Hartvale Ct [1] GU15 152 A8
Harvard Cl RG5 88 B8
Harvard Rd GU47 143 E1
Harvaston Par RG30 84 F7
Harvest Cl
Reading RG31 84 B6
Yateley GU46 149 B4
Harvest Cotts TW17 125 A5
Harvest Ct TW17 125 A5
Harvest Dr RG41 115 B7
Harvest Gn RG14 104 E1
Harvest Hill SL8 3 D2
Harvest Hill Rd SL6 39 F3
Harvest Lea RG42 119 A8
Harvest Pl RG10 36 E1
Harvest Rd TW20 95 D2
Harvest Ride
Bracknell RG42 91 C2
Winkfield RG12, RG42, SL5 119 A8
Harvey Ho
[11] Reading RG30 85 D6
Slough SL3 43 E7
Harvey Rd
Oatlands Park KT12 125 F2
Slough SL3 44 B4
Harveys Nurseries Pk Cvn Site RG4 59 C4
Harwell Int Bsns Ctr OX11 9 F8
Harwell International Bsns Ctr OX11 10 C8
Harwich Cl [4] RG6 87 D1
Harwich Rd SL1 42 A7
Harwood Gdns SL4 95 B8
Harwood Rd SL7 1 C1
Harwood Rise RG20 129 F2
Haslemere Cl GU16 152 C3
Haslemere Rd SL4 67 A6
Haslett Rd TW17 125 E7
Hasting Cl SL6 40 C2
Hastings Cl RG30 85 A4
Hastings Mdw SL2 23 A4
Hatch Cl RG7 108 C7
Hatch End GU20 146 C4
Hatchet La SL4, SL5 93 B5
Hatchets La RG18 80 C7
Hatchett Rd TW14 98 C7
Hatchgate Cl RG18 106 C7
Hatchgate Copse RG12 117 E3
Hatch Gate Ct RG10 88 E6
Hatchgate Gdns SL1 21 D1
Hatch Gate La RG10 37 A6
Hatch La
Bucklebury RG7 108 C7
Burghfield RG30 111 D6
Harmondsworth UB7 70 D7
Windsor SL4 67 A5
Hatch Pl SL6 19 E7
Hatch Ride
Crowthorne RG45 143 B7
Wokingham RG40 142 F8
Hatch Ride Prim Sch RG45 143 B7
Hatch The SL4 66 C7
Hatchway RG2 113 C7
Hatfield Cl SL6 39 C6
Hatfield Ct
Camberley GU15 151 B5
Reading RG31 84 B4
Hatfield Rd SL1 43 A4
Hatford Rd RG30 85 B4
Hatherley Rd RG1 86 E6
Hatherwood GU46 149 F5
Hatt Cl RG20 50 D7
HATTON 71 F2
Hatton Ave SL2 22 D1
Hatton Cross Rdbt TW6 71 F4
Hatton Cross Sta TW6 71 F3
Hatton Ct SL4 67 C5
HATTON HILL 146 C5
Hatton Hill
Ashampstead RG8 54 B7
Windlesham GU20 146 C5
Hatton Rd
East Bedfont TW14 98 D8
Hatton TW14, TW6 71 E2
Hatton Rd N TW6 71 D6
Haughurst Hill RG26 134 C1
Havelock Bsns Pk SL6 39 C7
Havelock Cres SL6 39 B7
Havelock Rd
Maidenhead SL6 39 B7
Wokingham RG41 116 A6
Havelock St RG41 116 A6
Haven Ct [11] RG1 86 D7
Haven Of Rest SL6 40 B7
Haven Rd TW15 98 B5
Haven The RG17 102 A1
Havergate Way RG2 86 A2
Haversham Dr RG12 118 B3
Hawkchurch Rd RG2 113 D8
Hawkedale Inf Sch TW16 125 F6
Hawkedon Prim Sch RG6 87 E2
Hawkedon Way RG6 87 E2
Hawker Ct SL3 44 A3
Hawker Way RG5 88 A7
Hawkesbury Dr RG31 84 E3
Hawkes Cl
Slough SL3 44 B3
Wokingham RG41 116 A7
Hawkes Leap GU20 146 B6
Hawkesworth Dr GU19 145 E1
Hawkins Cl
Bracknell RG12 119 A7
Yateley GU46 149 B5
Hawkins Way RG40 116 E6
Hawk La
Bracknell, Harmans Water RG12 118 D5
Bracknell RG12 118 C5
Hawkridge Ct RG12 118 E6
Hawks Hill SL8 3 C2
Hawkshill Rd SL2 22 A2
Hawksway TW18 96 F5
Hawkswood Ave GU16 151 F2
Hawkswood Gr SL3 23 F6
Hawkswood Ho RG42 117 E8
Hawkswood La SL9 23 F8
Hawksworth Rd RG7 111 B3
Haw La RG8, RG18 53 E7
HAWLEY 150 E3
Hawley Cl RG31 84 C4
Hawley Garden Cotts The GU17 150 D4
Hawley Gn GU17 150 E3
Hawley Gr GU17 150 E2
Hawley Lodge GU17 150 F2
Hawley Mews RG30 85 D6
Hawley Place Sch GU17 150 E1
Hawley Prim Sch GU17 150 E3
Hawley Rd GU14, GU17 150 E3
Hawley Way TW15 98 B3
Haws Hill Farm SL4 65 B3
Hawthorn Cl RG42 118 A8
Hawthorn Cotts RG7 112 C3
Hawthorn Ct [1] TW15 98 C1
Hawthorne Ave SL4 93 B6
Hawthorne Cl
Marlow SL7 1 E4
Thatcham RG18 106 D4
Hawthorne Cres
Blackwater GU17 150 E4
Slough SL1 42 F7
Hawthorne Ct TW19 97 D8
Hawthorne Dr SL4 93 B6
Hawthorne Rd
Caversham RG4 59 E4
Egham TW18 96 C4
Hawthornes RG31 57 B3
Hawthorne Way
Great Shefford RG17 48 B4
Stanwell TW19 97 D8
Winkfield SL4 93 B7
Hawthorn Gdns
Maidenhead SL6 39 E5
Reading RG2 86 E2
HAWTHORN HILL 64 C1
Hawthorn La
Farnham Royal SL2 22 A5
Newell Green, Hawthorn Hill RG42 91 E8
Newell Green SL4 92 A7
Hawthorn Rd
Frimley GU16 151 F2
Newbury RG14 105 A4
Hawthorns Prim Sch The RG41 115 E7
Hawthorns The
Charvil RG10 61 A3
Flackwell Heath HP10 3 B8
Poyle SL3 69 F6
Wooburn Green HP10 3 E6
Hawthorn Way
Sonning RG4 60 E3
Upper Halliford TW17 125 D5
Hawtrey Cl SL1 43 B4
Hawtrey Rd SL4 67 C5
Haydon Ct
Maidenhead SL6 39 E6
Twyford RG10 61 E4
Haydon La RG20 30 E7
Haydon Pl GU46 149 E6
Hayes La RG41 115 C4
Hayes Pl SL7 1 D1
Hayfield Cl RG31 84 C8
Hayfield Ct RG17 46 F6
Hay La SL3 23 D8
Hayley Gn RG42 91 F3
Haymill Rd SL1, SL2 21 D1
Haynes Cl SL3 43 F1
Hay Rd RG1 85 F5
Hayse Hill SL4 66 D6
Haysoms Dr RG19 131 B7
Hayward Pl SL8 3 C2
Haywards Cl RG9 15 C1
Haywards Mead SL4 41 F1
Haywards The RG18 106 D4
Haywood RG12 118 C2
Haywood Ct RG1 86 F7
Haywood Way RG30 84 F5
Hazelbank RG40 141 E6
Hazelbank Ct KT16 124 C1
Hazelbank Rd KT16 124 C2
Hazel Cl
Burghfield RG30 111 B5
Englefield Green TW20 95 B2
Marlow Bottom SL7 1 C6
Wokingham RG41 115 F5
Hazel Cres RG2 86 E2
Hazeldene RG20 51 B1
Hazel Dr RG5 87 C5
Hazel Gn RG26 134 D1
Hazel Gr
Staines TW18 97 C2
Thatcham RG18 106 D5
Hazelhurst Rd SL1 21 D3
Hazell Cl SL6 39 F8
Hazell Hill RG12 118 C6
Hazel Lodge TW20 96 A4
Hazell Way SL2 22 F6
Hazelmere Cl TW14 71 E1
Hazel Rd RG8 57 C4
Hazels Paddock RG18 106 C8
Hazelwood Cl RG31 57 C1
Hazelwood Ct SL6 20 C2
Hazelwood La RG42 90 F4
Hazlemere Rd SL2 43 B5
Heacham Cl RG6 114 A8
Headington Cl
Maidenhead SL6 39 A7
Wokingham RG40 116 D8
Headington Dr RG40 116 D8
Headington Rd SL6 39 A7
Headlands Ct RG7 110 F1
HEADLEY 132 D2
Headley Cl RG5 88 A8
Headley Park Ind Est RG5 87 F7
Headley Rd RG5 87 E7
Headley Rd E RG5 88 A7
HEAD'S HILL 132 B4
Heads La RG17 128 A5
Heardman Cl RG19 106 F2
Hearmon Cl GU46 149 E6
Hearne Dr SL6 40 A1
Hearn Rd RG5 87 E5
Hearn Wlk RG12 118 E8
Hearsey Gdns GU17 150 C6
Heathacre SL3 69 E6
Heath Cl
Harlington UB3 71 D7
Stanwell TW19 70 C1
Virginia Water GU25 122 D5
Wokingham RG41 116 B4
Heath Cnr GU15 152 A3
Heathcote SL6 40 B2
Heathcote Ct [2] SL4 67 D4
Heathcote Rd GU15 151 D5
Heathcroft Ave TW16 98 F1
Heath Ct RG26 134 E2
Heath Dr RG9 35 A1

HEATH END
Ball Hill 129 A1
Tadley 134 F1
Heath End Farm RG26 134 E1
Heath End Rd RG26 134 E1
Heather Cl RG40 141 E7
Heatherdale Rd GU15 151 D4
Heatherdene Ave RG45 142 E4
Heatherdene Cl RG2 113 C7
Heather Dr
Sunningdale SL5 121 B2
Tadley RG26 134 F2
Thatcham RG18 106 D5
Heather Gdns RG14 130 F7
Heather Hill Cl RG6 87 D4
Heatherlands SL5 120 E4
Heatherley Cl GU15 151 B5
Heatherley Rd GU15 151 B5
Heather Mead GU16 151 F2
Heather Mead Ct GU16 151 F2
Heathermount RG12 118 E5
Heathermount Dr RG45 143 A6
Heathermount Gdns RG45 142 F6
Heathermount Learning Ctr The SL5 120 D3
Heather Ridge Arc GU15 152 C4
Heather Ridge Inf Sch GU15 152 D4
HEATHERSIDE 152 B4
Heatherside Cnr GU15 152 D6
Heatherside Dr GU25 122 A3
Heathers The TW19 97 F8
Heatherway RG45 143 A5
Heatherwood Hospl SL5 119 E6
Heathfield RG7 137 A6
Heathfield Ave
Reading RG30 84 D6
Shiplake RG9 35 B2
Sunningdale SL5 120 E4
Heathfield Cl RG9 35 B2
Heathfield Ct TW15 97 E5
Heathfield Rd SL1 3 F1
Heathfields RG20 78 A8
Heathfield St Mary's Sch SL5 119 B7
Heath Flats GU19 145 E3
Heath Gr TW16 98 F1
Heath Hill Rd N RG45 143 B5
Heath Hill Rd S RG45 143 B4
Heath Ho 5 RG26 134 E1
Heath La RG18 106 C5
Heathland 1 RG26 134 E1
HEATHLANDS 142 E8
Heathlands Ct
Wokingham RG40 142 F8
Yateley GU46 149 E4
Heathlands Dr SL6 39 A6
Heathlands Rd RG40 116 E2
Heathlea Ho RG31 84 B7
Heathmoors RG12 118 C4
Heathpark Dr GU20 146 E4
Heath Rd
Bagshot GU19 145 E3
Pamber Heath RG26 135 E1
Reading RG6 87 A5
Southend RG7 82 A2
Wooburn Moor HP9 3 F8
Heath Ride RG40, RG45 142 C5
Heath Rise
Camberley GU15 151 D5
Virginia Water GU25 122 D5
Heathrow Airport London TW6 71 A5
Heathrow Airport Visitor Ctr* TW6 71 C6
Heathrow Bvd UB7 70 F7
Heathrow Cl TW6 70 B6
Heathrow Copse RG26 134 D1
Heathrow Prim Sch UB7 70 F8
Heathrow Terminal 4 Sta TW6 71 C1
Heathrow Terminal 5 Sta TW6 70 C4
Heathrow Terminals 1, 2, 3 TW6 71 B4
Heathside Pk GU15 152 C7
Heath Villa SL5 120 A6
Heathway
Camberley GU15 151 D5
North Ascot SL5 119 E8
Reading RG31 84 C8
Heathway Cl GU15 151 D5
Heathwood Cl GU46 149 D7
Heavens Lea SL8 3 C2
Hebbecastle Down RG42 91 C2
Hebden Cl RG19 106 C2
Hectors Way 1 RG14 105 B2
Hedge Croft GU46 149 B6
Hedge Lea HP10 3 D8
Hedgerows The RG5 87 D8
Hedgeway RG14 105 C4
Hedingham Mews SL6 39 D7
Hedley Rd HP10 3 B8
HEDSOR 3 F3
Hedsor Hill SL8 3 C1
Hedsor La HP10, SL1 3 F2
Hedsor Rd SL8 3 B2
Hedsor View Cotts SL6 19 F7
Heelas Rd RG41 116 A5
Heights The
Camberley GU15 151 E5
Marlow SL7 18 B8
Helena Rd SL4 67 D5
Helen Cotts SL4 66 D5
Helen Ct
20 Newbury RG14 104 F2
Reading RG30 85 A5
Helgiford Gdns TW16 98 E1
Helix Bsns Pk GU15 151 B3
Helksham Cl GU47 143 D1
Hellyer Way SL8 3 C3
Helmsdale RG12 118 E4
Helmsdale Cl RG30 85 B8
Helston Gdns RG2 86 B1
Helston La SL4 67 B6
Helvellyn Cl TW20 96 C1
Hemdean Hill RG4 59 A3
Hemdean House Sch RG4 59 A3
Hemdean Rd RG4 59 A3
Hemdean Rise RG4 59 A3
Hemming Way SL2 22 B2
Hemmyng Cnr RG42 91 C2
Hempson Ave SL3 43 C3
Hemsdale SL6 19 B1
Hemwood Rd SL4 66 D4
Hencroft Mews 14 SL1 42 F4
Hencroft St N SL1 42 F4
Hencroft St S SL1 42 F3
Hendons Way SL6 40 B1
Hendon Terr TW15 98 D2
Hendon Way TW19 70 D1
Hengrave Cl RG6 87 E2
Hengrove Cres TW15 97 D5
Henley Bsns Ctr RG9 35 F8
Henley Coll The (Deanfield Bldgs) RG9 15 D1
Henley Coll The (Rotherfield Bldgs) RG9 15 C1
Henley Ct
12 Egham TW20 96 A3
25 Reading RG1 86 D7
Henley Gdns GU46 149 D5
Henley Ho SL5 120 E4
Henley Lodge 12 SL6 39 F6
HENLEY-ON-THAMES 15 C1
Henley-on-Thames Sta RG9 15 E1
Henley Rd
Caversham RG9 59 D3
Hurley SL6 17 D3
Maidenhead SL6 38 E7
Marlow SL7 18 B8
Shiplake RG9 60 B6
Slough SL1 41 F7
Henley Wood Rd RG6 87 D4
Henry Ct 17 RG1 86 C7
Henry III Twr 4 SL4 67 D6
Henry Randell's Almshouses GU17 150 E3
Henry Rd SL1 42 D4
Henry St RG1 86 B6
Henrys The RG18 106 D4
Henshaw Cres RG14 130 D8
Hensworth Rd TW15 97 D3
Henwick Cl RG18 106 B6
Henwick La RG18 106 A4
Henwood Copse RG8 55 A6
Hepplewhite Cl 7 RG26 134 E1
Hepworth Croft GU47 150 E6
Hepworth Way KT12 125 F1
Herald Way RG5 88 A6
Herbert Cl RG12 118 B4
Hereford Cl TW18 124 B8
Herewood Cl RG14 104 F4
Heriot Ct
Camberley GU15 151 D3
Chertsey KT16 123 F2
Heriot Rd KT16 124 A2
Heritage Ct
8 Egham TW20 96 A3
15 Reading RG1 85 F7
Hermes Cl RG41 115 B7
HERMITAGE 79 B7
Hermitage Cl
Frimley GU16 151 F1
Littleton TW17 125 A5
Slough SL3 43 C3
Hermitage Ct TW18 96 F3
Hermitage Cvn Pk The RG42 91 D3
Hermitage Dr
North Ascot SL5 119 E7
Twyford RG10 61 D5
Hermitage Gn RG18 79 A6
Hermitage La SL4 67 A4
Hermitage Par SL5 120 A6
Hermitage Prim Sch RG18 79 B8
Hermitage Rd RG18 79 B2
Hermitage The
Eastbury RG17 46 E7
1 Feltham TW13 98 F5
Hermits Cl RG7 111 B3
Hermit's Hill RG7, RG30 111 D4
Herndon Cl TW20 96 A4
Herne Pl SL5 121 C4
Hernes Cl TW18 124 B8
Heroes Wlk RG2 113 B7
Heron Cl SL5 119 D8
Heron Ct
Sandhurst GU47 150 C7
Staines TW18 97 B4
Stanwell TW19 97 E7
Herondale RG12 118 C2
Heron Dr
Slough SL3 44 B2
Twyford RG10 61 E6
Heronfield TW20 95 C2
Herongate RG17 100 D7
Heron Ho RG14 105 D3
Heron Ind Est RG7 139 A8
Heron Island RG4 59 C1
Heron Rd RG41 115 E6
Heronsbrook SL5 120 F7
Heronscourt GU18 153 C8
Heron Shaw RG8 34 C7
Herons Pl
Maidenhead SL6 20 C3
Marlow SL7 1 E3
Herons Way RG19 106 B3
Heron's Way RG40 116 E7
Heron Way
Aldermaston Wharf RG7 109 B3
Reading RG1 85 E4
Herrick Cl GU16 152 C3
Herries Sch SL6 19 B8
Herrings La
Chertsey KT16 124 A3
Windlesham GU20 146 D4
Herriot Ct GU46 149 C4
Herschel Gram Sch SL1 42 C7
Herschel Grange RG42 91 D3
Herschel St SL1 42 F4
Hertford Cl
Caversham RG4 59 D6
Wokingham RG41 115 E5
Hetherington Cl SL2 21 F2
Hetherington Rd TW17 125 C7
Hever Cl SL6 39 C6
Hewett Ave RG4 58 D4
Hewett Cl RG4 58 D4
Hewgate Ct RG9 15 E1
Hewlett Pl GU19 145 F3
Hexham Cl GU47 143 D2
Hexham Rd RG2 86 C3
Heynes Gn SL6 39 B3
Heywod Dr GU19 145 D3
Heywood Ave SL6 39 A1
Heywood Court Cl SL6 39 A2
Heywood Farm Barns SL6 39 B1
Heywood Gdns SL6 39 A1
Hibbert Rd SL6 40 B4
Hibbert's Alley 20 SL4 67 D6
Hickox Ct HP10 3 F7
Hicks La GU17 150 B5
Hieatt Cl 21 RG1 86 B6
Higgs La GU19 145 D3
High Beech RG12 118 F5
High Beeches GU16 151 D2
High Beeches Cl SL7 1 C6
Highbridge Cl RG4 59 E5
Highbridge Wharf 9 RG1 86 B7
Highbury Cres GU15 152 A8
Highbury Rd RG31 84 B7
High Chimneys GU20 146 E7
Highclere SL5 120 D4
Highclere Cl RG12 118 E7
Highclere Ct RG2 86 E1
Highclere Dr GU15 152 A7
Highcliffe Cl RG5 60 F1
High Close Sch RG40 116 C7
Highdown Ave RG4 59 A6
Highdown Hill Rd RG4 59 A6
Highdown Sch & Sixth Form Ctr RG4 59 A5
Higher Alham RG12 118 E2
Highfield
Bracknell RG12 117 F3
Earley RG6 87 B2
Highfield Ave RG14 105 A2
Highfield Cl
Englefield Green TW20 95 C2
Wokingham RG40 116 B6
Highfield Ct
Burghfield Common RG7 111 B3
Burnham SL2 22 B4
Englefield Green TW20 95 D2
Twyford RG10 61 E4
Highfield La SL6 39 A4
Highfield Pk
Marlow SL7 1 B1
Wargrave RG10 36 F3
Highfield Pk (Cvn Pk) RG2 140 D8
Highfield Rd
Bourne End SL8 3 B4
Chertsey KT16 124 A1
Flackwell Heath HP10 3 A8
Maidenhead SL6 39 B8
Newbury RG14 104 F1
Purley on T RG31 57 B4
Upper Halliford TW16 125 F4
Windsor SL4 66 F4
High Fields SL5 120 F4
Highfields Sch SL6 39 E7
Highgate Rd RG5 87 D5
Highgrove RG41 88 C1
Highgrove Ave SL5 119 F8
Highgrove Pk SL6 39 E8
Highgrove Pl RG10 61 E5
Highgrove St RG1 86 C5
Highgrove Terr RG1 86 B6
High Heavens Wood SL7 1 C8
Highland Pk TW13 98 F4
Highland Rd GU15 151 E8
Highlands
Flackwell Heath HP10 3 B7
Newbury RG14 130 E7
Highlands Ave RG41 115 C5
Highlands La RG9 35 A8
Highlands Sch The RG31 57 D1
Highlands The SL2 22 C7
Highlea Ave HP10 3 A8
High Mdw RG4 58 D3
High Mdws SL6 20 C3
Highmead Cl RG2 86 E2
High Meadow Pl KT16 123 F3
Highmoor Rd RG4 58 F3
High Pines The RG42 92 B5
High Rd SL6 19 E6
High St Mall 1 SL6 39 F7
High St
Ascot SL5 120 A6
Ascot, Sunninghill SL5 120 D4
Bagshot GU19 145 E3
Boxford RG20 76 B2
Bracknell RG12 118 B7
Bray SL6 40 C4
Burnham SL1 21 C2
Camberley GU15 151 D6
Chalvey SL1 42 D3
Chieveley RG20 51 B1
Colnbrook SL3 69 C7
Compton RG20 31 D4
Cookham SL6 20 B7
Crowthorne RG45 143 C4
Datchet SL3 68 B6
East Ilsley RG20 30 E7
Egham TW20 96 A3
Eton SL4 67 D8
Feltham, Lower Feltham TW13 98 F5
Goring RG8 34 C6
Harlington UB3 71 D8
Harmondsworth UB7 70 D8
Hungerford RG17 100 D5
Iver SL0 44 F7
Kintbury RG17 102 A2
Lambourn RG17 25 B2
Lambourn, Upper Lambourn RG17 24 E6
Maidenhead SL6 39 F7
Marlow SL7 1 E1
4 Pangbourne RG8 56 C6
Reading RG1 86 B7
Sandhurst GU47 149 F8
Sandhurst, Little Sandhurst GU47 143 A1
Shepperton TW17 125 C3
Slough, Langley SL3 44 A2
Slough, Upton SL1 42 F4
Sonning RG4 60 D4
Staines TW18 96 F4
Stanwell TW19 70 D1
Streatley RG8 34 A6
Sunningdale SL5 121 A4
Taplow SL6 20 E1
Thatcham RG19 106 D3
Theale RG7 83 E3
Twyford RG10 61 D5
Wargrave RG10 36 D2
West End GU24 153 F7
Whitchurch-on-T RG8 56 C7
Windsor SL4 67 D6
Wraysbury TW19 68 F1
High Street Harlington TW6 71 D7
High Town Rd SL6 39 F7
High Tree Dr RG6 87 B6
Highview RG31 84 B5
High View Cl SL7 1 D8
Highview Cres GU15 144 F1
High View Rd GU18 152 F8
HIGHWAY 39 B7
Highway RG45 143 A5
Highway Ave SL6 39 A6
Highwayman's Ridge GU20 146 B6
Highway Rd SL6 39 B6
Highwood Cl
Newbury RG14 105 B6
Yateley GU46 149 D4
Highwood Prim Sch RG5 87 C6
Highwoods Cl SL7 1 C7
Highwoods Dr SL7 1 C7
Highworth Cotts RG26 134 C1
Highworth Way RG31 57 B2
Hilary Cl RG2 113 D7
Hilary Ho 2 RG14 105 A1
Hilborn Way RG2 115 A1
Hilbury Rd RG6 87 A3
Hilcot Rd RG30 85 D8
Hildens Dr RG31 84 C7
Hildesley Ct RG20 30 E7
Hilfield GU46 149 F5
Hilgrove Ho SL6 19 D1
Hillary Ct TW19 97 E7
Hillary Dr RG45 143 B6
Hillary Rd SL3 43 E4
Hillberry RG12 118 C2
Hillbrow RG2 86 E1
Hillbrow Ct SL5 121 A4
Hill Cl
Newbury RG14 130 D7
Wooburn Green HP10 3 F7
Hillcopse View RG12 118 E8
Hill Cres RG7 108 C3
Hillcrest
Binfield RG42 90 D3
Hampstead Norreys RG18 52 F6
Tadley RG26 135 B1
Hillcrest Ave SL6 19 E6
Hillcrest Cotts RG14 104 F7
Hillcrest Rd GU15 152 B7
Hilldrop La RG17 46 A3
Hillersdon SL2 43 B8
Hill Farm App HP10 3 F7
Hill Farm Rd
Marlow Bottom SL7 1 E6
Taplow SL6 20 E2
Hillfoot RG7 81 A1
Hill Gdns RG8 34 A6
HILLGREEN 50 C5
Hillgreen La RG20 50 C7
Hillhampton SL5 120 F2
Hill Ho SL6 20 D1
Hillhouse La RG19 133 A1
Hillingdon Ave TW19 97 E7
Hill Lands RG10 36 D2
Hillmead Ct SL6 40 F8
Hill Piece OX11 10 E7
Hill Pl SL2 22 B5
Hill Prim Sch The RG4 59 C5
Hill Rd
Arborfield Garrison RG2 114 F1
Newbury RG14 104 E4
Hillrise KT12 125 F2
Hill Rise SL3 69 A8
Hillsborough Pk GU15 152 C5
Hillside
Ascot SL5 120 C4
Burghfield Common RG7 111 C3
East Garston RG17 47 C6
Maidenhead SL6 39 D5
Sandhurst GU15 150 F7
Slough SL1 42 E4
Wentworth GU25 122 C3
Whitchurch-on-T RG8 56 D8
Hill Side RG1 86 C5
Hillside Dr RG42 90 C2
Hillside Pk
Earley RG2 86 F1
Sunningdale SL5 120 F1
Hillside Prim Sch RG6 113 F8
Hillside Rd
Earley RG6 87 D3
Hungerford RG17 100 D4
Marlow SL7 1 E4
Hills La SL6 19 D7
Hill St RG1 86 B6
Hilltop Cl SL5 120 E7
Hill Top Dr SL7 1 B2
Hilltop Fst Sch SL4 66 E4
Hilltop Rd
Caversham RG4 58 D5
Earley RG6 87 B8
Twyford RG10 61 E7
Hilltop View GU46 149 B5
Hill View RG7 113 A1
Hillview Cl RG31 57 B2
Hill View Mews RG30 84 E8
Hill View Rd TW19 68 D1
Hilmanton RG6 113 F8
Hilperton Rd 3 SL1 42 E4
Hindhay La SL6 19 C3
Hindhead Rd RG6 87 A3
Hind's Head 7 RG17 25 B2
Hinksey Cl SL3 44 B3
Hinton Cl RG45 143 B7
Hinton Dr RG45 143 B7
Hintonhatch Cnr RG10 62 A2
Hinton Rd
Hurst RG10 62 A1
Slough SL1 41 E6
Hirstwood RG30 57 E1
Hirtes Ave RG2 113 E5
Hitcham Grange SL6 20 E1
Hitcham Ho SL1 21 A1
Hitcham La SL1, SL6 20 F2
Hitcham Rd SL1, SL6 41 A8
Hitchcock Cl TW17 124 F6
Hitherhooks Hill RG42 90 E1
Hithermoor Rd TW19 70 A2
Hobart Ct SL7 2 A3
Hobbis Dr SL6 39 A6
Hobbs End RG9 35 B8
Hockett La SL6 19 A6
Hockford La RG7 134 A3
Hockham Rd RG20 31 E5
Hockley La SL2 23 B5
Hodcott Bglws RG20 30 B8
Hodgedale La RG10 37 D6
Hodge La SL5 93 A3
Hodges Cl GU19 145 E1
Hodsoll Rd RG1 85 F8
HOE BENHAM 102 F8
Hoe Benham La RG20 102 F7
Hoffman Cl RG42 91 D2
Hogarth Ave
Ashford TW15 98 C2
Reading RG30 84 F5
Hogarth Cl
Sandhurst GU47 150 E6
Slough SL1 41 E6
Hogfair La SL1 21 C1
Hogmoor La RG10 61 F1
Hogoak La SL4 92 A8
Hogwood Farm Ind Est RG40 141 A5
Hogwood Ind Est RG40 141 A6
Hogwood La RG40 141 A6
Holbeche Cl GU46 149 A6
Holbeck RG12 117 F3
Holberton Rd RG2 113 D8
Holborne Cl RG14 130 D5
Holborn Hill OX12 6 D7
Holbrook Ct TW20 96 C3
Holbrook Mdw TW20 96 C2
Holder Cl RG2 113 D5
Holford Cl RG31 84 C8
Holland Ct TW15 97 F2
Holland Gdns TW20 123 F7
Holland Pines RG12 117 F2
Holland Rd
Marlow SL7 1 F3
Reading RG30 84 D7
Hollands The RG19 106 E3
Hollerith Rise RG12 118 B3
Hollicombe Cl RG30 84 E7
Hollies The RG14 130 D5
HOLLINGSWORTH 52 E5
Hollington Pl RG19 106 C3
Hollins Wlk RG30 85 D6
HOLLOWAY 38 C5
Holloway Dr GU25 122 E5
Holloway Ho TW20 95 F2

Holloway La UB7 70 E8
Hollow Hill La SL0 44 C5
Hollow La
Shinfield RG2 113 E5
Virginia Water GU25 122 C6
Holly Acre 4 GU46 149 D5
Holly Ave GU16 152 B3
Hollybank GU24 153 F6
Holly Bush RG19 132 D2
Hollybush Hill SL2 23 B5
Hollybush La
Burghfield Common RG7 110 E3
Cookham Dean SL6 19 B6
Iver SL0 44 B7
Hollybush Ride RG40, RG45 142 C6
Hollybush Tk GU19, GU20 145 F6
Holly Cl
Brimpton RG19 133 B6
Englefield Green TW20 95 B2
Farnham Common SL2 22 C8
Holly Cnr RG7 140 B7
Hollycombe TW20 95 D4
Holly Cotts GU47 143 A1
Holly Cres SL4 66 D5
Hollycroft RG19 133 F1
Hollycroft Cl UB7 71 A8
Hollycroft Gdns UB7 71 A8
HOLLY CROSS 37 A6
Holly Ct
1 Chertsey KT16 124 A1
Crowthorne RG45 142 E4
Slough SL1 41 E6
Hollydale Cl RG2 86 E1
Holly Dr
Maidenhead SL6 39 F8
Windsor SL4 67 E2
Hollyfields Cl GU15 151 B5
Holly Hedge Cl GU16 151 E2
Holly Hedge Rd GU16 151 E2
Holly Ho
Bracknell RG12 118 B3
Caversham RG4 58 E3
Hollyhook Cl RG45 143 A6
Holly La
Ashampstead RG8 54 B6
Frilsham RG18 80 B3
Hollym Cl RG6 87 E2
Holly Rd RG5 88 A6
Holly Ridge GU24 153 E6
Holly Spring Inf Sch RG12 118 E7
Holly Spring Jun Sch RG12 118 E7
Holly Spring La RG12 118 D8
Holly Way GU17 150 D4
Holly Wlk SL4 93 E4
Holmanleaze SL6 40 A8
Holmbank Dr TW17 125 E5
Holmbury Ave RG45 143 A7
Holmdene RG7 111 B3
Holme Cl RG45 143 A7
Holmedale SL2 43 C6
Holme Grange Craft Village RG40 116 E2
Holme Grange Sch RG40 116 F3
HOLME GREEN 116 F3
Holmemoor Dr RG4 60 E2
Holme Park Farm La RG4 60 C2
Holmes Cl
Ascot SL5 120 C3
Wokingham RG41 116 A4
Holmes Cres RG41 116 A4
Holmes Rd RG6 87 A5
Holmewood Cl RG41 116 A2
Holmlea Rd
Datchet SL3 68 D6
Goring RG8 34 C5
Holmlea Wlk SL3 68 C6
Holmsdale Cl SL0 44 F7
Holmwood Ave RG30 84 F4
Holmwood Cl SL6 39 B5
Holsworthy Cl RG6 87 E3
Holt La
Brightwalton RG20 49 F8
Wokingham RG41 116 B7
Holton Heath 9 RG12 118 F5
Holt Rd RG17 102 B2
Holt Sch The RG41 116 B7
Holtspur Ave HP10 3 F7
Holtspur La HP10 3 F6
HOLT THE 73 E8
Holt The RG8 57 D4
HOLTWOOD 129 B5
Holtwood Rd RG20 129 B6
Holybrook Cres RG30 85 A4
Holybrook Rd RG1 85 F5
Holy Brook Sch The RG30 85 A4
Holy Family RC Prim Sch SL3 43 F1
Holyhead Mews SL1 41 D7
HOLYPORT 65 A7
Holyport CE Prim Sch SL6 65 B8
Holyport Manor Sch SL6 64 E6
Holyport Rd SL6 40 B1
Holyport St SL6 65 A8
Holyrood Cl RG4 59 D6
Holy Trinity CE Prim Sch
Cookham SL6 20 B7
Sunningdale SL5 121 A3
Holy Trinity CE Sch SL7 1 D3
Holywell Cl TW19 97 E7
Holywell Ct RG19 106 D3
Holywell Way TW19 97 E7
Hombrook Dr RG42 117 E8
Hombrook Ho RG42 117 E8
Home Cl GU25 122 D3
Home Croft RG31 57 B1
Home Ct 7 RG1 86 B6
Home Farm
Bagshot GU19 145 D4
Welford RG20 75 F6
Home Farm Barns RG14 77 F4
Home Farm Cl
Reading RG2 86 C4
Upper Halliford TW17 125 E5
Home Farm Cotts
Sindlesham RG41 115 B7
Yattendon RG18 53 E1
Home Farm Way SL3 23 C4
Homefield Way RG17 100 C5
Homelands Way RG9 15 D1
Home Mdw SL2 22 C3
Home Mead Cl RG14 130 E8
Home Meadow Dr HP10 3 B7
Home Park Rd GU46 149 D6
Homer Fst Sch SL4 66 D6
Homers Rd SL4 66 D6
Homeside Cl SL6 19 E2
Homestead Rd
Maidenhead SL6 39 D4
Staines TW18 97 B2
Homestead The RG9 35 B1
Homewaters Ave TW16 125 F8
Homewood SL3 43 D7
Home Wood SL7 17 F6
Hone Hill GU47 150 B8
Honesty Bottom RG20 28 D2
Honeybottom Rd RG26 135 B1
Honey End La RG30 85 A6
Honeyfields RG17 100 D5
Honey Hill
Lambourn RG17 25 B3
Wokingham RG40 117 A1
Honeyhill Rd RG42 118 A8
Honey La SL6 17 E2
Honey Meadow Cl RG4 59 E2
Honeysuckle Cl
Crowthorne RG45 143 A7
Iver SL0 44 C7
Yateley GU46 149 A6
Honeysuckle Ct SL3 69 C7
Honister Wlk GU15 152 D4
Honiton Rd RG2 86 C2
Honnor Rd TW18 97 D1
Hook Cl RG19 131 B7
Hook End La RG8 34 B2
Hook La GU24 153 C6
Hook Mill La GU18 146 D2
Hookstone La GU24 153 F8
Hooper Ho TW15 97 E5
Hoops Way RG2 112 F8
Hope Ave RG12 118 E2
Hope Cotts RG42 92 A5
Hope Fountain GU15 151 F4
Hopeman Cl GU47 150 D7
Hop Gdns
Henley-on-T RG9 15 D2
Kintbury RG17 102 B2
Hopper Vale RG12 118 A3
Hopwood Cl RG14 105 D4
Horatio Ave RG42 118 E8
Horewood Rd RG12 118 B3
Horizon West Ind Est RG14 105 D3
Hormer Cl GU47 143 D1
Hornbeam Cl
Purley on T RG8 57 C5
Sandhurst GU47 143 D1
Wokingham RG41 115 D3
Hornbeam Copse RG42 119 A8
Hornbeam Dr RG6 87 D1
Hornbeam Gdns 7 SL1 43 A3
Hornbeam Pightle RG7 111 B3
Hornbeams RG7 139 C6
Hornby Ave RG12 118 D2
HORNCASTLE 84 E5
Horndean Rd RG12 118 F3
Horne Rd
Littleton TW17 125 A5
Thatcham RG19 106 E2
Hornsea Cl RG30 57 E1
Horn St RG20 31 E5
Horris Hill Sch RG20 130 E3
Horrocks Ho RG30 84 F5
Horsebrass Dr GU19 145 E2
Horse Cl The RG4 59 C4
Horsecroft Way RG31 57 B4
Horse Gate Ride SL5 120 A3
Horseguards Dr SL6 40 B7
Horse Guards Way RG19 106 D1
Horsell Ct KT16 124 B2
HORSEMOOR 78 B8
Horsemoor Cl SL3 44 A2
Horseshoe Cl GU15 151 F8
Horseshoe Cloisters 2 SL4 67 D6
Horseshoe Cres
Burghfield Common RG7 111 B3
Camberley GU15 151 F8
Horseshoe End RG14 131 B7
Horseshoe Hill SL1 21 C8
Horseshoe Pk RG8 56 D5
Horseshoe Rd RG8 56 D5
Horsham Rd
East Bedfont TW14 71 C1
Sandhurst GU47 143 D1
Horsham Reach SL6 20 C2
Horsnape Gdns RG42 90 B2
Horsneile La RG42 118 B8
HORTON 69 A4
Horton Cl SL6 20 C1
Horton Depot SL3 69 C4
Horton Gdns SL3 68 F4
Horton Grange SL6 20 C1
Horton Rd
Datchet SL3 68 D6
Horton SL3 69 A6
Poyle SL3, TW19 69 E4
Stanwell TW19 70 A2
Horton Trad Est SL3 69 C4
Hose Hill RG7, RG30 111 A7
Hosier St RG1 86 A7
Hoskins Place Ind Est GU15 151 B3
Houlton Ct GU19 145 F2
Houston Ct 4 SL4 67 C5
Houston Way RG45 142 D5
Howard Ave SL2 42 E8
Howard Cl
Ashford TW16 98 F2
Bracknell RG12 118 A4
Howard Ct SL8 3 A3
Howard Mews SL3 69 B8
Howard Rd
Newbury RG14 105 A1
Wokingham RG40 116 C5
Howards Gate SL2 22 C2
Howard St 17 RG1 85 F7
Howard Villas RG2 113 C7
Howarth Ct RG14 131 B8
Howarth Rd SL6 40 A6
Howe La RG42 63 F2
Howell Cl
Arborfield Garrison RG2 140 E8
Bracknell RG42 91 C2
Howgate Dr RG8 34 C7
How Lane Farm SL6 64 A5
Howorth Ct RG12 118 E5
Howth Dr RG5 87 D7
Hoylake Cl SL1 41 E4
Hubbard Cl RG10 61 F2
Hubberholme RG12 118 A6
Hubert Rd SL3 43 D3
Hub The 7 SL6 40 A7
Huckleberry Cl RG8 57 C4
Huddington Glade GU46 149 A5
Huddlestone Ho SL5 120 D4
Hudson Pl 9 SL3 43 F1
Hudson Rd
Harlington UB7 71 D8
Woodley RG5 87 F6
Hughenden Cl SL6 39 C6
Hughenden Rd SL1 42 D7
Hughes Rd
Ashford TW15 98 C2
Wokingham RG40 116 E7
Hugh Fraser Dr RG31 84 C6
Hulbert Gate RG40 116 B6
Hull Cl SL1 42 C4
Humber Cl
Thatcham RG18 106 B5
Wokingham RG41 115 E7
Humber Way
Sandhurst GU47 150 D8
Slough SL3 44 A2
Hummer Rd TW20 96 A4
Humphrey's La RG17 47 C6
Humphries Yd RG12 118 C5
HUNGERFORD
100 E4
Waltham St Lawrence 62 E2
Hungerford Ave SL2 42 E8
Hungerford Cl GU47 150 C8
Hungerford Dr
Maidenhead SL6 19 E3
Reading RG1 85 E5
HUNGERFORD GREEN 32 F4
Hungerford Hill
East Garston RG17 47 F1
Lambourn RG17 25 A2
Hungerford La
Kintbury RG17 101 E3
Stanford Dingley RG7 81 F1
Waltham St L RG10 62 E2
HUNGERFORD NEWTOWN 74 A3
Hungerford Prim Sch RG17 100 D5
Hungerford Sta RG17 100 E6
Hungerford Trad Est RG17 100 C5
Hunsford Lodge SL4 67 A4
Hunstanton Cl SL3 69 C7
Huntercombe Cl SL6 41 C7
Huntercombe Hospl The SL6 41 C6
Huntercombe La N SL6 41 C7
Huntercombe La S SL6 41 C6
Huntercombe Spur SL1 41 C6
Hunter Ct SL1 41 C8
Hunters Chase RG4 58 F5
Hunters Ct 3 RG41 88 B2
Hunter's Ct RG5 87 E6
Hunter's Hill RG7 110 F3
Hunters Mdw RG17 48 A3
Hunters Mews SL4 67 C6
Hunters Way
Shinfield RG7 113 B1
Slough SL1 41 E4
Hunters Wharf 22 RG1 86 A6
Huntingdon Cl RG6 87 E2
Huntingdon Gdns RG14 105 E5
Huntingdonshire Cl RG41 115 D6
Huntingfield Way TW20 96 D2
Huntington Pl SL3 44 B3
Huntley Cl TW19 97 E8
Huntley Ct RG1 86 E6
Huntley The RG30 85 D6
Hunts Cotts RG14 104 E6
HUNT'S GREEN
Henley-on-Thames 35 B6
HUNT'S GREEN *continued*
Newbury 76 E1
Huntsgreen Ct RG12 118 C7
Hunt's La SL6 20 E3
Huntsmans Mdw SL5 119 F8
Huntsmoor Rd RG26 135 A1
Huntswood La SL1, SL6 20 F4
Hurford Dr RG19 106 F3
HURLEY 17 F4
Hurley Ct RG12 118 E5
Hurley High St SL6 17 F4
Hurley La SL6 18 B3
Hurley Riverside Pk Cvn Site SL6 17 D4
Hurricane Way
Slough SL3 44 B1
Woodley RG5 88 B8
Hursley Cl RG30 84 E7
HURST 88 F7
Hurst Com Coll The RG26 134 D1
Hurstdene Ave TW18 97 B2
Hurstfield Dr SL6 41 B7
Hurst Gr KT12 125 F1
Hurst La TW20 123 A7
Hurst Lodge Sch SL5 120 B1
Hurst Park Rd RG10 61 E2
Hurst Rd
Slough SL1 41 D8
Twyford RG10 61 E3
Hurst Way RG2 112 F8
Hurstwood SL5 120 A3
Hurworth Ave SL3 43 C3
Huscarle Way RG31 57 C4
Huson Rd RG42 91 C2
Hussars Dr RG19 106 D1
Hutsons Cl RG40 116 D8
Hutton Cl
Earley RG6 87 A2
Newbury RG14 105 B4
Windlesham GU20 146 D3
Huxley Cl SL2 23 B1
Hyde Cl TW15 98 E2
HYDE END 133 E4
Hyde End La
Brimpton RG7 133 D5
Shinfield RG7 113 C3
Hyde End Rd RG7 113 D2
Hyde Gn SL7 1 F1
Hyde La RG20 132 A1
Hydes The RG31 57 C4
Hyde Terr TW15 98 E2
Hydro Ho KT16 124 C1
Hyland Ho 5 SL8 3 B3
Hylle Cl SL4 66 E6
Hyperion Way RG2 86 B3
Hythe Cl RG12 118 E4
HYTHE END 96 B6
Hythe End Rd TW19 96 A5
Hythe Field Ave TW20 96 D2
Hythe Park Rd TW20 96 D2
Hythe Prim Sch TW18 96 D3
Hythe Rd TW18 96 D3
Hythe The TW18 96 E3

I

Ian Mikardo Way RG4 59 D2
Iberian Way GU15 152 B6
Ibotson Ct SL3 69 E6
Ibstock Cl RG30 85 B7
Ibstone Ave RG4 59 E5
Icarus Ct 6 RG1 86 D7
Icknield Cotts RG8 34 A6
Icknield Pl RG8 34 D8
Icknield Rd RG8 34 D8
Icon Ho 12 RG1 86 A8
Iden Ct RG14 105 B4
Iffley Ct 11 TW18 96 F3
Ilbury Cl RG2 113 E5
Ilchester Cl SL6 39 C5
Ilchester Ct 7 RG14 105 A2
Ilchester Mews RG4 59 E6
Ilex Cl
Englefield Green TW20 95 B1
Pamber Heath RG26 135 E1
Yateley GU46 149 B6
Ilfracombe Way RG6 87 E3
Iliffe Cl 20 RG1 86 B6
Ilkley Rd RG4 58 E3
Illkley Way RG19 106 C2
Il-libro Ct 7 RG1 86 B7
Illingworth SL4 66 E4
Illingworth Ave RG4 59 E6
Illingworth Gr RG12 118 F8
Ilsley Rd RG20 31 D4
Ilsleys' Prim Sch The RG20 30 E6
Imperial Ct
Henley-on-T RG9 15 E1
7 Newbury RG14 104 F2
Windsor SL4 67 A4
Imperial Ho GU25 122 E4
Imperial Rd
East Bedfont TW14 98 E8
Windsor SL4 67 A4
Imperial Way
Reading RG2 113 A7
Thatcham RG19 106 E2
Impstone Rd RG26 135 F1
Inch's Yd 9 RG14 105 A2
Inchwood RG12 118 C1
India Rd SL1 43 B4
Indigo Apartments 15 RG1 86 B6
Indigo Ct 9 TW13 98 F5
Infantry Dr 5 RG19 106 E2
Ingle Dell GU15 151 D4
Ingleglen SL2 22 B7
Ingle Glen RG40 142 A7
Ingles Edge RG17 127 E4
Ingleside SL3 69 F6
Ingleton RG12 118 A6
Inglewood Ave GU15 152 D5
Inglewood Ct RG30 85 C6
Inglewood Rd RG17 101 E2
Ingoldsby Copse RG14 105 E5
Inhurst La RG26 134 C1
Inhurst Way RG26 134 F1
Inkerman Rd SL4 41 F2
INKPEN 127 D5
Inkpen Cl RG30 85 A4
Inkpen Common Nature Reserve* RG17 128 A5
Inkpen Prim Sch RG17 127 D6
Inkpen Rd
Hungerford RG17 100 F3
Kintbury RG17 102 A1
Inner Ring E TW6 71 B4
Inner Ring W TW6 71 A4
Innings La
White Waltham SL6 63 D7
Winkfield RG12 118 E8
Inniscrown Ho SL3 68 B7
Institute Rd
Marlow SL7 1 E1
Taplow SL6 40 F7
Instow Rd RG6 87 B2
International Way TW16 125 E8
In The Ray SL6 40 B8
Invergordon Cl RG31 84 E4
Inverness Way GU47 150 D7
Invicta Cl TW14 98 F7
Inwood Cl SL6 19 B6
Iona Cres SL1 41 E7
iO Trade Ctr RG30 58 A1
Ipswich Rd SL1 42 A7
Iris Ct RG30 84 E7
Irish Hill Rd RG17 102 B2
Irvine Pl GU25 122 E4
Irvine Way RG6 114 C8
Irving Ho SL4 66 E5
Irwin Ct TW15 97 D5
Isaac Newton Rd RG2 115 A1
Isbury Almshouses RG17 25 B3
Isis Cl RG41 88 B1
Isis Ct 1 RG1 59 A1
Isis Ho KT16 124 C2
Isis Way
Bourne End SL8 3 B4
Sandhurst GU47 150 D8
Island Cl TW18 96 E4
Island Farm Rd RG7 110 D2
Island Ho UB7 70 B6
Island Rd RG2 85 F2
Islandstone La RG10 89 A6
Island The TW19 96 A5
Islet Park Dr SL6 20 C3
Islet Park Ho SL6 20 C3
Islet Pk SL6 20 C3
Islet Rd SL6 20 C3
Isobel Ho 11 TW16 98 F1
Ivanhoe Rd RG40 141 A6
Iveagh Ct RG12 118 C4
IVER 44 F7
Iverdale Cl SL0 44 C6
IVER HEATH 23 F3
Iver La SL0 44 F7
Iver Lodge SL0 44 F8
Iverna Gdns TW14 71 D2
Iver Sta SL0 44 F4
Iver Village Inf Sch SL0 44 F7
Iver Village Jun Sch The SL0 44 E7
Ives Cl GU46 149 B7
Ives Rd SL3 44 A3
Ivybank RG31 57 C1
Ivy Cl SL6 65 A7
Ivy Cres SL1 41 F6
Ivydene Rd RG30 58 C1
Ivy Dr GU18 153 A7

J

Jack Ct GU17 150 E4
Jack Price Ct 9 RG1 86 B5
Jackson Cl RG12 118 B4
Jackson Ind Est SL8 3 B2
Jacksons La RG4 58 C5
Jack St RG14 105 A3
Jacob Cl
Bracknell RG42 117 D7
Windsor SL4 66 E6
Jacob Rd GU15 151 A7
Jago Ct RG14 131 A8
Jakes Ho SL6 40 A8
James Butcher Dr RG7 83 F3
James Cl SL7 1 F4
James Ct RG30 85 D5
James Elliman Sch SL2 42 E6
James Mdw SL3 68 F8
James Rd GU15 151 B2
James's La RG7, RG30 111 E4
James St
Reading RG1 85 F7
Windsor SL4 67 D6
Jameston RG12 118 C1
James Watt Rd
Arborfield Garrison RG2 140 F7
Arborfield Garrison RG2 141 A8
James Way GU15 151 B2

Jamnagar Cl TW18 ...... 96 F2
Janson Ct RG1 .... 85 F6
Japonica Cl RG41 .... 115 D4
Jaques's La RG7 .... 111 A6
Jardine Cotts SL2 .... 23 A8
Jarratt Ho SL4 .... 67 B4
Jarry Ct SL7 .... 1 F3
Jarvis Dr RG10 .... 61 D6
Jasmine Cl RG41 .... 115 D7
Jasmine Way RG19 ...... 133 B6
Jay Cl RG6 .... 87 B1
Jays Ct SL5 .... 120 D5
Jays Nest Cl GU17 ...... 150 D4
Jayworth Ho RG1 .... 86 E8
Jealott's Hill RG42 .... 91 B7
Jedburgh Cl RG19 .... 106 F3
Jefferson Cl
Caversham RG4 .... 59 C7
Slough SL3 .... 44 A2
Jeffery Cl RG40 .... 116 D6
Jeffrey Pl 5 RG1 .... 86 A8
Jeffries Ct SL8 .... 3 B2
Jellicoe Cl SL1 .... 42 B4
Jenkins Cl RG30 .... 85 C6
Jenkins Ct GU19 .... 145 D2
Jenkins' Hill London Rd
GU19 .... 145 D2
Jenner Wlk RG31 .... 84 A7
Jennery La SL1 .... 21 C2
Jennetts Cl RG7 .... 81 E3
JENNETTS HILL 81 E3
Jennings Field HP10 ...... 3 C7
Jenny's Wlk GU46 .... 149 E6
Jerome Cl SL7 .... 1 F4
Jerome Cnr RG45 .... 143 C3
Jerome Rd RG5 .... 87 E6
Jerrymoor Hill RG40 .... 141 F8
Jersey Dr RG41 .... 88 A2
Jersey Pl SL5 .... 120 D3
Jesmond Dene RG14 .... 104 F4
Jesse Cl GU46 .... 149 F5
Jesse Terr RG1 .... 85 F7
Jessiman Terr TW17 .... 125 A4
Jesus Hospital SL6 .... 40 C3
Jetty Ho KT16 .... 124 C2
Jevington RG12 .... 118 C1
Jig's La N RG42 .... 91 E2
Jig's La S
Bracknell RG42 .... 91 E1
Winkfield RG42 .... 118 E8
Job's La SL6 .... 19 B8
Jock's La RG42 .... 90 F1
Joel Cl RG6 .... 87 A3
Johannes Ct 5 RG30 ...... 85 D6
John Balliol Ct 24 RG1 ... 86 D7
John Boys Ho RG14 ..... 130 C6
John Childs Cl RG14 .... 105 A1
John F Kennedy Meml★
TW20 .... 95 D6
John Hunt Cl RG19 ...... 106 E2
John Kaye Ct TW17 ..... 125 A4
John Kimber's Almshouses
1 RG14 .... 104 F2
John Madejeski Acad
RG2 .... 86 C1
John Nike Way RG12 .... 117 C7
John Norgate Ho RG14 .. 105 E3
John O'Gaunt Com Tech Coll
RG17 .... 100 D3
John Pl RG42 .... 91 E1
John Rankin Inf Sch
RG14 .... 130 D8
John Rankin Jun Sch
RG14 .... 130 D8
Johns Cl TW15 .... 98 C4
Johnson Dr RG40 .... 142 B7
Johnsons La RG18 ...... 106 C8
Jonathan Ct SL6 .... 39 E7
Jonathan Hill RG20 ..... 131 B3
Jones Cnr SL5 .... 119 E7
Jones Dr RG19 .... 131 F5
Jordan Cl
Caversham RG4 .... 59 E5
Shinfield RG7 .... 113 D1
Jordans Cl TW19 .... 97 C8
Jordan's La RG7 .... 110 F2
Joseph Ct RG42 .... 91 E2
Josephine Ct RG30 .... 85 E6
Jouldings La RG7 .... 140 D4
Jourdelay's Pas SL4 ...... 67 D8
Journeys End SL2 .... 42 E8
Joviel Ho TW18 .... 97 A1
Jubilee Ave
North Ascot SL5 .... 119 E8
Wokingham RG41 .... 116 B7
Jubilee Cl
North Ascot SL5 .... 119 E8
Pamber Heath RG26 ..... 135 E1
Stanwell TW19 .... 97 C8
Woodley RG5 .... 87 E6
Jubilee Cotts
Riseley RG7 .... 139 C3
Slough SL3 .... 44 B1
Jubilee Ct
Bracknell RG12 .... 118 C6
9 Staines TW18 .... 97 A4
Thatcham RG19 .... 106 A3
Jubilee Rd
Finchampstead RG40 .... 141 F3
Littlewick Green SL6 ..... 38 B5
Newbury RG14 .... 105 B2
Reading RG6 .... 87 A6
Jubilee Sq RG1 .... 86 B6
Jubilee Way
Datchet SL3 .... 68 C7
Jubilee Way *continued*
East Bedfont TW14 .... 98 F7
Juliet Gdns RG42 .... 118 F8
Julius Hill RG42 .... 118 F8
Julkes La RG2 .... 114 E7
Junction Rd
Ashford TW15 .... 98 D3
Lightwater GU18 .... 146 B1
Reading RG1 .... 86 E6
Junction Terr RG14 ..... 105 C2
Juniper RG12 .... 118 C1
Juniper Ct
Flackwell Heath HP10 ...... 3 C7
Slough, Cippenham SL1 .... 41 E6
Slough, Upton SL1 .... 43 A4
Juniper Dr SL6 .... 40 B8
Juniper Gdns TW16 ...... 98 F2
Juniper Hill Sch HP10 ..... 3 B7
Juniper La HP10 .... 3 D7
Juniper Pl RG19 .... 133 B6
Juniper Rd SL7 .... 1 D5
Junipers The RG41 ..... 115 D4
Juniper Way RG31 .... 57 D2
Jupiter Ho RG7 .... 134 E2
Jupiter Way RG41 .... 115 F6
Justice Cl RG19 .... 106 F2
Jutland Cl RG41 .... 115 E6
Jutland Ho SL4 .... 66 F5
Jutland Pl TW20 .... 96 C3

K

Katesgrove La RG1 .... 86 A6
Katesgrove Prim Sch RG1 86 A6
Katherine Ct 2 GU15 ... 151 D5
Kathleen Sanders Ct RG7. 83 E4
Kaynes Pk SL5 .... 119 E8
Kaywood Cl SL3 .... 43 C3
Keane Cl RG5 .... 87 E8
Kearsley Rd RG30 .... 85 C6
Keates Gn RG42 .... 118 B8
Keats Cl RG5 .... 87 E4
Keats La SL4 .... 67 C8
Keats Rd RG5 .... 87 E4
Keats Way
Crowthorne RG45 .... 143 B6
Yateley GU46 .... 149 B4
Keble Rd SL6 .... 39 E8
Keble Way GU47 .... 143 E2
Keeble Ho RG41 .... 116 A6
Keel KT16 .... 124 C2
Keel Dr SL1 .... 42 C4
Keeler Cl SL4 .... 66 E4
Keepers Coombe RG12 .. 118 D3
Keepers Farm Cl SL4 ..... 66 E5
Keepers Terr GU25 ..... 122 A4
Keepers Wlk GU25 ..... 122 D4
Keephatch Ho RG40 ..... 116 F7
Keep Hatch Prim Sch
RG40 .... 116 D7
Keephatch Rd RG40 ..... 116 E7
Keighley Cl RG30 .... 106 C2
Kelburne Cl RG41 .... 88 C3
Keldholme RG12 .... 118 A6
Kellie Ho SL5 .... 121 A1
Kelly Cl TW17 .... 125 E7
Kelmscott Cl RG4 .... 58 F3
Kelpatrick Rd SL1 .... 41 D7
Kelsall Pl SL5 .... 120 B2
Kelsey Ave RG40 .... 141 E6
Kelsey Cl SL6 .... 39 D3
Kelsey Gr GU46 .... 149 E5
Kelso Mews RG4 .... 59 E6
Kelton Cl RG6 .... 87 E2
Kelvedon Way RG4 .... 58 E5
Kelvin Cl RG2 .... 140 E7
Kelvin Gate RG12 .... 118 D7
Kelvin Rd RG14 .... 105 B4
Kemble Ct RG31 .... 84 D4
Kemerton Cl RG31 .... 84 D4
Kemp Ct GU19 .... 145 F2
Kempe Cl SL3 .... 44 C2
Kempton Cl RG14 .... 105 C1
Kemsley Chase SL2 ...... 22 C4
Kenavon Dr RG1 .... 86 C8
Kendal Ave
Caversham RG4 .... 59 E5
Shinfield RG2 .... 113 E6
Kendal Cl
East Bedfont TW14 .... 98 F7
Slough SL2 .... 43 A6
Thatcham RG18 .... 106 C4
Kendal Dr SL2 .... 43 A6
Kendal Gr GU15 .... 152 D4
Kendall Ct Bsns Pk GU15 150 F4
Kendall Pl SL6 .... 39 C5
Kendrick Cl RG40 .... 116 C5
Kendrick Ct 5 RG1 .... 86 C6
Kendrick Girls' Gram Sch
RG1 .... 86 C7
Kendrick Rd
Newbury RG14 .... 130 D5
Reading RG1 .... 86 C6
Slough SL3 .... 43 B3
Kenilworth Ave
Bracknell RG12 .... 118 D8
Reading RG30 .... 85 D5
Kenilworth Cl SL1 .... 42 F3
Kenilworth Gdns TW18 ... 97 C3
Kenilworth Rd TW15 ..... 97 D5
Kenley Ho RG12 .... 118 D6
Kenneally SL4 .... 66 C5
Kenneally Cl 11 SL4 ...... 66 C5
Kenneally Pl 12 SL4 ...... 66 C5
Kenneally Row 13 SL4 .... 66 C5
Kenneally Wlk 10 SL4 .... 66 C5
Kennedy Cl
Farnham Common SL2 ..... 22 C6
Maidenhead SL6 .... 39 C6
Marlow SL7 .... 1 E3
Newbury RG14 .... 130 D6
Kennedy Ct TW15 .... 98 C3
Kennedy Dr RG8 .... 56 E5
Kennedy Gdns RG6 ...... 87 B3
Kennedy Ho SL1 .... 41 D5
Kennedy Mdw RG17 ..... 100 C4
Kennel Ave SL5 .... 119 F8
Kennel Cl SL5 .... 92 F2
Kennel Gn SL5 .... 119 E8
Kennel La
Bracknell RG42 .... 91 B1
Cookham Dean SL6 .... 19 C7
Windlesham GU20 .... 146 C5
Kennel Lane Sch RG42 ... 91 B2
Kennel Ride SL5 .... 92 F1
Kennel Wood SL5 .... 119 F8
Kennet Cl RG19 .... 106 E3
Kennet Cotts RG30 .... 85 A1
Kennet Ct
Hungerford RG17 .... 100 E7
1 Newbury RG14 .... 105 A1
Wokingham RG41 .... 115 F6
Kennet Ctr The 12 RG14 . 105 A2
Kennet Ent Ctr RG17 .... 100 D7
Kennet Pl
Burghfield Common RG7 .. 111 B3
Chilton Foliat RG17 .... 73 A1
4 Newbury RG14 .... 105 B4
Kennet Rd
Bourne End SL8 .... 3 B4
Kintbury RG17 .... 102 B2
Maidenhead SL6 .... 39 F8
Newbury RG14 .... 104 F2
Kennet Sch RG19 .... 106 E3
Kennet Side
Newbury RG14 .... 105 C3
9 Reading RG1 .... 86 C7
Kennet St RG1 .... 86 C7
Kennett Rd SL3 .... 44 B3
Kennet Valley Prim Sch
RG31 .... 84 F4
Kennet Way RG17 .... 100 D7
Kennet Weir Bsns Pk RG7 83 F2
Kennet Wlk RG1 .... 86 D8
Kensington Cl RG6 .... 87 B1
Kensington Rd RG30 ..... 85 D7
Kent Ave SL1 .... 42 C8
Kent Cl
Staines TW18 .... 97 D2
Wokingham RG41 .... 115 D5
Kent Cotts RG7 .... 139 C3
Kent Folly RG42 .... 91 F2
Kentigern Dr RG45 ...... 143 E5
Kent Lodge 6 SL6 .... 39 F6
Kenton Cl
Bracknell RG12 .... 118 D7
Frimley GU16 .... 151 F1
Marlow SL7 .... 1 E2
Kenton Rd RG6 .... 87 C4
Kentons La SL4 .... 66 F5
Kenton's La RG10 .... 36 D7
Kent Rd
Reading RG30 .... 85 D7
Windlesham GU20 .... 146 D5
Kent Way SL6 .... 19 E1
Kentwood Cl RG30 .... 57 E1
Kentwood Farm RG40 ... 116 D8
Kentwood Hill RG31 ...... 57 E1
Kenwood Cl
Harmondsworth UB7 ...... 71 A8
Maidenhead SL6 .... 39 A7
Kenworth Gr GU18 ...... 146 A1
Keppel Spur SL4 .... 95 B8
Keppel St SL4 .... 67 D5
Kepple Pl GU19 .... 145 F3
Kernham Dr RG31 .... 57 C4
Kerria Way GU24 .... 153 F6
Kerris Way RG6 .... 87 B1
Kersey Cres RG14 ...... 104 E5
Kershope Ct RG2 .... 86 C3
Kersten Cl RG14 .... 131 C8
Kesteven Way RG41 ..... 115 E6
Keston Cl RG4 .... 59 C2
Kestrel Ave TW18 .... 96 F5
Kestrel Bldgs RG40 ..... 141 A6
Kestrel Cl RG19 .... 106 B3
Kestrel Path SL2 .... 21 E1
Kestrels Mead RG26 .... 135 B2
Kestrel Way
Burghfield Common RG7 .. 111 B3
Reading RG30 .... 85 A4
Wokingham RG41 .... 115 F5
Keswick Ave TW17 ...... 125 E6
Keswick Cl
Frimley GU15 .... 152 D4
Reading RG30 .... 84 D7
Keswick Ct SL2 .... 42 F6
Keswick Dr GU18 .... 153 B8
Keswick Gdns RG5 .... 87 E5
Keswick Rd TW20 .... 96 B1
Ketcher Gn RG42 .... 90 C4
Kettering Cl RG31 .... 84 E4
Kevins Dr GU46 .... 149 E7
Kew Cotts RG14 .... 104 E1
Kew Gdns SN8 .... 126 A3
Keynsham Way GU47 .... 143 D2
Keys Pl SL6 .... 39 F6
Khalsa Prim Sch SL2 ..... 43 A7
Kibble Gn RG12 .... 118 C3
Kibblewhite Cres RG10 ... 61 D6
Kidderminster Rd SL2 .... 22 A2
Kidmore End Rd RG4 ..... 59 B7
Kidmore Rd RG4 .... 58 F5
Kidwells Cl SL6 .... 39 F8
Kidwells Park Dr 13 SL6 .. 39 F7
Kielder Ct RG2 .... 86 C3
Kielder Wlk GU15 .... 152 C4
Kier Pk SL5 .... 120 C6
KIFF GREEN 108 C6
Kilburn Cl RG31 .... 84 D4
Kildare Gdns RG4 .... 59 C3
Killarney Dr SL6 .... 39 E7
Killigrew Ho 4 TW16 .... 98 E1
Kilmartin Gdns GU16 ... 151 F1
Kilmington Cl RG12 ..... 118 E2
Kilmiston Ave TW17 .... 125 C3
Kilmiston House TW17 .. 125 C3
Kilmore Dr GU15 .... 152 B4
Kilmuir Cl GU47 .... 150 D7
Kiln Cl
Harlington UB3 .... 71 D8
Hermitage RG18 .... 79 C7
Kiln Croft Cl SL7 .... 2 A3
Kiln Dr RG18 .... 78 E5
Kiln Fields HP10 .... 3 E2
KILN GREEN 37 D1
Kiln Hill RG7 .... 140 B7
Kiln La
Bracknell RG12 .... 118 A7
Mortimer RG7 .... 137 C5
Reading RG31 .... 84 B8
Shiplake RG9 .... 35 C2
Sunningdale SL5 .... 121 A4
Winkfield SL4 .... 93 B2
Wooburn SL8, HP10 .... 3 D3
Kiln Pl SL6 .... 19 A3
Kiln Rd
Caversham RG4 .... 59 D8
Newbury RG14 .... 105 C5
Kiln Ride
Upper Basildon RG8 ...... 54 F5
Wokingham RG40 .... 142 A8
Kiln Ride Extension
RG40 .... 142 A6
Kilnsea Dr RG6 .... 87 D1
Kilnside RG12 .... 91 D1
Kiln Terr RG18 .... 78 E5
Kiln View Rd RG2 .... 86 D2
Kilowna Cl RG10 .... 61 A4
Kilross Rd TW14 .... 98 E7
Kimber Cl SL4 .... 67 A4
Kimberley RG12 .... 118 C1
Kimberley Cl
1 Reading RG1 .... 85 E5
Slough SL3 .... 43 F2
Kimber's Cl RG14 .... 104 F3
Kimbers Dr
Burnham SL1 .... 21 D2
Newbury RG14 .... 104 C5
Kimber's La SL6 .... 39 E3
Kimbolton 3 SL6 .... 40 B8
Kimmeridge RG12 ...... 118 E3
Kimpton Cl RG6 .... 113 E8
Kinburn Dr TW20 .... 95 E3
King Acre Ct TW18 .... 96 E5
King Edward Ct 6 SL4 ... 67 D6
King Edwards Cl SL5 .... 119 E8
King Edwards Rd SL5 ... 119 E8
King Edwards Rise SL5 .. 119 E8
King Edward St SL1 ...... 42 D4
King Edward VII Ave SL4,
SL3 .... 67 E8
King Edward VII Hospl
SL4 .... 67 C4
Kingfisher Cl RG7 .... 109 B3
Kingfisher Court Ind Est
RG14 .... 105 D3
Kingfisher Ct
Slough SL2 .... 22 B1
Twyford RG10 .... 61 E3
Kingfisher Dr
Staines TW18 .... 96 F4
Woodley RG5 .... 87 C6
Yateley GU46 .... 149 B6
Kingfisher Gr RG7 ...... 113 A3
Kingfisher Ho SL7 .... 1 F2
Kingfisher Par GU17 .... 150 B5
Kingfisher Pl RG1 .... 86 B8
King George Cl TW16 .... 98 E3
Kinghorn La SL6 .... 19 D3
Kinghorn Pk SL6 .... 19 D3
King James Way RG9 .... 35 C8
King John's Cl TW19 ..... 68 C1
King John's Palace SL3 .. 69 D6
Kings Apartments GU15 . 151 C4
King's Ave TW16 .... 98 F2
Kingsbridge Cotts RG40 . 142 E7
Kingsbridge Hill RG7 .... 139 A6
Kingsbridge Rd
Newbury RG14 .... 104 E1
Reading RG2 .... 86 C2
Kingsbury Cres TW18 .... 96 D4
Kingsbury Dr SL4 .... 95 A8
Kings Chase 16 SL6 ...... 39 F6
Kings Cl RG9 .... 15 D2
King's Cl TW18 .... 97 D1
Kingsclear Pk GU15 ..... 151 D4
KINGSCLERE
WOODLANDS 133 B1
Kings Common Cl RG9 ... 35 B1
King's Court Fst Sch SL4 . 95 B8
Kings Cres GU15 .... 151 C8
Kingscroft Jun Sch TW18 . 97 A2
Kingscroft La RG42 ...... 92 A6
Kings Ct UB7 .... 70 B6
Kingsdown Cl RG6 .... 87 B2
Kingsfield SL4 .... 66 D6
Kingsford Cl RG5 .... 88 A5
Kingsgate Pl 8 RG1 ...... 86 D7
Kingsgate St RG1 .... 86 D7
Kings Gdns RG10 .... 61 D6
Kings Glade GU46 ...... 149 F6
Kings Gr SL6 .... 39 E6
Kings Grove Ind Est SL6 .. 39 E6
Kings International Coll for
Bsns & the Arts GU15 .. 151 C2
King's Keep GU47 ...... 143 B1
Kings La
Cookham Dean SL6 .... 19 B8
Englefield Green TW20 .... 95 A2
Windlesham GU20 .... 146 E5
Kingsland Ctr RG19 ..... 106 D3
Kingsland Grange RG14 . 130 E8
Kingsland Ho RG14 ..... 130 E8
Kingsley Ave
Camberley GU15 .... 151 D3
Englefield Green TW20 .... 95 B2
Kingsley Cl
Charvil RG10 .... 61 A5
Crowthorne RG45 .... 143 B3
Newbury RG14 .... 105 B5
Reading RG2 .... 113 B7
Kingsley Dr SL7 .... 1 C6
Kingsley Path SL2 .... 21 D1
Kings Mead RG14 ...... 130 C5
Kingsmead Ho SL1 .... 42 C5
KING'S MEADOW 86 C8
King's Meadow Rd RG1 .. 86 B8
Kingsmere Rd RG42 ..... 117 F8
Kingsoak Ct SL6 .... 39 B3
King's Oak Ct 4 RG1 ..... 86 C7
Kings Rd
Newbury RG14 .... 105 B2
Silchester RG7 .... 136 B2
West End GU24 .... 153 F5
Windsor SL4 .... 67 D5
King's Rd
Ascot SL5 .... 120 D4
Caversham RG4 .... 59 C2
Crowthorne RG45 .... 143 C5
Egham TW20 .... 96 A4
Henley-on-T RG9 .... 15 D2
Reading RG1 .... 86 D7
Slough SL1 .... 42 E3
Kings Rd W RG14 .... 105 A2
King's Reach Ct 11 RG1 ... 86 B7
King's Ride
Bracknell SL5 .... 119 D5
Camberley GU15 .... 151 D7
King's Ride Ho SL5 ..... 119 E5
Kings Ride Pk SL5 ...... 119 C4
King's Road Ho 3 SL4 ... 67 D5
King St
Chertsey KT16 .... 124 A1
Maidenhead SL6 .... 39 F6
Mortimer RG7 .... 137 A6
Reading RG1 .... 86 B7
King Stable St SL4 .... 67 D7
King's Terr SL3 .... 69 B8
Kingston Ave TW14 ...... 71 F1
Kingston Cres TW15 ..... 97 D2
Kingston Gdns RG2 ...... 86 C2
Kingston La RG7 .... 110 D6
Kingston Rd
Ashford TW15 .... 97 F2
Camberley GU15 .... 145 A1
Staines TW15, TW18 ...... 97 B2
King Street La RG41 ...... 88 C1
Kingsway
Blackwater GU17 .... 150 E5
Caversham RG4 .... 59 E6
Farnham Common SL2 ..... 22 C6
Slough SL3 .... 43 C3
Stanwell TW19 .... 97 E7
Kingsway Mews SL2 ..... 22 C6
Kingswick Cl SL5 .... 120 D5
Kingswick Dr SL5 .... 120 D5
Kings Wlk
Henley-on-T RG9 .... 15 D2
4 Maidenhead SL6 .... 39 F7
Reading RG1 .... 86 B7
King's Wlk GU15 .... 150 F6
Kings Wood SL7 .... 17 D6
Kingswood Cl
Camberley GU15 .... 152 A8
Englefield Green TW20 .... 95 D4
Kingswood Creek TW19 .. 68 D2
Kingswood Ct
Maidenhead SL6 .... 39 F5
17 Reading RG30 .... 85 D6
Kingswood Hall of Residence
TW20 .... 95 D4
Kingswood Ho SL1 .... 42 C8
Kingswood Par SL7 .... 1 D5
Kingswood Rise TW20 .... 95 D4
King's Yd SL5 .... 119 E5
Kingwood House Stables
RG17 .... 45 D7
Kinnaird Cl SL1 .... 41 C7
Kinross Ave SL5 .... 119 F4
Kinross Cl TW16 .... 98 F3
Kinross Ct SL5 .... 119 F4
Kinross Dr TW16 .... 98 F3
Kinson Rd RG30 .... 58 A1
KINTBURY 102 A1
Kintbury Mill RG17 ..... 102 B3
Kintbury Rd RG17 ...... 127 F6
Kintbury St Mary's CE Prim
Sch RG17 .... 102 B2
Kintbury Sq RG17 ...... 102 A2
Kintbury Sta RG17 ..... 102 B3
Kintbury Wlk RG30 .... 85 C4
Kinver Wlk 5 RG1 .... 86 B5
Kipling Cl
Thatcham RG18 .... 106 C5
1 Woodley RG5 .... 87 E4
Yateley GU46 .... 149 C4
Kipling Ct SL4 .... 67 B5
Kipling Hall RG45 ...... 143 B5
Kirkby Ct GU16 .... 151 E1

Kirkfell Cl RG31 . . . . 57 C2
Kirkham Cl
Caversham RG4 . . . . 59 E6
Sandhurst GU47 . . . . 143 D2
Kirkstall Ct RG31 . . . . 84 D4
Kirkstone Cl GU15 . . . . . 152 D4
Kirkwall Spur SL1 . . . . 42 E8
Kirkwood Cres RG7 . . . . . 110 F3
Kirton Cl RG30 . . . . 85 B7
Kirtons Farm Rd RG30 . . . . 85 C1
Kitsmead La GU25, KT16 . 122 C1
Kittiwake Cl RG5 . . . . 88 B7
Kitwood Dr RG6 . . . . 87 E1
Klondyke SL7 . . . . 1 D2
Knappe Cl RG9 . . . . 35 C8
Knapp Rd TW15 . . . . 97 F4
Knappswood Cl RG8 . . . . . 55 C4
Knapp The RG6 . . . . 87 B4
Knighton Cl RG4 . . . . 59 A3
Knightsbridge Cres TW18 97 B2
Knightsbridge Ct 7 SL3 . . 44 A2
Knightsbridge Dr RG19 . . 132 B3
Knightsbridge Rd GU15 . 151 E7
Knights Cl
Egham TW20 . . . . 96 D2
Windsor SL4 . . . . 66 D6
Knights La RG20 . . . . 129 C3
Knights Lea RG20 . . . . 129 B3
Knight's Pl 8 SL4 . . . . 67 C5
Knights Way
Caversham RG4 . . . . 59 B5
Frimley GU15 . . . . 152 C4
Knightswood RG12 . . . . . 118 B1
Knock The GU47 . . . . 150 D7
Knole Wood SL5 . . . . 120 E1
Knoll Cl OX12 . . . . 6 E7
Knoll Gdns RG20 . . . . 130 A4
Knollmead RG31 . . . . 84 D4
Knoll Park Rd KT16 . . . . . 123 F1
Knoll Rd GU15 . . . . 151 D6
Knoll The
Chertsey KT16 . . . . 123 F1
Purley on T RG31 . . . . 57 B2
Knollys Rd RG26 . . . . 135 F1
Knolton Way SL2 . . . . 43 C7
Knossington Cl RG6 . . . . . 87 C2
Knott La RG7 . . . . 109 B4
Knowle Cl RG4 . . . . 58 D4
Knowle Croft SL6 . . . . 39 E5
Knowle Gn TW18 . . . . 97 A3
Knowle Gr GU25 . . . . 122 C2
KNOWLE GREEN 97 A3
Knowle Grove Cl GU25 . . 122 C2
KNOWLE HILL 122 C2
Knowle Hill GU25 . . . . . . 122 C2
Knowle Park Ave TW18 . . . 97 B3
Knowle Park Inf Sch
TW18 . . . . 97 A3
Knowle Rd RG5 . . . . 87 E4
Knowles Ave RG45 . . . . . . 142 F5
KNOWL HILL 37 E4
Knowl Hill CE Prim Sch
RG10 . . . . 37 F4
Knowl Hill Common RG10 37 E3
Knowl Hill Terr RG10 . . . . 37 E4
Knowsley Cl SL6 . . . . 19 A1
Knowsley Rd RG31 . . . . . . 57 C3
Knox Gn RG42 . . . . 90 C3
Kola Ho SL2 . . . . 43 B6
Korda Cl TW17 . . . . 124 F6
Krooner Rd GU15 . . . . 151 B3
Kurnool Mortar Cross Roads
GU15 . . . . 151 A6
Kybes La RG7 . . . . 112 D5
Kyftle Court Flat 11
RG14 . . . . 104 F2
Kyle Cl RG12 . . . . 118 B6

L

Laburnham Rd SL6 . . . . 39 E6
Laburnum Cl SL7 . . . . 1 E4
Laburnum Ct 6 KT16 . . . 124 A1
Laburnum Gdns RG2 . . . . . 86 E1
Laburnum Gr
Brands Hill SL3 . . . . 69 B8
Newbury RG14 . . . . 105 A4
Laburnum Pl TW20 . . . . . . 95 B2
Laburnum Rd
Chertsey KT16 . . . . 124 A1
Winnersh RG41 . . . . 88 C1
Laburnum Rise RG19 . . . . 133 B5
Laburnums The GU17 . . . 150 B5
Laburnum Way TW19 . . . . 97 F7
Lacewood Gdns RG2 . . . . . 86 E1
Lacey Cl TW20 . . . . 96 D1
Ladbroke Cl RG5 . . . . 87 F6
Ladbroke Rd SL1 . . . . 42 D3
Ladwell Cl RG14 . . . . 130 D5
Ladybank RG12 . . . . 118 B1
Ladyday Pl SL1 . . . . 42 C5
Lady Elizabeth Ho 3 SL6 . 39 E7
Lady Jane Ct RG4 . . . . 59 C3
Lady Margaret Rd SL5 . . . 120 F2
Ladymask Cl RG31 . . . . . . 84 F4
Ladywood Grange SL5 . . 120 F1
Laffords The RG7 . . . . 82 A2
Laggan Rd SL6 . . . . 19 F1
Laggan Sq SL6 . . . . 19 F1
Laird Ct GU19 . . . . 145 E1
Lake Ave SL1 . . . . 42 D6
LAKE END 41 B4
Lake End Ct SL6 . . . . 41 A7
Lake End Rd SL4, SL6 . . . . 41 B5
Lake End Way RG45 . . . . . 143 A4
Lakeland Dr GU16 . . . . . . 151 E1
Lake Rd GU25 . . . . 122 B5
Lakeside
Bracknell RG42 . . . . 91 C1
Earley RG6 . . . . 87 B3
Maidenhead SL6 . . . . 20 B1
Lakeside Bsns Pk GU47 . . 150 A7
Lakeside Dr SL2 . . . . 22 F4
Lakeside Ind Est SL3 . . . . . 70 A8
Lakeside Pk KT16 . . . . . . 124 C1
Lakeside Prim Sch GU16 151 F1
Lakeside Rd SL3 . . . . 69 F7
Lakeside The GU17 . . . . . 150 D4
Lakes The SL7 . . . . 18 A6
Lakeview SL5 . . . . 119 D6
Lake View SL6 . . . . 20 A1
Lalande Cl RG41 . . . . 115 E6
LALEHAM 124 C6
Laleham Abbey TW18 . . . 124 C5
Laleham CE Prim Sch
TW18 . . . . 124 C7
Laleham Ho TW18 . . . . . . 124 C5
Laleham Nurseries
TW17 . . . . 124 E6
Laleham Rd
Littleton TW17 . . . . 125 A4
Staines TW18 . . . . 96 F2
Laleham Reach KT16 . . . . 124 A6
Lamb Cl RG18 . . . . 106 C5
Lambdens Hill RG7 . . . . . 109 D7
Lambert Ave SL3 . . . . 43 E3
Lambert Cres GU17 . . . . . 150 C4
Lambert Dr RG14 . . . . 105 E5
Lambeth Ct RG30 . . . . 84 F7
Lambfields RG7 . . . . 83 D3
Lambly Hill GU25 . . . . . . 122 E6
Lamborne Cl GU47 . . . . . 143 A1
LAMBOURN 25 C2
Lambourn CE Prim Sch
RG17 . . . . 25 B1
Lambourn Ct RG14 . . . . . 105 B4
Lambourne Cl RG31 . . . . . 84 D8
Lambourne Ct SL6 . . . . 40 C7
Lambourne Ct Cvn Site
RG17 . . . . 25 B2
Lambourne Dr
Bagshot GU19 . . . . 145 D2
Maidenhead SL6 . . . . 39 C3
Lambourne Gdns RG6 . . . . 87 D4
Lambourn Gr RG12 . . . . . 118 E7
Lambourn Pl RG17 . . . . . . 25 B3
Lambourn Rd RG20 . . . . . 104 C6
LAMBOURN
WOODLANDS 46 B4
Lambridge La RG9 . . . . 15 C3
Lambridge Wood Rd RG9 . 15 B4
Lambrook Haileybury Sch
RG42 . . . . 92 A3
Lambs Farm Bsns Pk
RG7 . . . . 139 B8
Lamb's La RG7 . . . . 139 A7
Lambs Lane Prim Sch
RG7 . . . . 139 A8
Lambton Ho SL4 . . . . 67 A4
Lambwood Hill RG7 . . . . . 112 D1
Lambwood Ind Est RG7 . 112 C1
Lamden Way RG7 . . . . 111 B3
Lamerton Rd RG2 . . . . 86 C1
Lamesley Ho SL6 . . . . 39 E6
Lammas Ave SL4 . . . . 67 D5
Lammas Ct TW18 . . . . 96 E5
Lammas Ct
Staines TW19 . . . . 96 D5
Windsor SL4 . . . . 67 C5
Lammas Dr TW18 . . . . 96 D4
Lammas Mead RG42 . . . . . 90 E1
Lammas Rd SL1 . . . . 41 D8
Lamorna Cres RG31 . . . . . 57 C1
Lamp Acres RG14 . . . . . . 105 B5
Lamplighters Wlk RG31 . . 84 F4
Lamtarra Way RG14 . . . . . 131 C8
Lanark Cl
Frimley GU16 . . . . 151 E2
Woodley RG5 . . . . 88 A6
Lancashire Hill RG42 . . . . 91 F2
Lancaster Ave SL2 . . . . . . 22 C1
Lancaster Cl
Ashford TW15 . . . . 97 E4
Englefield Green TW20 . . . . 95 D3
Hungerford RG17 . . . . . . 100 C4
2 Reading RG1 . . . . 86 C5
Stanwell TW19 . . . . 70 E1
Thatcham RG18 . . . . 106 C4
Lancaster Ct
Reading RG2 . . . . 86 E1
Stanwell TW19 . . . . 97 E7
Lancaster Dr GU15 . . . . . 151 D6
Lancaster Gdns RG6 . . . . . 87 B3
Lancaster Ho RG12 . . . . . 118 B4
Lancaster Rd SL6 . . . . 39 B8
Lancaster Sq RG17 . . . . . 100 D4
Lancastria Mews SL6 . . . . . 39 D7
Lancelot Cl SL1 . . . . 42 A4
Lancers Dr RG19 . . . . 106 E2
Lanchester Dr RG45 . . . . 143 C7
Lancing Cl RG30 . . . . 85 D7
Lancing Rd TW13 . . . . 98 F6
Landen Ct RG40 . . . . 116 B4
Landen Gr RG41 . . . . 115 E8
Landon Way TW15 . . . . . . 98 B2
Landrake Cres RG2 . . . . . . 86 C1
Landseer Cl GU47 . . . . . . 150 E6
Landseer Ct 6 RG26 . . . . 134 E1
Landsend La RG10 . . . . . . 61 B2
Lane End Cl RG2 . . . . 113 E6
Laneswood RG7 . . . . 136 E5
Lane The
Chertsey KT16 . . . . 124 A6
Chilton OX11 . . . . 10 E8
Virginia Water GU25 . . . . 122 E6
Langborough Rd RG40 . . 116 C5
Langdale Cl SL6 . . . . 40 A6
Langdale Dr SL5 . . . . 119 E7
Langdale Gdns RG6 . . . . . . 86 F2
Langdon Cl GU15 . . . . . . 152 C4
Langdown Way SL6 . . . . . . 39 D5
Langford Cl RG4 . . . . 59 C5
Langham Pl TW20 . . . . 95 F3
Langhams Way RG10 . . . . 36 E2
Lang Ho TW15 . . . . 97 E7
LANGLEY 44 A3
Langley Broom SL3 . . . . . . 43 F1
Langley Bsns Ct RG20 . . . . 51 C5
Langley Bsns Ctr SL3 . . . . 44 A4
Langley Bsns Pk SL3 . . . . 44 A4
Langley Cnr SL3 . . . . 23 F6
LANGLEY COMMON 115 A2
Langley Common Rd RG2,
RG41 . . . . 114 F1
Langley Cres UB3 . . . . 71 F7
Langley Dr GU15 . . . . 151 D6
Langley Farm Cotts RG20 . 51 E6
Langley Gram Sch SL3 . . . 43 F2
Langley Hall Dr RG31 . . . . 84 D4
Langley Hill RG31 . . . . 84 C5
Langley Hill Cl RG31 . . . . 84 C6
Langley Manor Sch SL3 . . 43 E5
Langley Park Rd SL0 . . . . . 44 C6
Langley Rd
Slough SL3 . . . . 43 E3
Staines TW18 . . . . 96 F2
Langley Sta SL3 . . . . 44 A4
Langley Way SL7 . . . . 1 C2
Langleywood Sch SL3 . . . . 43 E3
Langton Cl
Maidenhead SL6 . . . . 39 D8
Slough SL1 . . . . 41 D5
Langton's Mdw SL2 . . . . . . 22 C6
Langton Way TW20 . . . . . . 96 C2
Langworthy End SL6 . . . . . 65 B8
Langworthy La SL6 . . . . . . 65 A8
Laniver Cl RG6 . . . . 87 B1
Lansdowne Ave SL1 . . . . . . 42 E5
Lansdowne Ct
Slough SL1 . . . . 42 E5
Taplow SL6 . . . . 40 C7
Lansdowne Gdns RG7 . . . 113 C1
Lansdowne Rd
Reading RG30 . . . . 84 C7
Staines TW18 . . . . 97 B1
Lanterns Wlk SL6 . . . . 40 B7
Lapwing Cl RG31 . . . . 84 C6
Larbert Cotts SL6 . . . . 38 B5
Larch Ave
Sunningdale SL5 . . . . 120 E4
Wokingham RG41 . . . . . . 116 A7
Larch Cl
Burghfield RG30 . . . . 111 B4
Camberley GU15 . . . . 151 E8
Newbury RG14 . . . . 104 D5
Slough SL2 . . . . 42 B8
Larch Ct RG4 . . . . 59 B3
Larch Dr
Brimpton RG19 . . . . 133 B6
Woodley RG5 . . . . 87 E5
Larches The RG42 . . . . 92 A1
Larches Way GU17 . . . . . . 150 B5
Larchfield Prim Sch SL6 . . 39 E4
Larchfield Rd SL6 . . . . 39 E5
Larchmoor Pk SL2 . . . . 23 A7
Larchside Cl RG7 . . . . 113 B2
Larchwood 6 RG12 . . . . . 118 F5
Larchwood Dr TW20 . . . . . 95 B2
Larchwood Glade GU15 . 152 A7
Lardon Cotts RG8 . . . . 34 A6
Larges Bridge Dr RG12 . . 118 D6
Larges La RG12 . . . . 118 C7
Larissa Cl RG31 . . . . 57 E1
Lark Ave TW18 . . . . 96 F5
Larkes-Meade RG6 . . . . . . 87 A1
Larkfield SL6 . . . . 40 B1
Larkham Cl TW13 . . . . 98 E5
Larkings La SL2 . . . . 23 B4
Larksfield TW20 . . . . 95 C1
Larkspur Cl RG41 . . . . . . 115 D7
Larkspur Gdns RG18 . . . . 106 F4
Larkswood Cl
Reading RG31 . . . . 57 D3
Sandhurst GU47 . . . . 143 A1
Larkswood Dr RG45 . . . . 143 B5
La Roche Cl SL3 . . . . 43 C3
Lascelles Ho 4 SL1 . . . . . 43 A4
Lascelles Rd SL3 . . . . 43 B3
Lashbrook Mead RG9 . . . . 36 B3
Lashbrook Rd RG9 . . . . . . 36 B4
Lassell Gdns SL6 . . . . 40 B7
Lasswade Ct KT16 . . . . . . 123 F2
Lasswade Rd KT16 . . . . . 123 F2
Lastingham Ct TW18 . . . . 97 A2
Latham Ave GU16 . . . . . . 151 E2
Latimer RG12 . . . . 118 B1
Latimer Dr RG31 . . . . 84 C4
Latimer Rd RG41 . . . . 116 B5
Latitude KT16 . . . . 124 C1
Latton Cl OX11 . . . . 10 E8
Laud Cl
Newbury RG14 . . . . 105 D5
Reading RG2 . . . . 86 A6
Lauder Cl GU16 . . . . 151 E2
Lauderdale Ho 12 TW18 . . 96 F3
Laud's Cl RG9 . . . . 15 C1
Laud Way RG40 . . . . 116 E6
Launceston Ave RG4 . . . . . 59 E6
Launcestone Cl RG6 . . . . . 87 B2
Laundry Ct 5 RG14 . . . . 105 B2
Laundry La GU47 . . . . . . 150 E5
Lauradale RG12 . . . . 118 A5
Laurel Ave
Brimpton RG19 . . . . 133 A5
Englefield Green TW20 . . . . 95 B3
Slough SL3 . . . . 43 E4
Laurel Cl
Camberley GU15 . . . . 151 D4
Poyle SL3 . . . . 69 E7
Wokingham RG41 . . . . . . 115 F5
Laurel Ct 7 RG12 . . . . . . 118 F5
Laurel Dr RG31 . . . . 84 B8
Laurel Gdns RG19 . . . . . . 131 B6
Laurels The
Camberley GU15 . . . . 152 A7
Hungerford RG17 . . . . . . 100 E7
Pangbourne RG8 . . . . 56 D5
8 Slough SL3 . . . . 44 A2
Woodley RG5 . . . . 60 E1
Laurel Terr GU47 . . . . 142 F1
Laurence Ct 1 SL7 . . . . 1 D2
Laureston GU15 . . . . 152 A7
Lauser Rd TW19 . . . . 97 C8
Lautree Gdns SL6 . . . . 19 E7
Lavender Pk SL5 . . . . 119 C6
Lavender Row SL5 . . . . 92 E1
Lavenham Dr RG5 . . . . 87 F8
Lavershot Hall GU20 . . . . 146 C8
Lawford Cres GU46 . . . . . 149 D6
Lawkland SL2 . . . . 22 C2
Lawn Cl SL3 . . . . 68 C7
Lawns The
North Ascot SL5 . . . . 119 D6
Reading RG2 . . . . 86 D3
Lawn The SL3 . . . . 68 C6
Lawrence Alison Mews
RG4 . . . . 58 E2
Lawrence Cl RG40 . . . . . . 116 D6
Lawrence Cres GU20 . . . . 146 D4
Lawrence Ct SL4 . . . . 67 C5
Lawrence Ctr RG41 . . . . . 116 A4
Lawrence Gr RG42 . . . . . . 117 D8
Lawrence Lodge GU15 . . 151 D7
Lawrence Mead RG17 . . . 102 B2
Lawrence Pl RG14 . . . . . . 105 C5
Lawrence Rd RG30 . . . . . . 85 A8
Lawrences La RG18 . . . . . 106 D6
Lawrences Way RG18 . . . 106 D5
Lawrence Way
Camberley GU15 . . . . 150 F4
Slough SL1 . . . . 41 D8
Lawson Dr RG4 . . . . 58 E5
Lawson La OX11 . . . . 10 E8
Lawson Rd RG9 . . . . 35 F7
Lawson Way SL5 . . . . 121 B3
Laxton Gn SL6 . . . . 39 C3
Layburn Cres SL3 . . . . 69 B8
Laylands Gn RG17 . . . . . . 102 B1
Layland's Gn RG17 . . . . . 102 B1
Layleys Gn RG18 . . . . 78 F4
Laytom Rise RG31 . . . . 57 C3
Layton's La TW16 . . . . . . 125 F7
Lazare Ct 7 TW18 . . . . . . 96 F3
Lea Cl
Marlow Bottom SL7 . . . . . . 1 D6
Reading RG30 . . . . 85 A3
Leacroft
Staines TW18 . . . . 97 B4
Sunningdale SL5 . . . . 121 A4
Lea Croft RG45 . . . . 143 B6
Leacroft Cl TW18 . . . . 97 B4
Leacroft Rd SL0 . . . . 44 F7
Leafield Copse RG12 . . . 118 F5
Leafy Oak Farm GU17 . . . 150 A4
Lea Heath Way RG10 . . . . . 88 D5
Leaholme Gdns SL1 . . . . . . 41 D8
Lea Inf Sch SL2 . . . . 43 B6
Lea Jun Sch SL2 . . . . 43 B6
Leander Pl RG31 . . . . 84 D4
Lea Rd GU15 . . . . 151 B2
Leas Dr SL0 . . . . 44 E7
Lea The
Finchampstead RG40 . . . . 141 F8
Thorpe Lea TW20 . . . . 96 C1
Leaver Rd RG9 . . . . 15 C1
Leaves Gn RG12 . . . . 118 D3
Lea View RG18 . . . . 79 C8
LECKHAMPSTEAD 49 F5
LECKHAMPSTEAD
THICKET 49 E7
Ledbury Cl RG30 . . . . 58 C1
Ledbury Dr RG31 . . . . 84 D4
Ledger La SL6 . . . . 65 D5
Ledger's Rd SL1 . . . . 42 D4
Ledran Cl
Earley RG6 . . . . 87 C1
Lower Earley RG6 . . . . . . 114 C8
Lee Ct RG5 . . . . 87 E7
Leeds Rd SL1 . . . . 42 E6
Lee La SL6 . . . . 18 E2
Lees Cl SL6 . . . . 39 B5
Lee's Ct GU20 . . . . 146 D4
Lees Gdns SL6 . . . . 39 B5
Leeson Gdns SL4 . . . . 41 E2
Lees Wlk SL7 . . . . 1 C2
Legoland Windsor★ SL4 . . 66 D2
Leicester RG12 . . . . 118 E2
Leicester Cl RG9 . . . . 15 D3
Leigh Field RG7 . . . . 136 F6
Leigh Pk SL3 . . . . 68 B7
Leigh Rd SL1 . . . . 42 B6
Leigh Sq SL4 . . . . 66 D5
Leighton Ct RG2 . . . . 86 E3
Leighton Gdns SL6 . . . . . . 20 B1
Leighton Ho 6 SL7 . . . . 1 E2
Leighton Park Sch RG2 . . . 86 E4
Leiston Cl 3 RG6 . . . . 87 D1
Leiston Spur SL1 . . . . 42 E7
Leith Cl
Crowthorne RG45 . . . . . . 143 A7
Leith Cl continued
Slough SL1 . . . . 43 A5
Le Marchant Rd GU15,
GU16 . . . . 151 F3
Lemart Cl RG30 . . . . 84 E8
Lemington Gr RG12 . . . . . 118 B3
Leney Cl RG40 . . . . 116 D8
Lenham Cl RG41 . . . . 88 E1
Lennox Cl RG31 . . . . 84 B4
Lennox Rd RG6 . . . . 87 A5
LENT 21 B1
Lent Gn SL1 . . . . 21 B1
Lent Green La SL1 . . . . 21 B1
LENT RISE 41 A8
Lent Rise Comb Sch SL1 . 41 B8
Lent Rise Rd SL1 . . . . 21 B1
Leonard Ct RG7 . . . . 83 E3
Leonardslee Cres RG14 . . 105 D4
Leopold Mall 6 SL1 . . . . . 42 F4
Leopold Wlk RG1 . . . . 86 D7
Leppington RG12 . . . . . . 118 B2
Lerwick Dr SL1 . . . . 42 E8
Lesford Rd RG1 . . . . 85 E5
Lesley Ct 16 RG30 . . . . . . 85 D6
Leslie Dunne Ho SL4 . . . . . 66 E5
Leslie Southern Ct RG14 . 105 B4
Lesters Rd SL6 . . . . 19 D6
Letchworth Ave TW14 . . . . 98 F8
LETCOMBE BASSETT 6 E7
Letcombe Ct 6 RG1 . . . . . 86 B6
Letcombe Sq RG12 . . . . . 118 F5
Letcombe St RG1 . . . . 86 B7
Letts Gn RG5 . . . . 87 F5
Leverkusen Rd RG12 . . . . 118 B6
LEVERTON 73 C1
Leverton Farm Bldgs
RG17 . . . . 73 C1
Leverton La RG17 . . . . 73 B1
Lewendon Rd RG14 . . . . . 104 E5
Lewes Ct SL1 . . . . 42 C4
Lewington Mews RG17 . . 100 D4
Lewins Farm Ct SL1 . . . . . 41 F6
Lewins Way SL1 . . . . 41 F6
Lewin Terr TW14 . . . . 98 D8
Lewisham Way GU47 . . . 143 D2
Lewis Ind Est RG17 . . . . . . 48 A3
Lewis Wlk RG14 . . . . 130 C6
Lexington Ave SL6 . . . . 39 D5
Lexington Gr RG2 . . . . . . 113 C6
Leyburn Cl RG5 . . . . 88 A8
Leycester Cl GU20 . . . . . 146 B6
Leyland Gdns RG2 . . . . . 113 E6
Leylands La TW19 . . . . 70 A2
Leys Gdns RG14 . . . . 104 F4
Leyside RG45 . . . . 143 A5
Liberty Ho 2 KT16 . . . . . 123 F1
Liberty Ho RG19 . . . . 132 A5
Liberty Of Earley Ho 5
RG6 . . . . 87 C1
Libra Ho HP10 . . . . 3 A8
Library Par RG5 . . . . 87 E7
Licensed Victuallers Sch
SL5 . . . . 119 C7
Lichfield Cl 1 RG6 . . . . . . 87 C1
Lichfields RG12 . . . . 118 E7
Liddell SL4 . . . . 66 C4
Liddell Cl RG40 . . . . 141 E3
Liddell Pl SL4 . . . . 66 C4
Liddell Sq 14 SL4 . . . . 66 C5
Liddell Way SL4 . . . . 66 C4
Liddel Way SL5 . . . . 119 F5
Lido Rd OX11 . . . . 9 F8
Lidstone Cl RG6 . . . . 114 D8
Lidstone Ct SL3 . . . . 43 E7
Liebenrood Rd RG30 . . . . . 85 C6
Lightlands La SL6 . . . . 19 F5
LIGHTWATER 153 A8
Lightwater Ctry Pk★
GU18 . . . . 145 F1
Lightwater Mdw GU18 . . . 153 B8
Lightwater Rd GU18 . . . . 153 C8
Lightwater Village Sch
GU18 . . . . 146 A1
Lightwood RG12 . . . . 118 D3
Liguel Cl RG17 . . . . 100 D4
Lilac Cl RG8 . . . . 57 C5
Lilac Ct SL2 . . . . 21 F2
Lilacs The RG41 . . . . 115 C4
Lilac Wlk
Brimpton RG19 . . . . 133 B5
Reading RG31 . . . . 84 C5
LILLEY 29 A4
Lilley Way SL1 . . . . 41 E5
Lillibrooke Cres SL6 . . . . . 39 A3
Lily Ct RG41 . . . . 116 A6
Lily Hill Dr RG12 . . . . 118 E7
Lily Hill Rd RG12 . . . . 118 F7
Lima Ct RG1 . . . . 85 F6
Lime Ave
Camberley GU15 . . . . 152 A6
Windsor SL4 . . . . 67 F7
Winkfield SL4 . . . . 93 F5
Lime Cl
Brimpton RG19 . . . . 133 A5
Newbury RG14 . . . . 105 D4
Wokingham RG41 . . . . . . 115 F5
Limecroft GU46 . . . . 149 C5
Limefield Cl RG6 . . . . 87 E3
Lime Lodge 4 TW16 . . . . . 98 F1
Lime Mews TW20 . . . . 95 F3
Limerick Cl RG42 . . . . . . 118 A8
Limes Cl TW15 . . . . 98 A3
Limes Rd TW20 . . . . 95 F3
Limes The
Windsor SL4 . . . . 66 C6

Limes The *continued*
Winkfield Row RG42 . . . . . . 91 F3
Lime Tree Copse RG42 . . . 92 A1
Lime Tree Ct SL4 . . . . 95 C8
Lime Tree Rd RG8. . . . . 34 B6
Limetree Wlk GU25 . . . . . 122 E5
Lime Wlk
Bracknell RG12 . . . . 118 C5
Maidenhead SL6 . . . . 39 A8
Limmer Cl RG41 . . . . 115 C4
LIMMERHILL. 115 E5
Limmerhill Rd RG41. . . . . 115 E5
Linchfield Rd SL3 . . . . 68 C6
Lincoln Cl
Frimley GU15. . . . . 152 B4
Winnersh RG41 . . . . 88 A3
Lincoln Ct
Newbury RG14. . . . . 104 F2
[3] Slough SL1 . . . . 42 E3
Lincoln Gdns RG10. . . . . . . 61 D5
Lincoln Hatch La SL1. . . . . 21 C1
Lincoln Ho HP10 . . . . 3 D3
Lincoln Rd
Maidenhead SL6 . . . . 39 B8
Reading RG2 . . . . 86 C4
Lincolnshire Gdns RG42 . . 91 E1
Lincoln Way
Charlton TW16. . . . . 125 E8
Slough SL1. . . . . 41 D6
Lindale Cl GU25. . . . . 121 F5
Lindberg Way RG5 . . . . 61 B1
Lind Cl RG6. . . . . 87 B2
Linden [3] RG12 . . . . 118 F4
Linden Ave SL6 . . . . 19 D1
Linden Cl
Newbury RG14. . . . . 104 F4
Wokingham RG41 . . . . 115 F4
Linden Ct
Camberley GU15 . . . . 151 F7
Englefield Green TW20 . . . . 95 B2
Linden Dr SL2 . . . . 22 C4
Linden Hill La RG10 . . . . . . 37 C2
Lindenhill Rd RG42. . . . . . 117 F8
Linden Ho SL3 . . . . 44 B1
Lindenmuth Way RG19 . . 131 F5
Linden Pl TW18. . . . . 97 A4
Linden Rd
Reading RG2 . . . . 86 E2
Woodley RG5. . . . . 87 D4
Linden Way TW17. . . . . . . 125 C4
Lindisfarne Way RG2. . . . . 86 A2
Lindores Ho SL6 . . . . 65 B8
Lindores Rd SL6 . . . . 65 B8
Lindsay Cl TW19 . . . . 70 D2
Lindsay Ct TW17 . . . . 125 C4
Lindsay Dr TW17. . . . . 125 D3
Lindsey Cl RG41 . . . . 115 E6
Lindsey Gdns TW14 . . . . . . 98 D8
Lines Rd RG10 . . . . 88 F5
Ling Dr GU18 . . . . 152 F7
Lingholm Cl
Maidenhead SL6 . . . . 39 C6
Reading RG30 . . . . 84 F5
Lingwood RG12 . . . . 118 C3
LINKENHOLT. 147 D1
Link Ho [2] RG14 . . . . 105 A2
Link Rd
Datchet SL3 . . . . 68 C6
East Bedfont TW14 . . . . 98 F8
Newbury RG14. . . . . 105 A2
Links App HP10 . . . . 3 B8
Linkscroft Ave TW15 . . . . . 98 B2
Links Dr RG30 . . . . 85 A8
Links Rd
Ashford TW15 . . . . 97 E3
Flackwell Heath HP10 . . . . . . 3 C8
Links The SL5 . . . . 119 E7
Links Way HP10. . . . . 3 B8
Linkswood Rd SL1 . . . . 21 C3
Link The
Slough SL2. . . . . 43 B7
Yateley GU46. . . . . 149 C7
Link View RG14. . . . . 104 F7
Linkway
Camberley GU15 . . . . 151 C4
Crowthorne RG45 . . . . 142 F5
Link Way
Arborfield Cross RG2. . . . . 114 E2
Staines TW18. . . . . 97 B2
Thatcham RG18 . . . . 106 B4
Linnet Cl RG31. . . . . 84 B6
Linnet La RG20 . . . . 131 F3
Linnet Wlk RG41 . . . . 115 F6
Lintott Ct TW19. . . . . 70 D1
Lion Cl TW17 . . . . 124 E6
Lion Ct [3] RG1. . . . . 86 A8
Lionel Ct RG10. . . . . 61 D5
Lion Mews [3] RG17 . . . . . . 25 B2
Lip La
Wickham, Elcot RG20 . . . . 102 D8
Wickham RG20 . . . . 75 E2
Lippincote Ct RG31 . . . . . . 57 E3
Lipscomb Cl RG18. . . . . 79 B6
Lipscombe Cl RG14 . . . . . 104 E2
Liscombe RG12 . . . . 118 B2
Liscombe Ho RG12. . . . . . . 118 B2
Lisle Cl RG14 . . . . 104 F5
Lismore Cl RG5 . . . . 87 E4
Lismore Ct TW18. . . . . 97 B3
Lismore Pk SL2 . . . . 42 F7
Lister Cl RG8 . . . . 57 C5
Liston Ct [5] SL7 . . . . 1 D2
Liston Ho SL7. . . . . 1 D2
Liston Rd SL7. . . . . 1 D2
Litcham Spur SL1 . . . . 42 D7
Lithgow's Rd TW14, TW6 . . 71 F3
Litlington Cl RG6 . . . . 114 C8
Little Acre SL4. . . . . 67 A4
Little Acres SL3. . . . . 69 D7
Little Aldershot La RG26. 134 B2
Little Boltons [9] SL7 . . . . 1 E2
Little Bowden La RG8 . . . . 55 F4
Littlebrook Ave SL2 . . . . . . 41 E8
Little Buntings SL4. . . . . . . 66 F4
Little Cl HP10. . . . . 3 B6
Little Copse GU46. . . . . . . 149 D7
Littlecote Dr RG1 . . . . 85 E6
Littlecote Rd SN8 . . . . 99 B5
Little Croft GU46. . . . . 149 D4
Littlecroft Rd [2] TW20 . . . 95 F3
Little Croft Rd RG8. . . . . . . 34 C5
Littledale Cl RG12. . . . . . . 118 E6
Littledown Cotts SL1. . . . . 42 F5
Littledown Rd SL1 . . . . 42 F5
Littledown Sch SL1 . . . . . . 42 F6
Little Elms UB3 . . . . 71 D7
Littlefield Ct UB7 . . . . 70 D7
Littlefield Gn SL6 . . . . 63 F6
LITTLEFIELD GREEN 63 F6
Little Foxes RG40 . . . . 142 A7
Little Fryth RG40. . . . . 142 D6
Little Glebe RG4 . . . . 60 E3
LITTLE HEATH 84 B8
Little Heath Rd RG31. . . . . . 84 A7
Little Heath Sch RG31. . . . . 84 B7
Little Hill Rd RG10 . . . . 88 D4
Little Horse Cl RG5. . . . . . . 87 E4
LITTLE HUNGERFORD 79 C8
Littlejohn's La RG30. . . . . . 58 C1
Little John's La RG30. . . . . 85 C8
Little La RG7. . . . . 107 C6
Little London Rd RG7 . . . 136 B1
LITTLE MARLOW 2 D5
Little Marlow CE Sch SL7 . 2 C5
Little Marlow Rd SL7. . . . . . 1 E3
Little Moor GU47. . . . . 143 C1
Little Oak Cl TW17 . . . . . . 124 F5
Little Oaks Dr RG31 . . . . . . 84 C8
Little Paddock GU15 . . . . 152 A8
Littleport Spur SL1. . . . . . . 42 E7
Little Ringdale RG12 . . . . 118 E5
Little Saffron RG18. . . . . . . 79 B6
LITTLE SANDHURST 143 B1
Little St RG1. . . . . 85 E8
Littlestead Cl RG4. . . . . 59 E5
LITTLESTEAD GREEN 59 E7
Little Sutton La SL3 . . . . . . 44 C1
LITTLETON 125 A6
Littleton CE Inf Sch
TW17 . . . . 125 A6
LITTLETON COMMON 98 D1
Littleton Ho TW15. . . . . 98 C1
Littleton La TW17 . . . . 124 E4
Littleton Rd TW15. . . . . 98 C1
Little Vigo GU46 . . . . 149 B4
LITTLEWICK GREEN. 38 B4
Littlewick Green Montessori
Sch SL6 . . . . 38 C4
Little Woodlands SL4 . . . . 66 F4
Litton Rd RG2. . . . . 86 D2
Liverpool Rd
Reading RG1 . . . . 86 E8
Slough SL1. . . . . 42 B7
Livery Cl RG1 . . . . 86 B7
Living Rainforest The★
RG18. . . . . 53 C5
Livingstone Ct TW19 . . . . . 97 E7
Livingstone Gdns RG5. . . . 87 E5
Livingstone Rd RG14 . . . . 105 B2
Llangar Gr RG45 . . . . 143 A5
Llanvair Cl SL5 . . . . 120 A3
Llanvair Dr SL5 . . . . 119 F3
Llewellyn Pk RG10 . . . . 61 D6
Lochinvar Cl SL1. . . . . 42 B4
Lochinver RG12. . . . . 118 B2
Lock Ave SL6 . . . . 20 C2
Lockbridge Ct SL6 . . . . 40 C8
Lock Bridge Rd SL8 . . . . 3 A3
Locke Gdns SL3. . . . . 43 C4
Lockets Cl SL4. . . . . 66 D6
Lock La SL6 . . . . 39 C4
Lock Mead SL6 . . . . 20 C2
Lock Path SL4 . . . . 66 D8
Lock Pl RG1 . . . . 86 D7
Lockram La RG7 . . . . 111 C1
Lock Rd SL7 . . . . 1 F1
Lockside Ct RG7 . . . . 109 C3
Locksley Ct [4] SL1 . . . . 42 E3
Locksley Gdns RG41. . . . . . 88 D3
Locks Ride SL5 . . . . 92 C2
Lockstile Mead RG8. . . . . . 34 C7
Lockstile Way RG8 . . . . 34 C6
Lockton Chase SL5. . . . . . 119 D6
Lockton Ho RG40 . . . . 116 C6
Lockyer Cl RG41 . . . . 88 A2
Lodden View RG10. . . . . 61 E3
Loddon Bridge Rd RG5 . . . 87 F6
Loddon Cl GU15 . . . . 152 A6
Loddon Court Farm Park
Homes RG7 . . . . 138 F7
Loddon Ct RG6 . . . . 87 C4
Loddon Dr
Charvil RG10 . . . . 61 A8
Maidenhead SL6 . . . . 39 D8
Loddon Hall Rd RG10. . . . . 61 E5
Loddon Prim Sch RG6. . . . 87 D3
Loddon Rd SL8 . . . . 3 A4
Loddon Spur SL1 . . . . 42 E7
Loddon Vale Ctr RG5. . . . . 88 A7
Lodge Cl
Englefield Green TW20 . . . . 95 D3
Marlow SL7 . . . . 1 E1
Slough SL1. . . . . 42 C4
Lodge Gr GU46 . . . . 149 F6
Lodge Rd RG10 . . . . 88 E7
Lodge The
Englefield Green TW20 . . . . 95 C3
Newbury RG14. . . . . 105 A4
Slough SL2. . . . . 43 B8
Lodge Way
Charlton TW17. . . . . 125 C7
Stanwell TW15. . . . . 97 E6
Windsor SL4 . . . . 66 E4
Lodgings of the Military
Knights [3] SL4 . . . . 67 D6
Logan Cl RG30. . . . . 84 F7
Lois Dr TW17 . . . . 125 B4
Lomond Ave RG4 . . . . 59 E5
London Ct RG14 . . . . 105 C3
London Rd
Ascot SL5. . . . . 120 D5
Ashford TW15, TW18,
TW19 . . . . 97 D5
Bagshot GU15, GU19. . . . . 145 D2
Blackwater GU15, GU17 . . 150 E4
Blewbury OX11 . . . . 11 F8
Bracknell RG12, SL5 . . . . . 119 C6
Brands Hill SL3 . . . . 69 B8
Camberley GU15 . . . . 151 C6
Datchet SL3. . . . . 68 C7
Egham TW18 . . . . 96 F4
Englefield Green TW20 . . . . 95 C1
Newbury RG14. . . . . 105 C3
Reading RG1 . . . . 86 D7
Slough SL3. . . . . 43 D2
Sunningdale, Blacknest
SL5 . . . . 121 B6
Sunningdale, Shrubs Hill SL5,
GU25. . . . . 121 C4
Thatcham RG18, RG19. . . . 106 F3
Twyford RG10 . . . . 61 E6
Virginia Water GU25,
TW20 . . . . 122 B7
Windlesham GU19, GU20,
SL5 . . . . 146 C7
Wokingham RG40 . . . . 116 E6
Woodley RG6. . . . . 87 B8
London Road Ind Est
RG14. . . . . 105 B3
London St
Chertsey KT16. . . . . 124 A2
Reading RG1 . . . . 86 B7
Loneacre GU20 . . . . 146 E4
Longacre RG14 . . . . 130 D8
Long Barn La RG2. . . . . 86 C3
Longbourn SL4 . . . . 67 A4
Longbourne Way KT16 . . 123 F3
Longbridge Rd RG19 . . . . 106 F2
Longbrook Ct GU20 . . . . . 146 D4
Long Cl
Farnham Common SL2. . . . . 22 B5
Kintbury RG17 . . . . 102 B2
Long Close Prep Sch SL3. 43 A3
Longcroft Rd RG19. . . . . . 106 E2
Longcross Sta KT16 . . . . . 121 F1
Longdon Rd RG41. . . . . 88 C1
Longdown Lodge GU47. . 150 B8
Longdown Rd GU47 . . . . . 143 B1
Long Dr SL1 . . . . 21 C2
Longfield Rd RG10 . . . . 61 D6
LONGFORD 70 C6
Longford Ave
Feltham TW14 . . . . 71 F1
Stanwell TW19. . . . . 97 E7
Longford Cl GU15 . . . . 151 D4
Longford Com Sch TW14 . 98 F8
LONGFORDMOOR 70 A6
Longford Rdbt UB7 . . . . 70 B6
Longford Way TW19 . . . . . 97 E7
Long Furlong Dr SL2 . . . . . 21 E1
Long Gr
Tadley RG26. . . . . 134 D2
Upper Bucklebury RG7 . . . 107 C5
Long Half Acre SL6 . . . . . . 38 B4
Long Hedge RG17. . . . . 25 D2
Long Hill Rd RG12, SL5. . . 119 A7
Longhurst Cl RG4 . . . . 59 C3
Long La
Brightwalton RG20 . . . . 28 E3
Cookham Rise SL6. . . . . 19 D5
Hermitage RG14, RG18 . . . . 78 F2
Holyport, Braywoodside SL6 64 D4
Holyport, Touchen-end SL6 . 64 E6
Newbury RG18. . . . . 105 D7
Purley on T RG31. . . . . 57 B4
Stanwell TW19. . . . . 97 F7
Longlands Way GU15. . . . 152 D5
Long Lane Prim Sch RG31 57 B4
Longleat Dr RG31 . . . . 57 B3
Longleat Gdns SL6 . . . . 39 D6
Longleat Way TW14 . . . . . . 98 D8
Long Mdw RG8 . . . . 34 B5
Longmead
Ball Hill RG20 . . . . 129 F1
Windsor SL4 . . . . 66 E6
Longmead La SL1 . . . . 21 D5
Longmeadow GU15, GU16 151 F3
Long Mickle GU47 . . . . . . 143 B1
Longmoor Cl RG40 . . . . . . 141 E6
Longmoor La RG7. . . . . . . 137 A7
Longmoors RG42 . . . . 117 E8
Longmore Rd RG2 . . . . . . 113 D6
Long Readings La SL2. . . . 22 B2
Longridge Cl RG30 . . . . 85 B7
Long Row RG20. . . . . 49 A7
Longshot Ind Est RG12 . . . 117 E7
Longshot La RG12. . . . . . . 117 E7
Longside Cl TW20. . . . . . . 123 C8
Long's Way RG40 . . . . 116 E7
Longview HP9 . . . . 3 F8
Longwater Ave RG2,
RG30 . . . . 112 D8
Longwater La RG40 . . . . . 141 E2
Longwater Rd
Bracknell RG12 . . . . 118 C3
Finchampstead RG40. . . . . 141 E2
Long Wlk The SL4. . . . . 94 D7
Long Wlk The★ SL4 . . . . . . 67 D4
Longwood RG14 . . . . 105 B6
Longwood Ave SL3. . . . . . . 44 B1
Longworth Ave RG31. . . . . 84 B7
Longworth Dr SL6 . . . . 20 C1
Lonsdale Cl SL6. . . . . 20 A1
Lonsdale Way SL6 . . . . 40 C1
Look Ahead SL1 . . . . 42 E4
Look Out Discovery Ctr The★
RG12. . . . . 118 D1
Loosen Dr SL6. . . . . 39 A3
Lord Knyvett Cl TW19 . . . . 70 D1
Lord Knyvetts Ct [12] TW19 70 E1
Lord Mayors Dr SL2. . . . . . 22 A7
Lord Raglan Ho SL4 . . . . . . 67 C4
Lords Bridge Ct TW17 . . . 125 B2
Loring Rd SL4 . . . . 66 F6
Lorne Cl SL1. . . . . 42 B3
Lorne Pl [4] RG1 . . . . 85 E7
Lorne St RG1 . . . . 85 E7
Lorraine Rd GU15 . . . . 151 F8
Lorraine Sch GU15. . . . . . . 151 E8
Lory Ridge GU19. . . . . 145 E4
Losfield Rd SL4 . . . . 66 E6
Lossie Dr SL0. . . . . 44 B6
Loughborough RG12 . . . . 118 E3
Loundyes Cl RG18. . . . . . . 106 B4
Lovatt Cl RG31 . . . . 84 B7
Lovedean Ct RG12 . . . . . . 118 E3
LOVE GREEN. 44 D8
Love Green La SL0 . . . . 44 E8
Lovegrove Dr SL2 . . . . 21 F1
Love Hill La SL3. . . . . 44 A6
Lovejoy La SL4. . . . . 66 D5
Love La
Iver SL0. . . . . 44 D7
Newbury RG14. . . . . 105 A6
Lovelace Cl SL6. . . . . 17 F4
Lovelace Rd RG12. . . . . . . 117 E5
Lovel La SL4. . . . . 93 B3
Lovell Cl RG9 . . . . 35 C8
Lovells Cl GU18 . . . . 146 B1
Lovel Rd SL4 . . . . 93 A4
Loverock Rd RG30 . . . . 58 D1
Love's Cl RG7. . . . . 111 A3
Loves Wood RG7. . . . . 136 F5
Lovett Gdns SL6 . . . . 20 C3
Lovett Rd TW18. . . . . 96 C4
Lowbrook Dr SL6 . . . . 39 A3
Lowbrook Prim Sch SL6. . 39 A3
Lowbury RG12 . . . . 118 E5
Lower Armour Rd RG31 . . 57 D1
LOWER ASSENDON 15 A6
LOWER BASILDON. 34 E2
Lower Boyndon Rd SL6. . . 39 E6
Lower Britwell Rd SL2. . . . 21 D1
Lower Broadmoor Rd
RG45 . . . . 143 D4
Lower Brook St [21] RG1. . . 86 A6
Lower Canes GU46. . . . . . 149 A6
LOWER CAVERSHAM. 59 D1
Lower Charles St GU15 . . 151 C6
Lower Church Rd GU47. . 149 E8
Lower Cippenham La SL1 41 F6
Lower Comm RG27. . . . . . 140 F1
LOWER COMMON 140 F1
Lower Cookham Rd SL6 . . 20 C2
LOWER EARLEY 87 A1
Lower Earley Way RG6 . . 114 C8
Lower Earley Way N RG6 . 87 F2
Lower Earley Way W
Earley RG6. . . . . 113 F7
Lower Earley RG6 . . . . 114 A8
Lower Elmstone Dr RG31 . 57 C1
Lower Farm Ct RG19 . . . . 105 F1
LOWER FELTHAM 98 E5
Lower Field Rd RG1. . . . . . 86 A6
LOWER GREEN 127 B5
LOWER HALLIFORD 125 D2
Lower Henley Rd RG4 . . . . 59 D3
Lower Henwick Farm
RG18 . . . . 105 F5
Lower Lees Rd SL2. . . . . . . 22 B2
Lower Meadow Rd RG2. . . 86 D2
Lower Mill Field GU19. . . 145 D2
Lower Moor [2] GU46. . . . 149 D5
Lower Mount RG1. . . . . 86 D5
Lower Nursery SL5. . . . . . 121 A4
LOWER PADWORTH 109 C4
Lower Pound La SL7 . . . . . 18 D8
Lower Raymond Almshouses
[13] RG14. . . . . 104 F2
Lower Rd
Chilton OX11 . . . . 10 D8
Cookham Rise SL6. . . . . 19 E7
Lower Ridge SL8. . . . . 3 B4
Lower Sandhurst Rd RG40,
GU47 . . . . 142 C2
LOWER SHIPLAKE 36 A3
Lower Ventnor Cotts SL6. 19 C8
Lower Village Rd SL5 . . . 120 C4
Lower Ward SL4 . . . . 67 D7
Lower Way RG19. . . . . 106 B3
Lower Wokingham Rd RG40,
RG45 . . . . 142 D5
Lower Woodspeen Ct
RG20 . . . . 104 A7
Lowes Cl RG9. . . . . 36 B4
Lowesden Works RG17 . . . 46 A5
Lowestoft Cl RG6 . . . . 87 D2
Lowestoft Dr SL1 . . . . 41 D7
Loweswater Wlk GU15 . . 152 D4
Lowfield Cl GU18 . . . . 153 A8
Lowfield Ct RG4 . . . . 59 C5
Lowfield Gn RG4. . . . . 59 E4
Lowfield Rd RG4. . . . . 59 D5
Lowlands Dr TW19 . . . . 70 D2
Lowlands Rd GU17 . . . . . . 150 C4
Lowry Cl GU47 . . . . 150 D6
Lowther Cl RG41 . . . . 115 F8
Lowther Rd RG41 . . . . 115 F8
Loxwood RG6. . . . . 87 C2
Loxwood Cl
East Bedfont TW14 . . . . 98 D7
Three Mile Cross RG7 . . . . 113 A4
Lucan Dr TW18 . . . . 97 D1
Lucas Cl GU46 . . . . 149 D5
Lucas Gn GU24 . . . . 153 D4
LUCAS GREEN 153 E5
Lucas Green Rd GU24 . . . 153 E5
Lucey Cl RG31 . . . . 57 B3
Lucie Ave TW15. . . . . 98 B2
Luckley-Oakfield Sch
RG40. . . . . 116 B3
Luckley Path RG40 . . . . . . 116 C6
Luckley Rd RG41 . . . . 116 B3
Luckley Wood RG41. . . . . 116 B3
Luckmore Dr RG6. . . . . 87 A3
Luddington Ave GU25 . . . 122 F7
Ludgrove Sch RG40 . . . . . 116 D3
Lud Lodge TW15 . . . . 97 E6
Ludlow RG12 . . . . 118 B2
Ludlow Cl RG14. . . . . 105 E4
Ludlow Ho SL6 . . . . 39 E6
Ludlow Rd
Feltham TW13 . . . . 98 F5
Maidenhead SL6 . . . . 39 E6
Luff Cl SL4 . . . . 66 E4
Luker Ave RG9. . . . . 15 D3
Lulworth Rd RG2. . . . . 113 C8
Lunds Farm Rd RG5 . . . . . . 88 A8
Lundy Ct SL1 . . . . 41 E6
Lundy Ho RG2 . . . . 86 A2
Lundy La RG30. . . . . 85 C7
Lupin Cl GU19 . . . . 145 C1
Lupin Ride RG45 . . . . 143 B7
Luscina View RG1. . . . . 86 C8
Luscombe Cl RG4 . . . . 59 D2
Lutman La SL6. . . . . 19 F2
Lutman's Haven RG10. . . . . 37 E5
Lutterworth Cl RG42 . . . . . 91 C1
Lutton Cl RG6. . . . . 113 F8
Lych Gate Cl GU47 . . . . . . 149 F8
Lycroft Cl RG8 . . . . 34 C7
Lydbury RG12. . . . . 118 F6
Lydford Ave SL2 . . . . 42 D8
Lydford Rd RG1. . . . . 86 E6
Lydiaville Mobile Home Pk
[1] RG41. . . . . 88 A2
Lydney RG12. . . . . 118 B2
Lydsey Cl SL2. . . . . 22 A2
Lyefield Ct RG4 . . . . 59 B6
Lyell Pl E SL4. . . . . 66 C4
Lyell Pl W SL4 . . . . 66 C4
Lyell Rd SL4 . . . . 66 C4
Lyell Wlk E SL4 . . . . 66 C4
Lyell Wlk W SL4 . . . . 66 C4
Lyle Ho RG8 . . . . 55 F1
Lyme Gr RG31 . . . . 57 D1
Lymington Ave GU46 . . . . 149 C5
Lymington Gate RG4 . . . . . 58 E5
Lynchets View RG17. . . . . . 24 E5
Lynch Hill La SL1 . . . . 21 E2
Lynch Hill Prim Sch SL2. . 21 F2
Lynch La RG17 . . . . 25 B3
Lynden Cl SL6 . . . . 65 B8
Lynden Mews RG2 . . . . 86 B5
Lyndhurst Ave
Blackwater GU17. . . . . 150 C6
Cookham Rise SL6. . . . . 19 E6
Lyndhurst Cl RG12 . . . . . . 119 A6
Lyndhurst Rd
Ascot SL5. . . . . 120 A5
Goring RG8 . . . . 34 C7
Reading RG30 . . . . 58 A1
Lyndhurst Sch GU15 . . . . 151 B5
Lyndwood Dr SL4 . . . . 68 A1
Lyndwood Par SL4 . . . . 68 A1
LYNE 123 B1
Lyne Cl GU25 . . . . 122 F3
Lyne Crossing Rd KT16,
GU25 . . . . 123 B3
Lyne Ct KT16 . . . . 122 F2
Lynegrove Ave TW15 . . . . . 98 C3
Lyneham Gdns SL6. . . . . . . 19 B1
Lyneham Rd RG45. . . . . . . 143 B5
Lyne La
Lyne KT16 . . . . 123 A2
Virginia Water KT16, TW20,
GU25. . . . . 123 A3
Lyne Place Manor GU25 . 122 F2
Lyne Rd GU25. . . . . 122 E3
Lyngfield Pk SL6. . . . . 65 D8
Lynmouth Ct RG1 . . . . 59 B1
Lynmouth Rd RG1. . . . . 59 A1
Lynn Cl TW15 . . . . 98 D3
Lynton Cl RG5 . . . . 87 C5
Lynton Ct
[4] Newbury RG14. . . . . . . 105 A4
[4] Reading RG1 . . . . 59 A1
Lynton Gn SL6. . . . . 39 E7
Lynwood SL5 . . . . 120 E4
Lynwood Ave
Egham TW20 . . . . 95 E2
Slough SL3. . . . . 43 D3
Lynwood Chase RG42 . . . . 91 C1
Lynwood Cres SL5 . . . . . . 120 E3
Lynwood Ct TW15. . . . . 97 F3
Lyon Cl RG19 . . . . 106 F2

Lyon Oaks RG42 .... 91 B2
Lyon Rd RG45 .... 143 C6
Lyon Sq RG30 .... 85 A8
Lyon Way GU16 .... 151 C1
Lyon Way Ind Est GU16 .. 151 C1
Lysander Cl RG5 .... 88 A8
Lysander Dr RG12 .... 118 C5
Lysander Mead SL6 ...... 40 C8
Lytchett Minster Cl 4
RG12 .... 118 F4
Lytham RG12 .... 117 E3
Lytham Cl RG30 .... 85 C4
Lytham Ct SL5 .... 120 C4
Lytham End RG31 .... 57 B3
Lytham Rd RG5 .... 87 E7

M

Mabett Cl RG2 .... 140 E8
Mabley Ct RG12 .... 118 A3
MacAdam Ave RG45 ..... 143 C7
Mc Ardle Way SL3 .... 69 D7
MacArthur Cl RG30 ...... 84 F8
McAuliffe Dr SL1, SL2 ..... 21 F8
Macbeth Ct RG42 .... 118 E8
McCarthy Way RG40 .... 141 F8
McCrae's Wlk RG10 ...... 36 D2
MacDonald Rd GU18 .... 153 A8
Mace Cl RG6 .... 87 A1
McIlroys Bldg RG1 .... 86 A7
Mackay Cl RG31 .... 84 E3
McKay Trad Est SL3 ...... 69 E5
McKenzie Ct 4 RG14 .... 104 F4
Mackenzie Mall 3 SL1 ... 42 F4
Mackenzie St 2 SL1 ..... 42 F4
McKernan Ct GU47 ...... 149 F8
Macklin Cl RG17 .... 100 D5
MacLarens Dr RG42 ..... 119 A8
Macnaghten Woods
GU15 .... 151 E6
McNair Cl RG6 .... 87 A1
MacPhail Cl RG40 .... 116 E8
Macrae Rd GU46 .... 149 C6
Maddle Rd RG17 .... 24 D7
Maddock Cl RG2 .... 113 D4
Madeira Pl 8 RG14 ..... 105 A2
Madejski Stad (Reading FC)
RG2 .... 112 F8
Madingley RG12 .... 118 B1
Madox Brown End GU47 . 150 E6
Mafeking Rd TW19 .... 96 B6
Magdalene Rd
Littleton TW17 .... 124 F6
Sandhurst GU47 .... 143 F2
Magill Cl RG7 .... 113 B2
Magna Carta La TW19 .... 95 E7
Magna Carta Sch The
TW18 .... 96 D2
Magna Rd TW20 .... 95 B2
Magnolia Cl
Sandhurst GU47 .... 143 D1
Winkfield RG42 .... 119 A8
Magnolia Ct
Brimpton RG19 .... 133 B6
Woodley RG5 .... 88 A7
Magnolia Gdns SL3 ...... 43 C3
Magnolia Way
Wokingham RG41 .... 115 F5
Wooburn Green HP10 ...... 3 E7
Magpie Cl RG19 .... 106 B3
Magpie Way
Reading RG31 .... 84 B6
Slough SL2 .... 21 F1
Maguire Dr GU16 .... 152 C3
Mahonia Cl GU24 .... 153 F6
Maiden Erlegh Dr RG6 ... 87 B4
Maiden Erlegh Sch RG6 .. 87 B4
Maidenhatch RG8 .... 55 F1
MAIDENHEAD 39 F4
Maidenhead Bsns Campus
The SL6 .... 38 E3
MAIDENHEAD COURT 20 C4
Maidenhead Court Pk
SL6 .... 20 B3
Maidenhead Ho 21 RG14 104 F2
Maidenhead Office Pk
SL6 .... 38 E2
Maidenhead Rd
Binfield RG40 .... 89 E3
Cookham Rise SL6 .... 19 F6
Newell Green RG42 .... 91 B6
Windsor SL4 .... 66 E7
Maidenhead Sta SL6 ..... 39 F6
Maidenhead Trad Pk SL6 . 40 B2
Maiden Lane Ctr 1 RG6 .. 87 D1
Maiden Pl RG6 .... 87 D2
Maidensfield RG41 .... 88 D2
Maiden's Gn SL4 .... 92 B6
MAIDEN'S GREEN 92 B5
Main Ave RG31 .... 84 B6
Main Dr
Bracknell RG42 .... 91 F2
Iver SL0 .... 44 E3
Winkfield, Newell Green
RG42 .... 92 A1
Winkfield RG42, SL5 ..... 119 B8
Main Gate Lodges SL4 .... 94 F5
Mainprize Rd RG12 ...... 118 E7
Main St
Chaddleworth RG20 ...... 49 A7
Chilton OX11 .... 10 D8
Greenham RG19 .... 131 F5
Newtown RG19 .... 132 A5
West Ilsley RG20 .... 10 A2
Mainstone Rd GU24 ..... 153 F3
Maise Webster Cl TW19 .. 97 D8
Maisonettes The RG8 .... 34 D8
Maist Prep Sch The SL5 . 120 D5
Maist Senior Sch SL5 ... 120 D5
Maitland Rd RG1 .... 85 E7
Maiwand Gdns RG30 ..... 84 D7
Maize La RG42 .... 91 E2
Majendie Cl RG14 .... 104 D5
Major's Farm Rd SL3 ..... 68 D7
Makepiece Rd RG42 ...... 91 B1
Maker Cl RG30 .... 85 B5
Makins Rd RG9 .... 35 B7
Malcolm Pl 6 RG1 .... 86 A8
Malders La SL6 .... 19 C3
Maldon Cl RG30 .... 85 D6
Malet Cl TW20 .... 96 D2
Malham Fell RG12 ...... 118 A5
Malham Rd RG19 .... 106 C3
Mallard Cl
Burnham SL1 .... 21 B3
Earley RG6 .... 87 A3
Twyford RG10 .... 61 E3
Mallard Ct RG14 .... 104 F3
Mallard Dr SL1 .... 41 F6
Mallard Pl 2 GU14 ..... 151 A1
Mallard Row RG1 .... 86 A7
Mallards The
Frimley GU16 .... 151 F2
Great Shefford RG17 ..... 48 A3
Laleham TW18 .... 124 B7
Mallards Way GU18 ..... 153 A8
Mallard Way
Aldermaston Wharf RG7 .. 109 B3
Yateley GU46 .... 149 B6
Mallory Ave RG4 .... 59 D6
Mallowdale Rd RG12 .... 118 E2
Mallow Gdns RG18 ..... 106 D5
Mallow Pk SL6 .... 19 C1
Malone Rd RG5 .... 87 D6
MALPAS 83 E6
Malpas Rd SL2 .... 43 B6
Maltby Way RG6 .... 113 F8
Malt Ct 9 RG14 .... 104 F4
Malt Hill
Egham TW20 .... 95 E3
Newell Green RG42 ...... 91 E5
Malthouse Cl 8 RG19 ... 106 E2
Malt House Cl SL4 .... 95 B8
Malthouse Flats RG9 ..... 16 D6
Malthouse La
4 Reading RG1 .... 85 F8
West End GU24 .... 153 F7
Malthouse Way 2 SL7 .... 1 D1
Maltings Pl 6 RG1 .... 86 A7
Maltings The
19 Newbury RG14 ...... 104 F2
Staines TW18 .... 96 E4
Thatcham RG19 .... 106 F2
West Ilsley RG20 .... 10 B1
Malton Ave SL1 .... 42 B6
Malt Shovel La RG17 ..... 24 F4
Malvern Cl RG5 .... 87 F6
Malvern Ct
Brands Hill SL3 .... 69 A8
5 Newbury RG14 .... 104 F1
Reading RG1 .... 86 D6
Malvern Rd
Harlington UB3 .... 71 E7
Maidenhead SL6 .... 19 D1
Yateley GU17 .... 149 F1
Malvern Way RG10 .... 61 D7
Malyns Way RG31 .... 57 B4
Malyons The TW17 ..... 125 D3
Managua Cl RG4 .... 59 E2
Manchester Rd RG1 ...... 86 E7
Mandarin Ct RG14 ...... 105 C2
Mandarin Dr RG14 ...... 105 C1
Mandarin Rd RG2 .... 113 E4
Mandela Ct 2 RG1 .... 86 D7
Mander Ct RG4 .... 59 B3
Mandeville Cl RG30 ...... 84 F6
Mandeville Ct TW20 ...... 96 A4
Mandeville Rd TW17 .... 125 A4
Manea Cl RG6 .... 114 C8
Manfield Cl SL2 .... 22 A2
Manners Rd RG5 .... 87 D7
Mannock Way RG5 .... 88 B8
Manor Barns La RG40 ... 141 F2
Manor Bglws RG20 .... 31 D4
Manor Cl RG42 .... 91 A1
Manor Commercial Ctr
RG2 .... 86 A1
Manor Cres RG20 .... 31 D4
Manorcroft Prim Sch
TW20 .... 96 A2
Manorcrofts Rd TW20 .... 96 A2
Manor Ct
Egham TW18 .... 96 D3
Marlow SL7 .... 1 C3
Slough, Cippenham SL1 ... 41 F5
5 Slough, Upton Park SL1 . 42 F3
Manor Farm
20 Egham TW20 .... 96 A3
Froxfield SN8 .... 99 B4
Poyle SL3 .... 69 E5
Manor Farm Ave TW17 .. 125 B3
Manor Farm Cl SL4 ...... 66 F4
Manor Farm Cotts SL4 ... 68 A2
Manor Farm Ct TW20 .... 96 A3
Manor Farm Ho SL4 ...... 66 F4
Manor Farm La
Egham TW20 .... 96 A3
Tidmarsh RG8 .... 56 C2
Manor Farm Rd RG2 ..... 86 B2
Manor Gdns HP10 .... 3 E5
Manor Gr SL6 .... 65 D6
Manor Ho The GU15 .... 151 D6
Manor House Ct
Lower Halliford TW17 .... 125 B2
Reading RG6 .... 87 A5
Manor House Dr SL5 ..... 93 A1
Manor House La SL3 ..... 68 B6
Manor La
Brimpton RG7 .... 133 C6
Chieveley RG20 .... 51 B1
Harlington UB3 .... 71 D8
Hermitage RG18 .... 79 B8
Leckhampstead RG20 ..... 49 F4
Maidenhead SL6 .... 39 E4
Newbury RG14 .... 105 E5
Manor Leaze TW20 ...... 96 B3
Manor Mead Sch TW17 .. 125 B4
MANOR PARK 22 D1
Manor Park Cl RG30 ..... 84 C6
Manor Park Dr
Finchampstead RG40 .... 141 E6
Yateley GU46 .... 149 E6
Manor Pk
Froxfield SN8 .... 99 B4
Staines TW18 .... 96 D5
Manor Pl
Newbury RG14 .... 104 D5
Staines TW18 .... 97 B3
Manor Prim Sch RG30 ... 85 A4
Manor Rd
Ashford TW15 .... 98 A3
Goring RG8 .... 34 B5
Henley-on-T RG9 .... 35 D8
Letcombe Bassett OX12 .... 7 C5
Maidenhead SL6 .... 39 E4
Oatlands Park KT12 ..... 125 F2
Whitchurch-on-T RG8 ..... 56 C7
Windsor SL4 .... 66 E5
Wokingham RG41 .... 116 A2
Manor The RG2 .... 113 E5
Manor View RG7 .... 133 F7
Manor Way
Bagshot GU19 .... 145 F3
Egham TW20 .... 95 F2
Holyport SL6 .... 65 A8
Manor Wood Gate RG9 ... 36 A4
Manse Cl UB3 .... 71 D8
Mansel Cl SL2 .... 43 B8
Mansell Cl SL4 .... 66 E5
Mansell Ct RG2 .... 86 E2
Mansell Dr RG14 .... 130 C5
Mansfield Cl SL5 .... 119 D7
Mansfield Cres RG12 ... 118 B3
Mansfield Ho 4 TW18 ... 96 F3
Mansfield Pl SL5 .... 119 D8
Mansfield Rd
Reading RG1 .... 85 F6
Wokingham RG41 .... 116 A5
Man's Hill RG7 .... 111 C2
Mansion House St 7
RG14 .... 105 A3
Mansion La SL0 .... 44 C6
Manston Dr RG12 ...... 118 C3
Mant Cl RG20 .... 75 D5
Manuka Ct GU47 .... 149 F8
Manygate La TW17 ..... 125 C3
Manygate Mobile Home Site
TW17 .... 125 D3
Maple Bank RG10 .... 61 E6
Maple Cl
Blackwater GU17 .... 150 C5
Maidenhead SL6 .... 39 C5
Sandhurst GU47 .... 142 F1
Winnersh RG41 .... 88 D3
Maple Cres
Newbury RG14 .... 105 A4
Slough SL2 .... 43 B6
Maple Ct
Ashford TW15 .... 98 D1
3 Bracknell RG12 .... 118 F5
Englefield Green TW20 .... 95 B2
Goring RG8 .... 34 B6
Marlow SL7 .... 1 E3
Windsor SL4 .... 67 C4
Mapledene RG4 .... 58 E3
Maple Dr
Crowthorne RG45 ...... 143 C7
Lightwater GU18 .... 152 F8
Reading RG30 .... 84 D6
MAPLEDURHAM 57 E6
Mapledurham Dr RG8 .... 57 C5
Mapledurham Ho★ RG31 . 57 E6
Mapledurham View RG31 . 57 D2
Mapledurham Watermill★
RG31 .... 57 D6
Mapledurham Wlk SL6 ... 19 E3
Maple Gdns
Reading RG2 .... 86 E2
Stanwell TW19 .... 97 E6
Yateley GU46 .... 149 D5
Maple Gr RG4 .... 60 E1
Maple Ho RG4 .... 59 C3
Maple La RG8 .... 55 B5
Maple Rise SL7 .... 1 E3
Maplespeen Ct RG14 .... 104 F4
Maples The 10 SL8 .... 3 B3
Maplin Pk SL3 .... 44 B4
Marathon Cl RG5 .... 88 B8
Marbeck Cl SL4 .... 66 D6
Marbull Way RG42 ...... 91 B2
Marchant Cl RG19 ...... 131 D7
Marchant Ct SL7 .... 2 A3
Marcheria Cl RG12 ..... 118 B3
Marches The SL4 .... 42 D2
Marchmont Pl RG12 ..... 118 C6
Marchwood Ave RG4 ..... 59 C7
Marcia Ct SL1 .... 41 F5
Marconi Rd RG14 .... 105 B4
Marcus Cl RG30 .... 85 B7
Mardale GU15 .... 152 C4
Mardy RG4 .... 58 E5
Marefield RG6 .... 87 C2
Marefield Rd SL7 .... 1 D2
Mare La RG10 .... 63 E3
Marescroft Rd SL2 .... 21 E1
Mareshall Ave RG42 ..... 91 B2
Marfleet Cl 1 RG6 .... 87 E2
Margaret Cassidy Ho UB7 70 C6
Margaret Cl
Reading RG2 .... 113 C7
Staines TW18 .... 97 D2
Maria Ct 15 RG30 .... 85 D6
Marie Davis Ct 16 RG1 .... 86 B7
Marigold Cl RG45 ...... 142 F6
Marina Cl KT16 .... 124 C1
Marina Way
Burnham SL1 .... 41 D6
Iver SL0 .... 44 F6
Mariners La RG7 .... 82 B3
Marino Way RG40 ...... 141 A6
Marion Ave TW17 ...... 125 B4
Marish Ct SL3 .... 44 A3
Marish Prim Sch SL3 ..... 44 A3
Marish Wharf Ind Est SL3 43 E4
Marjory Kinnon Sch
TW14 .... 71 E2
Markby Way RG6 .... 87 E2
Market La SL3 .... 44 C3
Market Pl
Bracknell RG12 .... 118 B7
Colnbrook SL3 .... 69 C7
Henley-on-T RG9 .... 15 D2
Lambourn RG17 .... 25 B2
8 Newbury RG14 .... 105 A3
Reading RG1 .... 86 B7
Wokingham RG40 .... 116 C6
Market Place Mews RG9 . 15 D2
Market Sq
8 Marlow SL7 .... 1 D2
Staines TW18 .... 96 E4
Market St
Bracknell RG12 .... 118 B7
Maidenhead SL6 .... 39 F7
Newbury RG14 .... 105 A2
8 Windsor SL4 .... 67 D6
Market Way 2 RG1 ...... 86 B7
Markham Centre Trad Est
The RG7 .... 83 F2
Markham Ct GU15 ...... 151 D6
Marks Rd RG41 .... 116 A8
Marlborough Ave RG1 .... 86 D5
Marlborough Bsns Ctr
KT16 .... 123 F1
Marlborough Cl SL6 ...... 39 A6
Marlborough Cres UB3 ... 71 D7
Marlborough Ct
7 Hungerford RG17 ..... 100 D5
Reading RG1 .... 85 F6
Slough SL1 .... 41 E7
Wokingham RG40 .... 116 D7
Marlborough Ho
5 Maidenhead SL6 .... 39 F6
Reading RG1 .... 86 D5
Marlborough Rd
Ashford TW15 .... 97 E3
Maidenhead SL6 .... 39 A6
Slough SL3 .... 43 D2
Marlborough Rise GU15 . 151 E6
Marlborough Way RG31 .. 84 B4
Marley Croft TW18 .... 96 E5
Marlin Cl TW16 .... 98 E2
Marlin Ct SL7 .... 1 D1
Marling Cl RG31 .... 57 C2
MARLOW 1 B2
MARLOW BOTTOM 1 C6
Marlow Bridge La SL7 .... 18 E8
Marlow CE Inf Sch SL7 .... 1 D3
Marlow Com Hospl SL7 .... 1 E2
Marlow Ct RG4 .... 59 D3
Marlowes The RG14 ..... 130 F8
Marlow Ho SL7 .... 1 E1
Marlow Lodge 13 SL6 ..... 39 F6
Marlow Mill SL7 .... 1 E1
Marlow Rd
Bisham SL6 .... 18 E4
Bisham SL7 .... 18 E7
Henley-on-T RG9 .... 15 E3
Little Marlow SL7, SL8 ..... 2 D5
Maidenhead SL6 .... 39 F7
Marlow Bottom SL7 .... 1 B7
Marlow Sta SL7 .... 1 F2
Marlston Cotts RG18 ..... 79 F5
Marlston Rd RG18 .... 79 D5
Marmion Rd RG9 .... 35 E8
Marquis Ct TW19 .... 97 E7
Marquis Pl 4 RG1 .... 86 E7
Marriott Cl TW14 .... 71 D1
Marsack St RG4 .... 59 C2
Mars Cl RG41 .... 115 F6
Marshall Cl
Frimley GU16 .... 152 D2
Purley on T RG8 .... 57 D4
Marshall Ho 1 RG30 ..... 85 B7
Marshall Rd GU47 ...... 150 D6
Marshalls Ct RG14 ...... 104 D5
Marsham Ho RG42 .... 91 B1
Marshaw Ct RG2 .... 86 C3
MARSH BENHAM 103 D4
Marsh Ct RG30 .... 85 D8
Marshfield SL3 .... 68 C6
Marshgate Apartments
RG17 .... 100 B5
Marshgate Trad Est SL6 .. 41 A7
Marsh La
Curridge RG18 .... 78 D4
Hungerford RG17 .... 100 B5
Newbury RG14 .... 105 A3
Taplow SL6 .... 40 E6
Marshland Sq RG4 .... 59 B5
Marsh Mill RG9 .... 36 A8
Mars Ho RG7 .... 134 E2
Marsh Pl RG8 .... 56 D5
Marsh Rd RG18 .... 106 E4
Marshwood Rd GU18 .... 153 D8
Marston Dr RG14 .... 105 D5
Marston Way SL5 ...... 119 E7
Martel Cl GU15 .... 152 C7
Marten Pl RG31 .... 57 B3
Martin Cl
Windsor SL4 .... 66 D6
Woodley RG5 .... 87 E6
Martindale Ave GU15 ... 152 C4
Martineau La RG10 ...... 88 E7
Martingale Chase RG14 . 105 C4
Martin Rd
Maidenhead SL6 .... 39 F8
Slough SL1 .... 42 E3
Martins Cl GU17 .... 150 D4
Martins Dr RG41 .... 116 B7
MARTIN'S HERON 118 F6
Martin's Heron Sta RG12 118 F5
Martins La RG12 .... 118 E6
Martin's Plain SL2 .... 22 F3
Martins The RG19 ...... 106 F2
Martin Way GU16 ...... 151 E2
Marunden Gn SL2 .... 21 F2
Marvyn Cotts RG7 ...... 110 C3
Mary Drew Almshouses The
TW20 .... 95 D2
Mary Hare Gram Sch
RG14 .... 77 F3
Maryland RG40 .... 141 E8
Mary Lyne Almshouses
RG30 .... 84 F5
Mary Mead RG42 .... 91 D2
Mary Morgan Ct SL2 ..... 42 D8
Maryside SL3 .... 43 E4
Mascoll Path SL2 .... 21 F2
Masdar Gdns RG40 ..... 141 E6
Masefield Gdns RG45 ... 143 B3
Masefield Rd RG18 ..... 106 D4
Masefield Way TW19 ..... 97 F7
Mason Cl GU46 .... 149 E5
Mason Ct
Ball Hill RG20 .... 129 F1
3 Reading RG1 .... 85 F8
Masonic Hall Rd KT16 ... 123 F3
Mason Pl GU47 .... 149 F8
Mason's Ct SL1 .... 41 E6
Masons Rd SL1 .... 41 E6
Mason St RG1 .... 85 E8
Master Cl RG5 .... 88 B8
Mathisen Way SL3 .... 69 E6
Matlock Rd RG4 .... 58 E4
Matson Dr RG9 .... 15 F2
Matthew Arnold Cl TW18 . 97 C2
Matthew Arnold Sch The
TW18 .... 97 C2
Matthew Ct TW15 .... 97 E5
Matthews Chase RG42 .... 90 F1
Matthews Cl RG19 ...... 106 B4
Matthews Ct SL5 .... 120 D5
MATTHEWSGREEN 116 A8
Matthewsgreen Rd RG41 116 A8
Matthews La TW18 .... 96 F4
Matthews Rd GU15 ..... 151 C8
Maudsley Ho SL6 .... 40 B7
Maultway Cl GU15 ..... 152 B8
Maultway Cres GU15 .... 152 B8
Maultway N GU15 ...... 145 B1
Maultway The GU15,
GU16 .... 152 D6
Maureen Campbell Ct
TW17 .... 125 B4
Mawbray Cl RG6 .... 87 C2
Maxdata Ctr The RG12 ... 118 A7
Maxine Cl GU47 .... 143 B1
Maxwell Cl RG5 .... 87 E8
Maxwell Ct SL1 .... 21 C1
Maxwell Rd TW15 .... 98 C2
Maybrick Cl GU47 ...... 142 F1
Maybury Cl SL1 .... 41 D7
May Cl 2 GU47 .... 150 D8
Mayfair RG30 .... 84 D7
Mayfair Dr RG14 .... 104 E1
Mayfield Ave RG31 ...... 84 B4
Mayfield Cl TW15 .... 98 B2
Mayfield Cotts RG20 ..... 31 C4
Mayfield Dr
Caversham RG4 .... 59 D3
Windsor SL4 .... 67 A4
Mayfield Gdns TW18 ..... 96 F2
Mayfield Light Ind Est
SL4 .... 93 B5
Mayfield Mews RG41 .... 115 A8
Mayfield Rd
Camberley GU15 .... 151 B1
Wooburn Green HP10 ...... 3 E6
May Fields
Sindlesham RG41 .... 115 A8
Winnersh RG41 .... 88 A1
Mayflower Ct 10 RG1 .... 86 B7
Mayflower Dr GU46 .... 149 B7
Mayflower Way SL2 ..... 22 C8
Maying The RG2 .... 113 B6
Maynard Cl RG18 ...... 106 D5
Maynard Ct
6 Staines TW18 .... 97 A4
Windsor SL4 .... 67 A6
Mayo Rd KT12 .... 125 F2
Mayors La RG14 .... 105 A2
Mayow Cl RG19 .... 106 F2
May Pk RG31 .... 84 E4
Maypole Rd SL6 .... 41 A8
Mays Cl RG6 .... 87 B5
Mays Croft RG12 .... 118 A5

MAYS GREEN 35 B5
Mays La RG6 87 B5
May's La RG7 136 A7
Mays Rd RG40 116 E6
May Tree Cl SL7 1 C6
Maytree Wlk RG4 59 E4
Maywood Dr GU15 152 A7
Meachen Ct 2 RG40 116 C6
Mead Ave SL3 44 B4
Mead Cl
  Caversham RG4 59 D2
  Egham TW20 96 B2
  7 Marlow SL7 1 F3
  Reading RG31 84 B6
  Slough SL3 44 B4
Mead Ct TW20 96 C2
Meade Ct GU19 145 F3
Meadfield Ave SL3 44 A3
Meadfield Rd SL3 44 B3
Mead Haze SL6 20 C2
Meadhurst SL5 120 A6
Meadhurst Pk TW16 98 E2
Meadhurst Rd KT16 124 B1
Mead La
  Chertsey KT16 124 C1
  Upper Basildon RG8 55 D6
Meadowbank RG20 129 B7
Meadow Bank 11 SL8 3 B3
Meadowbank Rd GU18 146 C1
Meadowbrook Cl SL3 69 F6
Meadowbrook Montessori Sch RG42 91 F4
Meadow Cl
  Blackwater GU17 150 D4
  Compton RG20 31 E5
  Goring RG8 34 C6
  Marlow SL7 1 F1
  Moulsford OX10 13 F4
  Old Windsor SL4 68 B2
  Thatcham RG19 106 C3
Meadow Cotts
  Shepperton TW17 125 B3
  West End GU24 153 F7
Meadow Croft RG17 73 A1
Meadowcroft Rd RG2 113 C8
Meadow Ct TW18 96 E5
Meadow Gdns TW18 96 D3
Meadow Ho 4 GU17 150 E4
Meadow La
  Eton SL4 67 C7
  Pangbourne RG8 56 D5
Meadowlands RG7 81 D4
Meadowlea Cl UB7 70 D8
Meadow Rd
  Ashford TW15 98 D3
  Earley RG6 87 D3
  Henley-on-T RG9 15 E1
  Newbury RG14 130 F8
  Reading RG1 58 F1
  Slough SL3 43 E3
  Wentworth GU25 121 E4
  Wokingham RG41 116 A5
Meadows Bsns Pk The GU17 150 E4
Meadowside RG31 57 B1
Meadowside Rd RG8 56 D5
Meadows Sch The HP10 3 E6
Meadows (Superstores) The GU47 150 E5
Meadows The HP10 3 B8
Meadowsweet Cl RG18 106 E4
Meadow Vale Prim Sch RG42 117 F8
Meadowview
  Hungerford RG17 100 D6
  Shepperton TW17 125 C3
  Stanwell TW19 69 F2
Meadow View
  Chertsey KT16 124 C1
  Marlow Bottom SL7 1 E6
  Winnersh RG41 88 D3
Meadow View Ct RG1 58 E1
Meadow View La SL6 64 E8
Meadow Way
  Blackwater GU17 150 C5
  Bracknell RG42 91 A1
  Caversham RG4 59 D2
  Dorney SL6 40 F4
  Fifield SL6 65 D6
  Old Windsor SL4 68 B1
  Theale RG7 83 D3
  West End GU24 153 F6
  Wokingham RG41 116 A5
Meadow Wlk
  Bourne End SL8 3 A5
  Wokingham RG41 116 A6
Meads Cl RG20 50 D7
Meads The
  Stoke Poges SL2 23 A2
  4 Windsor SL4 67 A5
Mead The RG17 48 B3
Meadway
  Ashford TW15 98 A4
  Frimley GU16 151 F2
  Staines TW18 97 A1
Mead Way SL1 41 D8
Meadway Cl TW18 97 A1
Meadway Prec RG30 85 A6
Meadway The RG30 84 F7
Mead Wlk SL3 44 B4
Meare Est HP10 3 E8
Mearings The RG30 111 F5
Measham Way RG6 87 C2
Meashill Way OX11 9 F8
Meavy Gdns RG2 86 B2
Medallion Pl SL6 40 B7
Mede Cl TW19 95 D7
Mede Ct TW18 96 E5
Medina Cl RG41 115 E7
Medlake Rd TW20 96 C2
Medlar Dr GU17 150 F3
MEDMENHAM 17 A5
Medway Cl
  Thatcham RG18 106 B5
  Wokingham RG41 115 F7
Medway Ct RG30 85 D6
Melbourne Ave
  Slough SL1 42 C7
  Winnersh RG41 88 C1
Melbury Cl KT16 124 A2
Meldreth Way
  Earley RG6 87 C1
  Shinfield RG6 114 D8
Meldrum Cl RG14 130 C6
Melford Gn RG4 59 E6
Melksham Cl RG6 113 E8
Melling Cl RG6 87 E3
Mellor Wlk
  1 Reading RG1 86 B5
  17 Windsor SL4 67 D6
Melody Cl RG41 88 C3
Melrose RG12 118 B1
Melrose Ave RG6 87 A5
Melrose Gdns RG2 114 E2
Melton Ct SL6 39 F6
Melville Ave GU16 151 F1
Membury Bsns Pk RG17 45 E4
Membury Wlk RG12 118 F5
Memorial Ave RG9 35 E2
Mendip Cl
  Charvil RG10 61 B4
  Harlington UB3 71 D7
  Slough SL3 44 A1
Mendip Dr RG31 84 A6
Mendip Rd RG12 118 E4
Menpes Rd RG31 57 C4
Mentone Cotts RG10 62 F5
Meon Cl RG26 135 A1
Merchants Pl 9 RG1 86 A8
Mercia Ho TW15 125 C8
Mercian Way SL1 41 D5
Mercia Rd SL6 39 C4
Mercury Ave RG41 115 E6
Mercury Ho RG7 134 E2
Mercury Pk The HP10 3 E7
Mere Cl SL7 1 F2
Mereoak La
  Grazeley RG7 112 F4
  Three Mile Cross RG7 113 A5
Mereoak Orch RG7 113 A5
Mereoak Pk RG7 113 A5
Mere Rd
  Shepperton TW17 125 B3
  Slough SL1 42 F3
Mereside Pk TW15 98 C4
Meridian Ct SL5 120 B1
Meridian The RG1 86 C8
Merlewood RG12 118 D4
Merlin Cl SL3 69 B8
Merlin Clove RG42 92 B2
Merlin Ct
  Frimley GU16 151 D1
  3 Maidenhead SL6 39 B8
Merlin Lo RG30 85 D5
Mermaid Cl RG41 88 B2
Merrick Ho RG2 86 A2
Merrifield Cl RG6 114 D8
Merrivale Gdns RG2 86 B1
Merron Cl GU46 149 C5
MERRYHILL GREEN 88 D3
Merryhill Green La RG41 88 D3
Merryhill Rd RG42 118 B8
Merryman Dr RG45 143 A7
Merryweather Cl RG40 115 F1
Merrywood Pk GU15 151 F4
Mersey Way RG18 106 B5
Merston Ct RG4 59 B4
Merthyr Vale RG4 59 A6
Merton Cl
  Maidenhead SL6 39 C3
  Sandhurst GU47 143 F2
Merton Ct 10 SL1 43 A3
Mertonford RG40 116 D5
Merton Rd SL1 43 A3
Merton Rd N RG2 86 B1
Merton Rd S RG2 86 B1
Mervyn Rd TW17 125 C2
Merwin Way SL4 66 D4
Meryton Ho SL4 67 A4
Metcalf Rd TW15 98 B3
Meteor Cl RG5 88 A7
Metro Ctr The RG41 89 A2
Mews The
  Ascot SL5 120 C4
  Farley Hill RG7 140 C7
  Newbury RG14 104 E2
  Reading RG1 86 E6
  Sonning RG4 60 D4
Mey Cl RG31 84 C5
Meyrick Dr RG14 130 C5
Mezel Hill Cotts SL4 94 C3
Michael Cl SL6 39 C5
Michaelmas Cl GU46 149 D4
Michaels Chase RG4 59 C3
Micheldever Way RG12 118 F4
Michelet Cl GU18 146 B1
Micklands Prim Sch RG4 59 D4
Micklands Rd RG4 59 E3
Mickle Hill GU47 143 A1
Micro Ctr The RG2 86 B2
Midas Ho RG7 134 E2
Midcroft SL2 22 B1
Middle Cl
  Frimley GU15 152 C6
  Newbury RG14 130 D7
Middle Farm Cl RG20 51 B2
Middlefields RG10 61 E6
Middlefields Ct RG10 61 E6
Middle Gn
  Slough SL3 43 E6
  Staines TW18 97 D1
Middle Gordon Rd GU15 151 C5
MIDDLE GREEN 43 E5
Middlegreen Rd SL3 43 D5
Middlegreen Trad Est SL3 43 D4
Middle Hill TW20 95 D3
Middlemoor Rd GU16 151 E1
Middle Springs RG8 34 C8
Middleton Ct RG14 105 E5
Middleton Rd GU15 151 F7
Middletons Cl RG17 100 E7
Middle Wlk SL1 21 B2
MIDGHAM 107 E3
MIDGHAM GREEN 108 B4
Midgham Halt RG7 108 C2
Midsummer Mdw RG4 58 F6
Midway Ave
  Chertsey KT16 124 A6
  Thorpe TW20 123 B6
Midway Cl TW19 97 B5
Midwinter Cl RG30 84 E8
Milam Cl RG2 140 E8
Milbanke Ct RG12 117 F7
Milbanke Way RG12 117 F7
Mildenhall Cl RG6 87 D2
Mildenhall Rd SL1 42 E7
Mildridge Farmhouse SL3 69 B7
Mile Elm SL7 2 A3
MILE END 25 C6
MILES GREEN 153 F2
Miles Pl GU18 152 F7
Milestone Ave RG10 61 A5
Milestone Cres RG10 61 A4
Milestone View Ct RG4 59 E4
Milestone Way RG4 59 D6
Miles Way RG5 88 A7
Milford Ct SL1 43 A4
Milford Rd RG1 58 F1
Military Dr 1 RG19 106 E2
Milkhouse Rd RG20 103 D4
Millars Brook RG41 116 A4
Millars Bsns Ctr RG41 116 A4
Millbank SL7 1 F1
Mill Bank RG17 102 A3
Millbank Cres RG5 87 F6
Millboard Rd SL8 3 B3
Millbridge Rd GU46 149 B8
Millbrook Way SL3 69 E5
Mill Cl
  Bagshot GU19 145 D3
  Wokingham RG41 115 F7
Mill Cotts HP10 3 D5
Mill Ct SL3 69 C4
Milldown Ave RG8 34 C7
Milldown Rd RG8 34 C7
MILL END 16 D7
Millennium Ct RG2 86 C4
Millennium Mews SL1 42 E5
Millennium Way RG12 118 C8
Miller Dr RG41 88 A2
Millers Cl
  Goring RG8 34 B7
  Staines TW18 97 B3
Millers Ct RG4 59 D1
Miller's Ct TW20 96 D2
Miller's Field RG17 48 B3
Millers Gr RG31 84 E4
Miller's La SL4 68 A1
Millers Thumb RG12 118 E7
Milley La RG10 62 B8
Milley Rd RG10 62 E6
Mill Farm Ave TW16 98 E1
Millfield
  Charlton TW16 125 D8
  Lambourn RG17 25 B2
Mill Field GU19 145 D3
Millgate Ct RG10 61 E5
Mill Gn
  Bracknell RG42 90 E1
  Caversham RG4 59 C1
MILL GREEN 132 F2
Millgreen La RG19 132 F3
Mill Hall Sch RG19 131 D8
Millholme Wlk GU15 152 C4
Mill House La KT16 123 B5
Millington Cl RG2 86 D3
Millins Cl GU47 143 E1
Mill La
  Aldermaston Wharf RG7 109 C2
  Ascot SL5 121 A7
  Bracknell RG12 117 F5
  Colthrop RG19 107 B2
  Cookham SL6 20 C7
  Earley RG6 87 E3
  Henley-on-T RG9 35 F8
  Horton SL3 69 C4
  Hurley SL6 17 F4
  Lambourn RG17 25 C2
  Newbury RG14 105 B3
  Reading, Horncastle RG31 84 E4
  Reading RG1 86 B7
  Shiplake RG9 36 A2
  Sindlesham RG41 115 A8
  Taplow SL6 40 C8
  Thorpe TW20 123 C5
  Tidmarsh RG8 56 D2
  Windsor SL4 67 A7
  Winnersh RG41 87 F1
  Yateley GU46 149 D8
Millmead RG41 116 A7
Mill Mead TW18 96 F4
Millmere GU46 149 D7
Mill Pl SL3 68 D5
Mill Place Cvn Pk SL3 68 C5
Mill Pond Rd GU20 146 B6
Mill Rd
  Burghfield Common RG30 84 F2
  Caversham RG4 59 C1
  Goring RG8 34 C8
  Lower Shiplake RG9 36 B3
  Marlow SL7 1 E1
Mill Reef Cl RG19 105 F3
Mill Ride SL5 119 D8
Millside SL8 3 C3
Mills Spur SL4 95 B8
Mill St
  Colnbrook SL3 69 D7
  Slough SL2 42 F5
Millstream Ho RG14 105 D3
Millstream La SL1 41 E5
Millstream Way HP10 3 E8
Mill West SL2 42 F5
Millworth La RG2 113 E4
Milman Cl RG12 119 A7
Milman Rd RG2 86 B5
Milner Rd SL1 41 A8
Milsom Cl RG2 113 E5
Milton Cl
  Bracknell RG12 118 B3
  Henley-on-T RG9 15 D2
  Horton SL3 69 A4
Milton Ct RG40 116 B7
Milton Dr
  Littleton TW17 124 E5
  Wokingham RG40 116 B7
Milton Gdns
  Stanwell TW19 97 F7
  Wokingham RG40 116 B6
Milton Rd
  Earley RG6 87 A7
  Egham TW20 95 F3
  Slough SL2 22 D1
  Wokingham RG40, RG41 116 B6
Milton Way RG10 61 F5
Milverton Cl SL6 39 B3
Milward Ct RG2 86 C4
Milward Gdns RG12 117 C7
Mimosa Dr RG2 113 E6
Mina Ave SL3 43 D4
Minchin Gn RG42 90 C3
Minden Cl RG41 115 E6
Minerva Cl TW19 70 A2
Minerva Ho RG7 134 E2
Minister Ct 4 RG1 86 B7
Ministry Rd RG19 132 A5
MINLEY 149 F1
Minley Rd GU17 149 E1
Minniecroft Rd SL1 21 B2
Minorca Ave GU16 152 E2
Minorca Rd GU16 152 E1
Minoru Pl RG42 90 D3
Minstead Cl RG12 118 F6
Minstead Dr GU46 149 C5
Minster Ct
  Camberley GU15 151 D7
  Camberley, York Town GU15 150 F4
Minsterley Ave TW17 125 E5
Minster St RG1 86 B7
Minster Way SL3 43 F4
Mint Cl RG6 86 F1
Minter Ct RG26 134 F1
Minton Cl RG30 84 F8
Minton Rise SL6 41 B7
Mirador Cres SL2 43 B6
Mire La RG10 62 D4
Misbourne Ct SL3 44 A2
Missenden Cl TW14 98 F7
Missenden Gdns SL1 41 B7
Mistletoe Rd GU46 149 D4
Mitcham Cl RG2 86 B5
Mitcham Rd GU15 145 A1
Mitchell Bldgs GU46 149 B5
Mitchell Cl
  Pamber Heath RG26 135 E2
  Slough SL1 42 A4
Mitchell Way RG5 88 B7
Mitford Cl RG2 113 D8
Mitre Cl TW17 125 D3
Mitre Pl RG42 91 B2
Mixnams La KT16 124 A6
Moat Dr SL2 43 C8
Modbury Gdns RG2 86 C2
Moffats Cl GU47 150 A8
Moffy Hill SL6 19 E2
Mohawk Way RG5 88 B7
Mole Rd RG2, RG41 114 F6
Moles Cl RG40 116 D5
Mollison Cl RG5 88 B8
Molly Millar Bridge RG41 116 B4
Molly Millars Cl RG41 116 B4
Molly Millar's La RG41 116 A4
Molyneux Rd GU20 146 D4
Molyns Ho RG9 15 E3
Molyns Mews SL1 41 E5
Monarch Cl TW14 98 E8
Monarch Dr RG2 113 E6
Monastry The 22 RG30 85 D6
Monck Ct 7 RG30 85 D6
Mondial Way UB7 71 C7
Moneyrow Gn SL6 65 A7
MONEYROW GREEN 65 A7
Monica Gdns RG14 105 C5
Monkey Island Ct SL6 65 E8
Monkey Island La SL6 40 E2
Monkley Ct 5 RG4 59 C1
Monksbarn RG2 86 D2
Monks Cl SL5 120 B3
Monks Dr SL5 120 B3
Monksfield Way SL2 22 A2
Monks Hollow SL7 1 E5
Monkshood Cl RG40 116 E7
Monks La RG14 130 F7
Monks Rd
  Virginia Water GU25 122 D5
  Windsor SL4 66 D5
Monks Way
  Harmondsworth UB7 70 E8
  Reading RG30 85 D5
  Staines TW18 97 D1
Monks Wlk SL5 120 B3
Monkswood Cl RG14 130 E7
Monkswood Ct 7 SL7 1 E2
Monktons La RG7 137 C5
Monmouth Ct 5 RG1 59 A1
Mons Cl RG41 115 E6
Monsell Gdns TW18 96 E6
Mons Wlk TW20 96 C3
Montacute Dr RG19 106 F2
Montague Cl
  Camberley GU15 151 B5
  Lightwater GU18 146 A1
  Wokingham RG40 116 E7
Montague Dr RG19 131 B6
Montague Rd SL1 42 F6
Montague St
  Caversham RG4 59 C2
  Reading RG1 86 D7
Montague Terr RG14 131 A8
Montagu Rd SL3 68 B6
Montbatten Ct SL3 43 E3
Monteagle La
  Yateley GU46 149 A6
  Yateley GU46 149 B5
Montem La SL1 42 D4
Montem Prim Sch SL1 42 B4
Montgomery Cl GU47 150 B8
Montgomery Dr RG7 113 B2
Montgomery of Alamein Ct RG12 118 D8
Montgomery Pl SL2 43 C7
Montgomery Rd RG14 130 E8
Montpelier Dr RG4 59 D5
Montpellier Ct SL4 67 C5
Montreal Terr RG10 61 E4
Montrose Ave
  Datchet SL3 68 C7
  Slough SL1 42 B7
Montrose Cl
  Ashford TW15 98 C3
  Frimley GU16 151 E2
Montrose Dr SL6 39 A6
Montrose Ho 7 RG1 86 A8
Montrose Rd TW14 71 D1
Montrose Way SL3 68 D7
Montrose Wlk RG31 84 E4
Monument Cl RG14 130 D7
Monycrower Dr SL6 39 E7
Moorbridge Rd SL6 40 A7
Moor Cl
  Finchampstead RG40 141 E7
  Sandhurst GU47 143 E1
Moor Copse Cl RG6 87 B3
Moordale Ave RG42 90 F1
Moore Cl SL1 42 B4
Moore Grove Cres TW20 95 F1
Moor End SL6 40 C1
Moores Gn RG40 116 E8
Moores La SL4 41 F2
Moore's Pl RG17 100 C5
Moorfields Cl TW18 123 E8
Moorfield Terr SL6 40 A8
Moor Furlong SL1 41 E5
Moorhayes Dr TW18 124 C6
Moorhen Dr RG6 87 B1
Moorings The
  Old Windsor SL4 95 C8
  Windsor SL4 67 A7
Moor La
  Bracknell RG12 117 C6
  Harmondsworth UB7 70 C8
  Maidenhead SL6 19 F1
  Newbury RG14 104 E3
  Staines TW19 96 D6
Moorland Rd UB7 70 C8
Moorlands Dr SL6 38 F8
Moorlands Pl GU15 151 B5
Moorlands Prim Sch RG30 84 F7
Moorlands Rd GU15 151 B4
Moormede Cres TW18 96 F4
Moor Park Ho RG12 117 E3
Moor Pl GU20 146 B5
Moors Ct RG40 141 E8
Moorside HP10 3 E8
Moorside Cl
  1 Farnborough GU14 151 A1
  Maidenhead SL6 19 F1
Moors The
  Pangbourne RG8 56 D5
  Thatcham RG19 106 D2
Moorstown Ct 7 SL1 42 E4
Moor The SL7 2 D4
Moray Ave GU47 150 D7
Moray Dr SL2 43 A7
Mordaunt Dr RG45 143 B3
Morden Cl RG12 118 F5
Moreau Wlk SL3 43 E7
Morecambe Ave RG4 58 E5
Moreland Ave SL3 69 C7
Moreland Cl SL3 69 C7
Moreleigh Cl RG2 113 B8
Morella Cl GU25 122 D5
Morello Dr SL3 43 F5

Moretaine Rd TW15 97 D5
Moreton Ct RG1 86 D5
Moreton Way SL1 41 D5
Morgan Ct [2] TW15 98 B3
Morgan Rd RG1 86 C6
Moriston Cl RG30 85 B8
Morlais RG4 59 A5
Morlands Ave RG30 85 A5
Morley Cl
Slough SL3 43 F4
Yateley GU46 149 B5
Morley Ct SL5 120 F3
Morley Pl RG17 100 D5
Mornington Ave RG40 141 F8
Mornington Cl RG26 134 E1
Mornington Rd TW15 98 C3
Morpeth Cl RG2 86 C4
Morrell Ct TW18 97 B3
Morrice Cl [3] SL3 44 A2
Morris Ct SL4 66 E6
Morrish Gr RG17 102 B2
Morrison Cl RG8 55 D4
Morriss Ct [10] RG1 86 C7
MORTIMER 137 A5
Mortimer Cl RG2 113 C7
Mortimer Hall RG7 137 C5
Mortimer La
Mortimer RG7 137 D7
Silchester RG7 137 D1
Mortimer Rd
Grazeley RG7 112 D2
Slough SL3 43 D3
Mortimer St John's CE Sch RG7 137 A5
Mortimer St Mary's CE Jun Sch RG7 137 D5
Mortimer Sta RG7 137 E5
MORTIMER WEST END 136 D4
Morton Dr SL1 21 F8
Morton Pl RG7 83 E4
Mortons La RG7 107 C6
Morval Rd GU17 149 F1
Mosaic Apartments The SL1 42 E4
Moss Cl RG4 59 C3
MOSS END 91 C6
Mossy Vale SL6 19 D1
Mostyn Ho RG42 91 B1
Moulden Way RG7 110 F8
MOULSFORD 13 F4
Moulsford Prep Sch OX10 14 A5
Moulsham Copse La GU46 149 B7
MOULSHAM GREEN 149 B8
Moulsham La GU46 149 B7
Moundsfield Way SL1 41 E4
Mountain Ash SL7 1 D6
Mountbatten Cl
Newbury RG14 105 C5
[6] Slough SL1 43 A3
Mountbatten Mews GU15 151 D7
Mountbatten Rise GU47 142 F1
Mountbatten Sq [7] SL4 67 C6
Mount Cl
Farnham Common SL2 22 C8
Newbury RG14 105 A1
Mount Cl The GU25 122 D3
Mount Felix KT12 125 F2
Mountfield RG8 34 C7
Mount La
Bracknell RG12 118 C7
Chaddleworth RG20 49 A8
Mount Lee TW20 95 F3
Mount Pleasant
Beenham RG7 108 F6
Bracknell RG12 118 C6
Reading RG1 86 B6
Sandhurst GU47 143 A1
Tadley RG26 135 B1
Wokingham RG41 116 A6
Mount Pleasant Cl GU18 146 A1
Mount Pleasant Cotts
[7] Bourne End SL8 3 B3
Englefield Green TW20 95 D2
Mount Pleasant Gr RG1 86 B6
Mount Rd RG18 106 E4
Mountsfield Cl TW19 70 A2
Mounts Hill SL4 93 C3
Mount St RG2 86 B5
MOUNT THE 86 C5
Mount The
Caversham RG4 58 F3
Reading RG1 86 D5
Wentworth GU25 122 D3
Mount View RG9 15 D2
Mount View Ct RG9 15 D2
Mowbray Cres TW20 96 A3
Mowbray Dr RG30 85 A8
Mower Cl RG40 116 F7
Moyleen Rise SL7 1 C1
Mrs Bland's Inf Sch RG7 110 F2
Muckhatch La TW20 123 B7
Mud La
Finchampstead RG27 140 F1
Peasemore RG20 50 D6
Mud La Cotts RG27 140 F1
Muirfield Cl RG1 86 D7
Muirfield Ho
Bracknell RG12 117 E3
Sunningdale SL5 121 A1
Mulberry Ave
Stanwell TW19 97 E7
Windsor SL4 67 F5
Mulberry Bsns Pk RG41 116 A4
Mulberry Cl
Crowthorne RG45 143 C4
[1] Sandhurst GU47 150 D8
Mulberry Cl *continued*
Twyford RG10 61 E4
Woodley RG5 87 E6
Mulberry Ct
[1] Bracknell RG12 118 F4
[2] Newbury RG14 104 F2
[5] Wokingham RG40 116 C6
Mulberry Dr SL3 43 E1
Mulberry Ho RG42 91 B1
Mulberry Trees TW17 125 D2
Mulberry Way RG7 83 E3
Mulberry Wlk SL6 39 C8
Mulfords Hill RG26 135 B1
Mulgrave Rd GU16 151 F2
Mullens Rd TW20 96 C3
Mullens Terr RG4 58 D8
Mullion Ct [10] RG1 85 F7
Mulroy Dr GU15 152 A6
Mumbery Hill RG10 36 E1
Muncaster Cl TW15 98 A4
Muncaster Ho TW18 124 C6
Muncaster Rd TW15 98 B3
Munces Rd SL7 1 D6
Munday Ct RG42 90 E1
Mundaydean La SL7 1 B4
Mundesley Spur SL1 42 E7
Mundesley St RG1 86 B6
Munkle Marsh RG19 107 A3
Munnings Dr GU47 150 E6
Munro Ave RG5 87 F4
Murdoch Cl TW18 97 A3
Murdoch Ct RG40 116 D5
Murdoch Rd RG40 116 D5
Murray Ct SL5 120 C3
Murray Ho RG41 116 A6
Murray Rd RG41 116 A6
Murrellhill La
Binfield RG42 90 C1
Bracknell RG42 117 C8
Murrells La GU15 151 B3
Murrin Rd SL6 39 C8
Mushroom Castle RG42 92 B2
Mus of Berkshire Aviation The★ RG5 88 B6
Mus of Reading★ RG1 86 B8
Mustard La RG4 60 E2
Mustard Mill Rd TW18 96 F4
Muswell Cl RG7 83 E3
Mutton Oaks RG12 117 D8
Myers Way GU16 152 D2
Mylne Sq RG40 116 D6
Mylum Cl RG2 113 C6
MYRKE 42 F2
Myrke The SL3 42 F2
Myrtle Ave TW14 71 E2
Myrtle Cl
Burghfield Common RG7 111 B3
Lightwater GU18 153 B8
Poyle SL3 69 E6
Purley on T RG31 57 C3
Myrtle Cres SL2 42 F6
Myrtle Dr GU17 150 D5
Myton Wlk RG7 83 E3

N

Nabbs Hill Cl RG31 84 C5
Nairn Cl GU16 151 E2
Nalderhill Rd RG20 103 B6
Napier Cl RG45 143 D5
Napier Ct RG1 86 C8
Napier Dr GU15 152 A8
Napier Lodge TW15 98 D2
Napier Rd
Ashford TW15 98 D1
Crowthorne RG45 143 C4
Maidenhead SL6 39 B6
Reading RG1 86 C8
Napier Wlk TW15 98 D1
Napper Cl SL5 119 D7
Narromine Dr RG31 84 F4
Naseby RG12 118 B1
Naseby Rise RG14 105 D5
Nash Cl RG6 87 A3
Nashdom SL1 20 F5
Nashdom La SL1 21 A6
Nash Gdns SL5 119 E7
Nash Grove La RG40 115 E1
Nash Pk RG42 90 B2
Nash Rd SL3 44 A2
Natalie Cl TW14 98 D8
Nathan Ct [7] RG1 85 F7
Naylors The RG7 139 D6
Neath Gdns RG30 84 F7
Needham Cl SL4 66 E6
Neil Cl TW15 98 C3
Nell Gwynn Ave TW17 125 D3
Nell Gwynne Ave SL5 120 D5
Nell Gwynne Cl SL5 120 D5
Nelson Cl
Bracknell RG12 118 E7
East Bedfont TW14 98 F7
Slough SL3 43 D2
Nelson Ct [4] KT16 124 A1
Nelson Mews [8] RG1 86 B6
Nelson Rd
Ashford TW15 97 E3
Caversham RG4 59 C2
Harmondsworth TW6 70 F6
Windsor SL4 66 F4
Nelson's La RG10 89 B6
Nelson Terr [24] RG1 86 B6
Nelson Way GU15 150 F4
Nene Rd TW6, UB7 71 B6
Nene Rd Rdbt TW6 71 B6
Neo Apartments [2] SL1 43 A4
Neptune Cl RG41 115 E6
Neptune Rd TW6 71 C6
Neptune Way SL1 41 E4
Netherton RG12 118 A5
Netley Cl RG4 59 E6
Nettlecombe RG12 118 D3
Nettleton Rd TW6 71 B6
Neuman Cres RG12 118 A3
Neve Ho SL6 39 F8
Nevelle Cl RG42 117 D8
Nevil Ct RG19 106 D2
Neville Cl
Stoke Poges SL2 22 F6
Waltham St L RG10 62 F6
Neville Ct SL1 21 C2
Neville Dr RG19 106 E3
Nevis Rd RG31 57 D3
Newall Rd TW6 71 C6
Newalls Rise RG10 36 E2
Newark Rd
Windlesham GU20 146 B6
Yateley GU17 149 E2
Newark St RG1 86 B6
New Bath Rd RG10 61 C6
Newberry Cres SL4 66 D5
Newbery Cl RG31 57 D1
Newbery Way SL1 42 D4
Newbold Coll RG42 90 D1
Newbold Rd RG14 104 D5
Newbold Sch RG42 90 D1
Newbolt Cl RG18 106 C5
New Bright St [6] RG1 86 A6
NEWBURY 104 E3
Newbury Bsns Pk RG14 105 C4
Newbury Cl RG10 61 B4
Newbury Coll RG14 131 A7
Newbury Dr SL6 40 B6
Newbury Hill RG18 52 F5
Newbury Ho RG14 130 D6
Newbury La RG20 31 D4
Newbury Racecourse Sta RG14 105 C2
Newbury Rd
Great Shefford RG17 48 B2
Harmondsworth TW6 70 F6
Hermitage RG18 79 B6
Lambourn RG17 25 C1
Newbury Ret Pk RG14 131 B7
Newbury St
Kintbury RG17 102 B2
Lambourn RG17 25 B2
Newbury Sta RG14 105 A2
Newcastle Rd RG2 86 C4
New Christ Church CE Prim Sch RG1 86 B5
Newchurch Rd
Slough SL2 41 F8
Tadley RG26 135 A1
New Cl RG9 16 A8
New Cross RG9 35 F2
New Ct SL7 1 D2
Newdale Ct RG20 103 F6
Newell Gn RG42 91 C3
NEWELL GREEN 92 A1
Newell Hall RG42 91 C3
NEW ENGLAND 153 D7
Newfield Gdns SL7 1 F3
Newfield Rd SL7 1 F3
Newfield Way SL7 1 F2
New Forest Ride RG12 118 F4
New Greenham Pk RG19 131 F5
Newhaven Cres TW15 98 D3
Newhaven Spur SL2 22 B1
New Hill RG8 57 C5
New Hope Terr RG1 59 A1
New Horizon Ho RG19 132 A4
New Horton Manor SL3 69 A4
Newhurst Gdns RG42 91 D3
Newlands Ave RG4 59 B3
Newlands Cl GU46 149 D5
Newlands Cotts RG41 114 F7
Newlands Dr
Maidenhead SL6 39 A7
Poyle SL3 69 E4
Newlands Girls' Sch SL6 39 A7
Newlands Ho SL6 39 A6
Newlands Prim Sch GU46 149 C5
Newlands Rd GU15 151 B1
New Lane Hill RG30 84 E6
Newlyn Gdns RG2 86 B1
Newmans Pl SL5 121 B2
New Market [12] SL6 39 F7
Newmarket Cl RG6 87 D2
New Mdw SL5 119 D8
New Mile Rd SL5 120 C7
New Mill La RG27 140 E2
New Mill Rd RG40 140 E3
New Par TW15 97 F4
New Park Rd TW15 98 C3
Newport Cl [5] RG14 105 B4
Newport Dr RG42 91 B2
Newport Rd
Harmondsworth TW6 71 A6
Newbury RG14 105 B4
Reading RG1 59 A1
Slough SL2 21 E1
Newquay Dr RG6 87 B1
New Rd
Bagshot GU19 145 F3
Blackwater GU17 150 E4
Bourne End SL8 3 B4
Bracknell RG12 118 D7
Burghfield Common RG7 111 E1
Cookham Rise SL6 19 E7
Crowthorne RG45 143 C5
Datchet SL3 68 D6
East Bedfont TW14 71 D1
Egham TW18 96 C4
New Rd *continued*
Harlington TW6, UB7 71 C7
Holyport SL6 65 B8
Hurley SL6 17 F3
Littleton TW17 125 B6
Lower Shiplake RG9 36 A3
Marlow Bottom SL7 1 D6
Newbury RG14 105 C1
North Ascot SL5 92 F1
Reading RG1 86 D5
Sandhurst GU47 150 A8
Shiplake RG9 35 B2
Sindlesham RG41 115 B8
Slough SL3 44 A3
Twyford RG10 61 D7
Twyford, Ruscombe RG10 61 F6
Windlesham GU19, GU20 146 A4
New Road Hill RG7 108 B3
New Scotland Hill Prim Sch GU47 143 A2
New Sq
East Bedfont TW14 98 C7
Slough SL1 42 F4
New St
Beech Hill RG7 138 B1
Henley-on-T RG9 15 E2
Staines TW18 97 A4
Newstead Rise RG2 86 E1
Newton Ave RG4 59 D5
Newton Cl SL3 43 F4
Newton Ct SL4 68 A1
Newton La SL4 68 B1
Newtonside SL4 68 A1
Newton Side Orch SL4 68 A1
Newton's Mews RG17 100 D6
NEWTOWN
Henley-on-Thames 35 F8
Newbury 131 B4
NEW TOWN
Pangbourne 55 D4
Reading 86 F7
Newtown RG26 135 A1
Newtown Gdns RG9 35 E8
New Town Prim Sch RG1 86 D8
Newtown Rd
Henley-on-T RG9 35 F8
Marlow SL7 1 F3
Newbury RG14, RG19, RG20 131 A7
Sandhurst GU47 150 B8
New Villas RG20 129 B3
New Way RG7 82 A2
New Wickham La TW20 96 B1
New Wokingham Rd RG45 143 A6
New Zealand Ave KT12 125 F1
Niagara Rd RG9 35 E8
Nicholas Ct [11] RG1 85 F7
Nicholas Gdns SL1 41 E5
Nicholas Rd RG9 35 B8
Nicholas Winton Ct SL6 40 A8
Nicholls SL4 66 C4
Nicholls Wlk SL4 66 C4
Nicholsons Ctr [5] SL6 39 F7
Nicholsons La SL6 39 F7
Nicholson Wlk [2] TW20 96 A3
Nideggan Cl RG19 106 D3
Nightingale Cres RG12 118 D4
Nightingale Ct [9] SL1 43 A3
Nightingale Gdns GU47 150 B8
Nightingale Ho [1] RG1 85 F5
Nightingale La
Maidenhead SL6 19 D3
Mortimer RG7 137 D6
Nightingale Pk SL2 21 F5
Nightingale Pl SL6 19 F7
Nightingale Rd RG5 87 D4
Nightingale Shott TW20 95 F2
Nightingales The
Newbury RG14 131 B8
Stanwell TW19 97 F7
Nightingale Wlk SL4 67 C4
Night Owls RG19 131 C7
Nimrod Cl RG5 88 B7
Nimrod Ind Est RG1 86 B5
Nimrod Way RG2 86 B5
Nine Acres SL1 41 F5
Nine Elms Cl TW14 98 F7
Nine Mile Ride
Bracknell RG12, RG40 118 C1
Crowthorne RG40 142 D7
Finchampstead RG40 141 D6
Nine Mile Ride Ind RG40 141 D5
Nine Mile Ride Prim Sch RG40 141 F6
Ninth Ave RG31 84 B6
Niplands Cotts HP10 3 D2
Nire Rd RG4 59 E2
Nixey Cl SL1 43 A4
No 4 RG30 85 C6
Noakes Hill RG8 54 B7
Nobel Dr UB3 71 E7
Noble Ct SL2 42 F5
Noble Rd RG9 35 F7
Nobles Way TW20 95 E2
Nodmore RG20 49 B7
Norbury Rd TW13 98 F5
Norcot Rd RG30 84 F8
Norden Cl SL6 39 C4
Norden Mdws SL6 39 C5
Norden Rd SL6 39 C5
Norelands Dr SL1 21 C3
Nores Rd RG2 113 D7
Norfolk Ave SL1 42 C8
Norfolk Chase RG42 91 F1
Norfolk Cl RG41 115 E6
Norfolk Ho RG1 86 D5
Norfolk Park Cotts SL6 39 F8
Norfolk Rd
Maidenhead SL6 39 F8
Reading RG30 85 D7
Norland Dr HP10 3 C8
Norlands RG18 106 C5
Norlands La TW18, TW20 123 E7
Norman Ave RG9 15 E1
Norman Ct [4] TW18 97 A4
Normandy Wlk TW20 96 C3
Norman Ho RG9 15 E1
Norman House TW17 125 A2
Normanhurst TW15 98 A3
Norman Keep RG42 118 F8
Norman Pl RG1 59 B1
Norman Rd
Ashford TW15 98 D2
Caversham RG4 59 C4
Normanstead RG9 15 D1
Normanstead Rd RG31 84 C8
Normans The SL2 43 B7
Normay Rise RG14 130 C5
Normoor Rd RG7 110 F1
Norreys Ave RG40 116 D7
Norreys Dr SL6 39 D4
Norris Field RG20 49 B8
Norris Gn RG5 61 A1
Norris La RG20 49 B8
Norris Rd
Reading RG6 87 A6
Staines TW18 96 F4
Northam Cl RG6 87 E3
Northampton Ave SL1 42 C7
Northampton Cl RG12 118 E6
NORTH ASCOT 119 F8
Northborough Rd SL2 22 B1
Northbourne Cl RG6 87 B2
Northbrook Copse RG12 118 F3
Northbrook Pl RG14 105 A3
Northbrook Rd RG4 59 D6
Northbrook St RG14 105 A3
North Burnham Cl SL1 21 B3
Northbury Ave RG10 61 E5
Northbury La RG10 61 E6
North Cl
East Bedfont TW14 71 D1
Medmenham SL7 17 D7
Windsor SL4 66 F6
Northcott RG12 118 A1
North Cotts SL2 22 C2
Northcourt Ave RG2 86 D4
Northcroft
Slough SL2 22 B1
Wooburn Green HP10 3 F6
Northcroft Cl TW20 95 B3
Northcroft Gdns TW20 95 B3
Northcroft La RG14 104 F3
Northcroft Rd TW20 95 B3
Northcroft Terr RG14 104 F3
Northcroft Villas TW20 95 B3
North Ct RG40 141 F4
Northdean [5] SL6 19 F1
Northdene Ct TW20 95 E3
North Dr
Sulhamstead RG7 110 D7
Wentworth GU25 121 E4
NORTH END 129 A2
Northend Cl HP10 3 C7
North End La SL5 121 B2
Northern Ave RG14 105 A6
Northern Hts SL8 3 B5
Northern Perimeter Rd TW6 71 E6
Northern Perimeter Road W TW6 70 E6
Northern Rd SL2 22 D1
Northern Way RG2 85 F1
Northern Woods HP10 3 C7
North Farm Cl RG17 25 C3
Northfield GU18 153 B8
Northfield Ave RG9 36 A4
Northfield Ct
Henley-on-T RG9 15 D3
Staines TW18 124 B8
Northfield End RG9 15 D3
Northfield Farm Ind Est RG17 48 C6
Northfield Rd
Eton SL4 41 F2
Lower Shiplake RG9 36 B4
Maidenhead SL6 19 F1
Reading RG1 59 A1
Staines TW18 124 B8
Thatcham RG18 106 B4
NORTHFIELDS 61 E7
Northfields
Chieveley RG20 51 B4
Lambourn RG17 25 B3
Northfields Terr RG17 25 C3
North Fryerne GU46 149 D8
Northgate Dr GU15 152 A7
North Gn
Bracknell RG12 118 D8
[3] Maidenhead SL6 19 F1
Slough SL1 42 E6
North Gr KT16 123 F3
NORTH HEATH 50 D1
Northington Cl RG12 118 F3
North Links Rd HP10 3 B8
North Lodge Dr SL5 119 C7
North Lodge Mews RG30 85 D5
Northmead Rd SL2 41 F8
Northolt Rd
Harmondsworth TW6 70 E6
Harmondsworth UB7 70 D6
North Pk SL0 44 D3

North Rd
East Bedfont TW14 71 D1
Maidenhead SL6 39 E7
Moulsford OX10 13 F4
Winkfield SL5 119 B8
Northrop Rd TW6 71 E6
North Row SL3 23 E8
North St
Caversham RG4 59 B2
Egham TW20 95 F2
Reading RG1 85 F8
Winkfield SL4 93 A6
North Standen Rd RG17 100 A4
North Star La SL6 39 C6
NORTH STREET 83 D5
NORTH SYDMONTON 131 F1
North Terr SL4 67 E7
NORTH TOWN 19 F2
North Town Cl 1 SL6 19 F1
North Town Mead 4 SL6 19 F1
North Town Moor SL6 19 F1
North Town Rd SL6 19 F1
Northumberland Ave RG2 86 C3
Northumberland Cl
Bracknell RG42 91 F1
Stanwell TW19 70 E1
Northumberland Cres
TW14 71 E1
Northumbria Rd SL6 39 B4
Northview RG17 100 D5
North View RG12 117 C6
North View Gdns 2
RG14 105 B4
Northview Hts 2 RG17 100 D5
Northway
Newbury RG14 105 B2
Thatcham RG18 106 C5
Wokingham RG41 115 E7
North Wlk RG7 83 E4
Northwood Dr RG14 105 C4
Northwood Rd TW6 70 D6
Norton Cl RG14 130 C6
Norton Pk SL5 120 C4
Norton Rd
Frimley GU15 152 C4
Reading RG1 86 E7
Riseley RG7 139 C3
Wokingham RG40 116 C5
Woodley RG5 87 F5
Norway Dr SL2 43 B8
Norwich Ave GU15 151 E3
Norwich Dr RG5 87 C8
Norwich Ho SL6 39 E8
Norwood Cres TW6 71 C6
Norwood Rd RG1 86 E7
Notley End TW20 95 C1
Notley Pl RG4 59 B4
Notrees RG17 102 A2
Nottingham Fee OX11 11 F8
Notton Way RG6 113 F8
Nuffield Dr GU47 143 F1
Nuffield Rd
Arborfield Garrison RG2 140 F7
Arborfield Garrison RG2 141 A8
Nugee Ct RG45 143 B5
Nugent Ct SL7 1 F3
Nuneaton RG12 118 E3
Nunhide La RG8, RG31 83 F6
Nun's Acre RG8 34 B7
Nuns Wlk GU25 122 D4
NUPTOWN 91 F7
Nuptown La
Newell Green SL4 92 A8
Winkfield RG42 91 F7
Nursery Cl
Hurst RG10 88 E7
Lower Shiplake RG9 36 A4
Nursery Gdns
Purley on T RG8 57 B5
Staines TW18 97 B1
Sunbury TW16 125 F7
Nursery La
North Ascot SL5 119 E8
Slough SL3 43 D5
Nursery Pl SL4 68 B1
Nursery Rd
Burnham SL6 41 B7
Sunbury TW16 125 F7
Nursery Way TW19 68 D1
Nursery Wlk SL7 1 B1
Nutbean La RG7 139 F5
Nutbourne Ct TW18 96 F1
Nutfield Ct GU15 151 D7
Nuthatch Cl TW19 97 F7
Nuthatch Dr RG6 87 B4
Nuthurst RG12 118 E4
Nut La RG10 62 E6
Nutley RG12 118 A1
Nutley Cl GU46 149 D5
Nutmeg Cl RG6 86 F1
Nutter's La RG2 140 A8
Nuttingtons RG20 49 F6
Nutty La TW17 125 C6

O

Oak Apartments UB3 71 D7
Oak Ave
Egham TW20 96 D1
Sandhurst GU47 143 D1
Oak Cott RG10 63 A2
Oakdale
Bracknell RG12 118 D3
Windlesham GU20 146 D4
Oakdale Cl RG31 84 C8
Oakdale Wlk RG5 88 A8
Oakdene
Burghfield Common RG7 111 A2
Sunningdale SL5 120 F3
Oak Dr
Burghfield Common RG7 110 F2
Newbury RG14 104 F2
Woodley RG5 88 A6
Oaken Copse GU15 152 C7
Oak End Way RG7 109 C4
Oakengates RG12 118 A1
Oaken Gr
Maidenhead SL6 19 C1
Newbury RG14 130 D8
Oakes Ct RG17 100 D5
Oakey Dr RG40 116 B5
Oak Farm Cl GU17 150 C5
Oakfield RG1 86 D5
Oakfield Ave SL1 42 B5
Oakfield Ct RG41 116 A5
Oakfield Fst Sch SL4 67 B5
Oakfield Rd
Ashford TW15 98 B3
Blackwater GU17 150 F3
Bourne End SL8 3 A3
Pamber Heath RG26 135 E1
Oakfields GU15 151 B5
Oakfield Works GU47 150 E7
Oak Gn RG2 113 D8
Oak Grove Cres GU15 150 F6
Oakhall Ct TW16 98 F3
Oakhall Dr TW16 98 F3
Oakham Cl RG31 57 D2
Oak Hill SN8 99 C3
Oakhurst SL6 20 B4
Oak La
Englefield Green TW20 95 C5
Windsor SL4 67 A6
Oaklands
Curridge RG18 78 C3
Reading RG1 86 F6
4 Tadley RG26 134 E1
Yateley GU46 149 D6
Oaklands Bsns Ctr RG41 116 A4
Oaklands Cl SL5 92 F1
Oaklands Cvn Pk RG41 114 F1
Oaklands Dr
North Ascot SL5 92 F1
Wokingham RG41 116 A5
Oaklands Inf & Jun Schs
RG45 143 A6
Oaklands La RG45 143 B7
Oaklands Pk RG41 116 A4
Oaklea Dr RG27 140 E2
Oak Leaf Ct SL5 119 D8
Oakleigh GU18 153 C8
Oakley HP10 3 F7
Oakley Cres SL1 42 E6
Oakley Ct UB3 71 C7
OAKLEY GREEN 66 B5
Oakley Green Rd
Fifield SL4 65 E5
Oakley Green SL4 66 B5
Oakley Green SL4 66 B7
Oakley Rd
Camberley GU15 151 B4
Caversham RG4 58 F4
Newbury RG14 105 D4
Oak Lodge
5 Ashford TW16 98 F1
Crowthorne RG45 143 C5
Oakmede Pl RG42 90 C2
Oakridge
Newbury RG20 130 B4
West End GU24 153 F6
Oak Ridge Cl RG14 130 E8
Oakridge Pl SL2 22 C8
Oakside Way RG2 113 E8
Oaks Rd
Lower Shiplake RG9 36 A4
Stanwell TW19 70 D1
Oaks The
Blackwater GU17 150 E3
Bracknell RG12 118 D7
Newbury RG14 131 A7
Staines TW18 96 F4
Yateley GU46 149 D5
Oak Stubbs La SL6 40 F4
Oak The OX10 14 C6
Oaktree Ave RG19 133 B5
Oak Tree Ave SL7 1 D3
Oaktree Cl SL7 1 D3
Oak Tree Cl
Tadley RG26 135 B1
Wentworth GU25 122 D3
Oak Tree Copse RG31 57 E3
Oak Tree Dr
Englefield Green TW20 95 C3
Slough SL3 44 B1
Oak Tree Rd
Marlow SL7 1 D4
Reading RG31 57 E2
Thatcham RG19 106 E2
Oaktree Way GU47 143 A1
Oak Tree Wlk RG8 57 D5
Oakvew Gdns SL3 43 F2
Oakview RG40 116 B4
Oak View RG31 84 C8
Oak Way
East Bedfont TW14 98 E7
Woodley RG5 87 D4
Oakway Dr GU16 151 E1
Oakwood Ct SL1 42 E7
Oakwood Ho RG6 87 C4
Oakwood Pl RG45 143 A4
Oakwood Rd
Bracknell RG12 118 E7
Oakwood Rd *continued*
Virginia Water GU25 122 C4
Windlesham GU20 146 E4
OARE 79 B8
Oareborough RG12 118 E4
Oareborough La RG18 52 A1
Oast Ct TW18 96 F4
Oast House Cl TW19 95 E8
Oatlands Dr
Oatlands Park KT13 125 E1
Slough SL1 42 D7
OATLANDS PARK 125 E1
Oatlands Rd RG2 113 F5
Oban Ct SL1 42 D4
Oban Gdns RG5 87 E4
O'Bee Gdns RG26 134 F1
Obelisk Way GU15 151 C6
Oberon Way TW17 124 E6
Observatory The 6 RG30 85 E7
Observer Dr 3 RG19 106 E2
Ochre Ct 6 TW13 98 F5
Ockwells Rd SL6 39 C2
Octavia RG12 118 A1
Octavia Way TW18 97 A2
Oddfellows Rd RG14 104 F2
Odell Cl RG6 114 B8
Odencroft Rd SL2 22 A2
Odette Gdns RG26 135 C1
Odiham Ave RG4 59 E5
Odiham Rd RG7 139 D1
Odney La SL6 20 B7
Ogden Pk RG12 118 E6
Ogmore Cl RG30 84 E7
Okingham Cl GU47 143 D1
Oldacre GU24 153 F7
Oldacres SL6 40 B7
Old Acres La RG10 61 B5
Old Apple Yd The RG41 88 A3
Old Bakehouse Ct RG45 143 B4
Old Bakery Ct SL0 44 F7
Old Bakery The 10 TW20 96 A3
Old Barn Cl RG4 59 A6
Old Bath Rd
Charvil RG10 61 B5
Newbury RG14 104 F4
Reading RG31 84 C4
Sonning RG4 60 D1
Old Bisley Rd GU16 152 C3
Old Bix Rd RG9 15 A6
Old Bothampstead Rd
RG20 51 D6
Old Bracknell Cl RG12 118 B6
Old Bracknell La E RG12 118 B6
Old Bracknell La W
RG12 118 B6
Old Brewery La RG9 15 E2
Oldbury RG12 117 F6
Oldbury Rd KT16 123 E2
Old Chapel Cotts RG18 53 E1
Old Chapel The RG7 113 A2
Old Charlton Rd TW17 125 C4
Old Coach Works RG17 25 A2
Old Coalyard The TW20 95 F2
Old College Rd 2 RG14 104 F4
Oldcorne Hollow GU46 149 A5
Old Court Cl SL6 39 B3
Old Dean Rd GU15 151 D7
Oldean Cl RG31 57 C1
Olde Farm Dr GU17 150 B5
Old Elm Dr RG30 84 D7
Oldershaw Mews SL6 39 B8
Old Farm Cres RG31 57 C2
Old Farm Dr RG12 91 C1
Old Ferry Dr TW19 68 D1
Oldfield Cl RG6 87 B7
Oldfield Prim Sch SL6 40 B6
Oldfield Rd SL6 40 B7
Oldfield Rd Ind Est SL6 40 B7
Old Fives Ct SL1 21 B2
Old Forest Rd RG41 88 F1
Old Forge Cl SL6 40 A3
Old Forge Cres TW17 125 B3
Old Forge End GU47 150 B7
Old Forge The
Streatley RG8 34 A6
2 Tadley RG26 134 E1
Old Granary The 8
RG17 100 D5
Old Green La GU15 151 C7
Old Hayward La RG17 73 D2
Old House Ct SL3 43 D7
Oldhouse La GU18, GU20 146 C2
Old Kennels Ct RG30 85 A5
Old Kiln Ind Est SL6 19 A3
Old Kiln Rd HP10 3 A8
Old La
Hamstead Marshall
RG20 102 E1
Headley RG19 133 F1
Old Lands Hill RG12 118 D8
Old La The RG1 85 F5
Old Library The 10 RG14 105 A2
Old Marsh La SL6 40 F4
Old Mill Ct RG10 61 D5
Old Mill La SL6 40 D4
Old Mill Pl TW19 69 B1
Old Mill The RG8 56 D6
Old Monteagle La GU46 149 B5
Old Moor La HP10 3 E8
Old Newtown Rd RG14 104 F1
Old Nursery Pl TW15 98 B3
Old Nursery The RG18 79 A6
Old Orchard
Iver SL0 44 F7
Maidenhead SL6 39 E5
Old Orch The RG31 84 E4
Old Palace Ct SL3 69 D6
Old Papermill Cl HP10 3 E8
Old Pasture Rd GU16,
GU15 151 F3
Old Pharmacy Ct RG45 143 C4
Old Police Ho The 14
RG14 105 A4
Old Pond Cl GU15 151 C1
Old Portsmouth Rd
GU15 152 A5
Old Post Office La 10 SL6 39 F7
Old Priory La RG42 91 D2
Old Riseley Stores The
RG7 139 C3
Old Row Ct RG40 116 C6
Old Sawmill La RG45 143 C6
Old Sawmills The RG17 127 E6
Old School Ct TW19 95 E8
Old School La GU46 149 C6
Old School Mews TW20 96 D3
Old School The
Hampstead Norreys RG18 52 F5
Wooburn HP10 3 D4
Old School Yd The 4
RG17 25 B2
Old Silk Mill The RG10 61 D5
Old Slade La SL0 44 F2
Old St
Chieveley, Beedon Common
RG20 51 C5
Chieveley RG18 51 F1
Hermitage RG18 78 F8
Old Stanmore Rd RG20 30 E6
Old Station Bsns Pk RG20 31 E4
Old Station Way HP10 3 E5
Old Station Yd The RG17 25 B2
Oldstead RG12 118 D4
Old Stocks Ct RG8 54 F5
Old Thornford Rd RG19 132 E6
Old Vicarage Way HP10 3 D4
OLD WARREN 135 E5
Old Watery La HP10 3 E8
Oldway La SL1 41 D5
Old Welmore GU46 149 E5
Old Whitley Wood La
RG2 113 C6
OLD WINDSOR 95 A8
Old Wokingham Rd
RG45 143 C7
Old Woosehill La RG41 115 F7
Oleander Cl RG45 143 A7
Oliver Ct SL1 41 E6
Oliver Dr RG31 84 C5
Oliver Rd SL5 120 B5
Oliver's Paddock SL7 1 D5
Olivia Ct RG41 116 B6
Olivia Dr SL3 43 F1
Ollerton RG12 118 A1
Omega Way TW20 123 C8
Omer's Rise RG7 110 F3
Om Ho RG30 85 D8
One Pin La SL2 22 C8
Onslow Dr SL5 93 A1
Onslow Gdns RG4 59 C3
Onslow Lodge TW18 96 F1
Onslow Mews KT16 124 A3
Onslow Rd SL5 121 B2
Onyz The RG12 118 E6
Opal Ct SL3 23 C1
Opal Way RG41 115 E7
Opecks Cl SL2 23 B1
Opendale Rd SL1 41 B8
Opladen Way RG12 118 E4
Oppidan SL6 41 C7
Oracle Ctr The RG1 86 B7
Oracle Parkway RG6 60 A1
Oram Ct 2 SL7 1 D2
Orbit Cl RG40 141 E6
Orchard Ave
Ashford TW15 98 C2
Hatton TW14 71 D2
Slough SL1 41 D8
Windsor SL4 67 A6
Orchard Bungalow Mobile
Home Pk SL2 21 F5
Orchard Chase RG10 88 F7
Orchard Cl
Ashford TW15 98 C2
Egham TW20 96 B3
Farnborough GU17 150 F1
Henley-on-T RG9 15 E1
Hermitage RG18 79 C8
Maidenhead SL6 40 A3
Newbury RG14 105 C5
Purley on T RG31 57 B4
Shinfield RG7 113 B2
Shiplake RG9 35 E2
West End GU24 153 D6
Wokingham RG40 116 D6
Woolhampton RG7 108 C2
Orchard Cotts RG10 62 F6
Orchard Ct
Bracknell RG12 118 C7
Camberley GU15 151 B2
Harmondsworth UB7 70 C7
Oatlands Park KT12 125 F1
Reading RG2 113 C7
Thatcham RG19 106 E3
Orchard Dene Dr RG7 109 C2
Orchard Dr
Sunbury TW17 125 E6
Wooburn HP10 3 D4
Orchardene RG14 105 B4
Orchard Est RG10 61 E5
Orchard Gate
Farnham Common SL2 22 C7
Sandhurst GU47 150 B8
Orchard Gdns SL6 20 B7
Orchard Gn RG17 73 A1
Orchard Gr
Caversham RG4 59 E4
Flackwell Heath HP10 3 B7
Maidenhead SL6 39 C7
Orchard Hill GU20 146 D3
Orchard Ho 8 SL8 3 A4
Orchard Lea RG20 30 E7
Orchard Lodge SL1 41 E5
Orchard Mill SL8 3 B1
Orchard Park Cl RG17 100 D4
Orchard Pl RG40 116 C6
Orchard Rd
Hurst RG10 88 F7
Mortimer RG7 137 B5
Old Windsor SL4 68 B1
Orchards Residential Pk
SL3 43 F5
Orchard St RG1 86 B6
Orchard The
Flackwell Heath HP10 3 B7
Lightwater GU18 153 B8
Marlow SL7 1 E3
Theale RG7 83 E4
Virginia Water GU25 122 E4
Orchard View KT16 124 A3
ORCHARDVILLE 21 B1
Orchardville SL1 21 B1
Orchard Way
Ashford TW15 97 F6
Camberley GU15 151 B2
Slough SL3 43 E5
Orchardwood SL5 119 E7
Orchids The OX11 10 D7
Oregon Ave RG31 57 D3
Oregon Wlk RG40 141 E7
Oriel Hill GU15 151 D4
Oriental Rd SL5 120 D5
Orion RG12 118 A1
Orkney Cl RG31 84 E4
Orkney Ct SL6 20 E5
Ormathwaites Cnr RG42 91 E1
Ormonde Gdns 5 RG14 104 F4
Ormonde Rd RG41 116 A5
Ormsby St RG1 85 E7
Orpheus Ho RG7 134 E2
Orpington Cl RG10 61 E4
Orrin Cl RG30 85 B7
Orts Rd
Newbury RG14 105 B2
Reading RG1 86 D7
Orville Cl RG5 88 A7
Orwell Cl
Caversham RG4 58 F4
Windsor SL4 67 D4
Osbert Ho RG4 59 B4
Osborne Ave TW19 97 F7
Osborne Ct SL4 67 C5
Osborne Dr GU18 153 A8
Osborne La RG42 91 C4
Osborne Lodge 9 SL4 67 C5
Osborne Mews SL4 67 C5
Osborne Rd
Egham TW20 95 F2
Reading RG30 85 B8
Windsor SL4 67 D4
Wokingham RG40 116 C6
Osborne St SL1 42 F4
Osier Pl TW20 96 C2
Osman's Cl RG42 92 B1
Osnaburgh Hill GU15 151 B5
Osney Rd SL6 19 E2
Osprey Ave RG12 117 D5
Osprey Ct 5 RG1 86 C7
Osteriey Ct RG1 86 E6
Osterley Cl RG40 116 F5
Osterley Dr RG4 59 E6
Ostler Gate SL6 19 C1
Ostlers Dr TW15 98 C3
Oswald Cl RG42 91 D2
Othello Gr RG42 118 E8
Otter Cl RG45 143 A7
Otter Ct RG2 113 C7
Our Lady of Peace RC Inf Sch
SL1 41 C8
Our Lady of Peace RC Jun
Sch SL1 41 C8
Our Lady of the Rosary RC
Prim Sch TW18 97 A2
Our Lady's Prep Sch
RG45 143 B5
Ouseley Lodge SL4 95 C8
Ouseley Rd TW19 95 D8
Overbecks 3 RG14 105 D4
Overbridge Sq RG14 105 E3
Overbury Ave RG41 88 F1
Overdale Rise GU16 151 E3
Overdown Rd RG31 57 D3
Overlanders End RG31 57 E3
Overlord Cl GU15 151 C8
Owen Cl 5 SL3 43 F1
Owen Rd
Newbury RG14 105 B6
Windlesham GU20 146 D5
Owl Cl RG41 115 E5
Owletts Gr 4 RG14 105 D4
OWLSMOOR 143 E1
Owlsmoor Prim Sch
GU47 143 E1
Owlsmoor Rd GU47 143 D1
OWNHAM 76 C1
Owston RG6 87 C2
Oxenhope RG12 118 A5
Oxford Ave
Burnham SL1 21 B3
Harlington TW6 71 F7
Slough SL1 41 F8
Oxford Cl TW15 98 C1
Oxford Ho RG41 116 A6

Oxford Rd
Chieveley RG20 51 C1
Marlow SL7 1 D2
Newbury RG14 104 F5
Purley on T RG8, RG30,
RG31 57 D4
Reading RG30, RG1 85 D8
Sandhurst GU47 143 E2
Windsor SL4 67 C6
Wokingham RG41 116 A6
Oxford Rd E SL4 67 C6
Oxford Road Com Sch
RG1 85 F7
Oxfordshire Pl RG42 91 F1
Oxford St
Caversham RG4 59 A2
Hungerford RG17 100 E7
Lambourn RG17 25 B3
Newbury RG14 104 F4
Oyster Wharf 13 RG1 86 B7

P

Pacific Cl TW14 98 F7
Pack and Prime La RG9 15 C2
Packman Dr RG10 61 D6
Padbury Cl TW14 98 D7
Padbury Oaks UB7 70 B6
Paddick Cl RG4 60 E3
Paddick Dr
Earley RG6 87 D1
Lower Earley RG6 114 D8
Paddison Ct 6 RG19 106 E2
Paddock Cl
Camberley GU15 152 A6
Maidenhead SL6 39 A2
Paddock Cotts SL6 39 A2
Paddock Ho SL5 119 E6
Paddock Hts RG10 61 E4
Paddock Rd
Caversham RG4 59 D1
Newbury RG14 130 F8
Paddocks The HP10 3 B8
Paddocks Way KT16 124 B1
Paddock The
Chilton OX11 10 D8
Crowthorne RG45 143 A6
Datchet SL3 68 B6
Maidenhead SL6 19 C2
Newbury RG14 105 C2
Wentworth GU25 122 E3
Winkfield SL4 93 B7
Padley Ct 18 RG1 86 C7
Padstow Cl SL3 43 E3
Padstow Gdns RG2 86 B1
Padstow Wlk TW14 98 F7
PADWORTH 109 F1
Padworth Coll RG7 109 E1
Padworth La RG7 109 E3
Padworth Rd RG7 136 C7
Page Rd TW14 71 D1
Page's Croft RG40 116 D5
Pages Gdns RG8 56 D5
Pages Wharf SL6 40 C8
Paget Cl
Camberley GU15 152 B7
Marlow SL7 1 F4
Paget Dr SL6 39 A4
Paget Rd SL3 43 F2
Pagoda The SL6 20 B1
Paice Gn RG40 116 D7
Paices Hill RG7 135 A5
Painesfield Dr 8 KT15,
KT16 124 A1
Pakenham Rd RG12 118 D2
Palace Cl SL1 41 F5
Paley St SL6 64 B6
PALEY STREET 64 C5
Palgrave Ho RG45 143 C4
Palmera Ave RG31 84 C4
Palmer Cl
Crowthorne RG40 143 A8
Peasemore RG20 50 D7
Palmer Ct RG40 116 C6
Palmer Park Ave RG6 87 A6
Palmer School Rd RG40 116 C7
Palmers Cl SL6 39 A3
Palmer's Hill RG8 54 C5
Palmer's La
Burghfield Common,
Poundgreen RG7 112 A3
Burghfield Common RG7 111 A2
Palmerston Ave SL3 43 B3
Palmerstone Ct GU25 122 E4
Palmerstone Rd RG6 87 B6
Palmer The 23 RG30 85 D6
PAMBER HEATH 135 F1
Pamber Heath Rd RG26 135 E1
Pamber Rd RG7 136 B1
Pamela Row SL6 65 A8
PANGBOURNE 56 D6
Pangbourne Coll RG8 56 A4
Pangbourne Hill RG8 56 C5
Pangbourne Lodge Dr
RG8 56 C5
Pangbourne Mews RG8 56 D6
Pangbourne Pl RG8 56 D6
Pangbourne Prim Sch
RG8 56 E5
Pangbourne Rd RG8 55 C4
Pangbourne St 2 RG30 85 B8
Pangbourne Sta RG8 56 C6
Pankhurst Dr RG12 118 D4
Pannells Cl KT16 123 F1
Pan's Gdns GU15 151 F4
Pantile Cl RG30 84 F6
Pantile Row SL3 44 A2
Papist Way OX10 14 B8
Papplewick Sch SL5 120 A8
Paprika Cl RG6 86 F1
Parade Ct 7 SL8 3 A4
Parade The
Ashford TW16 98 F1
Bourne End SL8 3 A3
Earley RG6 87 B3
Egham TW18 96 D3
Farnham Common SL2 22 C6
Reading RG30 85 D5
Tadley RG26 135 B1
Wentworth GU25 122 D3
Windsor SL4 66 D6
Woodley RG5 87 E4
Woodley RG5 87 F8
Paradise La RG7 108 C7
Paradise Mews RG9 15 D2
Paradise Rd RG9 15 D1
Paradise Way RG7 108 C7
Park Ave
Camberley GU15 151 D4
Staines TW18 97 A2
Thatcham RG18 106 D4
Thorpe Lea TW20 96 C1
Upper Halliford TW17 125 E6
Wokingham RG40 116 B6
Wraysbury TW19 68 D3
Park Cl SL4 67 D5
Park Close Cotts TW20 94 F3
Park Cnr SL4 66 E4
Parkcorner La RG2, RG41 114 F6
Park Cotts
3 Camberley GU15 151 B3
Kintbury RG17 101 B3
Park Cres
Reading RG30 85 B6
Sunningdale SL5 120 F3
Park Dr SL5 120 F3
Park End RG14 105 A4
Parker Ct RG6 87 C4
Parker's Cnr RG7 83 A3
Parkers Ct GU19 145 E3
Parker's La RG42 92 B5
Park Farm Ind Est GU15 151 C1
Parkfield Ho RG45 143 C4
Parkfields GU46 149 D6
Parkgate SL1 21 C1
Park Gr RG30 85 B6
Parkham RG42 117 D8
Parkhill Cl GU17 150 D4
Parkhill Dr RG31 57 D2
Parkhill Rd GU17 150 D4
Park Ho
Englefield Green TW20 95 C2
Maidenhead SL6 39 E6
Parkhouse Ct 9 RG30 85 D6
Parkhouse La RG30 85 D6
Park House Sch & Sports
Coll RG14 130 E6
Parkhurst 20 RG30 85 D6
Park La
Arborfield Garrison
RG40 141 B5
Beech Hill RG7 138 C2
Bracknell RG42 90 E1
Burnham SL1 21 E7
Camberley GU15 151 C5
Charvil RG10 61 B3
Horton SL3 69 A4
Newbury RG14 105 A4
Reading RG31 84 C7
Silchester RG7 137 C2
Slough SL3 43 B3
Stockcross RG20 103 B2
Thatcham RG18 106 D4
Winkfield SL4 93 B7
Parkland Ave SL3 43 D2
Parkland Dr RG12 118 E8
Parkland Gr TW15 98 A4
Parkland Rd TW15 98 A4
Park Lane Prim Sch RG31 84 D8
Park Lane Prim Sch Annexe
RG31 84 D8
Park Lawn SL2 22 C2
Park Mews TW19 97 F8
Park Par SL2 22 C3
Park Pl GU17 150 F3
Park Rd
Ashford TW15 98 B3
Bracknell RG12 118 D8
Camberley GU15 151 C4
Egham TW20 96 A4
Henley-on-T RG9 15 E1
Lower Halliford TW17 125 A1
Sandhurst GU47 150 C8
Stanwell TW19 70 C1
Stoke Poges SL2 22 E3
Wokingham RG40 116 B6
Parkside
Henley-on-T RG9 15 C2
Maidenhead SL6 19 D1
Parkside Bsns Pk RG5 87 E7
Parkside Lodge 11 SL3 43 A3
Parkside Pl TW18 97 A2
Parkside Rd
Reading RG30 85 D6
Sunningdale SL5 121 A4
Thatcham RG18 106 D5
Parkside Wlk SL1 43 A3
Park St
Bagshot GU19 145 E3
Camberley GU15 151 C5
Hungerford RG17 100 D5
Maidenhead SL6 39 F7
Newbury RG14 105 A4
Poyle SL3 69 D6
Slough SL1 42 F4
Park St *continued*
Windsor SL4 67 D6
Parkstone Dr GU15 151 C4
Park Terr RG14 105 A3
Park The RG17 25 A3
Parkview
Flackwell Heath HP10 3 B7
Maidenhead SL6 39 F7
Park View
Ascot SL5 120 E8
Bagshot GU19 145 D3
Beech Hill RG7 138 D5
Burghfield Common RG7 111 A2
Reading RG1 86 A5
Parkview Chase SL1 41 E7
Park View Dr N RG10 61 A5
Park View Dr S RG10 61 A4
Park Wall La RG8 34 C1
Parkway
Camberley GU15 151 C3
Crowthorne RG45 143 A5
Marlow SL7 2 A3
Park Way
Hungerford RG17 100 E4
Newbury RG14 105 A3
Parkway Dr RG4 60 E3
Park Wlk RG8 57 D5
Parlaunt Park Prim Sch
SL3 44 B3
Parlaunt Rd SL3 44 B2
Parliament La SL1, SL6 20 F5
Parnham Ave GU18 153 D8
Parry Gn N SL3 43 F2
Parry Gn S SL3 44 A2
Parsley Cl RG6 86 F1
Parsonage Gdns SL7 1 E1
PARSONAGE GREEN 32 E4
Parsonage La
Farnham Common SL2 22 D4
Hungerford RG17 100 D6
Lambourn RG17 25 A3
Windsor SL4 67 A6
Parsonage Pl RG17 25 A3
Parsonage Rd TW20 95 D3
Parsonage Way GU16 151 E1
Parsons Cl
Arborfield Garrison RG2 141 A8
Newbury RG14 104 E2
Parsons Down Inf Sch
RG19 106 B3
Parsons Down Jun Sch
RG19 106 A3
Parsons Field GU47 150 B8
Parsons Rd
Datchet SL3 68 F8
Slough SL3 43 F1
Parson's Wood La SL2 22 D5
Parthia Cl RG1 86 A6
Part La RG7 139 E4
Partridge Ave GU46 149 B6
Partridge Cl
Bracknell RG12 117 E5
Frimley GU16 151 E1
Partridge Dr RG31 84 C6
Partridge Mead SL6 19 F2
Pascal Cres RG2 113 D7
Paschal Rd GU15 151 F8
Passfield Lodge GU18 146 B1
Pasture Cl RG6 114 B8
Patches Field SL7 1 E5
Paterson Cl GU16 152 C3
Pates Manor Dr TW14 98 D8
Pathway The RG42 90 C3
Patricia Cl SL1 41 E6
Patrick Gdns RG42 91 E1
Patrick Rd RG4 59 B2
Patriot Pl RG1 86 C7
Patten Ash Dr RG40 116 E7
Patten Ave GU46 149 C5
Patterson Ct HP10 3 E7
Pattinson Rd RG2 113 D6
Pavenham Cl RG6 114 B8
Pavilion Gdns TW18 97 B1
Pavilions End The GU15 151 D3
Pavilions The SL4 67 B6
Pavillions The RG10 61 E5
Pavy Cl RG19 106 F2
Paxton Ave SL1 42 C3
Payley Dr RG40 116 E8
Paynesdown Rd RG19 106 B4
Payton Hos SL6 19 E6
Peace La SL6 19 F6
Peachey Dr RG19 106 F2
Peach St RG40 116 C6
Peacock Ave TW14 98 D7
Peacock Cotts RG40 117 C5
Peacock La RG12 117 D6
Peacock Rd SL7 2 A3
Peacock Wlk RG41 115 E5
Pearce Cl SL6 19 F1
Pearce Dr SL6 19 F7
Pearce Rd SL6 19 F1
Pearce's Orch RG9 15 D3
Pearl Gdns SL1 42 B5
Pearmain Cl TW17 125 B4
Pearmans Glade RG2 113 E8
Pears Ave TW17 125 E6
Pearson Rd RG4 60 D3
Pearson Way RG5 87 E5
Peartree Cl SL1 41 F5
Pear Tree Ct GU15 152 B8
Pear Tree La RG14 105 C5
Pear Tree Rd TW15 98 C3
Peascod Pl 16 SL4 67 D6
Peascod St SL4 67 D6
Pease Hill RG7 107 F7
PEASEMORE 50 C7
Peasemore Hill RG20 50 B8
Pebble Hill RG17 128 B6
Peckmoor Dr RG19 131 C7
Peddlars Gr GU46 149 E6
Peel Cl
Caversham RG4 59 D2
Windsor SL4 67 B4
Woodley RG5 88 B8
Peel Ct SL1 42 B8
Peel Ctr The RG12 118 B7
Peel Ho TW20 95 F2
Pegasus Cl RG19 106 A4
Pegasus Ct
Egham TW20 96 B3
2 Lambourn RG17 25 B2
Reading RG31 84 C7
Peggotty Pl GU47 143 E2
Peg's Green Cl RG30 85 B6
Peket Cl TW18 123 E8
Pelham Ct
Maidenhead SL6 39 E7
12 Reading RG30 85 D6
Staines TW18 97 B3
Pelican Ho RG14 104 F3
Pelican La RG14 105 A4
Pelican Rd RG26 135 E2
Pelling Hill SL4 95 B7
Pell St RG1 86 B6
Pemberley Lodge SL4 67 A4
Pemberton Gdns RG31 84 D4
Pemberton Rd SL2 21 E1
Pembroke RG12 118 A1
Pembroke Broadway
GU15 151 C5
Pembroke Cl
Ascot SL5 120 D4
Burghfield Common RG7 111 C3
Pembroke Ho 3 RG4 59 C1
Pembroke Mews SL5 120 D4
Pembroke Pl RG4 59 C3
Pembroke Rd 4 RG14 105 A3
Pembury Ct UB3 71 D8
Penbere Cl RG26 135 E2
Pendals Cl RG18 52 F5
Pendeen Ct SL1 42 A5
Pendell Ave UB3 71 F7
Pendennis Ave RG4 59 E6
Pendine Pl RG12 118 B4
Pendlebury RG12 118 A2
Pendragon Ct RG30 85 D5
Pendragon Way GU15 152 D3
Pendred Rd RG2 113 D6
Penfurzen La RG42 91 D8
Peninsula Pl RG45 143 C4
Peninsular Cl
Camberley GU15 152 B7
Feltham TW14 71 E1
Penling Cl SL6 19 E6
Penn Cl RG4 59 A6
Penn Ct 10 SL7 1 E2
Pennethorne GU15 152 B8
Pennfields RG10 61 E6
Penn Ho SL1 21 C2
Pennine Cl RG31 84 B6
Pennine Rd SL2 42 A8
Pennine Way
Charvil RG10 61 B4
Harlington UB7 71 D7
Penn Mdw SL2 23 A4
Penn Rd
Datchet SL3 68 D6
Newbury RG14 104 D5
Slough SL2 22 D1
Penn Wood Prim Sch SL2 22 D1
Penny Hill Cvn Site
GU17 149 C2
Penny La TW17 125 E2
Pennylets Gn SL2 23 A5
Pennypiece RG8 34 C7
Pennyroyal Ct RG1 86 A6
Penroath Ave RG30 85 C6
Penrose Ave RG5 87 E6
Penrose Cl RG14 104 F5
Penrose Ct TW20 95 C2
Pensford Cl RG45 143 B7
Penshurst Rd SL6 39 D5
Pentangle The 12 RG14 105 A4
Pentland Ave TW17 125 A4
Pentland Cl RG30 84 F5
Pentland Pl 8 RG19 106 D2
Pentland Rd SL2 42 A8
Pentlands The RG17 102 C2
Penton Ave TW18 123 F8
Penton Ct TW18 96 F2
Penton Hall TW18 124 A8
Penton Hall Dr TW18 124 A8
Penton Hook Marina
KT16 124 A6
Penton Hook Rd TW18 124 A8
Penton Rd TW18 96 F1
Pentridge Ho 2 RG2 113 C8
Penwood Ct SL6 39 B7
Penwood Gdns RG12 117 D3
Penwood La SL7 1 C1
Penwood Rd RG20 130 C3
Penyston Rd SL6 39 C7
Penzance Spur SL2 22 B1
Pepler Way SL1 21 B2
Peppard La RG9 35 E7
Peppard Rd
Caversham, Emmer Green
RG4 59 C7
Caversham RG4 59 B3
Pepper La RG2 86 E3
Pepys Cl SL3 69 B8
Perch Cl SL7 18 C8
Percival Rd TW13 98 F6
Percy Ave TW15 98 A3
Percy Bryant Rd TW16 98 E1
Percy Pl SL3 68 B6
Peregrine Cl
Bracknell RG12 118 B4
Wokingham RG41 115 F5
Peregrine Rd TW16 125 F7
Periam Cl RG9 35 C8
Perigee RG2 113 E7
Perkins Ct TW15 97 F3
Perkins Way RG41 116 A5
Perpetual Park Dr RG9 35 F8
Perrin Cl TW15 97 F3
Perrin Ct TW15 98 A4
Perrycroft SL4 66 F4
Perryfields Way SL1 21 B1
Perryhill Dr GU47 142 F1
Perry Ho SL1 21 B1
Perryman Way SL2 21 F2
Perry Oaks RG12 118 E7
Perry Way
Bracknell RG12 118 E7
Lightwater GU18 152 F7
Perseverance Hill RG9 35 A5
Perth Ave SL1 42 B7
Perth Cl RG5 61 A1
Perth Trad Est SL1 42 B8
Peterhead Mews SL3 44 A1
Peterhouse Cl GU47 143 F2
Petersfield Ave
Slough SL2 43 A5
Staines TW15, TW18 97 C2
Petersfield Rd TW18 97 C3
Peters La SL6 65 B8
Petrel Cl RG41 115 E5
Petts La TW17 125 A5
Petty Cross SL1 41 E7
Petworth Ave RG30 84 F3
Petworth Ct
Frimley GU15 151 F4
Reading RG1 85 E6
Windsor SL4 67 A6
Pevensey Ave RG4 59 E5
Pevensey Ct RG2 86 E1
Pevensey Rd SL2 42 A8
Pewsey Vale RG12 118 F4
Pheasant Cl RG41 88 C2
Pheasant La RG20 131 F3
Pheasants Croft SL6 39 A4
Pheasants Ridge SL7 1 C7
Pheasant View RG12 117 D5
Philberds Lodge SL6 40 B1
Philbye Mews SL1 41 F4
Philip Cotts SL8 3 C3
Philip Dr HP10 3 C7
Philip Rd TW18 97 D2
Phillimore Rd RG4 59 C8
Phillip Copse RG12 118 D2
Phillips Cl RG5 61 B1
Phipps Cl SL6 39 A2
Phipps Rd SL1 41 E8
Phoebe Ct 19 RG1 86 A6
Phoenix Bsns Pk RG12 117 C7
Phoenix Cl RG41 115 E6
Phoenix Ct
Feltham TW13 98 E4
Maidenhead SL6 39 D4
Phoenix Pl
Reading RG1 85 F7
5 Staines TW18 97 A3
Phoenix Wlk RG14 130 C6
Phyllis Court Dr RG9 15 E3
Pickering RG12 118 A5
Picket Post Cl RG12 118 F6
Picketts La RG8 55 E4
Pickford Dr SL3 43 F5
Pickfords Gdns SL1 42 E5
Pickins Piece SL3 69 A5
Pickwell Cl RG6 87 C1
Pickwick Gdns GU15 152 B4
Pickwick Terr SL2 43 B6
Picton Cl GU15 152 B7
Picton Way RG4 59 B4
Picture Ho The 1 RG1 86 A7
Piercefield RG31 84 C4
Pierce's Hill RG31 57 C1
Pierson Rd SL4 66 D6
Pigeon Gr RG12 117 D5
Pigeonhouse La SL5 92 E4
Pigeons Farm Rd RG19 131 D8
Piggott Sch The RG10 61 C7
Piggott's Rd 4 RG4 59 C1
Pightle The
Burghfield Common RG7 111 F3
Peasemore RG20 50 D7
Pigott Ct RG40 116 D6
Pigott Rd RG40 116 E8
Pike Cl SL7 18 C8
Pikeshaw Way RG31 57 C2
Pike St RG14 105 B4
Pilgrims Way RG4 59 C6
Pilgrims Way The OX11 12 A7
Pimento Dr RG6 86 F1
Pimpernel Pl RG18 106 F4
Pincents Kiln Ind Pk
RG31 84 A4
Pincents La RG31 84 A4
Pinchcut RG7 111 A3
Pinchington La RG14,
RG19 131 B7
Pindar Pl RG14 105 E5
Pine Acre SL5 120 F2
Pine Ave GU15 151 D3
Pine Cl
Maidenhead SL6 39 B7
Sandhurst GU15 150 E7
Pinecote Dr SL5 120 F2

Pinecrest GU17 150 E1
Pinecroft SL7 1 D4
Pine Croft Rd RG41 116 A2
Pine Ct RG12 118 E5
Pine Dr
Blackwater GU17 150 E3
Mortimer RG7 136 F6
Wokingham RG40 142 A7
Pinefields Cl RG45 143 B4
Pine Gr
Twyford RG10 61 D5
Windlesham GU20 146 D4
Pinehill Rd RG45 143 C3
Pinehill Rise GU47 150 C8
Pinehurst
Ascot SL5 120 D4
Englefield Green TW20 95 C1
Pinelands Mobile Home Pk
RG7 135 F4
Pinel Cl GU25 122 E5
Pine Mount Rd GU15 151 D4
Piner Cotts SL4 66 E4
Pine Ridge RG14 105 C5
Pineridge Gdns 10 RG30 85 D6
Pine Ridge Inf Sch GU15 145 A1
Pine Ridge Rd RG7 111 A3
Pines Prim Sch The
RG12 118 A2
Pines The
Camberley GU15 151 F7
Slough SL3 43 F5
Twyford RG10 61 E7
Pinetree Ct RG4 59 A5
Pine Trees Bsns Pk TW18 96 E3
Pine Way TW20 95 B2
Pinewood Ave RG45 143 C6
Pinewood Cl
Sandhurst GU47 149 F8
Tadley RG26 134 D1
Pinewood Cotts RG45 143 A8
Pinewood Cres RG18 79 C8
Pinewood Dr
Caversham RG4 58 E5
Newtown RG20 131 A2
Staines TW18 97 A3
Pinewood Gdns GU19 145 C3
Pinewood Mews TW19 70 D1
Pinewood Pk Cvn Site
RG40 143 C8
Pinewood Rd GU25 122 A5
Pinfold La RG8, RG18 54 B5
PINGEWOOD 112 C7
Pingewood Cl RG30 85 A2
Pingewood Rd N RG30 85 A1
Pingewood Rd S RG7,
RG30 112 C7
Pinglestone Cl UB7 70 E7
Pink La SL1 21 B3
Pinkneys Dr SL6 38 F8
Pinkneys Farm SL6 19 B1
PINKNEYS GREEN 19 A1
Pinkneys Rd SL6 39 A8
Pinks La RG26 134 E1
Pinnacle The RG1 86 D7
Pipers Cl SL1 21 C2
Pipers Ct
Burnham SL1 21 C2
Thatcham RG19 107 A2
Piper's End GU25 122 D6
Pipers Ind Est RG19 106 F2
Pipers La RG19 106 F1
Pipers Way RG19 106 F2
Pipistrelle Way RG10 61 A4
Pipit Cl RG19 106 B3
Pippin Gr RG2 113 E6
Pippins Ct TW15 98 B2
Pippins Sch SL3 69 F6
Pippins The SL3 43 F5
Pipsons Cl GU46 149 D6
Pitch Pl RG42 90 D3
Pitcroft Ave RG6 87 A6
Pitfield La RG7 137 C4
Pitford Rd RG5 88 A8
Pitts Cl RG42 90 C2
Pitt's La RG6 87 B8
Pitts Rd SL1 42 C5
Plackett Way SL1 41 D5
Plaines Cl SL1 41 F5
Planes The KT16 124 C2
Plantagenet Pk RG42 118 F8
Plantation Cl RG18 78 F5
Plantation Rd
Chilton OX12 9 F8
Tadley RG26 134 F2
Plantation Row GU15 151 B5
Plantinum Apartments 17
RG1 86 B6
Plateau The RG42 92 A1
Platt Ct RG17 100 E3
Platt La RG17 45 C6
Players Gn RG5 87 E5
PLAY HATCH 60 A5
Playhatch Rd RG4 60 B5
Play Platt RG7 83 D4
Plough La
Shiplake RG9 35 E1
Stoke Poges SL2 23 B4
Wokingham RG40 116 F6
Ploughlands RG42 117 F8
Ploughlees La SL1 42 E6
Plough Rd GU46 149 E7
Plover Cl
Staines TW18 96 F5
Wokingham RG41 115 F5
Plover La RG27 140 E1
Plowden Way RG9 35 E1
Plummery The 1 RG1 86 C7
Plumpton Rd 1 RG14 105 C1
Plumtrees RG6 87 B2
Pluto Cl SL1 41 E4
Pluto Rd OX11 9 F8
Plymouth Ave RG5 87 C5
Plymouth Rd SL1 41 E8
Plympton Cl RG6 87 B2
Pocket Cl RG42 117 D7
Pocket Pl RG6 87 B4
Pocketts Yd SL6 20 B7
Pococks La SL4 42 E1
Poffley Pl RG19 107 A3
Pointers Cl RG20 51 B2
Point Royal RG12 118 B4
Points The SL6 39 B3
Polar Pk UB7 70 F7
Poldark Pl RG2 113 B7
Polehampton CE Inf Sch
RG10 61 D5
Polehampton Cl RG10 61 D4
Polehampton Ct RG10 61 D4
Polehampton Jun Sch
RG10 61 E6
Pollard Cl SL4 68 B2
Pollard Gr GU15 152 C4
Pollardrow Ave RG42 117 F8
Pollards Way RG31 84 D4
Polo Ctr The SL5 121 C6
Polsted Rd RG31 57 D1
Polyanthus Way RG45 143 B8
Polye Pk SL3 69 E4
Polygon Bsns Ctr SL3 69 F5
Pond Cl
Farnborough (Berks) OX12 8 E1
Newbury RG14 130 D7
Pond Croft GU46 149 E6
Ponderosa Cvn Site TW19 69 F3
Pond Head La RG6 87 D4
Pond Ho KT16 124 B2
Pond La
Hermitage RG18 79 C7
Mapledurham RG4 58 A6
Pondmoor Rd RG12 118 B4
Pond Rd TW20 96 C2
Pondside Cl UB3 71 D7
Poole Cl RG30 85 A7
Pool End Cl TW17 125 A4
Pooley Ave TW20 96 B3
POOLEY GREEN 96 C2
Pooley Green Cl TW20 96 C3
Pooley Green Rd TW20 96 C3
Pool La
Slough SL1 42 E6
Waltham St L RG10 63 A5
Poolmans Rd SL4 66 D4
Pope Cl TW14 98 F7
Popel's Cotts SL4 92 D5
Poperinghe Way RG2 140 D8
Popes Cl SL3 69 C7
Popes La SL6 19 C7
POPESWOOD 117 D8
Popeswood Lodge RG42 117 D8
Popeswood Rd RG42 117 D8
Popeswood Rdbt RG42 117 D8
Popham Cl RG12 118 F4
Poplar Ave
Reading RG30 84 F5
Windlesham GU20 146 B6
Poplar Cl
Bracknell RG12 118 D6
Brimpton RG19 133 A6
Poyle SL3 69 E6
Poplar Gdns RG2 86 E1
Poplar Gn RG2 113 D8
Poplar Ho SL3 43 F1
Poplar La
Hurst RG10 62 A2
Winnersh RG41 88 D3
Poplar Pl RG14 105 A5
Poplar Rd
Ashford TW15 98 C3
Wooburn Green HP10 3 E7
Poplars Gr SL6 20 B2
Poplars The SL5 120 A4
Poppy Dr RG18 106 F4
Poppyhills Rd GU15 151 F8
Poppy Pl RG40 116 B6
Poppy Way RG31 84 C5
Porchester SL5 120 A5
Porchester Rd RG14 105 A1
Porchfield Cl RG6 87 A1
Porlock Cl 5 RG19 106 D2
Porlock Pl RG31 84 C4
Port Down RG17 100 E5
Porter Cl RG6 114 C8
Porter End RG14 131 B8
Portesbery Hill Dr GU15 151 E6
Portesbery Rd GU15 151 E6
Portesbery Sch GU15 151 D6
Portia Gr RG42 118 E8
Portland Bsns Ctr SL3 68 B6
Portland Cl SL2 21 D1
Portland Cres TW13 98 D4
Portland Gdns
Marlow SL7 1 D1
Reading RG30 84 D7
Portland Rd TW15 97 E5
Portlands Mews 1 SL7 1 D1
Portlock Rd SL6 39 C7
Portman Cl 5 RG42 118 A8
Portman Ctr The RG30 58 D1
Portman Rd RG30 58 C1
Portman Way RG30 85 D8
Portmeirion Gdns RG30 57 F1
Portnall Cotts SL5 121 C4
Portnall Dr GU25 121 F4
Portnall Rd GU25 121 F4
Portnall Rise GU25 121 F3
Portrush Cl RG5 87 D6
Portsmouth Ct SL1 42 E6
Portsmouth Rd GU15 152 A7
Portway
Riseley RG7 139 C2
Tadley RG26 134 E1
Portway Cl RG1 85 E6
Post Horn Pl RG31 84 F4
Posting House Mews
RG14 104 E4
Post Office Cotts SL2 23 A5
Post Office La
Burghfield RG30 111 D5
Slough SL3 43 D7
Post Office Rd RG17 127 E5
Potbury Cl SL4 93 B2
Potley Hill Prim Sch
GU46 150 A5
Potley Hill Rd GU46 149 F5
Pottery La RG17 127 E5
Pottery Rd RG30 57 F1
Potts Pl 6 SL7 1 D2
POUGHLEY 73 F8
Poulcott TW19 68 E1
Pound Cotts RG8 34 A6
Pound Cres SL7 1 C1
Poundfield La SL6 19 F7
Poundfield Way RG10 61 F3
POUNDGREEN 112 C3
Pound Green Cotts RG7 111 B1
Pound La
Hurst RG10 89 B5
Little Marlow SL7 2 C4
Marlow SL7 1 D1
Newbury RG20 104 D4
Sonning RG4 60 E2
Thatcham RG18, RG19 106 A3
Windlesham GU20 146 C4
Pound Piece RG17 100 C5
Pound Pl RG42 90 C3
Pound Rd KT16 124 B2
Pound St RG14 104 F2
Pound The SL1 21 D1
Powis Cl SL6 39 B4
Powney Rd SL6 39 C7
POYLE 69 E6
Poyle 14 Trad Est SL3 69 E4
Poyle Gdns RG12 118 D8
Poyle La SL1 21 B3
Poyle New Cotts SL3 69 F5
Poyle Rd SL3 69 E5
Poyle Tech Ctr The SL3 69 E5
Poynings The SL0 44 F2
Prancing Horse Cl RG19 106 E3
Precincts The SL1 21 C1
Precinct The TW20 96 A3
Prescott RG12 117 F2
Prescott Rd SL3 69 E5
Presentation Coll RG30 85 D5
Preston Pl RG14 105 D5
Preston Rd
Littleton TW17 125 A4
Reading RG2 86 B5
Slough SL2 43 C6
Prestwick Ct 23 RG1 86 D7
Prestwood SL2 43 B7
Pretoria Rd KT16 123 F1
Price Gdns RG42 91 B2
Pride Ct RG30 85 E7
Prides Crossing SL5 93 A1
Priest Ave RG40 116 F5
Priest Hill
Caversham RG4 59 A3
Englefield Green SL4, TW20 95 C6
Farley Hill RG7 140 B6
Priest La GU24 153 C5
PRIESTWOOD 118 A8
Priestwood Ave RG42 117 F8
Priestwood Court Rd
RG42 118 A8
Priestwood Sq 1 RG42 118 A8
Primrose Cl RG8 57 C5
Primrose La RG41 88 C3
Primrose Lea SL7 1 D3
Primrose Walk GU46 149 B6
Primrose Way GU47 143 B1
Primrose Wlk RG12 118 C4
Prince Albert Ct 6 TW16 98 E1
Prince Albert Dr SL5 119 D4
Prince Albert's Wlk SL3,
SL4 68 B6
Prince Andrew Cl SL6 20 B1
Prince Andrew Rd SL6 20 B1
Prince Andrew Way SL5 119 D7
Prince Consort Cotts SL4 67 D5
Prince Consort Dr SL5 119 D5
Prince Consort's Dr
Old Windsor SL4 94 A6
Windsor SL4 67 A1
Prince Dr GU47 143 A1
Prince Hold Rd RG19 106 A3
Prince Of Wales Ave
RG30 85 D7
Prince of Wales Wlk
GU15 151 C6
Princes Cl SL4 41 F1
Princes Ct
Bourne End SL8 3 C4
Englefield Green TW20 95 C3
Prince's La RG20 50 D6
Princes Rd
Ashford TW15 97 F3
Bourne End SL8 3 C3
Egham TW20 95 F2
Feltham TW13 98 F5
Princess Ave SL4 67 B4
Princess Christians Hospl
SL4 67 C6
Princess Margaret Hospl The
SL4 67 D5
Princess Marina Dr
Arborfield Garrison RG2 115 A1
Arborfield Garrison RG2 140 F7
Princess Sq RG12 118 B7
Princess St 19 SL6 39 F6
Princes St SL1 43 B4
Prince's St RG1 86 C7
Princess Way GU15 151 C5
Princes Terr SL8 3 C3
Princes Way GU19 145 E1
Prince William Ct TW15 97 F3
Prince William Dr RG31 57 C1
Prior Croft Cl GU15 152 A4
Prior End GU15 152 A5
Prior Heath Inf Sch
GU15 152 A5
Prior Place Cross Roads
GU15 152 B4
Prior Rd GU15 152 A5
Priors Cl
Maidenhead SL6 40 B2
5 Slough SL1 43 A3
Priors Court Cotts
Chieveley RG18 78 D7
Hermitage RG18 78 F7
Priors Court Rd RG18 78 E7
Priors Court Sch RG18 78 D8
Priors Ct 16 RG1 86 B6
Prior's La GU17 150 A5
Priors Rd
Tadley RG26 135 A1
Windsor SL4 66 D4
Priors Way SL6 40 B2
Priors Way Ind Est SL6 40 B2
Priors Wood RG45 142 D4
Priory Ave
Caversham RG4 59 A2
Hungerford RG17 100 D4
Priory Cl
Hungerford RG17 100 D4
Sunningdale SL5 121 A2
Priory Ct
Camberley GU15 150 F5
Caversham RG4 59 A2
Egham TW20 96 C2
Winnersh RG41 88 C3
Priory Gdns TW15 98 D3
Priory Gn TW18 97 B3
Priory Hts SL1 41 E7
Priory La RG42 91 C2
Priory Mews
8 Chertsey KT16 124 A2
Staines TW18 97 B3
Priory Pl
6 Hungerford RG17 100 D5
Newbury RG19 131 B6
Priory Rd
Burnham SL1 41 C8
Hungerford RG17 100 D4
Newbury RG14 105 A1
Sunningdale SL5 121 A2
Winkfield SL5 119 B7
Priory Sch SL1 41 D8
Priory The RG41 88 C3
Priory Way
Datchet SL3 68 B7
Harmondsworth UB7 70 E8
Priory Wlk RG12 118 F5
Priscilla Ho 9 TW16 98 F1
Pritchard Cl RG19 131 D7
Privet Cl RG6 87 B1
Proctors Rd RG40 116 F6
Progress Bsns Ctr SL1 41 D7
Projection E 11 RG1 86 A8
Projection W 10 RG1 86 A8
Promenade Rd RG4 59 A2
Prospect Cotts RG42 117 D8
Prospect Ct SL2 22 C6
Prospect La TW20 95 A3
Prospect Mews 4 RG1 85 F7
Prospect Park Hospl
RG30 85 B6
Prospect Pl
Hurley SL6 17 F3
Newbury RG14 105 A1
Staines TW18 96 F3
3 Windsor SL4 67 D4
Prospect Rd
Hungerford RG17 100 D5
Marlow SL7 1 D2
Prospect Sch RG30 85 A5
Prospect St
Caversham RG4 59 B2
Reading RG1 85 F7
Providence Ct UB3 71 D7
Providence Ho GU19 145 E3
Providence La UB3 71 D7
Providence Pl 11 SL6 39 F7
Prudential Bldgs 1 SL1 42 F4
Prune Hill TW20 95 E1
Prunus Cl GU24 153 E6
Pryor Cl RG31 57 B4
Ptarmigan Hts RG12 117 D5
Puccinia Ct TW19 97 E7
Pudding Hill RG10 37 D6
Pudding La RG20 28 E1
Pudseys Cl SL6 19 B6
Puffers Way RG14 104 E2
Puffin Way RG2 86 A2
Pullmans Pl 6 TW18 97 A3
Pulse The 2 SL6 40 A7
Pumpkin Hill SL1 21 E6
Pump La
Ascot SL5 120 E8
Pump La *continued*
Grazeley RG7 112 C2
Pump La N SL7 1 F6
Pump La S SL7 2 A4
Pundles La SL6 63 C6
PUNT HILL 39 C6
Purbeck Ho 3 RG2 113 C8
Purbrook Ct RG12 118 E3
Purcell Rd RG45 143 B7
Purfield Dr RG10 36 E2
Purley CE Inf Sch RG8 57 C5
Purley Ind Est RG20 49 B7
Purley La RG8 57 C5
Purley Magna RG8 57 C4
PURLEY ON THAMES 57 B6
Purley Rise RG8 57 A5
Purley Village RG8 57 C5
Purley Way RG8 56 E5
Pursers Ct SL2 42 E6
Pursers Farm RG7 113 B3
Purslane RG40 116 D5
Purssell Cl SL6 39 A3
PURTON 51 D8
Purton Ct SL2 22 C5
Purton La SL2 22 C5
Putman Pl RG9 15 E1
Pyegrove Chase RG12 118 E2
Pyke Cl RG40 116 D6
Pykes Hill RG8 54 D4
Pyle Hill RG14 105 B1
Pyrcroft Ct KT16 123 F2
Pyrcroft Grange Prim Sch
KT16 123 E2
Pyrcroft Rd KT16 123 E2

Q

Quadrant Ct
Bracknell RG12 118 E6
23 Reading RG1 86 B6
Quadrant The SL6 40 A6
Quadrivium Point SL1 42 C5
Qualitas RG12 117 F1
Quantock Ave RG4 59 D5
Quantock Cl
Charvil RG10 61 B4
Harlington UB3 71 D7
Slough SL3 44 A1
Quantocks The RG19 106 D2
Quarrington Cl RG19 106 E2
Quarry Bank GU18 153 A8
Quarrydale Dr SL7 1 F2
Quarry La
Lower Shiplake RG9 36 A4
Yateley GU46 149 E5
Quarry Wood Rd SL6, SL7 19 A8
Quartz Cl RG41 115 D7
Quaves Rd SL3 43 C3
Quebec Gdns GU17 150 D4
Quebec Rd RG9 35 E8
Queen Anne Royal Free CE
Fst Sch The SL4 67 D4
Queen Anne's Cl SL4 94 B5
Queen Anne's Ct 9 SL4 67 C6
Queen Annes Gate RG4 59 C3
Queen Anne's Rd SL4 67 C3
Queen Anne's Sch RG4 59 B3
Queen Charlotte St 10
SL4 67 D6
Queen Cl RG9 15 E1
Queen Elizabeth Rd
GU15 144 D1
Queen Elizabeth's Wlk
SL4 67 F5
Queen Mary Ave GU15 151 A5
Queen Mary Ct TW19 97 E7
Queen Mary Rd TW17 125 C7
Queens Acre SL4 67 D3
Queens Acre Ho 6 SL4 67 D4
Queensborough Dr RG4 58 E5
Queensbury Pl GU17 150 C3
Queen's Cl
North Ascot SL5 119 E8
Old Windsor SL4 68 A2
Queen's Cotts
Reading RG1 86 B7
Wargrave RG10 36 D2
Queens Ct
Goring RG8 34 C6
3 Newbury RG14 105 A1
Slough SL1 42 F6
Queen's Ct TW18 97 D2
Queen's Dr SL3 23 F4
Queen's Dr The RG2, RG6 86 E4
Queens Gate Cotts SL4 67 D3
Queenshill Lodge SL5 120 B6
Queens Hill Rise SL5 120 C6
Queens Keep GU15 151 D5
Queen's La 8 SL6 39 F7
Queens Lawns RG1 86 D6
Queensmead
Ashford TW15 97 F3
Datchet SL3 68 B6
Queensmere Sh Ctr SL1 42 F4
Queens Park Gdns 3
TW13 98 F5
Queens Pine RG12 118 E3
Queen's Pl SL5 120 A6
Queens Rd
Bisley GU24 153 F1
Camberley GU15 151 B4
Eton SL4 41 F1
Slough SL1 42 F6
Windsor SL4 67 C5
Queen's Rd
Ascot SL5 120 D4
Caversham RG4 59 C1

Queen's Rd *continued*
Datchet SL3 68 B7
Egham TW20 95 F2
Marlow SL7 1 D2
Newbury RG14 105 B2
Reading RG1 86 C7
Queens Ride RG45 143 B7
Queen St
Caversham RG4 59 A3
Chertsey KT16 124 A1
Henley-on-T RG9 15 E1
Maidenhead SL6 39 F7
Queen's Terr 5 SL4 67 D4
Queensway
Caversham RG4 59 D6
Maidenhead SL6 19 E2
Queens Way RG17 102 C1
Queen's Wharf RG1 86 C7
Queens Wlk TW15 97 D4
Queens Wlk Mall 3 SL6 39 F7
Queen Victoria Cross Roads GU15 151 A6
Queen Victoria Ho RG40 116 D6
Queen Victoria St RG1 86 B8
Queen Victoria's Wlk SL4 67 F6
Quelm Park Rdbt RG42 91 B2
Quentin Rd RG5 87 D6
Quentin Way GU25 122 B5
QUICK'S GREEN 54 D5
Quinbrookes SL2 43 C7
Quince Cl SL5 120 D5
Quincy Rd TW20 96 A3
Quinn Ct 4 RG30 85 C7
Quintilis RG12 117 F1
Quoitings Dr SL7 1 C2
Quoitings Gdns SL7 1 C2
Quoiting Sq SL7 1 D2

R

Racecourse Rd RG14 105 B1
Raceview Bsns Ctr RG14 105 B2
Rachaels Lake View RG42 91 E1
Rackstraw Rd GU47 143 D2
Radbourne Rd RG31 84 D4
Radcliffe Way RG42 117 E8
Radcot Ave SL3 44 B3
Radcot Cl
Maidenhead SL6 19 E3
Woodley RG5 60 E1
Radical Ride RG40 141 F7
Radius Pk TW14 71 F3
Radley Bottom
Hungerford Newtown RG17 74 B3
Hungerford RG17 101 E7
Radley Cl TW14 98 F7
Radnor Cl RG9 15 E2
Radnor Ho 10 RG1 85 E5
Radnor Rd
Bracknell RG12 118 F6
Earley RG6 87 C3
Radnor Way SL3 43 E2
Radstock La RG6 87 A2
Radstock Prim Sch RG6 87 B2
Radstock Rd RG1 86 E7
Raeburn Way GU47 150 D6
Ragdale RG7 111 A3
Raggleswood Cl RG6 87 C3
Raghill RG7 135 D6
Raglan Ct RG2 86 D2
Raglan Gdns RG4 59 C4
Ragley Mews RG4 59 D6
Ragmans Cl SL7 1 D8
Ragstone Rd SL1 42 E3
Railside RG7 108 F2
Railton Cl RG2 113 D7
Railway Cotts RG8 34 C6
Railway Rd RG14 105 B2
Railway Terr
Egham TW18 96 D3
Mortimer RG7 137 E5
Slough SL2 42 F5
Rainbow Pk RG41 88 B2
Rainforest Wlk RG12 118 B4
Rainsborough Chase SL6 39 B3
Rainworth Cl RG6 114 A8
Raleigh Cl
Slough SL1 42 A5
Woodley RG5 87 E5
Raleigh Ct TW18 97 A4
Raleigh Rd TW13 98 F6
Raleigh Way GU16 151 F3
Ralphs Ride RG12 118 E6
Ralston Ct 25 25 67 D6
Ram Alley RG19 133 D1
Rambler Cl SL6 41 B7
Rambler La SL3 43 C3
Ramptons La RG7 136 B6
Ramsay Cl GU15 152 B8
Ramsay Rd GU20 146 E5
Ramsbury Cl RG12 117 E3
Ramsbury Cnr RG18 106 F8
Ramsbury Dr
Earley RG6 87 B4
Hungerford RG17 100 E5
Ramsbury Terr RG17 100 E5
Ramsey Cl RG6 87 E2
Ramsey Ct SL2 21 D1
Ramslade Cotts RG12 118 C6
Ranald Court Cotts SL5 92 F1
Ranald Ct SL5 92 F2
Rances La RG40 116 E5
Randall Cl SL3 43 F1
Randall Ct SL4 68 A1
Randall Mead RG42 90 B2
Randell Cl GU17 150 E1
Randolph Rd
Reading RG1 59 A1
Slough SL3 43 E3
Ranelagh CE Sch RG12 118 C6
Ranelagh Cres SL5 119 D8
Ranelagh Dr RG12 118 C6
Range Rd RG40 142 B7
Range Ride GU15 150 F7
Range View GU47 150 E8
Range Villas TW17 124 E2
Range Way TW17 125 A2
Rangewood Ave RG30 84 F3
Ranikhet Prim Sch RG30 85 A8
Rapley Cl GU15 151 F8
Rapley Gn RG12 118 C3
Ratby Cl RG6 87 C2
Raven Cl GU46 149 B6
Ravendale Rd TW16 125 F7
Ravenglass Cl RG6 87 C3
Ravensbourne Ave TW19 97 E7
Ravensbourne Dr RG5 87 E8
Ravenscote Com Jun Sch GU16 152 A3
Ravenscourt
Marlow SL7 2 A3
Sunbury TW16 125 F8
Ravenscroft Rd RG9 15 D2
Ravensdale Mews TW18 97 B2
Ravensdale Rd SL5 120 A4
Ravensfield TW20 95 C2
Ravens Field SL3 43 D4
Ravenshoe Cl SL8 3 A3
Ravenstone Rd GU15 152 D5
Ravenswing Pk RG7 135 D2
Ravenswood Ave RG45 142 E5
Ravenswood Dr GU15 152 A5
Ravenswood Village Settlement RG45 142 E6
Ravensworth Rd
Mortimer RG7 136 E5
Slough SL2 22 A2
Rawcliffe Ho SL6 40 A6
Rawdon Rise GU15 152 B5
Rawlinson Rd GU15 150 F6
Ray Dr SL6 40 B7
Rayfield SL6 40 B8
Ray Ho 5 SL8 3 A4
Ray Lea Cl SL6 40 B8
Ray Lea Rd SL6 40 B8
Ray Lodge SL6 40 B7
Ray Lodge Mews SL6 40 B7
Ray Mdw SL6 20 A1
Ray Mead Ct SL6 20 C1
Ray Mead Rd SL6 40 C8
Ray Mill Rd E SL6 20 B1
Ray Mill Rd W SL6 40 A8
Raymond Cl SL3 69 E6
Raymond Rd
Maidenhead SL6 39 D7
Slough SL3 44 A3
Rayner Dr RG2 140 E8
Rayners Cl SL3 69 C7
Ray Park Ave SL6 40 B8
Ray Park La SL6 40 B7
Ray Park Rd SL6 40 B8
Rays Ave SL4 66 F7
Ray St SL6 40 B7
Raywood Cl UB7 71 C7
Reade Ct SL2 22 C6
READING 86 B4
Reading Alternative Sch RG1 86 C5
Reading Blue Coat Sch RG4 60 C3
Reading Bridge RG1 86 B8
Reading Gate Ret Pk RG2 85 F1
Reading Girls Sch RG2 86 C3
Reading Green Park Station RG30 85 D1
Reading International Bsns Pk RG2 113 A6
Reading Link Ret Pk RG2 86 A5
Reading Rd
Aldermaston RG7 135 F5
Aldworth RG8 33 A2
Arborfield RG2 114 C3
Blackwater GU17 150 B4
Burghfield Common RG7 111 B2
Finchampstead RG27 140 F4
Goring RG8 34 E6
Henley-on-T RG9 15 E1
Moulsford OX10 14 A7
Pangbourne RG8 56 D5
Streatley RG8 34 A6
Winnersh RG41 88 C2
Wokingham RG41 115 E8
Woodley RG5 87 D8
Yateley GU46 149 D6
Reading Ret Pk RG30 58 B1
Reading Sch RG1 86 D6
Reading Sta RG1 86 A8
Reading Stadium (Speedway) RG2 85 F1
Reading West Sta RG30 85 E7
Recognition Ho 9 SL4 67 A5
Recreation Cl GU14 150 F1
Recreation La RG7 113 B2
Recreation Rd
Bourne End SL8 3 B3
Burghfield Common RG7 111 A2
Reading RG30 84 E8
Wargrave RG10 36 E2
Rectory Cl
Bracknell RG12 118 C5
Farnham Royal SL2 22 C2
Littleton TW17 125 A6
Newbury RG14 104 F1
Sandhurst GU47 149 F8
Rectory Cl *continued*
Windsor SL4 67 A6
Wokingham RG40 116 C6
Rectory La
Aston Tirrold OX11 12 F8
Bracknell RG12 118 B5
Letcombe Bassett OX12 6 E7
Windlesham GU20 146 C4
Rectory Rd
Caversham RG4 59 A2
Padworth RG7 135 F7
Streatley RG8 33 C7
Taplow SL6 20 E1
Wokingham RG40 116 C6
Rectory Row RG12 118 B5
Rectory Terr SL2 22 C3
Rectory The RG14 104 E2
Redberry Cl RG4 59 D5
Red Brick Cotts 13 SL4 67 D6
Red Cottage Dr RG31 84 C4
Red Cottage Mews SL3 43 C3
Redcrest Gdns GU15 151 F5
Red Cross Rd RG8 34 C6
Red Ct SL1 42 E5
Reddington Dr SL3 43 E2
Redditch RG12 118 D2
Redesdale Ct RG2 86 C3
Redfield Ct RG14 105 D4
Redfinch Mews RG18 106 E3
Redford Cl TW13 98 F6
Redford Rd SL4 66 D6
Redgauntlet RG40 141 D6
Redgrave Pl SL7 1 F3
Redhatch Dr RG6 87 A2
RED HILL 129 C5
Red Hill RG9 35 A5
Red House Cl RG6 114 B8
Red La RG7 135 D5
Redlake La RG40 116 F2
Redlands Pl RG40 115 F2
Redlands Prim Sch RG1 86 E5
Redlands Rd RG1 86 D6
Redlane Ct RG1 86 D5
Redlane Hill RG7 135 C6
Redlane Rd RG20 30 A3
Red Leaf Cl SL3 43 F5
Redleaves Ave TW15 98 B2
Red Lion Cotts SL2 23 B1
Red Lion Way HP10 3 E6
Redmayne GU15 152 C4
Redpitch Pk HP10 3 F6
Red Rd GU18, GU24, GU15 153 C7
Redriff Cl SL6 39 D6
Red Roofs SL6 40 C7
Red Rose RG42 90 C3
Redruth Gdns RG2 86 B1
Redshank Ct RG19 106 A3
Redshots Cl SL7 1 E4
Red Shute Hill RG18 79 A4
Red Shute Ind Est RG18 79 A4
Redvers Rd RG12 118 B4
Redwood
Burnham SL1 21 B3
Staines TW20 123 E7
Redwood Ave RG5 88 A6
Redwood Dr
Frimley GU15 152 D4
Sunningdale SL5 121 B3
Redwood Gdns SL1 42 D6
Redwood Mews TW15 98 D1
Redwoods The SL4 67 D4
Redwood Way RG31 57 D3
Reed Cl SL0 44 E7
Reed Pl TW17 124 F1
Reeds Ave
Lower Earley RG6 87 A3
Reading RG6 86 F3
Reedsfield Cl TW15 98 B5
Reedsfield Rd TW15 98 B4
Reed's Hill RG12 118 B4
Reed Wlk RG14 105 C4
Reeve Rd SL6 65 B8
Reeves Way RG41 116 A4
Reform Rd SL6 40 B7
Regal Ct
Maidenhead SL6 40 B2
8 Newbury RG14 105 B2
Regatta Ho 8 TW18 96 F3
Regency Ho 5 KT16 123 F1
Regency Hts RG4 58 E4
Regency Pl 7 KT16 124 A1
Regent Cl
Earley RG6 87 C1
Hungerford RG17 100 C5
Regent Ct
Bagshot GU19 145 F2
9 Maidenhead SL6 39 F7
Reading RG1 86 A8
Slough SL1 42 E7
Windsor SL4 67 D6
Regents Ct
Newbury RG14 104 F3
4 Newbury RG14 105 B3
Staines TW18 97 B2
Regents Ho 3 TW20 96 A3
Regents Pl
Maidenhead SL6 39 D7
Sandhurst GU47 150 C8
Regents Riverside RG1 59 A1
Regent St RG1 86 E7
Regents Wlk SL5 120 C2
Regent Way GU16 152 A1
Regional Ho SL1 43 A4
Regis Cl RG2 113 D7
Regis Ct TW14 71 D1
Regnum Dr RG14 105 B5
Reid Ave SL6 39 E5
Rembrandt Cl RG41 115 D6
Rembrandt Way RG1 85 E5
Remembrance Rd RG14 104 E2
R.E.M.E Mus of Technology* RG2 141 A8
REMENHAM 16 A5
Remenham Church La RG9 16 A4
REMENHAM HILL 16 C2
Remenham La RG9 15 F3
Remenham Row RG9 15 F2
Remenham Terr RG9 16 C2
Renault Rd RG5 88 A6
Renfree Way TW17 125 A2
Rennie Cl TW15 97 D5
Rennie Ct RG14 104 F4
Renshaw Ind Est TW18 96 F4
Repton Cl SL6 39 C3
Repton Rd RG6 87 C3
Restwold Cl RG30 85 C4
Retford Cl RG5 60 F1
Retreat The
Englefield Green TW20 95 E3
Fifield SL6 65 D7
Revel Rd HP10 3 D8
Revesby Cl
Maidenhead SL6 39 D3
West End GU24 153 D6
Rex Ave TW15 98 A3
Reynards Cl RG41 88 C2
Reynolds Ct RG18 106 D3
Reynolds Gn GU47 150 D6
Rhema Ct 9 RG1 85 F7
Rhigos RG4 58 F6
Rhine Cl RG4 59 D2
Rhodes Cl
Earley RG6 87 E3
Egham TW20 96 B3
Rhodes Ct TW20 96 C3
Rhododendron Cl SL5 92 E1
Rhododendron Cnr RG40 142 B4
Rhododendron Rd GU16 152 B1
Rhododendron Ride SL4, TW20 94 F3
Rhododendron Wlk
Brimpton RG19 133 B5
North Ascot SL5 92 E1
Ribbleton Cl RG6 87 E3
Ribstone Rd SL6 39 B3
Ricardo Rd SL4 68 B1
Richard Ct TW15 97 F3
Richard Dodd Pl 16 SL1 42 F4
Richard Nevill Ct 1 RG4 59 C2
Richards Cl UB3 71 D8
Richardson Ho TW20 95 C5
Richardson's Lawn Cotts SL4 94 B5
Richards Way SL1 42 A5
Richborough Cl RG6 87 B2
Richfield Ave RG1 58 F1
Richfield Pl RG1 58 F1
Richings Pl SL0 44 E3
Richings Way SL0 44 F3
Richmond Ave
Feltham TW14 71 E1
Thatcham RG19 106 A3
Richmond Cl GU16 151 F1
Richmond Cres
Slough SL1 43 A5
Staines TW18 96 F3
Richmond Dr TW17 125 D3
Richmond Ho
Sandhurst GU47 150 E7
Sunningdale SL5 120 F1
Richmond Rd
Caversham RG4 58 E4
Reading RG30 85 D8
Sandhurst GU47 150 E8
Staines TW18 96 F3
Richmond Rise RG41 115 E7
Richmond Wood SL5 121 B1
Rickman Cl
Arborfield Garrison RG2 114 E1
Bracknell RG12 118 C3
Woodley RG5 87 D5
Rickman's La SL2 22 E6
Riddings La RG19 133 C2
Rider's La RG7 112 A4
Rideway Cl GU15 151 B4
Ridgebank SL1 41 F6
Ridge Ct SL4 67 C4
Ridge Hall Cl RG4 58 E3
Ridgemead Rd TW20 95 B5
Ridgemount Cl RG31 57 B2
Ridge Mount Rd SL5 121 A1
RIDGES THE 142 B3
Ridge The
Cold Ash RG18 106 D8
Sunningdale SL5 121 A2
Upper Basildon RG8 55 F8
Ridgeway
Oatlands Park KT12 125 F1
Wargrave RG10 36 E2
Ridge Way
Iver SL0 44 F6
Virginia Water GU25 122 E4
Ridgeway Cl
Hermitage RG18 79 B7
Lightwater GU18 153 A8
Marlow SL7 1 E4
Ridgeway Prim Sch The RG2 86 D1
Ridgeway The
Bracknell RG12 118 C6
Caversham RG4 59 B3
Letcombe Bassett OX12 7 D5
Lightwater GU18 146 B1
Marlow SL7 1 E4
Ridgeway The *continued*
Woodley RG5 87 F5
Ridgeway Trad Est The SL0 44 E6
Ridgewood Ctr (Hospl) GU16 152 C3
Ridgewood Dr GU16 152 D3
Riding Court Rd SL3 68 D7
Riding Ct SL3 68 C8
Ridings The
Caversham RG4 59 C8
Frimley GU16 152 B3
Iver SL0 44 F2
Maidenhead SL6 39 A7
Riding Way RG41 115 E6
Ridleigh Ct TW15 98 A4
Ridlington Cl RG6 87 E2
Rigby Lodge SL1 42 E7
Righton Cl RG10 61 B3
Riley Rd
Marlow SL7 1 D2
Reading RG30 84 F8
Rimaud Ho 18 RG1 86 B6
Ringmead
Bracknell, Great Hollands RG12 117 E4
Bracknell, Hanworth RG12 118 B2
Ring The RG12 118 C7
Ringwood RG12 117 F2
Ringwood Cl SL5 120 B5
Ringwood Rd
Blackwater GU17 150 C6
Reading RG30 58 A1
Ripley Ave TW20 95 E2
Ripley Cl SL3 43 E2
Ripley Rd RG30 58 A1
RIPLEY SPRINGS 95 E2
Ripon Cl GU15 152 D3
Ripon Rd GU17 149 F1
Ripplesmere RG12 118 D5
Ripplesmore Cl GU47 150 B8
Ripston Rd TW15 98 D3
Risborough Rd SL6 39 E8
RISELEY 139 C3
Riseley Bsns Pk RG7 139 C3
Riseley Rd SL6 39 D7
Rise Rd SL5 120 F3
Rise The
Caversham RG4 59 B4
Cold Ash RG18 106 C7
Crowthorne RG45 142 F5
Finchampstead RG40 141 A2
Winkfield RG42 119 A8
Wokingham RG41 116 A7
Rissington Cl RG31 57 E3
Riverbank TW18 96 F2
Riverbank The SL4 67 B7
River Ct
Taplow SL6 40 C7
Twyford RG10 61 B5
Riverdale Ct RG14 105 C3
Riverdene Dr 4 RG41 88 A3
Riverfield Rd TW18 96 F2
River Gdns
Bray SL6 40 D4
Purley on T RG8 57 D5
Riverine SL6 40 C8
Rivermead Ct SL7 18 E8
Rivermead Ind Est RG19 106 F1
Rivermead Prim Sch RG5 87 F6
Rivermead Rd
Camberley GU15 151 B2
Woodley RG5 87 F5
River Mount KT12 125 F2
River Park Ave TW18 96 D4
Riverpark Dr SL7 1 F1
Riverpark Ind Est RG14 105 B3
River Rd
Caversham RG4 58 D3
18 Reading RG1 86 A6
Staines TW18 123 F8
Taplow SL6 40 C6
Yateley GU46 149 B8
River & Rowing Mus* RG9 15 F1
Riversdale SL8 3 B1
Riversdale Cotts SL8 3 B1
Riversdale Ct
Bourne End SL8 3 B1
Reading RG1 86 E8
Riversdell Cl KT16 123 F2
Riverside
Bradfield RG7 82 C6
Chilton Foliat RG17 72 F1
Egham TW20 96 A5
Marlow SL7 1 E1
Oatlands Park TW17 125 E2
Wraysbury TW19 95 C8
Riverside Ave GU18 153 C8
Riverside Cl TW18 123 F8
Riverside Cotts HP10 3 E8
Riverside Ct 1 RG4 59 A2
Riverside Dr
Egham TW18 96 E3
Staines TW18 123 F8
Riverside Ho RG1 86 A7
Riverside Mus* RG1 86 C8
Riverside Pk SL3 69 E5
Riverside Pk RG30 58 B2
Riverside Pl TW19 70 D1
Riverside Rd
Staines TW18 96 F1
Stanwell TW19 70 E1
Riverside Way GU15 151 A3
Riverside Wlk SL4 67 D7

River St SL4 67 D7
Riverview TW17 125 D2
River View
Flackwell Heath HP10 3 B7
Froxfield SN8 99 C5
Riverview Rd RG8 56 C5
Riverway
Eton SL4 67 C7
Great Shefford RG17 48 A3
Staines TW18 124 B8
River Wlk RG14 105 C4
Riverwood Ave SL7 2 A1
Riverwoods Dr SL7 2 A1
Rixman Cl SL6 39 D5
Rixon Cl SL3 43 E7
Robert Cort Ind Est RG2 86 B4
Robert Palmer Cotts The RG4 60 D3
Robert Piggott CE Inf Sch RG10 36 E1
Robert Piggott CE Jun Sch RG10 36 D1
Robert Sandilands Prim Sch RG14 104 E4
Roberts Cl TW19 70 C1
Robertsfield RG19 105 F3
Roberts Gr RG41 115 F4
Robertson Cl RG14 131 B8
Roberts Rd GU15 151 A6
Roberts Way TW20 95 C1
Robina Ho RG42 117 F8
Robin Cl RG7 111 B3
Robindale Ave RG6 87 D3
Robin Hill Dr GU15 152 A3
Robin Hill Ho GU46 149 B5
Robin Hood Cl SL1 41 F5
Robinhood La RG41 88 C3
Robin Hood Way RG41 88 C3
Robin La
Bishops Green RG20 131 F3
Sandhurst GU47 143 C1
Robin Par SL2 22 C7
Robin's Bow GU15 151 B4
Robins Cl RG14 130 F7
Robins Grove Cres GU46 149 B6
Robins Hill RG17 127 E6
Robinson Cl OX11 12 A8
Robinson Crusoe Pk RG40 141 B6
Robinson Ct
Earley RG6 87 A1
Maidenhead SL6 39 E4
Robin Way
Reading RG31 84 B6
Staines TW18 96 F5
Robin Willis Way SL4 68 A1
Robinwood 5 SL5 121 B2
Roby Dr RG12 118 D2
Rochester Ave
Feltham TW13 98 F6
Woodley RG5 60 E1
Rochester Rd TW20 96 D2
Rochfords Gdns SL2 43 C5
Rochford Way SL6 41 A7
Rockall Ct SL3 44 B3
Rockbourne Gdns RG30 58 A1
Rockfel Rd RG17 25 A2
Rockfield Way 7 GU47 150 D8
Rockingham Gate 17 RG14 104 F2
Rockingham Ho 18 RG14 104 F2
Rockingham Rd RG14 104 F2
Rockley Ct RG7 83 D2
Rockmoor La SP11 147 A1
Roddell Ct SL3 69 E6
Roddell Pl SL1 42 F6
Rodd Est TW17 125 D4
Roden Down Mews RG20 31 E5
Rodney Ct 13 RG1 86 A6
Rodney Way SL3 69 E6
Rodway Rd RG30 57 F1
Roebuck Est RG42 90 C1
Roebuck Gn SL1 41 E5
Roebuck Rise RG31 57 D3
Roebuts Cl RG14 130 F8
Rogers La SL2 22 F4
Rogers's La RG17 47 C6
Rokeby Cl
Bracknell RG12 118 D8
Newbury RG14 131 A7
Rokeby Dr RG4 58 D8
Rokesby Rd SL2 21 F2
Rokes Pl GU46 149 A6
Roland's Copse RG7 108 C2
Rolls La SL6 64 E8
Romana Ct TW18 97 A4
Roman Lea SL6 19 F7
Romano Ct 3 RG14 105 B2
Roman Pl SL6 39 C6
Roman Ride RG45 142 D5
Romans Field RG7 136 B1
Romans Gate RG26 135 F1
Roman Way
Bourne End SL8 3 B4
Earley RG6 87 D3
Thatcham RG18 106 B4
Winkfield RG42 118 F8
Romany Cl RG30 58 A1
Romany La RG30 58 A1
Romeo Hill RG42 118 F8
Romney Cl TW15 98 C3
Romney Ct 11 SL7 1 F3
Romney Ho RG12 118 E5
Romney Lock Rd SL4 67 D7
Romsey Cl
Blackwater GU17 150 C6
Slough SL3 43 F3
Romsey Rd RG30 58 A1
Rona Ct RG30 85 B8
Ronaldsay Spur SL1 42 E8
Ronita Ct RG1 86 F6
Rood Hill RG20 76 B4
Rook Cl RG41 115 E5
Rookery Ct RG40 141 A6
Rookery Ct SL7 1 D2
Rookery Rd TW18 97 B3
Rookery The RG20 50 D7
Rooke's Way RG18 105 E4
Rook Rd HP10 3 D4
Rooksfield RG20 132 A2
Rooksmead Rd TW16 125 F7
Rooksnest La RG17 128 A5
Rookswood
Bracknell RG42 91 B1
Stockcross RG20 103 F6
Rookwood Ave GU47 143 E2
Rope Wlk RG19 106 C3
Rosa Ave TW15 98 A4
Rosary Gdns
Ashford TW15 98 B4
Yateley GU46 149 D6
Roseacre Cl TW17 125 A4
Rosebank Cl SL6 19 E7
Rosebay RG40 116 E8
Rosebery Rd RG4 58 D7
Rose Bsns Est SL7 1 D5
Rose Cl RG5 88 B7
Rose Cotts
Maidenhead SL6 39 C3
Sandhurst GU47 143 A1
Rosecroft Way RG2 113 E5
Rose Ct 4 RG40 116 C6
Rosedale RG42 90 C3
Rosedale Cres RG6 87 A8
Rosedale Gdns
Bracknell RG12 118 A4
Thatcham RG19 106 C2
Rosedene La GU47 150 D7
Rosefield Rd TW18 97 A4
Rose Gdns
Stanwell TW19 97 D8
8 Wokingham RG40 116 C6
Rose Hill
Binfield RG42 90 C3
Burnham SL1 21 A5
Rosehill Ct SL1 43 A3
Rosehill Ho RG4 59 C7
Rosehill Pk RG4 59 C7
Rose Kiln La RG1, RG2 86 A4
Rose La RG10, RG9 37 A8
Roselawn Park Cvn Site RG30 111 D5
Roseleigh Cl SL6 39 A7
Rose Lodge TW20 96 A4
Rosemary Ave RG6 86 F1
Rosemary Gdns
Blackwater GU17 150 D5
Thatcham RG18 106 E4
Rosemary La
Blackwater GU17 150 D5
Thorpe TW20 123 B6
Rosemary Terr RG14 104 E2
Rosemead KT16 124 B2
Rosemead Ave
Feltham TW13 98 F6
Purley on T RG31 57 B3
Rosemoor Gdns RG14 105 D4
Rosen Ct RG19 106 E3
Rosery The SL8 3 A3
Roses La SL4 66 D5
Rose St RG40 116 C6
Rosevale Dr RG10 88 F8
Rose Wlk
Reading RG1 86 A7
Slough SL2 42 B8
Rosewood RG5 87 D4
Rose Wood SL5 119 E7
Rosewood Dr TW17 124 F4
Rosewood Way
Farnham Common SL2 22 C7
West End GU24 153 E6
Rosier Cl RG19 106 F2
Rosken Gr SL2 22 B3
Roslyn Rd RG5 87 D6
Rossby RG2 113 E7
Rossendale Rd RG4 59 D3
Rossett Cl RG12 118 B5
Ross Ho 2 RG30 85 D6
Rossington Pl 5 RG2 113 C8
Rossiter Cl SL3 43 E2
Rosslea GU20 146 A6
Rosslyn Cl TW16 98 E2
Ross Rd
Maidenhead SL6 39 E4
Reading RG1 59 A1
Rosyth Gdns RG14 131 D8
Rotary Way RG19 106 E1
Rothbury Ct RG2 86 D3
Rothbury Wlk GU15 152 C4
Rother Cl GU47 150 C8
Rotherfield Ave RG41 116 A7
Rotherfield Cl RG7 83 F4
Rotherfield Rd RG9 35 E7
Rotherfield Way RG4 59 B4
Rothwell Gdns RG5 61 A1
Rothwell Ho RG45 143 C4
Rothwell Wlk RG4 59 D2
ROTTEN ROW 81 F3
Rotten Row Hill RG7 81 F3
Roughgrove Copse RG42 90 B2
Rounce La GU24 153 D6
Roundabout La RG41 115 D8
Round Cl GU46 149 F5
Round End RG14 130 D5
Roundfield RG7 107 B6
Roundhead Rd RG7 83 D3
Roundshead Dr RG42 91 E1
Roundway
Egham TW20 96 C3
Frimley GU15 152 C6
Roundway Cl GU15 152 C6
Routh Ct TW14 98 D7
Routh La RG30 84 E6
Rowallan Cl RG4 59 D6
Rowan 2 RG12 118 F4
Rowan Ave TW20 96 C3
Rowan Cl
Ashford TW15 97 D4
Camberley GU15 151 F8
Wokingham RG41 115 F5
Rowan Ct
Bagshot GU19 145 D2
Earley RG6 87 B1
Reading RG2 113 E7
Rowan Dr
Crowthorne RG45 143 C6
Newbury RG14 105 A5
Woodley RG5 87 F8
Rowan Ho
1 Bourne End SL8 3 A4
East Bedfont TW14 71 D1
Rowanhurst Dr SL2 22 C7
Rowans Cl GU14 150 E1
Rowans The TW16 98 F3
Rowan Way
Burghfield RG30 111 B5
Slough SL2 42 B8
Rowanwood RG40 141 A6
Rowcroft Rd RG2 140 F7
Rowdell Dr RG2 86 D1
Rowdown RG17 24 E5
Rowe Ct RG30 85 B8
Row La RG4 59 E7
Rowland Cl SL4 66 D4
Rowland Hill Almshouses 8 TW15 98 A3
Rowland Pl RG41 116 A2
Rowland's Cl RG7 136 C5
Rowland Way
Earley RG6 86 F2
Littleton TW15 98 D1
Rowles Paddock RG20 10 A2
Rowley Cl RG12 118 E6
Rowley La SL3 23 D4
Rowley Rd RG2 86 B4
Rowlock Gdns RG18 79 C8
Roxborough Way SL6 38 F4
Roxburgh Cl GU15 152 C4
Roxeth Ct 7 TW15 98 A3
Roxford Cl TW17 125 E4
Roxwell Cl SL1 41 E5
Royal Ave RG31 84 C5
Royal Berkshire Hospl RG1 86 C6
Royal Cotts SL6 19 C7
Royal Ct 7 RG1 86 C7
Royal Free Ct 18 SL4 67 D6
Royal Fst Sch The SL4 94 C3
Royal Holloway Univ of London TW20 95 D2
Royal Hunt Ho SL5 119 D8
Royal Mans RG9 15 E1
Royal Mews SL4 67 D6
Royal Military Acad GU15 150 F6
Royal Oak Cl GU46 149 E6
Royal Oak Dr RG45 143 B8
Royal Station Ct RG10 61 D4
Royal Victoria Gdns SL5 120 A4
Royal Way RG2 112 F8
Roy Cl RG18 78 F6
Roycroft La RG40 141 E8
Roydon Ct TW20 96 D2
Royston Cl RG30 84 F7
Royston Way SL1 41 D8
Rubus Cl GU24 153 E6
Ruby Cl
Slough SL1 42 A4
Wokingham RG41 115 E7
Ruby Ct 5 TW13 98 F5
Rudd Hall Rise GU15 151 E4
Ruddlesway SL4 66 D6
Rudland Cl RG19 106 D2
Rudsworth Cl SL3 69 D7
Rufus Isaacs Rd RG4 59 B2
Rugby Cl GU47 143 E1
Ruggles-Brise Rd TW15 97 D3
Rugosa Rd GU24 153 E6
Rumsey's La OX11 12 A8
Runnemede Rd TW20 96 A4
Runnymede* TW20 95 F5
Runnymede Cotts TW19 96 D7
Runnymede Ct TW20 96 A4
Runnymede Ho 13 TW20 96 A3
Runnymede Rdbt TW20 96 B4
Rupert Cl RG9 15 E3
Rupert House Sch RG9 15 E2
Rupert Rd RG14 130 F7
Rupert's La RG9 15 E3
Rupert Sq 7 RG1 86 D7
Rupert St RG1 86 D7
Rupert Wlk 5 RG1 86 D7
RUSCOMBE 61 F6
Ruscombe Bsns Pk RG10 61 E5
Ruscombe Gdns SL3 68 A7
Ruscombe La RG10 61 E5
Ruscombe Pk RG10 61 E5
Ruscombe Rd RG10 61 E5
Ruscombe Turn RG10 61 F4
Ruscombe Way TW14 98 F8
Rushall Cl RG6 113 E7
Rusham Park Ave TW20 96 A2
Rusham Rd TW20 95 F2
Rusham Terr TW20 96 A2
Rushbrook Rd RG5 87 C7
Rushburn HP10 3 F6
Rushden Dr RG2 86 E1
Rushes The
Maidenhead SL6 40 C6
Marlow SL7 18 C8
Rushey Way
Earley RG6 87 C2
Lower Earley RG6 114 A8
Rushington Ave SL6 39 F5
Rushmere Cotts RG5 88 A5
Rushmere Pl TW20 95 E3
Rushmon Ct KT16 123 F2
Rushmoor Gdns RG31 84 B4
Rushy Ho RG12 118 E5
Ruskin RG4 59 D3
Ruskin Ave TW14 71 F1
Ruskin Ct RG45 142 F4
Ruskin Rd TW18 96 F2
Ruskin Way RG41 115 D6
Russell Cl RG12 118 D2
Russell Ct
Blackwater GU17 150 D5
Maidenhead SL6 39 F7
Newbury RG14 104 E3
Russell Dr TW19 70 D1
Russell Gdns UB7 71 A8
Russell Ho 4 SL8 3 A4
Russell Rd
Lower Halliford TW17 125 C2
Newbury RG14 104 E2
Tokers Green RG4 58 D7
Russell St
Reading RG1 85 F7
Windsor SL4 67 D5
Russell Way RG41 88 B1
Russet Ave TW17 125 E6
Russet Cl TW19 69 F1
Russet Gdns GU15 151 D3
Russet Glade
Burghfield Common RG7 111 B2
Caversham RG4 59 C7
Russet Rd SL6 39 C3
Russett Gdns RG10 61 E6
Russet Way RG20 51 C5
Russington Rd TW17 125 D3
Russley Gn RG40 116 A1
Rustington Cl 5 RG6 87 B1
Ruston Way SL5 119 E7
Rutherford Cl SL4 66 F6
Rutherford Wlk RG31 84 A7
Rutherwyk Rd KT16 123 E2
Rutland Ave SL1 42 C8
Rutland Gate SL6 39 C6
Rutland Pl SL6 39 C6
Rutland Rd
Maidenhead SL6 39 D6
Reading RG30 85 D7
Ruxbury Ct TW15 97 E5
Ruxbury Rd KT16 123 D3
Ruxley Gdns TW17 125 C4
Ryan Mount GU47 150 A8
Ryans Mount SL7 1 C2
Rycroft SL4 66 F4
Rydal Ave RG30 57 F2
Rydal Cl GU15 152 D5
Rydal Dr RG19 106 A3
Rydal Pl GU18 153 B8
Rydal Way TW20 96 B1
Ryde Gdns GU46 149 B6
Ryde The TW18 124 B8
Rydings SL4 66 F4
Rye Cl
Bracknell RG12 91 D1
Maidenhead SL6 39 A4
Winkfield RG12 118 D8
Ryecroft Cl
Wargrave RG10 36 E2
Woodley RG5 60 E1
Ryecroft Gdns GU17 150 E4
Rye Ct 1 SL1 43 A3
Ryefield Terr SL3 69 D7
Rye Gr GU20, GU18 146 F2
Ryehurst La RG42 90 F5
RYEISH GREEN 113 C4
Ryeish Green Sch RG7 113 C4
Ryeish La RG7 113 C3
Ryemead La SL4 92 C5
Ryhill Way RG6 113 F8
Ryland Cl TW13 98 F4
Rylstone Cl SL6 39 C3
Rylstone Rd RG30 85 D8
Ryvers End SL3 43 F3
Ryvers Prim Sch SL3 43 D3
Ryvers Rd SL3 43 F3
Ryves Ave GU46 149 A5

S

Sabah Ct TW15 98 A4
Sabin Gates RG12 118 B6
Sackville St RG1 86 A8
Sacred Heart RC Prim Sch RG9 15 D1
Saddleback Rd GU15 151 E8
Saddlebrook Pk TW16 98 E1
Saddler Cnr 4 GU47 150 B7
Saddlewood GU15 151 C4
Sadlers Ct RG41 88 D1
Sadlers End RG41 115 C7
Sadlers La RG41 115 D8
Sadlers Mews SL6 40 B7
Sadlers Rd RG17 127 A6
Sadlers The RG31 57 B1
Saffron Cl
Datchet SL3 68 B6
Earley RG6 87 C4
Newbury RG14 104 F3
Saffron Ct TW14 98 C8
Saffron Rd RG12 118 B5
Sage Cl RG6 87 A1
Sagecroft Rd RG18 106 C5
Sage Ct SL4 95 A8
Sage Rd RG31 57 C3
Sage Wlk RG42 91 D1
Sailing Club Rd SL8 3 A3
Sainsbury Ctr The KT16 124 A2
St Adrian's Cl SL6 39 B4
St Agnes Mews RG2 86 C2
St Agnes Terr RG17 25 B2
St Albans Cl 12 SL4 67 D6
St Alban's St SL4 67 D6
St Andrews RG12 117 E3
St Andrew's Ave SL4 66 F5
St Andrews Cl
Bradfield RG7 82 C6
Crowthorne RG45 142 F6
St Andrew's Cl
Old Windsor SL4 68 A1
Upper Halliford TW17 125 D5
Wraysbury TW19 68 E1
St Andrews Cotts 1 SL4 67 A5
St Andrew's Cres SL4 66 F5
St Andrews Ct
Ascot SL5 120 C4
Colnbrook SL3 69 D7
22 Reading RG1 86 D7
2 Slough SL1 42 E3
St Andrew's Hall (Mus of English Rural Life)* RG2 86 C6
St Andrew's Rd
Caversham RG4 58 F4
Henley-on-T RG9 35 D8
St Andrew's Sch RG8 55 C1
St Andrew's Way SL1 41 D6
St Anne's Ave TW19 97 D8
St Anne's Cl RG9 15 D1
St Annes Dr RG40 117 A6
St Annes Glade GU19 145 D3
St Anne's RC Prim Sch
Caversham RG4 59 B2
Chertsey KT16 124 A1
St Anne's Rd RG4 59 A2
St Ann's Cl KT16 123 F3
ST ANN'S HEATH 122 F5
St Ann's Heath Jun Sch GU25 122 E4
St Ann's Hill Rd KT16 123 D3
St Ann's Rd KT16 123 F3
St Anthonys Cl RG42 118 A8
St Anthony's RC Prim Sch SL2 22 C1
St Anthony's Way TW14 71 F3
St Augustine's RC Prim Sch GU16 151 F2
St Barnabas Rd
Caversham RG4 59 A6
Earley RG2 86 F1
St Bartholomews Rd RG1 86 F7
St Bartholomew's Sch RG14 104 E1
St Benets Way RG4 59 C6
St Bernard's Prep Sch SL1 43 B4
St Bernard's RC Gram Sch SL3 43 C4
St Bernards Rd SL3 43 C3
St Birinus Rd RG31 84 C5
St Catherine's Cl RG41 88 B1
St Catherines Ct
2 Staines TW18 97 A4
3 Windsor SL4 67 A5
St Catherine's Hill RG7 136 E6
St Catherines Pl 1 TW20 96 A3
St Catherines Rd GU16 151 F1
St Catherines Wood GU15 151 C4
St Cecelia Ct RG2 86 C2
St Chad's Rd SL6 39 B4
St Christophers Gdns SL5 119 D8
St Clements Cl RG6 87 C1
Saint-Cloud Way SL6 40 A7
St Columba's Cl SL6 39 B4
St Crispin's Sch RG40 116 E6
St Cuthbert's Cl TW20 95 D2
St Cuthbert's RC Prim Sch TW20 95 C1
St David's Cl
Caversham RG4 58 F5
Maidenhead SL6 39 A4
St Davids Ct TW15 97 F6
St Davids Dr TW20 95 C1
St David's Rd RG14 104 F2
St David's Sch TW15 97 F5
St Dominic Savio RC Prim Sch RG5 87 D8
St Donats Pl RG14 105 A2
St Dunstan's Rd TW13 98 F5
St Edmund Campion RC Prim Sch SL6 39 B6
St Edward's RC Fst Sch SL4 67 A6
St Edward's Rd RG6 87 A6
St Edward's Royal Free Ecumenical Mid Sch SL4 67 A6
St Edward's Sch RG30 85 D7
St Elizabeth Cl RG2 113 B7
St Elmo Cl SL2 22 D1

St Elmo Cres SL2 22 D1
St Ethelbert's RC Prim Sch SL2 43 A7
St Finian's RC Prim Sch RG18 106 D8
St Francis Cl RG45 142 E4
St Francis RC Prim Sch SL5 120 A3
St Gabriels Ct GU15 151 D5
St Gabriel's Sch RG20 131 B5
St George's Ave RG14 104 E2
St George's Cl SL4 66 E6
St George's Cres SL1 41 D6
St George's Ct GU47 143 E2
St Georges Ind Est GU15 151 B3
St George's La SL5 120 B5
St Georges Lodge SL6 20 B7
St George's Rd
Camberley GU15 151 D6
Reading RG30 85 C8
St George's Sch
Ascot SL5 120 B6
Windsor SL4 67 D7
St George's Terr
[8] Lambourn RG17 25 B2
Reading RG30 85 B8
St Giles Cl RG1 86 B6
St Giles Ct [1] RG1 86 B6
St Helens Cres GU47 150 B8
St Helier Cl RG41 116 B3
St Hilda's Ave TW15 97 E3
St Ives Cl RG7 83 D2
St Ives Rd SL6 40 A7
St James Cl
Pangbourne RG8 56 C6
Twyford RG10 61 E5
St James Ct TW18 97 A4
St James Ctyd [5] SL7 1 E2
St James Gate SL5 121 A2
St James Pl SL1 41 C7
St James Rd RG40 141 E8
St James Wharf [8] RG1 86 C7
St James Wlk SL0 44 E4
St John's Beaumont Sch SL4 95 B6
St John's CE Prim Sch RG1 86 D7
St Johns Cl RG5 87 F8
St Johns Ct TW20 96 A3
St Johns Dr SL4 67 A5
St John's Gdns [3] RG14 104 F1
St John's Hill RG1 86 C7
St Johns Rd
Slough SL2 43 A6
Windsor SL4 67 A5
St John's Rd
Caversham RG4 59 C2
Mortimer RG7 137 A5
Newbury RG14 105 A1
North Ascot SL5 92 F1
Reading RG1 86 C7
Sandhurst GU47 150 C7
Thatcham RG19 106 C3
St Johns St RG45 143 B4
St John's St RG1 86 C7
St Johns Way KT16 124 A1
St John the Evangelist CE Inf Sch RG14 104 F1
St Joseph's Convent Sch RG1 86 E5
St Josephs Ct [1] RG14 105 B4
St Joseph's RC High Sch SL2 43 A7
St Joseph's RC Prim Sch
Bracknell RG12 118 D7
Newbury RG14 105 B4
St Jude's CE Sch TW20 95 C2
St Jude's Cl TW20 95 C3
St Jude's Cotts TW20 95 C3
St Jude's Rd TW20 95 C3
St Katherine's Rd RG9 35 D7
St Laurence Way SL1 43 A3
St Lawrence Sq RG17 100 C6
St Leger Ct RG14 104 E4
St Leonard's Ave SL4 67 C5
St Leonards Hill SL4 66 E4
St Leonard's Rd
Windsor, Clewer Green SL4 66 D1
Windsor SL4 67 C4
St Leonards Wlk SL0 44 F3
St Luke's CE Prim Sch SL6 39 F8
St Lukes Ct RG4 59 B4
St Luke's Rd
Maidenhead SL6 39 F8
Old Windsor SL4 68 A1
St Lukes Way RG4 59 B5
St Margaret Clitherow RC Prim Sch RG12 117 F2
St Margarets Ave TW15 98 B3
St Margaret's Rd SL6 39 A7
St Marks Cl RG19 106 C3
St Mark's Cl RG7 83 B5
St Mark's Cres SL6 39 B7
St Mark's Hospl SL6 39 C7
St Mark's Pl SL4 67 C5
St Mark's Rd
Bracknell RG42 117 C8
Henley-on-T RG9 35 D8
Maidenhead SL6 39 D7
Windsor SL4 67 C5
St Martins Cl [3] RG6 87 C1
St Martin's Ct TW15 97 C3
St Martins Prec RG4 59 A2
St Martin's RC Prim Sch RG4 59 E6
St Mary's All Saints CE Prim Sch RG1 85 E5
St Mary's Ave
Purley on T RG8 57 D5
Stanwell TW19 97 D8
St Mary's Butts RG1 86 A7
St Mary's CE Prim Sch SL1 43 A3
St Marys Cl GU47 150 C8
St Mary's Cl
Henley-on-T RG9 35 A8
Maidenhead SL6 40 A7
Stanwell TW19 97 D8
St Mary's Cres TW19 97 D8
St Mary's Ct [6] RG14 105 A4
St Mary's Dr TW14 98 C8
St Mary's Farnham Royal CE Prim Sch SL2 22 C2
St Mary's Gdns GU19 145 E3
St Mary's Gr RG1 86 A7
St Mary's Hill SL5 120 C4
St Mary's Ho RG18 79 C1
St Marys La SL4 92 D5
St Marys Lodge TW19 97 D8
St Mary's Pl [8] RG14 105 A4
St Mary's RC Prim Sch SL6 19 F2
St Mary's Rd
Ascot SL5 120 B3
Camberley GU15 151 C6
Mortimer RG7 137 A5
Newbury RG14 105 A4
Sindlesham RG41 115 B8
Slough SL3 43 E4
Winnersh RG41 88 B1
St Mary's Sch
Ascot SL5 120 B2
Henley-on-T RG9 35 E8
St Mary's Way RG7 111 B3
St Mary's Wlk [16] SL6 39 F7
St Matthew's Ct [9] TW15 98 A3
St Michaels CE Prim Sch GU47 149 F8
St Michael's CE Prim Sch SL5 120 D4
St Michaels Cl RG17 25 A2
St Michaels Cotts RG40 143 C8
St Michaels Ct RG10 61 E6
St Michael's Ct SL2 21 D1
St Michael's Easthampstead CE Prim Sch RG12 118 A4
St Michaels La RG7 110 D5
St Michael's Pl GU15 151 B5
St Michael's Prim Sch RG30 85 A7
St Michael's RC Prim Sch TW15 98 A3
St Michaels Rd
Ashford TW15 98 A3
Camberley GU15 151 B5
St Michael's Rd
Newbury RG14 104 F2
Reading RG30 84 D7
Sandhurst GU47 149 F8
St Nazaire Cl TW20 96 C3
St Nicholas' CE Comb Sch SL6 20 E1
St Nicholas CE Prim Sch
Hurst RG10 88 F7
Shepperton TW17 125 B3
St Nicholas Dr TW17 125 A2
St Nicholas' Rd RG14 104 F2
St Nicolas CE Jun Sch RG14 105 A2
St Olave's Cl TW18 96 F1
St Patrick's Ave RG10 61 A5
St Patricks Cl RG20 30 E7
St Patrick's Cl SL6 39 B4
St Pauls Ave SL2 43 A5
St Paul's CE Comb Sch, Wooburn HP10 3 D4
St Paul's CE Jun Sch RG41 116 A6
St Paul's Cl TW15 98 C3
St Paul's Ct
[20] Maidenhead SL6 39 F6
Reading RG1 86 A6
St Paul's Gate RG41 116 A6
St Paul's Mews RG2 113 B7
St Paul's RC Prim Sch RG31 84 C7
St Paul's Rd TW18 96 D2
St Peter's Ave RG4 58 E3
St Peter's CE Comb Sch SL1 21 B2
St Peter's CE Jun Sch GU46 149 E6
St Peter's CE Mid Sch SL4 67 F1
St Peter's CE Prim Sch RG6 87 B5
St Peters Cl RG19 132 D2
St Peter's Cl
Burnham SL1 21 B1
Old Windsor SL4 68 A2
Staines TW18 96 F2
St Peter's Gdns GU46 149 D6
St Peter's Hill RG4 58 F3
St Peter's Lodge SL6 39 E5
St Peter's RC Prim Sch SL7 1 D3
St Peters Rd RG6 87 A5
St Peter's Rd
Maidenhead SL6 19 D2
Reading RG6 87 A5
St Peter St SL7 1 E1
St Peters Way UB3 71 D8
St Pinnock Ave TW18 124 A8
St Pirans Sch SL6 19 E1
St Piran's Sch SL6 18 E1
St Richards Rd RG14 105 B4
St Ronans Rd RG30 85 B8
St Saviour's Rd RG1 85 F5
St Saviour's Terr [11] RG1 86 A6
Saint Sebastian's CE Prim Sch RG40 142 E8
St Sebastian's Cl RG40 142 E7
St Sebastian's Ct RG40 142 E7
St Stephens Cl RG4 59 A2
St Stephens Ct [9] RG1 86 D7
St Swithins Cl RG20 75 D4
St Swithuns Ct RG10 61 D4
St Teresa's RC Prim Sch RG40 116 D5
St Theresa's Rd TW14 71 F3
St Thomas Ct RG18 106 E3
St Thomas Wlk SL3 69 D7
Salamanca RG45 142 E5
Salcombe Dr RG6 87 B4
Salcombe Rd
Ashford TW15 97 E5
Newbury RG14 104 E1
Reading RG2 86 D3
Saleby Cl RG6 87 E2
Sale Garden Cotts RG40 116 C5
Salesian Gdns KT16 124 A1
Salesian Sch KT16 124 A1
Salford Cl RG2 113 C7
Salisbury Ave SL2 42 C8
Salisbury Cl RG41 116 A2
Salisbury Ct SL6 39 E5
Salisbury Mews SL2 22 C1
Salisbury Rd
Blackwater GU17 150 C5
Harlington TW6 71 C1
Hungerford RG17 100 C3
Reading RG30 85 E8
Salisbury Row [4] RG17 100 D5
Salix Gdns RG10 61 D6
Salmon Cl RG7 113 B2
Salmond Rd RG2 113 C6
Salters Cl SL6 40 A7
Saltersgate Cl RG6 87 D2
Salters Rd SL6 40 A7
SALT HILL 42 D5
Salt Hill Ave SL1 42 C5
Salt Hill Dr SL1 42 C5
Salt Hill Mans SL1 42 C5
Salt Hill Way SL1 42 D5
Saltire Gdns [2] RG42 118 A8
Salwey Cl RG12 118 B3
Samarkand Cl GU15 152 B4
Samian Pl RG42 90 E1
Sampage Cl RG2 113 C6
Sampson Bsns Pk GU15 151 B3
Sampson Ct TW17 125 C4
Sampson Pk RG42 117 D8
Sampsons Gn SL2 21 F2
Sanctuary Cl RG30 84 F8
Sanctuary Rd TW19, TW6 71 A1
Sandbrooke Wlk RG7 111 A3
Sandcroft Rd RG4 58 E6
Sandells Ave TW15 98 C4
Sanden Cl RG17 100 C5
Sandford Ct RG41 88 C1
Sandford Down RG12 118 F4
Sandford Dr RG5 60 F1
Sandford La RG5, RG10 88 C6
SANDFORD PARK 88 B7
Sandgate Ave RG30 57 F2
Sandgates KT16 123 E1
Sandhills RG10 37 D3
Sandhills Ct GU25 122 E4
Sandhills La GU25 122 F4
Sandhills Mdw TW17 125 C2
Sandhills Way RG31 84 F4
SANDHURST 150 C7
Sandhurst La GU17 150 B6
Sandhurst Lodge RG45 142 E3
Sandhurst Rd
Crowthorne RG45 143 B3
Wokingham RG40 142 B8
Yateley GU46 149 F7
Sandhurst Royal Military Acad Hospl GU15 151 A8
Sandhurst Sch GU47 150 E8
Sandhurst Sta GU47 150 A7
Sandisplatt Rd SL6 39 A6
Sandleford Cl RG2 113 C6
Sandleford La RG19 131 B6
Sandleford Lodge Pk RG19 131 B6
Sandlers End SL2 22 B1
Sandown Ave RG31 84 B4
Sandown Cl GU17 150 D5
Sandown Dr GU16 151 E2
Sandown Rd SL2 41 F8
Sandown Way RG14 105 C1
Sandpipers Pl SL6 19 E6
Sandpit Hill RG14, RG20 130 C4
Sandpit La
Caversham RG4 59 F8
Farley Hill RG7 140 B5
Sandringham Ct SL1 41 D7
Sandringham Dr TW15 97 D4
Sandringham Rd
Maidenhead SL6 19 E2
Stanwell TW6 70 E2
Sandringham Way RG31 84 B4
Sands Farm Dr SL1 21 C1
Sandstone Cl RG41 88 C1
Sandstone Gr RG18 79 C8
Sandy Cl RG18 79 A4
Sandy Dr TW14 98 E7
Sandygate Cl SL7 1 D3
Sandygate Rd SL7 1 D3
Sandy La
Bracknell RG12 118 C8
Camberley GU15 151 E6
Hermitage RG18 78 F4
North Ascot SL5 119 C8
Sandhurst GU47 143 A2
Sunningdale SL5 121 A4
Virginia Water GU25 122 E5
Wokingham RG41 115 D4
Sandy Lane Prim Sch RG12 91 C1
Sandy Mead SL6 40 C1
Sandy Ride SL5 120 E5
Sandy Way KT12 125 F1
SANHAM GREEN 100 D2
Sapphire Cl RG41 115 E7
Sargood Cl RG19 106 E2
Sarsby Dr TW19 96 A6
Sarum RG12 117 F1
Sarum Cres RG40 116 D7
Sarum Ct [1] RG30 85 D6
Sarum Rd RG26 135 A1
Sarum Way RG17 100 D4
Satis Ho SL3 68 C7
Saturn Cl RG41 115 E6
Saturn Croft RG42 92 B2
Saturn Ho RG7 134 E2
Saunders Cl RG10 61 F3
Saunders Ct RG8 57 B5
Saunton Ave UB3 71 F7
Savernake Cl RG30 84 F7
Savernake Way RG12 118 F4
Saville Cres TW15 98 D2
Saville Gdns GU15 152 B5
Saville Ho [5] TW20 96 A3
Savill Gardens The★ TW20 94 E2
Savill Mews TW20 95 D2
Savill Way SL7 1 F2
Savory Wlk RG42 90 C2
Savoy Ct SL6 19 F1
Savoy Gr GU17 150 D3
Sawmill Cotts SL3 23 F2
Sawmill Rd RG18 79 A4
Sawpit Rd RG10 88 E7
Sawtry Cl RG6 87 E2
Sawyers Cl SL6 39 A2
Sawyer's Cl SL4 66 E7
Sawyers Cres SL6 39 A2
Sawyers Ley RG7 137 D8
Saxby Cl RG7 111 B3
Saxham Lodge RG40 116 C5
Saxon Cl SL3 43 F4
Saxon Ct
[10] Reading RG1 86 D7
Stanwell TW19 70 A2
Thatcham RG19 106 A3
Saxon Dr RG42 118 F8
Saxon Gate RG30 111 B5
Saxon Gdns SL6 20 D1
Saxon Lodge SL1 41 F5
Saxon Pl RG8 56 D5
Saxon Prim Sch TW17 125 A4
Saxon Rd TW15 98 D2
Saxons Acre RG20 28 D3
Saxon Way
Harmondsworth UB7 70 C8
Old Windsor SL4 68 B1
Saxon Way Trad Est UB7 70 C8
Saxony Way GU46 149 C4
Sayers Cl RG14 131 B8
Scafell Cl RG31 57 B2
Scafell Rd SL2 41 F8
Scania Wlk RG42 92 B2
Scarborough Rd TW6 71 C1
Scarborough Way SL1 42 B4
Scarlet Oaks GU15 151 E3
Scarletts La RG10 37 C1
Scholars Cl
Caversham RG4 58 F3
Great Shefford RG17 48 A3
Scholars Wlk SL3 44 A4
School Cl GU24 153 F4
School Dr RG5 87 E5
School Gn RG2 113 E4
SCHOOLGREEN 113 F4
School Hill
Crowthorne RG45 143 D4
Midgham RG7 107 F3
Sandhurst GU47 143 A1
Wargrave RG10 36 D1
School Ho TW19 70 C1
School La
Bagshot GU19 145 E2
Boxford RG20 76 E4
Burghfield Common RG7 110 F2
Caversham, Emmer Green RG4 59 B6
Caversham RG4 59 A2
Cookham Dean SL6 19 B7
Cookham SL6 20 B7
East Garston RG17 47 D6
Egham TW20 96 A3
Froxfield SN8 99 A1
Little Marlow SL7 2 C5
Littlewick Green SL6 38 B4
Lower Halliford TW17 125 B2
Maidenhead SL6 19 E1
Medmenham SL7 17 B6
North Ascot SL5 119 D8
Riseley RG7 139 E3
Silchester RG7 136 B1
Slough SL2 42 F6
Stoke Poges SL2 23 B5
Wargrave RG10 36 D2
Windlesham GU20 146 D4
Yateley GU46 149 B6
School of Electronic Engineering RG2 114 F1
School of Military Survey RG18 78 F7
School Rd
Arborfield Cross RG2, RG41 114 F2
Ascot SL5 120 D4
Ashford TW15 98 B2
Burghfield RG30 111 C6
Chieveley RG20 77 F8
Compton RG20 31 E4
Harmondsworth UB7 70 D8
Hurst RG10 88 F8
Padworth RG7 109 F1
Reading RG31 84 D8
Riseley RG7 139 E3
Waltham St L RG10 62 F3
Windlesham GU20 146 B5
Wokingham RG40 116 D6
Wooburn Green HP10 3 E6
School Terr RG1 86 E8
Schroder Ct TW20 95 B3
Scobell Cl RG2 113 D5
Scotland Hill GU47 150 A8
Scotlands Dr SL2 22 B6
Scots Cl TW19 97 D7
Scots Dr RG41 115 E7
Scotswood SL5 120 E1
Scottalls La RG18 52 F5
Scott Cl
Caversham RG4 59 A5
Farnham Common SL2 22 C7
Woodley RG5 88 A7
Scott's Ave TW16 98 E1
Scotts Mews SL5 119 B8
Scott's Way TW16 98 E1
Scott Terr RG12 118 E8
Scours La RG30 58 B1
Scratchface La RG7 81 E7
Scrivens Mead RG19 106 F3
Scutley La GU20 146 E3
Scylla Cres TW6, TW14 98 B8
Scylla Rd TW14, TW6 71 B1
Seacourt Rd SL3 44 B2
Seafield Ct [14] RG1 85 F7
Seaford Gdns RG5 87 E6
Seaford Rd
Stanwell TW6 70 D2
Wokingham RG40 116 D6
Sealand Rd TW6 71 A1
Searing Way RG26 135 A1
Searles Farm La RG30 85 B1
Searlwood Ct GU24 153 F5
Seaton Dr TW15 97 E6
Seaton Gdns RG2 86 C2
Seaton Rd GU15 151 B5
Second Ave
Reading RG31 84 B6
Tadley RG7 135 C2
Second Cres SL1 42 C8
Seddon Hill RG42 91 B2
Sedgefield Rd RG14 131 C8
Sedge Gr RG18 106 E4
Sedgmoor Cl HP10 3 A7
Sedgmoor Gdns HP10 3 A8
Sedgmoor La HP10 3 B7
Sedgmoor Rd HP10 3 A8
Seebys Oak GU47 150 E6
Seer Green Ho SL1 21 C2
Sefton Cl
Stoke Poges SL2 22 F4
West End GU24 153 F6
Sefton Paddock SL2 23 A5
Sefton Park Cotts SL2 23 A4
Sefton Park Sch SL2 23 B5
Segrave Cl RG4 60 E2
Segsbury Gr RG12 118 F5
Selborne RG12 118 B6
Selborne Cl GU17 150 C6
Selborne Ct [2] RG1 86 C7
Selborne Gdns RG30 58 A1
Selborne Ho [10] SL8 3 A4
Selby Rd TW15 98 C2
Selcourt Cl RG5 87 D8
Selim Ct [5] SL1 43 A4
Sellafield Way RG6 87 C2
Selsdon Ave RG5 87 F8
Selsey Way RG6 114 B8
Selva Ct [6] RG1 86 C6
Selwood Cl TW19 70 C1
Selwood Gdns TW19 70 C1
Selwyn Cl SL4 66 E5
Selwyn Dr GU46 149 B6
Selwyn Pl SL1 41 F6
Sen Cl RG42 91 C2
Send Rd RG4 59 C1
Sermed Ct SL2 43 C5
Servite Ho SL6 40 B8
Setley Way RG12 118 F6
Seton Dr RG31 84 F5
Setter Combe RG42 91 D2
Settrington Cl [3] RG6 87 E2
Sett The GU46 149 B5
Sevenoaks Dr RG7 113 B3
Sevenoaks Rd RG6 87 B3
Seventh Ave RG31 84 B6
Seventh St RG19 131 F5
Severalls The SN8 126 D3
Severn Cl
Sandhurst GU47 150 C8
Thatcham RG18 106 B5
Severn Cres SL3 69 B8
Severn Way RG30 84 F6
Sewell Ave RG41 116 A8

Sewell Cl RG18 . . . . 79 B1
Seymour Ave RG2. . . . . . . 113 E5
Seymour Cl SL6. . . . . 39 B3
Seymour Court La SL7 . . . . .1 B5
Seymour Court Rd SL7 . . . . 1 C4
Seymour Ct RG45 . . . . 142 E4
Seymour Dr GU15. . . . . . . 152 B8
Seymour Ho SL3. . . . . 43 E4
Seymour Park Rd SL7 . . . . . 1 D3
Seymour Plain SL7. . . . . 1 C5
Seymour Rd SL1 . . . . 42 D4
Seymour Way TW16. . . . . . 98 E1
Shackleton Ct 6 TW19. . . 70 E1
Shackleton Rd SL1. . . . . . . 42 F6
Shackleton Way RG5. . . . . 88 A7
Shafer Ct RG14 . . . . 105 A1
Shaftesbury Cl RG12 . . . . 118 D4
Shaftesbury Cres TW18 . . 97 D1
Shaftesbury Ct
Maidenhead SL6 . . . . 39 E5
6 Slough SL1. . . . . 42 E4
Wokingham RG40 . . . . . . .116 D7
Shaftesbury Mount
GU17 . . . . .150 D3
Shaftesbury Rd
Bisley GU24. . . . . 153 F3
Reading RG30 . . . . 85 B8
Shaggy Calf La SL2 . . . . . . 43 A6
Shakespeare Cl RG4 . . . . . 59 D5
Shakespeare Lodge SL1. . 41 F5
Shakespeare Rd RG18. . . 106 C4
Shakespeare Way RG42 . 118 E8
Shalbourne Cl RG17. . . . . 100 B5
Shalbourne Rise GU15 . . 151 D5
Shamaa Ho 15 SL1 . . . . 42 F4
Sharman Row 11 SL3. . . . . 43 F1
Sharney Ave SL3. . . . . 44 B3
Sharnwood Dr RG31 . . . . . 84 F5
Sharonelle Ct RG40 . . . . . 116 B6
Sharpthorpe Cl 2 RG6 . . . 87 B1
SHAW. 105 C5
Shaw Ct SL4. . . . . 68 A2
Shaw-cum-Donnington CE Prim Sch RG14 . . . . 105 A6
SHAW FARM. 67 E3
Shaw Farm Rd RG14 . . . . 105 B6
Shaw Gdns 13 SL3 . . . . 43 F1
Shaw Hill RG14 . . . . 105 B5
Shaw Mill RG14. . . . . 105 B5
Shaw Pk RG45 . . . . 143 B3
Shaw Rd
Newbury RG14. . . . . 105 B4
Reading RG1 . . . . 85 F5
Shaw The SL6 . . . . 19 E6
Shears Ct TW16. . . . . 98 E1
Sheehy Way SL2 . . . . 43 B6
Sheepcote La
Holyport SL6 . . . . 64 C4
Wooburn SL1. . . . . .3 F1
Sheepcote Rd
Eton SL4. . . . . 42 A1
Windsor SL4 . . . . 66 E5
Sheepdown RG20 . . . . 30 E7
Sheepdrove Rd RG17. . . . . . 25 C3
Sheep Fair Way RG17 . . . . 25 B2
Sheephouse Rd SL6. . . . . . 20 B2
Sheephouse Way RG20. . . 49 A6
Sheeplands Farm RG10. . . 61 D8
Sheep Leaze La RG20 . . . . 29 D2
SHEEPRIDGE 2 E7
Sheepridge La SL7, HP10. . . .2 E7
Sheepwalk TW17 . . . . 124 F3
Sheepwash La RG20. . . . . 131 A2
Sheepways La RG4. . . . . . . 58 B8
Sheep Wlk
Caversham RG4. . . . . 59 B4
Littleton TW17 . . . . 125 A4
Sheerlands Rd RG2 . . . . . 140 F7
Sheet St SL4. . . . . 67 D6
Sheet Street Rd SL4. . . . . . 94 A7
SHEFFIELD BOTTOM 110 F8
Sheffield Rd
Harlington TW14, TW6. . . . . 71 C2
Slough SL1. . . . . 42 C7
Sheffield Way TW14, TW6 . 71 D2
Shefford CE Prim Sch RG17. . . . . 48 B4
Shefford Cres RG40 . . . . . 116 D8
Shefford Lodge 3 RG14. 105 A2
SHEFFORD WOODLANDS. 74 D7
Sheldon Gdns RG2. . . . . . . 86 C1
Shelgate Wlk RG5. . . . . 87 C7
Shelley Ave RG12 . . . . 118 E7
Shelley Cl
Medmenham SL7. . . . . 17 D7
16 Slough SL3 . . . . 43 F1
Wooburn Green HP10 . . . . . . 3 E8
2 Woodley RG5 . . . . 87 E4
Shelley Ct
Camberley GU15 . . . . 151 C5
Reading RG1 . . . . 86 D6
Shelley Rd
12 Marlow SL7 . . . . .1 F3
Thatcham RG18 . . . . 106 C4
Shelley Wlk GU46 . . . . 149 B5
Shellfield Cl TW19 . . . . 70 A2
Shelson Ave TW13 . . . . 98 F4
Shelton Ct SL3. . . . . 43 C3
Shenston Ct 23 SL4 . . . . . . 67 D6
Shenstone Cl RG40. . . . . . . 142 A8
Shenstone Dr SL1. . . . . 21 D1
Shenstone Pk SL5. . . . . 120 E5
Shenstone Rd RG2 . . . . 86 B4
Shepherds Ave RG6 . . . . . . 87 B8
Shepherds Chase GU19. . 145 E2
Shepherds Cl
Hurley SL6. . . . . 17 F3
Shepperton TW17 . . . . 125 B3
Shepherds Ct SL4. . . . . 66 E5
Shepherds Hill
Bracknell RG12 . . . . 118 C8
Compton RG20. . . . . 31 E3
Earley RG6. . . . . 87 C8
Shepherd's Hill RG20. . . . . 76 E4
Shepherd's House La RG6 87 A8
Shepherds La
Bracknell RG42 . . . . 91 B1
Caversham RG4. . . . . 58 D6
Hurley SL6. . . . . 17 E4
Shepherds Mount RG20 . . 31 E3
Shepherds Rise RG20 . . . . 31 E4
Shepherds Way RG45 . . . 142 E4
Shepherds Wlk RG6. . . . . . 87 C8
Shepley Dr
Reading RG30 . . . . 85 C4
Wentworth SL5 . . . . 121 D3
Shepley End SL5. . . . . 121 D4
Sheppard Ct RG31 . . . . 84 C7
Sheppee Rdbt RG42. . . . . . 91 E1
SHEPPERTON. 125 C3
Shepperton Bsns Park TW17 . . . . 125 C4
Shepperton Court Dr TW17. . . . . 125 B4
Shepperton Ct TW17 . . . . 125 B3
SHEPPERTON GREEN 125 A5
Shepperton Ho TW17 . . . 125 C3
Shepperton Rd TW17, TW18. . . . . 124 D5
Shepperton Sta TW17 . . . 125 C4
Shepperton Studios TW17 . . . . 124 F6
Shepton Ho 12 RG1 . . . . . . 86 C7
Sheraton Cl GU17 . . . . 150 E4
Sheraton Dr RG31. . . . . 57 B1
Sherborne Cl SL3 . . . . 69 E6
Sherborne Ct SL6. . . . . 39 E6
Sherborne Rd TW14. . . . . . 98 D7
Sherbourne Dr
Maidenhead SL6 . . . . 39 C3
Wentworth SL5 . . . . 121 D4
Windsor SL4 . . . . 66 F3
Woodley RG5. . . . . 87 F8
Sherbourne Gdns TW17 . 125 E2
Sherbourne Wlk SL2 . . . . . 22 C8
Sherfield Cl RG2. . . . . 86 D4
Sherfield Dr RG2. . . . . 86 D4
Shergold Way SL6 . . . . 19 F6
Sheridan Ave RG4. . . . . 59 A4
Sheridan Cres RG26. . . . . 134 E1
Sheridan Ct
4 Maidenhead SL6. . . . . . . 40 B8
Newbury RG14. . . . . 105 C3
Slough SL1. . . . . 41 E6
Sheridan Grange SL5 . . . 121 A3
Sheridan Way RG41 . . . . 115 E5
Sheringham Ct
5 Maidenhead SL6. . . . . . . 39 E7
3 Reading RG1 . . . . 86 C5
Sherman Pl 14 RG1 . . . . . . 86 B6
Sherman Rd
Reading RG1 . . . . 86 B6
Slough SL1. . . . . 42 E8
Sherrardmead RG14 . . . . 105 B5
Sherring Cl RG42 . . . . 91 C1
Sherwood Cl
Bracknell RG12 . . . . 119 A7
Slough SL3. . . . . 43 E3
Sherwood Ct
Colnbrook SL3 . . . . 69 D7
Slough SL3. . . . . 43 F1
Sherwood Dr SL6 . . . . 39 A6
Sherwood Gdns RG9 . . . . . 35 C8
Sherwood Ho 8 RG1. . . . . . 85 E5
Sherwood Pl RG8 . . . . 57 B4
Sherwood Rd RG41 . . . . . . 88 C2
Sherwood Rise RG8. . . . . . 57 B5
Sherwood St RG30 . . . . 85 C8
Shetland Rd TW6 . . . . 71 C1
Shield Rd TW15. . . . . 98 C4
Shifford Cres SL6 . . . . 19 E3
Shildon Cl GU15 . . . . 152 D3
Shilling Cl RG30 . . . . 85 B6
SHINFIELD 113 E4
Shinfield Inf Sch RG2 . . . 113 E4
Shinfield Rd
Earley RG2. . . . . 113 E8
Reading RG2 . . . . 86 E3
Shinfield Rise RG2 . . . . 86 E1
Shinfield St Mary's CE Jun Sch RG2. . . . . 113 F4
SHIPLAKE 35 F2
Shiplake CE Sch RG9. . . . . 35 E2
Shiplake Coll RG9. . . . . 35 F1
Shiplake Ho
Bourne End SL8. . . . . 3 B4
Bracknell RG12 . . . . 118 F5
SHIPLAKE ROW 35 C2
Shiplake Sta RG9 . . . . 36 B4
Shipley Cl RG5. . . . . 61 A1
Shipton Cl RG31 . . . . 57 C2
Shire Cl GU19. . . . . 145 E2
Shire Cotts RG7. . . . . 108 F6
Shire's Head Cl RG30. . . . . 85 D6
Shires The RG41 . . . . 115 D4
Shires Way GU46 . . . . 149 D7
Shirley Ave
Reading RG2 . . . . 113 C7
Windsor SL4 . . . . 66 F6
Shirley Rd SL6. . . . . 39 C5
Shooter's Hill RG8 . . . . 56 B7
Shooters Way RG2. . . . . . . 112 F8
Shop La
Leckhampstead RG20 . . . . . 49 F5
Newbury RG14. . . . . 104 E6
Shoppenhangers Rd SL6 . 39 C3
Shoppenhanger's Rd SL6. 39 E4
Shoreham Rd E TW6 . . . . . 70 E2
Shoreham Rd W TW6 . . . . . 70 E2
Shoreham Rise SL2 . . . . . . 21 D1
Shorland Oaks RG42 . . . . . 91 C2
Shortfern SL2 . . . . 43 C7
Shortheath La RG7. . . . . . 110 E3
Short La TW15, TW19 . . . . . 97 F7
Shortlands UB3. . . . . 71 D8
Shortlands Hill OX10 . . . . . 13 D4
Short Rd TW19. . . . . 70 E1
Short St
Caversham RG4. . . . . 59 B2
Pangbourne RG8 . . . . 56 D5
Reading RG1 . . . . 86 B6
Short The RG8. . . . . 57 D5
Shortwood Ave TW18 . . . . 97 B5
Shortwood Comm TW18. . 97 B4
Shortwood Inf Sch TW18 . 97 B5
SHOTTESBROOKE PARK. . . 63 C7
SHREDING GREEN 44 C7
Shrewsbury Rd TW14, TW6. . . . . 71 D1
Shrewsbury Terr RG14 . . 104 E1
Shrivenham Cl 3 GU47 . 150 D8
Shropshire Gdns RG42 . . . 91 F1
Shrubbs Hill La SL5 . . . . . 121 C3
Shrubland Dr RG30 . . . . . . 85 A4
Shrublands Dr GU18 . . . . 153 B8
SHRUBS HILL 121 C3
SHURLOCK ROW 63 A1
Shute End RG40, RG41 . . . 116 B6
Shyshack La RG26 . . . . . . 134 F1
Sibley Park Rd RG6 . . . . . . 87 A2
Sibson RG6. . . . . 87 C2
Sidbury Cl SL5. . . . . 121 A4
Sidestrand Rd RG14 . . . . . 130 E7
Sidings The TW18. . . . . 97 B4
Sidmouth Ct 18 RG1. . . . . . 86 C7
Sidmouth Grange Cl RG6 . 87 B7
Sidmouth Grange Rd RG6 87 B7
Sidmouth St RG1 . . . . 86 C7
Sidney Harrison Ho RG9. . 36 B4
Sidney Rd
Staines TW18. . . . . 97 A4
Windsor SL4 . . . . 66 C4
Sienna Ct 7 TW13 . . . . 98 F5
Signals Cl RG19. . . . . 106 D1
Silbury Cl RG31 . . . . 84 B4
SILCHESTER 136 C1
Silchester CE Prim Sch RG7. . . . . 136 B1
Silchester Ct TW15. . . . . . . 97 E6
Silchester Ho SL6. . . . . 40 B8
Silchester Manor Sch SL6 . . . . 40 D7
Silchester Pl RG7 . . . . 113 B5
Silchester Rd
Reading RG30 . . . . 85 C4
Tadley RG26. . . . . 135 D1
Silco Dr SL6 . . . . 39 E6
Silk Pl RG40 . . . . 116 D7
Silverbeck Way TW19 . . . . 70 A2
Silver Birches RG41 . . . . . 115 D3
Silver Cl SL6. . . . . 39 A5
Silverdale Ct TW18. . . . . . . 97 B3
Silverdale Rd
Earley RG6. . . . . 87 C3
Tadley RG26. . . . . 135 B1
Wargrave RG10. . . . . 36 E1
Silver Dr GU16. . . . . 152 C3
Silver Fox Cres RG5 . . . . . . 87 D6
Silverglades GU46 . . . . . . 149 C4
Silver Hill GU47 . . . . 150 E8
Silver La RG7 . . . . 136 B8
Silver St RG1 . . . . 86 B6
Silverstone Mews SL6. . . . 39 C4
Silver Street Flats 25 RG1 86 B6
Silverthorne Dr RG4 . . . . . 58 E6
Silvertrees Dr SL6 . . . . 39 A5
Silverwood Dr GU15. . . . . 152 A7
Silverwood Grange SL5 . 120 F2
Silwood RG12. . . . . 117 E1
Silwood Cl SL5 . . . . 120 D7
Silwood Park (Imperial Coll) SL5 . . . . 120 F6
Silwood Rd SL5. . . . . 120 F5
Simkins Cl RG42 . . . . 92 B2
Simmonds Cl RG42. . . . . . 117 E8
Simmonds Cres RG6 . . . . . 87 E1
Simmonds Malthouse 5 RG1 . . . . 86 A6
Simmonds St RG1. . . . . 86 A7
Simmons Cl 6 SL3. . . . . . . 44 A2
Simmons Field RG18 . . . . 106 F4
Simmons Fields RG10 . . . . 61 B3
Simmons Pl TW18 . . . . 96 E3
Simmons Rd RG9 . . . . 15 D3
Simms Farm La RG7 . . . . 136 F4
Simod Ct 3 RG30. . . . . 85 C7
Simons Cl RG31. . . . . 57 C4
Simons La RG41 . . . . 115 D8
Simons Wlk TW20. . . . . 95 C1
Simpson Cl SL6. . . . . 40 B8
Simpsons Way SL1. . . . . . . 42 E5
Sinclair Rd SL4 . . . . 67 C4
Sindle Cl RG41. . . . . 88 B2
SINDLESHAM 115 A8
Sindlesham Farm Cotts 2 RG6 . . . . 87 E2
Sindlesham Rd RG2 . . . . . 114 E3
Singers Cl RG9 . . . . 35 E8
Singers La RG9 . . . . 35 E8
Sinhurst Rd GU15 . . . . . . 151 B4
SIPSON 71 A8
Sipson Cl UB7 . . . . 71 A8
Sipson La UB3, UB7 . . . . . . 71 B8
Sipson Rd UB7. . . . . 71 A7
Sipson Way UB7 . . . . 71 A7
Sir Henry Peakes Dr SL2 . 22 A6
Sirius Cl RG41 . . . . 115 F6
Sirl Cotts SL5. . . . . 120 C5
Sir Robert Mews SL3. . . . . 44 A1
Sir Sydney Camm Ho SL4. 67 B6
Sir William Borlase's Gram Sch SL7 . . . . 1 C1
Sir William Perkins's Sch KT16. . . . . 123 F1
Six Acre La RG17. . . . . 126 A5
Sixth Ave RG31 . . . . 84 B6
Sixth St RG19 . . . . 131 F5
Skarries View RG4 . . . . 58 D8
Skeffling Cl 4 RG6 . . . . . . 87 E2
Skelmerdale Way RG6. . . . 87 E3
Skelton Ct RG30 . . . . 85 D7
Skelton Fields RG42. . . . . . 91 C1
Skerries Ct 5 SL3 . . . . 44 A2
Skerritt Way RG8 . . . . 57 D4
Skillman Dr RG19 . . . . 106 F3
Skilton Rd RG31 . . . . 57 C3
SKIMPEDHILL. 118 B7
Skimpedhill La RG12 . . . . 118 B7
SKINNERS GREEN 130 B7
Skinners Green La RG14. 130 B7
Skippons Cl RG14 . . . . 130 C6
Sky Bsns Pk TW20 . . . . . . 123 C7
Skydmore Path SL2 . . . . . . 21 F2
Skye Cl RG31 . . . . 84 E4
Skylark Way RG2. . . . . 113 E5
Skylings RG14 . . . . 105 C4
Skyport Dr UB7 . . . . 70 D7
Skyway 14 Trad Est SL3 . . 69 F4
Slade Hill Gdns RG20. . . . 129 F2
Slaidburn Gn RG12. . . . . . 118 E2
Slanting Hill RG18 . . . . 79 B4
Sledmere Ct TW14 . . . . 98 E7
Slim Rd GU15. . . . . 151 C7
Sloane Cl RG8 . . . . 34 C6
Slopes The RG4. . . . . 59 D2
SLOUGH. 42 D5
Slough Bsns Ctr SL1 . . . . . 42 E5
Slough & Eton CE Coll SL1 . . . . 42 D3
Slough Gram Sch SL3. . . . 43 B3
Slough Interchange Ind Est SL2 . . . . 43 A5
Slough Mus* SL1. . . . . 43 A4
Slough Rd
Datchet SL3 . . . . 68 B8
Eton SL4. . . . . 42 E2
Slough Sta SL1 . . . . 42 F5
Slough Trad Est SL1. . . . . . 42 B7
Smalley Cl RG41 . . . . 115 E4
Smallholdings TW15 . . . . . 98 B4
Smallmead Rd
Burghfield Common RG30 . . 85 D1
Reading RG2 . . . . 86 A1
Smallridge RG14. . . . . 130 C4
Smallwood Dr RG26. . . . . 135 B1
Smeaton Ct 7 RG14 . . . . 104 F4
Smewins Rd RG10, SL6. . . . 63 D5
Smitham Bridge Rd RG17 . . . . 100 C5
Smithfield Cl SL6 . . . . 38 F3
Smithfield Rd SL6. . . . . 39 A3
Smith's Hill OX12 . . . . .6 F5
Smiths La SL4 . . . . 66 E6
Smith Sq RG12. . . . . 118 D7
Smithy's Gn GU20. . . . . . . 146 D4
Snake La RG20. . . . . 104 A7
Snape Spur SL1. . . . . 42 E7
Snelsmore Common Ctry Pk* RG14. . . . . .77 D2
Snipe La RG20. . . . . 131 F2
Snowball Hill
Maidenhead SL6 . . . . 39 A1
White Waltham SL6 . . . . 64 B8
Snowberry Cl RG41 . . . . . 115 F5
Snowden Cl SL4 . . . . 66 D3
Snowden Dr RG31. . . . . 84 A6
Snowdon Cl RG19. . . . . . . 106 D2
Snowdon Rd TW6. . . . . 71 C1
Snowdrop Copse RG18 . . 106 F4
Snowdrop Gr RG41. . . . . . . 88 C3
Snows Paddock GU20 . . . 146 B7
Snows Ride GU20 . . . . 146 B6
Soane End RG4 . . . . 59 A7
Soham Cl RG6 . . . . 114 C8
Soho Cres HP10 . . . . 3 D4
Soho Mills Ind Est HP10. . . 3 D4
Soke Rd RG7 . . . . 135 E3
Soldiers Rise RG40. . . . . . 142 D7
Solent Ct 3 RG1. . . . . 86 B6
Somerford Cl SL6. . . . . 40 B8
Somerlea SL6 . . . . 20 C3
Somersby Cres SL6 . . . . . . 39 E3
Somerset Cl
Hungerford RG17 . . . . 100 C5
Wokingham RG41 . . . . 115 D6
Somerset Gr RG42 . . . . 91 F1
Somerset Hospl SN8 . . . . . 99 B5
Somerset Lodge 3 SL6 . . 39 F6
Somerset Way SL0. . . . . . . 44 F4
Somerset Wlk RG31. . . . . . 84 B6
Somersham 2 SL6. . . . . . . 40 B8
Somerstown Ct RG1. . . . . . 85 F7
Somerton Gdns RG6 . . . . . 87 A2
Somerton Gr RG19 . . . . . . 106 C2
Somerville Cl RG41 . . . . . 115 D4
Somerville Cres GU46 . . . 149 E6
Somerville Rd SL4 . . . . 42 C1
Somerville Rise RG12 . . . 118 B4
Songbird Cl RG2. . . . . 113 E5
SONNING. 60 D4
Sonning CE Prim Sch RG4. . . . . 60 D3
Sonninge Cl GU47. . . . . . 150 D8
SONNING EYE. 60 C5
Sonning Gate RG4 . . . . 60 E2
Sonning La RG4. . . . . 60 C2
Sonning Mdws RG4 . . . . . . 60 C1
Sophie Gdns SL3. . . . . 43 D4
Sopwith Cl RG5 . . . . 88 A7
Sorrel Cl
Burghfield Common RG7 . . 111 B3
Newbury RG14. . . . . 105 D5
Wokingham RG40 . . . . 116 E8
Sorrel Dr GU18 . . . . 152 F7
Sospel Ct SL2. . . . . 22 C3
Southampton Cl GU17. . . 150 C6
Southampton Rd
Stanwell TW6. . . . . 70 F1
Stanwell TW19. . . . . 70 E1
Southampton St RG1. . . . . 86 B6
SOUTH ASCOT 120 B4
South Ascot Village Prim Sch SL5 . . . . 120 A4
South Ave
Egham TW20 . . . . 96 C2
Henley-on-T RG9 . . . . 35 E8
South Bank RG8 . . . . 14 C3
Southbank Gdns RG17. . . . 25 C2
Southbourne Dr SL8 . . . . . . 3 A3
Southbury La RG10. . . . . . . 61 F5
South Cl
Burnham SL1. . . . . 41 D6
Medmenham SL7. . . . . 17 D7
Wokingham RG40 . . . . 116 D4
SOUTHCOTE 85 C4
Southcote Ave TW13 . . . . . 98 F6
Southcote Dr GU15 . . . . . 152 A5
Southcote Farm La RG30 . 85 D4
Southcote La RG30. . . . . . . 85 C4
Southcote Lodge RG30. . . 85 A4
Southcote Prim Sch RG30 85 C4
Southcote Rd RG30 . . . . . . 85 D6
Southcroft
Englefield Green TW20 . . . . 95 B3
Slough SL2. . . . . 22 B1
Southdown Rd
Caversham RG4. . . . . 59 B5
Tadley RG26. . . . . 135 A1
Thatcham RG19 . . . . 105 F4
South Dr
Reading RG2 . . . . 86 F2
Sonning RG4 . . . . 60 C1
Sulhamstead RG7 . . . . 110 D7
Wentworth GU25. . . . . 122 A2
Wokingham RG40 . . . . 116 C5
SOUTHEND
Bradfield 82 A2
Brightwalton 28 C1
Southend RG18 . . . . 106 D6
Southend Rd RG7 . . . . 82 B2
Southern Cotts TW19 . . . . 70 A2
Southern Ct 18 RG1 . . . . . . 86 B7
Southerndene Cl RG31 . . . 57 C2
Southern Gate Pk RG2 . . 113 A8
Southern Hill RG1. . . . . 86 D5
Southern Ind Area RG12. 117 F6
Southern Perimeter Rd
East Bedfont TW6 . . . . 71 B1
Harlington TW14, TW6. . . . . 71 D2
Stanwell TW19, TW6 . . . . . . 70 D2
Southern Rd GU15 . . . . . . 151 C6
South Farm La GU19 . . . . 146 A2
SOUTH FAWLEY 27 C5
South Field Cl SL4 . . . . 41 C3
Southfield Gdns SL1 . . . . . 41 B8
Southfields
Boxford RG20 . . . . 76 C3
Chieveley RG20 . . . . 78 B8
Southfields Ave TW15. . . . 98 B2
Southfield Sch RG40 . . . . 116 D5
South Gate Ave TW13 . . . . 98 D4
Southgate Ho SL6. . . . . 39 F7
Southglade RG2 . . . . 113 D8
South Gn SL1. . . . . 42 E6
South Gr KT16 . . . . 123 F3
South Groves RG17 . . . . . . 73 A2
South Hill Rd RG12. . . . . . 118 B3
South Lake Cres RG5. . . . . 87 E5
Southlake Ct RG5 . . . . 87 D5
South Lake Prim Sch RG5 87 D5
Southlands Cl RG40 . . . . . 116 D5
Southlands Rd RG40 . . . . 116 D4
Southlea Rd SL3 . . . . 68 B5
South Lynn Cres RG12. . . 118 B4
South Mdw RG45 . . . . 143 D3
South Meadow La SL4. . . . 67 C8
South Oak Way RG2. . . . . 112 F7
South Pl SL7. . . . . .1 E1
South Rd
Bisley GU24. . . . . 153 F3
Bracknell RG40, RG12 . . . . 117 E1
Crowthorne RG45 . . . . 143 E3
Englefield Green TW20 . . . . 95 D2
Maidenhead SL6 . . . . 39 E6
South Row
Chilton OX11 . . . . 10 D7
Fulmer SL3. . . . . 23 E8
Southside KT16 . . . . 124 A6
South St
Blewbury OX11 . . . . 12 A8
Caversham RG4. . . . . 59 B2
Reading RG1 . . . . 86 C7
Staines TW18. . . . . 96 F3
SOUTH STOKE 14 C4
South Stoke Prim Sch RG8. . . . . 14 B4

South Terr SL4 .... 67 E6
South View
Bracknell RG12 .... 117 D6
Cookham Rise SL6 .... 19 E7
Hungerford RG17 .... 100 D5
South View Ave RG4 .... 59 C2
Southview Cl RG10 .... 61 E6
South View Gdns 3
RG14 .... 105 B4
South View Pk RG4 .... 59 C2
Southview Rd SL7 .... 1 E4
Southville Cl TW14 .... 98 E7
Southville Cres TW14 .... 98 E7
Southville Jun & Inf Schs
TW14 .... 98 F7
Southville Rd TW14 .... 98 E8
Southwark Cl GU46 .... 149 C6
Southway GU15 .... 151 B4
Southwell Park Rd GU15 151 C5
Southwick GU19 .... 145 E1
Southwick Ct RG12 .... 118 E3
Southwold RG12 .... 117 E1
Southwold Cl RG6 .... 87 D1
Southwold Spur SL3 .... 44 C4
Southwood RG40 .... 116 D4
Southwood Gdns
Burghfield Common RG7 .. 111 A3
Cookham Rise SL6 .... 19 E5
Southwood Rd
Cookham Rise SL6 .... 19 E5
Yateley GU17 .... 149 E1
Sovereign Beeches SL2 .. 22 B6
Sovereign Ct 4 SL5 .... 121 B2
Sovereign Dr GU15 .... 152 B7
Sovereign Ho TW15 .... 97 E4
Sovereign Hts SL3 .... 69 A8
Sovereign Pk 3 RG31 .... 84 D8
Sovereign Way RG31 .... 84 C5
Sovoy Ct GU15 .... 151 C5
Sowbury Pk RG20 .... 78 A8
Spackman Cl RG19 .... 106 D2
Spackmans Way SL1 .... 42 D3
Spade Oak Farm SL8 .... 2 E3
Spade Oak Mdw SL8 .... 2 E4
Spa Meadow Cl RG19 .... 131 C8
Span Hill RG4 .... 60 B7
Sparrowbill RG20 .... 28 E2
Sparrow Cl RG41 .... 115 E5
Sparvell Way GU15 .... 151 C6
Speedbird Way UB7 .... 70 C7
Speedwell Way RG18 .... 106 F4
SPEEN 104 C5
Speenhamland Ct 5
RG14 .... 105 A4
Speenhamland Prim Sch
RG14 .... 104 F4
Speen Hill Cl RG14 .... 104 E4
Speen La RG14 .... 104 D4
Speen Lodge Ct RG14 .... 104 E4
Speen Pl RG14 .... 104 E4
Spelthorne Gr TW16 .... 98 F1
Spelthorne Inf Sch TW15 . 98 E2
Spelthorne Jun Sch
TW15 .... 98 D2
Spelthorne La TW15,
TW17 .... 125 C8
Spelthorne Mus★ TW18 .. 96 F3
Spencer Cl
Pamber Heath RG26 .... 135 E1
Wokingham RG41 .... 115 D6
Spencer Gdns TW20 .... 95 D3
Spencer Rd
Bracknell RG42 .... 117 F8
Newbury RG14 .... 130 D6
Reading RG2 .... 113 B7
Slough SL3 .... 43 F3
Spencers Cl SL6 .... 39 D8
Spencers Ct RG7 .... 113 A3
Spencers La SL6 .... 19 E7
Spencers Rd SL6 .... 39 D8
SPENCERS WOOD 113 A1
Spenwood Cl RG7 .... 113 B2
Sperling Rd SL6 .... 19 F1
Spey Rd RG30 .... 85 A7
Spinfield La SL7 .... 1 B2
Spinfield La W SL7 .... 1 C1
Spinfield Mount SL7 .... 1 B1
Spinfield Pk SL7 .... 1 C1
Spinfield Sch SL7 .... 1 B2
Spinis RG12 .... 117 F1
Spinner Gn RG12 .... 118 B4
Spinners Wlk
Marlow SL7 .... 1 C1
Windsor SL4 .... 67 C6
Spinney SL1 .... 42 B5
Spinney Cl RG4 .... 59 B7
Spinney Dr TW14 .... 98 C8
Spinney La SL4 .... 93 B7
Spinney The
Finchampstead RG40 .... 141 F8
Frimley GU15 .... 152 C6
Reading RG31 .... 84 E4
Sunningdale SL5 .... 120 E4
Yateley GU46 .... 149 C7
Spinningwheel La RG42 .. 90 C8
Spires Ct KT16 .... 124 A3
Spire View 3 TW19 .... 70 D1
SPITAL 67 B3
Spitfire Cl SL3 .... 44 A2
Spitfire Way RG5 .... 88 A7
Spittal St SL7 .... 1 D2
Splash The RG42 .... 91 B2
Spode Cl RG30 .... 84 E8
Spout La TW19 .... 70 A3
Spout La N TW19 .... 70 B3
Spray La RG20 .... 28 C1
Spray Rd SN8, RG17 .... 126 E3
Spriggs Cl RG19 .... 106 D2
Springate Field SL3 .... 43 E4
Spring Ave TW20 .... 95 F2
Spring Cl
Maidenhead SL6 .... 19 F2
Pangbourne RG8 .... 55 D5
Spring Cnr 2 TW13 .... 98 F5
Spring Cross Ave GU17 .. 150 D4
Springdale
Earley RG6 .... 87 B2
Finchampstead RG40 .... 141 E8
Springdale Cotts SL8 .... 3 B2
Spring Farm Mews RG8 .. 14 C1
Springfield
Lightwater GU18 .... 153 D8
Slough SL1 .... 43 A3
Springfield Cl SL4 .... 67 B5
Springfield Ct
Maidenhead SL6 .... 40 B7
Twyford RG10 .... 61 E5
Springfield End RG8 .... 34 C8
Springfield Gr TW16 .... 125 F8
Springfield La RG14 .... 131 B8
Springfield Mews RG4 .... 59 B4
Springfield Pk
Maidenhead SL6 .... 40 C1
Twyford RG10 .... 61 E4
Springfield Prim Sch
Reading RG31 .... 84 B7
Sunbury TW16 .... 125 F7
Springfield Rd
Ashford TW15 .... 97 F3
Bracknell RG12 .... 117 C8
Brands Hill SL3 .... 69 B7
Frimley GU15 .... 152 B5
Pamber Heath RG26 .... 135 E1
Windsor SL4 .... 67 B5
Springfields Cl KT16 .... 124 B1
Spring Gdns
Ascot SL5 .... 120 B5
Bourne End SL8 .... 3 A4
Frimley GU15 .... 152 A5
Marlow SL7 .... 1 E3
Newbury RG20 .... 130 B3
Shinfield RG7 .... 113 B2
Theale RG7 .... 83 D3
Wooburn Green HP10 .... 3 E8
Spring Gr
Reading RG1 .... 86 B6
Sunningdale SL5 .... 120 F2
Spring Hill SL6 .... 39 E3
Springhill Ct 5 RG12 .... 118 B5
Springhill Rd RG8 .... 34 C8
Springhurst RG14 .... 131 B8
Spring La
Aldermaston RG7 .... 135 C6
Aston Tirrold OX11 .... 12 E8
Caversham RG4 .... 60 B5
Cold Ash RG18 .... 106 C8
Cookham Dean SL6 .... 19 C5
Farnham Common SL2 .... 22 C5
Mortimer RG7 .... 137 A6
Riseley RG7 .... 139 A4
Slough SL1 .... 41 F5
Spring Mdws RG17 .... 48 B4
Springmead Ct GU47 .... 143 E1
Spring Meadow RG12 .... 118 D8
Spring Meadows Bsns Ctr
RG10 .... 36 F5
Spring Rd TW13 .... 98 F5
Spring Rise TW20 .... 95 E2
Spring Terr 4 RG1 .... 86 B5
Spring Wlk RG10 .... 36 D1
Spring Wood La RG7 .... 111 A2
Spring Woods
Sandhurst GU47 .... 143 C1
Virginia Water GU25 .... 122 B5
Sproggit Ind Est TW19 .... 70 F1
Spruce Ct 1 SL1 .... 42 F3
Spruce Dr GU18 .... 153 A7
Spruce Rd RG5 .... 88 A6
Spurcroft Prim Sch
RG19 .... 106 D2
Spurcroft Rd RG19 .... 106 D2
Spur The
Slough SL1 .... 41 D8
Wargrave RG10 .... 36 E3
Square The
Bagshot GU19 .... 145 E3
Bracknell RG12 .... 118 E5
Earley RG6 .... 114 A8
Harmondsworth TW6 .... 70 B6
Lightwater GU18 .... 146 C1
Newtown RG19 .... 132 A4
Pangbourne RG8 .... 56 D6
Shinfield RG7 .... 113 B2
Yattendon RG18 .... 53 E1
Squires Bridge Rd KT17 . 124 F5
Squire's Bridge Rd
TW17 .... 125 A6
Squires Ct
Camberley GU15 .... 151 C3
Chertsey KT16 .... 124 B1
Squire's Rd TW17 .... 125 A5
Squires Wlk TW15 .... 98 D1
Squirrel Cl GU47 .... 150 B8
Squirrel Dr SL4 .... 93 B7
Squirrel Rise SL7 .... 1 D6
Squirrels Drey RG45 .... 142 F5
Squirrels Way RG6 .... 87 B2
Squirrel Wlk RG41 .... 115 F7
Stable Cl RG7 .... 111 A3
Stable Cotts SL7 .... 18 C5
Stable Croft GU19 .... 145 D2
Stable Ct RG14 .... 105 B6
Stables Ct SL7 .... 1 B1
Stables The SL5 .... 121 B1
Stable View GU46 .... 149 D7
Staddlestone Cl RG31 .... 57 C2
Stadium Way RG30 .... 58 B1
Staff College Rd GU15 .. 151 B6
Stafferton Way SL6 .... 40 A6
Stafford Ave SL2 .... 22 C1
Stafford Cl
Burnham SL6 .... 41 B7
Woodley RG5 .... 87 F7
Stafford Lake GU21,
GU24 .... 153 F1
Staffordshire Cl RG30 .... 84 F8
Staffordshire Croft RG42 . 91 F2
Stag Hill RG17 .... 73 A2
Stainash Cres TW18 .... 97 B3
Stainash Par TW18 .... 97 B3
STAINES 96 E6
Staines By-Pass TW15,
TW18 .... 97 C3
Staines La KT16 .... 124 A3
Staines Lane Cl KT16 .... 123 F4
Staines Prep Sch TW18 .. 97 A3
Staines Rd
Chertsey KT16 .... 124 A5
East Bedfont TW14 .... 98 D8
Laleham TW18 .... 124 B7
Wraysbury TW19 .... 95 F7
Staines Rd W TW15 .... 98 D1
Staines Sta TW18 .... 97 A3
Stainford Cl TW15 .... 98 D3
Stamford Ave GU16 .... 151 F1
Stamford Rd SL6 .... 39 C6
Stanbrook Cl RG7 .... 82 A2
Stanbury Gate RG7 .... 113 A3
Stanfield RG26 .... 135 B1
STANFORD DINGLEY 81 C4
Stanford Dingley Circular
Wlks★ RG18 .... 80 E7
STANFORD END 138 F3
Stanham Rd RG30 .... 84 F8
Stanhope Gate GU15 .... 151 A5
Stanhope Heath TW19 .... 70 C1
Stanhope Rd
Camberley GU15 .... 150 F4
Reading RG2 .... 86 D3
Slough SL1 .... 41 D7
Stanhope Way TW19 .... 70 C1
Stanlake La RG10 .... 61 F4
Stanley Cl SL7 .... 1 F3
Stanley Cotts SL2 .... 42 F5
Stanley Gn E SL3 .... 43 F2
Stanley Gn W SL3 .... 43 F2
Stanley Gr 1 RG1 .... 85 F7
Stanley Ho SL4 .... 68 A2
Stanley Rd
Ashford TW15 .... 97 E3
Newbury RG14 .... 105 B2
Wokingham RG40 .... 116 E6
Stanley Spencer Art Gall★
SL6 .... 20 B7
Stanley St RG1 .... 85 F8
Stanley Wlk RG12 .... 118 C7
STANMORE 30 B2
Stanmore Cl SL5 .... 120 A5
Stanmore Gdns RG7 .... 136 F5
Stanmore Rd RG20 .... 30 C2
Stanshawe Rd RG1 .... 86 A8
Stansted Rd TW6 .... 70 F1
Stanton Cl RG6 .... 87 C4
Stanton Way SL3 .... 43 E2
Stanway Cotts RG1 .... 86 F6
Stanway Pl KT16 .... 123 F2
STANWELL 97 C7
Stanwell Cl TW19 .... 70 D1
Stanwell Fields CE Prim Sch
TW19 .... 70 E1
Stanwell Gdns TW19 .... 70 D1
STANWELL MOOR 70 A1
Stanwell Moor Rd TW19, TW6,
UB7 .... 70 B4
Stanwell New Rd TW18 .. 97 B5
STANWELL PLACE 70 B1
Stanwell Rd
Ashford TW15 .... 97 E3
East Bedfont TW14, TW19,
TW6 .... 98 B8
Horton SL3 .... 69 C4
Stapleford Rd RG30 .... 85 C4
Staplehurst RG12 .... 117 E2
Stapleton Cl
Marlow SL7 .... 1 F4
Newbury RG14 .... 130 C6
Star Cotts RG20 .... 30 E6
Star La
Knowl Hill RG10 .... 37 E4
Reading RG1 .... 86 B7
Starling Ct RG41 .... 115 F5
Starlings Dr RG31 .... 84 B6
Starmead Dr RG40 .... 116 E5
Star Post Rd GU15 .... 151 F8
Star Rd RG4 .... 59 C2
Starting Gates 3 RG14 .. 105 C1
Starting Gate The SL5 .. 120 A4
Startins La SL6 .... 19 C8
Starwood Ct SL3 .... 43 C3
Statham Ct RG42 .... 117 E8
Station App
Ashford TW15 .... 97 F4
Blackwater GU17 .... 150 E4
17 Maidenhead SL6 .... 39 F6
Marlow SL7 .... 1 E1
Reading RG1 .... 86 A8
Shepperton TW17 .... 125 C4
Staines TW18 .... 97 A3
Virginia Water GU25 .... 122 D5
Station Cres TW15 .... 97 E4
Station Hill
Ascot SL5 .... 120 A5
Cookham Rise SL6 .... 19 F7
Hampstead Norreys RG18 .. 52 F6
Station Hill *continued*
Reading RG1 .... 86 A8
Station Ho SL3 .... 68 B6
Station Ind Est RG40 .... 116 B6
Station Par
Ashford TW15 .... 97 F4
Cookham Rise SL6 .... 19 F6
Sunningdale SL5 .... 121 A2
Virginia Water GU25 .... 122 E4
Station Path TW18 .... 96 F4
Station Rd
Ashford TW15 .... 97 F4
Bagshot GU19 .... 145 E4
Bourne End SL8 .... 3 A3
Bracknell RG12 .... 118 B7
Broad Laying RG20 .... 130 A3
Chertsey KT16 .... 124 A1
Cookham Rise SL6 .... 19 F7
Earley RG6 .... 87 C4
East Garston RG17 .... 47 C6
Egham TW20 .... 96 A3
Frimley GU16 .... 151 C1
Goring RG8 .... 34 C6
Great Shefford RG17 .... 48 A3
Henley-on-T RG9 .... 15 E1
Hungerford RG17 .... 100 D6
Kintbury RG17 .... 102 B2
Lambourn RG17 .... 25 B2
Lower Shiplake RG9 .... 36 A4
Marlow SL7 .... 1 E1
Mortimer RG7 .... 137 E5
Newbury RG14 .... 105 A2
1 Pangbourne RG8 .... 56 C6
Reading RG1 .... 86 B8
Shepperton TW17 .... 125 C4
Slough, Langley SL3 .... 44 A4
Slough SL1 .... 41 E7
Speen RG14 .... 104 D5
Sunningdale SL5 .... 121 A4
Taplow SL6 .... 40 F7
Thatcham RG19 .... 106 E2
Theale RG7 .... 83 E2
Twyford RG10 .... 61 D4
Wargrave RG10 .... 36 C1
Wokingham RG40 .... 116 B6
Woolhampton RG7 .... 108 C2
Wraysbury TW19 .... 69 A1
Station Rd N 5 TW20 .... 95 F3
Station Rise SL7 .... 1 E2
Station Road Ind Est
RG19 .... 106 F1
Station Terr RG10 .... 61 E4
Station Way RG12 .... 118 C7
Station Yard Ind Est
RG17 .... 100 E5
Staunton Rd SL2 .... 42 D8
Staveley Rd TW15 .... 98 D2
Staverton Cl
Bracknell RG42 .... 91 B1
Wokingham RG40 .... 116 F6
Staverton Rd RG2 .... 86 D3
Stayne End GU25 .... 122 A5
Steam Farm La TW14 .... 71 F3
Steeple Ct 18 TW20 .... 96 A3
Steeple Point SL5 .... 120 B6
Steeple Wlk RG6 .... 113 F8
Steerforth Copse GU47 .. 143 E2
Steggles Cl RG5 .... 87 D8
Stepgates KT16 .... 124 B2
Stepgates Cl KT16 .... 124 B2
Stepgates Com Prim Sch
KT16 .... 124 B2
Stephanie Chase Ct
RG40 .... 116 D7
Stephen Cl
Egham TW20 .... 96 C2
Twyford RG10 .... 61 F3
Stephens Cl RG7 .... 136 F6
Stephens Firs RG7 .... 136 F6
Stephenson Cl RG18 .... 106 D4
Stephenson Ct
8 Newbury RG14 .... 104 F4
13 Slough SL1 .... 42 F4
Stephenson Dr SL4 .... 67 B7
Stephenson Rd RG2 .... 141 A7
Stephens Rd RG7 .... 136 F6
Sterling Ctr The RG12 .. 118 D6
Sterling Gdns GU47 .... 150 E8
Sterling Ind Est RG14 .... 105 B2
Sterling Way RG30 .... 58 B1
Stern Ct KT16 .... 124 C1
Stevens Ct 2 RG41 .... 88 C2
Stevens Hill GU46 .... 149 E5
Stevenson Dr RG42 .... 90 C3
Stewart Ave
Littleton TW17 .... 125 A5
Slough SL1 .... 42 F8
Stewart Cl SL6 .... 65 D6
Stewarts Dr SL2 .... 22 B8
Stewarts Way SL7 .... 1 D7
Stile Rd SL3 .... 43 D3
Stilton Cl RG6 .... 87 E2
Stilwell Cl GU46 .... 149 E6
Stirling Ave TW17 .... 125 E6
Stirling Cl
Caversham RG4 .... 59 D6
Frimley GU16 .... 151 E2
Windsor SL4 .... 66 D5
Stirling Gr SL6 .... 39 B8
Stirling Ho 26 RG1 .... 86 B6
Stirling Pl 1 SL6 .... 39 B8
Stirling Rd
Slough SL1 .... 42 B8
Stanwell TW6 .... 70 F1
Stirling Way RG18 .... 106 C4
Stirrup Cl RG14 .... 131 B7
STITCHENS GREEN 33 F3
Stockbridge Way GU46 .. 149 D4
Stockbury Cl RG6 .... 87 B1
STOCKCROSS 103 E6
Stockcross CE Sch RG20 103 E6
Stockdales Rd SL4 .... 41 F2
Stockton Rd RG2 .... 86 C1
Stockwells SL6 .... 20 D1
Stockwood Rise GU15 .... 151 F5
Stoke Common Rd SL3 .. 23 B8
Stoke Court Dr SL2 .... 22 F4
Stoke Ct RG2 .... 86 B1
Stokeford Cl 5 RG12 .... 118 F4
Stoke Gdns SL1 .... 42 F5
Stoke Gn SL2 .... 23 A1
STOKE GREEN 23 B1
Stoke Park Ave SL2 .... 22 C2
STOKE POGES 22 F3
Stoke Poges La SL1, SL2 .. 42 E7
Stoke Poges Sch The SL2. 22 F5
Stoke Rd SL2 .... 42 F7
Stokesay SL2 .... 42 F6
Stokes Farm RG40 .... 116 F8
Stokes La RG26 .... 134 C1
Stokesley Rise HP10 .... 3 E8
Stokes View RG8 .... 56 C5
Stoke View SL1 .... 42 F5
Stoke Wood SL2 .... 22 F8
Stompits Rd SL6 .... 65 C8
Stomp Rd SL1 .... 41 C8
Stonea Cl RG6 .... 114 C8
Stonebridge Field SL4 .. 42 B1
STONE COPSE 105 E7
Stone Copse RG14 .... 105 E7
Stone Cres TW14 .... 98 F8
Stonecroft Ave SL0 .... 44 E7
Stonefield Pk SL6 .... 39 C7
Stonegate GU15 .... 152 C6
Stoneham Cl RG30 .... 85 A6
Stonehaven Dr RG5 .... 88 A6
Stonehill Gate SL5 .... 120 D3
Stonehill Ho GU19 .... 145 F2
Stonehill Rd GU18 .... 146 A1
Stonehouse RG8 .... 34 E2
Stone House La SL6 .... 2 C1
Stonehouse Rise GU16 .. 151 E1
Stoneleigh Ct
Frimley GU16 .... 151 F1
Theale RG7 .... 83 D2
Stonemasons Ct 6
RG14 .... 104 F1
Stone St RG30 .... 58 B1
Stone's Wlk RG7 .... 111 A3
Stoney Cl GU46 .... 149 D4
Stoneyfield RG7 .... 109 A6
Stoney La
Farnham Royal SL2 .... 22 A4
Newbury RG14, RG18 .... 105 D6
Thatcham RG19 .... 106 E3
Stoneyland Ct 6 TW20 .. 95 F3
Stoneylands Rd TW20 .... 95 F3
Stoney Meade SL1 .... 42 B5
Stoney Rd RG42 .... 118 A8
Stoney Ware SL7 .... 18 E8
Stoney Ware Cl SL7 .... 18 D8
Stony La RG17 .... 46 D3
Stookes Way GU46 .... 149 B4
Stork House Dr RG17 .... 25 A2
Stornaway Rd SL3 .... 44 C2
Stour Cl
Reading RG30 .... 85 A8
Slough SL1 .... 42 B3
Stovell Rd SL4 .... 67 B7
Stowe Rd SL1 .... 41 E6
Stowmarket Cl RG6 .... 87 D2
Strachay Cl RG8 .... 56 C2
Straight Bit HP10 .... 3 B8
Straight La RG17 .... 46 F4
Straight Mile The
Hurst RG10, RG40 .... 89 D6
Waltham St L RG10 .... 62 E1
Straight Rd SL4 .... 68 B1
STRAIGHT SOLEY 73 A5
Strande La SL6 .... 19 F5
Strande Pk SL6 .... 19 F5
Strande View Wlk SL6 .... 19 F5
Strand Way RG6 .... 87 C1
Stranraer Gdns SL1 .... 42 E5
Stranraer Way 1 TW6 .... 70 E1
Stratfield RG12 .... 117 E1
Stratfield Ct SL6 .... 40 B8
STRATFIELD
MORTIMER 137 D5
Stratfield Rd SL1 .... 43 A4
Stratford Cl SL2 .... 21 D1
Stratford Dr HP10 .... 3 D4
Stratford Gdns SL6 .... 39 C4
Stratford Rd TW6 .... 71 C2
Stratford Way RG31 .... 84 A6
Strathcona Cl HP10 .... 3 C7
Strathcona Way HP10 .... 3 C7
Strathearn Ave UB3 .... 71 F7
Stratheden Pl 6 RG1 .... 85 F8
Strathmore Ct 3 GU15 .. 151 D5
Strathmore Dr RG10 .... 61 A4
Strathy Cl RG30 .... 85 B8
Stratton Gdns RG2 .... 86 C1
Stratton Rd TW16 .... 125 F7
Strawberry Fields RG7 .. 137 B6
Strawberry Hill
Newbury RG14 .... 104 F4
Newell Green RG42 .... 91 E2
Streamside SL1 .... 41 F5
STREATLEY 34 A7
Streatley CE Sch RG8 .... 33 F6
Streatley Farm Cotts RG8 34 A8

Streatley & Goring Bridge RG8 .... 34 B6
Streatley Hill RG8 .... 33 F6
Streets Heath GU24 .... 153 F7
Street The
Aldermaston RG7 .... 135 A7
Englefield RG7 .... 83 B5
Mortimer RG7 .... 137 D5
Moulsford OX10 .... 14 A6
South Stoke RG8 .... 14 B3
Swallowfield RG7 .... 139 C6
Tidmarsh RG8 .... 56 D2
Waltham St L RG10 .... 63 A6
Stretcher Dr RG18 .... 79 C8
Stretton RG7 .... 82 A1
Stretton Cl RG7 .... 82 A1
Strode's Coll TW20 .... 95 F3
Strodes College La TW20 . 95 F3
Strode's Cres TW18 .... 97 C3
Strode St TW20 .... 96 A4
Stroller Cl RG19 .... 105 F4
Stroma Ct SL1 .... 41 D6
Strongrove Hill RG17 .... 100 C6
Strood La SL5 .... 93 C2
Stroud Cl
Pamber Heath RG26 .... 135 E1
Windsor SL4 .... 66 D4
STROUDE 122 F7
Stroude Rd
Egham TW20 .... 96 A1
Virginia Water GU25, TW20 .... 122 E6
Stroud Farm Rd SL6 .... 65 B8
STROUD GREEN 105 B1
Stroud La GU17 .... 150 A4
Strouds Mdw RG18 .... 106 C7
Strouds The RG7 .... 108 F6
Stroud Way TW15 .... 98 B2
Stuart Cl
Caversham RG4 .... 59 B5
Windsor SL4 .... 66 F5
Stuart Ho RG42 .... 117 F8
Stuart Rd RG14 .... 130 D6
Stuart Way
Staines TW18 .... 97 B2
Virginia Water GU25 .... 122 A5
Windsor SL4 .... 66 F5
STUBBINGS 38 D8
STUBBLES 54 C6
Stubbles RG8 .... 54 C6
Stubbles La SL6 .... 19 B6
Stubbs Folly GU47 .... 150 D7
STUD GREEN 64 F7
Studios Rd TW17 .... 124 F6
Studland Cl RG2 .... 113 C7
Studland Ind Est RG20 .. 129 B3
Sturbridge Cl RG6 .... 87 C1
Sturdee Cl GU16 .... 151 E1
Sturges Ct RG40 .... 116 D5
Sturges Rd RG40 .... 116 C5
Sturt Gn SL6 .... 64 E8
Styles SL5 .... 120 F2
Styventon Pl KT16 .... 123 F2
Suck's La RG8 .... 54 D3
Suffolk Cl
Bagshot GU19 .... 145 E2
Slough SL1 .... 41 E7
Wokingham RG41 .... 115 D6
Suffolk Combe RG42 .... 91 F1
Suffolk Ct 2 SL6 .... 39 F8
Suffolk Ho RG1 .... 86 D5
Suffolk Rd
Maidenhead SL6 .... 39 D4
Reading RG30 .... 85 D7
SULHAM 56 E2
Sulham La RG8 .... 56 E3
SULHAMSTEAD 110 C6
SULHAMSTEAD ABBOTS 110 F4
SULHAMSTEAD BANNISTER UPPER END 110 E5
Sulhamstead Hill RG7 ... 110 C6
Sulhamstead Rd
Burghfield RG7, RG30 .... 111 B5
Ufton Nervet RG7 .... 110 D4
Sulhamstead & Ufton Nervet CE Prim Sch RG7 .... 110 C4
Sulham Wlk RG30 .... 85 B4
Sullivan Rd GU15 .... 151 A5
Sullivans Reach KT12 ... 125 F2
Sumburgh Way SL1 .... 42 E8
Summer Ct RG41 .... 115 A8
Summerfield Cl RG41 .... 88 F1
Summerfield Rise RG8 ... 34 D7
Summer Gdns GU15 .... 152 C5
Summerhouse La UB7 .... 70 D8
Summerlea SL1 .... 42 B5
Summerleaze Rd SL6 .... 20 A1
Summer Pl RG12 .... 118 A7
Summers Rd SL1 .... 21 C2
Summit Cl RG40 .... 141 F7
Summit Ctr UB7 .... 70 D7
SUNBURY 125 F6
SUNBURY COMMON 98 E1
Sunbury Cres TW13 .... 98 F4
Sunbury Cross Ctr 10 TW16 .... 98 F1
Sunbury Ct SL4 .... 67 D8
Sunbury Int Bsns Ctr TW16 .... 125 E8
Sunbury Manor Sch TW16 .... 125 F8
Sunbury Rd
Eton SL4 .... 67 D8
Feltham TW13 .... 98 F4
Sun Cl SL4 .... 67 D8
Sunderland Cl RG5 .... 88 B8
Sunderland Ct 11 TW19 .. 70 E1
Sunderland Gdns RG14 .. 104 D2
Sunderland Pl RG18 .... 106 C4
Sunderland Rd SL6 .... 39 B8
Sundew Cl
Lightwater GU18 .... 153 D8
Wokingham RG40 .... 116 E7
Sundial Cl RG30 .... 85 A6
Sundon Cres GU25 .... 122 C4
Sundown Rd TW15 .... 98 C3
Sunfield Bsns Pk RG40 .. 140 F3
Sun Gdns RG7 .... 111 A1
Sun Hill RG7 .... 108 F2
Sun La
Maidenhead SL6 .... 39 F7
Riseley RG7 .... 139 B2
Sunley Cl RG14 .... 130 D6
Sunmead Rd TW16 .... 125 F6
Sunna Lodge TW16 .... 98 F1
Sunning Ave SL5 .... 120 E2
SUNNINGDALE 121 B4
Sunningdale Park (Civil Service Coll) SL5 .... 120 F4
Sunningdale Sch SL5 ... 120 F3
Sunningdale Sta SL5 .... 121 A2
SUNNINGHILL 120 C4
Sunninghill Cl SL5 .... 120 D5
Sunninghill Ct SL5 .... 120 D5
Sunninghill Lodge
Ascot SL5 .... 120 C7
Ascot, Sunninghill SL5 ... 120 D5
Sunninghill Rd
Ascot SL5 .... 120 D5
Windlesham GU20 .... 146 A7
Winkfield SL4, SL5 .... 93 E2
Sunning Ho
Ascot SL5 .... 120 C5
Windlesham GU20 .... 146 F8
Sunnybank
Ascot SL5 .... 120 A5
Marlow SL7 .... 1 D4
SUNNYMEADS 68 E4
Sunnymeads Sta TW19 ... 68 E4
Sunnymede Cotts SL6 .... 20 B1
Sunnyside RG14 .... 104 E6
Sun Pas 19 SL4 .... 67 D6
Sun Ray Est GU47 .... 150 A8
Sunrise Hill RG20 .... 30 F7
Sun St RG1 .... 86 D7
Superity Cotts RG20 .... 31 D6
Surbiton Rd GU15 .... 145 A1
Surley Row RG4 .... 59 A5
Surly Hall Wlk SL4 .... 66 F6
Surrey Ave
Camberley GU15 .... 151 A4
Slough SL2 .... 22 C1
Surrey Ct RG42 .... 91 F1
Surrey Heath Mus★ GU15 .... 151 D6
Surrey Rd RG2 .... 86 B4
Surridge Ct GU19 .... 145 E2
Sussex Cl SL1 .... 43 B4
Sussex Gdns RG5 .... 87 E7
Sussex Ho SL2 .... 22 C6
Sussex Keep SL1 .... 43 B4
Sussex La RG7 .... 113 C1
Sussex Lodge 7 SL6 .... 39 F6
Sussex Pl SL1, SL3 .... 43 B3
Sutcliffe Ave RG6 .... 87 D3
Sutherland Ave TW16 .... 125 F7
Sutherland Chase SL5 ... 119 E7
Sutherland Gdns TW16 .. 125 F7
Sutherland Gr RG31 .... 84 E4
Sutherland Grange SL4 .. 66 D7
Sutherlands RG14 .... 130 E7
Sutherlands Ave RG1 .... 86 C5
SUTTON 44 C1
Sutton Ave SL3 .... 43 C4
Sutton Cl
Cookham SL6 .... 20 B7
Maidenhead SL6 .... 39 C5
Sutton Ct RG6 .... 87 B7
Sutton La
Brands Hill SL3 .... 69 B8
Slough SL3 .... 44 C1
Sutton Pl SL3 .... 69 B8
Sutton Rd
Camberley GU15 .... 145 A1
Cookham SL6 .... 20 B6
Newbury RG14 .... 104 D5
Suttons Bsns Pk RG1 .... 86 F8
Suttons Park Ave RG6 .... 86 E8
Sutton Wlk RG1 .... 86 C5
Swabey Rd SL3 .... 44 A2
Swainstone Rd RG2 .... 86 B5
Swaledale RG12 .... 118 A4
Swallow Cl
Reading RG31 .... 84 C6
Staines TW18 .... 96 F4
Yateley GU46 .... 149 B6
SWALLOWFIELD 139 C6
Swallowfield TW20 .... 95 B2
Swallowfield Dr RG2 .... 113 C6
Swallowfield Gdns RG7 .. 83 E4
Swallowfield Pk RG7 .... 139 E7
Swallowfield Rd RG2 .... 114 D2
Swallowfield St RG7 .... 139 C7
Swallow Ho SL7 .... 2 A2
Swallows Croft RG1 .... 85 E5
Swallow St SL0 .... 44 D8
Swallow Way RG41 .... 115 E5
Swanbrook Ct 6 SL6 .... 40 A7
Swancote Gn RG12 .... 118 B4
Swan Ct
3 Blackwater GU17 .... 150 E4
Newbury RG14 .... 104 F3
Swan Dr RG7 .... 109 C3
Swandrift TW18 .... 96 F1
Swangate RG17 .... 100 D7
Swan Ho GU47 .... 150 B7
Swanholm Gdns RG31 .... 84 F4
Swan La GU17, GU47 .... 150 B7
Swanmore Cl RG6 .... 87 E1
Swan Pl 5 RG1 .... 86 A7
Swan Rd SL0 .... 44 F7
Swanscourt RG10 .... 61 E3
Swansdown Wlk RG19 ... 106 B3
Swansea Rd
Harlington TW14, TW6 .... 71 D1
Reading RG1 .... 59 A1
Swansea Terr RG31 .... 57 D1
Swanston Field RG8 .... 56 D7
Swan Terr SL4 .... 67 B7
Swan Wlk TW17 .... 125 E2
Swedish Hos RG20 .... 76 B5
Sweeps Ditch Cl TW18 .. 124 A8
Sweeps La TW20 .... 95 F3
Sweetbriar RG45 .... 143 A7
Sweet Briar Dr RG31 .... 84 C4
Sweetzer's Piece RG7 ... 136 E6
Swepstone Cl RG6 .... 87 C2
Swift Cl RG41 .... 115 E5
Swift Ho SL7 .... 2 A2
Swift La GU19 .... 145 F3
Swinbrook Cl RG31 .... 57 D3
Swindon Rd TW6 .... 71 C2
Swinley Rd SL5 .... 119 C4
Swinnerton Ho RG9 .... 15 E3
Swiss Cottage Cl RG31 ... 84 C8
Swiss Ct GU17 .... 150 C4
Swiss Farm Park Homes RG9 .... 15 D3
Switchback Cl SL6 .... 19 D2
Switchback Rd N SL6 .... 19 E3
Switchback Rd S SL6 .... 19 D2
Switchback The SL6 .... 19 D2
Swithin Chase RG42 .... 91 E1
Sycamore Cl
8 Bourne End SL8 .... 3 B3
Burghfield RG30 .... 111 B4
Frimley GU16 .... 151 E1
Maidenhead SL6 .... 39 C3
Sandhurst GU47 .... 150 B8
Woodley RG5 .... 87 C5
Sycamore Ct
Pangbourne RG8 .... 56 C6
Windsor SL4 .... 67 C4
Sycamore Dr
Frimley GU16 .... 151 E1
Marlow Bottom SL7 .... 1 D5
Twyford RG10 .... 61 E5
Sycamore Lodge 8 TW16 98 F1
Sycamore Rd RG2 .... 86 E2
Sycamore Rise
Bracknell RG12 .... 118 D6
Newbury RG14 .... 105 C5
Sycamores The GU17 .... 150 B5
Sycamore Wlk
Englefield Green TW20 .... 95 B2
Slough SL3 .... 43 E7
Sydenham Gdns SL1 .... 42 C4
Sydenham Ho 4 RG1 .... 86 D7
Sydings The RG14 .... 104 D5
Sydney Cl
Crowthorne RG45 .... 143 C7
Thatcham RG19 .... 106 E3
Sydney Cres TW15 .... 98 B2
Sydney Gr SL1 .... 42 C7
Sydney Loader Pl GU17 .. 150 A5
Sydney Lodge RG19 .... 106 E3
Syke Cluan SL0 .... 44 E4
Syke Ings SL0 .... 44 F4
Sykes Cotts RG12 .... 118 E2
Sykes Dr TW18 .... 97 B3
Sykes Rd SL1 .... 42 B7
Sylvan Ridge GU47 .... 143 A1
Sylvanus RG12 .... 117 F2
Sylvan Wlk RG30 .... 85 C4
Sylverns Ct RG42 .... 91 D1
Sylvester Cl
Newbury RG14 .... 104 E5
Winnersh RG41 .... 88 D3
Sylvester Rd SL6 .... 19 E2
Symeon Pl RG4 .... 58 F3
Symondson Mews RG42 .. 90 C4
Sympson Rd RG26 .... 135 D1

T

Tachbrook Rd TW14 .... 98 F8
Tadcroft Wlk RG31 .... 84 E3
Tadham Pl RG19 .... 106 C2
TADLEY 135 B1
Tadley Common Rd RG26 .... 135 C1
Tadmor Cl TW16 .... 125 F5
Taff Way RG30 .... 85 A7
Tag La RG10 .... 37 A1
Talavera Cl RG45 .... 142 F4
Talbot Ave SL3 .... 43 F4
Talbot Cl
Caversham RG4 .... 59 D2
Newbury RG14 .... 104 E5
Talbot Ct
Reading RG1 .... 86 A7
Windsor SL4 .... 67 B4
Talbot Pl
Bagshot GU19 .... 145 E4
Datchet SL3 .... 68 C6
Talbot Rd TW15 .... 97 E3
Talbots Dr SL6 .... 39 B6
Talbot Way RG31 .... 57 C3
Talfourd Ave RG6 .... 87 A5
Talisman Cl RG45 .... 142 D5
Tallis La RG30 .... 85 D4
Tall Trees SL3 .... 69 E6
Tamar Ct RG30 .... 85 D6
Tamar Gdns RG2 .... 86 C3
Tamarind Ct 3 TW20 .... 95 F3
Tamarind Way RG6 .... 86 F1
Tamarisk Ave RG2 .... 86 E1
Tamarisk Ct RG18 .... 106 F4
Tamarisk Rise RG40 .... 116 C7
Tamarisk Way SL1 .... 42 A5
Tamar Way
Slough SL3 .... 44 B2
Wokingham RG41 .... 115 E7
Tamesa House TW17 .... 125 A2
Tamesis Pl RG4 .... 59 B1
Tamworth RG12 .... 118 D2
Tamworth Cl 2 RG6 .... 87 C1
Tangier Ct SL4 .... 67 D8
Tangier La SL4 .... 67 D8
Tanglewood RG40 .... 142 A7
Tanglewood Ride GU24 . 153 D7
Tangley Dr RG41 .... 116 B4
Tanglyn Ave TW17 .... 125 B4
Tanhouse La RG41 .... 116 A5
Tank Rd GU15 .... 150 F5
Tanner Ct RG14 .... 105 A4
Tanners Cl RG7 .... 110 F1
Tanners La RG4 .... 58 F8
Tanners Row RG41 .... 116 A3
Tanners Yd GU19 .... 145 E3
Tape La RG10 .... 88 F8
Tapestries Hall SL4 .... 68 A2
Tapestries The SL4 .... 68 A2
TAPLOW 20 E1
Taplow Common Rd SL1 . 21 A3
Taplow Quay SL6 .... 40 C7
Taplow Rd SL6 .... 41 A7
Taplow Sta SL6 .... 40 F7
Tarbat Ct 6 GU47 .... 150 D8
Tarbay La SL4 .... 66 B5
Target Cl TW14 .... 71 E1
Target Hill RG42 .... 91 D1
Targett Ct RG41 .... 88 B2
Tarlton Ct RG30 .... 84 F6
Tarmac Way UB7 .... 70 B7
Tarnbrook Way RG12 .... 118 E2
Tarn Howes Cl RG19 .... 106 A3
Tarn La RG14 .... 130 F8
Tarragon Cl
Bracknell RG42 .... 91 D1
Earley RG6 .... 86 F1
Tarragon Way RG7 .... 111 B3
Tarrant Ct GU25 .... 122 E4
Tarrant Gn RG42 .... 91 C1
Tarrant's Hill RG17 .... 100 D5
TASIS-The American Sch in England TW20 .... 123 C6
Tasker Cl UB7 .... 71 C7
Tasman Ct TW16 .... 98 E1
Tatchbrook Cl SL6 .... 40 A8
Tattersall Cl RG40 .... 116 E5
Tavistock Cl
Maidenhead SL6 .... 39 A8
Staines TW18 .... 97 D1
Tavistock Ind Est RG10 ... 61 F5
Tavistock Rd RG2 .... 86 B3
Tawfield RG12 .... 117 E2
Tayberry Gr RG7 .... 137 B6
Taylor Ct 8 RG1 .... 85 E7
Taylor's Cl SL7 .... 1 F2
Taylors Ct SL6 .... 39 B8
Taynton Wlk 3 RG1 .... 86 B5
Tay Rd RG30 .... 85 A7
Tazewell Ct RG1 .... 85 F6
Tealgate RG17 .... 100 D7
Teal Gr RG2 .... 113 E5
Tean Ho RG2 .... 86 A2
Tebbit Cl RG12 .... 118 D7
Teesdale Rd SL2 .... 41 F8
Teikyo Sch (UK) SL3 .... 23 D5
Tekels Ave GU15 .... 151 D4
Tekels Ct GU15 .... 151 E4
Tekels Way GU15 .... 151 F3
Telford Ave RG45 .... 143 C8
Telford Cres RG5 .... 60 F1
Telford Ct 3 RG14 .... 104 F4
Telford Dr SL1 .... 42 A4
Telston Cl SL8 .... 3 A5
Tempest Rd TW20 .... 96 C2
Templar Cl GU47 .... 150 A8
Templars Lodge RG12 ... 118 D3
Templars Pl 1 SL7 .... 1 E1
TEMPLE 18 C5
Templecroft TW15 .... 98 D2
Templedene Ave TW18 ... 97 C2
Templegate SL4 .... 67 C5
Temple Gdns TW18 .... 123 F8
Temple Ho RG9 .... 15 E3
Temple La SL7 .... 18 D6
Temple Mews RG5 .... 87 F7
Temple Mill Cotts SL7 .... 18 C5
Temple Mill Island SL7 ... 18 C5
TEMPLE PARK 90 E1
Temple Park Rdbt RG42 .. 90 F2
Temple Pk SL6 .... 17 F3
Temple Pl 20 RG1 .... 86 A6
Temple Rd SL4 .... 67 D5
TEMPLETON 101 B1
Templeton Gdns RG2 .... 86 C1
Templeton Ho RG9 .... 35 F8
Temple Way
Bracknell RG42 .... 90 E1
Farnham Common SL2 .... 22 C7
Templewood Gate SL2 .... 22 C7
Templewood La SL2 .... 22 D8
Ten Acre La TW20 .... 123 C7
Tenaplas Dr RG8 .... 54 F5
Tenby Ave RG4 .... 59 D5
Tenby Dr SL5 .... 120 D4
Tennyson Cl TW14 .... 71 F1
Tennyson Rd
Ashford TW15 .... 97 E3
Thatcham RG18 .... 106 C4
Woodley RG5 .... 87 E4
Tennyson Way SL2 .... 21 E1
Tensing Ct TW19 .... 97 E7
Tenth Ave RG31 .... 84 B6
Teresa Vale RG42 .... 91 E2
Tern Cl RG30 .... 85 A6
Terrace Rd N RG42 .... 90 C4
Terrace Rd S RG42 .... 90 C2
Terrace The
Ascot SL5 .... 120 D4
Bray SL6 .... 40 C3
Camberley GU15 .... 151 A5
Wokingham RG40 .... 116 B6
Terrent Ct SL4 .... 67 A5
Terrington Hill SL7 .... 1 C2
Terry's La SL6 .... 19 F8
Tesimond Dr GU46 .... 149 A6
Tessa Rd RG1 .... 58 F1
Test Cl RG30 .... 85 A8
Testwood Rd SL4 .... 66 D6
Tetbury Ct 9 RG1 .... 85 E7
Teviot Rd RG30 .... 84 E7
Thackery Lodge TW14 .... 71 D1
Thakerays The RG19 .... 106 D2
Thamebridge Ct 5 SL6 ... 40 B8
Thames Ave
Chertsey KT16 .... 124 A6
Pangbourne RG8 .... 56 D6
Reading RG1 .... 59 A1
Windsor SL4 .... 67 D7
Thames Bank
Goring RG8 .... 34 B7
Staines TW18 .... 96 F1
Taplow SL6 .... 40 C7
Thamesbourne Mews SL8 . 3 A3
Thames Cl
Bourne End SL8 .... 3 A4
Chertsey KT16 .... 124 C2
Thames Cres SL6 .... 20 B2
Thames Ct
Goring RG8 .... 34 B6
Reading RG1 .... 59 B1
Thames Dr RG10 .... 60 F7
Thames Edge Ct 2 TW18 . 96 E4
Thamesfield Ct TW17 ... 125 C2
Thamesfield Gdns SL7 ..... 1 E1
Thamesfield Ho TW17 .... 125 C2
Thamesfield Mews TW17 .... 125 C2
Thamesgate TW18 .... 124 B8
Thames Ho RG9 .... 15 E3
Thameside Prim Sch RG4 59 B2
Thameside Reach RG8 ... 14 A4
Thames Ind Est SL7 .... 1 F2
Thames Mead SL4 .... 66 E6
Thames Meadow TW17 ... 125 E1
Thamesmead Sch TW17 . 125 D3
Thames Rd
Goring RG8 .... 34 B6
Slough SL3 .... 44 B3
Thatcham RG18 .... 106 B5
Thames Reach
Medmenham SL7 .... 17 D6
Purley on T RG8 .... 57 D5
Thames Side
Henley-on-T RG9 .... 15 E2
Laleham KT16, TW18 .... 124 C4
Reading RG1 .... 59 A1
Windsor SL4 .... 67 D7
Thames Side Prom RG1 .. 59 A2
Thames St
Oatlands Park KT12 .... 125 F2
Sonning RG4 .... 60 D4
Staines TW18 .... 96 F3
Windsor SL4 .... 67 D7
Thames Terr RG4 .... 60 D4
Thames Valley Bsns Pk RG6 .... 60 A1
Thames Valley Nuffield Hospl The SL3 .... 23 C4
Thames Valley Univ SL1 .. 42 E5
Thames Valley Univ (Reading Campus)
Reading RG1 .... 86 D7
Reading RG1 .... 86 F6
Thanington Way RG6 .... 87 B2
THATCHAM 106 E5
Thatcham Nature Discovery Ctr★ RG19 .... 106 A2
Thatcham Park CE Prim Sch RG18 .... 106 D4
Thatcham Sta RG19 .... 106 F1
Thatchers Dr SL6 .... 39 A5
Theal Cl GU47 .... 150 D8
THEALE 83 D4
Theale CE Prim Sch RG7 . 83 D3
Theale Green Com Sch RG7 .... 83 D3
Theale Lakes Bsns Pk RG7 .... 110 F8
Theale Rd RG30 .... 111 C6
Theale Sta RG7 .... 83 E2
THE HOLT 37 B1
Theobald Dr RG31 .... 57 D4
Theobalds Way GU16 .... 152 C3
Thetford Ho 7 RG1 .... 85 E5
Thetford Mews RG4 .... 59 D6
Thetford Rd TW15 .... 97 E5
Thibet Rd GU47 .... 150 C8
Thicket Gr SL6 .... 38 F7
Thicket Rd RG30 .... 84 E8
Thickthorne La TW18 .... 97 C1

Third Ave
Marlow SL7 1 F2
Reading RG31 84 B6
Tadley RG7 135 C2
Third Cres SL1 42 C8
Third St E RG19 132 A5
Thirkleby Cl SL1 42 C5
Thirlmere Ave
Burnham SL1 41 C8
Reading RG30 57 F1
Thirlmere Cl TW20 96 B1
Thirlmere Wlk GU15 152 D4
Thirtover RG18 79 B1
Thistledown RG31 57 C1
Thistleton Way RG6 87 E2
Thomas Askew Ho 1 RG14 104 E1
Thomas Ct SL6 39 A2
Thomas Dr RG42 91 E1
Thomas Knyvett Coll TW15 97 E5
Thomas La RG40 141 E8
Thomas Merriman Ct RG14 105 A2
Thomas Rd HP10 3 D4
Thompkins La SL2 22 A5
Thompson Cl
Hermitage RG18 78 F6
Slough SL3 44 A2
Thompson Dr RG19 106 E2
Thompsons Yd 13 RG1 86 B6
Thomson Wlk RG31 84 E4
Thorburn Chase GU47 150 E6
Thornaby Pl HP10 3 E8
Thornbank Cl TW19 70 A2
Thornbers Way RG10 61 B5
Thornbridge Rd RG2 113 B8
Thornbury Cl RG45 143 B5
Thornbury Gn RG10 61 D5
Thorn Cl RG41 115 C3
Thorncroft TW20 95 C1
Thorndike SL2 42 B8
Thorndown La GU20 146 D3
Thorn Dr SL3 43 E7
Thorne Cl
Crowthorne RG45 143 A7
Henley-on-T RG9 35 B8
Littleton TW15 98 C1
Thorney Cl RG6 87 E2
Thorney Ho RG2 86 A2
Thorney La N SL0 44 F6
Thorney La S SL0 44 F5
Thornfield RG19 132 D3
Thornfield Gn GU17 150 F3
Thornford Rd RG19 132 E3
Thornhill RG12 118 E5
Thornhill Way TW17 125 A4
Thorningdown OX11 10 D8
Thorn La 6 RG1 86 B7
Thorn St RG1 86 A7
Thornton Mews
Crowthorne RG45 143 C4
Reading RG30 85 C8
Thornton Rd RG30 85 C8
Thornycroft Cl 1 RG14 105 B3
Thorp Cl RG42 90 C3
THORPE 123 C6
Thorpe By-Pass TW20 123 B6
Thorpe CE Inf Sch TW20 123 B6
Thorpe Cl RG41 116 A3
THORPE GREEN 123 A5
Thorpe Ho 4 RG30 85 B7
Thorpe Ind Est TW20 123 C7
Thorpe Ind Pk TW20 123 C8
THORPE LEA 96 B1
Thorpe Lea Prim Sch TW20 96 D2
Thorpe Lea Rd TW20 96 C2
Thorpe Park★ TW20 123 E5
Thorpe Rd
Chertsey KT16 123 D4
Egham TW18, TW20 96 D3
Thorpeside Cl TW18, TW20 123 E7
Thrale Mews RG30 85 B8
Three Acre Rd RG14 130 F8
Three Firs Way RG7 110 F1
Three Gables La RG8 34 A7
THREE MILE CROSS 113 B4
Three Post La 1 RG17 25 B2
Threshfield RG12 118 A4
Thrift La SL6 39 D1
Throgmorton Rd GU46 149 A5
Thrush Cl RG7 111 B3
Thurlby Way SL6 39 D3
Thurlestone Cl TW17 125 C3
Thurlestone Gdns RG2 86 C2
Thurlestone Par TW17 125 C3
Thurley Bsns Units RG7 112 C1
Thurley Cotts SL3 23 B3
Thurlow Grange 4 RG14 104 F1
Thurnscoe Cl RG6 113 F8
Thurso Cl RG30 85 A8
Thurston Rd SL1 42 E7
Thyme Cl RG6 87 A1
Tichborne Cl GU17 150 D5
Tichbourne Cl GU16 151 F3
Tickenor Dr RG40 141 F7
Tickhill Cl RG6 113 F7
Tickleback Row RG42 91 B6
Tides End Ct GU15 151 F4
TIDMARSH 56 C2
Tidmarsh Barns RG8 56 C2
Tidmarsh Ct RG8 56 C1
Tidmarsh Grange RG8 56 C1
Tidmarsh La RG8 56 B2
Tidmarsh Rd RG8 56 C4
Tidmarsh St 1 RG30 85 B8
Tidwells Lea RG12 118 E8
Tierney Ct 2 SL7 1 E1
Tiffany Cl RG41 115 D6
Tiger Cl RG5 88 B7
Tigerseye Cl RG41 115 D7
Tiggell Cl RG6 87 D4
Tilbury Cl RG4 59 C3
Tilbury Wlk SL3 44 B3
Tilebarn Cl RG9 15 C1
Tile Barn Row RG20 129 E1
Tilecotes Cl SL7 1 D2
TILEHURST 57 E1
Tilehurst La RG42 90 D3
Tilehurst Rd RG1, RG30 85 D7
Tilehurst Sta RG31 57 E3
Tilling Cl RG31 57 B2
Tilly's La TW18 96 F4
Tilney Way
Earley RG6 113 F8
Lower Earley RG6 114 A8
Tilstone Ave SL4 41 E2
Tilstone Cl SL4 41 E1
Timberley Pl RG45 142 E4
Timbers Wlk SL6 39 B5
Timber Yd The GU24 153 D4
Timline Gn RG12 118 F7
Timson Ct RG14 105 B3
Timsway TW18 96 F3
Tindal Cl GU46 149 D6
Tinkers La SL4 66 D5
Tinsey Cl TW20 96 B3
Tinsley Cl RG6 113 F8
Tintagel Dr 1 GU16 151 F1
Tintagel Farm Cl RG40 142 B8
Tintagel Ho SL1 42 C5
Tintagel Rd RG40 142 A8
Tintern Cl SL1 42 C3
Tintern Cres RG1 85 F5
Tinwell Cl RG6 87 E2
Tippett Rise RG2 86 B5
Tippings La RG5 88 A8
Tippits Mead RG42 117 D8
Tiptree Cl RG6 113 F8
Tiree Ho SL2 42 B8
Titan Ho RG7 134 E2
TITCOMB 127 F7
Titcombe Way RG17 102 A2
Tite Hill TW20 95 D3
Tithe Barn Dr SL6 40 E1
Tithebarn Gr RG31 84 F4
Tithe Cl
Maidenhead SL6 40 C1
Wentworth GU25 122 D3
Tithe Ct
Slough SL3 44 A2
Wokingham RG40 116 C7
Tithe La TW19 69 A1
Tithe Mdws GU25 122 D3
Titlarks Hill Rd SL5 121 B1
TITTLE ROW 39 A5
Tiverton Cl RG5 60 E1
Tiverton Way GU16 151 F1
Toad La GU17 150 E4
Tobermory Cl SL3 43 E2
Tocker Gdns RG42 91 B2
Tockington Ct GU46 149 D6
Tockley Rd SL1 21 B2
Tofrek Terr RG30 85 C7
TOKERS GREEN 58 D8
Tokers Green La RG4 58 D7
Tollgate SL6 39 A6
Toll Gdns RG12 118 F6
Tolpuddle Way GU46 149 F5
Tomlin Cl RG19 106 E2
Tomlin Rd SL2 21 E1
Tomlins Ave GU16 151 F2
Tomlinscote Sch & Sixth Form Coll GU16 152 A2
Tomlinscote Way GU16 152 A2
Tomlinson Dr RG40 142 A7
Tonkins Dr RG19 106 E2
Toogood Pl RG42 91 D3
Topaz Cl
Slough SL1 42 B5
Wokingham RG41 115 E7
Topaz Ct 11 TW13 98 F5
Top Common RG42 91 D1
Tope Cres RG2 140 F7
Tope Rd RG2 140 F8
Torcross Gr RG31 84 B4
Torin Ct TW20 95 C3
Torleven Hts RG42 90 D3
Torquay Spur SL2 22 B2
Torridge Rd SL3 69 B8
Torrington Rd RG2 86 C2
Toseland Way RG6 87 E3
Totale Rise RG42 91 B2
TOT HILL 130 E1
Totnes Rd RG2 86 C2
Tottenham Wlk GU47 143 D1
Totterdown RG7 110 F1
TOUCHEN-END 64 D5
Toulouse Cl GU15 152 B7
Toutley Cl RG41 88 F1
Toutley Rd RG41 89 A1
Toutley Works RG41 89 A2
Tower Cl
Caversham RG4 59 C8
Flackwell Heath HP10 3 C7
Tower Ct 14 TW20 96 A3
Tower Hill RG20 49 A8
Tower Ho
Iver SL0 44 E7
Marlow SL7 1 B1
4 Slough SL1 42 E4
Towers Dr RG45 143 B4
Town Farm Prim Sch TW19 97 D8
Town Farm Way TW19 97 D8
Town Hall (Mus)★ KT15 124 A2
Town La
Stanwell TW19 97 D7
Wooburn HP10 3 D4
Townlands Hospl RG9 15 D2
Town Mills 6 RG14 105 A3
Town Pl 13 RG1 86 D7
Town Quay TW18 124 C6
Townsend Cl RG12 118 E4
Townsend Rd
Aldworth RG8 32 E3
Ashford TW15 97 E3
Streatley RG8 34 A7
Townside Pl GU15 151 D6
Town Sq
Bracknell RG12 118 C7
Camberley GU15 151 C6
9 Slough SL1 42 F4
Town Tree Rd TW15 98 A3
Tozer Wlk SL4 66 D4
Tracey Ave 12 SL3 43 F1
Tracy Ave SL3 68 F8
Trafalgar Cl RG41 115 E6
Trafalgar Ct RG1 85 D6
Trafalgar Way GU15 150 F4
Trafford Rd RG1 58 E1
Transcend 6 SL4 67 C5
TRAPSHILL 127 F4
TRASH GREEN 111 B7
Travic Rd SL2 21 F2
Travis Ct SL2 22 B2
Travis La GU47 150 C7
Treacher Ct RG10 61 E5
Treble Ho Terr OX11 12 A8
Tredegar Rd RG4 59 A6
Tree Cl RG30 84 D8
Treesmill Dr SL6 39 C3
Trees Rd SL8 3 B3
Treeton Cl RG6 113 F8
Treetops RG4 58 F2
Tree Tops Ave GU15 152 B8
Trefoil Cl RG40 116 E7
Trefoil Dro RG18 106 F4
Treforgan RG4 58 F5
Trelawney Ave SL3 43 F3
Trelawney Dr RG31 57 B1
Trelawney Ind Ct SL3 43 E3
Trelleck Rd RG1 85 F5
Tremayne Wlk GU15 152 C4
Trenchard Rd SL6 65 B8
Trenches La SL0, SL3 44 A6
TRENCH GREEN 58 A8
Trent Cl RG41 115 E7
Trent Cres RG18 106 B5
Trenthams Cl RG8 57 B5
Trenton Cl GU16 152 A1
Trent Rd SL3 69 B8
Trent Villas Est SL3 68 B6
Tresham Cres GU46 149 A6
Tressell The SL6 39 D6
Trevelyan RG12 117 E2
Trevelyan Ct SL4 67 B5
Trevelyan Mid Sch SL4 67 C3
Trevithick Cl TW14 98 F7
Trevor Ct TW19 70 A2
Trevor Ho 2 RG30 85 B7
Trevose Ho SL2 22 B1
Treyarnon Ct RG1 86 E6
Triangle The
Newbury RG14 131 B7
Reading RG30 84 D8
Trident Ho TW19 97 E8
Trident Ind Est SL3 69 E4
Trilakes Ctry Pk★ GU46, GU47 149 E8
Trimble Hall SL5 120 D2
Trindledown RG42 91 A2
Tringham Cotts GU24 153 F7
Tring Rd RG31 57 C2
Trinity GU47 143 E2
Trinity Ave SL7 1 D3
Trinity CE Prim Sch RG9 15 D1
Trinity Cl TW19 70 C1
Trinity Cres SL5 121 A4
Trinity Ct
Bracknell RG12 117 F7
Marlow SL7 1 D3
16 Newbury RG14 104 F2
Theale RG7 83 D3
Trinity Ho SL6 19 F6
Trinity Pl
Reading RG1 85 F7
Windsor SL4 67 C5
Trinity Rd SL7 1 D2
Trinity St Stephens CE Fst Sch SL4 67 B6
Trinity Sch RG14 105 B5
Triumph Cl
Harlington UB7 71 C6
Woodley RG5 87 F5
Troon Ct
Ascot SL5 120 C4
21 Reading RG1 86 D7
Troston Ct 10 TW18 96 F3
Trotsford Mdw GU17 150 C4
Trotsworth Ave GU25 122 E5
Trotsworth Ct GU25 122 D5
Trotwood Cl GU47 143 E2
Troutbeck Cl
Slough SL2 43 A6
Twyford RG10 61 D6
Troutbeck Wlk GU15 152 D3
Trout Cl
Earley RG6 87 A8
Marlow SL7 18 C8
Trout Wlk RG14 105 C4
Trowe's La
Beech Hill RG7 138 D4
Swallowfield RG7 139 D5
Trumbull Rd RG42 91 A1
Trumper Way SL1 41 F5
TRUMPS GREEN 122 D3
Trumps Green Ave GU25 122 D3
Trumps Green Cl GU25 122 E4
Trumps Green Inf Sch GU25 122 D3
Trumpsgreen Rd GU25 122 D3
Trumps Mill La GU25 122 F4
Truro Cl SL6 39 A7
Truss Hill Rd SL5 120 C4
Trust Cnr RG9 35 E8
Trusthorpe Cl RG6 87 E2
Tubbs Farm Cl RG17 25 B2
Tubwell Rd SL2 23 B4
Tudor Ave RG20 51 C4
Tudor Cl
Ashford TW15 97 E4
Wokingham RG40 116 F5
Tudor Ct
21 Egham TW20 96 A3
18 Egham TW20 96 A3
Maidenhead SL6 20 C2
3 Stanwell TW19 70 E1
Thatcham RG18 106 C4
Windlesham GU20 146 B7
Tudor Dr
Wooburn Green HP10 3 D7
Yateley GU46 149 D4
Tudor Gdns SL1 41 C8
Tudor Hall GU15 151 F6
Tudor Ho RG12 118 B4
Tudor La SL4 95 C8
Tudor Mill HP10 3 E6
Tudor Rd
Ashford TW15 98 D2
Newbury RG14 105 A1
Reading RG1 86 A8
Tudor Way SL4 66 E6
Tulip Ho RG18 106 E3
Tull Way RG18 105 F5
Tunnel Link Rd TW6 71 A1
Tunnel Rd E TW6 71 B6
Tunnel Rd W TW6 71 B6
Tuns Hill Cotts RG6 87 A5
Tuns La
Henley-on-T RG9 15 E2
Slough SL1 42 C4
Tupsley Rd RG1 85 F5
Turbary Gdns RG26 135 B1
Turf Hill Rd GU15 151 F8
Turing Dr RG12 118 A4
Turks Head Ct SL4 67 D7
Turk's La RG7 137 A4
Turmeric Cl RG6 86 F1
Turnberry RG12 117 E2
Turnberry Ct 19 RG1 86 D7
Turnberry Ho SL5 121 A1
Turnbridge Cl RG6 114 B8
Turner Pl GU47 150 D6
Turner Rd SL3 43 C4
Turners Cl TW18 97 B3
Turners Dr RG19 106 E2
Turnery The RG19 106 C3
Turnfields RG19 106 D3
Turnoak Pk SL4 66 E3
Turnpike Ind Est RG14 105 D5
Turnpike Rd
Bracknell RG42 117 D7
Newbury RG14, RG18 105 E4
Turnstone Cl RG41 88 B3
Turnstone End GU46 149 B6
Turnville Cl GU18 146 A1
Turpin Rd TW14 71 F1
Turpins Gn SL6 39 A5
Turpins Rise GU20 146 B6
Turtle Twrs RG1 86 A7
Turton Way SL1 42 D3
Tuscam Way GU15 150 F4
Tuscan Cl RG30 57 E1
Tuscany Ct 2 SL6 39 E7
Tuscany Villas GU18 146 B1
Tuscany Way GU46 149 C4
TUTTS CLUMP 81 F3
Tuxford Mews RG30 85 B7
Tweed Ct RG30 85 B7
Tweed Rd SL3 69 B8
Twelve Trees Ho RG45 143 C4
Twinches La SL1 42 B5
Twin Oaks RG4 59 B6
Twinwoods RG20 49 A4
Two Mile Dr SL1 41 E4
Two Rivers Sh Ctr TW18 96 E4
Two Rivers Way RG14 105 D3
Two Tree Hill RG9 35 B8
Twycross Rd RG40 116 E7
TWYFORD 61 D5
Twyford Bsns Pk RG10 61 D4
Twyford Orchards Cvn Pk RG10 61 F7
Twyford Rd
Binfield RG10, RG42 90 C7
Waltham St L RG10 62 E6
Wokingham RG40 89 B2
Twyford Sta RG10 61 E4
Twynersh Ave KT16 123 F3
Twynham Rd SL6 39 B7
Tyberton Pl RG1 85 F5
Tydehams RG14 130 F7
Tyle Pl SL4 68 A2
Tyler Cl RG4 58 E5
Tyle Rd RG30 84 D8
Tyler Dr RG2 140 E7
Tyler's La RG7 80 B1
Tylers Pl RG30 84 F8
Tyler Wlk 4 SL3 43 F1
Tylorstown RG4 58 F5
Tymawr RG4 58 F5
Tyndale Mews SL1 42 B4
Tyne Way RG18 106 B5
Tyrell Gdns SL4 66 F4
Tyrrel Ct 20 RG1 86 C7
Tytherton RG12 118 C7

U

Uffcott Cl RG6 113 F7
Uffington Cl RG31 84 C8
Uffington Dr RG12 118 E5
Ufton Court Yd SL8 3 B4
Ufton Ct SL8 3 B4
UFTON GREEN 110 B5
UFTON NERVET 110 D3
Ullswater RG12 117 F2
Ullswater Cl
Burnham SL1 41 C8
Lightwater GU18 146 B1
Thatcham RG19 106 A3
Ullswater Dr RG31 57 D3
Ullswater Rd GU18 146 B1
Ulster Cl RG4 59 D5
Umberstone GU25 122 D3
Umberville Way SL2 21 F2
Underhill OX10 14 A4
Underhill Cl SL6 39 E6
Underwood RG12 117 E3
Underwood Cotts RG8 33 F6
Underwood Ct RG42 90 C1
Underwood Rd RG30 85 A4
Underwood Sh Ctr RG30 84 F4
Union Cl GU47 143 E2
Union Rd RG7 82 D4
Union St RG1 86 A8
Unity Cl RG4 59 B6
Unity Ct RG4 59 B6
Unity Ho RG19 132 A4
Univ of Reading
Earley RG6 87 B6
Reading RG1 86 C6
Reading, Whiteknights RG6 86 F4
Unwin Ave TW14 71 D2
Upavon Dr RG1 85 F6
Upavon Gdns RG12 118 F4
Upcroft SL4 67 B4
Upcroft Prim Sch RG30 84 F8
Updown Hill GU20 146 D4
Upland Rd GU15 151 D7
Uplands
Hungerford RG17 100 C5
Marlow Bottom SL7 1 D6
Uplands Cl GU47 150 B8
Uplands Prim Sch GU47 150 B8
Uplands Rd RG4 58 E5
UPPER BASILDON 55 A5
Upper Bray Rd SL6 40 C3
Upper Broadmoor Rd RG45 143 D5
UPPER BUCKLEBURY 107 C6
Upper Chobham Rd GU15 152 B4
Upper College Ride GU15 151 E8
Upper Crown St RG1 86 B6
Upper Culham Farm RG10 36 E8
Upper Eddington RG17 100 E7
Upper End RG20 49 A8
Upper Gordon Rd GU15 151 D5
UPPER GREEN 127 D3
UPPER HALLIFORD 125 D5
Upper Halliford Rd TW17 125 E5
Upper Halliford Sta TW17 125 E7
UPPER LAMBOURN 24 F6
Upper Lambourn Rd RG17 25 A3
Upper Lees Rd SL2 22 B2
Upper Meadow Rd RG2 86 D2
Upper Nursery SL5 121 A4
Upper Park Rd GU15 151 E6
Upper Raymond Almshouses 14 RG14 104 F2
Upper Red Cross Rd RG8 34 C7
Upper Redlands Rd RG1 86 E5
Upper Terr RG41 115 B8
Upper Thames Way SL8 2 F3
Upper Ventnor Cotts SL6 19 C8
Upper Verran Rd GU15 151 D3
Upper Village Rd SL5 120 D4
UPPER WARGRAVE 36 F2
Upper Warren Ave RG4 58 D3
Upper Wlk GU25 122 E5
Upper Woodcote Rd RG4 58 D5
UPPER WOOLHAMPTON 108 C4
Uppingham Dr RG5 60 F1
Uppingham Gdns RG4 59 D6
Upshire Gdns RG12 118 F5
UPTON 43 A3
Upton Cl
Henley-on-T RG9 15 E1
Slough SL1 42 F3
Upton Court Rd SL3 43 B2
Upton Hospl SL1 42 F3
Upton House Sch SL4 67 C5
UPTON LEA 43 A6
Upton Lea Par SL2 43 B6
UPTON PARK 42 F3
Upton Pk SL1 42 F3

Upton Rd
Reading RG30 . . . 85 B7
Slough SL1, SL3 . . . 43 A3
Urbis Apartments SL4 . . . 66 E5
Urquhart Rd RG19 . . . 106 E2
Usk Rd RG30 . . . 84 F6
Uxbridge Rd SL1, SL2, SL3 . 43 C6

V

Vachel Rd RG1 . . . 86 A8
Vale Cres RG30 . . . 57 E1
Vale Gr SL1 . . . 42 E3
Valentia Rd RG30 . . . 85 D8
Valentine Cl RG6 . . . 86 F1
Valentine Cres RG4 . . . 59 C4
Vale Rd
Camberley GU15 . . . 151 A4
Windsor SL4 . . . 66 F6
Valerie Ct RG1 . . . 85 E6
Vale View RG10 . . . 61 B4
Vale View Dr RG7 . . . 138 D5
Valley Cl
Caversham RG4 . . . 59 A4
Goring RG8 . . . 34 C6
Valley Cres RG41 . . . 116 A8
Valley End SL3 . . . 23 C1
Valley Gardens★ TW20 . . 121 E7
Valley Rd
Burghfield Common RG7 . . 111 A3
Frimley GU16 . . . 152 C1
Henley-on-T RG9 . . . 35 B8
Newbury RG14 . . . 130 E8
Valley Road Sch RG9 . . . 35 C8
Valley View GU47 . . . 150 A7
Valley Vineyards★ RG10 . . 62 A3
Valley Way RG26 . . . 135 E1
Valon Rd RG2 . . . 140 F8
Valpy St RG1 . . . 86 B8
Valroy Cl GU15 . . . 151 D6
Vanbrugh Ct 1 RG1 . . . 86 E7
Vandyke RG12 . . . 117 E3
Vanguard Ho 5 TW19 . . . 70 E1
Vanguard Way TW6 . . . 71 E5
Vanlore Way RG31 . . . 84 C5
Vanners La RG20 . . . 129 D5
Vansittart Est SL4 . . . 67 C6
Vansittart Rd
Bisham SL7 . . . 18 E7
Windsor SL4 . . . 67 B6
Vantage Ct UB3 . . . 71 E7
Vantage Rd SL1 . . . 42 B5
Vanwall Bsns Pk SL6 . . . 39 C5
Vanwall Rd SL6 . . . 39 C4
Vastern Rd RG1 . . . 59 B1
Vaughan Almshouses 1
TW15 . . . 98 B3
Vaughan Copse SL4 . . . 42 D2
Vaughan Gdns SL4 . . . 41 F2
Vaughan Way SL2 . . . 21 E1
Vauxhall Dr RG5 . . . 88 A6
Vegal Cres TW20 . . . 95 C3
Veitch Cl TW14 . . . 98 F8
Venetia Cl RG4 . . . 59 C7
Venning Rd RG2 . . . 140 F8
Ventnor Rd RG31 . . . 57 D1
Venture Ho TW18 . . . 97 A4
Venus Cl
Slough SL2 . . . 21 F1
Wokingham RG41 . . . 115 F6
Verbena Cl RG41 . . . 88 A3
Verdon Ct SL2 . . . 22 B2
Verey Cl RG10 . . . 61 F3
Verica Gdns RG26 . . . 135 E2
Vermillion Ct 13 TW13 . . . 98 F5
Vermont Rd SL2 . . . 21 F1
Vermont Woods RG40 . . . 141 E7
Verney Cl SL7 . . . 1 D2
Verney Mews RG30 . . . 85 C7
Verney Rd SL3 . . . 44 A2
Vernon Cl TW19 . . . 97 E7
Vernon Cres RG2 . . . 113 B7
Vernon Ct SL5 . . . 119 D6
Vernon Dr SL5 . . . 119 E7
Vernon Rd TW13 . . . 98 F6
Verran Rd GU15 . . . 151 D3
Vibia Cl TW19 . . . 97 D8
Viburnum Ct GU24 . . . 153 E6
Vicarage Ave TW20 . . . 96 B3
Vicarage Cl
Cookham SL6 . . . 20 B7
Finchampstead RG40 . . . 141 F6
Vicarage Cres TW20 . . . 96 B3
Vicarage Ct
East Bedfont TW14 . . . 98 C8
Egham TW20 . . . 96 B2
Shinfield RG2 . . . 113 D5
Vicarage Dr SL6 . . . 40 C4
Vicarage Flats SL4 . . . 67 D8
Vicarage Gdns
Ascot SL5 . . . 120 A4
White Waltham SL6 . . . 63 F8
Vicarage La
Cold Ash RG18 . . . 106 C8
Laleham TW18 . . . 124 C6
Wraysbury TW19 . . . 95 F7
Yateley GU46 . . . 149 C7
Vicarage Rd
Ashford TW16 . . . 98 F2
Bagshot GU19 . . . 145 C3
Blackwater GU17 . . . 150 E4
Egham TW20 . . . 96 B3
Henley-on-T RG9 . . . 35 E8
Maidenhead SL6 . . . 39 F8
Vicarage Rd *continued*
Reading RG2 . . . 86 C5
Staines TW18 . . . 96 E5
Yateley GU46 . . . 149 C7
Vicarage Way SL3 . . . 69 D7
Vicarage Wlk SL6 . . . 40 C4
Vicarage Wood Way RG31 57 B1
Vickers Cl
Shinfield RG2 . . . 113 F4
Woodley RG5 . . . 88 B7
Vickers Ct 9 TW19 . . . 70 E1
Vicount Ct 2 TW15 . . . 98 C1
Victor Cl SL6 . . . 39 B8
Victoria Ave GU15 . . . 151 A5
Victoria Cotts SL6 . . . 19 C8
Victoria Cres SL0 . . . 44 F6
Victoria Ct
Bagshot GU19 . . . 145 E1
Camberley GU15 . . . 151 A5
Henley-on-T RG9 . . . 15 E1
3 Marlow SL7 . . . 1 E2
Slough SL1 . . . 42 E5
Victoria Dr
Blackwater GU17 . . . 150 C4
Burnham SL1, SL2 . . . 21 F6
Victoria Gdns
Marlow SL7 . . . 1 E2
Newbury RG14 . . . 105 A4
Wokingham RG40 . . . 116 E8
Victoria Gr 6 RG14 . . . 105 B2
Victoria Ho SL4 . . . 68 A2
Victoria La UB7 . . . 71 D8
Victoria Mews RG30 . . . 85 C7
Victoria News TW20 . . . 95 C2
Victoria Rd
Ascot SL5 . . . 120 A4
Caversham RG4 . . . 59 A3
Eton SL4 . . . 41 F1
Marlow SL7 . . . 1 E2
Mortimer RG7 . . . 136 F6
Reading RG31 . . . 84 D8
Sandhurst GU47 . . . 143 E1
Slough SL2 . . . 43 B5
Staines TW18 . . . 96 E5
Wargrave RG10 . . . 36 E2
Victoria St
Englefield Green TW20 . . . 95 C2
Reading RG1 . . . 86 D7
10 Slough SL1 . . . 42 F4
Windsor SL4 . . . 67 D6
Victoria Way 3 RG1 . . . 86 D7
Victoria Wlk RG40 . . . 116 E8
Victor Pl RG7 . . . 108 C2
Victor Rd
Thatcham RG19 . . . 106 E3
Windsor SL4 . . . 67 C4
Victor Way RG5 . . . 88 A7
Victory Cl
Reading RG30 . . . 85 A6
Stanwell TW15, TW19 . . . 97 E7
Victory Rd KT16 . . . 124 A1
Vigo La GU46 . . . 149 C3
Viking RG12 . . . 117 E4
Village Cl
Reading RG2 . . . 113 B6
Wokingham RG41 . . . 115 F8
Village Ct SL5 . . . 120 C4
Village Gate TW17 . . . 125 B4
Village Mews SL5 . . . 120 C5
Village Rd
Dorney SL4 . . . 41 B3
Thorpe TW20 . . . 123 C6
Village Sh Ctr The 5 SL1 . 42 F4
VILLAGE THE . . . 94 B5
Village The
Finchampstead RG40 . . . 141 E3
Old Windsor SL4 . . . 94 B5
Village Way
Ashford TW15 . . . 98 A4
Yateley GU46 . . . 149 D7
Villa Mews 2 RG1 . . . 86 E7
Villa Pl RG7 . . . 139 C6
Villiers Ct SL4 . . . 67 B7
Villiers Mead RG41 . . . 116 A6
Villiers Rd SL2 . . . 42 D8
Villiers Way RG14 . . . 130 C6
Villiers Wlk RG14 . . . 130 C6
Vincent Cl
Chertsey KT16 . . . 123 E2
Harmondsworth UB7 . . . 71 A8
Woodley RG5 . . . 87 F6
Vincent Dr TW17 . . . 125 E6
Vincent Ho 8 RG1 . . . 85 F8
Vincent Rd
Chertsey KT16 . . . 123 E2
Thatcham RG18 . . . 106 E4
Vincent Rise RG12 . . . 118 E6
Vine Cl TW19 . . . 70 A2
Vine Cres RG30 . . . 85 A4
Vine Ct
Newbury RG14 . . . 105 B1
Stoke Poges SL2 . . . 23 A6
Vine Rd SL2 . . . 22 F6
Vineries Cl UB7 . . . 71 A8
Vinery The RG10 . . . 36 D2
Vines The RG41 . . . 115 C3
Vineyard Dr SL8 . . . 3 A5
Vinter Ct TW17 . . . 125 A4
Vintners Ho RG31 . . . 57 D1
Viola Ave TW19 . . . 97 E7
Viola Croft RG42 . . . 118 F8
Violet Gr RG18 . . . 106 E5
Virginia Ave GU25 . . . 122 C4
Virginia Beeches GU25 . . 122 C6
Virginia Cl TW18 . . . 124 C6
Virginia Ct
Ashford TW15 . . . 97 E4
Virginia Water GU25 . . . 122 D5
Virginia Dr GU25 . . . 122 C5
VIRGINIA WATER . . . 122 C6
Virginia Water★ SL5 . . . 121 E6
Virginia Water Sta GU25 . 122 E4
Virginia Way RG30 . . . 85 B5
Viridian Ct 10 TW13 . . . 98 F5
Viscount Ct SL4 . . . 67 C6
Viscount Ind Est SL3 . . . 69 E4
Viscount Rd TW19 . . . 97 E7
Viscount Way
Hatton TW6 . . . 71 E3
Woodley RG5 . . . 88 A7
Vivien Cl SL6 . . . 19 F6
Vivienne Ho TW18 . . . 97 A3
Voller Dr RG31 . . . 84 C6
Volunteer Rd RG7 . . . 83 D2
Vo-Tec Ctr RG14 . . . 105 E2
Vulcan Cl
Sandhurst GU47 . . . 150 A7
Woodley RG5 . . . 61 B1
Vulcan Ct GU47 . . . 150 A7
Vulcan Dr RG12 . . . 118 D6
Vulcan Ho RG7 . . . 134 E2
Vulcan Way GU47 . . . 150 B7

W

Waborne Rd SL8 . . . 3 B4
Wade Dr SL1 . . . 42 A5
Wadham GU47 . . . 143 F1
Wadham Cl TW17 . . . 125 C2
Wagbullock Rise RG12 . . 118 C3
Waggoners Hollow
GU19 . . . 145 E2
Wagner Cl SL6 . . . 38 F3
Wagtail Cl RG10 . . . 61 E4
Waingel's Copse Sch RG5 61 A2
Waingels Rd RG5, RG10 . . . 61 A2
Wainscot SL5 . . . 120 F3
Wainwright Cl RG40 . . . 117 A6
Wakefield Cres SL2 . . . 22 F6
Wakeford Cl RG26 . . . 135 E1
Wakeford Ct RG26 . . . 135 E2
Wakelins End SL6 . . . 19 E7
Wakeman Rd SL8 . . . 3 A3
Wakemans RG8 . . . 55 D4
Walbury RG12 . . . 118 E5
Waldeck Ho SL6 . . . 40 A7
Waldeck Rd SL6 . . . 40 A7
Waldeck St RG1 . . . 86 B5
Walden Ave RG2 . . . 114 C3
Waldens Cl SL8 . . . 3 A3
Waldorf Hts GU17 . . . 150 D3
Waldron Hill RG12 . . . 118 F8
Waldrons The RG17 . . . 47 C6
Waleys Pl 2 RG4 . . . 59 C2
Walgrove Gdns SL6 . . . 63 E7
Walker Cl TW14 . . . 98 F8
Walker Cres SL3 . . . 43 F1
Walker Ct SL6 . . . 39 D7
Walker Rd SL6 . . . 40 A4
Walker's La RG17 . . . 25 B3
Walkers Pl RG30 . . . 85 C7
Walker's Ridge GU15 . . . 151 E5
Walk The
Ashford TW16 . . . 98 F1
Eton SL4 . . . 42 A1
Wallace Cl
Marlow SL7 . . . 1 F4
Upper Halliford TW17 . . . 125 D5
Woodley RG5 . . . 87 D5
Wallace Gr RG7 . . . 113 A4
Wallace Wlk SL4 . . . 42 F1
Wallcroft Cl RG42 . . . 90 E1
Walled Garden The SL7 . . 18 A6
Walled Gdn The
Beech Hill RG7 . . . 138 E5
Wargrave RG10 . . . 36 D2
Waller Ct RG4 . . . 59 B2
Waller Dr RG14 . . . 105 E5
Wallingford Cl RG12 . . . 118 E5
Wallingford Rd
Compton RG20 . . . 31 E5
Moulsford RG8, OX10 . . . 14 A1
South Stoke RG8, OX10 . . . 14 C5
Streatley RG8 . . . 34 A7
Wallington Rd GU15 . . . 145 A1
Wallingtons Rd RG17 . . . 101 F1
Wallis Ct SL1 . . . 43 A4
Wallis Gdns RG14 . . . 131 B8
Wall La RG7 . . . 136 D2
Wallner Way RG40 . . . 116 E5
Walmer Cl
Crowthorne RG45 . . . 143 C5
Reading RG30 . . . 85 A6
Walmer Rd RG5 . . . 60 F1
Walnut Cl
Thatcham RG18 . . . 106 C4
Wokingham RG41 . . . 115 F5
Yateley GU46 . . . 149 D4
Walnut Ct 3 RG40 . . . 116 C6
Walnut Gr HP10 . . . 3 E6
Walnut Lo SL1 . . . 42 D3
Walnut Mews RG42 . . . 117 F8
Walnut Tree Cl
Bourne End SL8 . . . 3 B2
Twyford RG10 . . . 61 F6
Walnut Tree Cotts RG20 . . 75 D8
Walnut Tree Ct RG8 . . . 34 C6
Walnut Tree Ho TW20 . . . 95 F3
Walnut Tree Rd TW17 . . . 125 C7
Walnut Way
Bourne End SL8 . . . 3 B2
Reading RG30 . . . 84 D8
Walpole Rd
Old Windsor SL4 . . . 95 B8
Slough SL1 . . . 41 D7
Walrus Cl RG5 . . . 88 B7
Walsh Ave RG42 . . . 91 E1
Walter Inf Sch RG41 . . . 116 A6
Walter Rd RG41 . . . 115 E7
Walters Cl RG18 . . . 106 C8
Waltham Cl
Maidenhead SL6 . . . 38 F2
Sandhurst GU47 . . . 143 D1
Waltham Ct
Goring RG8 . . . 34 C8
Wargrave RG10 . . . 62 B8
Waltham Rd
Maidenhead SL6 . . . 38 F1
Twyford RG10 . . . 61 E4
Twyford, Ruscombe RG10 . . 62 B5
WALTHAM ST
LAWRENCE . . . 62 F6
Waltham St Lawrence Prim
Sch RG10 . . . 62 F3
Walton Ave RG9 . . . 35 E8
Walton Bridge Rd KT12,
TW17 . . . 125 E2
Walton Cl RG5 . . . 87 C7
Walton Dr SL5 . . . 119 F8
Walton Gdns TW13 . . . 98 F4
Walton La
Burnham SL2 . . . 21 F3
Lower Halliford TW17 . . . 125 D2
Oatlands Park TW17 . . . 125 E1
Walton Lodge KT12 . . . 125 F1
Walton Manor KT12 . . . 125 F2
Walton Way RG14 . . . 105 C4
Wandhope Way RG31 . . . 57 C2
Wansey Gdns RG14 . . . 105 D5
Wanstraw Gr RG12 . . . 118 E2
Wantage Cl RG12 . . . 118 E4
Wantage Rd
Great Shefford RG17 . . . 48 C5
Hungerford RG17 . . . 100 E7
Lambourn RG17 . . . 25 C5
Reading RG30 . . . 85 C7
Sandhurst GU47 . . . 150 D8
Streatley RG8 . . . 33 F8
Wapshott Rd TW18 . . . 96 E3
Waram Cl RG17 . . . 100 E7
Warbler Cl RG31 . . . 84 B6
Warbler Dr RG6 . . . 87 B1
Warborough Ave RG31 . . . 84 B8
Warborough Rd OX12 . . . 7 A7
Warbreck Dr RG31 . . . 57 B3
Warbrook La RG27 . . . 141 A1
Ward Cl
Iver SL0 . . . 44 F7
Wokingham RG40 . . . 116 D8
Ward Gdns SL1 . . . 41 E6
Wardle Ave RG31 . . . 57 D1
Wardle Cl GU19 . . . 145 E3
Wardour Lodge SL5 . . . 120 F3
Ward Royal 5 SL4 . . . 67 C6
Ward Royal Par 2 SL4 . . 67 C6
Wards Cotts TW19 . . . 97 F8
Wards Pl TW20 . . . 96 C2
Wards Stone Pk RG12 . . . 118 E2
Wareham Rd RG12 . . . 118 F4
Warehouse Rd RG19 . . . 131 F5
WARFIELD . . . 91 E5
Warfield CE Prim Sch
RG42 . . . 91 E1
Warfield Rd
Bracknell RG12, RG42 . . . 91 C1
East Bedfont TW14 . . . 98 E8
Warfield Rdbt RG42 . . . 91 C2
Warfield St RG42 . . . 91 D3
WARGRAVE . . . 36 D1
Wargrave Hill RG10 . . . 36 D2
Wargrave Rd
Henley-on-T RG9, RG10 . . . 36 B8
Twyford RG10 . . . 61 D5
Wargrave Sta RG10 . . . 36 C1
Wargrove Dr GU47 . . . 150 D8
Waring Cl RG6 . . . 114 C8
Warings The RG7 . . . 109 A7
Warley Rise RG31 . . . 57 C3
War Memorial Pl RG9 . . . 35 E7
Warner Cl
Harlington UB3 . . . 71 D7
Slough SL1 . . . 41 E5
Warner Ct GU47 . . . 150 E7
Warners Hill SL6 . . . 19 C8
Warnford Rd RG30 . . . 84 F7
Warnham La RG20 . . . 31 B2
Warnsham Cl 1 RG6 . . . 87 B1
Warren Cl
Burghfield Common RG7 . . 111 A3
Finchampstead RG40 . . . 141 F6
Sandhurst GU47 . . . 150 A8
Slough SL3 . . . 43 E3
Warren Ct
Caversham RG4 . . . 58 F2
Farnham Common SL2 . . . 22 C7
9 Lambourn RG17 . . . 25 B2
Warren Down RG42 . . . 117 E8
Warren Farm RG17 . . . 26 B8
Warren Ho RG4 . . . 58 F2
Warren House Ct RG4 . . . 58 F2
Warren House Rd RG40 . 116 D8
Warren La RG40 . . . 141 E5
Warren Rd
Ashford TW15 . . . 98 E1
Newbury RG14 . . . 130 D6
Woodley RG4, RG5 . . . 60 D1
Warren Rise GU16 . . . 151 F3
WARREN ROW . . . 37 C6
Warren Row SL5 . . . 119 D7
Warren Row Rd
Knowl Hill RG10 . . . 37 C6
Wargrave RG10 . . . 36 F7
Warrenside RG4 . . . 58 E2
Warren The RG4 . . . 58 D3
Warrington Ave SL1 . . . 42 C7
Warrington Spur SL4 . . . 95 B8
Warwick RG12 . . . 118 E3
Warwick Ave
Slough SL2 . . . 22 C1
Staines TW18 . . . 97 C2
Thorpe TW20 . . . 123 C8
Warwick Cl
Frimley GU15 . . . 152 B3
Maidenhead SL6 . . . 39 B4
Warwick Ct 2 SL4 . . . 67 C5
Warwick Dr RG14 . . . 105 B1
Warwick Ho RG2 . . . 86 C4
Warwick Rd
Ashford TW15 . . . 97 E3
Reading RG2 . . . 86 C4
Warwick Villas TW20 . . . 123 C8
Wasdale Cl GU47 . . . 143 D2
Washbury Ho RG14 . . . 130 E7
WASH COMMON . . . 130 D5
Wash Hill HP10 . . . 3 E3
Wash Hill Lea HP10 . . . 3 E4
Wash Hill Mobile Home Pk
HP10 . . . 3 E3
Washington Ct
Marlow SL7 . . . 2 A2
Thatcham RG19 . . . 106 A3
Washington Dr
Slough SL1 . . . 41 D6
Windsor SL4 . . . 66 E4
Washington Gdns RG40 . 142 A8
Washington Rd RG4 . . . 59 B2
WASH WATER . . . 130 D4
Wash Water RG20 . . . 130 B3
WASING . . . 134 D5
Wasing Cnr RG7 . . . 134 B6
Wasing La RG7 . . . 134 D6
Watchetts Dr GU15 . . . 151 C2
Watchetts Jun Sch
GU15 . . . 151 C2
Watchetts Lake Cl GU15 151 D3
Watchetts Rd GU15 . . . 151 B4
Watchmoor Pk GU15 . . . 151 B4
Watchmoor Rd GU15 . . . 151 A4
Watchmoor Trade Ctr
GU15 . . . 151 A3
Waterbeach Cl SL1 . . . 42 D7
Waterbeach Rd SL1 . . . 42 D7
Waterfall Cl GU25 . . . 122 A6
Waterford Way RG40 . . . 116 C6
Waterham Rd RG12 . . . 118 B3
Waterhouse Mead GU47 150 D7
Water La RG19 . . . 131 C7
Waterloo Cl
Camberley GU15 . . . 152 B7
East Bedfont TW14 . . . 98 F7
Moulsford OX10 . . . 14 A7
Waterloo Cres RG40 . . . 116 E4
Waterloo Rd
Crowthorne RG45 . . . 143 B4
Reading RG2 . . . 86 B5
Wokingham RG40 . . . 116 F5
Waterloo Rise RG2 . . . 86 B4
Waterman Ct SL1 . . . 41 E5
Waterman Pl RG1 . . . 59 A1
Watermans Bsns Pk
TW18 . . . 96 D4
Waterman's Rd RG9 . . . 35 E8
Watermans Way RG10 . . . 36 C1
Watermead TW14 . . . 98 E7
Watermeadows The
RG14 . . . 105 B4
Watermill Ct RG7 . . . 108 C2
WATER OAKLEY . . . 65 F8
Water Oakley Cotts SL4 . . 65 F8
Water Oakley Farm Cotts
SL4 . . . 65 F8
Water Rd RG30 . . . 85 B7
Waters Dr TW18 . . . 96 F4
Watersfield Cl 4 RG6 . . . 87 B1
Waterside HP10 . . . 3 E7
Waterside Cotts RG4 . . . 60 B4
Waterside Ct
Newbury RG14 . . . 105 B3
Twyford RG10 . . . 61 C5
Waterside Dr
Langley SL3 . . . 43 F4
Purley on T RG8 . . . 57 D5
Theale RG7 . . . 83 F3
Waterside Gdns 4 RG1 . . 86 A7
Waterside Lodge SL6 . . . 40 C8
Watersplash La RG42 . . . 91 B2
Water Splash La SL5 . . . 120 E8
Watersplash Rd TW17 . . . 125 A5
Waters Reach SL6 . . . 20 A1
Water St RG18 . . . 52 F6
Watery La
Chertsey KT16 . . . 123 D2
Kintbury RG20 . . . 128 F5
Wooburn Green HP10 . . . 3 E8
Watkins Cl RG40 . . . 141 E7
Watlington St RG1 . . . 86 C7
Watmore La RG41 . . . 88 D2
Watson Cl
Aldermaston Wharf RG7 . . 109 C3
Finchampstead RG40 . . . 115 F1
Watt's La OX11 . . . 12 A8
Wavell Cl RG2 . . . 86 F1
Wavell Gdns SL2 . . . 21 F2
Wavell Rd SL6 . . . 39 B6
Wavendene Ave TW20 . . . 96 C1
Waverley RG12 . . . 117 E4
Waverley Cl GU15 . . . 151 F4
Waverley Ct 18 RG30 . . . 85 D6
Waverley Dr
Camberley GU15 . . . 151 F5
Virginia Water GU25 . . . 122 A5

Waverley Rd
Bagshot GU19 **145** E3
Reading RG30 **85** C7
Slough SL1 **42** C8
Waverley Sch RG40 **115** E1
Waverleys The RG18 **106** D4
Waverley Way RG40 **115** F1
WAWCOTT **102** C5
Wawcott Farm Cotts
RG20 **102** C4
Waybrook Cres RG1 **86** F6
Wayewood GU15 **151** E6
Wayland Cl
Bracknell RG12 **118** F5
Bradfield RG7 **82** D4
Waylands TW19 **68** E1
Waylen St RG1 **85** F7
Ways End GU15 **151** E4
Waysend Ho GU15 **151** E4
Wayside Cotts GU20 **146** F6
Wayside Mews SL6 **39** F8
Wealden Way RG30 **84** F8
Weald Rise RG30 **57** F2
Weardale Cl RG2 **86** D4
Weathervane Cotts
RG17 **100** C5
Weather Way RG12 **118** C7
Weaver Moss GU47 **150** B7
Weavers Ct
27 Reading RG1 **86** D7
Wokingham RG40 **116** C6
Weavers La RG17 **127** C6
Weavers Way RG10 **61** D4
Weavers Wlk 2 RG14 **105** A3
Webb Cl
Bagshot GU19 **145** E1
Bracknell RG42 **90** E1
Slough SL3 **43** D2
Webb Ct RG40 **116** E8
Webbs Acre RG19 **106** F2
Webb's Cl RG1 **85** F6
Webbs La RG7 **109** B7
Webster Cl SL6 **39** A5
Wedderburn Cl RG41 **88** D2
Wedgewood Way RG30 **57** F1
Weedon Cl OX10 **14** A8
Weekes Dr SL1 **42** B4
Weighbridge Row RG1 **58** F1
Weint The SL3 **69** C7
Weir Cl RG31 **84** F4
Weir Pl TW18 **123** E8
Weir Pool Ct RG10 **61** C4
Weir Rd KT16 **124** B2
Weirside Ct 1 RG1 **86** D7
Welbeck RG12 **117** E4
Welbeck Rd SL6 **39** D5
Welby Cl SL6 **39** A4
Welby Cres RG41 **88** B1
Weldale St RG1 **85** F8
Welden SL2 **43** C7
WELFORD **76** A7
Welford Park Gdns★
RG20 **75** F7
Welford Pk RG20 **75** E7
Welford Rd
Wickham RG20 **75** D4
Woodley RG5 **88** A8
Welford & Wickham CE Prim
Sch RG20 **75** D4
Welland Cl
Brands Hill SL3 **69** B8
Reading RG31 **57** C1
Wellbank SL6 **20** E1
Wellburn Cl GU47 **150** B7
Well Cl GU15 **151** B4
Wellcroft Rd SL1 **42** B5
WELL END **2** F5
Well End Cotts SL8 **2** F5
Weller Dr
Arborfield Garrison
RG40 **141** A6
Camberley GU15 **151** C3
Weller's La RG42 **91** C7
Wellesley Ave SL0 **44** F4
Wellesley Cl GU19 **145** C3
Wellesley Ct
Crowthorne RG45 **142** F4
Iver SL0 **44** F4
Wellesley Dr RG45 **142** E5
Wellesley Ho SL4 **67** B6
Wellesley Path SL1 **43** A4
Wellesley Rd SL1 **43** A4
Welley Ave TW19 **68** E3
Welley Rd TW19 **68** E3
Wellfield Cl RG31 **84** C7
Wellhill Rd OX12 **27** C6
WELLHOUSE **79** E6
Wellhouse La RG18 **79** E6
Well House La RG27 **140** B3
Wellhouse Rd SL6 **19** E2
Wellington Ave
Reading RG2 **86** D4
Virginia Water GU25 **122** B4
Wellington Bsns Pk
RG45 **142** E4
Wellington Cl
4 Maidenhead SL6 **39** B8
Newbury RG14 **105** C5
Oatlands Park KT12 **125** F1
Sandhurst GU47 **150** C8
Wellington Coll RG45 **143** A3
Wellington Cotts
Ball Hill RG20 **129** B2
Knowl Hill RG10 **37** C6
Wellington Cres RG26 **134** D1
Wellington Ct
Ashford TW15 **97** E3
Camberley GU15 **151** C5

Wellington Ct *continued*
Shinfield RG7 **113** A3
Stanwell TW19 **97** E8
Wellington Ctry Pk★
RG7 **139** D1
Wellington Dr RG12 **118** E4
Wellington Gdns RG7 **82** A1
Wellingtonia Ave RG45,
RG40 **142** C3
Wellingtonia Ho 25 RG30 **85** D6
Wellingtonia Rdbt RG45 **142** E4
Wellingtonias RG42 **92** A1
Wellington Ind Est RG7 **113** A1
Wellington Lodge SL4 **93** B6
Wellington Rd
Ashford TW15 **97** E3
Crowthorne RG45 **143** C4
Hatton TW14 **71** E2
Maidenhead SL6 **39** D7
Sandhurst GU47 **150** C8
Wokingham RG40 **116** B5
Wellington St SL1 **43** A4
Wellington Terr GU47 **150** D8
Well Mdw RG14 **105** B5
Wells Cl SL4 **67** A7
Wells La SL5 **120** B5
Wellswood SL5 **120** B6
Welsh La RG7, RG7 **139** A2
Welshman's Rd RG7 **136** A5
Welwick Cl RG6 **87** E2
Welwyn Ave TW14 **71** F1
Wendan Rd RG14 **130** F8
Wendover Ct TW18 **96** C3
Wendover Dr GU16 **152** C3
Wendover Pl TW18 **96** D3
Wendover Rd
Bourne End SL8 **3** A5
Burnham SL1 **41** B8
Egham TW18 **96** D3
Wendover Way RG30 **84** D7
Wenlock Edge RG10 **61** B4
Wenlock Way RG19 **106** D2
Wensley Cl RG10 **61** D5
Wensleydale Dr GU15 **152** D5
Wensley Rd RG1 **85** E5
WENTWORTH **121** F3
Wentworth Ave
North Ascot SL5 **119** C7
Reading RG2 **113** D8
Slough SL2 **22** A2
Wentworth Cl
Ashford TW15 **98** B4
Crowthorne RG45 **142** F6
Yateley GU46 **149** D5
Wentworth Cres SL6 **39** C6
Wentworth Ct RG14 **105** B1
Wentworth Dr GU25 **121** F5
Wentworth Golf Club
GU25 **122** A4
Wentworth Ind Ct 1 SL2 **22** A2
Wentworth Lodge RG14 **104** E2
Wentworth Pl GU15 **151** A4
Wentworth Way SL5 **119** C7
Wescott Inf Sch RG40 **116** D6
Wescott Rd RG40 **116** D6
Wesley Dr TW20 **96** A2
Wesley Pl SL4 **93** B6
Wessex Cl RG17 **100** C5
Wessex Ct
4 Stanwell TW19 **70** E1
Tadley RG26 **135** B1
24 Windsor SL4 **67** D6
Wessex Gdns RG10 **61** E3
Wessex Prim Sch SL6 **39** B4
Wessex Rd
Bourne End SL8 **3** B2
Harmondsworth TW19, TW6 **70** E4
Wessex Road Ind Est SL8 **3** B2
Wessex Way SL6 **39** B4
Wessons Hill SL6 **19** C7
Westacott Bsns Ctr SL6 **38** E2
Westacott Way SL6 **38** D4
WEST BEDFONT **97** F8
West Berkshire Com Hospl
RG18 **105** E4
West Berkshire Mus★
RG14 **105** A3
Westborough Ct SL6 **39** C6
Westborough Rd SL6 **39** C6
Westbourne Rd
Feltham TW13 **98** F5
Sandhurst GU47 **150** E7
Staines TW18 **97** B1
Westbourne Terr
3 Newbury RG14 **105** A4
Reading RG30 **85** C7
WESTBROOK **76** D5
Westbrook SL6 **40** E1
Westbrook Cl RG17 **100** C5
Westbrook Ct 1 RG41 **88** B2
Westbrook Gdns RG12 **118** D8
Westbrook Gn OX11 **11** F8
Westbrook Rd
Reading RG30 **58** C1
2 Staines TW18 **96** F3
Westbrook St OX11 **11** F8
Westbury Cl
Crowthorne RG45 **143** B6
Shepperton TW17 **125** B3
Westbury La RG8 **57** A6
West Cl
Ashford TW15 **97** E4
Medmenham SL7 **17** D7
Westcoign Ho SL6 **40** B8
Westcombe Cl RG12 **118** E2
Westcote Rd RG30 **85** D6
Westcotts Gn RG42 **91** D1
West Cres SL4 **66** F6

Westcroft SL2 **22** B1
West Ct
Bray SL6 **40** C4
Sonning RG4 **60** E2
West Dean SL6 **39** F8
Westdene Cres RG4 **58** E4
West Dr
Reading RG31 **84** E5
Sonning RG4 **60** D1
Wentworth GU25, SL5 **121** E2
WEST END
Bisley **153** F6
Bracknell **91** B3
Waltham St Lawrence **62** E3
West End Ct SL2 **22** F4
Westende RG40 **116** D6
Westende Jun Sch RG40 **116** D6
West End Ho RG14 **105** B5
West End La
Harlington UB7 **71** C7
Newell Green RG42 **91** B3
Stoke Poges SL2 **22** E4
West End Rd RG7 **136** F5
Westerdale RG19 **106** D2
Westerdale Dr GU16 **152** B3
Westerham Wlk 7 RG1 **86** B5
Western Ave
Chertsey KT16 **124** A6
Henley-on-T RG9 **35** E8
Newbury RG14 **104** E4
Thorpe TW20 **123** B6
Woodley RG5 **60** E1
Western Cl
Chertsey KT16 **124** A6
Henley-on-T RG9 **35** E8
Western Ctr The RG12 **117** F7
Western Dr
Shepperton TW17 **125** D3
Wooburn Green HP10 **3** E5
Western Elms Ave RG30 **85** E7
Western End RG14 **104** E2
Western House Prim Sch
SL1 **41** F4
Western Ind Area RG12 **117** F7
Western Oaks RG31 **57** E2
Western Perimeter Rd TW19,
TW6, UB7 **70** B4
Western Perimeter Rd Rdbt
TW19 **70** C2
Western Rd
Bracknell RG12 **117** F7
Henley-on-T RG9 **35** E8
Reading RG1 **85** E6
Westfield Bglws SL7 **16** F6
Westfield Cotts SL7 **16** F6
Westfield Cres
Lower Shiplake RG9 **36** B3
Thatcham RG18 **106** B4
Westfield Rd
Camberley GU15 **151** B2
Caversham RG4 **59** B2
Cholsey OX10 **13** D6
Maidenhead SL6 **39** B7
Slough SL2 **22** B1
Thatcham RG18 **106** B5
Winnersh RG41 **88** B2
WEST FIELDS **104** E2
Westfields
Compton RG20 **31** D4
Kintbury RG20 **128** A3
Westfield Sch SL8 **3** B4
Westfields Inf Sch GU46 **149** B5
Westfields Jun Sch
GU46 **149** B5
Westfield Way RG14 **104** E2
West Fryerne
Reading RG30 **85** D6
Yateley GU46 **149** D8
Westgate Cres SL1 **41** F6
Westgate Ct
Newbury RG14 **104** E1
Reading RG30 **85** C8
Westgate Rd RG14 **104** E2
Westgate Ret Pk SL1 **42** A6
Westgate Sch The SL1 **42** A5
West Gn GU46 **149** B7
West Green Ct RG1 **85** F5
Westhatch Cnr RG42 **91** C5
Westhatch La RG42 **91** C5
West Hill RG1 **86** B6
Westhorpe Park Cvn Site
SL7 **2** B3
Westhorpe Rd SL7 **1** F3
WEST ILSLEY **10** B1
West Ilsley Ho RG20 **10** A1
West La RG9 **15** D2
Westland RG18 **106** B4
Westland Cl TW19 **70** E1
Westlands Ave
Earley RG2 **86** E1
Slough SL1 **41** C7
Westlands Cl SL1 **41** C7
Westlands Rd RG14 **131** A8
West Lawn RG41 **115** A7
Westleigh Ho RG31 **84** B7
Westley Mill
Binfield RG42 **90** E8
Holyport RG42 **63** F1
Westlyn Rd RG26 **135** E1
Westmacott Dr TW14 **98** F7
Westmead SL4 **67** B4
West Mead SL6 **19** F2
Westmead Dr RG14 **131** A8
West Mills RG14 **104** F3
West Mills Yd RG14 **104** F3
Westminster Way RG6 **87** C1
Westmorland Cl RG41 **115** D6

Westmorland Dr
Bracknell RG42 **91** F1
Frimley GU15 **152** B3
Westmorland Rd SL6 **39** D6
WESTON **75** D8
Westonbirt Dr RG4 **58** E3
Weston Gr GU19 **145** F2
Weston Rd SL1 **41** F8
Weston's RG20 **51** D8
West Point SL1 **41** D5
West Ramp TW6 **71** A6
West Rd
Bracknell RG40 **117** D2
Camberley GU15 **151** D5
East Bedfont TW14 **98** D8
Maidenhead SL6 **39** E7
West Ridge SL8 **3** B4
Westridge Ave RG8 **57** C5
WESTRIDGE GREEN **33** B4
Westside GU24 **153** E6
West Sq SL0 **44** F7
West St
Henley-on-T RG9 **15** D2
Maidenhead SL6 **39** F7
Marlow SL7 **1** D1
Newbury RG14 **104** F3
Reading RG1 **86** A7
West Surrey Estates
TW15 **125** C8
West View
East Bedfont TW14 **98** C8
Peasemore RG20 **50** C7
West View Cotts RG18 **52** F6
West View Ct RG17 **100** D6
Westview Dr RG10 **61** E6
Westward Rd RG41 **115** F7
Westwates Cl RG12 **118** D8
West Way
Goring RG8 **34** C8
Shepperton TW17 **125** D3
Westwood Farm Inf Sch
RG31 **57** C3
Westwood Farm Jun Sch
RG31 **57** C3
Westwood Glen RG31 **57** C1
Westwood Gn SL6 **19** F6
WEST WOODHAY **128** C3
Westwood Rd
Marlow SL7 **1** C1
Newbury RG14 **105** B1
Reading RG31 **57** D1
Windlesham GU20 **146** E6
Westwood Row RG31 **57** C2
Wetherby Cl RG4 **59** C6
Wetherby Ho GU15 **151** D7
Wethered Pk SL7 **1** D1
Wethered Rd
Marlow SL7 **1** D2
Slough SL1 **41** B8
Wetton Pl TW20 **95** F3
Wexford Ct SL6 **40** B7
Wexham Court Prim Sch
SL2 **43** C7
Wexham Park Hospl SL2 **23** C1
Wexham Park La SL3 **23** C5
Wexham Pl SL2 **23** D6
Wexham Rd SL1, SL2 **43** B6
Wexham Sch SL2 **43** C8
Wexham St SL3 **23** B3
WEXHAM STREET **23** C4
Wexham Woods SL3 **43** C8
Wey Ave KT16 **124** A6
Weybridge Mead GU46 **149** E7
Wey Cl GU15 **151** B5
Weycrofts RG42 **90** F1
Weymead Cl KT16 **124** C1
Whale Ave RG2 **86** A2
Whaley Rd RG40 **116** D8
Wharf Bsns Ctr SL8 **3** A3
Wharfedale Rd RG41 **88** A3
Wharfe La RG9 **15** E2
Wharf La SL8 **3** A3
Wharf Rd
Newbury RG14 **105** A3
Wraysbury TW19 **95** D8
Wharfside RG7 **109** C3
Wharf St RG14 **105** A3
Wharf The
Newbury RG14 **105** A3
Pangbourne RG8 **56** C6
Whatley Gn RG12 **118** B3
Whatmore Cl TW19 **70** A1
Wheatash Rd KT15 **124** B1
Wheatbutts The SL4 **41** F2
Wheatfield Cl SL6 **39** A4
Wheatfields Rd RG2 **113** E5
Wheat Ho TW19 **97** E7
Wheatlands Cl RG31 **84** E4
Wheatlands La RG14 **130** B6
Wheatlands Rd SL3 **43** C3
Wheatley RG12 **117** E4
Wheatley Cl RG2 **86** E1
Wheatsheaf Cl RG41 **115** A7
Wheatsheaf La
Newbury RG14 **105** B4
Staines TW18 **96** F1
Wheatsheaf Par SL4 **68** A2
Wheatstone Cl SL3 **43** A3
Wheble Dr RG5 **87** D8
Wheeler Cl
Burghfield Common RG7 **111** B3
Wokingham RG41 **115** F5
Wheeler Ct RG31 **57** E1
Wheelers Green Way
RG19 **106** F2
Wheelton Cl RG6 **87** E3
Wheelwrights Pl SL3 **69** C7
Whins Cl GU15 **151** B4

Whins Dr GU15 **151** B4
Whinshill Ct SL5 **121** A1
Whistler Gr GU47 **150** D6
Whistlers La RG7 **136** B1
Whistley Cl RG12 **118** E6
Whistley Court Farm
RG10 **61** E1
WHISTLEY GREEN **61** E1
Whitaker Cl RG18 **106** B4
Whitamore Row RG9 **35** E8
Whitby Ct RG4 **59** D6
Whitby Dr 1 RG1 **86** C5
Whitby Gn RG4 **59** D6
Whitby Rd SL1 **42** C6
Whitchurch Cl SL6 **19** E3
WHITCHURCH-ON-
THAMES **56** C7
Whitchurch Prim Sch
RG8 **56** E7
Whitchurch Rd RG8 **56** D6
Whiteacres Dr SL6 **40** C1
Whitebeam Cl RG41 **115** D3
White Bridge Cl TW14 **71** F1
Whitebrook Pk SL6 **20** C4
White City RG45 **143** D5
White Cl
Hermitage RG18 **78** F6
Slough SL1 **42** D5
Whitefields Cotts RG14 **104** F7
Whiteford Rd SL2 **42** E8
White Gates RG20 **75** D5
Whitegates La RG6 **87** A7
WHITEGROVE **91** E2
Whitegrove Prim Sch
RG42 **91** F1
Whitegrove Rdbt RG42 **91** D2
Whitehall SL6 **20** B1
Whitehall Dr RG2 **140** E8
Whitehall Farm La GU25 **122** E6
Whitehall La
Egham TW20 **95** F1
Wraysbury TW19 **69** A1
Whitehart Cl RG7 **83** E4
White Hart Ho 2 GU17 **150** E4
White Hart Ind Est 1
GU17 **150** E4
White Hart Rd
2 Maidenhead SL6 **39** F7
Slough SL1 **42** D3
White Hart Row 3 KT16 **124** A2
Whitehaven SL1 **42** F6
White Hermitage SL4 **68** C2
White Hill
Ashampstead RG8 **54** D6
Remenham Hill RG9 **16** A2
Shiplake RG9 **35** A5
Windlesham GU20 **146** B6
Wooburn Moor HP9 **3** F8
Whitehill Cl
Camberley GU15 **151** D7
Marlow SL7 **1** C6
Whitehill Pl GU25 **122** E4
Whitehills Gn RG8 **34** C6
White Horse La RG40 **141** D5
White Horse Rd SL4 **66** D5
Whitehouse Farm RG26 **135** D2
White House Gdns GU46 **149** C7
WHITEHOUSE GREEN **110** F6
White House La RG7 **138** F8
White House Prep Sch
RG40 **116** A3
White House Rd OX10 **14** F8
Whitehouse Way SL3 **43** D3
WHITEKNIGHTS **86** F5
Whiteknights Prim Sch
RG6 **86** F1
Whiteknights Rd RG6 **86** F5
Whitelands Dr SL5 **119** D8
Whitelands Park Prim Sch
RG18 **106** C5
Whitelands Rd RG18 **106** D4
Whiteley SL4 **66** E7
White Lilies Island SL4 **67** B7
White Lion Way GU46 **149** D7
Whitelock Ho RG9 **15** E3
Whitelocks Piece RG17 **73** A2
White Lodge Cl
Marlow Bottom SL7 **1** C6
Purley on T RG31 **57** B3
Whitemoor La
Lower Basildon RG8 **34** C1
Upper Basildon RG8 **54** E5
White Paddock SL6 **39** A2
Whitepit La HP10 **3** D7
White Rd
Chilton OX11 **10** D8
Sandhurst GU15 **150** F6
White Rock SL6 **20** B1
White's Hill RG7 **110** D5
White Shoot OX11 **12** A5
Whites La
Beenham RG7 **109** B7
Datchet SL3 **68** B8
Whitestone Cl RG6 **87** E3
Whitewalls Cl RG20 **31** E5
WHITE WALTHAM **63** E7
White Waltham CE Sch
SL6 **63** D7
Whiteways Ct TW18 **97** B1
Whitewell Cl RG2 **114** E2
WHITLEY **86** C1
Whitley Cl TW19 **70** E1
Whitley Park Inf Sch RG2 **86** B2
Whitley Park Jun Sch
RG2 **86** B2

Whitley Park La RG2 . . . . . 86 D4
Whitley Rd GU46 . . . . 149 D4
Whitley St RG2 . . . . 86 B5
WHITLEY WOOD 113 C7
Whitley Wood La RG2 . . . 113 C7
Whitley Wood Rd RG2 . . . 113 C7
Whitmoor Rd GU19 . . . . . 145 F2
Whitmore Cl GU47 . . . . . . 143 D1
Whitmore La SL5 . . . . 121 A5
Whitstone Gdns RG2 . . . . . 86 C1
Whittaker Rd SL2 . . . . 21 E1
Whittenham Cl SL2 . . . . . . 43 A5
Whittle Cl
Finchampstead RG40 . . . . . 141 E7
Sandhurst GU47 . . . . 143 A1
Whittle Parkway SL1 . . . . . 41 D7
Whitton Cl 2 RG6 . . . . 87 D1
WHITTONDITCH 72 A5
Whittonditch Works SN8 . 72 A5
Whitton Rd RG12 . . . . 118 F6
Whitworth Rd RG2 . . . . . . 141 A7
Whurley Way SL6 . . . . 19 E2
Whybrow Ct RG18 . . . . 106 D3
Whynstones Rd SL5 . . . . . 120 A4
Whyteladyes La SL6 . . . . . . 19 E6
Wickens Cnr RG7 . . . . 109 A6
Wickets The
Ashford TW15 . . . . 97 E4
Maidenhead SL6 . . . . 39 C7
Wickford Way RG6 . . . . . . 113 F8
WICKHAM 75 C4
WICKHAM HEATH 103 B8
Wickham La TW20 . . . . 96 A1
Wickham Rd
Camberley GU15 . . . . 151 E8
Earley RG6 . . . . 87 E1
Stockcross RG20 . . . . 103 E6
Wickham Vale RG12 . . . . . 117 E3
WICK HILL
Bracknell 118 C8
Finchampstead 142 A6
Wick Hill Ho RG12 . . . . . . 118 C8
Wick Hill La RG40 . . . . 142 A5
Wickhurst Cotts SL6 . . . . . 38 B5
Wick La TW20 . . . . 94 F3
Wick Rd TW20 . . . . 95 B1
Wicks Gn RG42 . . . . 90 B3
Wicks La RG10 . . . . 62 E2
Widbrook Rd SL6 . . . . 20 B3
Widecroft Rd SL0 . . . . 44 E7
Widmere La SL7 . . . . 1 A6
Wield Ct RG6 . . . . 87 E1
Wiggett Gr RG42 . . . . 90 C2
Wiggington Ho SL4 . . . . . . 67 D7
Wigmore La
Reading RG30 . . . . 58 B1
Reading RG30 . . . . 58 C1
Theale RG7 . . . . 83 C1
Wigmore Rd RG26 . . . . . . 134 F1
Wilberforce Mews 15 SL6 39 F7
Wilberforce Way RG12 . . 118 D4
Wilbury Lodge SL5 . . . . . . 120 F3
Wilcox Gdns TW17 . . . . . . 124 F6
Wild Briar RG40 . . . . 141 F7
Wild Cl RG6 . . . . 114 C8
Wildcroft Dr RG40 . . . . . . 116 A1
Wilder Ave RG8 . . . . 56 E5
Wilderness Ct RG6 . . . . 87 A3
Wilderness Rd
Earley RG6 . . . . 87 A4
Frimley GU16 . . . . 151 E2
Wilders Cl
Bracknell RG42 . . . . 91 A1
Frimley GU16 . . . . 151 E3
Wilde Theatre RG12 . . . . . 118 C2
Wildgreen N 1 SL3 . . . . . . 44 A2
Wildgreen S 2 SL3 . . . . . . 44 A2
Wildoaks TW18 . . . . 97 B3
WILDRIDINGS 118 A5
Wildridings Prim Sch
RG12 . . . . 118 A5
Wildridings Rd RG12 . . . . 118 A5
Wildridings Sq RG12 . . . . 118 A5
Wildwood Dr RG26 . . . . . . 134 D1
Wildwood Gdns GU46 . . . . 149 C4
Wilford Rd SL3 . . . . 43 F2
Wilfred Way RG19 . . . . 107 A3
Wilfrids Wood Cl HP10 . . . . . 3 B6
Willant Cl SL6 . . . . 38 F2
Willats Cl KT16 . . . . 124 A3
William Byrd Sch UB7 . . . . 71 C8
William Cl RG19 . . . . 106 D2
William Ellis Cl SL4 . . . . . . 68 A1
William Hartley Yd SL3 . . . 23 B1
Williams Ct RG17 . . . . 100 D5
William Sim Wood RG42 . . 92 B2
Williamson Cl RG41 . . . . . . 88 B3
William St
Reading RG1 . . . . 85 F8
Slough SL1 . . . . 42 F5
Windsor SL4 . . . . 67 D6
Willington Cl GU15 . . . . . . 151 B6
Willink Sch The RG7 . . . . 110 F2
Willis Cl RG18 . . . . 79 B3
Willoners SL2 . . . . 42 A7
Willoughby Rd
Bracknell RG12 . . . . 117 F6
Slough SL3 . . . . 44 A3
Willow Bank SL7 . . . . 1 D5
Willow Bank Inf Sch RG5 . 60 F1
Willow Bank Jun Sch RG5 60 F1
Willowbrook SL4 . . . . 42 D2
Willowbrook Ct 11 TW20 . 96 A3
Willowbrook Rd TW19 . . . . 97 E6
Willow Cl
Burghfield RG30 . . . . 111 B5
Colnbrook SL3 . . . . 69 C7
Flackwell Heath HP10 . . . . . . 3 C6
Maidenhead SL6 . . . . 19 D1
Newbury RG14 . . . . 104 F1
Willow Cotts OX10 . . . . 13 F5
Willow Court La OX10 . . . . 13 F5
Willow Ct
2 Ashford TW16 . . . . 98 E1
Frimley GU16 . . . . 151 D1
Wokingham RG41 . . . . 116 B6
Willowdale RG40 . . . . 141 F8
Willow Dr
Bracknell RG12 . . . . 118 C8
Maidenhead SL6 . . . . 40 B2
Twyford RG10 . . . . 61 D6
Willowford GU46 . . . . 149 D6
Willow Gdns
Purley on T RG31 . . . . 57 B2
Reading RG2 . . . . 86 E1
Willow Gn GU24 . . . . 153 F6
Willowherb Cl RG40 . . . . . 116 E7
Willow Ho RG14 . . . . 130 E8
Willow La
Blackwater GU17 . . . . 150 D4
Wargrave RG10 . . . . 36 C4
Willow Lodge 7 TW16 . . . 98 F1
Willowmead TW18 . . . . . . 124 B8
Willowmead Cl
10 Marlow SL7 . . . . 1 F3
Newbury RG14 . . . . 130 C5
Willowmead Gdns SL7 . . . . . 1 F3
Willowmead Rd 8 SL7 . . . . . 1 F3
Willowmead Sq 9 SL7 . . . . . 1 F3
Willow Par SL3 . . . . 44 A3
Willow Pk SL2 . . . . 23 A5
Willow Pl SL4 . . . . 67 C8
Willow Rd
Bishops Green RG20 . . . . . 131 F2
Poyle SL3 . . . . 69 E5
Willows Ct 2 RG8 . . . . 56 C6
Willows End GU47 . . . . . . 150 B8
Willowside RG5 . . . . 60 F1
Willows Prim Sch The
RG14 . . . . 131 B8
Willows Rd SL8 . . . . 3 B4
Willows Riverside Pk The
SL4 . . . . 66 C7
Willow St 3 RG1 . . . . 86 A6
Willows The
9 Bourne End SL8 . . . . 3 B3
1 Bracknell RG12 . . . . 118 F5
Brimpton RG7 . . . . 133 F6
Caversham RG4 . . . . 59 A2
Lightwater GU18 . . . . 146 C1
Windsor SL4 . . . . 66 D7
Willow Tree Glade RG31 . . 84 C4
Willow Way GU47 . . . . 142 F1
Willow Wlk
Chertsey KT16 . . . . 124 B2
Englefield Green TW20 . . . . 95 C3
Willow Wood Cl SL1 . . . . . . 21 B3
Willson Rd TW20 . . . . 95 B3
Wilmington Cl RG5 . . . . 87 F8
Wilmot Cl RG42 . . . . 90 C2
Wilmot Rd SL1 . . . . 21 B2
Wilmot Way GU15 . . . . 151 F3
Wilmot Wlk RG14 . . . . 130 C6
Wilsford Cl RG6 . . . . 113 E7
Wilson Ave RG9 . . . . 35 E8
Wilson Cl RG20 . . . . 31 E4
Wilson Ct RG41 . . . . 88 B1
Wilson Prim Sch RG30 . . . 85 C7
Wilson Rd RG30 . . . . 85 C7
Wilson Valkenburg Ct
RG14 . . . . 104 E4
Wilstrode Ave RG42 . . . . . . 90 F1
Wilton Cl UB7 . . . . 70 D8
Wilton Cres SL4 . . . . 66 D4
Wilton Rd
Camberley GU15 . . . . 151 B3
Reading RG30 . . . . 85 D8
Wiltshire Ave
Crowthorne RG45 . . . . 143 B5
Slough SL2 . . . . 22 C1
Wiltshire Cl RG17 . . . . 100 C5
Wiltshire Dr RG40 . . . . 116 D7
Wiltshire Gr RG42 . . . . 91 F2
Wiltshire Lodge 2 SL6 . . . 39 F6
Wiltshire Rd
Marlow SL7 . . . . 1 F4
Marlow SL7 . . . . 2 A3
Wokingham RG40 . . . . 116 C7
Wiltshire Wlk RG31 . . . . . . 84 B6
Wilwood Rd RG42 . . . . 117 E8
Wilwyne Cl RG4 . . . . 59 C4
Wimbledon Cl GU15 . . . . . 144 F1
Wimbledon Rd GU15 . . . . 144 F1
Wimblington Dr RG6 . . . . 114 C8
Wimborne Gdns RG30 . . . . 58 A1
Wimbushes RG40 . . . . 141 D6
Winbury Ct SL6 . . . . 39 E7
Winbury Sch SL6 . . . . 40 B4
Wincanton Rd RG2 . . . . . . 113 C7
Winchbottom La SL7, HP10 . 2 B6
Winch Cl RG42 . . . . 90 C3
Winchcombe Rd
Newbury RG14 . . . . 105 A2
Twyford RG10 . . . . 61 E4
Winchcombe Sch The
RG14 . . . . 105 A4
Winchendon Pl RG4 . . . . . . 59 B6
Winchester Cl SL3 . . . . 69 E6
Winchester Dr SL6 . . . . 39 B3
Winchester Ho 5 RG14 . 105 A2
Winchester Rd
Harlington UB3 . . . . 71 E7
Winchester Rd *continued*
Reading RG2 . . . . 86 B4
Winchester Way GU17 . . . 150 C6
Winchgrove Rd RG42 . . . . . 91 A1
Winchstone Cl TW17 . . . . 124 F5
Winch Terr SL4 . . . . 66 D5
Wincroft Rd RG4 . . . . 58 E5
Windermere Cl
East Bedfont TW14 . . . . 98 F7
Stanwell TW19 . . . . 97 D6
1 Thorpe Lea TW20 . . . . . . 96 B1
Winnersh RG41 . . . . 88 C3
Windermere Rd
Lightwater GU18 . . . . 146 B1
Reading RG2 . . . . 86 D3
Windermere Way
Slough SL1 . . . . 41 C7
Thatcham RG19 . . . . 106 A3
Windermere Wlk GU15 . . 152 D5
WINDING WOOD 74 F2
Winding Wood Dr GU15 . 152 B3
Windlebrook Gn 3
RG42 . . . . 118 A8
Windle Cl GU20 . . . . 146 D4
WINDLESHAM 146 C4
Windlesham Ct GU20 . . . . 146 C6
Windlesham Rd
Bracknell RG42 . . . . 117 F8
West End GU24 . . . . 153 F7
Windlesham Village Inf Sch
GU20 . . . . 146 B6
Windmill Ave RG41 . . . . . . 115 E8
Windmill Bsns Village
TW16 . . . . 125 E8
Windmill Cl
Charlton TW16 . . . . 98 E1
Windsor SL4 . . . . 67 B5
Wokingham RG41 . . . . 115 E8
Windmill Cnr RG7 . . . . 137 A6
Windmill Ct
Earley RG6 . . . . 87 C4
Mortimer RG7 . . . . 137 A6
Windmill Field GU20 . . . . 146 D4
Windmill Ho TW16 . . . . . . 125 E8
Windmill La RG7 . . . . 108 A5
Windmill Lodge TW16 . . . 125 E8
Windmill Rd
Bracknell RG42 . . . . 118 A8
Charlton TW16 . . . . 125 E8
Cookham Rise SL6 . . . . 19 E6
Fulmer SL3 . . . . 23 D7
Mortimer RG7 . . . . 137 A6
Slough SL1 . . . . 42 D5
Windmill Rd W TW16 . . . . 125 E8
Windmill Shott TW20 . . . . . 95 F2
Windmill Terr TW17 . . . . . 125 E2
Windrush Ave SL3 . . . . 44 B3
Windrush Ct 5 RG30 . . . . . 85 B7
Windrush Ho SL8 . . . . 3 A4
Windrush Hts GU47 . . . . . 150 B8
Windrush Way
Maidenhead SL6 . . . . 39 F8
Reading RG30 . . . . 85 B7
WINDSOR 67 E6
Windsor Boys' Sch The
SL4 . . . . 67 B6
Windsor Bsns Ctr The
SL4 . . . . 67 C7
Windsor Castle* SL4 . . . . 67 E7
Windsor Cl SL1 . . . . 21 C1
Windsor Ct
Camberley GU15 . . . . 151 C3
Newbury RG14 . . . . 105 B2
11 Reading RG1 . . . . 85 E7
Windsor Dr TW15 . . . . 97 D4
Windsor & Eton Central Sta
SL4 . . . . 67 D6
Windsor & Eton Riverside Sta
SL4 . . . . 67 D7
Windsor Forest Ct SL5 . . 119 D8
Windsor Girls' Sch SL4 . . . 67 A4
Windsor Great Pk* SL4 . . 94 D4
Windsor Hall SL4 . . . . 67 F4
Windsor Hill HP10 . . . . 3 F5
Windsor Ho
4 Egham TW20 . . . . 96 A3
Henley-on-T RG9 . . . . 35 E8
Windsor La SL1 . . . . 21 C1
Windsor Park Rd UB3 . . . . 71 F7
Windsor Pl KT16 . . . . 124 A3
Windsor Rd
Datchet SL3 . . . . 68 A7
Englefield Green SL4, TW19,
TW20 . . . . 95 E6
Fulmer SL2 . . . . 23 A8
Maidenhead SL6 . . . . 40 C1
North Ascot SL5 . . . . 120 A8
Oakley Green SL4 . . . . 66 A7
Slough SL1 . . . . 42 E4
Wraysbury TW19 . . . . 68 E1
Windsor Ride
Bracknell RG12 . . . . 118 E1
Bracknell SL5 . . . . 119 C4
Sandhurst GU15 . . . . 151 A8
Wokingham RG40 . . . . 142 A7
Windsor Rise RG14 . . . . . . 131 C8
Windsor Royal Sta 5 SL4 67 D6
Windsor Sq 27 RG1 . . . . . . 86 B6
Windsor St KT16 . . . . 124 A3
Windsor Way RG31 . . . . 84 B4
Winfield Dr RG19 . . . . 131 C7
Wingate Rd RG5 . . . . 87 E6
Wing Cl SL7 . . . . 1 C1
Wingfield Gdns GU16 . . . 152 D3
Wingrove Rd RG30 . . . . 85 C6
WINKFIELD 92 D5
Winkfield Cl RG41 . . . . . . 116 B3
Winkfield La SL4 . . . . 92 D7
Winkfield Manor SL5 . . . . . 92 D2
Winkfield Rd
Ascot, Brookside SL5 . . . . . 93 A1
Ascot SL5 . . . . 120 B7
Windsor SL4 . . . . 66 E2
WINKFIELD ROW 92 B2
Winkfield Row RG42 . . . . . 92 B3
Winkfield St Mary's CE Prim
Sch RG42 . . . . 92 B3
Winkfield St SL4 . . . . 92 C6
Winkworth La RG7, RG26 . 135 C2
WINNERSH 88 B3
Winnersh Gate RG41 . . . . . 88 D2
Winnersh Gr RG41 . . . . 88 C1
Winnersh Prim Sch RG41 . 88 D3
Winnersh Sta RG41 . . . . . . 88 C2
Winnersh Triangle Ind Est
RG41 . . . . 88 B3
Winnersh Triangle Sta
RG41 . . . . 88 A3
Winscombe RG12 . . . . 117 E4
Winser Dr RG30 . . . . 85 D5
Winsford Par 4 SL1 . . . . . 42 F3
Winslet Pl RG30 . . . . 58 B1
Winston Cl RG7 . . . . 113 D2
Winston Ct SL6 . . . . 39 B8
Winston Way
Purley on T RG8 . . . . 57 B5
Thatcham RG19 . . . . 105 F4
Winterberry Way RG4 . . . . 58 E6
WINTERBOURNE 77 C5
Winterbourne Ct RG12 . . 118 D7
Winterbourne Rd RG20 . . . 76 E4
Winter Ct 11 SL7 . . . . 1 E2
Winter Hill SL6 . . . . 2 C1
Winter Hill Rd SL6 . . . . 19 A4
Winterton Dr RG14 . . . . . . 104 D5
Winton Cres GU46 . . . . . . 149 D5
Winton Rd RG2 . . . . 113 D8
Wintoun Path SL2 . . . . 21 E1
Wintringham Way RG8 . . . 57 D5
Winvale SL1 . . . . 42 E3
Winwood
Slough SL2 . . . . 43 C7
Windsor SL4 . . . . 66 F6
Wisdom Ct 14 RG30 . . . . . 85 D6
Wise's Firs RG7 . . . . 110 D3
Wishmoor Cl GU15 . . . . . . 151 E8
Wishmoor Rd GU15 . . . . . 151 E8
Wispington Cl RG6 . . . . 87 D2
Wistaria La GU46 . . . . 149 C5
Wisteria Cl RG41 . . . . 115 F5
Wiston Terr RG1 . . . . 86 B8
Witcham Cl RG6 . . . . 114 D8
Withey Cl SL4 . . . . 66 E6
Witheygate Ave TW18 . . . . 97 B2
Withybed La RG17 . . . . . . 101 E3
Withybed Way RG18 . . . . . 106 E5
Withy Cl
Lightwater GU18 . . . . 146 C1
Reading RG31 . . . . 84 C5
Withycroft SL3 . . . . 43 E7
Withys The RG18 . . . . 53 E1
Wittenham Ave RG31 . . . . . 84 B8
Wittenham Rd RG12 . . . . . 118 F8
Wittington Cotts SL7 . . . . . 17 D6
Woburn Cl
Caversham RG4 . . . . 58 E4
Frimley GU16 . . . . 152 A1
Woburn Ho SL5 . . . . 121 A1
Woden Ho RG8 . . . . 34 B5
Wofford Way RG19 . . . . . . 132 A5
Wokefield Row RG7 . . . . . 137 D8
WOKINGHAM 116 B5
Wokingham Hospl RG41 116 A6
Wokingham Rd
Bracknell RG42 . . . . 117 F8
Earley RG6 . . . . 87 C4
Hurst RG10 . . . . 88 F8
Sandhurst RG45, GU47 . . . 142 E2
Wokingham Sta RG40 . . . 116 B6
Wolf La SL4 . . . . 66 E4
Wolseley St RG1 . . . . 86 A6
Wolsey Ct 2 TW16 . . . . 98 F1
Wolsey Rd
Ashford, Felthamhill TW16 . 98 F1
Ashford TW15 . . . . 97 E4
Caversham RG4 . . . . 59 B2
Wolsingham Way RG19 . . 106 D2
Wolsley Ho RG8 . . . . 34 C6
Wondesford Dale RG42 . . . 90 C4
WOOBURN 3 D4
Wooburn Grange HP10 . . . . 3 D3
WOOBURN GREEN 3 F7
Wooburn Manor Pk HP10 . . 3 E5
Wooburn Mead HP10 . . . . . . 3 E6
Wooburn Mews HP10 . . . . . . 3 E5
WOOBURN MOOR 3 F8
Wooburn Town HP10 . . . . . . 3 D4
Woodavon Gdns RG18 . . . 106 D5
Woodberry Cl RG4 . . . . 59 A5
Woodbine Cl
Earley RG6 . . . . 87 C1
Sandhurst GU47 . . . . 150 C7
Woodbine Cotts TW20 . . . . 95 F2
Woodbine La RG20 . . . . . . 130 F1
Woodbourne Cl GU46 . . . 149 D6
Woodbridge Dr GU15 . . . 151 D7
Woodbridge Manor
GU15 . . . . 151 D7
Woodbridge Rd
Blackwater GU17 . . . . 150 B5
Reading RG31 . . . . 84 B6
Woodbury RG17 . . . . 25 C1
Woodbury Cl SL8 . . . . 3 C4
Woodbury Ct RG7 . . . . 140 D4
Woodby Dr SL5 . . . . 120 F2
Wood Cl SL4 . . . . 67 C3
Woodcock Ct RG7 . . . . 113 A4
Woodcote SL6 . . . . 39 D6
Woodcote House Sch
GU20 . . . . 146 B5
Woodcote Pl SL5 . . . . 119 F8
Woodcote Rd
Caversham RG4 . . . . 58 E4
South Stoke RG8 . . . . 14 E4
Woodcote Way RG4 . . . . . . 58 D5
Woodcott Ho RG26 . . . . . . 135 A1
Woodend GU15 . . . . 152 A7
Wood End RG45 . . . . 142 F4
Wood End Cl SL5 . . . . 119 E8
Woodend Dr SL5 . . . . 120 B4
Woodenhill RG12 . . . . 117 E1
Wooden Hill Prim Sch
RG12 . . . . 117 E2
Woodfield Cl RG20 . . . . . . 130 B4
Woodfield Cotts RG8 . . . . . 34 A6
Woodfield Dr SL6 . . . . 39 A6
Woodfield Way RG7 . . . . . . 83 E4
Woodford Cl RG4 . . . . 58 E4
Woodford Gn RG12 . . . . . 118 F5
WOODFORD PARK 87 E8
Woodford Way SL2 . . . . 22 A2
Wood Gn RG2 . . . . 113 D8
Wood Green Cl RG30 . . . . . 85 E7
Wood Hall SL5 . . . . 146 E8
Woodhall La SL5 . . . . 146 E8
Woodhaw TW20 . . . . 96 B4
Woodhouse La RG19 . . . . 133 E2
Woodhouse St RG42 . . . . . . 90 E1
Woodhurst La RG41 . . . . . 115 F8
Woodhurst Rd SL6 . . . . 20 B1
Woodhurst South SL6 . . . . . 20 C1
Woodies Cl RG42 . . . . 90 C1
Wood La
Arborfield RG41 . . . . 114 F3
Beech Hill RG7 . . . . 138 E5
Binfield RG42 . . . . 90 D1
Iver SL0 . . . . 44 C8
Slough SL1 . . . . 42 A4
Woodland Ave
Slough SL1 . . . . 42 D6
Windsor SL4 . . . . 66 F3
Woodland Cl SL7 . . . . 1 E4
Woodland Cres RG42 . . . . . 91 C1
Woodland Dr RG30 . . . . 84 D7
Woodland Grange SL0 . . . 44 E3
Woodlands GU46 . . . . 149 D4
Woodlands Ave
Burghfield Common RG7 . 111 A3
Wokingham RG41 . . . . 115 E8
Woodley RG5 . . . . 87 C7
Woodlands Bsns Pk SL6 . 39 A2
Woodlands Cl
Ascot SL5 . . . . 119 F3
Curridge RG18 . . . . 78 D5
Farnborough GU17 . . . . . . 150 E1
Woodlands Cotts SL2 . . . . 22 C7
Woodlands Ct
Sandhurst GU47 . . . . 143 F1
Woodley RG5 . . . . 87 D8
Woodlands Farm SL6 . . . . 19 C6
Woodlands Gr RG4 . . . . 59 E4
Woodlands La GU20,
GU24 . . . . 146 E3
Woodlands Par TW15 . . . . 98 C2
WOODLANDS PARK 38 F2
Woodlands Park Ave SL6 . 39 A2
Woodlands Park Prim Sch
SL6 . . . . 39 A1
Woodlands Park Rd SL6 . . 39 A2
Woodlands Rd
Camberley GU15 . . . . 151 B5
Shiplake RG9 . . . . 35 E4
Tadley RG26 . . . . 134 D1
Virginia Water GU25 . . . . 122 C5
Woodlands Rd E GU25 . . . 122 C5
Woodlands Rd W GU25 . . 122 C5
Woodlands Ride SL5 . . . . 120 A3
WOODLANDS ST MARY 46 E2
Woodlands The RG41 . . . 115 D4
Woodlands Wlk GU17 . . . 150 E1
Woodland Way SL7 . . . . 1 E4
Woodlark Glade GU15 . . . 151 D7
Woodlee Cl GU25 . . . . 122 C7
Woodleigh Mans SL5 . . . . 120 E4
WOODLEY 87 D7
Woodley CE Prim Sch
RG5 . . . . 88 B8
Woodley Gn RG5 . . . . 87 F8
WOODLEY GREEN 88 A7
Woodley Park Est RG5 . . . 87 D8
Woodman Cl RG2 . . . . 113 C6
Woodmancott Cl RG12 . . 118 F3
Woodman's La RG7 . . . . . 110 F3
Woodmere RG12 . . . . 118 E5
Woodmere Cl RG6 . . . . 87 B2
Woodmill Ct SL5 . . . . 119 D6
Wood Moor RG40 . . . . 141 F2
Woodmoor End SL6 . . . . . . 20 B7
Woodpecker Cl RG10 . . . . . 61 E3
Woodpeckers 1 RG12 . . . 118 B5
Woodpecker Wlk RG41 . . 115 F5
Wood Rd
Camberley GU15 . . . . 151 B1
Littleton TW17 . . . . 125 A5
Wood Ridge RG14 . . . . 130 E7
Woodridge Cl RG12 . . . . . 118 C6
Woodridge Ho
Bracknell RG12 . . . . 118 C6
Newbury RG14 . . . . 130 E7
Woodrow Ct RG4 . . . . 58 F2
Woodrow Dr RG40 . . . . . . 116 F6
Woodsend Cl RG6 . . . . 113 E8
Woodshore Cl GU25 . . . . . 122 B3
WOODSIDE 93 C4

Woodside
Blackwater GU17 150 C3
Cold Ash RG18 79 C1
Flackwell Heath HP10 3 C6
Newbury RG14 130 D7
Sandhurst GU15 150 F7
Woodside Ave HP10 3 C7
Woodside Bsns Pk RG2 113 B7
Woodside Cl
Finchampstead RG40 141 E8
Mortimer RG7 137 A6
Upper Bucklebury RG7 107 C5
Woodside Dr RG18 79 B6
Woodside La SL4 93 C3
Woodside Rd SL4 93 B2
Woodside Way
Reading RG2 113 D7
Virginia Water GU25 122 B6
WOODSPEEN 104 B7
Woods Rd RG4 59 E4
Woodstock 1 RG40 116 C6
Woodstock Ave SL3 43 D2
Woodstock Cl SL6 19 F1
Woodstock St RG1 86 E7
Woodthorne Cl RG31 57 B4
Woodthorpe Rd TW15 97 D4
Woodview Rd RG8 56 D5
Woodville Cl GU17 150 B5
Woodville Ct 14 RG1 86 A6
Woodward Cl RG41 88 D1
Woodway GU15 151 B5
Woodwaye RG5 87 D7
Woodway Rd OX11 12 A7
Woodyer Cl RG5 87 E5
Woolacombe Dr RG6 86 F2
Wooldridge Cl TW14 98 C7
Woolf Dr RG40 116 C7
Woolf Memorial Cotts
RG40 116 C7
Woolford Cl RG42 92 C1
WOOLHAMPTON 108 D2
Woolhampton CE Prim Sch
RG7 108 D4
Woolhampton Hill RG7 108 C3
Woolhampton Way
RG12 118 D4
Woolley Firs SL6 38 E5
WOOLLEY GREEN 38 D5
Woolton Lodge Gdns
RG20 129 F2
WOOSE HILL 115 F6
Woosehill RG41 115 E6
Woosehill Ct RG41 115 F7
Woosehill La RG41 115 F6
Wootton Cl RG31 84 C8
Wootton Dr HP10 3 E8
Wootton Rd RG9 35 C8
Wootton Way SL6 39 C6
Worcester Cl
Maidenhead SL6 39 D3
Reading RG30 85 A5
Worcester Ct
4 Ashford TW15 98 B3
5 Camberley GU15 151 B3
9 Staines TW18 97 A3
Worcester Dr TW15 98 B3
Worcester Gdns SL1 42 D4
Worcestershire Lea RG42 91 F1
Wordsworth RG12 117 F4
Wordsworth Ave GU46 149 B4
Wordsworth Ct RG4 59 C7
Wordsworth Rd
Slough SL2 21 D1
Thatcham RG18 106 C4
World Bsns Ctr TW6 71 C6
WORLD'S END 51 D6
Worlds End Hill RG12 118 F3
Wormersley Rd RG19 131 D7
Worple Ave TW18 97 B2
Worple Rd TW18 97 B1
Worple The TW19 68 F1
Worrall Way RG6 113 F8
Worsley Pl RG7 83 E4
Worster Rd SL6 19 E6
Worton Dr RG2 113 A8
Worton Grange Ind Est
RG2 113 A8
Wrabness Way TW18 124 B8
WRAYSBURY 68 E1
Wraysbury Gdns TW18 96 E4
Wraysbury Prim Sch
TW19 68 E1
Wraysbury Rd TW18,
TW19 96 C5
Wraysbury Sta TW19 69 A1
Wren Cl
Burghfield Common RG7 111 B3
Wokingham RG41 115 E5
Yateley GU46 149 B6
Wren Ct
Egham TW20 96 A3
Slough SL3 44 A3
Wrenfield Dr RG4 58 F5
Wrens Ave TW15 98 C4
Wrensfield SL7 1 C2
Wrenswood Cl RG2 113 B7
Wright SL4 66 C4
Wright Cl RG5 88 A7
Wright Gdns TW17 125 A4
Wright Sq SL4 66 C4
Wright Way SL4 66 C4
Wroxeter Ct RG2 86 E1
Wroxham RG12 117 F4
Wroxham Rd RG5 87 D8
Wulwyn Ct RG45 142 F5
Wyatt Cres RG6 87 D1
Wyatt Ct GU47 150 D7
Wyatt Rd
Staines TW18 97 A3
Windsor SL4 66 D4
Wychcotes RG4 58 F3
Wychelm Rd
Lightwater GU18 153 C8
Shinfield RG2 113 E5
Wychwood GU15 151 D7
Wychwood Ave RG12 118 F5
Wychwood Cl RG6 86 F2
Wychwood Cres RG6 86 F2
Wychwood Pl GU15 152 B8
Wycombe La HP10 3 E7
Wycombe Rd
Marlow Bottom SL7 1 E6
Marlow SL7 1 E4
Wye Cl
Ashford TW15 98 B4
Reading RG30 84 F6
Wye Ct SL8 3 A3
Wye Rd HP10 3 D8
Wye Valley Sch The SL8 3 B4
Wykeham Cl UB7 71 A8
Wykeham Rd RG6 87 A6
Wylam RG12 117 F4
Wylands Rd SL3 44 A2
Wyld Court Hill RG18 53 B5
Wyldewood SL5 120 D3
Wymers Cl SL1 21 B3
Wymers Wood Rd SL1 21 A3
Wyncote Cl RG2 86 F1
Wyndale Cl RG9 15 E1
Wyndham Cl GU46 149 D7
Wyndham Cres
Burnham SL1 21 B3
Woodley RG5 60 D1
Wyndham Rd RG14 105 D5
Wynford Cl RG30 85 C4
Wynnstay Gdns SL7 1 E5
Wynsham Way GU20 146 B6
Wyre Ct RG31 57 C3
Wyresdale RG12 118 F2
Wythe Cl RG18 79 C8
Wythegate TW18 96 F1
Wythemede RG42 90 B2
Wyvern Cl RG12 118 A5
Wyvern Ct TW15 97 E5

Y

Yale Cl GU47 143 F2
Yardley RG12 117 F4
Yard Mead TW20 96 A5
Yarmouth Rd SL1 42 C6
Yarnold Cl RG40 116 F7
Yarnton Cl RG4 59 C6
Yarrow Cl RG18 106 D5
YATELEY 149 D6
Yateley Common Ctry Pk*
GU17, GU46 149 F3
YATELEY GREEN 149 C7
Yateley Industries GU46 149 D7
Yateley Inf Sch GU46 149 D6
Yateley Manor Sch
GU46 149 D6
Yateley Rd GU47 149 F8
Yateley Sch GU46 149 C5
Yates Copse RG14 105 E5
YATTENDON 53 F1
Yattendon CE Prim Sch
RG18 53 F2
Yattendon Ct RG18 53 F2
Yattendon La RG8, RG18 54 D2
Yattendon Rd RG18 79 C7
Yaverland Dr GU19 145 D2
Yelverton Rd RG2 86 C3
Ye Meads SL6 40 F5
Ye Meads Cotts SL6 40 F5
Yeoman Dr TW15 97 E7
Yeoman Pl RG5 87 C7
Yeomanry Cl 2 RG19 106 E2
Yeomans La RG20 131 A1
Yeomans Way GU15 151 E5
Yeosfield RG7 139 C3
Yeoveney Cl TW19 96 D6
Yeovil Ent Ctr SL1 41 F8
Yeovil Rd
Sandhurst GU47 143 E1
Slough SL1 41 E8
Yew Cl
Newell Green RG42 92 A1
Wokingham RG41 115 F5
Yew Cnr RG12 118 C6
Yew Gate RG14 104 F6
Yewhurst Cl RG10 61 D6
Yew La RG1 85 F5
Yews The TW15 98 B4
Yew Tree Cl SL6 39 E8
Yew Tree Ct RG8 34 C6
Yew Tree Mews RG20 31 E4
Yew Tree Rd SL1 43 A3
Yew Tree Rise RG31 84 C5
Yewtrees TW20 123 C6
Yew Trees TW17 124 F5
Yew Tree Stables RG20 31 E4
Yew Tree Wlk GU16 151 F1
Yield Hall La 5 RG1 86 B7
Yield Hall Pl RG1 86 B7
Yockley Cl GU15 152 D3
Yoreham Cl RG6 87 E1
York Ave
Slough SL1 42 D7
Windsor SL4 67 B5
York Cl RG14 105 B2
York Ho
Bracknell RG42 117 F8
Reading RG31 84 B4
York Pl GU15 151 D7
York Rd
Binfield RG42 90 D3
Camberley GU15 151 D7
Henley-on-T RG9 15 D2
Hungerford RG17 100 D4
Maidenhead SL6 40 A7
Marlow SL7 1 D2
Newbury RG14 105 B2
Reading RG1 59 A1
Windsor SL4 67 B5
Yorkshire Pl RG42 91 F2
York Terrace La GU15 151 A5
YORK TOWN 151 A5
York Town Ind Est GU15 151 A4
Yorktown Rd
Sandhurst GU47 150 C7
Sandhurst GU47 150 E7
York Way GU47 150 B8
Youlden Cl GU15 152 A5
Youlden Dr GU15 152 B6
Young Cres RG19 131 D8
Young's Ind Est RG7 134 F4

Z

Zealand Ave UB7 70 E7
Zenith Ave RG2 113 D7
Zenith Ct GU47 143 E1
Zephyr Ho RG7 134 E2
Zetland Ct SL6 40 B8
Zinnia Cl RG41 115 D7
Zinzan St RG1 85 F7
Zodiac Ho RG7 134 E2

PHILIP'S MAPS

the Gold Standard for drivers

◆ **Philip's street atlases cover every county in England, Wales, Northern Ireland and much of Scotland**

- ◆ Every named street is shown, including alleys, lanes and walkways
- ◆ Thousands of additional features marked: stations, public buildings, car parks, places of interest
- ◆ Route-planning maps to get you close to your destination
- ◆ Postcodes on the maps and in the index
- ◆ Widely used by the emergency services, transport companies and local authorities

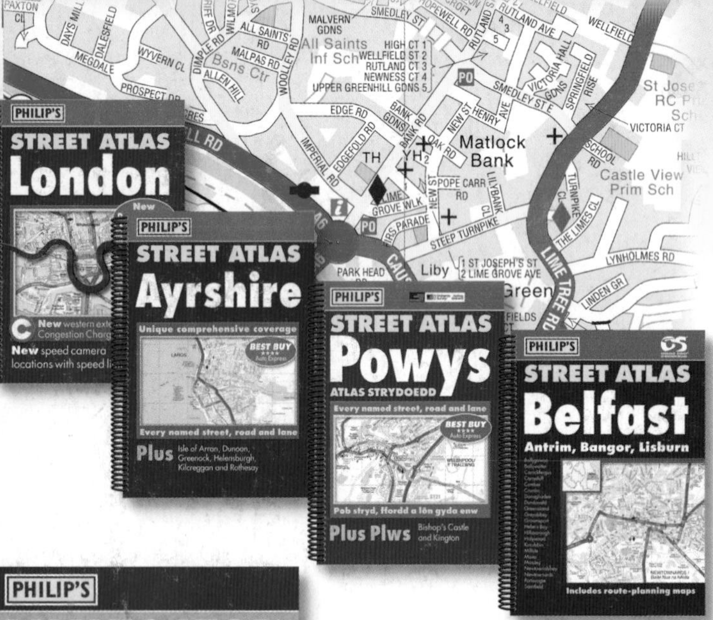

PHILIP'S NAVIGATOR Britain

New speed camera sites, now with speed limits

Major roads named as well as numbered

Thousands of farms, houses, tracks and footpaths

'The ultimate in UK mapping'
The Sunday Times

For national mapping, choose **Philip's Navigator Britain** the most detailed road atlas available of England, Wales and Scotland. Hailed by Auto Express as 'the ultimate road atlas', the atlas shows every road and lane in Britain.

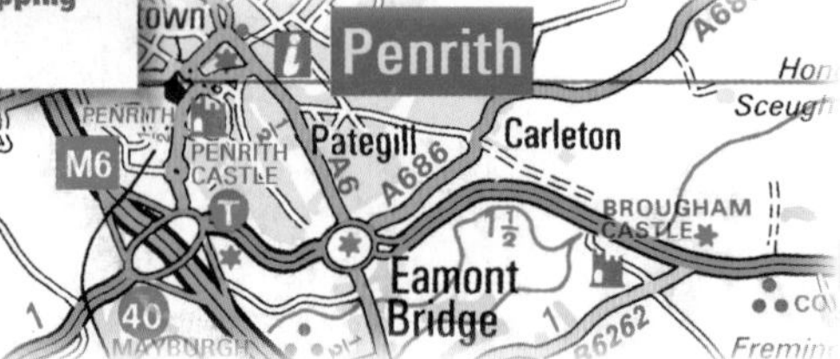

Street atlases currently available

England

- Bedfordshire and Luton
- Berkshire
- Birmingham and West Midlands
- Bristol and Bath
- Buckinghamshire and Milton Keynes
- Cambridgeshire and Peterborough
- Cheshire
- Cornwall
- Cumbria
- Derbyshire
- Devon
- Dorset
- County Durham and Teesside
- Essex
- North Essex
- South Essex
- Gloucestershire and Bristol
- Hampshire
- North Hampshire
- South Hampshire
- Herefordshire Monmouthshire
- Hertfordshire
- Isle of Wight
- Kent
- East Kent
- West Kent
- Lancashire
- Leicestershire and Rutland
- Lincolnshire
- Liverpool and Merseyside
- London
- Greater Manchester
- Norfolk
- Northamptonshire
- Northumberland
- Nottinghamshire
- Oxfordshire
- Shropshire
- Somerset
- Staffordshire
- Suffolk
- Surrey
- East Sussex
- West Sussex
- Tyne and Wear
- Warwickshire and Coventry
- Wiltshire and Swindon
- Worcestershire
- East Yorkshire Northern Lincolnshire
- North Yorkshire
- South Yorkshire
- West Yorkshire

Wales

- Anglesey, Conwy and Gwynedd
- Cardiff, Swansea and The Valleys
- Carmarthenshire, Pembrokeshire and Swansea
- Ceredigion and South Gwynedd
- Denbighshire, Flintshire, Wrexham
- Herefordshire Monmouthshire
- Powys

Scotland

- Aberdeenshire
- Ayrshire
- Dumfries and Galloway
- Edinburgh and East Central Scotland
- Fife and Tayside
- Glasgow and West Central Scotland
- Inverness and Moray
- Lanarkshire
- Scottish Borders

Northern Ireland

- County Antrim and County Londonderry
- County Armagh and County Down
- Belfast
- County Tyrone and County Fermanagh

How to order

Philip's maps and atlases are available from bookshops, motorway services and petrol stations. You can order direc from the publisher by phoning **0207 531 8473** or online at **www.philips-maps.co.uk**
For bulk orders only, e-mail philips@philips-maps.co.uk